Applied Research in Business and Education

ICOBI 2025 marks the eighth international conference organized by the Faculty of Business at NSBM Green University in Sri Lanka. Guided by the timely theme, “Innovating for Resilience: Redefining Business and Education beyond Boundaries”, the conference serves as a dynamic research platform for a global community of scholars, researchers, and practitioners to share and explore outcome-based research across various disciplines including Business, Law, Education and Media. The conference is designed to inspire transformative thinking and foster cross disciplinary dialogue through engaging keynote speeches of international scholars, paper presentations and interactive workshops. What makes ICOBI stands out is its strong emphasis on real-world impact and its inclusive space for both established academics and novice researchers. It provides a pivotal opportunity to disseminate knowledge, exchange pioneering research ideas, and build meaningful collaborations that drive resilience and forward thinking in business and education.

Dr. W A Piyumi Udeshinee (Lead Editor) is a Senior Lecturer attached to the Faculty of Business at NSBM Green University, Sri Lanka. She is currently the Dean of the Faculty of Postgraduate Studies and Professional Advancement. She holds a PhD from Stockholm University, Sweden where her research focused on dynamic assessment as a feedback strategy in technology-enhanced language learning.

Ms. Sashini Gayanika (Associate Editor) is a Senior Lecturer at the Faculty of Business, NSBM Green University, Sri Lanka, with expertise in Economics and Business Administration. She has completed her master’s in Economics at University of Colombo and reading for her PhD at University of Colombo. Her research interests lie in Economics and Behavioural Finance and has published in local and international journals.

Ms. Thilini De Silva (Editor) is the Dean of the Faculty of Business at NSBM Green University and a pioneer academic of the faculty. A first-class graduate in Banking and Finance from Wayamba University and a dual gold medallist, she holds an MBA from the Postgraduate Institute of Management and is currently pursuing a PhD at Stockholm University, Sweden on women empowerment, entrepreneurship, gender, and social media.

Applied Research in Business and Education

Proceedings of the International Conference on Business Innovation (ICOBI 2025), October 17, 2025, Colombo, Sri Lanka

Edited by

Dr. W A Piyumi Udeshinee [ORCID: 0000-0001-5427-4582]

Ms. Sashini Gayanika [ORCID: 0009-0004-3338-0174]

Ms. Thilini De Silva [ORCID: 0000-0002-7925-3232]

Routledge
Taylor & Francis Group

First edition published 2026
by Routledge
44 Park Square, Milton Park, Abingdon, Oxon, OX14 4RN

and by Routledge
605 Third Avenue, New York, NY 10158

Routledge is an imprint of the Taylor & Francis Group, an informa business

British Library Cataloguing-in-Publication Data
A catalogue record for this book is available from the British Library

ISBN: 9781041240679 (pbk)
ISBN: 9781041240464 (hbk)
ISBN: 9781003739920 (ebk)

DOI: 10.4324/9781003739920

Typeset in Times New Roman
by HBK Digital

Keynote Address 1

Pavithra Kailasapathy (PhD)
Professor
Department of Human Resources Management
Faculty of Management and Finance
University of Colombo, Sri Lanka

Growth Through Adversity: The Architecture of Resilience

Abstract

In a world marked by volatility, uncertainty, and rapid change, resilience is no longer a luxury—it is a necessity. This talk explores the transformative power of resilience across individual, organisational, and societal levels, drawing on stories from Sri Lanka and beyond to illustrate how adversity can become a catalyst for innovation and growth.

This talk explores the dynamic and multifaceted nature of resilience, positioning it as a critical capability for individuals, organisations, and communities navigating adversity. Drawing from Sri Lanka's post-tsunami recovery in 2004, grassroots innovation and collective action, illustrating how resilience sometimes can emerge organically in the absence of formal plans. The talk then traces the etymology of resilience and synthesises key scholarly definitions, framing it as the ability to rebound, adapt, and grow stronger through setbacks.

At the individual level, the talk highlights the pivotal role of mindset—particularly Carol Dweck's growth mindset theory—as a foundational element of resilience. It argues that resilience is not innate but developable, supported by both natural mechanisms (e.g., emotional regulation, supportive relationships) and induced mechanisms (e.g., training, coaching, mindfulness). The feedback we give to children and employees.

Organisational resilience is examined through case studies, including Toyota's post-tsunami supply chain restructuring and Sri Lankan apparel firms' move to PPE production during the COVID-19 pandemic. These examples underscore resilience as a strategic advantage, enabling firms to adapt, innovate, and thrive under pressure. The talk draws on contemporary research to show how resilience enhances organisational performance, competitiveness, and long-term sustainability.

The talk also articulates the innovation–resilience loop, where resilience fuels innovation and vice versa, creating a continuous cycle of adaptation and growth. Practical frameworks are proposed for building resilience at both individual and organisational levels, including anticipation, absorption, recovery, and growth.

The Sri Lankan context is woven throughout, from ancient irrigation systems to modern-day educational goals, reinforcing that resilience is embedded in the nation's cultural and historical DNA. The talk concludes with a call to action: in an era of volatility and uncertainty (VUCA), resilience must be cultivated intentionally across all sectors of society. It is not merely about bouncing back—but bouncing forward, stronger and wiser.

Keynote Address 2

Linda Bradley (PhD)
Associate Professor in Education
Department of Education, Communication and Learning
University of Gothenburg, Sweden

Empowering students through adaptive pedagogies and technology-enhanced learning: Strategies for inclusive and reflective higher education

Abstract

This keynote addresses the evolving landscape of higher education confronting challenges of digital transformation and increasingly diverse student populations. It is essential to reimagine teaching, learning, and assessment in ways that promote engagement, inclusion, and lifelong learning. The focus is on strategies that foster critical teaching, student agency, and professional development for educators. Central to this discussion is the integration of collaborative and inclusive pedagogies, where students take responsibility for their learning, co-construct knowledge in diverse groups and develop a sense of belonging. These approaches support both cognitive and social development, reinforcing student engagement and motivation.

Drawing on technology-enhanced learning environments, the importance of active student participation and the dynamic interplay between teaching and learning will be highlighted. The role of student-led projects and reflective practices in higher education will be addressed, showing how learning activities can align with content while promoting autonomy. Digital tools are not peripheral but essential to fostering inclusive classrooms, supporting differentiated instruction, and expanding access. Examples from academic professional development courses and international master's programs in information technology provide insights into cross-cultural communication and multilingual learning, illustrating how technology bridges geographic and linguistic boundaries.

A particular emphasis is placed on student-led projects and reflective practices—including podcasts, video journals, and peer response work that promote autonomy, intercultural competence, and linguistic development. These activities exemplify how content, communication, and critical reflection can be meaningfully aligned in diverse educational settings.

Technology-enhanced language learning is also addressed for its transformative potential, enabling institutions to personalize instruction, promote multilingualism, and support engagement beyond the classroom. From mobile apps and learning management systems to AI-driven platforms, digital tools are showcased as catalysts for inclusive and adaptable learning. A key focus is placed on inclusive teaching practices, where differentiated instruction and formative assessment strategies can create equitable learning environments. The role of generative AI is critically examined with attention to how it can be designed as a tool for learning.

Throughout, the keynote emphasizes reflective practice, for both students and educators, as a cornerstone of effective pedagogy. By integrating reflection into the curriculum through portfolios, peer review, and metacognitive tasks, higher education can nurture deeper learning and professional development. In conclusion, the role of higher education is shaping inclusive, collaborative, and future-ready learning environments. This calls for adaptive and technologically enhanced practices as core elements of a dynamic, globalized, and learner-driven educational environments that empower learners to thrive.

Keynote Address 3

Christopher Agyapong Siaw (PhD)
Lecturer in Marketing
Plymouth Business School University of Plymouth, UK

Building Collective Resilience through Co-Creation and Innovation

Abstract

The consequences of the Covid-19 pandemic and recent global geopolitical tensions have revealed an undeniable fact that disruptions anywhere ripple everywhere. If what affects one affects all, recovery cannot be individual, it must be collective. Accordingly, resilience cannot be built in isolation, it must be built together. Lessons from the Covid-19 pandemic remind us that resilience is no longer about bouncing back to the past, but bouncing forward to something stronger, smarter, and more sustainable through innovation. As policymakers, managers, academics, or students facing disruptions from artificial intelligence (AI) and the demands of sustainability, our resilience will come not from silos, but from how we collaborate, reimagine, and reinvent together. This is why redefining business and education beyond boundaries, through the co-creation of innovation, is not just important—it is essential for building true resilience.

Innovation today is no longer the work of lone geniuses, single labs, or isolated firms. It is co-created in ecosystems where problems are defined with users, expertise is pooled across suppliers, partners and manufacturers, and researchers collaborate with managers and entrepreneurs. Ecosystems thrive on networks—firms, customers, researchers, regulators, governments, and communities—because no single actor holds all the resources to tackle today's challenges, whether in low-carbon technologies, artificial intelligence, or global value chains. Co-creation in ecosystems provide the scaffolding—social, economic, and governance structures—that brings interdependent capabilities together. Co-creation mechanisms make ecosystems resilient because ecosystems reconfigure when one actor fails, absorb shocks through shared risks, adapt through continuous learning, and stay agile with modular platforms.

To thrive in resilient ecosystems, businesses need to develop dynamic capabilities—the ability to adapt, reconfigure, and renew from within—more than ever before. Nonetheless, in today's networked digital economy, internal agility alone is not enough. Bouncing forward with resilience that drives innovation also depends on openness—the ability to connect, exchange, and co-create value across boundaries. This is the essence of open innovation. Firms must develop *dynamic exchange capabilities* (DEC) that allow them to collaborate meaningfully with universities, start-ups, suppliers, and even competitors. DEC means building connectivity with the right partners, creating mutual value through shared action, and sustaining long-term participation that fuels continuous co-innovation.

For universities to thrive in resilient ecosystems, stronger ties with industry that go beyond one-way knowledge transfer are essential. Platforms like *Konfer* in the UK, which connects academics and businesses to co-create solutions in the UK innovation ecosystems, show how digital tools can accelerate innovation and create vital feedback loops. These loops ensure industry insights inform curricula, while university research fuels new products, services, and policies. With strong industry ties, universities must evolve from one-time destinations into lifelong learning hubs. That means offering flexible formats—short courses, modular programmes, part-time study—that meet the needs of professionals who are time-poor but knowledge-hungry. Crucially, these formats must cultivate adaptive mindsets with a resilience curriculum that teaches adaptive leadership, systems thinking, and crisis management across disciplines to prepare learners not just to perform, but to pivot in a world of constant disruption.

Today, the most critical disruptions to education and business come from the growth of AI technologies and demands of sustainability. Clearly, these challenges cannot be addressed in isolation. Rather, they require co-created innovations that build resilience not to return to old ways, but to leap forward towards a smarter and a more sustainable future.

Contents

List of Figures

List of Tables

Preface

On behalf of the organizing committee of the 8th International Conference on Business Innovation (ICOBI) 2025, it is our great pleasure to welcome all the authors and delegates of this esteemed event hosted by the Faculty of Business of NSBM Green University, Sri Lanka. We trust that the contents within will prove to be not only insightful but also transformative. For the eighth consecutive year, NSBM Green University proudly hosts the International Conference on Business Innovation (ICOBI), pushing the boundaries of academic discourse. This conference is a testament to the continuous commitment towards addressing the pressing global challenges through research and innovation while exploring the intersection of business and technology.

This year, under the theme "Innovating for Resilience: Redefining Business and Education Beyond Boundaries," the conference provides a dynamic platform for academics, researchers, and professionals to present and exchange their ideas, and discuss cutting-edge research that spans a wide range of disciplines to reshape communities and industries. Over the course of the event, we aim to foster dialogue and explore innovative solutions on a variety of themes that drive progress in the modern world. ICOBI 2025 serves as a vital platform to bring together local and international researchers, academics, and industry experts to discuss the profound impact of redefining business in the global innovative landscape.

The papers included in these proceedings underwent a rigorous double blind review process, ensuring that the contribution reflects the highest standards of scholarship and innovation.

We are also pleased to highlight that the highest-scoring papers will be published in a special issue by Taylor & Francis, further amplifying the impact of research presented at the conference. These efforts demonstrate the conference's commitment to academic integrity.

We extend our heartfelt gratitude to our keynote speakers, panelists, and participants whose insights and experiences have greatly enriched our discussions. We also wish to acknowledge the tireless efforts of the organizing committee, the reviewers and the volunteers who made this conference a success. We are confident that the research shared here will inspire new ideas and collaborations that will pave the way for more sustainable and innovative future in business.

We wish all participants a stimulating and rewarding conference experience.

The Conference Organizing Committee
ICOBI 2025

Message from the Vice-Chancellor

It is with great honour and pride that I extend my warmest welcome to the International Conference on Business Innovation (ICOBI) 2025, organized by NSBM Green University. As we gather for the eighth edition of this distinguished conference, we are reminded of the vital role academic inquiry and innovation play in shaping resilient and sustainable futures.

The theme of ICOBI 2025, "Innovating for Resilience: Redefining Business and Education Beyond Boundaries," reflects the pressing need to strengthen our ability to adapt and thrive amidst global uncertainties. In today's interconnected world, resilience has become a cornerstone for businesses, economies, and educational institutions alike. This conference provides a timely platform to explore how innovation can break traditional boundaries and redefine the way we approach challenges in business and education.

Building on the successes of previous conferences, ICOBI 2025 brings together scholars, researchers, and industry experts from diverse disciplines to share insights and foster dialogue on strategies that cultivate resilience. In doing so, we collectively contribute to advancing knowledge and practices that are not only innovative but also impactful in addressing contemporary global challenges.

Universities bear a profound responsibility to be hubs of research, knowledge creation, and transformative leadership. At NSBM, we remain committed to nurturing an environment where such discourse can flourish and where academic excellence directly informs societal and economic progress. ICOBI 2025 stands as a reflection of this commitment, serving as a platform where new ideas and cross-disciplinary collaborations can emerge.

I extend my heartfelt appreciation to the organizing committee for their dedication in curating this year's conference, as well as to all the presenters and participants whose contributions enrich the quality and impact of ICOBI. Your valuable research, innovative thinking, and shared expertise are essential in building a future that is resilient, inclusive, and forward-looking.

May ICOBI 2025 inspire fruitful collaborations and pioneering solutions that will redefine the boundaries of business and education, ultimately shaping a world better prepared to face the challenges of tomorrow.

Thank you.
Prof. E. A. Weerasinghe
Vice Chancellor
NSBM Green University

Message from the Deputy Vice-Chancellor

It gives me immense pleasure to extend my warm greetings to all participants of the eighth International Conference on Business Innovation (ICOBI 2025), hosted by NSBM Green University. This year's theme, "Innovating for Resilience: Redefining Business and Education Beyond Boundaries," reflects a bold and forward-looking vision at a time when the world is being tested by rapid transformations and unforeseen challenges.

Resilience is no longer a passive response to adversity but a proactive pursuit of strength, adaptability, and innovation. Through ICOBI 2025, we aim to highlight how research and knowledge creation can inspire solutions that cross geographical, disciplinary, and institutional boundaries, paving the way for sustainable progress in both business and education.

NSBM takes pride in its commitment to nurturing a culture of research and development. Conferences such as ICOBI not only provide an arena for academic discourse but also encourage the building of networks that connect ideas with action. This gathering is a testament to our shared belief that collaboration and innovation are vital to overcoming global challenges and reimagining the future.

I extend my heartfelt gratitude to the organizing team for their tireless efforts and to every contributor for enriching this event with your valuable insights. I trust that ICOBI 2025 will be an inspiring experience that sparks resilience-driven innovations and long-lasting collaborations.

Thank you.
Prof. Chaminda Rathnayake
Deputy Vice Chancellor
NSBM Green University

Message from the Head of Academic Development and Quality Assurance

It is my great pleasure to welcome all participants, scholars, and industry experts to the eighth International Conference on Business Innovation (ICOBI 2025), hosted by NSBM Green University. This year's theme, "Innovating for Resilience: Redefining Business and Education Beyond Boundaries," emphasizes the need to rethink traditional approaches and embrace forward-looking strategies in both business and education.

In today's rapidly changing world, resilience is more than an aspiration - it is a necessity. Businesses and educational institutions must continuously adapt, innovate, and collaborate to navigate uncertainties and emerging challenges. ICOBI 2025 offers an ideal platform to showcase research, share insights, and explore innovative solutions that transcend conventional boundaries.

At NSBM, we are committed to fostering a culture of academic excellence, critical inquiry, and applied innovation. Conferences like ICOBI not only provide opportunities to disseminate knowledge but also inspire actionable ideas that can transform organizations, industries, and communities.

I would like to extend my sincere appreciation to the organizing committee, and all contributors whose efforts have made this event possible. Your dedication ensures that ICOBI continues to serve as a hub for meaningful dialogue, cross-disciplinary collaboration, and pioneering thought leadership.

I encourage all participants to engage fully in the conference sessions, exchange ideas freely, and cultivate connections that will foster long-term collaborations. May ICOBI 2025 inspire creativity, innovation, and resilience that extend far beyond the confines of this conference.

Thank you.
Prof. Baratha Dodankotuwa
Head of Academic Development and Quality Assurance
NSBM Green University

Message from the Dean of the Faculty of Business

It is my great pleasure to welcome you to the eighth International Conference on Business Innovation (ICOBI 2025), organized by NSBM Green University. This year's theme, "Innovating for Resilience: Redefining Business and Education Beyond Boundaries," reflects the urgent need for organizations and educational institutions to adapt, innovate, and thrive in a rapidly changing global environment.

The concept of resilience goes beyond merely responding to challenges, emphasizes the capacity to anticipate, innovate, and transform in the face of uncertainty. ICOBI 2025 provides an invaluable platform to explore how businesses and educational institutions can embrace innovative strategies, leverage cross-disciplinary knowledge, and redefine conventional practices to ensure sustainable success.

The papers, presentations, and discussions shared during this conference will highlight diverse perspectives and creative approaches that are shaping the future of business and education. From building adaptive organizational cultures to integrating novel technologies and methodologies, the insights generated here will inspire actionable solutions that extend well beyond the academic sphere.

I encourage all participants to actively engage in dialogue, share your expertise, and cultivate meaningful collaborations. It is through such knowledge exchange that we can collectively address complex challenges, foster resilience, and drive positive change across industries and societies.

I extend my sincere gratitude to the organizing committee, speakers, and participants for their dedication in making ICOBI 2025 a success. I am confident that this conference will spark innovative ideas and pave the way for a resilient, forward-looking, and boundary-breaking future in business and education.

Thank you.
Thilini De Silva
Dean, Faculty of Business
NSBM Green University

Message from the Conference Chair

It is my honour and privilege to extend this message for the Eighth International Conference on Business Innovation (ICOBI 2025), to be held on 17 October 2025 at NSBM Green University of Sri Lanka. ICOBI has been convened annually since 2018, evolving into a premier forum for exploring cutting-edge intersections of business innovation, education, and sustainable development.

This year's conference is themed "Innovating for Resilience: Redefining Business and Education Beyond Boundaries." In a world marked by rapid change, uncertainty, and disruption, we believe that resilience is no longer optional; it is essential. Through this theme, ICOBI 2025 seeks to foster exploration of how business models, educational systems, and institutional practices can be reimagined to thrive across borders, constraints, and unpredictable environments.

ICOBI 2025 is attended by academics, industry leaders, entrepreneurs, and policy-makers from around the globe. We have invited submissions across a broad set of domains, including Economics & Business Analytics, Entrepreneurial Ecosystems, Governance & Compliance, Human Resource Management, Logistics & Supply Chain, Marketing & Branding, Strategic Business Transformation, Global & Sustainable Business, Adaptive Learning and Education Practices, Technology Enhanced Language Learning, and more.

I owe a deep gratitude to the organizing committee for their dedication and perseverance in bringing this event to life. I wish to extend my heartfelt thanks to our esteemed leadership, Prof. E. A. Weerasinghe, whose continuous guidance has been instrumental to the success of this event. I am also grateful to Prof. Chaminda Rathnayake, Deputy Vice Chancellor, and Prof. Baratha Dodankotuwa, Head of Academic Development & Quality Assurance, for their support in strengthening the research culture at NSBM. A special note of thanks is also due to Ms. Thilini De Silva, Dean of the Faculty of Business, whose leadership and guidance have been a driving force behind this endeavour.

I also wish to recognize our keynote speakers, Prof. Pavithra Kailasapathy (University of Colombo), Prof. Linda Bradley (University of Gothenburg), and Dr. Christopher Agyapong Siaw (Plymouth Business School), whose expertise will greatly enrich the discourse.

On behalf of the Organizing Committee, I offer my sincere thanks to all authors, reviewers, panelists, presenters, and attendees. I encourage you to engage fully, challenge assumptions, share bold ideas, and build collaborations that extend beyond this conference.

Let us together make ICOBI 2025 a catalyst for new thinking and resilient innovation, reimagining business and education beyond boundaries for a better tomorrow.

Dr. W A Piyumi Udeshinee
Conference Chair
ICOBI 2025

1 FreshSight: a convolutional neural network approach for real-time produce freshness and shelf-life assessment

W. P. R. Fernando[a] *and A. Kirupananda*[b]

School of Business, Informatics Institute of Technology, Sri Lanka

Abstract

Color-blind individuals encounter daily challenges, particularly in distinguishing color-based indicators of food spoilage. This limitation significantly impacts their ability to assess the freshness and safety of fruits and vegetables accurately. Concurrently, global concerns regarding food spoilage have intensified, with millions worldwide affected by foodborne illnesses each year. The modern lifestyle, characterized by its rapid pace and time constraints, exacerbates this issue, often leading to unnoticed spoilage and substantial waste. The resulting annual waste, estimated at one-third of all edible food, imposes significant societal and environmental burdens, underscoring the urgency for effective solutions. FreshSight enables users, including those with color vision deficiencies, to assess the condition of fruits and vegetables through a convolutional neural network (CNN)-based real-time image analysis engine and an intuitive interface. This system provides immediate visual feedback to help users make informed decisions and avoid the consumption of spoiled produce. It also offers inclusive design features that support individuals with visual impairments. Beyond individual benefits, FreshSight promotes responsible food handling and contributes to the broader goal of sustainable food systems. By combining advanced technology with user-centered design, the solution enhances both safety and accessibility in everyday food-related decisions. In addressing the critical challenges of food safety, inclusivity, and waste reduction, FreshSight aims to support healthier lifestyles and contribute positively to environmental and societal well-being in the modern world.

Keywords: Accessibility, color vision deficiency, food safety, food spoilage, image analysis, responsible consumption, sustainability

Introduction

Color-blind individuals face unique challenges in daily life, with their difficulties often overlooked by those with normal color vision. One notable challenge is the inability to recognize spoiled food based on color changes [1]. In the modern world, food spoilage is a major issue due to its harmful consequences for consumers [2]. Foodborne illnesses have become a significant global concern, affecting millions of people worldwide. More than 200 diseases result from consuming spoiled food contaminated with harmful bacteria like Salmonella and Shigella. Each year, approximately 3-5 billion people suffer from infectious diarrhea, and nearly 1.8 million people die due to food contamination [1]. The fast-paced, work-centric lifestyle of modern society often leaves individuals with inadequate time to monitor their daily food consumption. As a result, individuals often become unaware of both the quantity and quality of food stored inside their refrigerators [3]. In many households, food can remain in refrigerators, undergoing color changes and developing foul odors due to bacterial growth. Unfortunately, people often discover the spoilage long after it occurs, leading to significant food waste [1]. This food wastage poses a substantial societal burden, with roughly one-third of all edible human food being wasted annually [4]. The underlying causes and challenges associated with color-blindness in recognizing spoiled food are highlighted below:

Color-blindness: Color-blind individuals face challenges in recognizing freshness cues for produce, such as color changes, because of their condition, which affects their ability to perceive certain colors. This difficulty in distinguishing between fresh and spoiled produce can lead to color-blind individuals unintentionally consuming items that have gone bad, posing potential health risks [1].

[a]poorni.f@iit.ac.lk, [b]abarnah.k@iit.ac.lk

DOI: 10.4324/9781003739920-1

Foodborne illnesses: Color-blind individuals and others may unknowingly consume produce that has deteriorated or become contaminated due to the challenge of recognizing freshness based on visual cues. This can increase the risk of foodborne illnesses. The lack of recognition and subsequent consumption of spoiled produce can lead to a higher frequency of foodborne illnesses among color-blind individuals and anyone else who, by mistake, consumes spoiled food. These illnesses may have monetary costs as individuals require medical treatment, medication, and may need to take time off work, impacting their finances and overall well-being. Additionally, it can place a burden on healthcare systems [5].

Modern, fast-paced lifestyle: Today's fast-paced lifestyles leave individuals with minimal time to assess the freshness of produce. Demanding work schedules and busy routines often leave little time for proper monitoring. To cope with their fast-paced lives, many individuals rely on pre-packaged produce, which may not always have visible freshness indicators. This reliance can complicate the assessment of freshness of the produce [6].

Unawareness of produce quantity and quality: In households, produce items may linger in refrigerators for extended periods without being consumed. This extended storage affects the freshness and quality of the produce. The lack of awareness about the quantity and quality of stored produce often results in the frequent disposal of significant amounts of food. This leads to financial wastage and contributes to environmental concerns related to food waste [7].

Background and Related Work

Freshness assessment of fruits and vegetables

The term "fresh" is commonly used, especially concerning food, and holds significant importance for consumers, particularly in the acceptance of fruits and vegetables. It creates specific consumer expectations as a crucial factor impacting the quality of the fruits and vegetables [8]. A remarkable 59% of consumers give priority to the freshness of products when making their purchasing decisions [9].

Fruits and vegetables play a vital role in daily human meals, and as the incidence of diseases rises, people have become more attentive to natural and organic products, especially fruits and vegetables. The emphasis on the freshness of these products is driven by the growing awareness of their impact on human health [10]. The quality of fruits and vegetables has a direct influence on human health. With the increase in diseases in contemporary times, people are increasingly concerned about the freshness of the fruits and vegetables they consume [10]. Additionally, the nutritional value of perishable food items, like fruits and vegetables, is closely tied to their freshness levels [11]. The issue of waste in fresh fruits and vegetables (FFVs) is a significant challenge in the food supply chain industry, contributing to a substantial portion of annual food losses. Approximately one-third of all edible human food is wasted annually, posing a burden on society [4]. This underscores the critical importance of assessing and managing the freshness of fruits and vegetables throughout the supply chain.

Color blindness and freshness perception

Colorblind people or people with a color vision deficiency face many challenges in their daily activities [12]. Color blindness, a condition affecting the ability to see certain colors like red, green, blue, or their combinations, presents challenges for individuals. The most prevalent type is red- green color blindness, where these colors appear the same, while another common type is blue- yellow color blindness, making it difficult to distinguish between these hues. Unfortunately, there is currently no known treatment for color blindness [13]. This condition poses unique challenges for individuals, particularly in recognizing color changes indicative of freshness. For those with color blindness, identifying spoiled fruits and vegetables based on color becomes a challenge, highlighting an aspect often overlooked by those with normal color vision [1]. The difficulties faced by color-blind individuals in perceiving freshness add a layer of complexity to their overall experience [14].

Global and local consumption patterns of fruits and vegetables

The significance of fresh vegetables and fruits in human nutrition lies in their rich nutrient content, encompassing essential vitamins (B, C, K) and minerals (calcium, potassium, magnesium), along with dietary fibre. This nutritional profile contributes to a balanced diet, aiding in the prevention of chronic diseases like heart disease, cancer, diabetes, and obesity, particularly in developing countries. Over recent years, global production of fresh vegetables and fruits has surged by 30%, escalating from 30 million tons to 60 million metric tons [14]. In the context of Sri Lankan agriculture, fruits and vegetables hold pivotal importance for both farmers and consumers. A significant portion of the Sri Lankan population incorporates vegetables into their daily diet, often accompanying the staple food, rice. According to the Household Income and Expenditure Survey 2016, approximately 8% of the total household expenditure on food and beverages in Sri Lanka is allocated to vegetables. This underscores the frequent purchase of fresh vegetables as a dietary staple in the country [15]. Additionally, the HIES (2009/10) reveals that an average Sri Lankan household spent Rs. 13,267 on food, with Rs. 386 allocated to fruits, constituting a budget share of 2.91%. Further, the allocation of the food budget to fruits in urban, rural, and estate sector households stood at 3.4%, 2.9%, and 1.5%, respectively. This implies that urban areas accord greater significance to fruits in their budgetary considerations [16].

Limitations of existing methods and the novelty of FreshSight

The consumption of fruits and vegetables plays a pivotal role in daily human diets. With the rise in health-related concerns, individuals are becoming more cautious about consuming natural products, particularly fruits and vegetables. Among these, the freshness of fruits and uncooked vegetables is crucial, as it directly impacts human health [10]. The quality of fruits is closely associated with their freshness. Consumers often assess quality based on visual cues such as blemishes, color, size, and texture, as well as ripeness, aroma, and taste. These quality indicators fluctuate significantly throughout the growth cycle; pre-harvest, post-harvest, and during storage [17].

Traditional methods for assessing the quality of fruits and vegetables involve sensory evaluation or chemical analysis. However, these approaches have notable limitations, including susceptibility to environmental influences, lack of precision, slow processing, and resource intensiveness. In response, advanced non-destructive technologies have emerged, such as Raman spectroscopy, near-infrared spectroscopy, RGB vision detection, electronic nose, acoustic analysis, and dielectric property evaluation. Each method offers unique advantages: near-infrared spectroscopy examines internal composition; RGB vision detection supports automated visual analysis; electronic noses simulate olfactory sensing; acoustic analysis interprets maturity through sound; dielectric property methods estimate moisture and firmness; and Raman spectroscopy provides detailed chemical profiling while being unaffected by water interference [18].

Despite their value, these methods often require expensive, specialized equipment and trained operators, making them less accessible and scalable [19]. In contrast, FreshSight introduces a novel, accessible alternative by utilizing a CNN-based real-time image analysis engine within a user-friendly mobile platform. Unlike traditional sensor-heavy approaches, FreshSight requires only a smartphone camera to deliver accurate freshness and shelf-life predictions. It stands out by incorporating inclusive design for color-blind users and minimizing reliance on costly instrumentation or complex procedures. This combination of affordability, accessibility, and inclusive positions FreshSight as a unique and scalable solution to freshness assessment challenges in both domestic and commercial settings.

Implications of freshness on produce quality

Freshness plays an important role in the overall quality of produce, impacting economic considerations, health and safety, environmental sustainability, consumer satisfaction, and food wastage. The interconnectedness of these factors underscores the need for effective management throughout the supply chain.

Economic considerations

The economic implications of managing fruit and vegetable waste are substantial, with global findings indicating a significant strain on financial resources. According to [17] fruit waste accounts for approximately 12% and vegetable waste for 24%, resulting in an estimated global annual loss of 54.89 million USD. Seasonal patterns further intensify these losses; fruit waste peaks during the summer at 15%, while vegetable waste reaches 28% in summer and 24% in spring highlighting the seasonal variability in produce spoilage and its financial impact. Retailers, in particular, face persistent challenges in managing fresh inventory, often losing up to twice the value of their profit margins annually due to wastage. The difficulty of preserving freshness from the distribution center to the store shelf contributes heavily to these losses. Furthermore, economic repercussions extend beyond retail outlets and affect the entire supply chain. Maintaining consistent temperatures during transportation and storage remains a significant challenge, leading to the rejection of over 10% of fresh food shipments globally each year. These rejections add to the economic burden and highlight the critical importance of freshness management across all supply chain stages [9].

Health and safety

The paramount importance of food safety in human life cannot be overstated, as highlighted by [18]. Foodborne illness constitutes a significant global health challenge, affecting one in ten people annually according to the World Health Organization. In the United States alone, the Centres for Disease Control and Prevention (CDC) reports an alarming statistic of approximately 48 million people falling victim to foodborne illnesses each year, with 128,000 individuals requiring hospitalization. Contaminated foods, primarily caused by the consumption of fresh produce, contribute significantly to these incidents [19]. emphasize the need for pre-monitoring the freshness state of food to mitigate the magnitude of foodborne illnesses. However, a notable challenge exists in the absence of a simple system for accurately assessing the freshness of food before consumption. Consuming contaminated fruits poses severe health risks due to the presence of various disease-causing microbes and pathogens. These contaminants can originate from water, soil, manure, wildlife, birds, or other sources, especially when consumers handle or prepare food. The consequences of consuming non-fresh fruits include a range of diseases such as vomiting, diarrhea, abdominal cramps, nausea, fever, joint/backaches, and fatigue. Certain demographic groups face higher risks of foodborne illnesses. Individuals suffering from diseases like AIDS, cancer, kidney issues, or other chronic diseases are particularly vulnerable. Senior citizens are also at an elevated risk of these illnesses. Additionally, individuals with autoimmune disorders such as lupus, those on immune-suppressing medications, newborns, unborn babies, children under 5 years, pregnant women, and individuals with a history of drug or alcohol addiction are considered high-risk groups [10].

Consumer satisfaction

Consumer satisfaction is intricately linked to the freshness of produce, with a profound impact on individuals' choices when selecting fruits and vegetables. [8] emphasize that the nutritional value of perishable items, such as fruits and vegetables, is directly correlated with their freshness. Fresh produce tends to be richer in essential nutrients, contributing significantly to overall consumer health. When deciding where to purchase food, consumers heavily prioritize freshness. Notably, 59% of consumers place a remarkable emphasis on the quality of fresh offerings during their purchasing decisions. This emphasis on freshness, however, often leads to inconsistent experiences for shoppers. The discrepancy arises when products labelled as "fresh" fail to meet consumers' expectations, creating a challenge in ensuring consistent quality across the spectrum of fresh produce [9]. Addressing this inconsistency is important for enhancing overall consumer satisfaction in the realm of fresh food.

Food wastage

The issue of food wastage poses a significant global concern. A staggering one-third of the food produced worldwide is discarded, despite the alarming fact that there are a billion people facing malnutrition. The potential impact is noteworthy — the saved food could provide sustenance for nearly two billion more individuals [17]. According to the Food and Agriculture Organization (FAO) of the United Nations, food waste encompasses anything altering the accessibility, edibility, health, safety, or quality of a product, rendering it unsuitable for consumer consumption [20]. Particularly troubling is the wastage of fruits and vegetables, accounting for over 42% of the discarded food. These items, being the most consumed globally, face significant losses throughout the food supply chain, with an estimated 40–50% of them being wasted [17]. In simpler terms, more than one-third of the fruits and vegetables produced globally end up as waste, equivalent to a staggering 28 million tons [17]. The problem of food wastage extends beyond the broader supply chain and reaches our households. Often, unnoticed food in our refrigerators goes bad, changes color, and emits unpleasant odors due to bacterial formation [1]. Addressing this issue and embracing sustainable practices in assessing food freshness is not only crucial for reducing food wastage but also plays a pivotal role in resource conservation and minimizing the ecological footprint associated with food production and consumption [26] training.

Environmental impact

Examining food waste from an environmental standpoint reveals hidden costs and substantial impacts on the ecosystem. As reported by [17], the generation and disposal of food waste result in not only economic losses but also pollution problems due to unpleasant odors, the release of leachate into the environment, and pollution in landfills. The environmental toll extends throughout the entire food supply chain, where significant flows of resources, including water, fossil fuels, and chemicals, are utilized for the production, transportation, processing, storage, and preservation of food [21]. At each stage of the food supply chain, there are substantial emissions and environmental impacts, both locally and globally, as noted by [22]. Agricultural practices significantly contribute to environmental pollution, often stemming from a lack of awareness regarding the freshness levels of produce. Farmers, when informed of the optimal freshness levels, can adopt a more environmentally friendly approach by reducing the use of excessive fertilizers, pesticides, and water. Furthermore, knowledge of the ideal freshness levels enables precise harvesting, mitigating overharvesting or underharvesting risks and promoting resource conservation, thereby minimizing unnecessary environmental impact. The accumulation of wet organic materials in landfills has further adverse consequences, including leachate leakage, the attraction of insects, unpleasant odors [23], and the production of harmful greenhouse gases [17]. The overall environmental impact underscores the need for sustainable practices throughout the food supply chain to mitigate these adverse effects on the ecosystem [24][25].

Existing solutions and limitations

There have been significant technological advancements in assessing produce freshness, leading to the development of several software applications designed to assist consumers and businesses. Notable solutions such as FarmSoft, Clarifruit, and GoMicro [36] use various innovative approaches to evaluate the quality and freshness of fruits and vegetables. For example, FarmSoft is a comprehensive farm management tool that tracks produce quality from planting to harvest by utilizing historical data and monitoring environmental conditions. Clarifruit leverages computer vision technology to analyze visual attributes like color, size, and defects, providing real-time quality assessments through photographic analysis. Similarly, GoMicro [36] enhances smartphone camera capabilities with an attachment that allows detailed image capture, which is then analyzed using machine learning algorithms to detect spoilage and defects. Despite the potential of these applications, they face several limitations that hinder their widespread adoption and effectiveness. One significant limitation is the accuracy and reliability of the assessments. External factors such as lighting conditions and the quality of the smartphone camera can significantly impact the accuracy of visual analysis performed by applications like Clarifruit and GoMicro [36]. These variations can lead to inconsistent results, reducing the overall reliability of the freshness assessments. Another critical issue is user accessibility. Many existing solutions are not specifically designed to accommodate individuals with color vision deficiencies, who face challenges in distinguishing color-based freshness indicators. This lack of inclusivity limits the usability of these applications for a considerable portion of the population, making it difficult for color-blind users to interpret the visual cues provided by the software. Moreover, the dependency on user input presents another layer of complexity. Applications such as FarmSoft and ScanEat often require manual data entry and user interaction, which can introduce human error and affect the reliability of the freshness assessments. The necessity for user engagement also means that the effectiveness of these tools is contingent on the user's diligence and accuracy in providing input, which is not always guaranteed. The need for extensive databases and constant updates further complicates the functionality of these applications. The dynamic nature of produce characteristics means that databases need to be frequently updated to reflect new data on different fruit and vegetable varieties, environmental conditions, and spoilage patterns. This requirement for continuous data management and updates can be resource-intensive and challenging to maintain. While current software applications like FarmSoft, Clarifruit, and GoMicro [36] represent significant strides in the technology-assisted assessment of produce freshness, they are limited by issues related to accuracy, user accessibility, and dependency on user input. These limitations underscore the need for more advanced, inclusive, and reliable solutions that can provide consistent and accurate freshness assessments, catering to the diverse needs of all users, including those with color vision deficiencies.

Future innovations should focus on addressing these challenges by integrating more robust data analysis techniques, enhancing user interfaces for greater inclusivity, and reducing the dependency on manual input to improve overall effectiveness and user experience.

Methodology

Use of machine learning for freshness and shelf-life assessment

Dataset description

The dataset used in this study was curated to provide comprehensive coverage of freshness levels for fruits and vegetables, categorized into three main criteria: fresh, moderate, and spoiled. This dataset was obtained from a combination of sources, including a dataset provided by Dr. Fahad Tahir [11], which detailed freshness categorization, and an additional shelf-life dataset sourced from Kaggle [27]. By combining and refining these datasets, a unified dataset was created, comprising 25,115 images. This dataset was split into 70% for training and 30% for testing, ensuring robust model development and evaluation.

Model development

Data Preprocessing: Images were preprocessed to adjust for lighting and background variations, ensuring consistency in the data used for model training. This involved several steps. Image Resizing: All images were resized to a standard dimension of 128 × 128 pixels to maintain uniformity across the dataset. This resolution was chosen to balance computational efficiency and model performance small enough for faster training yet large enough to preserve key visual features relevant for classification [28]. Preprocessing included normalization (scaling pixel values to [0, 1]) to facilitate convergence and reduce variance across images [29]. To improve generalizability, image augmentation techniques such as rotation, flipping, and brightness adjustment were applied, which helped reduce overfitting in CNNs by synthetically expanding the training set [30].

Model architecture

The CNN architecture used for this study included multiple layers designed to extract and learn hierarchical features from the images:

Convolutional layers: These layers apply filters to the input images to detect local features such as edges, textures, and patterns. Pooling layers: Pooling layers reduce the dimensionality of the feature maps, retaining the most important information while reducing computational load. Fully connected layers: These layers integrate the extracted features and perform the final classification, determining the freshness and shelf life of the producer. Activation Functions: ReLU activation functions were used in the convolutional layers to introduce non-linearity, and a softmax activation function was applied in the output layer to produce probabilistic predictions. This architecture was selected based on its proven performance in image classification tasks, with simplicity to reduce overfitting and training time [31] [32]. Trade-offs included limiting the depth of the network to avoid excessive computation and potential overfitting, considering the dataset size. CNNs were employed for image analysis and classification. The models were trained using the annotated dataset, with the freshness scores paired with shelf lives, serving as the ground truth. The model uses layers to detect patterns and features in these images, enabling it to classify new images into the appropriate freshness category along with the corresponding shelf life.

Model training

The model was trained using the Adam optimizer, known for its efficiency in handling large datasets and its adaptive learning rate capabilities. Adam optimizer was selected for its adaptive learning rate and computational efficiency, particularly with large and noisy datasets [33]. The loss function used was categorical cross-entropy, suitable for multi-class classification problems. The training process involved iterating over the dataset in batches, updating the model parameters to minimize the loss function. Grid search was employed to tune hyperparameters like learning rate, batch size, and epoch count. Grid search offers exhaustive search across parameter combinations, ensuring optimal model configuration [34]. Additionally, k-fold cross-validation (k=5) was implemented to ensure the model's performance was consistent across different subsets of the data, further refining the model's accuracy and robustness.

Model testing

The effectiveness of the CNN model in predicting the freshness and shelf life of fruits and vegetables was evaluated using the confusion matrix. This matrix provides insights into how accurately the model predicts values compared to the actual ones. Model performance was evaluated using both validation and test accuracy. Validation accuracy reached 88.6%, while test accuracy was 90%, demonstrating good generalization. In Figure 1.1, the confusion matrix displays high values along the diagonal, indicating strong predictive accuracy [35]. This analysis suggests that the prediction model exhibits considerable accuracy in its predictions. Out of the dataset, 30 images were used for testing, of which 27 were correctly identified, resulting in a system accuracy rate of 90%. This accuracy rate was determined using the following formula.

Accuracy level = (Number of correctly recognized images/number of total tested images) × 100%

A visual illustration of the four-tier architecture of the proposed solution illustrates the constituents and connection between the functional architecture and the database design.

The proposed solution has been developed as a mobile responsive web application. The high-level architecture of FreshSight consists of several interconnected components, each playing a crucial role in delivering a seamless and effective user experience:

The proposed solution has been developed as a mobile responsive web application. The high-level architecture of FreshSight consists of several interconnected components, each playing a crucial role in delivering a seamless and effective user experience:

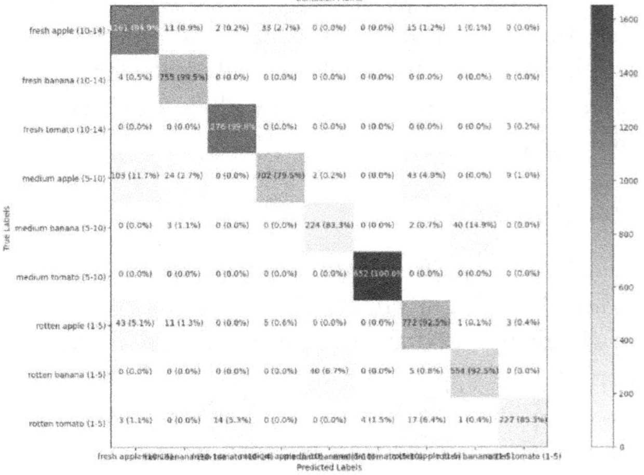

Figure 1.1 Confusion matrix for freshness and shelf-life prediction

Source: Author

User interface (UI): The UI is the front-end component that allows users to interact with FreshSight. It is designed to be intuitive and accessible, providing clear instructions and real time feedback on producing freshness. The interface includes options for capturing images, viewing freshness scores, and accessing additional information or settings.

Camera module: The camera module enables users to capture images of produce. It utilizes the smartphone's built-in camera to take photos under different lighting conditions. The module is optimized to ensure high-quality image capture, crucial for accurate freshness assessment.

Image processing engine: This component is responsible for analyzing the captured images. It employs advanced algorithms to detect color variations and other visual indicators of freshness. The engine processes the image data to identify spoilage signs such as discoloration or bruising.

Color analysis algorithm: The color analysis algorithm plays a critical role in evaluating produce freshness. It uses color correction techniques to adjust for variations in lighting and then analyzes the corrected image to determine freshness levels. The algorithm is designed to cater specifically to the needs of color-blind users by translating color information into actionable freshness scores.

Database: The database stores information about various types of produce and their freshness characteristics. It includes reference images and freshness criteria for different fruits and vegetables. The database is regularly updated to ensure accurate and relevant assessments.

Feedback system: The feedback system delivers results to the user through the UI. It provides a freshness score, and actionable recommendations based on image analysis. Users receive real-time feedback on the quality of their produce, helping them make informed decisions.

Cloud integration: FreshSight incorporates cloud integration for data storage and processing. Cloud services handle large-scale data operations, such as updating the produce database and refining image analysis algorithms based on user feedback. Cloud integration ensures that the app remains up to date with the latest freshness criteria and technological advancements.

Data privacy and security module: This component ensures the security of user data, including captured images and personal preferences. It employs

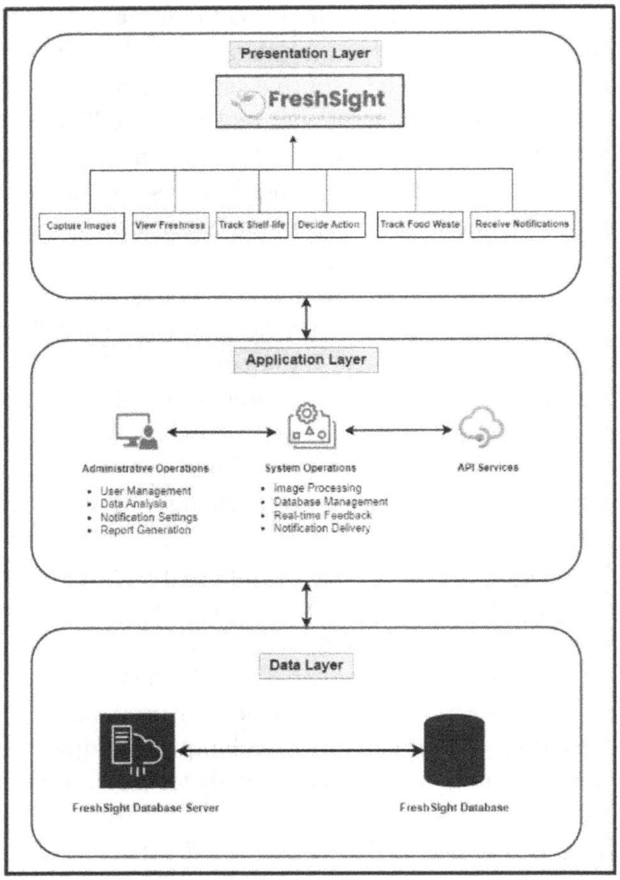

Figure 1.2 High-level architecture of the FreshSight system
Source: Author

encryption and secure communication protocols to protect user information from unauthorized access.

Analytics and reporting: FreshSight includes analytics capabilities to track usage patterns and user feedback. This data helps in refining the app and enhancing its performance. Reports generated from analytics provide insights into user behavior and app effectiveness.

The FreshSight solution thus integrates these components to deliver a comprehensive tool for assessing produce freshness. It leverages advanced image processing, color analysis, and cloud technologies to provide accurate, real-time feedback, empowering color-blind individuals to make better food choices.

Results and Findings

Following functional testing, the prototype underwent evaluation by both experts and non-experts. The aim was to assess the overall suitability and completeness of the solution in addressing the defined problem and meeting user expectations. The evaluation process surfaced several key insights. The concept was praised for aligning well with current consumer demands, particularly in promoting transparency and quality in food products. Suggestions were made to enhance the system by integrating real-time data and exploring technologies like blockchain to improve consumer trust. The inclusive design was highlighted as a valuable feature, especially for users with color vision deficiencies, reinforcing its importance in supporting informed choices and health-conscious decisions. Feedback from participants involved in distribution and agriculture emphasized the system's potential to revolutionize distribution processes and promote sustainability through more accurate freshness assessments.

On the usability front, the prototype's interface was regarded as intuitive and accessible to a broad range of users. Nevertheless, recommendations were given to introduce customizable visual themes and additional cues to further enhance accessibility for all users. The system's potential for widespread adoption was recognized, particularly due to its user-centric design and relevance to the retail and food industries. Additional emphasis was placed on the importance of making the solution adaptable for various user needs and retail environments. Overall, the evaluation reflected positively on the system's ability to meet key objectives such as enhancing transparency, promoting inclusivity, and delivering reliable freshness assessments. Consistent suggestions for improvement included stronger real-time integration, customizable interface elements, and enriched accessibility support. These insights provide a clear direction for further refinement and optimization, helping to ensure the solution meets real-world needs effectively and remain aligned with user expectations in diverse contexts.

Conclusion

Limitations of the current system

While FreshSight effectively aids color-blind users in assessing produce freshness, several limitations persist. The application's reliance on visual indicators may not account for all spoilage factors, such as microbial growth or internal decay. Variations in lighting conditions and camera quality can also affect the accuracy of color detection. Moreover, FreshSight's current focus on color may overlook other sensory cues like texture or smell. The app's effectiveness in diverse environmental conditions and its scalability to accommodate a wider range of produce types are areas that require further research and development to enhance reliability and user trust.

Future work

Further improvements recommended by industry experts and feedback from end users will be considered in future work. Introducing customization features will allow users to tailor freshness assessments and shelf-life parameters to their specific needs. Expanding the deep learning model to detect freshness and shelf life across a broader range of produce will provide more comprehensive insights. Future iterations will also aim to incorporate additional food quality indicators, such as texture and aroma, to offer a more holistic assessment of produce quality. Enhancing user engagement through gamification and sustainable food management challenges is another area of focus. Ensuring cross-platform compatibility and the inclusion of a language selection feature will further enhance accessibility. Additionally, gathering user feedback will remain crucial for continuous improvement, and the implementation of accessibility features will promote inclusiveness, particularly for users with visual impairments, ensuring the solution is adaptable for a wide and diverse audience.

Concluding remarks

The primary objective of this research is to validate FreshSight as an effective tool for color-blind individuals in assessing produce freshness, thereby enhancing their ability to make informed food safety decisions. The implications of this study are significant. Firstly, FreshSight offers a practical solution to the challenge of identifying produce quality for color-blind consumers, which can improve food safety practices and reduce food waste. The insights gained from this research underscore the potential of smartphone-based applications to assist underserved groups by leveraging accessible technology. As smartphone usage continues to rise, FreshSight can provide an essential service, enabling users to make safer and more efficient food choices. The benefits of this application are substantial, promising improved food safety outcomes and contributing to a reduction in food waste, thus supporting overall community health and sustainability.

References

[1] Megalingam, R. K., Sree, G., Reddy, M., Krishna, I., & Suriya, L. U. (2019). *Food spoilage detection using convolutional neural networks and k-means clustering.* In 2019 IEEE 4th International Conference on Recent Developments in Control, Automation & Power Engineering (RDCAPE) (pp. 493–498). IEEE. doi: 10.1109/RDCAPE47089.2019.8979114.

[2] Hebbar, N. (2020). Freshness of food detection using IoT and machine learning. In 2020 International Conference on Emerging Trends in Information Technology and Engineering (ic-ETITE), (pp. 1–3). doi: 10.1109/ic-ETITE47903.2020.80.

[3] Anand, G., & Prakash, L. (2018). IoT based novel smart refrigerator to curb food wastage. In 2018 3rd International Conference on Contemporary Computing and Informatics (IC3I), (pp. 268–272). doi: 10.1109/IC3I44769.2018.9007271.

[4] Abougharib, A., Awad, M., & Ndiaye, M. (2023). Remaining shelf-life estimation of fresh fruits and vegetables during transportation. *IEEE Access*, 11, 8845–8859. doi: 10.1109/ACCESS.2023.3239584.

[5] Nyachuba, D. G. (2010). Foodborne illness: is it on the rise?. *Nutrition Reviews*, 68(5), 257–269. doi: 10.1111/j.1753-4887.2010.00286.x.

[6] Monika, A., & Unnamalai, T. (2023). A study on growth and progress of instant food products industries in India. *Journal of Research Administration*, 5(2), 2.

[7] Hebrok, M., & Boks, C. (2017). Household food waste: drivers and potential intervention points for design – an extensive review. *Journal of Cleaner Production*, 151, 380–392. doi: 10.1016/j.jclepro.2017.03.069.

[8] Péneau, S., Brockhoff, P. B., Escher, F., & Nuessli, J. (2007). A comprehensive approach to evaluate the freshness of strawberries and carrots. *Postharvest Biology and Technology*, 45(1), 20–29. doi: 10.1016/j.postharvbio.2007.02.001.

[9] Freshness Challenge. (n.d.). *The freshness challenge: navigating the complexities of fresh food management.* LinkedIn. Retrieved November 20, 2023, from https://www.linkedin.com/pulse/freshness-challenge-navigating-complexities-fresh-mxbzf.

[10] Jayasinghe, P. K. S. C., & Sammani, S. (2022). Detection of freshness of the fruits using machine learning techniques. Accessed on Dec. 03, 2023. Available from: http://ir.lib.seu.ac.lk/handle/123456789/6413.

[11] Gilani, L., Tahir, S. F., Rasheed, U., Saqib, H., Hassan, M., & Alquhayz, H. (2022). Fruits and vegetables freshness categorization using deep learning. *Computers, Materials and Continua*, 71, 5083–5098. doi: 10.32604/cmc.2022.023357.

[12] Lausegger, G., Spitzer, M., & Ebner, M. (2017). OmniColor – a smart glasses app to support colorblind people. *International Journal of Interactive Mobile Technologies*, 11(5), 5. doi: 10.3991/ijim.v11i5.6922.

[13] Nigam, P. K., & Bhattacharya, M. (2013). Colour vision deficiency correction in image processing. In 2013 IEEE International Conference on Bioinformatics and Biomedicine, (pp. 79–79). doi: 10.1109/BIBM.2013.6732581.

[14] Balali, G. I., Yar, D. D., Afua Dela, V. G., & Adjei-Kusi, P. (2020). Microbial contamination, an increasing threat to the consumption of fresh fruits and vegetables in today's world. *International Journal of Microbiology*, 2020, e3029295. doi: 10.1155/2020/3029295.

[15] Herath, U. (2019). Consumer behavior and attitudes in purchasing vegetables. *Agricultural Research and Technology: Open Access Journal*, 20(2), 90–95. doi: 10.19080/ARTOAJ.2019.20.556123.

[16] Weerahewa, J., Rajapakse, C., & Pushpakumara, G. (2013). An analysis of consumer demand for fruits in Sri Lanka. 1981–2010. *Appetite*, 60, 252–258. doi: 10.1016/j.appet.2012.09.017.

[17] Baietto, M., & Wilson, A. D. (2015). Electronic-nose applications for fruit identification, ripeness and quality grading. *Sensors*, 15(1), 899–931. doi: 10.3390/s150100899.

[18] Xu, S., Huang, X., & Lu, H. (2023). Advancements and applications of raman spectroscopy in rapid quality and safety detection of fruits and vegetables. *Horticulturae*, 9(7), 843. doi: 10.3390/horticulturae9070843.

[19] Chauhan, O., Lakshmi, S., Pandey, A., Ravi, N., Gopalan, N., & Sharma, R. (2017). Non-destructive quality monitoring of fresh fruits and vegetables. *Defence Life Science Journal*, 2, 103. doi: 10.14429/dlsj.2.11379.

[20] Parsafar, B., Ahmadi, M., Jahed Khaniki, G. R., Shariatifar, N., & Rahimi Foroushani, A. (2023). The impact of fruit and vegetable waste on economic loss estimation. *Global Journal of Environmental Science and Management*, 9(4), 871–884. doi: 10.22034/gjesm.2023.04.14.

[21] Ahmadi, M., Jahed Khaniki, G., Shariatifar, N., & Molaee-Aghaee, E. (2022). Investigation of aflatoxins level in some packaged and bulk legumes collected from Tehran market of Iran. *International Journal of Environmental Analytical Chemistry*, 102(16), 4804–4813. doi: 10.1080/03067319.2020.1789614.

[22] Lee, S., & Chung, J. Y. (2019). The machine learning-based dropout early warning system for improving the performance of dropout prediction. *Applied Sciences*, 9(15), 3093. doi: 10.3390/app9153093.

[23] Girotto, F., Alibardi, L., & Cossu, R. (2015). Food waste generation and industrial uses: a review. *Waste Management*, 45, 32–41. doi: 10.1016/j.wasman.2015.06.008.

[24] Skaf, L., Franzese, P. P., Capone, R., & Buonocore, E. (2021). Unfolding hidden environmental impacts of food waste: an assessment for fifteen countries of the world. *Journal of Cleaner Production*, 310, 127523. doi: 10.1016/j.jclepro.2021.127523.

[25] Read, Q. D., Brown, S., Cuéllar, A. D., Finn, S. M., Gephart, J. A., Marston, L. T., et al. (2020). Assessing the environmental impacts of halving food loss and waste along the food supply chain. *Science of The Total Environment*, 712, 136255. doi: 10.1016/j.scitotenv.2019.136255.

[26] Neff, R. A., Kanter, R., & Vandevijvere, S. (2015). Reducing food loss and waste while improving the public's health. *Health Affairs*, 34(11), 1821–1829. doi: 10.1377/hlthaff.2015.0647.

[27] Kavumpadi, S. (2021). Fruit and vegetable dataset for shelf life. Kaggle. Available from: https://www.kaggle.com/datasets/soorajkavumpadi/fruit-and-vegetable-dataset-for-shelf-life (Accessed: 24 July 2025).

[28] LeCun, Y., Bengio, Y., & Hinton, G. (2015). Deep learning. *Nature*, 521, 436–444.

[29] Goodfellow, I., Bengio, Y., & Courville, A. (2016). Deep Learning. MIT Press, ch. 6.

[30] Shorten, A., & Khoshgoftaar, T. M. (2019). A survey on image data augmentation for deep learning. *Journal of Big Data*, 6(1), 1–48.

[31] Simonyan, K., & Zisserman, A. (2015). Very deep convolutional networks for large-scale image recognition. In Proceedings International Conference on Learning Representations (ICLR).

[32] Krizhevsky, A., Sutskever, I., & Hinton, G. (2012). ImageNet classification with deep convolutional neural networks. In Proceedings Advances in Neural Information Processing Systems (NeurIPS), (Vol. 25, pp. 1097–1105).

[33] Kingma, D. P., & Ba, J. (2015). Adam: a method for stochastic optimization. In Proceedings International Conference Learning Representations (ICLR).

[34] Bergstra, J., & Bengio, Y. (2012). Random search for hyper-parameter optimization. *Journal of Machine Learning Research*, 13, 281–305.

[35] Fawcett, T. (2006). An introduction to ROC analysis. *Pattern Recognition Letters*, 27(8), 861–874.

[36] GoMicro. (n.d.). *GoMicro – accurate, affordable, and accessible AI.* Retrieved July 24, 2025, from https://www.gomicro.co/.

2 Exploring how mobile learning impacts student motivation among university undergraduates in Sri Lanka

Asanthika Melanie Upananda[1,a] *and Dinamithrage Ruwanie Prasanthika Upananda*[2,b]

[1]University of Peradeniya, Sri Lanka

[2]The Open University of Sri Lanka, Sri Lanka

Abstract

In the 21st century, digital technology has become integral to every aspect of our lives, including the evolving landscape of education. Learners and teachers should identify emerging technological paradigms to create a mutually beneficial learning environment. In the Sri Lankan context, exploring whether we are adopting these methods is vital. Although teachers and learners accept these modern technologies, literature lacks empirical findings on how these cutting-edge technologies enhance student motivation, especially in the Asian context. Mobile learning is a personalized learning method that uses mobile devices to access educational content anytime and anywhere. Hence, this study keeps a keen eye on how mobile learning impacts student motivation. The sample was drawn from four state universities in Sri Lanka using the convenience sampling method and is perceived as suitable for the investigation. The participants were undergraduates who were studying in different faculties, representing the four universities. Researchers' main investigation is to explore how mobile learning affects student motivation. Thus, perceptions of students were considered as the foremost significant factors, and therefore, a purely qualitative study was incorporated. Student motivation was investigated concerning intrinsic and extrinsic motivation. To collect the primary data, structured interviews and questionnaires were used and analyzed using thematic analysis. Findings indicate that mobile learning is a personalized learning experience that can be effectively implemented to amplify student motivation. Furthermore, findings expand the literature by delivering additional insights in the Asian context.

Keywords: Extrinsic motivation, intrinsic motivation, mobile learning, student motivation

Introduction

Technology is everywhere, shaping the way we live, work, and interact. In today's interconnected world, it has transformed nearly every aspect of our lifestyle, from how we communicate to how we access information and perform daily tasks. With mobile phones in every hand, the digital world is now just a tap away. This allows instant access to services, entertainment, and information. This rapid technological advancement has also made a significant impact on the educational landscape. Traditional learning methods are increasingly being complemented or replaced by digital tools and mobile learning platforms, which offer students greater flexibility, accessibility, and personalized learning experiences.

Students who were born into the era of digital technology have a markedly different approach to learning [1]. They have instant access to diverse sources of information, multitasking, and staying socially connected with peers through mobile devices. The integration of mobile technologies with this new generation's digitally developed cognitive and social abilities calls for innovative approaches to modern learning concepts [2]. Mobile learning (M-learning) is the exploitation of ubiquitous handheld technologies, together with wireless and mobile phone networks, to facilitate, support, enhance and extend the reach of teaching and learning [3]. It offers enormous potential as a tool to be used in situations where learners are geographically dispersed, to promote collaborative learning, to engage learners with content, as an alternative to books or computers, as an alternative to attending campus lectures and for 'just-in-time' delivery of information. With mobile technology, we can "push" and "pull" information and deliver learning to anyone at any time and from any place. It

[a]asanthika.u@gmail.com, [b]drupa@ou.ac.lk

DOI: 10.4324/9781003739920-2

provides learning on the go or just-in-time learning [4]. According to the another study [5] M-learning was defined as a type of learning that enables learners to learn anywhere and anytime using wireless technologies. Portability, immediacy, individuality, connectivity and accessibility are among the important features of mobile devices. Mobile learning is an advanced form of electronic learning (e-learning); it has the goal of facilitating learning that cannot be interrupted by space and time; it incorporates the achievement of learning outcomes [6].

The m-learning framework consists of three core components: the device aspect, the learner aspect, and social interaction. It also highlights the intersections among these elements. Specifically, the device-learner (DL) intersection, which focuses on device usability; the device-social (DS) intersection, which emphasizes social technological interaction; and the learner-social (LS) intersection, which relates to interaction and learning. When all three aspects: device, learner, and social interconnect (DLS), they create an effective mobile learning experience [7]. According to the same study, mobile learning enhances cognitive engagement by enabling distance learners to easily communicate and collaborate within a supportive learning environment.

Motivation is the drive that moves an individual into consciously guided activities. It propels students to learn and stimulates the cognitive, affective and psychomotor abilities of the students to realize the learning outcomes [8]. Motivation also refers to a mental process and hence cannot be directly observed from outside; can be inferred from its products such as behaviors including choice of task, effort, desire, persistence, engagement, initiating and sustaining of activities, etc. [9]. Also, motivation is students' willingness to participate in adaptive mobile learning viewing it as an integral part of the study journey [10]. Lack of motivation affects the gaining of knowledge and skills by students, even if they have the most outstanding abilities. Motivation is the first condition for completing a learning task and the driving force behind the educational mobile process [11]. Consequently, the 21st-century scholars have shown serious interest in the study of students' Motivation in the teaching and learning environment [12]. But considering the Asian context, specifically in Sri Lankan context, there are lack of studies theoretically grounded studies has been done. Hence, this empirical study attempts to fill the existing literature gap in the context of Sri Lanka.

This study is mainly grounded on two types of motivations: intrinsic and extrinsic motivation. Intrinsic motivation is defined as performing an activity for its inherent satisfaction, rather than for the sake of any particular consequences [13]. Intrinsic motivation often arises from the challenge, interest, or enjoyment a person experiences while engaging in an activity [14]. It is linked to the desire to learn and acquire new knowledge, to feel inspired and find enjoyment in engaging with interesting educational materials, and to successfully complete challenging tasks [15]. In contrast, extrinsic motivation is the performance of an activity to achieve a particular outcome [13]. This kind of motivation is linked with the desire to receive a reward or avoid punishment and a bad situation, and to receive a benefit after the completion of learning. This is also affected by social status, learning conditions, family status and supportive opportunities [15]. Motivation in this regard means the absence of both intrinsic and extrinsic motivation, that is when students show reluctance or lack of motivation to learn. They have low self-efficacy and feel incapable because learning will not lead to the desired outcome, and completing tasks has no value as well [16].

In the technology-enabled world, teachers have a greater role in boosting the motivation of the students. Researchers emphasize that teachers play a crucial role in enhancing student engagement in the learning process by offering timely, high-quality feedback and providing essential support and guidance [10]. Instructors can leverage various tools in the classroom, such as multimedia systems, breakout rooms for in-depth discussions during video conferences, screen sharing for presenting class materials, and downloadable presentations to boost student motivation [17].

This study mainly focuses on achieving three main research objectives:

- To explore how university undergraduates in Sri Lanka perceive the role of mobile learning in shaping their academic motivation.
- To investigate the ways in which mobile learning tools and environments influence students' intrinsic and extrinsic motivational factors.
- To understand the experiences of undergraduates in using mobile learning for academic purposes and how these experiences affect their engagement and motivation.

This study grounded on achieving following research questions:

- How do university undergraduates in Sri Lanka perceive the role of mobile learning in influencing their academic motivation?
- In what ways do mobile learning tools and environments affect students' intrinsic and extrinsic motivation?
- How do undergraduate students describe their experiences with mobile learning, and how do these experiences impact their academic engagement and motivation?

Materials and Methodology

Materials

This research was designed as a qualitative study. Semi-structured interviews and questionnaires were used to gain deeper insight as the primary data collection methods. Interviews were conducted which enabled the researchers to explore how mobile learning impacts student motivation among university undergraduates. A self-administered online questionnaire was also used to gather data. It was comprised of several open-ended questions, and it was conducted using Google Forms to collect the insights on students' perceptions.

Following are the open-ended questions included in the self-administered questionnaire and these were asked from the students after briefing them about Mobile learning and internal and external motivational factors.

- Do you use mobile devices for educational purposes? (screening question)
  If yes, why?
- What internal motivational factors influence your interest in mobile learning?
- What external motivational factors influence your interest in mobile learning?
- What are the demotivating factors that influence your interest in mobile learning?
- What are your suggestions to overcome these factors?

This research aims to understand how mobile learning impacts student motivation and their perceptions of mobile learning on their motivation in their academic work.

The respondents of the study are first-year undergraduates studying in different faculties representing four universities in Sri Lanka. The selected respondents of the study who are first-year undergraduates were deemed appropriate due to the fact that mobile learning is an upcoming trend in education in the context of the COVID-19 pandemic and they have experienced a replacement of traditional learning with mobile learning during the later part of their school education. Hence, the mobile learning method can be applied effectively among the university students who are in their early phase.

In this research study, 25 students were selected for the interviews and 48 students were selected as participants for the questionnaire. These participants were first-year students at the University of Peradeniya, University of Moratuwa, University of the Visual and Performing Arts and The Open University of Sri Lanka representing different faculties such as faculty of engineering, faculty of management, faculty of music and faculty of dance and drama. The participants were chosen based on their willingness to be involved in the research.

The inquiry was carried out in strict compliance with ethical guidelines. Steps were taken to protect participants' identities and ensure confidentiality, and informed consent was secured from all involved. Transparency was maintained throughout every stage of the process, including the procedures, data analysis, and reporting. These efforts were made to maintain the integrity of the research, further the trust between participants and the academic community, and generate accurate, respectful knowledge.

Methodology

Interviews were the main method of collecting data [18], semi-structured interviews were chosen due to their increased flexibility over structured interviews. Physical interviews were conducted at all four universities representing students from different faculties. Moreover, the questionnaire was the other method of data collection and the Google Forms survey link was sent to students at the four universities representing various faculties. The survey link was sent through multiple media such as WhatsApp Groups, Messenger, and Instagram. The questions were developed based on the on the theory of motivation in learning and intrinsic and extrinsic motivational factors. Semi-structured (open-ended) questions in both interviews and

Table 2.1 Themes of analysis.

Theme	Theme definition
Intrinsic motivational factors influencing the interest in mobile learning	Statements or examples about internal motivational factors that influence the interest in mobile learning.
Extrinsic motivational factors influencing the interest in mobile learning	Statements or examples about external motivational factors that influence the interest in mobile learning.
Demotivating factors influencing interest in mobile learning	Statements or examples about demotivating factors that influence the interest in mobile learning.
M-Learning platforms	M-learning platforms used by university undergraduates.
Suggestions to overcome the demotivating factors	Statements, examples, and suggestions about how demotivating factors can be minimized in mobile learning

Source: Author

questionnaire were designed to allow respondents to answer in their own words. Unlike structured questions, they do not require a checkmark in a pre-designed list of options aimed to collect statistical data [17]. Using these strategies, answers from a varied range of students of different universities studying at different faculties were obtained in order to better understand how mobile learning impacts student motivation among university undergraduates in Sri Lanka.

Answers from the semi-structured interviews with the first-year undergraduates of the four universities, and the answers from the open-ended questions of the questionnaire were coded according to the themes that emerged and they allowed for an initial summary of the data (Table 2.1). This allowed the summaries to be grouped into themes and analyze data using thematic analysis.

Results and Discussion

Sample collection

The questionnaire was circulated to 75 students. However, only 48 respondents were entitled to the survey, and 27 respondents were eliminated from the screening question. Comments from the

Table 2.2 Comments expressed by the respondents.

Theme	Comments
Intrinsic motivational factors influencing the interest in mobile learning	• The desire to learn and gain new knowledge • Interest in using digital platforms • Self-regulation • Enjoyable and engaging nature • Interactive elements that stimulate curiosity • Ability to overcome challenges
Extrinsic motivational factors influencing the interest in mobile learning	• Teachers • Friends and batchmates • Built-in, mechanisms • Desire to receive external rewards • Practical application and perceived usefulness of the knowledge • Availability of resources
Demotivating factors influencing interest in mobile learning	• Situational problems • Technical issues • Workload and time constraints • Lack of engagement and social interaction • Negative attitudes
M-Learning platforms	• Google search/scholar • Google Classroom • Zoom • Teams • Moodle • YouTube • Coursera • WhatsApp group • ResearchGate • LinkedIn
Suggestions to overcome the demotivating factors	• Provide technical support • Allocate time for mobile learning • Make the learning engaging and create interaction • Create a positive attitude

Source: Author

semi-structured interviews with the undergraduates from the four universities and the answers to the open-ended questions from the questionnaire were coded according to the themes that emerged and were categorized in the form of a table for ease of reference (Table 2.2). These focused on how the intrinsic motivational factors influencing the interest in mobile learning, extrinsic motivational factors influencing the interest in mobile learning, demotivating factors influencing the interest in mobile learning and suggestions to overcome the demotivating factors.

Sample analysis

Table 2.2 highlights how m-learning impacts students' motivation. The majority of participants mentioned that m-learning is an effective method to enhance motivation in terms of academic success. They stated that several intrinsic motivational factors influence the interest in m-learning. One of the main reasons for this is the desire to learn and gain new knowledge. This is one of the strongest intrinsic motivational factors stated by students. This inner drive results from curiosity and personal growth rather than external factors. Students described m-learning as a convenient and accessible way to enhance knowledge beyond the traditional classroom. A Student stated that "it makes me feel like I am improving my knowledge every day". Another student mentioned that I started using m-learning during the pandemic, and now it has become a habit for me as I improve my knowledge and skills". Moreover, many students expressed their interest in using digital platforms. The familiarity and ease of use of mobile devices encourage students to engage in academic content using them. Another student noted, "I have always loved using my phone for my studies, and they are very interesting". Another student mentioned that "this is an interesting method because I use my phone a lot. This is like I have everything in my hands on time". These findings reflect how technological interest can enhance intrinsic motivation by making the learning process fun and enjoyable. Next, the students valued the ability to self-regulate their studies, choosing when, where, and how long to engage with content. This control over learning time and methods creates a sense of responsibility and ownership over their education. A Student stated that "with m-learning I can plan my own study time. I don't have to wait for someone to tell me what to do". Therefore, self-regulation turns out to be one of the decisive internal factors influencing students' motivation [17]. Further, many students highlighted the entertaining aspect of interactive components of m-learning like quizzes, videos, and interactive exercises, which stimulate students' curiosity and engagement. A student mentioned that "some activities make learning feel like a game. I don't get bored like in regular lectures. It is actually fun". Another student mentioned that" when I do an online quiz, I get curious to see the results". Those activities support intrinsic motivation by associating learning with positive emotional experiences. Finally, m-learning offered students the opportunity to revisit difficult materials and practice them repeatedly until they feel confident about their learning. A student noted that "when I don't understand something, I just replay the video or read it again and it helps to understand things properly". This ability to address and overcome academic challenges independently enhances their confidence and motivation.

Secondly, the students mentioned certain extrinsic motivational factors that influence the interest in mobile learning. Out of them, most of them stated that lecturers and instructors play a significant role in shaping their attitudes towards mobile learning. When teachers actively integrate mobile tools into their teaching and encourage their use, students become more motivated to engage with these platforms. Some students mentioned that their motivation increased when lecturers shared mobile-friendly resources. One student stated, "Our lecturers always upload videos and notes on moodle and tell us to check them". However, certain participants said teachers have both positive and negative external impacts on their motivation as some do not encourage this. This reflects how teacher encouragement and instructional design can act as external motivational factors that influence student motivation. Then, peer influence is another powerful extrinsic motivator. Students often adopted mobile learning apps and strategies after seeing their friends or batchmates using them. This peer-driven learning environment also fosters competition and collaboration, motivating students to learn more. One student said, "We have a WhatsApp group where we post links to videos or short notes and we learn a lot from them". Desire for receiving external rewards is another factor mentioned by many participants. They were motivated by the external rewards associated with mobile learning, such as better grades, certifications, or the chance to stand out academically. These rewards acted as tangible outcomes that encouraged students to spend time and effort in mobile learning. One participant mentioned, "When I complete a course on coursera and get a certificate, I can add it to my CV. That's a big motivation". Further, Students were more likely to engage in mobile learning when they perceived the content as directly useful or applicable to real-life tasks, future employment, or current academic needs. As stated by one student, "Some YouTube videos explain things in a way that's directly related to our exams. It saves time and helps a lot". Thus, learners are motivated by how beneficial the knowledge is for achieving goals. Finally, availability of resources such as internet access, mobile data, and free content is another factor highlighted by the students. Accessibility of content, particularly cost-free or low-data options, played a critical role in increasing students' interest in mobile learning. On student said, "I use apps that don't use much data because I don't have Wi-Fi all the time. If it's free, I'll try it". Another one stated, "Our university has free Wi-Fi, so I download all the videos and study offline later."

While mobile learning presents numerous benefits, the study also identified a range of demotivating factors that hinder students' interest and engagement in mobile learning. These factors, drawn from student interviews, provide insight into the practical and emotional barriers that reduce the effectiveness of mobile learning in the Sri Lankan undergraduate context. The most common and the frustrating demotivating factor involved is technical barriers, such as poor internet connection, and lack of access to reliable devices. These issues discouraged students from fully utilizing mobile learning tools. Most students highlighted, "The app disconnects a lot on my phone, and I get frustrated. I just give up after trying a few times" while another one stated, "Sometimes the video doesn't load properly due to bad network signals in our area." Students also pointed out the cost of mobile data as a technical and financial limitation, especially when accessing content in the internet. One said, "Watching lectures on YouTube uses too much data. I can't afford to do that often". After that, situational problems were another factor mentioned by many students. They said that their personal environments were not always conducive to focused mobile learning. Distractions at home or hostels, unstable study routines, and responsibilities outside academics made it difficult to stay engaged. One student highlighted, "Sometimes there's no quiet place to study, and using mobile apps in such noisy settings just doesn't work for me." Another participant said, "I'm always nervous when I attend online lectures at home because my parents usually forget that I have a lecture. So, I'm afraid that something inappropriate will happen". Therefore, the problem with online learning is the presence of a huge number of distractions such as noise, siblings, pets, and parents [17]. Students say they need a quiet environment to focus on their lessons and these situational constraints reveal how external conditions can disrupt learning even if the student is motivated. The, several students expressed that the pressure of university coursework left little time to explore mobile learning tools meaningfully. With lectures, assignments, quizzes, presentations and other responsibilities, mobile learning felt like an additional burden rather than a support tool. Many participants said, "We already have a heavy workload, so I don't have time to use extra apps unless it's for an assignment." Some others stated, "Sometimes I plan to use a learning app, but then I'm too tired after lectures". Next, some students mentioned that certain mobile learning apps or content formats felt boring, repetitive, or impersonal, which made them lose interest quickly. Another recurring concern was the absence of peer interaction and collaborative experiences in mobile learning. Students missed the group discussions, real-time questions, and social aspects of classroom-based learning. One student said, "When I learn through mobile apps, I feel like I'm learning alone. There's no one to ask or discuss with." This social isolation limits opportunities for peer support and feedback which are important in learning. In fact, there was evidence of negative perceptions toward mobile learning, especially from students who preferred traditional classroom instruction. Some believed that mobile learning was less effective or felt uncomfortable relying solely on devices for learning. A few students said, "I feel like I don't learn properly through apps. I prefer listening to a lecturer explain things" and "Staring at a screen for too long gives me a headache, and I feel less connected to what I'm learning."

Students in this era are well equipped with technological tools, and they are way more ahead of teachers. The survey and interview findings offered valuable insights into the key mobile learning platforms utilized by students throughout their academic journey. On top, students use YouTube video tutorials more frequently as YouTube offers more attractive videos related to academic activities. Apart from that, Moodle platform is also a widely used platform among students as this platform offers all the lecture materials and videos related to a particular subject. Google Search and Google Scholar were frequently mentioned as essential tools for quickly accessing information and academic articles, especially during assignment preparation. Google Classroom served as a central hub for course materials, announcements, and assignment submissions, facilitating seamless communication between students and lecturers.

Zoom and Microsoft Teams were widely used for attending online lectures and virtual discussions, with students appreciating the real-time interaction these platforms enabled. Platforms like Coursera were used to supplement university learning, offering structured courses and certificates that added value to students' academic profiles. Additionally, WhatsApp groups emerged as informal but powerful learning tools where students shared notes, clarified doubts, and stayed updated on academic tasks. Some students also referred to ResearchGate as a useful platform for accessing research papers and following subject experts. These findings highlight the diverse ways in which students integrate multiple mobile platforms into their learning routines, often blending formal and informal tools to enhance their motivation and academic engagement.

Finally, the students not only identified barriers to effective mobile learning but also offered practical and insightful suggestions to overcome those demotivating factors. A major suggestion was the need for improved technical infrastructure and support services. Students proposed that universities should provide help in proper training, and digital orientation sessions to assist those unfamiliar with mobile platforms. Additionally, they stressed the need for reliable internet access and devices. Many students pointed out, "If the university can provide better Wi-Fi in hostels and canteens or free data packages, that would remove many issues we face when learning through mobile." One student pointed out, "Some students don't know how to use apps like Moodle or even how to upload assignments." Students also emphasized the importance of recognizing mobile learning as part of academic time. They said if mobile learning is part of the timetable or assignments, they will actually make time for it. Further, many students felt that the content in mobile learning platforms should be more interactive, visually appealing, and diverse. They suggested using videos, quizzes, games, and real-life examples to keep learners interested as they help them understand quickly. Another significant factor was the integration of social interaction and collaborative opportunities within mobile learning environments. Students missed discussions, peer engagement, and the chance to learn from others. One student mentioned, "When we work in groups, we stay more motivated." At last, students emphasized the need to build confidence and awareness among their peers about the benefits of mobile learning. They believed that many students remain demotivated because they have negative perceptions or fear that mobile learning is difficult or ineffective. Many believe that mobile learning is not serious learning. Therefore, the lecturers should explain how it actually helps and if they talk positively about mobile learning and show how to use it, students will feel more motivated to try.

Conclusion

This qualitative study explored the impact of mobile learning (m-learning) on student motivation among undergraduates in Sri Lanka. The findings revealed that mobile learning positively influences both intrinsic and extrinsic motivational factors. Intrinsically, students expressed a strong desire to learn, self-regulate, and engage with content that is flexible, interactive, and accessible. Mobile learning platforms allowed students to take control of their academic journey, offering them opportunities for personal growth and intellectual satisfaction. Extrinsically, factors such as lecturer encouragement, peer influence, access to useful resources, and external rewards further enhanced their motivation to adopt mobile learning strategies.

However, the study also highlighted several demotivating factors, including technical issues, poor internet access, high data costs, situational distractions, heavy academic workload, and limited social interaction in mobile learning environments. These challenges often undermined students' ability to fully benefit from mobile learning tools. Despite these barriers, students offered practical and insightful suggestions to improve the mobile learning experience, such as providing technical support, making learning content more interactive, allocating dedicated time for mobile learning, promoting collaborative learning, and raising awareness of its benefits.

Overall, the study concludes that mobile learning holds strong potential to enhance student motivation when it is strategically integrated into the academic ecosystem and supported through institutional infrastructure and pedagogy.

To maximize the motivational benefits of mobile learning, several strategic actions are recommended based on the findings of this study. First and foremost, it is essential to improve the technical infrastructure available to students. Many participants expressed frustration with poor internet connectivity, lack of access to reliable devices, and the high cost of mobile data. Therefore, universities should consider providing better Wi-Fi facilities in lecture halls, hostels, and common areas. Institutions could also explore partnerships with service providers to offer free or discounted data packages and ensure access to devices through digital resource centers or lending schemes. These improvements would remove key barriers and allow students to engage more effectively with mobile learning content.

Another crucial recommendation is to enhance the role of lecturers and academic staff in the mobile learning environment. Students indicated that their motivation increased when lecturers actively used and recommended mobile learning tools. Institutions should therefore provide faculty training on integrating m-learning into their teaching strategies. When lecturers demonstrate the value of mobile learning and incorporate it meaningfully into lessons, students are more likely to adopt and engage with such tools. Additionally, lecturers should be encouraged to design and share mobile-friendly content, such as short videos, summaries, and online quizzes, to support continuous learning outside the classroom.

The design of mobile learning content must also be prioritised. To keep students engaged and motivated, the learning materials provided through mobile platforms should be interactive, visually appealing, and tailored to students' academic needs. Content formats such as gamified quizzes, animated explanations, and real-life case studies were particularly appreciated by students in this study. These engaging formats not only make the learning process enjoyable but also improve retention and application of knowledge. Universities can collaborate with educational technologists or instructional designers to ensure mobile content is developed with these principles in mind.

In addition, there is a need to formally recognize mobile learning as a legitimate and integral part of academic planning. Many students reported difficulty in allocating time for m-learning due to heavy workloads and the perception that it is not essential. If mobile learning activities are embedded into the academic calendar such as being part of coursework, assessments, or class discussions, students are more likely to treat them seriously and prioritize them accordingly. Institutions should therefore consider incorporating mobile-based tasks and assignments into course syllabus.

Peer collaboration and social interaction also emerged as important motivators. To address the feeling of isolation some students experience in mobile learning, universities should promote group-based mobile activities, such as collaborative assignments, discussion forums, or WhatsApp learning circles. These platforms can foster a sense of community and provide opportunities for students to support and learn from one another.

Finally, it is important to address the negative attitudes and misconceptions surrounding mobile learning. Some students view it as less effective or more difficult than traditional classroom learning. Universities should conduct awareness programs, orientation sessions, or student-led workshops to highlight the benefits and practical value of m-learning. By showcasing success stories, providing hands-on demonstrations, and emphasizing the skills students can gain, institutions can build a more positive perception and encourage broader adoption.

By implementing these recommendations, universities in Sri Lanka can create a more inclusive, engaging, and motivating mobile learning environment that better supports undergraduate students' academic success and digital literacy.

Further, future research should address the limitations of this study by employing larger and more diverse samples to enhance generalizability and enable the use of inferential statistical analysis for stronger conclusions. Studies could also differentiate more clearly between mobile-only and multi-platform usage by collecting data on the specific devices students use to access learning materials. Additionally, incorporating mixed-methods approaches would allow for a deeper understanding of how mobile learning uniquely impacts student motivation while quantitatively validating these effects. Investigating technical barriers and contextual factors in greater detail, as well as focusing on platforms designed specifically for mobile use, would provide more nuanced insights to inform effective mobile learning strategies.

References

[1] Barbaux, M.-T. (2006). From lifelong learning to m-learning. *Association for Learning Technology*. 132.

[2] Uzunboylu, H., Bicen, H., & Cavus, N. (2011). The efficient virtual learning environment: a case study of web 2.0 tools and Windows live spaces. *Computers*

and Education, 56(3), 720–726. doi: 10.1016/j.compedu.2010.10.014.

[3] Taleb, Z., Ahmadi, A., & Musavi, M. (2015). The Effect of M-learning on mathematics learning. *Procedia - Social and Behavioral Sciences*, 171, 83–89. doi: 10.1016/j.sbspro.2015.01.092.

[4] Abas, Z. W., Peng, C. L., & Mansor, N. (2009). A study on learner readiness for mobile learning at Open University Malaysia. In Proceedings of the IADIS International Conference Mobile Learning 2009, ML 2009.

[5] Zawacki-Richter, O. (2009). Mobile learning: transforming the delivery of education and training. The International Review of Research in Open and Distributed Learning, 10(4). 1–3. doi: 10.19173/irrodl.v10i4.751.

[6] Bamidele, A., & Aremu, B. V. (2021). The use of mobile learning to improve students' motivation and the achievement of learning outcomes, 175–183. doi: https://www.researchgate.net/publication/360422974.

[7] Koole, M. L. (2009). Mobile learning - a model for framing mobile learning. *Mobile Learning: Transforming the Delivery of Education and Training*, 1(2), 25–47.

[8] Sogunro, O. A. (2014). Motivating factors for adult learners in higher education. *International Journal of Higher Education*, 4(1), 22–37. doi: 10.5430/ijhe.v4n1p22.

[9] Sha, L., Looi, C. K., Chen, W., Seow, P., & Wong, L. H. (2012). Recognizing and measuring self-regulated learning in a mobile learning environment. *Computers in Human Behavior*, 28(2), 718–728. doi: 10.1016/j.chb.2011.11.019.

[10] Harati, H., Yen, C. J., Tu, C. H., Cruickshank, B. J., & Armfield, S. W. J. (2020). Online adaptive learning: a study of score validity of the adaptive self-regulated learning model. *International Journal of Web-Based Learning and Teaching Technologies*, 15(4), 18–35. doi: 10.4018/IJWLTT.2020100102.

[11] Lazowski, R. A., & Hulleman, C. S. (2016). Motivation interventions in education: a meta-analytic review. *Review of Educational Research*, 86(2), 602–640. doi: 10.3102/0034654315617832.

[12] Sengkey, V. G., & Galag, E. H. (2018). Student attitudes and motivation in learning English. Catalyst, 17. 2–6.

[13] Stefaniak, J., Peck, L., Stefaniak, J. E., & Shah, S. J. (2018). IAP PROOFS © 2018 the correlation of self-regulation and motivation with retention and attrition in distance education. Quarterly Review of Distance Education 19.3: 1–80.

[14] Li, L. Y., & Tsai, C. C. (2017). Accessing online learning material: quantitative behavior patterns and their effects on motivation and learning performance. *Computers and Education*, 114, 286–297. doi: 10.1016/j.compedu.2017.07.007.

[15] Ryan, R. M., & Deci, E. L. (2020). Intrinsic and extrinsic motivation from a self-determination theory perspective: definitions, theory, practices, and future directions. *Contemporary Educational Psychology*, 61, 101860. doi: 10.1016/j.cedpsych.2020.101860.

[16] Ucar, H., & Kumtepe, A. T. (2020). Effects of the ARCS-V-based motivational strategies on online learners' academic performance, motivation, volition, and course interest. *Journal of Computer Assisted Learning*, 36(3), 335–349. doi: 10.1111/jcal.12404.

[17] Al-Said, K. (2023). Influence of teacher on student motivation: opportunities to increase motivational factors during mobile learning. *Education and Information Technologies (Dordr)*, 28(10), 13439–13457. doi: 10.1007/s10639-023-11720-w.

[18] Bikowski, D., & Vithanage, R. (2016). Effects of web-based collaborative writing on individual L2 writing development. doi: http://llt.msu. edu/issues/february2016/bikowskivithanage.pdf.

3 A comprehensive study: exploring the underlying causes of mental disorders in children

Vathsala J. Karunanayake[1,a] *and Nipuni Wijesinghe*[2,b]

[1]Department of Information Technology, National Institute of Education, Sri Lanka

[2]Department of Marketing Management, Faculty Management Studies and Commerce, University of Sri Jayewardenepura, Sri Lanka

Abstract

This paper aims to determine factors that lead to mental disorders among children of age between 5 and 19 years using the quantitative research method. Understanding the increasing prevalence of child mental health problems, particularly in Sri Lanka, the study intends to address existing research gaps by examining selected socio-economic, familial and educational factors affecting children's mental health. Collected data for this study have been gathered from the counseling units of the Maharagama Divisional Secretariat during the years 2018 and 2019. The study employed structured questionnaires and quantitative research methods on the responses of children who underwent counseling. In order to find out the significant factors related to mental disorders; 31 cases were analyzed. The findings of the study indicated that sample children with mental disorders had higher likelihood of having experienced parental separation, low family economic status, non-family care living arrangement, inconsistent education and social isolation. Thus, it can be concluded that the treatment and prevention of the causes of mental disorders involve the support of the family, educational systems and the community. This paper concludes by suggesting that there is a need for policymakers as well as child welfare institutions to provide early intervention programs together with continuous monitoring. Finally, this study recommends that future studies should increase the sample size and employ sophisticated quantitative methods in order to create models for predicting child mental health problems, which can be useful in establishing long-term mental health care policies and strategies.

Keywords: Child mental health, family factors, mental disorders, Sri Lanka

Introduction

Background of study

Mental health disorders among children and adolescents have become a growing global concern, with a marked increase in prevalence across both developed and developing nations. These types of disorders are usually emotional, behavioral, cognitive or developmental in nature and they greatly limit a child's happiness, learning and ability to fit in with others. The World Health Organization claims that if mental health problems in children are not treated, they can continue into adulthood and result in ongoing mental, social and economic effects [1].

Childhood mental health matters are gaining significance in Sri Lanka within the field of public health [2] found that many children in residential care institutions in Colombo had trouble managing their emotions and behaviors which was likely due to their limited family support and access to therapy. Furthermore [3], discovered that anxiety disorders are very common among school-aged children (13–15 years) in the Colombo District, showing that this issue is found in both institutionalized and non-institutionalized youth groups.

According to studies worldwide, problems with mental health in children are commonly connected to various risks, including substance use in the family, poor behavior control, experiencing violence and trauma and lacking educational assistance [4, 5]. Moreover, children affected by conflict or poverty tend to be more vulnerable because these circumstances can cause psychological difficulties and hinder their growth and development [6].

[a]vathsalak@nie.edu.lk, [b]nipunitharushika909@gmail.com

DOI: 10.4324/9781003739920-3

Sri Lanka continues to encounter serious difficulties in handling the mental health of its children, despite more awareness. These factors are limited access to treatment, having to face social stigma over mental illness, not having enough mental health professionals and lacking community-based preventive actions [7]. Consequently, thorough studies based on reliable data are immediately needed to explore the socio-environmental and behavioral determinants of mental disorders in children. The research aims to address this gap by examining the role of substance use, behavioral difficulties, environment at home and schooling and then uses these insights to prepare evidence-based strategies that can be applied to Sri Lankan context.

Research problem outline

The growing number of mental health problems in children in Sri Lanka is a major issue for the public health system, education institutions and families. While people are becoming more aware of childhood mental health, not much evidence proves which socio-environmental factors contribute to mental disorders in children [2]. Although studies reveal that unfavorable family conditions, behavioral problems and lack of involvement in education are contributing factors, these aspects are often analyzed individually [3]. A lack of awareness about the links between these influences makes it difficult to design and implement effective strategies to prevent or intervene in this issue [7].

Problem statement

Although there is growing awareness about mental disorders affecting children in Sri Lanka, little research is done to uncover their causes from different angles. While previous research has pointed out specific problems like behavior problems, unstable families and inadequate education [2], less attention has been given to how they all interact to affect children's mental health. In addition, having to cope with socio-economic stressors, exposure to addictive substances and delayed intervention can make these problems worse [4]. Since there is a research gap, it becomes difficult for policymakers, educators and health professionals to create proper, evidence-based strategies to prevent and handle childhood mental disorders [7]. So, it is important to do more research about how behavioral, family and education concerns collectively shape the mental health of children in Sri Lanka.

Significance of the research

Identifying the main causes of mental disorders in children plays a key role in developing good prevention methods which is especially important in Sri Lanka, a country with few mental health resources. This study adds to the field by investigating the collective impact of behavior issues, substance abuse, family influences and education on children's mental health [2]. It gives information that shapes actions needed at both the government and community levels. These findings help guide policies and local actions meant to address the issue. The findings from this study can provide mental health professionals and educators with guidance to find and address anxiety, behavioral issues and emotional stress among these children. In addition, it helps achieve the national goal of child welfare by informing child-focused programs which are consistent with international mental health goals [7]. In the end, this research strengthens the proof for effective sustainable methods in mental health.

Self-location with the research process

Colombo and Maharagama were chosen as the main places for this research to take place. Colombo is the commercial and administrative headquarters of Sri Lanka and shows a wide variety of socio-economic backgrounds. Located in the Colombo District, Maharagama is a residential area where several child counseling and welfare departments are based. They were chosen because they offered organized mental health support and a chance to meet children who are in counseling. Paying attention to these aspects makes it possible for the study to get consistent information about mental health in children living in Sri Lankan urban and semi-urban contexts.

Aims and objectives

Aim

The aim of this research is to explore the underlying causes of mental disorders in children.

Objectives

- To analyze the impact of substance use on the mental disorder status of children.
- To analyze the impact behavioral challenges on disorder status in children.
- To analyze the impact of family environment on the mental disorder status of children.
- To analyze the impact educational involvement on mental disorder status in children.

Materials and Methodology

Materials

Data was mainly collected through the use of structured questionnaires. To develop the questionnaire, existing studies on mental disorders in children were reviewed and sections focused on substance use, behavior problems, family dynamics and learning were added. The questionnaire featured both closed-ended questions and scaled questions so that results could be measured consistently. The design made sure that the study met its objectives and analyzed the main causes of mental disorders in children between the ages of 5 and 19 in Sri Lanka.

Data was taken from counseling units located in the Maharagama Divisional Secretariat serving children who had earlier benefited from mental health care. It was important to ensure all children had the same chance to be chosen, so a simple random sampling method was applied to reduce selection bias and improve how well the study results represent the target population [8].

All questionnaire data were processed and analyzed with the software SPSS (Statistical Package for the Social Sciences). It was decided to use SPSS because it allows researchers to handle large amounts of data and run a variety of statistical tests, making it ideal for work in psychology and social science [9]. To find out how independent variables are connected to the mental disorder status of children, descriptive statistics, correlation analyses and regression techniques were applied.

In total, 31 valid responses were included in the final analysis, representing all children who went through counseling while data were collected. Everyone involved in the study was treated according to ethical guidelines and their anonymity was safeguarded.

The research methodology followed the structured approach provided by Saunders' Research Onion Model (Figure 3.1) [10]. This is a six-layered conceptual framework in research methodology that was developed by Saunders to help in researching the right approach to a given study. The model is organized in layers, like an onion that was presented by Saunders, Lewis, and Thornhill in 2019. Research scholars follow such a manner systematically so that they can design and conduct the research properly.

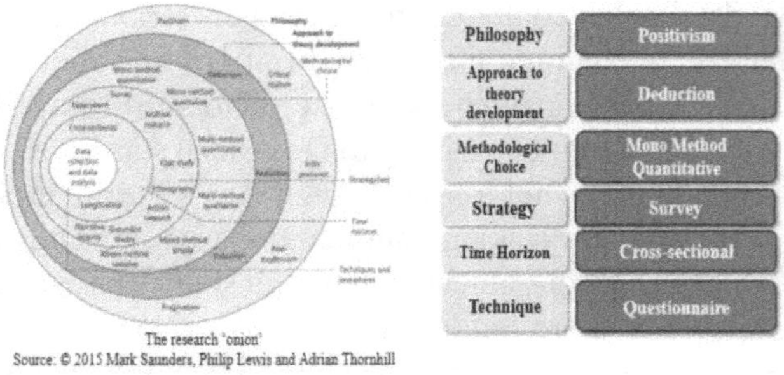

Figure 3.1 The research onion framework
Source: Author

Research philosophy: positivism

For this study, a positive approach was used, based on the belief that reality is objective and can be analyzed through collecting data and carrying out statistics. Studies interested in finding links between variables can use positivism when the data are quantifiable and can be measured statistically [10]. It supports researchers in coming to conclusions through useful facts which helps find main factors affecting mental disorders in children.

Research approach: deductive

This research used a deductive approach, starting by looking at general theories about child mental health and then creating specific hypotheses that could be tested with the collected data. This process is most effective when the study involves testing hypotheses using theories and empirical data [12].

Research strategy: survey

The choice of the survey strategy came from the efficiency it provides in collecting identical information from many people within a short period. Understanding trends in mental health and related social factors is made easier with questionnaires [13]. The survey helped identify how mental disorders in children might be influenced by behavioral, educational, family-related and substance factors.

Methodological choice: mono method quantitative

The research employed a mono method quantitative design, concentrating on collecting and analyzing numerical data. Since it is objective and can be used to generalize across similar populations, quantitative research was used for this study [11]. It allowed

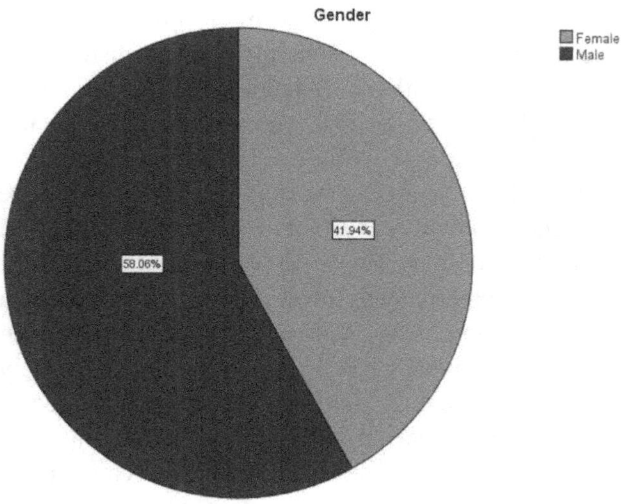

Figure 3.2 Gender analysis
Source: Author

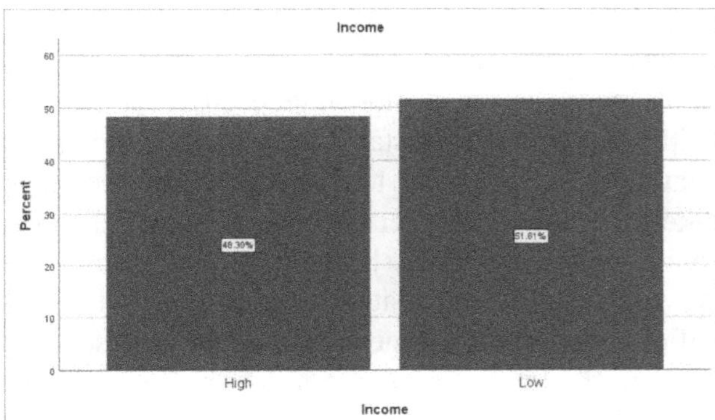

Figure 3.3 Income analysis
Source: Author

researchers to document the impact each independent factor had on the mental disorder of participants.

Time horizon: cross-sectional
The study was done with a cross-sectional time horizon which means that data were gathered in one time period. Such is frequently used in social science where the focus is to describe the current situation for a phenomenon like a person's mental health status, not to follow it over time. It proved helpful for examining the instant relationships among the selected variables present in the counseling dataset.

Sampling technique: simple random sampling
Each child in the counseling database had a fair possibility of being picked through a simple random sampling process. Applying this method helps prevent bias and makes sure the findings are based on solid statistics [8]. Counselors randomly chose respondents from a list of children who received counseling in the years 2018 and 2019 through a computerized system.

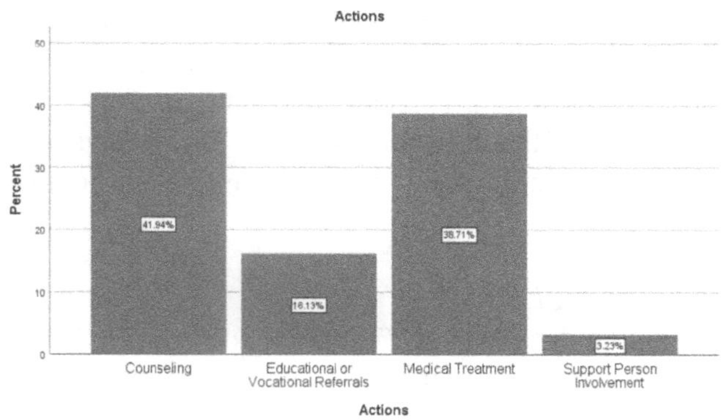

Figure 3.4 Actions taken analysis
Source: Author

Data collection and analysis
Participants took the survey in person, and their answers were recorded safely. Following collection, the data were then coded and added to SPSS for analysis. The program was used to calculate data such as how often certain things occurred (in descriptive statistics), the strength and statistical significance of correlations (inferential statistics) and to study how powerful the relationships were between the chosen independent variables (variables such as family environment or educational involvement) and the dependent variable (mental disorder status).

Overall, this methodological design ensured a rigorous, transparent, and replicable research process. With the help of Saunders' research onion and a well-structured quantitative approach, the study created findings that could direct improvements in the mental health of children.

Results and Discussion

Sample collection
Data for this study were collected from 31 children aged between 5 and 19 years who had received counseling services at the Maharagama Divisional Secretariat between 2018 and 2019. By using simple random sampling, every eligible child got the same opportunity to be chosen which increased the sample's representativeness and decreased the likelihood of selection bias [8]. The researchers used set questionnaires to gather important information about

the group's demographics as well as factors like substance use, behavioral challenges, home environment and school involvement. Strict guidelines were followed in the collection stage to ensure that both privacy and child safety were guaranteed throughout the study.

Sample analysis

Demographic Analysis (Table 3.1)

The sample consisted of 18 males (58.1%) and 13 females (41.9%). This indicates that a slightly higher number of boys were identified with mental disorder-related concerns. Gender distribution suggests the need to examine gender-specific causes and intervention strategies.

Among the children, 16 (51.6%) came from low-income backgrounds, while 15 (48.4%) were from high-income families. The near-equal distribution highlights that mental health issues affect children across economic levels, though slightly more are from financially constrained households, indicating potential socioeconomic stressors as contributing factors.

Counseling was the most common response, provided to 13 children (41.9%), followed by medical treatment (38.7%). Educational or vocational referrals were given to 5 children (16.1%), and only 1 case (3.2%) involved support person intervention. This emphasizes the reliance on psychological and medical solutions over holistic or family-based support.

The descriptive statistics (Table 3.2) reveal varying levels of influence across the four independent variables on mental disorder status. Substance use has a low mean (0.10), indicating it was present in few cases, but its high skewness (2.868) and kurtosis (6.654) suggest a positively skewed distribution with extreme outliers. Behavioral challenges, with the highest mean (0.52), were the most frequently observed factor, showing a relatively normal distribution. Family environment issues had a moderate presence (mean = 0.23) and a positively skewed distribution (skewness = 1.379), implying that most children experienced fewer family issues, with a few extreme cases. Educational involvement problems had a mean of 0.16 and were also positively skewed, indicating limited but impactful occurrences. The mental disorder status itself had a mean of 2.10, suggesting most children were categorized in moderate disorder types, with a near-normal distribution. Overall, behavioral challenges appear most common, while substance use and education-related problems are less frequent but skewed toward isolated high cases.

The correlation analysis (Table 3.3) reveals that substance use has a moderate positive correlation with mental disorder status (r = 0.503), indicating that children exposed to substance use are more likely to exhibit higher levels of mental disorder symptoms. Conversely, behavioral challenges show a weak negative correlation (r = -0.170) with mental disorder status, suggesting a slight inverse association, though not strong. Family environment and educational involvement show very weak correlations (r = 0.042 and r = -0.221, respectively), indicating limited direct relationship with mental disorder severity in this dataset. Interestingly, behavioral challenges are strongly negatively correlated with family environment (r = -0.558) and educational

Table 3.1 Demographic analysis.

Variable	Category	Frequency (N)	Percent (%)	Cumulative percent (%)
Gender	Female	13	41.9%	41.9%
	Male	18	58.1%	100.0%
Income	High	15	48.4%	48.4%
	Low	16	51.6%	100.0%
Actions taken	Counseling	13	41.9%	41.9%
	Educational or Vocational Referrals	5	16.1%	58.1%
	Medical Treatment	12	38.7%	96.8%
	Support Person Involvement	1	3.2%	100.0%

Source: Author

involvement (r = -0.453), implying that poorer family or educational support is linked to more behavioral issues. The correlation between substance use and behavioral challenges is moderately negative (r = -0.338), possibly reflecting that these issues may not co-occur as frequently in this sample. Overall, substance use emerges as the most significant factor positively linked to mental disorder status.

The Chi-square analysis provides critical insights into the factors associated with mental disorders in children. The results indicate that substance use ($\chi^2 = 11.388$, $p = 0.003$), behavioral challenges ($\chi^2 = 7.747$, $p = 0.021$), and educational involvement ($\chi^2 = 14.895$, $p = 0.001$) are all statistically significant contributors to children's mental disorder status. This means these factors are meaningfully associated with the type or severity of mental health issues observed. In contrast, family environment ($\chi^2 = 2.072$, $p = 0.355$) was not statistically significant, suggesting that in this dataset, family-related issues were not strongly linked to mental disorder outcomes. The overall chi-square test combining all factors was highly significant ($\chi^2 = 28.131$, $p = 0.000$), reinforcing that multiple variables together strongly influence the development of mental health disorders in children. These findings align with the study's objective of exploring the underlying causes and highlight the urgent need to address substance exposure, behavioral issues, and educational support in child mental health interventions.

Hypothesis testing (Table 3.4)

Conclusion

Objective 1: To analyze the association of substance, use on the mental disorder status of children.

The analysis revealed that substance use is connected to having a mental disorder in children ($\chi^2 = 11.388$, $p = 0.003$), meaning children at risk for substances often have severe mental health problems. The same idea is supported in literature from all over the world, where being exposed to drugs causes mental and emotional issues in young people [4, 6]. According to WHO [1], early contact with drugs can worsen anxiety and behavior problems. Unlike Mojtabai et al. [14], who found an increase in mental health treatment among young children living in institutions, this study only looked at a small, local area in Sri Lanka and thus may not represent such trends on a large scale.

Table 3.2 Descriptive statistics.

Variable	N	Mean	Std. Deviation	Variance	Skewness	Kurtosis
Substance Use	31	0.10	0.301	0.090	2.868	6.654
Behavioral Challenges	31	0.52	0.508	0.258	-0.068	-2.138
Family Environment	31	0.23	0.425	0.181	1.379	-0.109
Educational Involvement	31	0.16	0.374	0.140	1.937	1.868
Mental Disorder Status	31	2.10	0.597	0.357	-0.023	0.014

Source: Author

Table 3.3 Correlation analysis.

	Substance use	Behavioral challenges	Family Environment	Educational involvement	Mental disorder status
Substance use	1				
Behavioral challenges	-0.338	1			
Family environment	-0.177	-0.558	1		
Educational Involvement	-0.144	*-0.453*	-0.237	1	
Mental disorder status	0.503	-0.170	0.042	-0.221	1

Source: Author

Table 3.4 Hypothesis testing.

Objective	H_0 (Null Hypothesis)	H_1 (Alternative Hypothesis)	Chi-Square Value	df	p-value	Decision	Conclusion
To examine the impact of substance use	There is no association between substance use and mental disorder status in Children.	There is a significant association between substance use and mental disorder status in Children.	11.388	2	0.003	Reject H_0	Substance use significantly affects mental disorder status in Children.
To assess behavioral challenges	There is no association between behavioral challenges and mental disorder status in Children.	There is a significant association between behavioral challenges and mental disorder status in Children.	7.747	2	0.021	Reject H_0	Behavioral challenges significantly affect mental disorder status in Children.
To evaluate family environment influence	There is no association between family environment and mental disorder status in Children.	There is a significant association between family environment and mental disorder status in Children.	2.072	2	0.355	Fail to Reject H_0	No significant effect of family environment on mental disorder status in Children.
To analyze educational involvement	There is no association between educational involvement and mental disorder status in Children.	There is a significant association between educational involvement and mental disorder status in Children.	14.895	2	0.001	Reject H_0	Educational involvement significantly affects mental disorder status in Children.
To examine overall factor contribution	There is no combined effect of all factors on mental disorder status in Children.	There is a significant combined effect of all factors on mental disorder status in Children.	28.131	6	0.000	Reject H_0	All factors together have a highly significant effect on mental disorder status in Children.

Source: Author

Objective 2: To analyze the association of behavioral challenges on mental disorder status in children.

The analysis found that there is a strong link between behavioral challenges and mental disorder status ($\chi^2 = 7.747$, $p = 0.021$). This corroborates the conclusions of Rohanachandra et al. [2] regarding the high rate of emotional and behavioral problems among children living in institutions in Colombo. Similarly, De Silva et al. [3] noticed that certain behaviors in children were related to their higher risk of anxiety disorders. These outcomes show that issues with behavioral regulation often signal the beginning of mental health problems and are noticed worldwide [7]. Unlike the way ADHD is often studied internationally, this study combines several behavioral characteristics into one description that fits the way these disorders are diagnosed locally.

Objective 3: To analyze the association of family environment on the mental disorder status of children.

Despite the hypothesis, there was not a significant relationship identified between the family environment and the state of mental disorders ($\chi^2 = 2.072$, $p = 0.355$). This contrasts with Ganie et al. [6] and Otorkpa et al. [8], who say that disrupted caregiving and issues within the household are key reasons for these challenges. The difference may happen since some family matters are not fully considered or accurately reflected in this data or perhaps because the number of participants is limited. In addition, institutions and schools in Sri Lanka may give top priority to what children do at school and how they behave, rather than considering the conditions at home [2].

Objective 4: To analyze the association of educational involvement on mental disorder status in children.

The analysis revealed that mental disorder status is related to how involved someone is in education ($\chi^2 = 14.895$, $p = 0.001$). De Silva et al. [2] demonstrated that academic results, chances of dropping out of school and anxiety disorders are strongly associated among adolescents, a finding confirmed by this study. The results in this study are also supported by Depaoli et al. [12], who found that stress in school and underdeveloped thinking skills raise people's risk of psychological distress. Lim [11] also states that education is rarely looked at in detail in quantitative mental health research which makes this study's inclusion of education as a predictor important for the field.

Limitations of the research

It is important to acknowledge the limitations of this study. The research's sample size (n = 31) is relatively small, which makes it hard to apply the findings to a larger group. In addition, because cross-sectional research does not follow individuals over time, it makes it difficult to show a cause-and-effect relationship between the variables and mental disorder status. The research did not fully examine important influences such as a person's background, their exposure to stressful events or their genetic makeup. Besides, depending on institutions' archive and self-provided data brings a risk of bias, where information about sensitive concerns such as substance abuse and family issues, might not be given accurately. The accuracy of responses might have also been affected by social desirability and recall bias. Furthermore, several statistical findings were influenced by the problem of low cell frequency which could affect the reliability of some results and make further analysis difficult.

Contribution to knowledge

This analysis helps to expand the understanding of child mental health by adding real-life evidence from Sri Lanka which is seldom featured in global mental health research. The study points out that key factors such as substance use, bad behavior and low education, are primary causes of mental health problems among children. As a result of these findings, teachers, mental health caregivers and politicians may better understand early detection strategies. In addition, the results stress that local programs should be designed by bringing together both the educational and health sectors. Because the research concentrates on local information, it helps identify mental health problems unique to the region and supports designing programs that fit the culture and needs of vulnerable children.

Suggestions for future research

It would be beneficial to conduct future studies using a diverse group produced by multiple districts so more generalizable results can be found. More studies are needed to understand the links between social and psychological aspects and mental health over the years. Including qualitative interviews with both children and caregivers could reveal further details about contextual factors such as emotional abuse or stigma. Introducing physical and neurological assessments could bring together the signs of behavior and biological changes in children with different mental disorders.

Recommendations

Implement school-based mental health screenings

Since educational involvement often relates to mental disorders, schools ought to regularly look for learning difficulties, exam stress and troubled emotions through psychological assessments.

Strengthen substance abuse prevention programs

Since mental health problems are strongly linked to substance use, extra attention and time should be given through workshops, counseling and access to rehabilitation to at-risk youth in low-income communities.

Integrate behavioral therapy into child welfare services
Mental health difficulties were strongly linked to issues with behavior. Child psychologists should be included in each institution and divisional secretariats to give CBT and other programs for support.

Develop multi-sectoral collaboration
For mental health interventions to succeed, they should bring together health, education and social service professionals. Using a common system for referring patients would speed up support and cut down on the separation of services.

Promote mental health literacy among parents and guardians
Family background was not found to be important, but sharing parenting tips, improving family communication and noticing any potential distress in youngsters can help their emotional well-being.

References

[1] WHO (2024). Mental Health of Adolescents. World Health Organization. https://www.who.int/newsroom/fact-sheets/detail/adolescent-mental-health.

[2] Rohanachandra, Y. M., Nanayakkara, K. A. S. D., & Vipulanandan, S. (2022). Emotional and behavioral problems among children and adolescents in a residential care institution in Colombo, Sri Lanka – Implications for service delivery. *Asian Journal of Psychiatry*, 74, 103193. doi: https://doi.org/10.1016/j.ajp.2022.103193.

[3] De Silva, S., Peris, R., Senaviratne, S., & Samaranayake, D. (2024). Effectiveness of a cognitive behavioural therapy (CBT)-based intervention for reducing anxiety among adolescents in the Colombo District, Sri Lanka: cluster randomized controlled trial. *Child and Adolescent Psychiatry and Mental Health*, 18(1), 108. doi: https://doi.org/10.1186/s13034-024-00799-9.

[4] Otorkpa, C., Otorkpa, O. J., Olaniyan, O. E., & Adebola, O. A. (2024). Mental health issues of children and young people displaced by conflict: a scoping review. *PLOS Mental Health*, 1(6), e0000076. doi: https://doi.org/10.1371/journal.pmen.0000076.

[5] Mojtabai, R., & Olfson, M. (2024). Trends in mental disorders in children and adolescents receiving treatment in the state mental health system. *Journal of the American Academy of Child and Adolescent Psychiatry*, 64(8), 906–920. doi: https://doi.org/10.1016/j.jaac.2024.08.008.

[6] Ganie, A. U. R., Thirumoorthy, A., Jangam, K. V., & John Vijay Sagar, K. (2025). Exploring psychosocial factors in the functional recovery of children with severe mental disorders: a qualitative content analysis. *Clinical Child Psychology and Psychiatry*, 30(1), 95–115. doi: https://doi.org/10.1177/13591045241286106.

[7] Tai, Y. (2024). Analysis of the current status of children's mental health. In SHS Web of Conferences, (Vol. 199, p. 02023). doi: https://doi.org/10.1051/shsconf/202419902023.

[8] S. Noor, O. Tajik, and J. Golzar, "Simple Random Sampling," *International Journal of Education & Language Studies,* vol. 1, no. 2, pp. 78–82, Dec. 2022, doi: https://doi.org/10.22034/ijels.2022.162982.

[9] A. Rahman and G. Muktadir, "SPSS: An Imperative Quantitative Data Analysis Tool for Social Science Research," *International Journal of Research and Innovation in Social Science,* vol. 05, no. 10, pp. 300–302, 2021, doi: http://dx.doi.org/10.47772/IJRISS.2021.51012.

[10] M. Saunders, P. Lewis, and A. Thornhill, *Research Methods for Business Students,* 9th ed. Pearson, 2023.

[11] W. M. Lim, "What is quantitative research? An overview and guidelines," *Australasian Marketing Journal (AMJ),* vol. 1, no. 1, 2024, doi: https://doi.org/10.1177/14413582241264622.

[12] Depaoli, S., Agtarap, S., Choi, A. Y., Coburn, K. M., & Yu, J. (2018). Advances in quantitative research within the psychological sciences. *Translational Issues in Psychological Science*, 4(4), 335–339. doi: https://doi.org/10.1037/tps0000183.

[13] Singh, S., & Sagar, R. (2021). A critical look at online survey or questionnaire-based research studies during COVID-19. *Asian Journal of Psychiatry*, 65, 102850. doi: https://doi.org/10.1016/j.ajp.2021.102850.

[14] R. Mojtabai and M. Olfson, "Trends in Mental Disorders in Children and Adolescents Receiving Treatment in the State Mental Health System," *Journal of the American Academy of Child & Adolescent Psychiatry,* vol. 64, no. 8, pp. 906–920, Aug. 2025. doi:10.1016/j.jaac.2024.08.008.

4 Exploring the impact of perceived digital infrastructure on the work satisfaction of digital nomads in Sri Lanka

Dakshini Ganepola[1,a] *and Rasika Ranaweera*[2,b]

[1]Faculty of Postgraduate Studies and Professional Advancement, NSBM Green University, Homagama, Sri Lanka

[2]Faculty of Computing, NSBM Green University, Homagama, Sri Lanka

Abstract

Digital nomadism is a lifestyle of workers who use the internet and digital technologies to work remotely while traveling or living in different locations without being tied to a fixed office. It promotes a new category of professionals that need a robust digital infrastructure to support their work remotely. As Sri Lanka seeks to market itself as a potential hotspot for these workers, it becomes imperative to investigate their perceptions regarding the country's digital infrastructure and its impact on their work satisfaction. The purpose of this research is to assess the perception of digital infrastructure and the work satisfaction of digital nomads in Sri Lanka. The study took a qualitative form and carried out semi-structured interviews with digital nomads residing and working in different parts of the country. Thematic analysis was used to reveal patterns regarding the availability of, and the access to, an infrastructure, co-working spaces, and ICT services as well as other barriers to servicing. There are hopes that this research will be of value to some stakeholders, especially policymakers and tourism authorities and providers of digital services, so that these experts implement plans aimed at increasing the attractiveness of Sri Lanka among the users of remote work services. This research intends to assist the country in transforming its digital ecosystem to suit contemporary requirements of remotely working professionals.

Keywords: Digital infrastructure, digital nomads, remote work, work satisfaction

Introduction

Digital nomads are individuals who embrace a location-independent lifestyle, leveraging technology to perform their work remotely while traveling and exploring different parts of the world [1, 2]. The ascendance of digital nomadism represents a profound shift in the global understanding of work, lifestyle, and mobility, challenging conventional paradigms of employment and geographical constraints [1]. Digital nomads, can also be characterized by their tech-enabled lifestyle that transcends the geographical constraints, blend remote work with travel, leveraging digital technologies to work from various locations with reliable internet access [3]. The phenomenon of digital nomadism has garnered increasing attention in recent years, emerging as a significant trend that is reshaping the landscape of work and travel. This growing movement has also influenced tourism patterns, driven changes in urban development, and led to the emergence of specialized services and infrastructure designed to meet the unique needs of this mobile demographic [2, 3].

Enabled by the proliferation of digital technologies and the increasing feasibility of remote work, digital nomads are individuals who leverage technology to perform their work from various locations all around the world, often prioritizing travel and mainly the location independence [2]. The digital infrastructure encompasses the availability, affordability, and consistency of internet connectivity, mobile networks, and other technological resources crucial for enabling seamless remote work [4]. Sri Lanka, with its attractive tropical climate, cultural richness, and relatively low cost of living, has emerged as an increasingly popular destination for digital nomads who are seeking a blend of both work and leisure [5]. The viability and attractiveness of Sri Lanka as a digital nomad hub are very intrinsically linked to the quality and the reliability of its digital infrastructure.

The growing popularity of digital nomadism has prompted a need for deeper understanding of the factors that contribute to the success and satisfaction of these remote workers. Then the increasing prevalence of digital nomadism, also marks a significant transformation in the way which the individuals

[a]adrganepola@students.nsbm.ac.lk, [b]ranaweera.r@nsbm.ac.lk

DOI: 10.4324/9781003739920-4

approach work, lifestyle, and their travel [6]. This transformation is being propelled mainly by technological advancements, particularly in the realm of digital infrastructure, which enables seamless remote work and global connectivity. The viability and attractiveness of Sri Lanka as a digital nomad hub are intrinsically linked to the quality and reliability of its digital infrastructure.

The research delves into the nuanced relationship between digital nomads' perceptions of digital infrastructure in Sri Lanka and their overall work satisfaction, recognizing that these perceptions significantly influence their experiences and choices.

Background on digital nomadism in Sri Lanka
Sri Lanka's allure of being a destination fit for digital nomads is multifaceted, which will be encompassing not only its natural beauty and cultural heritage, but also the growing awareness of the need for robust digital infrastructure island wide. The nomad lifestyle represents a balanced convergence of work and leisure, which is then also enabled by technological advancements that facilitate the remote work and global connectivity [2].

Research aim and objectives
This research seeks to comprehensively investigate the impact of perceived digital infrastructure on the work satisfaction of digital nomads in Sri Lanka. It also aims to understand the multifaceted ways in which digital nomads in Sri Lanka perceive the availability, reliability, and also the quality of the country's digital infrastructure, and to ascertain how these perceptions subsequently influence their overall work satisfaction. The research is driven by the need to understand the specific challenges and opportunities faced by digital nomads in Sri Lanka, particularly in relation to digital infrastructure.

Many sources of information regarding digital nomads come from online blogs, interviews, and newspapers rather than academic papers [7]. The study also seeks to address a critical gap in existing literature by providing empirical insights into the specific challenges and opportunities that are being encountered by digital nomads in a developing country context. The study is also being grounded in the recognition that digital infrastructure is a foundational enabler of digital nomadism, which will be facilitating seamless connectivity, communication, and access to global networks that are essential for remote work [6]. The authors also seek to address a gap in the existing literature by focusing specifically on the experiences of digital nomads in Sri Lanka and their perceptions of the country's digital infrastructure.

Research problem and specific research questions
Despite the growing interest in digital nomadism, there is a lack of research specifically focused on the experiences of digital nomads in Sri Lanka compared to others.

- What are the perceptions of digital nomads in Sri Lanka regarding the availability, reliability, and quality of digital infrastructure?
- How does the perceived digital infrastructure influence the work satisfaction of digital nomads in Sri Lanka?
- Are there specific aspects of digital infrastructure that are particularly important to the work satisfaction of digital nomads in Sri Lanka?

Literature Review

Digital nomads, driven by societal changes such as increased mobility, technological ubiquity, and flexible employment, navigates a lifestyle marked by both its own opportunities and set of challenges [2]. Furthermore, the digital nomad lifestyle is also mainly characterized by the integration of work and travel, enabled by technological advancements.

Role of digital infrastructure in remote work settings
Digital infrastructure serves as the foundational bedrock upon which all the remote work arrangements are being constructed, wielding substantial influence over the efficacy and overall contentment which is being experienced by digital nomads [3]. In addition to be served as a mere facilitator, the quality and the resilience of digital infrastructure significantly shapes the productivity levels, perceived work satisfaction, and also the holistic experiences of digital nomads, thereby exerting considerable influence on their locational preferences and migratory patterns [6].

Beyond the realm of mere connectivity, the ambit of digital infrastructure encompasses an intricate web of digital services, encompassing secure online payment gateways, dependable cloud storage solutions, and robust cybersecurity protocols, all of which are very indispensable for digital nomads to manage their financial affairs, safeguard their sensitive data, and to even conduct their professional endeavors with confidence and security. The importance of digital infrastructure extends beyond mere accessibility; it encompasses the resilience and redundancy of the network, ensuring uninterrupted connectivity even in the face of any unforeseen disruptions such as natural disasters or technical malfunctions [2]. This necessitates investments in backup power systems, redundant internet connections, and geographically diverse data storage facilities to minimize the downtime and to maintain business continuity for digital nomads who rely on these services for their livelihoods.

Theoretical framework or models related to work satisfaction and technology acceptance

Several theoretical frameworks and models offer valuable insights into the relationship between work satisfaction and technology acceptance, providing a lens through which to examine the experiences of digital nomads.

"Technology acceptance model," states that the perceived usefulness and perceived ease of use of a technology are the primary determinants of its acceptance and adoption [8]. Which suggests that if digital nomads perceive digital infrastructure as useful for their work and also becomes easy to use, they are more likely to be satisfied with their work and the overall digital nomad experience.

The "job characteristics model" emphasizes the importance of skill variety, task identity, task significance, autonomy, and feedback in shaping job satisfaction. Because, once the digital infrastructure enables digital nomads to experience these job characteristics, they are more likely to be satisfied with their work.

The "expectation confirmation theory" can suggest that the satisfaction is determined by the extent to which expectations are confirmed or disconfirmed. So, if digital nomads' expectations regarding the availability, reliability, and the quality of digital infrastructure are met or exceeded, they are more likely to be satisfied.

Organizational support theory highlights the significance of an individual's perception concerning the degree to which an organization values their contributions and cares about their well-being [9]. Where social support can be linked to reducing the impact of stressors that may occur at work [10]. Because, then workers perceive that they are supported by their organizations, which makes them feel more obligated to help the organization to achieve its goals [11].

Methodology

The research methodology employed in this study is rooted in an interpretivist philosophy, which emphasizes the subjective and context-dependent nature of human experiences and its meanings. Therefore, this philosophical stance recognizes that individuals construct their own understanding of reality based on their unique perspectives, values, and their social interactions. Therefore, the research seeks to explore both the lived experiences and the current experiences of digital nomads in Sri Lanka to understand how they perceive and interpret the availability, reliability, and the quality of digital infrastructure.

Given the exploratory nature of the research question and the desire to gain in-depth insights into the experiences of digital nomads, a qualitative research approach was deemed most appropriate. Qualitative research methods are particularly well-suited for exploring complex social phenomena, understanding individual perspectives, and generating rich, descriptive data [12]. The study was initially designed to incorporate semi-structured interviews with 10–15 digital nomads in Sri Lanka. This method would have allowed for flexibility in data collection and would have made it easier to explore emerging themes and ideas. However, due to many unforeseen circumstances, including the low response rates and mainly the off-season nature of the data collection period, the number of interviews conducted was very limited. The primary data collection method involved participant observation at Outpost Weligama, a well-known co-working and co-living space that caters specifically to digital nomads.

As participants themselves, authors also immersed in the daily routines and social interactions of the digital nomad community, observing their work habits, communication patterns, and experiences with the local digital infrastructure with a very limited timeframe. During this period, field journals were maintained which was helpful in documenting the observations, reflections, and informal conversations with digital nomads. This firsthand experience itself allowed the authors a deeper understanding of the challenges and opportunities faced by digital nomads in Sri Lanka, as well as the impact of digital infrastructure on their work satisfaction and overall well-being for them.

The study's reliance on observational data and limited interview data presents certain limitations that should be acknowledged. The small sample size of five may limit the generalizability of the findings to the broader population of digital nomads in Sri Lanka. However, the depth of the observational data and the researcher's firsthand experience as a digital nomad provide valuable insights into the lived realities of this unique population. Furthermore, researchers may encounter difficulties during data collection [13]. For example, one study faced challenges because there were only a few Global South expatriates known, but the researcher still felt confident that the exploratory study had reached saturation [14].

In conducting this research, ethical considerations were carefully addressed to ensure the privacy, confidentiality, and well-being of all participants. Informed consent was obtained from all digital nomads who participated in informal conversations, and their identities were protected by using pseudonyms in the research report.

Findings and Analysis

Outpost Weligama, being the primary site of observation for this study due to many physical limitations and time crunch, serves as a microcosm of the digital nomad lifestyle in Sri Lanka. This co-working and co-living space attracts digital nomads from all over the world, drawn by its stunning beachfront location, vibrant community, and promise of a productive and fulfilling work-life balance.

The authors' observations were gathered at Outpost Weligama revealed a complex interplay between the allure of the location and the realities of the local digital infrastructure. Digital nomads were observed actively using social media applications like TikTok[a] and Instagram[b]; to share their experiences, promote the location, and communicate with the global digital nomad community which is the most crucial and noticeable part.

While the space offers a range of amenities, including comfortable workstations, high-speed internet, and communal areas, along with their own café/restaurant; the reliability and quality of the digital infrastructure emerged as a recurring concern among the digital nomads. Many digital nomads expressed frustration with the frequent internet outages, slow download speeds, and limited bandwidth, which often disrupted their work and hindered their ability to meet deadlines. These findings corroborate that there can be negative impacts and risks attached along with them to the remote working; such as the work overload and pressures that comes along to perform them on time [15].

"During periods of peak usage, such as every afternoon, weekday's mainly. The internet connection would often become congested, making it difficult to participate in video conferences, upload large files, or even browse the web effectively."

Several digital nomads reported having to adjust their work schedules to accommodate the unreliable internet, working during off-peak hours or seeking out alternative internet sources, such as mobile hotspots or moving to local cafes which didn't make the issue any lesser.

The digital infrastructure challenges encountered at Outpost Weligama in the past had had a direct impact on the work satisfaction of the digital nomads. Many had reported feeling stressed, frustrated, and unproductive when the internet was unreliable, which led to decreased motivation and overall job satisfaction. Despite the challenges posed by the digital infrastructure, the digital nomads at Outpost Weligama demonstrated a remarkable degree of adaptability and resilience. They actively sought out solutions to mitigate the impact of internet outages, such as using offline work tools, collaborating on projects in person, and developing backup plans for critical tasks and their latest addition was to have multiple connection lines where they were able to group all the nomads and evenly distribute a strong connection for them to continue with their work seamlessly.

Furthermore, the strong sense of community at Outpost Weligama provided a very valuable source of support and encouragement. Digital nomads often shared tips and tricks for navigating the local digital infrastructure, offered assistance with technical issues, and provided emotional support during times of frustration when they had their weekly meetups or during their random chit chats.

The communal spaces facilitated impromptu knowledge sharing and problem-solving sessions,

[a]https://www.tiktok.com/en/

[b]https://www.instagram.com/

where digital nomads could exchange ideas, troubleshoot all technical issues, and learn from each other's experiences which is a great opportunity one can have. This was also something they had continually each Tuesday morning in their communal space where they even offered free Food & Beverage for all participants.

One of the most striking observations from Outpost Weligama was the importance of social interaction and community for digital nomads, and Outpost stood out with the multiple activities they host on premises for both co-working and co-living individuals which included:

- Morning yoga sessions
- Wednesday Sri Lankan buffet at the rooftop
- Other informative sessions
- Surfing lessons
- Weekly movie nights

The co-working and co-living environment fostered a sense of belonging and camaraderie even though there was only a handful during my visit, which in a way helped the authors to buffer the negative effects of unreliable situations. The nomads have been actively participating in social events, group activities, and informal gatherings, which provided opportunities for networking, collaboration, and emotional support according to the management at Outpost Weligama. This is increasingly important, given that people are working in these locations far away from their physical office buildings or home base, requiring them to be able to carry out productive work in less-than-optimal environments [16].

The digital nomads at Outpost Weligama also leveraged their online networks to stay connected with colleagues, clients, and friends back home. They actively participated in online communities, forums, and social media groups, which provided a sense of connection and belonging, even when they were physically separated from their traditional support networks and even after their stay in Sri Lanka. The combination of both physical and virtual social interactions helped immensely to create a sense of community and counteract the common feelings of isolation and loneliness that can sometimes accompany the digital nomad lifestyle.

In addition to the observational insights from Outpost Weligama, this study also draws upon the researcher's firsthand experiences as a "Remote Worker" in Sri Lanka. During the period of data collection, the authors immersed themselves in the digital nomad lifestyle, living and working in Weligama. This was increasingly important, given that people were working in locations far from their physical office buildings or home bases, requiring them to be able to carry out productive work in less-than-optimal environments. The authors experiences as remote workers in Sri Lanka provided valuable insights into the challenges and opportunities of working remotely in a developing country like Sri Lanka.

The authors encountered firsthand the frustrations of unreliable internet, power outages, and limited access to digital resources, with the constant power outages for long hours and also the difficulties faced during the recent economic crisis. They also had the chance to witness the resilience, adaptability, and the resourcefulness of the local digital nomad community in Sri Lanka as well.

Observational Insights from outpost Weligama

Outpost Weligama, a well-known co-working and co-living hub, served as the primary location for observation during the research period. The insights gathered from this location offered me a very valuable understanding of the digital nomad experience in Sri Lanka. The facilities are designed to cater to the specific needs of digital nomads, providing a comfortable and productive work environment, incorporating comfortable workstations, reliable Wi-Fi, and communal spaces for collaboration and networking along with their own café/restaurant.

The reliability of Wi-Fi has emerged as a critical factor influencing the work satisfaction of digital nomads. During the past, where the Wi-Fi connectivity at Outpost Weligama experienced fluctuations, with occasional outages and slow speeds during peak hours. These disruptions impacted the productivity and overall satisfaction of digital nomads, causing frustration and mainly hindering their ability to meet their deadlines.

The work conditions at Outpost Weligama were generally conducive to productivity, with a quiet and focused atmosphere during work hours. Lack of privacy in the communal workspaces was a concern for some digital nomads, particularly those who required confidential or focused work environments.

The community aspect of Outpost Weligama played a significant role in the overall satisfaction of digital nomads. The hub fostered a sense of belonging and connection among its members, organizing social events, workshops, and networking opportunities to facilitate interaction and collaboration which were scattered throughout the week keeping the community thriving.

The opportunity to connect with like-minded individuals from diverse backgrounds was highly valued by digital nomads, providing them with a support system they very much needs, a source of inspiration, and a sense of community as well.

"*The social interaction between the nomads in co-living increases knowledge sharing and reduces loneliness of everyone.*"

The general satisfaction levels among digital nomads at Outpost Weligama were influenced by various factors, including the quality of facilities, the reliability of Wi-Fi, the work conditions, quality of food, affordability and the community atmosphere mainly. While the majority of digital nomads expressed satisfaction with their overall experience, there were also concerns raised at the same time.

Perceptions

Digital nomads' perceptions of the digital infrastructure significantly impact their work satisfaction and overall experience in Sri Lanka. The availability, reliability, and the quality of digital infrastructure are mainly the critical factors that influence their ability to work effectively and enjoy their nomadic lifestyle. Mainly the ability to connect to the internet from anywhere and at any time is essential for digital nomads to conduct their work, communicate with clients and colleagues, and access online resources at the same time they are living their tropical dream here in paradise.

The lack of reliable internet connectivity can significantly hinder their productivity and limit their ability to work effectively. Therefore, digital nomads seek digital equity and justice to diminish all the digital divide that is in there in tourism, advocating for digital inclusion and the infrastructure that caters to many diverse needs.

The reliability of digital infrastructure is another critical factor when it comes to influencing the work satisfaction of digital nomads. Unreliable internet connectivity, frequent power outages, and limited access to technology-related services can easily disrupt their work and cause frustration. Digital nomads mainly rely on stable and dependable digital infrastructure where they are able to meet deadlines, attend virtual meetings, and maintain communication with their clients and colleagues. The quality of digital infrastructure also plays a significant role when it comes to shaping digital nomads' perceptions and their experiences.

High-speed internet, modern co-working spaces, and access to the latest technology are the key essentials for digital nomads to work efficiently and effectively. The lack of quality digital infrastructure can easily limit their ability to perform their work and can negatively impact their overall satisfaction as well. The digital connectivity in developing countries like Sri Lanka faces many infrastructure challenges, including the lack of connectivity, electricity, and access to necessary devices, that has hindering digital access for a significant portion of their populations [16, 17].

The COVID-19 pandemic underscored the critical importance of technology for daily life, exacerbating the challenges for those lacking high-speed internet access, which is now an essential infrastructure [18, 19].

The digital divide is also particularly evident in many rural areas in Sri Lanka, where it is exacerbated by inadequate infrastructure and very limited digital skills, impacting the access to essential services and remote work opportunities [20]. Addressing the digital divide requires ensuring equitable access to technology and the internet, which is essential for the development and social inclusion [21, 22]. The digital divide has also made implications for developing countries because those with none or limited access to technology may be denied by many socioeconomic opportunities [23] when it comes to countries like Sri Lanka. Bridging the digital divide into rural areas is a key essential to ensure access to the public services and also up-to-date information, addressing all the challenges such as poor education, inadequate healthcare, and even challenges like the economic disparities [24, 25].

Research implications

The rise of remote work has enabled individuals to access many job opportunities beyond their local markets, leading to increased mobility and migration to areas with better amenities or lower costs of living [26]. Therefore, by addressing the challenges of digital infrastructure, Sri Lanka can position itself as a more attractive destination for digital nomads, thereby boosting its economy and promoting sustainable tourism.

As technology continues to evolve and the digital nomad lifestyle becomes more and more mainstream, there is a growing need for further research on the experiences, challenges, and the opportunities of digital nomads in different parts of the world. Investing in digital infrastructure and then expanding internet connectivity should be a priority in order to reduce the digital divide [26]. Digital infrastructure improvements are also to be made crucial in many similar developing countries as well [16]. The internet acts as a supportive agent in the migration patterns of the people seeking clearer migration paths [27].

Future research should also explore the long-term impacts of digital nomadism on individuals, communities, and the environment. Despite its limitations, this study offers valuable insights into the experiences of the digital nomads in Sri Lanka and contributes to the growing body of knowledge on the digital nomad phenomenon incurring. Yet, the impact of digital financial services in rural communities highlights the importance of infrastructure to support these financial activities [28]. The presence of digital nomads can lead to enhanced local infrastructure and then become improved services [6].

Policymakers can utilize research findings to create regulatory frameworks that can recognize digital nomads as a distinct group of visitors, addressing their unique needs and contributions to the local economy [29]. The rise of digital nomadism has underscored the need for updated legal frameworks. Therefore, the concept of digital nomadism has gained traction ever since, coinciding with advancements in digital technologies and the increasing feasibility of combining remote work with travel [3].

Discussion

The study's findings provide many valuable insights into the impact of perceived digital infrastructure on the work satisfaction of digital nomads in Sri Lanka. The observational insights from Outpost Weligama highlight the importance of reliable Wi-Fi, conducive work conditions, and a strong sense of community in shaping digital nomads' experiences. The study also reveals that the digital nomads' perceptions of digital infrastructure significantly influence their work satisfaction, emphasizing the need for improved digital infrastructure in Sri Lanka.

The research also revealed how the digital infrastructure influenced work satisfaction among the digital nomads in Sri Lanka, with reliable Wi-Fi, conducive work conditions, and a strong community sense being its key factors. The findings also indicated that digital nomads' perceptions of digital infrastructure greatly affect their work satisfaction, highlighting the need for Sri Lanka to improve its digital infrastructure. These findings underscore the necessity for many targeted interventions to address the digital divide in Sri Lanka and enhance digital literacy and promote the inclusive digital practices to improve digital equity in Sri Lanka as well [30].

The study's revelations are very critical because they shed light on the lived experiences of digital nomads who mainly depend on the internet for their income, compelling digital infrastructure improvements. The Sri Lankan government should invest in expanding and improving digital infrastructure to attract more digital similar nomads and support the growth of the digital economy at the same time.

Policy implications and recommendations

Investing in digital infrastructure, especially in underserved areas, is crucial when fostering digital inclusion and driving socio-economic development [31, 32]. Prioritizing digital infrastructure investments, especially in the underserved areas, is crucial for digital inclusion and its socio-economic development.

The government should also implement policies which can be useful to promote digital literacy and ensure that all citizens have the needed basic skills and knowledge to use digital technologies effectively [19]. By addressing the digital divide and enhancing digital literacy, Sri Lanka can create a more inclusive digital economy that benefits all citizens at the same time as well. The governments can also provide support and resources to the local businesses and entrepreneurs to help them adopt digital technologies and compete in the global market. While Policymakers can use the research findings to formulate strategies that support the digital transformation of both small and medium-sized enterprises through investments in digital infrastructure and digital literacy programs [33].

Furthermore, initiatives should also be able to focus on developing many user-friendly digital platforms and strengthening the cybersecurity measures to promote greater trust and participation in the digital economy which is very crucial and beneficial at the same time [34].

Limitations

The study acknowledges many limitations due to the small sample size, which may restrict the generalizability of the findings to the broader population of digital nomads in Sri Lanka. The reliance on observational data and personal experiences may also introduce subjectivity, which should be considered when interpreting the results. Future research should aim to include a larger and more diverse sample to be able to provide a more comprehensive understanding of the experiences of digital nomads in Sri Lanka.

Future research directions

Future research can focus on exploring the experiences of digital nomads mainly in other regions of Sri Lanka to gain a more of a comprehensive understanding of the challenges they face. Additionally, the research should examine the impact of government policies and regulations on the digital nomad lifestyle in Sri Lanka.

Both Quantitative and Qualitative methods can provide rich insights into the lived experiences of digital nomads, complementing the quantitative studies on technology adoption and economic impact [35]. Furthermore, future studies should investigate the correlation between digital financial literacy and financial inclusion in developing economies, in light of the fact that as mentioned earlier research has mostly been concentrated on specific technologies in isolation [36]. Also, research in understanding the social and economic impacts of digital transformation on the broader Sri Lankan society is also very critical for creating inclusive digital policies.

Conclusion

This study has highlighted the importance of perceived digital infrastructure on the work satisfaction of digital nomads in Sri Lanka. The findings underscore the need for improved digital infrastructure and policies to support the growth of the digital economy in Sri Lanka. The research suggests a need for tourism destinations to be able to adopt a proactive approach to attract digital nomads by providing digital infrastructure.

This research has provided many insights into the experiences of digital nomads in Sri Lanka, revealing the complex relationship between digital infrastructure and their work satisfaction. Despite the challenges posed by the unreliable internet connectivity, digital nomads however find ways to adapt, connect, and thrive in these types of environments/situations. The findings suggest that the sense of community, the flexibility of the digital nomad lifestyle, and the allure of the location contribute to their overall satisfaction, even in the face of digital infrastructure limitations. Theoretically, this research contributes to the understanding of the factors that can influence work satisfaction among the digital nomads, highlighting the importance of digital infrastructure, social connections, and also their individual adaptability. Practically, the findings can inform the development of policies and initiatives aimed at improving the digital infrastructure in Sri Lanka, attracting more digital nomads to the country with the rapid trend, and enhancing their overall experience.

By addressing the challenges faced by digital nomads and investing in digital infrastructure, Sri Lanka can attract more remote workers and create a more vibrant and inclusive digital economy right here on this island, Sri Lanka.

References

[1] Pretsch, J., Saretzki, J., Jernigan, A., & Cantor, D. (2022). Navigating the world: challenges within the relocation process - an empirical investigation. *Deleted Journal*, 5(1), 71. doi: 10.26417/153mdm82.

[2] Orel, M. (2020). Life is better in flip flops. digital nomads and their transformational travels to Thailand. *International Journal of Culture Tourism and Hospitality Research*, 15(1), 3. doi: 10.1108/Ijcthr-12-2019-0229.

[3] Bozzi, A. D. (2024). Digital nomadism from the perspective of places and mobilities: a literature review. *European Transport Research Review*, 16(1), 50. Springer Science+Business Media. doi: 10.1186/S12544-024-00663-Z.

[4] Ji, Y., Kim, S.-M., & Kim, Y. (2024). A way to attract digital nomads to tourist destinations in the new normal era. *Sustainability*, 16(6), 2336. doi: 10.3390/Su16062336.

[5] Hermann, I., & Paris, C. M. (2020). Digital nomadism: the nexus of remote working and travel mobility. *Information Technology and Tourism*, 22(3), 329. doi: 10.1007/S40558-020-00188-W.

[6] Hannonen, O. (2024). Emergent geographies of digital nomadism: conceptual framing, insights and implications for tourism. *Tourism Geographies*, 27(3–4), 568–578 . doi: 10.1080/14616688.2023.2299845.

[7] Šímová, T. (2022). A research framework for digital nomadism: a bibliometric study. *World Leisure Journal*, 65(2), 175. doi: 10.1080/16078055.2022.2134200.

[8] Mustajab, D. (2024). Exploring the effectiveness of remote and hybrid work policies: a literature review on workforce management practices. *Jurnal Manajemen Bisnis*, 11(2), 891. doi: 10.33096/Jmb.V11i2.798.

[9] Trenerry, B., Chng, S., Wang, Y., Suhaila, Z. S., Lim, S. S., Lu, H. Y., et al. (2021). Preparing workplaces for digital transformation: an integrative review and framework of multi-level factors. *Frontiers In Psychology*, 12, 620766. doi: 10.3389/Fpsyg.2021.620766.

[10] Ali, A. D., Narine, L., Hill, P., & Bria, D. C. (2023). Factors affecting remote workers' job satisfaction in Utah: an exploratory study. *International Journal of Environmental Research And Public Health*, 20(9), 5736. doi: 10.3390/Ijerph20095736.

[11] Härtel, T. M., Hüttemann, D., & Müller, J. (2023). Associations between the implementation of telework strategies and job performance: moderating influences of boundary management preferences and telework experience. *Frontiers in Psychology*, 14, 1099138. doi: 10.3389/Fpsyg.2023.1099138.

[12] Hossain, M. A., Tiwari, A., Saha, S., Ghimire, A., Imran, M. A. U., & Khatoon, R. (2024). Applying the technology acceptance model (tam) in information technology system to evaluate the adoption of decision support system. *Journal Of Computer and Communications*, 12(8), 242. doi: 10.4236/Jcc.2024.128015.

[13] Rashid, N. A., Lee, K., & Jamil, N. A. (2021). Conducting qualitative research in the new norms: are we ready?. *Nursing And Health Sciences*, 23(4), 967. doi: 10.1111/Nhs.12872.

[14] Hack-Polay, D. (2020). Global south expatriates, homesickness and adjustment approaches. *Public Health Reviews*, 41(1), 11. doi: 10.1186/S40985-020-00122-9.

[15] Matli, W. (2020). The changing work landscape as a result of the covid-19 pandemic: insights from remote workers life situations in South Africa. *International Journal of Sociology And Social Policy*, 40, 1237. doi: 10.1108/Ijssp-082020-0386.

[16] Ofek, E., Grubert, J., Pahud, M., Phillips, M., & Kristensson, P. O. (2020). Towards a practical virtual office for mobile knowledge workers. arxiv (Cornell University). doi: 10.48550/Arxiv.2009.02947.

[17] Herath, V. (2021). Starlink : a solution to the digital connectivity divide in education in the global south. arxiv (Cornell University). doi:10.48550/Arxiv.2110.09225.

[18] Fernando, I. (2021). Tourism amid covid-19 pandemic in Sri Lanka way-forwarding strategies through the porters' diamond model. *Sri Lanka Journal of Marketing*, 7(1), 22. doi: 10.4038/Sljmuok.V7i1.55.

[19] Weerarathna, R. S., Rathnayake, N., Yasara, I., Jayasekara, P., Ruwanpura, D., & Nambugoda, S. (2022). Towards work-life balance or away? the impact of work from home factors on work-life balance among software engineers during Covid-19 pandemic. *Plos One*, 17(12), e0277931. doi: 10.1371/Journal.Pone.0277931.

[20] Torabi, Z.-A., Rezvani, M. R., Hall, C. M., & Allam, Z. (2023). On the post-pandemic travel boom: how capacity building and smart tourism technologies in rural areas can help - evidence from Iran. *Technological Forecasting and Social Change*, 193, 122633. doi: 10.1016/J.Techfore.2023.122633.

[21] Molala, T. S., & Makhubele, J. C. (2021). The connection between digital divide and social exclusion: implications for social work. *Humanities and Social Sciences Reviews*, 9(4), 194. doi: 10.18510/Hssr.2021.9427.

[22] Sanders, C. K., & Scanlon, E. (2021). The digital divide is a human rights issue: advancing social inclusion through social work advocacy. *Journal of Human Rights and Social Work*, 6(2), 130. doi: 10.1007/S41134-020-00147-9.

[23] Esteban, A. M., & Cruz, M. J. P. (2021). Digital divide in times of pandemic among teacher education students. *Oalib*, 8(4), 1. doi: 10.4236/Oalib.1107323.

[24] Aruleba, K., & Jere, N. (2022). Exploring digital transforming challenges in rural areas of south africa through a systematic review of empirical studies. *Scientific African*, 16, e01190. doi: 10.1016/J.Sciaf.2022.E01190.

[25] Rangasubramanian, K. (2021). Towards a digital India: an overview of challenges, successes and opportunities. *International Journal of Advanced Research*, 9(2), 874. doi: 10.21474/Ijar01/12528.

[26] Ozimek, A. (2020). Remote workers on the move. SSRN Electronic Journal. doi: 10.2139/Ssrn.3790004.

[27] Pesando, L. M., Rotondi, V., Stranges, M., Kashyap, R., & Billari, F. C. (2020). The internetization of international migration. *Population and Development Review*, 47(1), 79. doi: 10.1111/Padr.12371.

[28] Somasundari, K. M., & Mukil, M. S. (2021). Impact of digital financial services among rural dwellers during covid pandemicv. *Emperor Journal of Economics and Social Science Research*, 3(5), 69. doi: 10.35338/Ejessr.2021.3508.

[29] Jiwasiddi, A., Schlagwein, D., Cahalane, M., Ćećez-Kecmanović, D., Leong, C., & Ractham, P. (2024). Digital nomadism as a new part of the visitor economy: the case of the 'digital nomad capital'chiang mai, Thailand. *Information Systems Journal*, 34(5), 1493. doi: 10.1111/Isj.12496.

[30] Jehan, S. N., & Alahakoon, M. U. I. (2020). Digitalization of public services —an input output logit analysis. *Applied System Innovation*, 3(4), 56. doi: 10.3390/Asi3040056.

[31] Alahakoon, M. U. I., & Jehan, S. N. (2020). Efficiency of public service delivery—a post-Ict deployment analysis. *Economies*, 8(4), 97. doi: 10.3390/Economies8040097.

[32] Maji, S. K., & Laha, A. (2021). The role of digital skill in mitigating digital divide: evidences from asiapacific region. *Rajagiri Management Journal*, 16(3), 260. doi: 10.1108/Ramj-05-20210035.

[33] Öztürk, İ., Alqassimi, O., & Ullah, S. (2024). Digitalization and smes development in the context of sustainable development: a china perspective. *Heliyon* , 10(6). doi: 10.1016/J.Heliyon.2024.E27936.

[34] Binaluyo, J. P., Santos, A. R., & Agustin, N. B. (2024). Challenges and opportunities for digital transformation in philippine microfinance institutions. *International Journal of Economics and Financial Issues*, 14(5), 269. doi: 10.32479/Ijefi.16526.

[35] Sosale, S., Hong, S. Y., Subasinghe, S., & Herat, H. (2023). Enhancing skills in Sri Lanka for inclusion, recovery, and resilience. doi: 10.1596/40663.

[36] Adel, N. (2024). The impact of digital literacy and technology adoption on financial inclusion in Africa, Asia, and Latin America. *Heliyon*, 10(24). doi: 10.1016/J.Heliyon.2024.E40951.

5 The role of workplace ostracism and negative reciprocity beliefs in shaping knowledge hiding in Sri Lanka's information technology sector

L. Mayuran[a] *and T. Thasika*[b]

Department of Human Resource Management, Faculty of Management Studies and Commerce, University of Jaffna, Sri Lanka

Abstract

In knowledge-intensive environments, such as Sri Lanka's Information Technology (IT) sector, the intentional concealment of information, known as knowledge hiding, poses a significant threat to organizational collaboration and innovation. Grounded in Social Exchange Theory (SET), this study investigates workplace ostracism as an interpersonal antecedent of knowledge hiding. Specifically, it examines how Negative Reciprocity Beliefs (NRBs) moderate the relationship between workplace ostracism and three dimensions of knowledge hiding: evasive hiding, playing dumb, and rationalized hiding. Utilizing a deductive, quantitative approach, data were collected from 250 IT professionals across eight Colombo-based organizations (92.6% response rate). Results from regression and moderation analyses revealed that workplace ostracism significantly predicts evasive hiding ($\beta = .42$, $p < .01$) and playing dumb ($\beta = .39$, $p < .01$), but not rationalized hiding ($\beta = .08$, n.s.). Moreover, NRBs significantly strengthen the positive association between ostracism and both evasive hiding ($\beta = .17$, $p < .01$) and playing dumb ($\beta = .15$, $p < .05$), but not rationalized hiding ($\beta = .02$, n.s.). Practical implications suggest that IT organizations should address exclusionary practices, foster inclusive environments, and consider employees' reciprocity beliefs in talent management to mitigate knowledge withholding. Furthermore, since data were drawn solely from IT firms in Sri Lanka, the generalizability of findings to other industries may be constrained. Future research should explore cross-cultural generalizability and adopt longitudinal designs to establish causality.

Keywords: Evasive hiding, knowledge hiding, negative reciprocity beliefs, playing dumb, rationalized hiding, Sri Lanka IT sector, workplace ostracism

Introduction

In the prevailing knowledge economy, continuous innovation is essential for the sustained prosperity and growth of organizations. Innovation not only strengthens customer confidence but also serves as a key driver of long-term enterprise success. This process relies heavily on effective knowledge transfer [1]. Consequently, efficient knowledge sharing plays a critical role in improving the innovation performance of organizations [2, 3].

While knowledge sharing is widely recognized as essential for organizational success, research by [4] highlights a persistent challenge: knowledge hiding. This phenomenon, common in knowledge-based organizations, significantly impedes effective knowledge transfer, undermining processes vital for growth and innovation. Despite extensive evidence on the detrimental effects of knowledge hiding, research on its antecedents remains less comprehensive compared to studies on its consequences [5]. We argue that workplace ostracism is a prevalent issue in contemporary organizations that diminishes employee engagement and performance [6, 7] and contributes to this problem. [8] suggest that workplace ostracism disrupts interpersonal dynamics, increasing the likelihood that excluded employees will withhold requested knowledge. However, the relationship between workplace ostracism and knowledge hiding remains underexplored.

Beyond the direct relationship between workplace ostracism and knowledge hiding, our study investigates the factors that influence this connection. Examining these boundary conditions allows us to determine the particular situations in which knowledge hiding tends to occur with greater or lesser

[a]mayuranl@univ.jfn.ac.lk, [b]ythasika@univ.jfn.ac.lk

DOI: 10.4324/9781003739920-5

frequency. Still, there is a scarcity of empirical studies exploring these moderating influences [9]. To address this gap, we focus on the moderating role of NRBs in the association between workplace ostracism and knowledge hiding. This focus is justified for two key reasons. First, NRBs may play a distinct role in shaping how workplace ostracism leads to knowledge hiding. Second, when individuals face negative treatment such as ostracism, their subsequent behavior - whether ethical or unethical - can differ significantly based on their NRBs. These arguments are supported by [10] and [11], who found that NRBs amplify the link between workplace aggression and the likelihood of employees engaging in unethical behaviors.

Through this inquiry, we provide two notable insights to the existing body of research. First, we contribute to the discourse on knowledge hiding [12, 11, 13, 14] by offering empirical evidence that highlights workplace ostracism as a relational trigger for such behavior. Second, this study deepens insights into the situational factors that influence whether employees experiencing ostracism are inclined to conceal knowledge. It does so through an investigation of individual differences, specifically NRBs, as moderating variables in the association between workplace ostracism and knowledge hiding.

Theory and Hypotheses

Workplace ostracism and knowledge hiding

Knowledge hiding, defined as "an intentional attempt by an individual to withhold or conceal knowledge that has been requested by another person" [4, p. 65], has gained increasing attention among scholars and practitioners [2, 15–17]. [12] emphasized the need to clearly differentiate knowledge hiding from other forms of behavior observed in organizational settings, including knowledge hoarding and Counterproductive Workplace Behaviors (CWBs). Although these behaviors share the common feature of information withholding, there are distinct differences between knowledge hiding and hoarding. Knowledge hiding occurs when an individual deliberately conceals knowledge that has been explicitly requested, whereas knowledge hoarding refers to the accumulation of knowledge without necessarily being asked to share it [18, 19].

Both knowledge hiding and CWBs may appear similar, as both can conflict with moral standards [20]. CWBs involve deliberate employee actions that "harm or intend to harm organizations and their stakeholders, such as clients, coworkers, customers, and supervisors" [21, p. 151]. Nonetheless, the act of knowledge hiding isn't always driven by harmful intentions. In certain scenarios, individuals adopt rationalized hiding to safeguard their own well-being or to prevent emotional harm to others [4]. Additionally, while CWBs can target either individuals (e.g., verbal abuse) or organizations (e.g., theft), knowledge hiding occurs exclusively in interpersonal interactions [22, 20].

Knowledge hiding consists of three key dimensions: evasive hiding, playing dumb, and rationalized hiding [4]. Evasive hiding involves deception, defined as "providing incorrect information or a misleading promise of a complete answer in the future, even with no intention of actually providing it" [23, p. 480]. Similarly, playing dumb is a deceptive tactic where individuals pretend ignorance about the requester's inquiry to avoid sharing knowledge [23]. In contrast, rationalized hiding does not always rely on deception. Instead, individuals justify withholding knowledge by claiming inability or shifting responsibility to others [23].

In some cases, individuals who conceal knowledge may genuinely believe they are acting with good intentions [22]. For instance, a project manager might withhold information selectively, not out of deceit, but to strategically manage expectations or avoid causing undue alarm among team members. However, knowledge hiding ultimately harms organizational performance and team effectiveness by undermining collaboration, stifling innovation, and hindering the execution of organizational policies [24]. The financial impact is substantial. [25] estimated that Fortune 500 companies lose $31.5 billion annually due to knowledge hiding. While its detrimental effects on organizations are well-documented [12], there remains a significant gap in understanding the interpersonal factors that drive knowledge hiding and the specific conditions that predict its occurrence.

Ostracism, a concept rooted in negative interpersonal treatment, has gained increasing attention in organizational research [26, 27]. [Another study defined it as "the extent to which an individual perceives that he or she is ignored or excluded by others in the workplace" [28]. Workplace ostracism, considered a type of emotional mistreatment, typically presents itself through three distinct patterns [29,

8]. First, it can stem from multiple groups within an organization, not just a single source. Employees may feel excluded by people across hierarchical levels, including those in managerial roles, peers, junior staff, or even clients. Second, the experience of ostracism is inherently subjective, varying from person to person. Third, experiencing ostracism often leads individuals to endure strained and emotionally uncomfortable interactions with others.

Research widely shown that experiencing ostracism can lead to serious detriments in both mental and physical health, lower levels of job satisfaction and commitment to the organization, a decline in organizational citizenship behaviors, and reduced effectiveness in service delivery [30–32]. Recent studies have increasingly focused on how workplace ostracism influences employees' interpersonal conduct [33]. For instance, researcher found that workplace ostracism heightens interpersonal deviance [34], while another study demonstrated a positive link between ostracism and interpersonal CWBs [2].

Building on prior evidence, we argue that workplace ostracism can play a role in fostering knowledge hiding, a link underpinned by the principle of reciprocal norms. Another theory suggests that individuals tend to reciprocate the treatment they receive either by returning kindness (positive reciprocity) or by retaliating against harm (negative reciprocity) [35]. Given that workplace ostracism is a negative interpersonal experience, ostracized employees are likely to perceive their colleagues as sources of mistreatment. This perception fosters NRBs, making it justifiable for the excluded employee to respond with interpersonal retaliation. Such retaliation could take the form of ostracism, knowledge hiding, or other CWBs.

Study suggested that employees' likelihood of hiding knowledge depends on how colleagues have reciprocated in the past [25]. Ostracized employees often respond to knowledge requests uncooperatively, withholding information through tactics like evasive answers or playing dumb. However, this does not apply to rationalized hiding, which stems from more positive intentions such as protecting others' feelings or safeguarding a third party's interests [25]. Norms of reciprocity, ostracized employees who hide knowledge as retaliation for exclusion are less likely to provide a rationalized justification [35]. Thus, unfavorable interpersonal experiences may not significantly increase rationalized hiding. The hypothesized research model is presented in Figure 5.1. Based on this reasoning, we hypothesize:

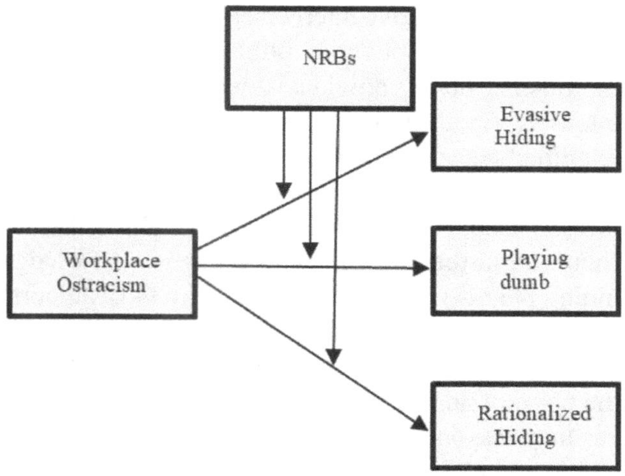

Figure 5.1 Hypothesized research model
Source: Author

H1a: There is a positive relationship between workplace ostracism and evasive hiding.

H1b: There is a positive relationship between workplace ostracism and playing dumb.

H1c: There is no significant relationship between workplace ostracism and rationalized hiding.

The moderating role of NRBs

The concept of reciprocity has been extensively explored in multiple academic fields, including sociology, psychology, philosophy, and organizational behavior. It is defined as "a mutually gratifying pattern of exchanging goods and services" [35 170]. Reciprocity plays a vital role in reinforcing interpersonal networks and promoting mutual interactions.

Reciprocity is commonly classified as either positive or negative [36]. Positive reciprocity reflects an altruistic principle, where individuals respond to kindness with kindness. In contrast, negative reciprocity embodies a self-serving principle, where individuals retaliate against perceived unfriendliness. Given that our research examines knowledge hiding, a negative organizational behavior, we specifically employ negative reciprocity to explain the effects of workplace ostracism. Empirical studies further support this perspective, demonstrating that negative reciprocity plays a pivotal role in determining when and why employees engage in unethical conduct [37, 11, 38].

NRBs reflect an individual's conviction that negative actions warrant negative reactions [39]. Those with high levels of such beliefs exhibit heightened sensitivity to negative interpersonal cues and a stronger self-serving motivation [40, 41]. When excluded by others, these individuals tend to react more intensely - both psychologically (e.g., experiencing amplified negative emotions) and behaviorally (e.g., displaying greater retaliation tendencies or reduced job satisfaction) [42, 47, 30]. This heightened reactivity can further drive them to engage in knowledge hiding [43, 44]. Empirical research by [45] supports this, showing that individuals with strong NRBs often retaliate directly when mistreated. Guided by the norm of negative reciprocity, ostracized employees may respond to workplace exclusion by deliberately withholding requested knowledge or engaging in other interpersonal mistreatment. Such behaviors allow them to vent negative emotions, reinforcing their belief that retaliation restores a sense of control over their work environment [10].

On the other hand, individuals with low NRBs tend to prioritize collective interests and cooperation. When faced with ostracism, these individuals respond more constructively, thereby diminishing their inclination to withhold information sought by others. We propose that NRBs act as a moderator in the relationship between workplace ostracism and evasive hiding or playing dumb. However, distinct from other aspects of knowledge hiding, rationalized hiding does not appear to be moderated by NRBs. This may be attributed to the fact that rationalized hiding is frequently motivated by prosocial emotional reasoning, rather than driven by retaliatory inclinations. Accordingly, we propose the following hypotheses:

H2a: NRBs strengthen the positive relationship between workplace ostracism and evasive hiding, such that the effect is more pronounced among employees with stronger (vs. weaker) NRBs.

H2b: NRBs strengthen the positive relationship between workplace ostracism and playing dumb, such that the effect is more pronounced among employees with stronger (vs. weaker) NRBs.

H2c: There is no significant moderating effect of NRBs on the link between workplace ostracism and rationalized knowledge hiding.

Methodology

This study examines Sri Lanka's IT industry, an ideal context for investigating the relationship between workplace ostracism and knowledge hiding, moderated by negative reciprocity. The sector plays a crucial role in the national economy, contributing over $1.5 billion in export revenue (2022) and employing approximately 175,000 skilled professionals [46]. As a knowledge-driven field where collaboration is essential for innovation, IT firms provide a relevant setting to explore how workplace ostracism may increase knowledge hiding, particularly among employees with a strong tendency toward negative reciprocity, where perceived exclusion may trigger retaliatory behaviors [47]. While knowledge hiding is often driven by competitive pressures and intellectual property concerns [48], the moderating role of negative reciprocity in this relationship remains unexplored in Sri Lanka.

Data were collected from employees across eight Colombo-based IT organizations, representing diverse roles, including software development, network administration, quality assurance, cybersecurity, and database management. After obtaining HR department approval, participants were selected via convenience sampling through workplace interactions. While this method may limit generalizability, it was practical given Colombo's concentration of IT firms and the accessibility of professional networks [49]. A standardized protocol was followed: participants received a package containing a cover letter (detailing study objectives), a questionnaire, a confidentiality agreement, and a return envelope. Completed surveys were returned to HR departments for later collection. The survey was administered in English, the industry's primary working language. Although Sinhala and Tamil are Sri Lanka's official languages, IT professionals typically exhibit high English proficiency, reducing potential language barriers that could affect response accuracy or participation rates.

Descriptive statistics were computed to summarize the demographic characteristics of the sample and provide an overview of the key study variables. A total of 270 questionnaires were distributed, and 250 completed questionnaires were returned, yielding a response rate of 92.6%. Out of the 250 participants, 158 were male (63.2%) and 92 were female (36.8%). The average age of respondents was 30.6 years (SD = 5.2), and the average organizational tenure was 5.8 years (SD = 3.4). Regarding marital status, 140 participants (56%) were single, while 110 (44%) were married. In terms of occupational roles,

105 participants (42%) were employed in software development, 45 (18%) in network administration, 35 (14%) in quality assurance, 33 (13.2%) in cybersecurity, and the remaining 32 (12.8%) in database management.

Measures

We employed established measures to gather data on the study variables. Responses were recorded using a five-point rating scale, with 1 representing "strongly disagree" and 5 indicating "strongly agree."

Workplace ostracism
We assessed this variable using the ten-item scale developed by [28]. An example item is "others at work did not invite you or ask if you wanted anything when they went out for a coffee break." The scale demonstrated high reliability, with a Cronbach's alpha coefficient of 0.93.

NRBs
We measured NRBs using [50] seven-item scale. A sample item reads: "My organization only cares about its own benefits and never considers my career or well-being." The scale demonstrated high reliability, with a Cronbach's alpha of 0.98.

Knowledge hiding
We measured knowledge hiding using [25] twelve-item scale, which consists of three sub-dimensions: evasive hiding (four items, e.g., "Agreed to help but never really intended to"), playing dumb (four items, e.g., "Said I did not know, even though I did"), and rationalized hiding (four items, e.g., "Explained that I would like to share but was not supposed to"). The scale exhibited strong internal reliability, with Cronbach's alpha values of 0.88, 0.92, and 0.88 for the respective sub-dimensions.

Control variables
Previous studies [51–53] suggest that knowledge-based behaviors can be shaped by individual demographic factors, such as gender, age, marital status, job category and the prevailing organizational climate. Given their potential impact on the study variables, we controlled for these factors. Gender was coded as a dummy variable (1 = male, 0 = female), marital status as categorical (1 = single, 2 = married, 3 = divorced), and job category as nominal (software development = 1, network administration = 2, quality assurance = 3, cybersecurity = 4, database management = 5). Age was measured in years.

Results

To examine the relationships between workplace ostracism and the three dimensions of knowledge hiding, a Pearson correlation analysis was conducted. The results are presented in Table 5.1.

The results of the correlation analysis indicated a positive significant relationship between workplace ostracism and both evasive hiding ($r = .42$, $p < .01$) and playing dumb ($r = .39$, $p < .01$), thereby lending support to hypotheses H1a and H1b. These findings suggest that employees who perceive themselves as being ostracized are more likely to engage in deceptive knowledge-hiding tactics, such as providing misleading responses or feigning ignorance when knowledge is requested.

In contrast, no significant correlation emerged between workplace ostracism and rationalized hiding ($r = .08$), thus supporting hypothesis H1c. This indicates that ostracized employees are less likely to engage in knowledge hiding that is justified with socially acceptable reasons, such as protecting others or adhering to confidentiality norms.

The results of the correlation analysis indicated a positive significant relationship between workplace

Table 5.1 Correlation matrix of study variables (SPSS output).

Variables	Workplace ostracism	Evasive hiding	Playing Dumb	Rationalized hiding
Workplace ostracism	1			
Evasive hiding	.42**	1		
Playing dumb	.39**	.56**	1	
Rationalized hiding	.08	.21**	.24**	1

Source: Author

Table 5.2 Moderation analysis – the role of NRBs (SPSS output).

Dependent Variable	Path	β	p-Value	Result
Evasive Hiding	Ostracism × NRBs → Evasive Hiding	.17	< .01	Significant
Playing Dumb	Ostracism × NRBs → Playing Dumb	.15	< .05	Significant
Rationalized Hiding	Ostracism × NRBs → Rationalized Hiding	.02	.34	Not Significant

Source: Author

Table 5.3 Conditional effects of workplace ostracism on knowledge hiding at different levels of NRBs (SPSS output).

Dimension of knowledge hiding	Level of NRBs	Effect of ostracism (β)	p-value	Significance
Evasive hiding	Low (−1 SD)	.08	< .05	Significant
	High (+1 SD)	.26	< .001	Highly Significant
Playing dumb	Low (−1 SD)	.06	< .10	Marginally Significant
	High (+1 SD)	.22	< .01	Significant
Rationalized hiding	Low (−1 SD)	.12	< .05	Significant
	High (+1 SD)	.13	< .05	Significant (no moderation)

Source: Author

ostracism and both evasive hiding (r = .42, p < .01) and playing dumb (r = .39, p < .01), thereby lending support to hypotheses H1a and H1b. These findings suggest that employees who perceive themselves as being ostracized are more likely to engage in deceptive knowledge-hiding tactics, such as providing misleading responses or feigning ignorance when knowledge is requested.

In contrast, no significant correlation emerged between workplace ostracism and rationalized hiding (r = .08), thus supporting hypothesis H1c. This indicates that ostracized employees are less likely to engage in knowledge hiding that is justified with socially acceptable reasons, such as protecting others or adhering to confidentiality norms.

Moderation analysis

To investigate the potential moderating role of NRBs, moderated regression analyses were performed, focusing on the associations linking workplace ostracism with the three facets of knowledge hiding, namely, evasive hiding, playing dumb, and rationalized hiding. The results of the moderation analysis are presented in Table 5.2. The variables were mean-centered, and interaction terms were created between workplace ostracism and NRBs for each regression model. The results are summarized in Table 5.3. The findings empirically validate all three sub-hypotheses (H2a, H2b, and H2c), affirming the moderating influence of NRBs on the associations between workplace ostracism and the distinct dimensions of knowledge hiding. Consistent with H2a, the interaction between workplace ostracism and NRBs was significant in predicting evasive hiding ($\beta = .17$, $p < .01$), indicating that the positive association between ostracism and evasive hiding is stronger among employees with higher levels of NRBs. Similarly, in support of H2b, the interaction between ostracism and NRBs also significantly predicted playing dumb ($\beta = .15$, $p < .05$), highlighting that ostracized employees with high NRBs are more inclined to feign ignorance as a form of retaliation. Finally, H2c was supported as the interaction effect between ostracism and NRBs on rationalized hiding was not significant ($\beta = .02$, $p = .34$), reinforcing the idea that this form of knowledge hiding is not driven by retaliatory motives and is less influenced by beliefs about negative reciprocity. The conditional effects analysis revealed that the impact of workplace ostracism on knowledge hiding varies depending on employees' levels of NRBs, supporting H2a and H2b, but not H2c. For evasive hiding, the relationship between ostracism and knowledge hiding was stronger among employees with high NRBs ($\beta = .26$, $p < .001$) compared to those with low NRBs ($\beta = .08$, $p <$

.05), indicating that individuals with stronger retaliatory tendencies are more likely to engage in evasive tactics in response to exclusion. Similarly, for playing dumb, the effect of ostracism was more pronounced among employees with high NRBs ($\beta = .22, p < .01$) than those with low NRBs ($\beta = .06, p < .10$), suggesting a moderating effect in line with H2b. However, for rationalized hiding, ostracism had a relatively similar and significant effect across both low ($\beta = .12, p < .05$) and high NRBs levels ($\beta = .13, p < .05$), indicating no meaningful moderation effect, thus supporting H2c. These findings confirm that the retaliatory nature of certain forms of knowledge hiding, such as evasive hiding and playing dumb, is more prevalent among employees who hold strong NRBs, whereas rationalized hiding remains unaffected by such beliefs.

Discussions

The study investigated the conditions of negative reciprocity that drive ostracized employees in IT organizations to hide knowledge. Consistent with our hypothesis, the analysis revealed that workplace ostracism was positively linked to knowledge workers' involvement in both evasive knowledge hiding and playing dumb. In contrast, its association with rationalized knowledge hiding was not statistically significant. Moreover, NRBs amplified the positive influence of workplace ostracism on evasive hiding and playing dumb, while exerting no moderating effect on rationalized hiding.

Theoretical Implications

This research contributes to the current body of knowledge in two distinct respects. Although numerous studies have investigated the antecedents of knowledge hiding through diverse lenses [54, 55], factors rooted in interpersonal dynamics remain relatively underexplored [12]. Given that daily work inherently involves employee interactions, these exchanges provide valuable interpersonal cues. Such cues serve a dual purpose: they offer social context and shape how employees interpret and respond to information [56]. Hence, exploring interpersonal dynamics plays a vital role in identifying the underlying factors that contribute to knowledge hiding.

Addressing this claim, existing studies [25, 15, 57] have investigated interpersonal elements, such as distrust, abusive supervision, and leader-member exchange, as influential factors contributing to knowledge hiding. Although these findings are valuable, the scope of interpersonal interactions influencing knowledge hiding remains underexplored. Extending this line of reasoning, our study seeks to enhance the existing body of research by proposing workplace ostracism as a distinct interpersonal driver of knowledge hiding. Recognized as a detrimental social experience, workplace ostracism has the potential to shape employees' behavioral patterns, attitudes, and job-related outcomes [29], and has been used as a proxy for interpersonal dynamics in prior studies [e.g., 30]. We therefore posit that experiences of workplace ostracism may incite knowledge hiding behaviors, as employees subjected to such exclusion, particularly when shaped by NRBs, might respond by intentionally withholding knowledge. By conceptualizing workplace ostracism as a relational precursor, this study contributes to the advancement of the knowledge hiding literature [58, 25, 23, 15].

Second, this research not only focuses on the direct impact of workplace ostracism on knowledge hiding but also delves into how NRBs may influence this relationship. Responding to [58] recommendations, the research explores the specific conditions under which knowledge hiding occurs, thereby contributing to a deeper understanding of the "why" and "when" behind ostracized employees' knowledge-hiding behavior. As anticipated, NRBs intensified the positive association between workplace ostracism and knowledge hiding. Specifically, the connection involving ostracism and both evasive hiding and playing dumb was more evident among employees with higher levels of NRBs. In contrast, for those with low levels of such beliefs, the effect was less significant. In other words, strong NRBs may amplify detrimental outcomes. Ostracized employees with high NRBs may perceive ostracism as justification for retaliation, leading them to engage in evasive hiding or playing dumb. On the other hand, employees with low NRBs may respond to mistreatment with greater tolerance and self-sacrifice, reducing their likelihood of retaliatory knowledge-hiding behaviors.

Practical Implications

Despite considerable theoretical and practical interest in knowledge sharing [12, 59], empirical research on knowledge hiding in the IT sector remains limited, underscoring this study's importance. The findings reveal that workplace ostracism significantly predicts employees' knowledge-hiding behaviors, urging IT managers to prioritize reducing exclusionary practices. While fostering a culture of openness, transparency, and fair competition can mitigate ostracism, such efforts often face challenges like resource constraints, poor communication infrastructure, and systemic inequities. Thus, where ostracism persists, IT organizations should provide timely psychological support to alleviate affected employees' stress and implement accessible complaint mechanisms to address their concerns effectively.

Given that individuals with weak political skills or inadequate organizational socialization are more vulnerable to ostracism [60, 61], exploring individual-focused strategies to reduce its prevalence is valuable. Managers can address this by offering targeted training and continuous counseling to enhance employees' political skills. Useful techniques consist of incorporating theatrical exercises, conducting evaluation discussions, utilizing video-based role-play followed by feedback, and applying behavioral modeling strategies [62]. Additionally, managers should facilitate employees' organizational adaptation through socialization tactics, such as providing role models and encouraging alignment with organizational values [63].

Our findings further underscore that how workplace ostracism influences knowledge hiding varies according to employees' NRBs. Those with stronger beliefs are more sensitive to ostracism and more likely to hide knowledge than their less reciprocally negative peers. To curb knowledge hiding, IT managers should consider these beliefs in employee management. Organizations can proactively screen for low negative reciprocity during recruitment, using questionnaires or scenario-based simulations while balancing other factors. While excluding candidates with high reciprocity beliefs is impractical, targeted interventions like ethics training can strengthen moral self-regulation among at-risk employees. Mentoring and training programs should also teach constructive responses to ostracism, such as pursuing forgiveness, seeking clarity, and engaging in mediation [64], to promote a healthier workplace environment.

Limitations and Future Research Directions

The present research contributes meaningfully to the existing body of knowledge, although certain limitations should be acknowledged. A primary limitation lies in the extent to which the findings can be generalized. Although the study was designed to minimize cultural bias, its exclusive focus on data collected from Sri Lankan organizations may limit the broader applicability of the results. Sri Lankan and Western cultures differ significantly, particularly in dimensions such as collectivism and individualism, which could shape the mental and behavioral responses of ostracized individuals. A key distinction lies in Sri Lanka's collectivist culture, which prioritizes group harmony, whereas Western cultures tend to emphasize individualism [65]. In collectivist settings, individuals place high value on social bonds and often respond to workplace exclusion with covert tactics, such as knowledge hoarding, to regain control while preserving interpersonal harmony [66]. In contrast, individualist cultures, which prioritize self-interest, may provoke more direct retaliation, such as overt ostracism, rather than subtle interpersonal mistreatment [53]. Thus, examining our model across diverse cultural contexts and samples could yield further insightful findings.

Second, due to the correlational design of this study, causal relationships cannot be definitively established. It is crucial to note that the link connecting ostracism and knowledge hiding might operate in both directions. In some cases, knowledge hiding may actually lead to ostracism, resulting in a recurring cycle. Both of these phenomena are commonly acknowledged as harmful forms of interpersonal behavior [25, 58, 29]. According to the norm of reciprocity [35], when individuals encounter knowledge hiding, they may interpret it as a relational violation by the instigator, potentially leading them to respond with retaliatory behaviors, including exclusion. Examining this two-way dynamic enhances our grasp of the interplay between ostracism and knowledge hiding and contributes meaningfully to the expanding body of research in this area. However, to conclusively determine causality between these variables, future research should adopt longitudinal methodologies.

Third, our findings highlight the role of NRBs in explaining the relationship between workplace ostracism and knowledge hiding. This boundary condition may also prove relevant for studying other forms of workplace mistreatment, such as abusive supervision. Previous research suggests that employees subjected to abusive supervision often retaliate as a means of reclaiming their personal identity [67]. Supporting this, another study [54] demonstrated that employees with strong NRBs engaged in higher levels of supervisor-directed deviance following abusive supervision compared to those with weaker beliefs. Future research could extend these insights by examining how NRBs moderate employee responses to abusive supervision, thereby contributing to the broader abusive supervision literature.

References

[1] Iqbal, A. (2021). Innovation speed and quality in higher education institutions: the role of knowledge management enablers and knowledge sharing process. *Journal of Knowledge Management*, 25(9), 2334–2360.

[2] Hussain, K., Konar, R., & Ali, F. (2016). Measuring service innovation performance through team culture and knowledge sharing behaviour in hotel services: a PLS approach. *Procedia-Social and Behavioral Sciences*, 224, 35–43.

[3] Kumar, M., Mamgain, P., Pasumarti, S. S., & Singh, P. K. (2024). Organizational IT support and knowledge sharing behaviour affecting service innovation performance: empirical evidence from the hospitality industry. *VINE Journal of Information and Knowledge Management Systems*, 54(2), 256–279.

[4] Connelly, C. E., Zweig, D., Webster, J., & Trougakos, J. P. (2012). Knowledge hiding in organizations. *Journal of Organizational Behavior*, 33(1), 64–88.

[5] Chen, L., Luo, X., Zhou, F., & Zhang, T. (2022). Knowledge hiding and Hider's innovative behavior in Chinese organizations: the mediating role of silence behavior and the moderating role of Zhongyong thinking. *Management and Organization Review*, 18(3), 491–518.

[6] Haldorai, K., Kim, W. G., Phetvaroon, K., & Li, J. (2020). Left out of the office "tribe": The influence of workplace ostracism on employee work engagement. *International Journal of Contemporary Hospitality Management*, 32(8), 2717–2735.

[7] Mattar, D. M., Haddad, J. J., & Haddad, C. J. (2025). Workplace ostracism and service performance: the mediating role of job tension, organizational identification, and work engagement. *Journal of General Management*, 50(3), 240–256.

[8] Jahanzeb, S., & Fatima, T. (2018). How workplace ostracism influences interpersonal deviance: the mediating role of defensive silence and emotional exhaustion. *Journal of Business and Psychology*, 33(6), 779–791.

[9] Zhao, H., Xia, Q., He, P., Sheard, G., & Wan, P. (2016). Workplace ostracism and knowledge hiding in service organizations. *International Journal of Hospitality Management*, 59, 84–94.

[10] Yao, L., Ayub, A., Ishaq, M., Arif, S., Fatima, T., & Sohail, H. M. (2022). Workplace ostracism and employee silence in service organizations: the moderating role of NRBs. *International Journal of Manpower*, 43(6), 1378–1404.

[11] Faldetta, G. (2021). Abusive supervision and workplace deviance: the role of negative reciprocity. *International Journal of Organizational Analysis*, 29(4), 935–949.

[12] Černe, M., Nerstad, C. G., Dysvik, A., & Škerlavaj, M. (2014). What goes around comes around: knowledge hiding, perceived motivational climate, and creativity. *Academy of Management Journal*, 57(1), 172–192.

[13] Liao, G., Li, M., Li, Y., & Yin, J. (2024). How does knowledge hiding play a role in the relationship between leader–member exchange differentiation and employee creativity? a cross-level model. *Journal of Knowledge Management*, 28(1), 69–84.

[14] Farooq, R., & Sultana, A. (2021). Abusive supervision and its relationship with knowledge hiding: the mediating role of distrust. *International Journal of Innovation Science*, 13(5), 709–731.

[15] Connelly, C. E., Černe, M., Dysvik, A., & Škerlavaj, M. (2019). Understanding knowledge hiding in organizations. *Journal of Organizational Behavior*, 40(7), 779–782.

[16] Anand, A., Centobelli, P., & Cerchione, R. (2020). Why should I share knowledge with others? a review-based framework on events leading to knowledge hiding. *Journal of Organizational Change Management*, 33(2), 379–399.

[17] Shrivastava, S., Pazzaglia, F., & Sonpar, K. (2021). The role of nature of knowledge and knowledge creating processes in knowledge hiding: reframing knowledge hiding. *Journal of Business Research*, 136, 644–651.

[18] Jalonen, H. (2024). Ignorance in organisations–a systematic literature review. *Management Review Quarterly*, 74(2), 909–950.

[19] Oliveira, M., Curado, C., & de Garcia, P. S. (2021). Knowledge hiding and knowledge hoarding: a systematic literature review. *Knowledge and Process Management*, 28(3), 277–294.

[20] Peng, H. (2012). Counterproductive work behavior among Chinese knowledge workers. *International Journal of Selection and Assessment*, 20(2), 119–138.

[21] Spector, P. E., & Fox, S. (2005). The stressor-emotion model of counterproductive work behavior. In Spector, P. E., & Fox, S. (Eds.), *Counterproductive Work Behavior: Investigations of Actors and Targets*, (pp. 151–174). American Psychological Association.

[22] Bari, M. W., Khan, Q., & Waqas, A. (2023). Person related workplace bullying and knowledge hiding behaviors: relational psychological contract breach as an underlying mechanism. *Journal of Knowledge Management*, 27(5), 1299–1318.

[23] Connelly, C. E., & Zweig, D. (2015). How perpetrators and targets construe knowledge hiding in organizations. *European Journal of Work and Organizational Psychology*, 24(3), 479–489.

[24] Donate, M. J., González-Mohíno, M., Appio, F. P., & Bernhard, F. (2022). Dealing with knowledge hiding to improve innovation capabilities in the hotel industry: the unconventional role of knowledge-oriented leadership. *Journal of Business Research*, 144, 572–586.

[25] Babcock, P. (2004). Shedding light on knowledge management. *HR Magazine*, 49(5), 46–51.

[26] Howard, M. C., Cogswell, J. E., & Smith, M. B. (2020). The antecedents and outcomes of workplace ostracism: a meta-analysis. *Journal of Applied Psychology*, 105(6), 577–596.

[27] Sharma, N., & Dhar, R. L. (2022). From curse to cure of workplace ostracism: a systematic review and future research agenda. *Human Resource Management Review*, 32(3), 100836.

[28] Ferris, D. L., Brown, D. J., Berry, J. W., & Lian, H. (2008). The development and validation of the workplace Ostracism Scale. *Journal of Applied Psychology*, 93(6), 1348–1366.

[29] Robinson, S. L., O'Reilly, J., & Wang, W. (2013). Invisible at work: an integrated model of workplace ostracism. *Journal of Management*, 39(1), 203–231.

[30] Manninen, S. M., Koponen, S., Sinervo, T., & Laulainen, S. (2024). Workplace ostracism in healthcare: Association with job satisfaction, stress, and perceived health. *Journal of Advanced Nursing*, 80(5), 1813–1825.

[31] Wang, D., Qin, Y., & Zhou, W. (2021). The effects of leaders' prosocial orientation on employees' organizational citizenship behavior–the roles of affective commitment and workplace ostracism. *Psychology Research and Behavior Management*, 14, 1171–1185.

[32] Zhu, H., Lyu, Y., Deng, X., & Ye, Y. (2017). Workplace ostracism and proactive customer service performance: A conservation of resources perspective. *International Journal of Hospitality Management*, 64, 62–72.

[33] Mao, Y., Liu, Y., Jiang, C., & Zhang, I. D. (2018). Why am I ostracized and how would I react? a review of workplace ostracism research. *Asia Pacific Journal of Management*, 35, 745–767.

[34] Hua, C., Zhao, L., He, Q., & Chen, Z. (2023). When and how workplace ostracism leads to interpersonal deviance: the moderating effects of self-control and negative affect. *Journal of Business Research*, 156, 113554.

[35] Gouldner, A. W. (1960). The norm of reciprocity: a preliminary statement. *American Sociological Review*, 25(2), 161 –178.

[36] Uhl-Bien, M., & Maslyn, J. M. (2003). Reciprocity in manager-subordinate relationships: components, configurations, and outcomes. *Journal of Management*, 29(4), 511–532.

[37] Koay, K. Y., Lim, V. K., Soh, P. C. H., Ong, D. L. T., Ho, J. S. Y., & Lim, P. K. (2022). Abusive supervision and cyberloafing: a moderated moderation model of moral disengagement and NRBs. *Information and Management*, 59(2), 103600.

[38] Selem, K. M., Khan, M. A., Elayan, M. B., Shehata, A. E., & Mkheimer, I. M. (2024). Tit-for-Tat! does negative reciprocity mitigate supervisors' abusive behaviors on hotel employee outcomes?. *Journal of Quality Assurance in Hospitality & Tourism*, 25(5), 1438–1464.

[39] Mo, S., Lupoli, M. J., Newman, A., & Umphress, E. E. (2023). Good intentions, bad behavior: a review and synthesis of the literature on unethical prosocial behavior (UPB) at work. *Journal of Organizational Behavior*, 44(2), 335–354.

[40] Zhu, Q., Cheng, K., & Zou, N. (2025). How does negative workplace gossip influence receivers' interaction avoidance and willingness to cooperate? the role of attributed self-serving motives. *Journal of Managerial Psychology*, 40(3), 303–318.

[41] Liu, X., Zhang, H., & Yu, X. (2023). Effects of workplace ostracism on pro-job unethical behavior: the role of moral disengagement, interpersonal sensitivity and self-serving political will. *Psychological Reports*, 00332941231207775.

[42] Poon, K. T., Jiang, Y., & Teng, F. (2020). Putting oneself in someone's shoes: the effect of observing ostracism on physical pain, social pain, negative emotion, and self-regulation. *Personality and Individual Differences*, 166, 110217.

[43] Ren, D., Wesselmann, E. D., & Williams, K. D. (2018). Hurt people hurt people: ostracism and aggression. *Current Opinion in Psychology*, 19, 34–38.

[44] Bhatti, S. H., Hussain, M., Santoro, G., & Culasso, F. (2023). The impact of organizational ostracism on knowledge hiding: analysing the sequential mediating role of efficacy needs and psychological distress. *Journal of Knowledge Management*, 27(2), 485–505.

[45] Wu, L. Z., Zhang, H., Chiu, R. K., Kwan, H. K., & He, X. (2014). Hostile attribution bias and NRBs exacerbate incivility's effects on interpersonal deviance. *Journal of Business Ethics*, 120, 189–199.

[46] U.S. Commercial Service (2023). *Sri Lanka - Country Commercial Guide: Telecommunications and*

Information Technology. U.S. Department of Commerce. https://www.trade.gov/country-commercial-guides/sri-lanka-telecommunications-and-information-technology.

[47] Mitchell, M. S., & Ambrose, M. L. (2007). Abusive supervision and workplace deviance and the moderating effects of NRBs. *Journal of Applied Psychology*, 92(4), 1159–1168.

[48] Fong, P. S., Men, C., Luo, J., & Jia, R. (2018). Knowledge hiding and team creativity: the contingent role of task interdependence. *Management Decision*, 56(2), 329–343.

[49] Etikan, I., Musa, S. A., & Alkassim, R. S. (2016). Comparison of convenience sampling and purposive sampling. *American Journal of Theoretical and Applied Statistics*, 5(1), 1–4.

[50] Wu, J. B., Hom, P. W., Tetrick, L. E., Shore, L. M., Jia, L., Li, C., et al. (2006). The norm of reciprocity: scale development and validation in the Chinese context. *Management and Organization Review*, 2(3), 377–402.

[51] Lin, C. P. (2006). Gender differs: Modelling knowledge sharing from a perspective of social network ties. *Asian Journal of Social Psychology*, 9(3), 236–241.

[52] Lazazzara, A., & Za, S. (2020). The effect of subjective age on knowledge sharing in the public sector. *Personnel Review*, 49(1), 303–323.

[53] Liu, C., Yang, J., & Gu, X. (2021). Antecedents of workplace ostracism. In C. Liu & J. Ma (Eds.), *Workplace ostracism* (Palgrave Explorations in Workplace Stigma, pp. 65–99).

[54] Chatterjee, S., Chaudhuri, R., Thrassou, A., & Vrontis, D. (2021). Antecedents and consequences of knowledge hiding: the moderating role of knowledge hiders and knowledge seekers in organizations. *Journal of Business Research*, 128, 303–313.

[55] Butt, A. S. (2019). Antecedents of knowledge hiding in a buyer–supplier relationship. *Knowledge and Process Management*, 26(4), 346–354.

[56] Yee, D. J., Wiggins, M. W., & Searle, B. J. (2020). Higher social cue utilisation improves communication, reduces perceived workload, and improves performance amongst ad hoc dyads in simulated rail control. *Ergonomics*, 63(1), 31–47.

[57] Zhao, H., Liu, W., Li, J., & Yu, X. (2019). Leader–member exchange, organizational identification, and knowledge hiding: the moderating role of relative leader–member exchange. *Journal of Organizational Behavior*, 40(7), 834–848.

[58] Uhl-Bien, M., & Maslyn, J. M. (2003). Reciprocity in manager-subordinate relationships: components, configurations, and outcomes. *Journal of Management*, 29(4), 511–532.

[59] Atapattu, M. M., & Huybers, T. (2022). Motivational antecedents, employee engagement and knowledge management performance. *Journal of Knowledge Management*, 26(3), 528–547.

[60] Wu, L. Z., Yim, F. H. K., Kwan, H. K., & Zhang, X. (2012). Coping with workplace ostracism: the roles of ingratiation and political skill in employee psychological distress. *Journal of Management Studies*, 49(1), 178–199.

[61] Wang, Y. (2023). The impact mechanism of constructive deviance on workplace ostracism: the roles of political skill and workplace friendship. *Current Psychology*, 42(27), 23323–23331.

[62] Zhang, L., & Huo, X. (2015). The impact of interpersonal conflict on construction project performance: a moderated mediation study from China. *International Journal of Conflict Management*, 26(4), 479–498.

[63] Saks, A., & A. Gruman, J. (2014). Making organizations more effective through organizational socialization. *Journal of Organizational Effectiveness: People and Performance*, 1(3), 261–280.

[64] Flanagan, K. S., Vanden Hoek, K. K., Ranter, J. M., & Reich, H. A. (2012). The potential of forgiveness as a response for coping with negative peer experiences. *Journal of Adolescence*, 35(5), 1215–1223.

[65] Chandrasekara, R., & Wijetunga, D. (2016). Tension between values of traditional and consumerist cultures in a Sri Lankan context: a self-discrepancy perspective. *Journal of International Consumer Marketing*, 28(5), 309–322.

[66] Gherghel, C., & Akamatsu, D. (2023). Interpersonal harmony pursuit in Japan and the United States: culture shapes motivation and goal content. *Current Psychology*, 42(24), 20474–20484.

[67] Quratulain, S. (2020). Trust violation and recovery dynamics in the context of differential supervisor-subordinate relationships: a study of public service employees. *Public Integrity*, 22(2), 111–133.

6 Enhancing argumentative writing skills through structured asynchronous forum debates in English as a second language (ESL) context

T.M.B.N. Thennakoon[a]

Department of Marketing Management, Faculty of Commerce and Management Studies, University of Kelaniya, Sri Lanka

Abstract

As digital technologies continue to reshape the landscape of language education, asynchronous online platforms have garnered growing recognition as effective mechanisms for fostering academic writing proficiency within English as a Second Language (ESL) contexts. This study critically examines the efficacy of structured asynchronous forum debates in advancing argumentative writing skills among undergraduate ESL learners. It specifically investigates the extent to which engagement in these debates enhances students' ability to formulate logically coherent arguments, employ appropriate academic language, and effectively address opposing viewpoints. Adopting a mixed-methods approach, the study was conducted with a cohort of 40 ESL undergraduates enrolled in Advanced English for Commerce and Management Studies course at the Department of Marketing Management, University of Kelaniya. Over a six-week period, participants engaged in weekly forum debates centered on discipline-specific topics. Quantitative data were gathered through pre- and post-intervention writing tasks, evaluated using five-dimensional analytic rubric. Qualitative data were derived from a content analysis of forum contributions and semi-structured interviews conducted with a representative sample of participants. The findings reveal statistically significant improvements across all assessed dimensions of argumentative writing, with the most pronounced gains observed in logical organization and textual cohesion. The asynchronous format facilitated opportunities for reflection, iterative revision, and meaningful peer interaction. Qualitative insights further highlighted enhanced learner confidence, deeper engagement with academic discourse conventions, and the development of critical reasoning skills. This study highlights the pedagogical value of integrating structured asynchronous debates into technology-enhanced writing instruction for ESL learners. The results offer practical implications for curriculum designers and educators and point to future research directions on long-term skill development and differentiated implementation across varying proficiency levels.

Keywords: Argumentative writing, Asynchronous learning, forum debates, English as a second language, technology-enhanced language learning

Introduction

In recent years, the role of English as a Second Language (ESL) instruction has undergone a substantial transformation, driven by the increasing emphasis on academic communication, critical thinking, and digital engagement in contemporary educational contexts. Among the core competencies required in academic settings, argumentative writing emerges as a critical skill, enabling learners to formulate coherent, evidence-based arguments, address opposing viewpoints, and actively participate in academic discourse. However, many ESL learners face challenges in mastering this genre due to limited exposure to authentic academic debates, restricted opportunities for peer interaction, and difficulties in organizing ideas cohesively [1, 2].

With the proliferation of digital platforms in academic contexts, asynchronous learning contexts have emerged as promising avenues for language development. Such environments facilitate learner engagement at an individual pace, fostering deeper reflection and the development of more thoughtfully structured responses. Forum-based asynchronous discussions have gained considerable recognition for their capacity to foster critical engagement and enhance the development of academic writing skills [3, 4]. Unlike synchronous interactions, asynchronous formats provide learners with extended time to plan, draft, revise, and refine their arguments—processes that are fundamental to the development of effective argumentative writing.

[a]tmbnt201@kln.ac.lk

DOI: 10.4324/9781003739920-6

Despite the increasing emphasis on Technology-Enhanced Language Learning (TELL), a significant portion of existing research has predominantly concentrated on synchronous tools, including live chat, videoconferencing, and collaborative writing platforms [5]. Empirical studies focusing on structured asynchronous debate formats as a pedagogical intervention remain scarce, particularly within the ESL context of South Asia. This gap is especially relevant in Sri Lanka, where many undergraduates possess intermediate proficiency in English but often lack confidence and competence in producing structured argumentative essays in academic settings [6].

To address this gap, the present study investigates the use of structured asynchronous forum debates as a tool for enhancing argumentative writing skills among ESL undergraduates. The intervention, implemented over a six-week period, was integrated into an academic English course offered to second-year students at the Department of Marketing Management, University of Kelaniya. Through weekly debates on discipline-relevant topics, students engaged in the process of constructing claims, providing evidence, countering opposing views, and integrating peer feedback—core elements of argumentative writing pedagogy [7].

The design of the intervention draws on social constructivist theories of learning, which emphasize the role of interaction and scaffolding in knowledge construction [8]. Structured forum debates align with this paradigm by promoting dialogic engagement, reflective reasoning, and collaborative meaning-making. Furthermore, the asynchronous nature of the debates provided students with the opportunity to engage in metacognitive reflection and self-editing, contributing to greater lexical accuracy and cohesion in their written output [9].

This paper aims to explore three key research questions:

1. To what extent do structured asynchronous forum debates enhance the logical organization of students' argumentative writing?
2. How do these debates impact the use of academic language and cohesive devices?
3. What are students' perceptions of their argumentative writing development through this digital intervention?

By addressing these questions through a mixed-methods approach, the study seeks to offer empirical evidence on the effectiveness of asynchronous forum debates as a language learning tool. Pre- and post-intervention writing tasks were quantitatively assessed using an analytic rubric, while content analysis and semi-structured interviews were employed to capture the qualitative dimensions of students' learning experiences.

By adopting this focus, the study advances the growing body of scholarship on technology-enhanced writing instruction in ESL contexts, offering evidence-based insights for curriculum designers, language educators, and educational technologists. Furthermore, the findings have broader implications for pedagogical practices in higher education, particularly in light of the increasing integration of asynchronous digital tools within blended and online learning frameworks.

Materials and Methodology

Materials

The instructional intervention was implemented as part of the Advanced English for Commerce and Management Studies module offered to second-year undergraduates in the Department of Marketing Management, University of Kelaniya. The course's core objective was to strengthen students' academic communication skills in English, with particular emphasis on argumentative writing, critical thinking, and academic discourse.

To implement the intervention, the university's Learning Management System (LMS), was utilized as the primary medium for asynchronous forum-based discussions.

The system facilitated organized weekly discussion threads, time-stamped posts, and threaded replies, thereby enabling systematic monitoring of interaction patterns and the depth of argumentative engagement. Each forum debate was hosted under a designated heading accompanied by structured prompts and detailed instructions. Learners were provided with a clear schedule specifying the debate topic, participation deadlines, and expectations for the quality and quantity of contributions.

Each forum debate adhered to a structured format, introduced with a brief contextual paragraph, a clearly defined debate prompt, and two contrasting positions designed to guide and frame learner responses. Topics were drawn from marketing and business contexts, including:

- 'Influencer marketing promotes unrealistic consumption habits.'
- 'Personalized advertising is ethical when based on customer data.'

- 'Surveillance in remote workplaces enhances productivity.'

To support and guide students' writing, a comprehensive resource packet was distributed at the outset of the intervention. This packet includes:

- A model of the Toulmin argument structure [7]
- Sample forum posts demonstrating effective argumentation and counterargument integration
- Guidelines on academic tone, citation etiquette (where applicable), and cohesive devices

An analytic scoring rubric was developed based on existing academic writing assessment tools [10]. It covered five key dimensions:

1. Logical organization and coherence
2. Use of evidence and examples
3. Academic language use
4. Engagement with counterarguments
5. Lexical accuracy and cohesive devices

Each dimension was scored on a 5-point scale (1 = weak, 5 = excellent), generating a composite score out of 25. The rubric was used for both the pre- and post-intervention writing assessments.

Furthermore, semi-structured interview protocols were created to explore students' perceptions of the forum debates. These were used in the post-intervention phase with a selected subset of participants.

Methodology

This study employed a mixed-methods approach, integrating quantitative and qualitative data to evaluate the impact of asynchronous forum debates on ESL learners' argumentative writing.

Participants

A purposive sample of 40 second-year undergraduates (65% female, 35% male; age 20–23) was selected from a cohort enrolled in the Advanced English for Commerce and Management Studies module. All participants had a minimum B grade in their previous English course and demonstrated intermediate proficiency.

Research design

The study was implemented over three phases:

- Pre-intervention phase: Students completed a baseline argumentative writing task in response to a standard prompt. This task was completed individually under timed, exam-like conditions and assessed using the rubric described above. A preparatory session was also held to introduce students to asynchronous debate etiquette, the LMS interface, and argumentation structures.
- Intervention phase: Spanning six weeks, this phase required students to participate in weekly structured forum debates. Each week, students:
  - Posted one initial argument (150–200 words)
  - Replied to two peers (100–150 words each)
  - Had the option to revise their initial post based on feedback

Instructors monitored the discussions for relevance and decorum but did not directly participate to preserve the authenticity of peer-led interaction. Participation was part of a formative assessment, worth 10% of the course grade.

- Post-Intervention Phase: At the conclusion of the sixth week, students completed a second argumentative writing task. This prompt differed from the pre-test but followed similar complexity and structure. The writing was assessed using the same rubric for comparative analysis.

Data collection

- Quantitative Data: Pre- and post-writing scores were collected for all 40 students. Scores were entered into SPSS for statistical analysis.
- Qualitative Data:
  - Forum posts (initial and replies) were extracted and coded using NVivo software.
  - 12 students were randomly selected for semi-structured interviews, which were transcribed and analyzed for emerging themes.

Data analysis

Paired sample t-tests were conducted to compare pre- and post-intervention scores. Statistical significance was set at $p < 0.05$. Each of the five rubric dimensions was tested independently to identify specific areas of improvement.

The forum content was analyzed using thematic coding. Categories including argument depth, engagement with counterarguments, use of academic tone, and self-revision behaviors were identified inductively [11]. The thematic overlap between student reflections and written performance was noted to support triangulation.

Interview data were coded for perceptions of:

- Writing improvement
- Interaction with peers
- Usefulness of asynchronous structure
- Challenges in online debate formats

This triangulated design ensured a robust understanding of both the learning gains and student experiences associated with the intervention.

Results and Discussion

Sample collection

The data collection process was structured to capture both quantitative measures of student writing improvement and qualitative insights into learners' engagement and perceptions. Data were drawn from three primary sources:

1. Pre- and post-intervention writing samples: All 40 participants completed two timed argumentative writing tasks, one at the beginning and one at the end of the six-week intervention. These were evaluated using a five-dimensional analytic rubric, scoring performance on logical organization and coherence, use of evidence and examples, academic language use, engagement with counterarguments, and cohesion &lexical accuracy. Each dimension was rated on a 5-point scale, producing a maximum total score of 25.
2. Forum debate contributions: Students engaged in six structured asynchronous debates, posting a total of 240 initial arguments and 480 peer replies. The average per student was six initial posts and twelve replies. Forum threads were downloaded from the LMS and prepared for thematic coding using NVivo software.
3. Semi-structured interviews: A subset of 12 participants were randomly selected for post-intervention interviews. Each interview, lasting approximately 25 minutes, was transcribed and analyzed to explore students' perceptions of the forum debates and their impact on writing proficiency.

The use of these three data types enabled triangulation, strengthening the validity of the findings and ensuring a holistic analysis of student outcomes.

Sample analysis

Quantitative analysis

A comparison of pre- and post-intervention writing scores showed statistically significant improvements across all rubric dimensions. The greatest gains were observed in logical organization and cohesion, followed closely by counterarguments and use of academic language.

The data in Table 6.1 highlights consistent improvement across all assessed areas. Students showed the most substantial gains in logical organization and cohesion & lexical accuracy, suggesting that the structured and reflective nature of asynchronous forum debates contributed significantly to their ability to logically structure arguments and use cohesive devices more effectively. The gains in counterarguments and academic language also indicate an increased capacity to engage with multiple viewpoints and to communicate with greater formality and precision.

To understand individual variation and the spread of improvements across the cohort, descriptive statistics were calculated for each dimension.

Table 6.2 reveals that while most students improved significantly, the degree of improvement varied. The standard deviations indicate moderate variation, with some students achieving over 1.5-point improvements in individual areas. The minimum values of 0.0 in a few dimensions indicate that a small number of

Table 6.1 Argumentative writing improvement summary.

Rubric dimension	Pre-test mean	Post-test mean	Mean improvement
Logical organization	2.86	3.68	0.82
Use of evidence	2.94	3.56	0.62
Academic language	2.81	3.42	0.61
Counterarguments	2.77	3.40	0.63
Cohesion & lexical accuracy	2.89	3.67	0.78

Source: Author

Table 6.2 Improvement summary statistics by dimension.

Rubric dimension	Mean improvement	Std Dev	Min	Max
Logical organization	0.82	0.35	0.10	1.60
Use of evidence	0.62	0.33	0.00	1.40
Academic language	0.61	0.32	0.00	1.20
Counterarguments	0.63	0.31	0.00	1.20
Cohesion & lexical accuracy	0.78	0.30	0.10	1.50
Total improvement	3.46	1.23	1.20	6.30

Source: Author

Table 6.3 Correlation matrix of improvement across rubric dimensions.

	Logical	Evidence	Language	Counterarg	Cohesion	Total
Logical organization	1.00	0.69	0.72	0.64	0.75	0.88
Use of evidence	0.69	1.00	0.66	0.71	0.68	0.84
Academic language	0.72	0.66	1.00	0.67	0.74	0.86
Counterarguments	0.64	0.71	0.67	1.00	0.65	0.82
Cohesion & lexical use	0.75	0.68	0.74	0.65	1.00	0.90
Total improvement	0.88	0.84	0.86	0.82	0.90	1.00

Source: Author

learners showed little or no gain in specific aspects, particularly in the use of evidence and academic language. These results highlight that although the intervention was broadly effective, individual learner differences—such as motivation, prior knowledge, or engagement level—likely influenced outcomes.

To examine how gains in one area related to others, a correlation matrix was developed.

Table 6.3 shows strong positive correlations among all five writing dimensions. Notably, Cohesion has a high correlation with Total Improvement ($r = 0.90$), followed closely by logical organization ($r = 0.88$). This suggests that students who became better at logically organizing their writing and using appropriate linking expressions also tended to improve across other dimensions. These correlations support the idea that writing skills develop in interconnected ways, and improvements in one area—such as vocabulary or organization—can reinforce gains in others. This reinforces the relevance of holistic approaches to writing instruction in ESL contexts [12].

Qualitative analysis

To complement the quantitative data, qualitative insights were gathered through two key sources: (1) content analysis of students' forum contributions over six weeks, and (2) semi-structured interviews conducted with 12 randomly selected students. This dual approach provided rich contextual evidence of the learning process and the perceived value of the structured asynchronous forum debates.

a) Evolution in Forum Contributions

The content analysis of 240 initial posts and 480 peer replies revealed clear progression in students' argumentative writing over time. In the initial weeks, posts were generally shorter, informally worded, and lacked structural clarity. Many students relied on personal opinions without supporting evidence, and counterarguments were often absent.

However, by weeks 4 to 6, several patterns of improvement were observed:

- Improved structure: Students began following a logical flow in their writing, including clear thesis statements, supporting points, and conclusions.
- Use of Evidence: A greater number of posts cited examples, case studies, and statistics. While not all were referenced formally, this shift indicated a growing awareness of evidence-based reasoning.

- Engagement with Counterarguments: In later posts, many students acknowledged and addressed opposing views. For example, one student wrote, *"While personalised advertising improves user experience, it can also lead to privacy violations. Therefore, regulation is essential."*
- Academic tone and formality: The language of forum posts became increasingly formal. Informal expressions such as "I feel like" and "this is bad" were replaced with academic phrases such as "It can be argued that..." or "A key concern associated with this practice is..."

This evolution suggests that sustained practice in a structured, low stakes setting allowed learners to internalize the components of effective academic argumentation.

b) Insights from student interviews
Thematic analysis of interview transcripts generated three major themes:

Theme 1: Increased confidence in argument construction
Most participants indicated that they felt significantly more confident in constructing and expressing their opinions in English after participating in the debates. This was particularly notable among students who initially hesitated to express their views due to fear of grammatical errors or lack of vocabulary.

"Earlier, I used to worry about whether my opinion was correct or if I used the wrong word. But with the debates, I learned that what matters is how I explain my idea clearly."*(Student 7)*

This sense of confidence extended to their performance in formal academic writing tasks, suggesting a transfer of skills from the discussion forum to traditional writing contexts.

Theme 2: Appreciation of reflective time and peer learning
A distinctive advantage of the asynchronous format, as noted by all participants, was the time to reflect before responding. Unlike in face-to-face debates, where immediate replies are expected, students had the opportunity to read peers' posts, process ideas, and construct thoughtful responses.

"When I saw what others wrote, I realised how to make my point stronger or how to organise better. Also, I had time to read it again and make changes before I posted."*(Student 11)*

Students also acknowledged the role of peer modeling, where exposure to strong posts influenced their own writing. Many adapted useful expressions, logical structures, and even counterargument formats they saw in their classmates' posts.

Theme 3: Initial reluctance to critique and gradual development of academic disagreement skills
Several students initially reported hesitation in disagreeing with their peers' opinions, often due to cultural factors or fear of sounding rude. However, the clear expectations set by the instructor, along with weekly exposure to respectful disagreement practices, helped students overcome this challenge.

"In the first week, I just agreed with everyone. But later, I learned it's okay to disagree if we do it in a polite and logical way." *(Student 3)*

By the final weeks, students were confidently offering alternative viewpoints, using hedging language such as "While I understand your perspective..." or "Another way to consider this is...". This shift marks a significant development in students' academic discourse competence, an essential skill in higher education settings.

c) Observed pedagogical impact
The qualitative data overall supports the conclusion that structured asynchronous forum debates not only improved students' writing skills but also influenced their academic identity. The forum functioned as a "safe rehearsal space" where learners could experiment with new structures, vocabulary, and argument forms without the pressure of immediate judgment or grades.

The gradual and visible improvement in both written output and self-perception aligns with Vygotskian theories of social learning and the zone of proximal development (ZPD), which suggest that students learn most effectively when scaffolded in peer-supported, reflective environments [13].

Conclusion

This study investigated the impact of structured asynchronous forum debates on the development of argumentative writing skills among ESL undergraduates. Conducted over a six-week intervention within an academic English course, the research combined quantitative and qualitative methods to assess improvements in students' ability to construct logical, evidence-based arguments, use academic language, and engage with counterarguments.

Quantitative findings indicated statistically significant improvements across all five assessed writing dimensions: Logical organization, use of evidence, academic language, engagement with counterarguments, and cohesion & lexical accuracy. The most notable gains were observed in organizational clarity and lexical cohesion, underscoring the effectiveness of the structured and reflective nature of asynchronous engagement. Correlation analysis further revealed that writing competencies developed interdependently, suggesting that holistic instructional approaches yield more meaningful outcomes than isolated skill instruction.

Qualitative data from forum content and semi-structured interviews reinforced these findings. Students demonstrated progressive mastery of academic discourse conventions, shifting from informal, opinion-based writing to well-structured, balanced arguments. Interview responses revealed increased learner confidence, appreciation for reflective time, and greater comfort in expressing disagreement constructively—skills often underdeveloped in ESL academic contexts.

Collectively, these findings underscore the pedagogical value of integrating asynchronous forum debates into ESL writing instruction, particularly in promoting critical thinking, structured argumentation, and sustained learner engagement.

The asynchronous format provides not only flexibility but also cognitive space for deeper thought, self-editing, and dialogic interaction. It serves as an accessible and low-pressure environment for students to practice and refine essential academic writing strategies.

From a curricular standpoint, this study advocates for the strategic incorporation of structured online forums into writing pedagogy, particularly for learners navigating English-medium academic environments. Educators and curriculum designers are encouraged to view asynchronous digital platforms not as supplemental tools, but as core spaces for the development of argumentation, reflection, and academic voice.

Future research may explore the longitudinal effects of such interventions, their adaptability across varying proficiency levels, and the impact of instructor presence and scaffolding on discourse quality. Additionally, comparative studies between synchronous and asynchronous formats could provide further insight into optimal digital writing environments for diverse ESL learner populations.

References

[1] Kaplan, R. B. (1966). Cultural thought patterns in intercultural education. *Language Learning*, 16(1–2), 1–20.

[2] Hyland, G. (2003). Second Language Writing. Cambridge: Cambridge University Press.

[3] Warschauer, J. (2017). The role of culture in second language learning with technology. In The Handbook of Technology and Second Language Teaching and Learning, (pp. 120–135). Wiley-Blackwell.

[4] Ertmer, P. A., & Newby, T. J. (2013). Behaviorism, cognitivism, constructivism: comparing critical features from an instructional design perspective. *Performance Improvement Quarterly*, 26(2), 43–71.

[5] Hampel, M., & Stickler, U. (2005). New skills for new classrooms: training tutors to teach languages online. *Computer Assisted Language Learning*, 18(4), 311–326.

[6] Jayasinghe, A., & Wickramasinghe, U. (2021). Academic literacy challenges among Sri Lankan undergraduates: a case from the management faculty. *Sri Lanka Journal of English Language Teaching*, 32(2), 25–39.

[7] Toulmin, S. (2003). The Uses of Argument, (2nd edn.). Cambridge: Cambridge University Press.

[8] Vygotsky, L. S. (1978). Mind in Society: The Development of Higher Psychological Processes. Cambridge, MA: Harvard University Press.

[9] Yang, S. Y. (2013). Exploring students' perceptions of using asynchronous discussion forums. *Journal of Educational Computing Research*, 49(2), 207–221.

[10] Weigle, A. (2002). Assessing Writing. Cambridge: Cambridge University Press.

[11] Saldaña, J. (2016). The Coding Manual for Qualitative Researchers, (3rd edn.). London: Sage.

[12] Coffin, C. (2003). Teaching Academic Writing: A Toolkit for Higher Education. London: Routledge.

[13] Silva, T., & Matsuda, P. (2010). On Second Language Writing. New York: Routledge.

[14] Cumming, J. (2011). Integrating writing instruction and language learning for international and generation 1.5 students. *TESL Canada Journal*, 28(2), 123–138.

7 Balancing innovation and public health: a critical analysis of Sri Lanka's patent law regime and its impact on medicine accessibility

Tharinsa Gamage[a]

Department of Legal Studies, Faculty of Business, NSBM Green University, Sri Lanka

Abstract

The intersection of the laws governing patents and public health presents a crucial global challenge when patent rights granted for essential medicines manufactured by multinational pharmaceutical companies often result in monopolies that undermine accessibility and affordability for patients. This article narrows its scope to critically examine Sri Lanka's patent system, evaluating whether its legal framework awarding patents for essential medicines strikes an appropriate balance between protecting innovation and upholding the right to health of the public. This study investigates whether the relevant provisions of Sri Lanka's Intellectual Property Act No. 36 of 2003 are aligned with TRIPS standards adequately and addresses the impact of patent protection on access to quality medicines in Sri Lanka. The qualitative research undertaken through library-based desk research, referring to primary and secondary sources explores the shortcomings of the Sri Lankan patent laws in terms of granting patents for essential medicines which lead to high prices and the limited use of International IP standards that hinder equitable access to patented medicines developments as opposed to the approaches followed by India and South Africa. This study concludes by proposing legal reforms to strengthened use of International IP flexibilities including enhancing the adherence to Compulsory Licensing and Parallel Importing in the patent law regime and recommending adjustments to revise the International IP standards particularly TRIPS Agreement in order to balance innovation incentives with equitable access, ensuring that Sri Lanka's patent law framework supports both economic growth through innovation and the right to health of the public by reinforcing the country's dual commitment to innovation and the right to health.

Keywords: International intellectual property standards, multi-national companies, patentability, right to health

Introduction

The critical role played by Intellectual Property to foster innovation while driving economic competitiveness in the complex global landscape of the 21st century has been a vital asset in propelling innovation, creativity, and competitiveness. Thus, the protection and efficient management of intellectual property has become paramount to meet the requirements of an era marked by scientific and technological advancements [1]. Parallel to the focus on innovation and intellectual property, the interplay between intellectual property (IP) protection and public health considerations has long been a topic of contention, particularly in the realm of patents and their access to medicines. The monopolistic nature of patented medicinal products leads to high prices for essential medicines, increasing the unaffordability, especially for the low- and middle-income countries.

As Sri Lanka pertain to access essential medicines, despite their longstanding commitment to affordable healthcare through its National Pharmaceuticals Policy, the State Pharmaceuticals Corporation's central procurement model and section 86 of the IP Act No.36 of 2003, providing for the compulsory licensing and parallel importation to legally empower the state to override patent monopolies in public health emergencies, no such licenses have ever been issued. To illustrate early 2023, the unaffordable prices of 164 out of 383 tracked essential medicines denoted the lack of deployment of IP flexibilities. Thus, this paper analyzes the gaps in patent law regime hindering the affordability of essential medicines, highlighting a critical tension between innovation policy and public health outcomes.

Research Methodology

This study adopted a qualitative research paradigm to systematically analyze Sri Lanka's legal framework on patents applicable to essential medicines. Rooted in a library-based approach, the research critically

[a]tharinsa.g@nsbm.ac.lk

DOI: 10.4324/9781003739920-7

examines primary legal sources alongside authoritative secondary literature. The doctrinal research is conducted to analyze the extent to which Sri Lanka's patent standards align with TRIPS benchmarks, assessing the extent to which legal provisions for compulsory licensing and parallel importing are operationalized. Where Sri Lankan jurisprudence is scarce, comparative analysis is conducted drawing lessons from India and South Africa that have actively deployed TRIPS flexibilities in advancing public health, to recalibrate Sri Lanka's patent law to better balance innovation with equitable medicine access.

Analysis and Discussion

Patents and access to medicine

"The patent system adds the fuel of interest to the fire of genius in the discovery and production of new and useful things"

Abraham Lincoln

Affirming to Lincoln's idea, IP is tangentially related to developing new vaccines and drugs and seeking mechanisms to allow their wide-scale distribution to safeguard public health. This collaboration is nurtured mainly through patents, which protect new inventions by giving an incentive to the inventor in technological inventions [2]. According to Chief Justice Burger, patents act as an absolute right to regulate the misappropriation of an invention by stimulating research and aiding the development and commercialization of new products [3]. Additionally, patents permit authoritative excessive pricing as they preclude potential competitors' entry [4]. Whether this is being practiced in Sri Lanka is one of the questions that prompted this research.

Patent protection becomes crucial when new medicines especially vaccines and treatments that are unique to a serious disease in the efficacy of the inventors are introduced [4]. Most of the newer drugs demonstrate a minor performance improvement, a dosage modification, or no improvement [5]. The introduction of new treatments and vaccines advances treatment, negatively affecting substitutes. The absence of alternatives encourages the supplier to raise the price, even though he/it may justify the imposing of a high price considering the overall business model [5]. Neither the patients nor the government health services can afford extreme prices in a developing country like Sri Lanka. Two billion people across the world in low and middle-income countries do not have regular access to essential medicines.

It is to be noted that according to Article 12 of ICESCR, [6] every human has a right to the enjoyment of the highest attainable standard of physical and mental health and the benefits of scientific progress [6]. Article 25 [7] establishes the right to a standard of living that allows healthy well-being. Therefore, everyone has the right to access life-saving health products and technologies, including vaccines, pharmaceuticals, personal protective equipment, and diagnostics. It is disturbing to note that Sri Lankans do not enjoy these rights in reality.

Although total free medical care is available in Sri Lanka, the right to health is not explicitly stated in the chapter on Fundamental Rights of the Sri Lankan Constitution [7] and the Report on Public Representations on Constitutional Reform incorporated several submissions on the inadequacy of healthcare through the supreme law of Sri Lanka. Although the chapter on Directive Principles indirectly mentions the right to health through article 27(2)(c), it is not justiciable and unenforceable in a court of law [8]. In Harindra v CEB, [8] the individual's right to health was recognized giving weight to the directive principles.

Conversely right to health is enshrined under the articles 14 and 21 of the chapter on Fundamental Rights and articles 39, 41, 42 of the Directive Principles of State Policy and Fundamental Duties chapter of the Constitution of India [9]. The state's obligation in providing access to health as a mean of investing of human dignity under article 21 was established in the case of Bandhua Mukti Morcha v Union of India [10]. Moreover in the case of State of Panjab v Mohinder Chawla, [11] the importance of right to health was elaborated. The Supreme Court held in State of Punjab v. Ram Lubhaya Bagga, [12] that even though the financial resources of the state are not unlimited, failure to adopt a policy to provide medical facility is violation of the constitution. It is emphasized here that Sri Lankan lacks the strengths that India has on this matter.

Sri Lankan patent law

Sri Lanka's patent law has evolved significantly since the enactment of the Intellectual Property Act, which aligned the nation's legal framework with the TRIPS.

Prior to this, patent protection was relatively weak, limiting incentives for innovation. The adoption of TRIPS brought substantial changes, including standardized patent durations and protections. Despite these advancements, the patent regime remains underdeveloped, with few judicial decisions and limited awareness among stakeholders. Weak practices adopted for medicinal patents is one of those,

This article is limited to assess the Sri Lankan patent law concerning medicine accessibility. Sri Lanka's patent law under the Intellectual Property Act of 2003 provides a 20-year exclusivity period for patent holders, aiming to encourage innovation. The two main mechanisms introduced by the Act are compulsory licensing and parallel importation. Compulsory licensing is a legal mechanism that allows a government or authorized body to grant permission to a third party to use a patented invention without the consent of the patent holder. This is done in exchange for a set fee under the law. The patent owner retains their intellectual property rights but must allow others to produce, use, or sell the invention under specific conditions.

Compulsory licensing, outlined in Section 86 of the Act, allows the government or authorized entities to permit third parties to use patented inventions without the patent holder's consent, typically to address pressing health concerns. Parallel importation, meanwhile, enables the import of legitimately sold patented products from other countries, potentially offering cost-effective alternatives.

However, despite the existence of such a legal framework, these mechanisms remain underutilized meaning they are legally available but have rarely been applied in practice. For instance, no compulsory licenses have been issued to date, and there's scant evidence of parallel importation being strategically employed. This disconnection between legal provisions and implementation points to systemic challenges such as limited institutional capacity, low stakeholder awareness, and an absence of clearly defined public health priorities. While the Act aligns with international standards, its real-world impact on medicine accessibility remains modest.

International intellectual property standards and their application in Sri Lanka

In response to the conflicting interests of Intellectual Property and public health, the Agreement on Trade-Related Aspects of Intellectual Property Rights (TRIPS), established under the auspices of the World Trade Organization (WTO), has set the stage for global IP standards. However, the rigid enforcement of these standards often conflicts with the pressing need for affordable and accessible healthcare, especially in developing countries [13]. The Doha Declaration on the TRIPS Agreement and Public Health, introduced in 2001, sought to bridge this gap by affirming the flexibility of TRIPS provisions to protect public health [14].

In particular, Articles 30 and 31 of the TRIPs Agreement permit states to make provision for the use of a patent in the domestic market without the prior authorization of the patent holder in situations of national emergency. Further, the Doha Declaration made provision for the compulsory licensing and parallel importing of any pharmaceutical drugs needed to meet national health emergencies [14]. The compulsory licensing has been introduced to facilitate the access to medicine by low-income consumers through prematurely shifting the company from monopolistic pricing to a competitive prolong structure through the introduction of generic drugs [15]. This system of compulsory licensing enables the state to assume control over the inventor's licensing rights, granting authorization to a third party to utilize the patent. As the new licensee determines the product's price based solely on production costs, excluding expenses related to research and development, the resulting price is typically significantly lower than that of the original. This benefits consumers by making the product more affordable.

Insights from India and South Africa

India has effectively addressed the conflict of patentability and access to medicines. The Patent Act [16] through its section 3(d) has limited the granting patents for exclusively new productions. In Norvatis v Union of India, [17] the court refused in granting patents for the new type of 'beta crystalline' for a known drug 'imatinib mesylate' as it did not show any improved therapeutic efficiency. Further under section 47, patented medicines or drugs can be imported to the country and be used or distributed.

Significantly as per section 84, any interested persons may apply to the Controller for the Grant of a compulsory license on a patent after three years from the date of grant of the patent when facilitating the reasonable requirements of the public, when the patented invention is not available for the public at a reasonably affordable price or when the patented invention is not performed within India. Section 85 has restricted the opportunities to revoke compulsory patent when the invention has not worked within the territory. This initiative helps to sustain the continuous flow of pharmaceutical goods and prevents fraudulent entrepreneurs from generating artificial crises and growing costs for essential medicines. In Nacto Pharma Ltd v Bayer Corporation and Compulsory Licensing Regime in India [18] issued compulsory license for cancer drugs.

Not only an individual application but also the Central Government may grant a compulsory license in the circumstances of a national emergency, extremely urgent situation or in public health crises including HIV, tuberculosis, malaria or other epidemics. Further by section 92A, compulsory license is issued for the manufacture and to export to any country that has insufficient pharmaceutical resources. The Supreme Court highlighted in All India Drug Action Network v Union of India [19] that state actions must provide its people with access to life saving medicines.

In addition to the compulsory licensing, India is termed as the 'pharmacy of the poor' as its pharmaceutical companies have acquired expertise in generic medicines production. With nearly 60000 generic brands, the Indian pharmaceutical industry has strong generic basis, fostered by its legal patent structure. This has lead India becoming one of the world's major medicinal production countries with about 20–22% stake in the world.

South Africa is in the forefront of using parallel imports and compulsory licensing demonstrating how bold legislation can turn legal tools into life-saving measures. Faced with the HIV/AIDS crisis, the government invoked TRIPS flexibilities to allow the production and importation of affordable antiretroviral drugs—at a fraction of the cost of branded versions. The Medicines and Related Substances Amendment Act [20] (Act 59 of 2002) gave teeth to these efforts, despite fierce opposition from global pharmaceutical companies. Forty major manufacturers sued South Africa, but the government stood firm, supported by the Doha Declaration, which affirmed the right of countries to prioritize public health over patent protections.

Loopholes in Sri Lanka's patent law

The influence created by International Intellectual Property Standards in maintaining a fair balance between Intellectual Property and global health is reflected in the attempts made by Sri Lanka to adjust their legislation in line with line with India and South Africa. However, it is prudent in the deep analysis that several loopholes can negatively impact access to essential medicines and healthcare technologies.

Although the compulsory licensing mechanism allows governments to authorize the production of generic versions of patented drugs without the patent holder's consent, it is often underutilized due to political and economic pressures. Furthermore, the TRIPS Agreement includes flexibility like compulsory licensing and parallel importing, but these are not always fully utilized or supported by all countries. Despite its alignment with TRIPS, Sri Lanka's patent law contains several loopholes, including vague provisions for compulsory licensing and a lack of clear criteria to prevent "evergreening."

Sri Lanka has theoretically adopted these provisions but has rarely utilized them in practice. No compulsory licenses have been issued yet, which could be attributed to several factors. Our market is relatively small, potentially resulting in fewer drug patents being filed domestically. Additionally, our well-established generic manufacturing capabilities, along with the ability to import generics from India, may have reduced the necessity for compulsory licensing.

Nonetheless, having these provisions in place is beneficial, as they ensure that if a genuine need arises, for example, compulsory licensing could be leveraged more effectively during health crises to ensure the availability of affordable generic medicines. Additionally, parallel importation could reduce costs for patented drugs, but the necessary legal framework is not fully operational.

The accessibility of medicine in Sri Lanka is hindered by high costs associated with patented drugs, which disproportionately affect vulnerable populations. Regulatory efforts, such as price controls by the NMRA, [21] have been introduced to mitigate these challenges, but they are insufficient to ensure equitable access. The country's reliance on imported pharmaceuticals further complicates the situation, underscoring the need for stronger public health safeguards in patent law. Addressing these gaps is crucial to improving medicine accessibility and fostering innovation.

Recommendations

The endeavors placed in weighing a sufficient balance in Intellectual Property rights and global health are satisfactory, yet, to mitigate the drawbacks discussed and to increase efficiency in the procedures, potential recommendations listed below will be discussed in detail. Why not give recommendations using bullets. So that it's clearer

Sri Lankan patent regime requires to improve the flexibility of the voluntary licensing, compulsory licensing and parallel importation.to combine the interests of patentees with the needs of general public. The use of compulsory licenses must be encouraged in public health emergencies to allow the production or importation of generic versions of patented medicines. Parallel importation can be exercised by supporting policies that enable parallel importation, allowing countries to import more affordable versions of patented medicines from other markets. In the mission of limiting patent extensions, evergreening, where patents for minor modifications are granted, must be prevented by implementing strict criteria for patentability to ensure that only genuine innovations are patented. Moreover, the patent term extensions for medicines must be prevented to delay the entry of generic medicines into the market.

Through the technique of voluntary licensing pharmaceutical companies can specify the conditions under which a generic version of a proprietary drug to be made available from other vendors. Promoting generic medicines is another recommendation that would reduce the deficiency in medicines. Generic competition must be encouraged to facilitate the timely market entry of generic medicines by streamlining the regulatory approval process.

Since Sri Lanka as well as India are parties to the TRIPS and adheres its flexibilities by introducing them into their domestic laws, TRIPS has not been successful in granting equal access to medicines specially to the developing and least developed countries. It is evidenced in the deep analysis that its aim should not be to discourage the invention of medicines but to encourage the availability of the medicines at affordable prices to meet the national public health requirements.

Henceforth, TRIPS should be revised with a few amendments to mark the efficiency in tackling the battle of right to patents and right to health. Firstly, TRIPS should be restructured to include a drug pricing system to oblige patentees to sell medicines at a low cost to provide access to life saving drugs to the poor in the developing world. The TRIPS should provide freedom by incorporating molding patent rules to increase access to medicines to the member states to form their patent laws meeting to socio-economic needs and priorities while respecting international obligations. The Trips should introduce a simple procedure to issue compulsory licenses, especially to facilitate productive patent regime to operate quickly in disease crises under a health responsive legal regime. It should further direct the countries to adopt parallel importing for essential life medicines.

Conclusion

In conclusion, this study highlights the requirement of a delicate balance in the critical intersection between patent laws and public health, particularly within the Sri Lankan context. It underscores the challenges posed by monopolistic control over essential medicines, which restricts accessibility and affordability for the public. By comparing Sri Lanka's approach with those of India and South Africa, the research identifies key shortcomings in the nation's patent framework, especially regarding the limited application of International Intellectual Property (IP) standards. To address these issues, the study advocates for legal reforms that promote the use of IP flexibilities, such as Compulsory Licensing and Parallel Importing, while also recommending adjustments to the TRIPS agreement. These measures aim to strike a balance between fostering innovation and ensuring equitable access to medicines, ultimately supporting both economic development and the fundamental right to health in Sri Lanka.

References

[1] Karapapa, S., & McDonagh, L. (2019). Intellectual Property Law, (1st edn.). Oxford University Press).

[2] Kodithuwakku, R. (2024). A balancing approach on right to patent and right to health during the Covid-19 pandemic.

[3] Diamond v Chakrabarty 447 U.S. 303[1980].

[4] Attorney General (Cth) v Adelaide Steamship Co [1913]18CLR30.

[5] Torremans, P. (2019). Holyoak and Torremans Intellectual Property Law, (9th edn.). Oxford University Press.

[6] United Nations, Universal Declaration of Human Rights, Article 25, 1948. [Online]. Available: https://www.un.org/en/about-us/universal-declaration-of-human-rights.

[7] Parliament of Sri Lanka, The Constitution of the Democratic Socialist Republic of Sri Lanka, 1978.

[Online]. Available: https://parliament.lk/constitution/1978-constitution.

[8] D. Harindra (A Minor) v. Ceylon Electricity Board, [1998] 5(4) SAELR 116.

[9] Government of India, The Constitution of India, 1950. [Online]. Available: https://legislative.gov.in/constitution-of-india/.

[10] Bandhua Mukti Morcha v. Union of India, AIR 1984 SC 802.

[11] State of Punjab v. Mohinder Singh Chawla, AIR 1997 SC 1225.

[12] State of Punjab v. Ram Lubhaya Bagga, (1998) 1 SCR 1120.

[13] P. Ranjan and P. Gour, "The TRIPS waiver decision at the World Trade Organization: Too little too late!," Infojustice.org, 2022. [Online]. Available: https://infojustice.org/archives/43762.

[14] B. Mercurio and P. N. Upreti, "The legality of a TRIPS waiver for COVID-19 vaccines under international investment law," Int. Comp. Law Q., vol. 71, no. 2, pp. 323–355, 2022. [Online]. Available: https://www.cambridge.org/core/services/aop-cambridge-core/content/view/C5065D1883F85B0655593BC7BDC5B8DD/S0020589322000082a.pdf.

[15] J. Kohler, A. Wong, and L. Tailor, "Improving access to COVID-19 vaccines: An analysis of TRIPS waiver discourse among WTO members, civil society organizations, and pharmaceutical industry stakeholders," Health and Human Rights Journal, vol. 24, no. 2, pp. 159–175, Dec. 2022. [Online]. Available: https://www.hhrjournal.org/2022/12/06/improving-access-to-covid-19-vaccines-an-analysis-of-trips-waiver-discourse-among-wto-members-civil-society-organizations-and-pharmaceutical-industry-stakeholders/.

[16] Government of India, The Patents (Amendment) Act, 2005, No. 15 of 2005, Apr. 4, 2005. [Online]. Available: https://www.ipindia.gov.in/writereaddata/Portal/IPOAct/1_69_1_patent_2005.pdf.

[17] Novartis AG v. Union of India, AIR 2013 SC 1311 [Online]. Available: https://blog.ipleaders.in/analysis-novartis-g-vs-union-india/.

[18] Bayer Corporation v. Natco Pharma Ltd., 2013. [Online]. Available: https://www.intepat.com/blog/natco-vs-bayer-indias-bold-move-on-compulsory-licensing-and-the-backlash-from-foreign-nations.

[19] All India Drug Action Network and Others v. Union of India and Others, Writ Petition (C) No. 423 of 2003, Supreme Court of India, Oct. 11, 2012. [Online]. Available: https://www.casemine.com/judgement/in/58117ed62713e179478c1837.

[20] Republic of South Africa, Medicines and Related Substances Amendment Act, No. 59 of 2002, Jan. 17, 2003. [Online]. Available: https://www.gov.za/sites/default/files/gcis_document/201409/a59-020.pdf.

[21] Parliament of Sri Lanka, National Medicines Regulatory Authority Act, No. 5 of 2015, Mar. 19, 2015. [Online]. Available: https://lawnet.gov.lk/wp-content/uploads/act_word/2015/5of2015.docx [lawnet.gov.lk].

8 Lean management in the apparel sector: a systematic literature review

J.H.P.K. Sithumini Jayasekara[1,a], *G.R.S. Kulasekara*[1] *and T.S.M. Amarasena*[1]

[1]Department of Operations and Logistics, NSBM Green University, Sri Lanka

Abstract

Lean management has developed as a transformative strategy to boost efficiency, eliminate wastage, and increase competitiveness in a variety of industries, including the apparel sector. Hence, the main purpose of this study is to examine the implementation, practices, benefits, and challenges of lean management mainly in the apparel industry. This comprehensive systematic literature review focuses on studies published between 2010 and 2025. The study is based on papers retrieved from major academic databases such as Emerald, Taylor and Francis and Google Scholar The entire research process was conducted through the systematic literature review methodology. The research papers selection criteria were implemented according to the PRISMA article selection flowchart procedures. An analysis of 50 academic papers was conducted to examine how lean Management has been absorbed in the apparel sector globally for this study. The findings revealed that lean management improves operational excellence significantly in the apparel sector. The review highlights improvements in productivity, cost reduction, and quality assurance achieved through lean practices, while also identifying barriers such as cultural resistance, lack of skilled labor, and inconsistent supply chain integration. Emerging trends, including the integration of lean principles with Industry 4.0 technologies and sustainable manufacturing practices, are discussed to illustrate how the sector is evolving in response to market demands and environmental concerns. The primary implication of this study is that the systematic literature evaluation encompasses only research papers published between 2010 and 2025, focusing exclusively on the engagement of lean management within the apparel sector.

Keywords: Apparel sector, lean management, productivity, systematic literature review, waste reduction

Introduction

The apparel sector is one of the world's largest manufacturing industries, providing a variety of career opportunities for people all around the world. It covers the basic needs of every human and has a very dynamic environment. The apparel sector has a significant impact on the economies of some countries, including Sri Lanka, Bangladesh, China, Vietnam, India, Indonesia, etc. [1]. The global apparel market is expected to generate $1.84 trillion in revenue by 2025. From 2025 to 2029, this market is expected to increase at a 2.64% annual rate (CAGR). The largest section of the Apparel market is Women's Apparel, which is expected to generate US$963.39 billion in 2025. When comparing global revenue generated in the apparel market, the United States leads with a projected revenue of $366 billion in 2025 [2]. Therefore, most of the apparel sector companies have adopted Lean management to improve efficiency, reduce costs, and enhance product quality [3]. Lean management has been increasingly applied in the apparel sector, including developed and developing countries like India, Bangladesh, Sri Lanka, and China to reduce waste and improve efficiency [4]. According to [5] Lean Management originated from the Toyota Production System developed in Japan. Further, he revealed that the foundation of Lean was laid by Sakichi Toyoda, Kiichiro Toyoda, and Taiichi Ohno. The rise of fast fashion pushed businesses to shorten manufacturing cycles and reduce waste. The expansion of Lean management to the garment business occurred between the 1990s and the 2000s. With increased sustainability concerns, textile manufacturers began adopting lean concepts to reduce fabric waste, energy use, and excess inventory [6]. Prakash [67] stated that 5S, Kanban, Poka-Yoke, Value Stream Mapping, and Just-in-Time are the main Lean tools that are used to enhance the productivity and quality in the apparel sector companies. Not only that Lean Management involve reducing the cost and improving the efficiency but it helps to enhance the sustainability across the industries while using cost reduction and waste management [7]. Most of the

[a]sithumini.j@nsbm.ac.lk

DOI: 10.4324/9781003739920-8

SME are struggling to implement Lean due to limited financial resources and a lack of expertise [8]. Therefore, the majority of the reputed and large-scale companies are focusing more on Lean Management applications in their process [9] highlighted the difficulties in balancing standardization with employee autonomy in a Lean workplace. Also, this study emphasized that the longer a firm operates under Lean principles, the higher the job performance of employees. Digital Lean is an emerging concept in the apparel industry. Digital lean optimizes production schedules through machine learning and predictive analytics, minimizing delays and improving resource allocation. This study highlighted that the efficiency increase through automation is 30%. Not only that IoT smart factories ensure the continuous improvement and reduce inefficiencies in the apparel sector [10].

When implementing the lean techniques, most of the developing countries face several challenges, like outdated machinery, limited skilled labor, and financial constraints. Most of the developed countries use digital Lean, which means that they are using automation, AI for optimized production.

Maware et al. [11] provided a systematic literature review on lean management in developed and developing countries. The lean management specifically of India is addressed in healthcare, construction, and supply chain sectors [12]. Despite the importance of theoretical foundation in research, only about 37% of studies in the field of lean management performance are theoretically underpinned [13]. Even though most of the articles have been discussed about lean management, no specific article has been discussed about lean management for the apparel sector.

However, these studies are typically limited to single case studies or regional focuses, and there is a scarcity of comprehensive syntheses that assess broad trends, common obstacles, and gaps in lean adoption across the apparel industry. This systematic literature review study seeks to address that gap by carefully analyzing available literature to provide a more comprehensive picture. This research differs from previous lean management literature review studies in that it focuses on how lean management was used in the apparel industry between 2010 and 2025. Furthermore, the study analyzed how Lean Management methods are implemented, as well as the difficulties and opportunities associated with their implementation.

The objective of this systematic research is to provide an extensive comprehension of lean management practices in the apparel sector. Specifically, this study intends to identify the various lean tools and approaches utilized in the apparel manufacturing sector, assess the benefits achieved and challenges encountered as provided in existing research articles, and highlight important research gaps while making recommendations for future research.

Methodology

This study mainly focuses on a systematic literature review (SLR) approach, and it can be used to analyze and synthesis the existing body of knowledge specifically on lean management in the apparel industry from 2010 to 2025. The methodology follows the structured way of framework [11], which provides a structured and transparent method for carrying out and reporting literature reviews. Researchers use the PRISMA model in academic research studies to ensure rigor and clarity when finding, screening, and selecting research articles for the analysis. The use of the PRISMA model in this particular study ensures that the sources are both comprehensive and unbiased, resulting in an accurate reflection of the current state of Lean Management implementation in the global apparel sector [14].

The main objective of using PRISMA is to improve the reproducibility, transparency clarity in literature review reporting. Its application in this specific study enables systematic identification, screening, eligibility assessment, and also final inclusion of research articles. This methodological structure reduces bias and supports an accurate reflection of how Lean Management has been applied and developed in the apparel industry globally during the selected time frame [14].

The review was initiated with a carefully structured search strategy designed to gather a broad and representative sample of literature on lean management within the global apparel manufacturing industry. To execute this, a comprehensive search was carried out by the researchers using Google Scholar, Emerald Insight, and Taylor and Francis, three well-established academic databases. These platforms were chosen due to their extensive indexing of peer-reviewed journals and conference papers in domains mostly linked to business management, industrial engineering, operations and manufacturing. Keywords were intentionally picked and combined based on Boolean operators (AND/OR) to improve the search precision and depth. Key terms include "Lean Management in the Apparel Industry", "Lean Management and the Apparel Sector", "5S in Apparel", "Kanban", "Just-in-Time", "Poka-Yoke", "TQM", and "Value Stream Mapping".

The article criteria are shown in Table 8.1. The inclusion criteria for selecting articles were clearly defined to ensure that only relevant, high-quality sources were considered. Eligible studies were mainly published in English, issued between January 2010 and March 2025, focused explicitly on the apparel industry, and based on empirical research, theoretical frameworks, or detailed case studies involving lean management. Conversely, the exclusion criteria eliminated articles published before 2010, non-English publications, review articles, book chapters, and early cite articles, studies for which full-text access was not available, and irrelevant articles that are not relevant to the area of study but were suggested during the initial search.

Table 8.1 Research Paper selection process.

Criteria	Details
Keywords used	"Lean Management", "Apparel Industry", " TQM", "5S", "Kanban", "JIT", "VSM"
Boolean operators	AND, OR
Databases searched	Google Scholar, Emerald Insight, Taylor & Francis
Inclusion criteria	Case studies, empirical research and conceptual papers Focus on Lean tools applied in the apparel industry Published between 2010 and 2025 Articles available in full text Written in English
Exclusion criteria	Studies focused on service industries and/or unrelated sectors Articles not specifying industry type or country Book chapters, review articles and early cite works Articles published before 2010 Duplicates
Document type	Published academic journal articles and conference papers
Publication timeframe	January 2010 – March 2025
Screening protocol	PRISMA 2020 – Identification, Screening, Eligibility and Inclusion

Source: Author

The article selection process is shown in Figure 8.1. The selection process was conducted in four distinct stages in accordance with the PRISMA model, which are Identification, Screening, Eligibility, and Inclusion. In the identification phase, an initial total of 225,789 records were retrieved from the above-mentioned three databases, where 165,026 from Taylor and Francis, 58,800 from Google Scholar, and 1,963 from Emerald Insight. These were exported for further screening and assessment. At this point, 24,269 entries were discarded as they were identified as review papers, book chapters, or early cite articles from Emerald Insight and Taylor and Francis. Additionally, 107,474 records were removed for being published before 2010, while another 62,898 were excluded due to lack of access to full-text documents, leaving 31,148 articles for the next phase.

A data extraction framework was developed to facilitate the organization and analysis of the selected studies. For each article, key information was extracted and categorized under the following attributes by the researchers manually including details of author(s) and year of publication, country or region of study, research design or methodology used, Lean tools discussed, benefits and outcomes reported, and implementation challenges identified,

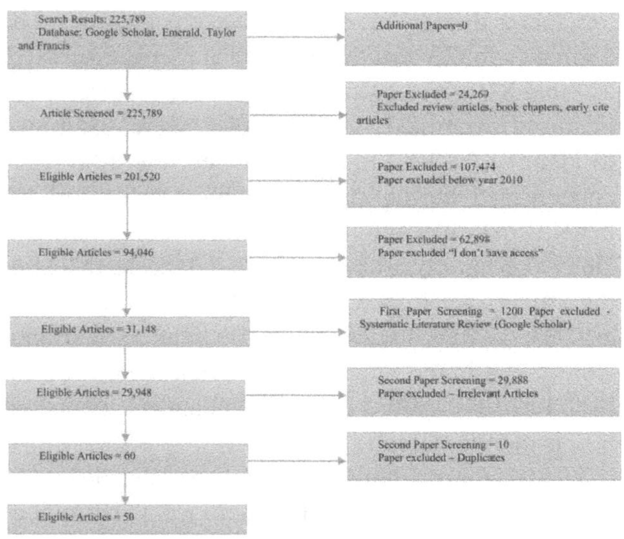

Figure 8.1 Article selection process
Source: Author

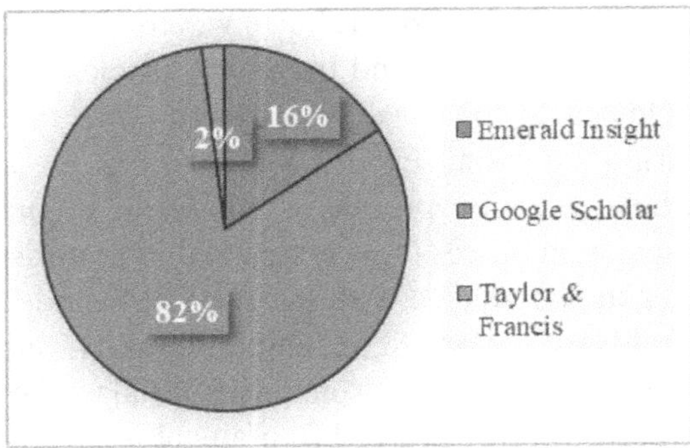

Figure 8.2 Percentage of database
Source: Author

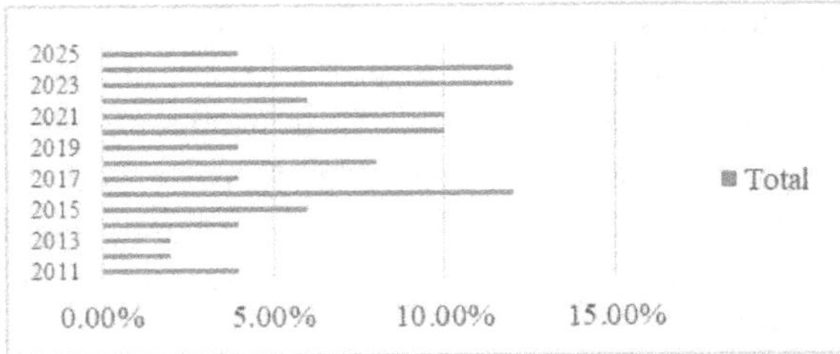

Figure 8.3 Year wise overview of articles
Source: Author

In summary, the methodology employed in this research combines rigorous screening with a structured synthesis process to deliver a holistic understanding of lean management in the apparel sector.

By focusing on the PRISMA 2020 model and leveraging data from a diverse set of global research studies, the review offers useful, actionable insights mainly for different practitioners, academics, and policymakers. It also provides a foundation for future research to focus on digital Lean innovations, sustainable practices, and lean adoption in apparel organizations. The analysis part is conduced based on the Excel software tool.

Results

The concept of Lean Management has been applied in different ways in the apparel sector, and companies have used different tools for process improvements and other objectives. Based on the analysis, most of authors mentioned that 5S is the main Lean tool that is used by the apparel sector companies. The 5S makes for 23% of the overall lean tools discussed.

Table 8.2 gives an overview of the research publications examined. Fifty articles were examined to identify the lean tools mentioned, the difficulties encountered during their implementation, and the benefits that they emphasized. The discussed 50 articles were mainly from the three databases. Most of the articles are from Google Scholar. Out of the 50 articles, 41 were found on Google Scholar, 8 articles were found in the Emerald, and one article was published in Taylor and Francis. The database contribution is mentioned in Figure 8.2.

The top journal with three published articles is the International Journal of Productivity Performance Management. Additional publications from other journals, as well as one journal with a single study paper. The 12 papers are from International Journals. 6 research papers are coming from the conference proceedings.

In this study, the authors from different countries determined the leading researchers who have worked in the lean management domain. Each author's country contribution is determined by the main author's country. When the analysis is done based on the geographical spread of the main authors, 19 research articles' authors are from Bangladesh. The second-largest author contribution comes from Sri Lanka. The distribution of research articles by country is shown in Figure 8.4.

38.7% research articles from Bangladesh, 26.53% research articles from Sri Lanka, 8.16% research articles from India. Peru, Ethiopia, Pakistan, Taiwan, Brazil, Denmark, Philippines, and Ghana contributed 26.53% form the total contribution. Based on this analysis, apparel production shifted from Europe/North America to Asia, making Asia the main manufacturing hub [15].

Figure 8.3 provides a year-wise overview of the published articles relating to Lean Management in the Apparel Sector. The majority of research publications were completed in the years 2023, 2024, and 2016. There were very few research articles published in 2013, 2014, and 2019. As a percentage, 12% of the research articles from 2023, 2024, and 2016. 88% of research publications were published between 2015 and 2025, while 12% of research articles were published between 2010 and 2015. From 2020-2023, there has been a steady output of publications. In the years 2013, 2012, and 2011, there was only one publication, indicating minimal research interest on the lean management side of the apparel sector.

The majority of the published articles mentioned 5S lean tools used in the apparel sector. With 31 research articles (62%) mentioned, 5S is the most

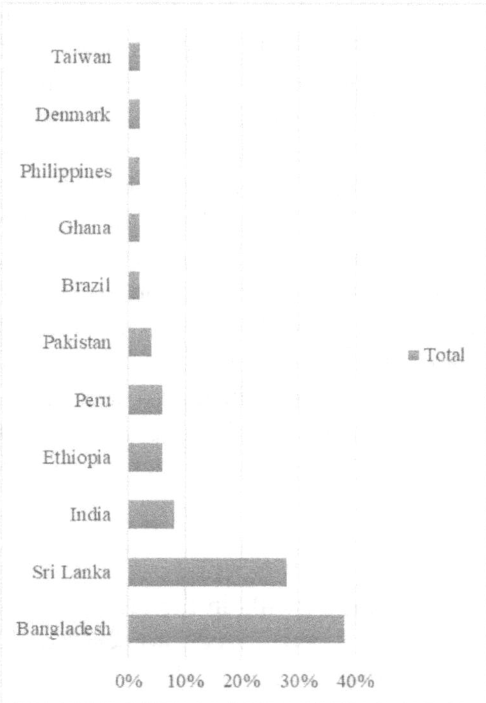

Figure 8.4 Geographic distribution of published articles
Source: Author

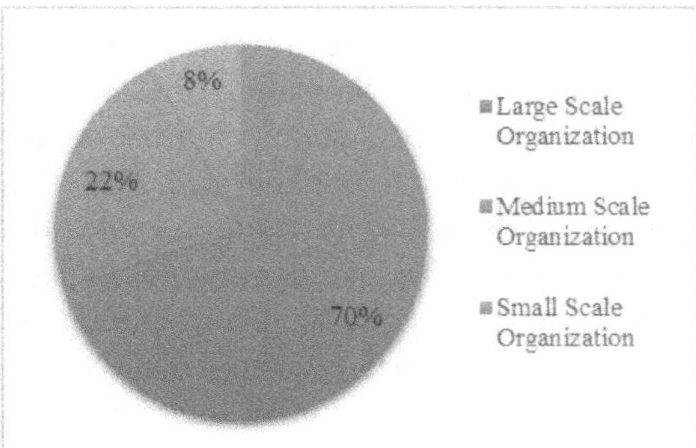

Figure 8.5 Organization type
Source: Author

commonly used Lean Management tool in the apparel industry, emphasizing the popularity of workplace organization and reducing wastages. Value Stream mapping and Kaizen are the other top two tools used, collectively contributing to the apparel industry. The image highlighted the use of Lean Tools in the apparel industry based on the count of the research articles out of 50.

Based on the Figure 8.5, the lean tools used in the apparel sector are shown in Figure 8.6. The majority of the research articles - 35 out of 50- are based on

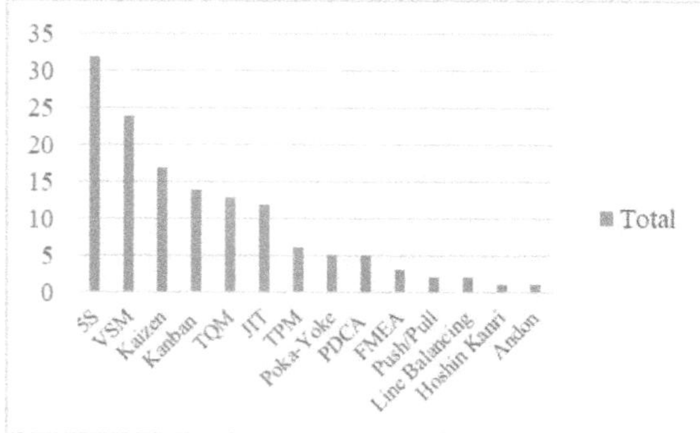

Figure 8.6 Lean Tools used in organizations
Source: Author

investigations that were carried out by large-scale organizations. 22% of research articles are from medium-scale organization scale organizations. Small-scale organizations are the subject of fewer research articles.

The challenges of lean implementation are shown in Figure 8.7. After analyzing all challenges, the study categorized the challenges into six main areas they are skill gap and lack of training, high waste and low productivity, resistance to change and cultural barriers, inadequate leadership, competitiveness and cost pressure, poor layout and lack of standardization. Most of the research articles have highlighted that the lack of training and skills of the workers is the main challenge for implementing Lean in apparel sector organizations. 35 research articles have highlighted that the skill gap is the main challenge. The main other challenge is the high waste and low productivity in organizations when implementing Lean management. Resistance to change and the cultural barriers are also significant challenges when implementing lean in apparel sector companies. The image below shows the challenges when implementing lean in the apparel sector organization.

In order to facilitate the study, all of the benefits of Lean Management that were discussed in the articles have been broken down into the seven primary categories. Reducing waste and defects, increasing productivity, improving quality, saving money and increasing efficiency.

Based on that, most of the research articles have been highlighted, and reducing waste and defects is the main benefit of Lean Management. Out of 50 articles, 34 articles have been highlighted to reduce defects and waste as the main benefit of lean management for the apparel sector organizations.

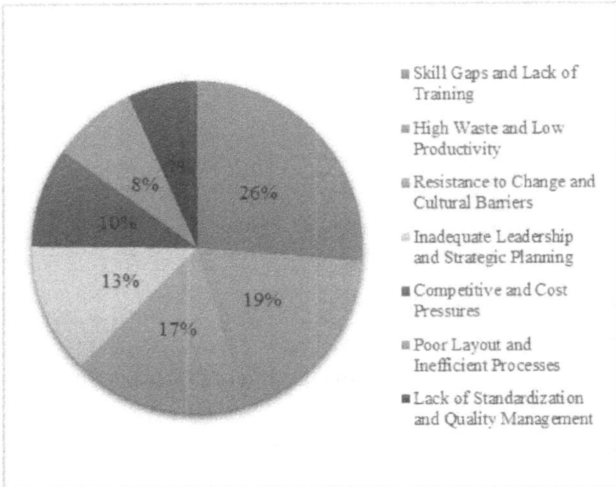

Figure 8.7 Challenges of lean implementation
Source: Author

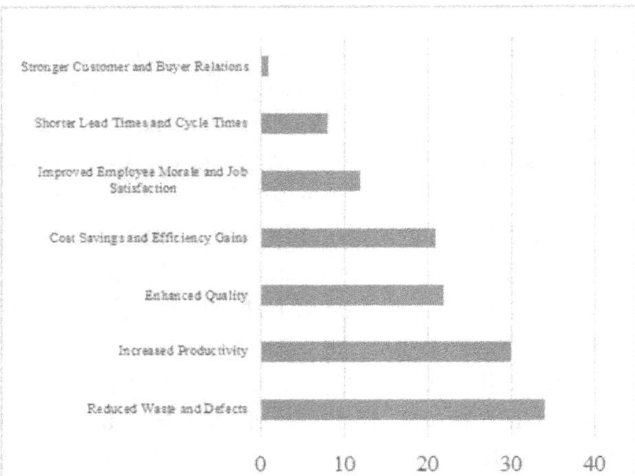

Figure 8.8 Benefits of lean implementation
Source: Author

The second top highlighted benefit is to increase productivity. One article among fifty articles highlighted that the relationship between the customer and the buyer will improve by implementing lean management. The studies highlighted that employee morale and job satisfaction will also improve with the lean implementation in the apparel sector. The benefit of the lean implementation is shown in Figure 8.8.

Discussion

Adoption of lean tools in the apparel sector

According to the review articles, 62% of the reviewed articles emphasized that 5S is the most widely used Lean tool in the apparel sector. This finding is supported by the [16]. Not only that, this article highlights that 5S is comparatively simple to apply and easy to understand, but it also provides quick advantages for the workplace organization. Additionally, JIT, Kaizen, and value stream mapping also widely used reduce the WIP and the seven wastages [17].

Most large-scale organizations use the Kanban system, which promotes inventory control and flow efficiency, whereas smaller businesses, with fewer resources, are more likely to concentrate on 5S and Kaizen. Most of the research articles [18] demonstrate growing interest in digital lean, combining workflow automation, IoT, and simulation for increased efficiency, especially in technologically advanced regions like Taiwan and Peru.

Lean benefits

After analyzing all the benefits in the research articles, the benefits were categorized into seven main categories. They reduce waste and defects, increase productivity, enhance the quality, save cost, improve employee morale, shorten lead time, and strengthen customer and buyer relations. Based on these benefits, waste reduction and productivity increases is the most frequently mentioned benefits in the research articles [19].

As evidenced by case studies from Sri Lanka and Bangladesh, and India, eliminating the non-value-adding activities helps apparel industry organizations to improve their throughput and streamline their operations [20, 21]. Furthermore, studies that combined lean tools with total quality management reported higher-quality products, demonstrating that integrated strategies typically comprehensive the operational results. A rising number of studies, [22] highlights the beneficial impact of lean on employee satisfaction and workplace morale, especially when employees are empowered via kaizen or team-oriented initiatives. This goes against the common belief that lean can be too strict and stressful since some employees are not willing to change the culture.

Key challenges in lean implementation

Even with many benefits for the lean management to the apparel industry, implementing lean is not easy. Most articles mentioned that the skill gap and lack of training in the biggest challenges encountered when implementing lean [23] have noted lot of developing countries don't have proper training for their employees. Cultural resistance to change, poor leadership, and poor factory layout and standardization are also big problems. Many apparel manufacturers have a hierarchical culture, and workers are often afraid of losing their jobs, which makes them resistant to lean-driven restructuring efforts. Financial limitations were also noted as a significant obstacle, particularly for SMEs [24]. The capital expenditures necessary for equipment upgrades, software adoption, and layout redesign are frequently difficult for smaller businesses to afford.

The role of organization type

According to the review, large-scale organizations are good at implementing lean systems into the workplace because they have access to resources and access to global buyers since they are adhering to lean practices as a compliance measure [25]. Small and medium-sized businesses (SMEs), on the other hand, frequently implement lean in a piecemeal manner. SMEs usually use one or two fundamental lean tools, such as VSM or 5S, but lack the training or strategic integration required for a complete transformation [26]

Regional focus and research gap

Due to the region's dominance in global apparel exports, the majority of the reviewed studies origin from South Asian countries, particularly Bangladesh and Sri Lanka. The lack of research from Africa, Latin America, and Eastern Europe limits the generalizability of findings, despite the fact that this provides rich insight into lean practices in developing economies. Furthermore, there aren't many studies comparing large and small businesses or lean maturity levels, nor are there many longitudinal studies monitoring the effects of lean over time.

Future Directions

Future studies should also delve deeper into the human side of lean, specifically how worker engagement, leadership philosophies, and organizational culture affect lean results. Particularly in the labor-intensive apparel industry, studies that concentrate on gender dynamics, worker safety, and well-being in lean environments can also be very beneficial.

Conclusion

This comprehensive literature review emphasizes how lean management significantly improved operational efficiency in the apparel industry globally, considering the articles published between the years 2010 and 2025. Key Lean tools, namely 5S, Kaizen, Kanban, Value Stream Mapping, Just-in-Time, and Total Quality Management, have been widely adopted to reduce waste, increase productivity, and improve product quality. In addition to promoting sustainability by reducing wastage in the apparel sector and optimizing resource usage of the industry, the above review also validates the beneficial effects of Lean on cost savings, shorter lead times, improved quality, and employee morale. Common difficulties such as cultural resistance, insufficient training, a lack of skills, inefficient leadership, and ineffective supply chain integration persist despite the above-mentioned advantages. According to current trends, these challenges can be overcome and digital Lean implementations made possible by merging Lean with Industry 4.0 technologies such as IoT and predictive analytics. Finally, lean management is still an important and evolving strategy that promotes sustainability and competition in the apparel industry while also offering insightful information for both practitioners and scholars.

References

[1] Kennemer, J. (2025). Cosmo Sourcing. Available from: https://www.cosmosourcing.com/blog/the-top-12-countries-for-clothing-garment-and-apparel-manufacturing.

[2] Statista (2025). Statista. Available from: https://www.statista.com/outlook/cmo/apparel/worldwide.

[3] Gamage, J., Vilasini, N., Perera, C., & Wijenatha, L. (2012). Impact of lean manufacturing on performance and organizational culture: a case study of an apparel manufacturer in Sri Lanka. Academia.

[4] Alam, S. M. M., & Islam, S. (2020). Clothing manufacturing and exporting countries of the world: a review. *Journal of Textile Engineering and Fashion Technology*, 6(5), 179–184.

[5] Dekier, L. (2012). The origin and evolution of lean management system. *Journal of International Studies*, 5(1), 46–51.

[6] Begum, S., Khan, S. M., Akash, S. A., & Bhuiyan, M. R. (2024). A framework for lean manufacturing implementation in the textile industry: a research study. *International Journal of Science and Engineering*, 1(04), 17–31.

[7] Raj, D., Ma, Y. J., Banning, J., & Gam, H. J. (2017). Implementation of Lean Production and Environmental Sustainability in the Indian Apparel Manufacturing Industry: A Way to Reach the Triple Bottom Line. Taylor and Francis.

[8] Bruce, M., Daly, L., & Towers, N. (2004). Lean or Agile. Emerald Group Publishing Limited.

[9] Wickramasinghe, V., & Wickamasinghe, G. (2017). Autonomysupport, Need Fulfilment and Job Performance in Lean Implementedtextile Andapparel Firms. Emerald Publishing Limited.

[10] Căsăneanu, N.-M., & Pîslaru, M. (2024). Digital lean manufacturing in the textile industry. In The 19th Romanian Textiles and Leather Conference, Iaşi.

[11] Maware, C., Okwu, O. M., & Adetunji, O. (2021). Asystematicliterature review of lean manufacturing implementation in manufacturing- based sectors of the developing anddevelopedcountries. *International Journal of Lean Six Sigma*, 16(8), 36.

[12] Shankar, U., Koushik, R., Jacob, J. S., Athul, C., & Ranjith, P. V. (2025). The systematic review of lean practices in India. *Journal of International Conference Proceedings,* 7(5), 15.

[13] Aripin, M. N., Nawanir, G., Mahmud, F., Fauzi, A. M., Hussain, S., & Lee, K. L. (2023). Systematic literature review: theory perspective in lean manufacturing performance. *Management Systems in Production Engineering*, 31(2), 230–241.

[14] PRISMA (2020). PRISMA Statemnet. Available from: https://www.prisma-statement.org/.

[15] Barrientos, S. (2019). 7 - Contested Terrain: The Limits of Social Compliance in Asian Apparel, (pp. 167–193). Cambridge University Press.

[16] Mothilal, B., & Prakash, C. (2018). Implementation of lean tools in apparel industry to improve productivity and quality. *Current Trends in Fashion Technology and Textile Engineering,* 4(1), 1-7.

[17] Rahman, Q., Hossain, M. F., Paul, S., & Rahi, A. A. (2022). An approach to reduce process wastages of an apparel manufacturing organization using value stream mapping. In 7th International Conference on Engineering Research, Innovation and Education, Sylhet.

[18] Schwarz, M., & Lee, W. J. (2020). Amplify Lean Performance Gains with Digital Lean Management. AVEVA.

[19] Saha, P., Talapatra, S. Belal, H., Jackson, V., Mason, A., & Durowoju, O. (2023). Examining the viability of lean production practices in the Industry 4.0 era: an empirical evidence based on B2B garment manufacturing sector. *Journal of Business and Industrial Marketing*, 38(12), 2694–2712.

[20] Islam, M. I., Rahman, T. T., Rajkumar, M. P. J., & Ahmed, A. (2016). Applying 5S method on trims store's documentation system in an apparel industry. In 2016 International Conference on Industrial Engineering and Operations Management, Kuala Lumpur.

[21] Rathod, B., Shinde, P., Raut, D., & Waghmare, G. (2016). Optimization of cycle time by lean manufacturing techniques-line balancing approach. *International Journal for Research in Applied Science and Engineering Technology*, 4(5), 224–229.

[22] Karunarathne, N., & Samarasinghe, H. M. U. S. R. (2019). Impact of lean implementation on employees' job satisfaction in the ABC apparel manufacturing firm. *International Business Research*, 12(11), 48–56.

[23] Khan, A. M., & Islam, M. M. (2013). Application of 5S system in the sample section of an apparel industry for smooth sample dispatch. *Research Journal of Management Sciences*, 2(7), 28–32.

[24] Bashar, A., & Hasin, M. A. A. (2018). Lean implementation: the progress and the future challenges of apparel industry to achieve the manufacturing competitiveness. *Journal of Mechanical Engineering*, 48, 30–36.

[25] Hoque, I., Hasle, P., & Maalouf, M. M. (2020). Lean meeting buyer's expectations, enhanced supplier productivity and compliance capabilities in garment industry. *International Journal of Productivity and Performance Management*, 53(1), 1–35.

[26] Pavletich-Gonzalo, D., Mera-Reategui, A., Quiroz-Flores, U. C., & Collao-Diaz, M. (2023). Production model based on lean manufacturing and SLP to increase productivity in an apparel sector MSME. In Leadership in Education and Innovation in Engineering in the Framework of Global Transformations: Integration and Alliances for Integral Development, Buenos Aires.

[27] Silva, S. K. P. N. (2011). Applicability of lean manufacturing on operational performance - a case study in the apparel industry in Sri Lanka. *Indian Journal of Management*, 4(10), 12.

[28] Nunesca, R. M., & Amorado, A. T. (2015). Application of lean manufacturing tools in a garment industry as a strategy for productivity improvement. *Asia Pacific Journal of Multidisciplinary Research*, 3(4), 8.

[29] Tahiduzzaman, M., Rahman, M., Dey, K. S., & Kapuria, K. T. (2018). Minimization of sewing defects of an apparel industry in Bangladesh with 5S & PDCA. *American Journal of Industrial Engineering*, 5(1), 17–24.

[30] Amanullah, A., & Raaz, M. N. N. (2020). Study on 7 wastes of lean in garments manufacturing. *International Journal of Multidisciplinary Informative Research and Review,* 1(1), 49–60.

[31] Legesse, D. A., & Singh, A. P. (2014). Productivity improvement through lean manufacturing tools: a case study on ethiopian garment industry.

International Journal of Engineering Research and Technology, 3(9), 1037–1045.

[32] Salman, S., Ahmed, T., Taqi, H. M. M., Frederico, G. F., Dip, A. S., & Ali, S. M. (2023). An integrated approach to explore the barriers to lean manufacturing in the context of the COVID-19 pandemic: implications for sustainability. *International Journal of Industrial Engineering and Operations Management*, 6(2), 165–184.

[33] Ukey, P., Deshmukh, A., & Arora, A. (2021). Implementation of lean tools in apparel industry for improving productivity. *Proceedings on Engineering Sciences*, 3(2), 241–245.

[34] Atsegeba, B. D., Melkamu, M., Lemma , N., Yemane, A., Dugassa , E., & Feyissa , N. (2024). Analysis of sewing defects through an integrated approach of 5s and PDCA cycle. *Journal of Engineering, Management and Information Technology*, 75–86.

[35] Mridha, H. J., Alam, A. R., Mahmud, T., & Ahmed, T. (2020). Contrivance of 5s system to effectuate higher productivity in apparel industries. *Global Journal of Engineering Research*, 20(1).

[36] Shamsi, H. S. (2014). 5S conditions and improvement methodology in apparel industry in Pakistan. *Journal of Polymer and Textile Engineering*, 1(2), 15–21.

[37] Abeykoon, M. W. B., & De Alwis, C. (2015). The impact of total quality management practices on export performance of apparel exporters in Sri Lanka. *Kelaniya Journal of Human Resource Management*, 10(1), 104–127.

[38] Riojas, P. A. B., Chumpitaz, F. R., & Ugaz, R. C. (2024). Supply chain management applying VSM, 5S and standardized work in an SME: a case study of an apparel manufacturing company. In 7th Bangladesh Conference on Industrial Engineering and Operations Management.

[39] de Soysa, J. P., & Silva, J. I. A. D. O. (2025). Lean manufacturing and the apparel industry: an assessment model for sustainability. *Lumen Et Virtus*, 16(46).

[40] M. Syduzzaman, Biswas, M. A. S., & Yeasmin, D. (2016). Developing a framework for implementing total quality management in the apparel industry: case study on a bangladeshi apparel manufacturing factory. *International Journal of Textile Science*, 5(5), 89–95.

[41] Syduzzaman, M., Islam, M. M., Habib, M. A., & Yeasmin, D. (2016). Effects of implementing TQM principles in the apparel manufacturing industry: case study on a Bangladeshi clothing factory. *Science and Technology*, 6(3), 68–75.

[42] Zanu, J. A., Appiah, N. A., & Adu-Gyamfi, V. (2023). Implementing total quality management principles in the apparel manufacturing sector: Ghana in perspective. *British Journal of Multidisciplinary and Advanced Studie*, 4(3), 81–97.

[43] Kapuria, T. K., Rahman, M., & Haldar, S. (2017). Root cause analysis and productivity improvement of an apparel industry in Bangladesh through kaizen implementation. *Journal of Applied Research on Industrial Engineering*, 4(4), 227–239.

[44] Ratnayake, R. M. V. S., Lanarolle, W. D. G., & Ratnayake, R. M. D. T. (2021). Kanban in apparel manufacturing: a case study. *International Journal of Emerging Science and Engineering*, 7(3), 1–9.

[45] Joy, R. A., Hawlader, M. S., Rahman, M. S., & Hossain, M. R. (n.d.). Improving quality, productivity, and cost aspects of a sewing line of apparel industry using TQM approach. *Mathematical Problems in Engineering*.

[46] Ashraf, S. R. B., Mahmud, M. I., Akram, M. A., Rashid, D. A. R. M. H., Rahman, M. T., & Tanvir, M. H. (2017). The practice of kaizen tool in the apparel industry of Bangladesh for process improvement and development of ergonomics standard. *International Research Journal of Engineering and Technology*, 4(10), 1747–1754.

[47] Dandeniya, G., Perera, R., & Amarasena, T. (2021). Application of the Lean Tools towards the Process Improvements of the Label Quarantine Process in the Warehouse Operations– A Case Study Based on ABC Apparel (Pvt.) Ltd in Sri Lanka. *Journal of Purchasing, Logistics and Supply Chain Management system.*

[48] Silva, S. K. P. N. (2022). Applicability of value stream mapping (VSM) to the apparel industry in Sri Lanka. Research Gate.

[49] Jayawardane, K., Musthaffa, S., & Dias, M. (2022). Impact of lean manufacturing on inventory turnover performances: evidence from the Sri Lankan apparel industry. In 2022 Moratuwa Engineering Research Conference (MERCon), Moratuwa.

[50] Kumar, D. V., Mohan, G. M., & Mohanasundaram, K. (2019). Lean tool implementation in the garment industry. In 6th World congress on Smart Materials and Polymer Technology, Helsinki.

[51] Fernandez-Diaz, L., Vera-Rojas, N., & Quiroz-Flores, J. C. (2024). Productivity enhancement by layout redesign and application of lean principles in the apparel industry. In Industrial Engineering and Industrial Management, Nice, France.

[52] Mohammad, A., Ahmad, S., & Iqbal, M. (2015). Identification of retention time & information delays applying value stream mapping technique in apparel manufacturing organization. In 2015 International Conference on Operations Excellence and Service Engineering, Florida, USA.

[53] Wang, C.-N., Chau Vo, T. T. B., Hsu, H.-P., Nguyen, N. T., & Nhieu, N.-L. (2024). Improving processing efficiency through workflow process reengineering, simulation and value stream mapping: a case study of business process reengineering. *Business Process Management Journal*, 30(7), 2482–2515.

[54] Galahitiyawe, N., & Aryarathne, S. (2020). Impact of lean manufacturing practices on operational performance: a study in Sri Lankan apparel sector. *Peradeniya Management Review*, 2(2), 99–120.

[55] Dissanayake, T., & Wijesingha, K. (2017). The Relationship Between People-Related Elements of Total Quality Management (TQM) Practices and Employees' Job Satisfaction in Apparel Industry in Gampaha District. *Wayamba Journal of Management.*

[56] Sabeen Shaheen. (2022). Quality Management and Operational Performance: A Case Study from Pakistan. *South Asian Journal of Operations and Logistics,* 14–19.

[57] Bashar, A., & Hasin, M. A. (2016). The Effect of Continuous Improvement on Waste Elimination for Implementing Lean Manufacturing in the Apparel Industry of Bangladesh. Independent Business Review, 98–109.

[58] Ratnayake, R., & Dinosha, V. (2018). Effectiveness of lean manufacturing layout of a firm within the apparel industry of Sri Lanka: a case study.

[59] Bizuneh, B., & Ome, R. (2024). Lean waste prioritisation and reduction in the apparel industry: application of waste assessment model and value stream mapping. *Cognet Journal*, 11(1), 2341538.

[60] Gamage, J. R., Vilasini, P. P. G. N., Wijenatha, L., & x Perea, L. (2012). Impact of lean manufacturing on performance and organisational culture: a case study of an apparel manufacturer in Sri Lanka. Research Papers - SLIIT Staff Publications, Colombo.

[61] De Silva, K., Peelikumbura, P., Gunathilaka, S., Jayawardena, H., De Silva, P., & Abeysiri, L. (2017). Applicability of lean concept in improving the human resourcing practice in the context of Sri Lankan apparel industry. In Proceedings of International HR Conference, Colombo.

[62] Kulasekara, R., & Ranaweera, P. (2023). Impact of lean manufacturing practices on sustainability performances in SMEs in Sri Lanka special reference to apparel industry: concept paper. In Annual International Conference on Business Innovation (ICOBI) 2023, Colombo.

[63] Hoque, I., Maalouf, M. M., Tanha, M., Islam, M. S., & Alam, M. Z. (2023). Implementing and sustaining lean, buyer-supplier role, and COVID-19 pandemic: insights from the garment industry of Bangladesh. *International Journal of Lean Six Sigma,* 1010–1034.

[64] Bashar, A., Hasin, A., & Adnan, Z. H. (2021). Impact of lean manufacturing: evidence from apparel industry in Bangladesh. *International Journal of Lean Six Sigma,* 923–943.

[65] Hoque, I., Hasle, P., & Maalouf, M. M. (2021). Transfer mechanisms lean implementation with integrated OHS in garment supplier factories. *International Journal of Productivity and Performance Management*, 71(8).

[66] Madhusa, W. A. S. S. W. K. T. G. P. (2020). Impact of lean manufacturing practices on sustainability performance: evidence from Sri Lankan apparel industry. *Journal of Accounting Research, Business and Finance Management*, 2020(1), 20–22.

[67] Prakash, C. (2018). Implementation of Lean Tools in Apparel Industry to Improve Productivity and Quality. Juniper Publishers.

[68] Google Trends (2025). Explore. [Online]. Available from: https://trends.google.com/trends/explore?-date=all&q=Lean%20Management&hl=en-GB.

[69] Anrony, J., Garza-Reyes, J. A., & Hines, P. (2021). Practical implications and future research agenda of lean manufacturing: a systematic literature review. *Production Planning and Control*.

Appendix

Table 8.2 Research Paper selection process.

Author	Country	Study	Type of Article	Org Type	LM tools	Challenges Faced	Benefits
[27]	Sri Lanka	Applicability of Lean Manufacturing on Operational Performance - A Case Study In The Apparel Industry In Sri Lanka	Case Study	Large	5S, JIT, VSM, Kaizen	Competitive and Cost Pressures. Skill Gaps and Lack of Training.	Increased Productivity, Shorter Lead Times and Cycle Times, Cost Savings and Efficiency Gains
[28]	Philippines	Application of Lean Manufacturing Tools in a Garment Industry as a Strategy for Productivity Improvement.	Journal Article	Medium	5S, Kaizen, Kanban, JIT, VSM, Push/Pull	No standard time, defects, high WIP, and unbalanced workload.	Cost Savings and Efficiency Gains, Reduced Waste and Defects
[17]	Bangladesh	An approach to reduce process wastages of an apparel manufacturing organization using value stream mapping	Conference Paper	Large	VSM, 5S	High WIP, poor layout, excess transport, long lead time	Shorter Lead Times and Cycle Times
[29]	Bangladesh	Minimization of Sewing Defects of an Apparel Industry in Bangladesh with 5S & PDCA	Journal Article	Large	5S, PDCA	Skill Gaps and Lack of Training, High Waste and Low Productivity	Reduced Waste and Defects, Increased Productivity
[21]	India	Optimization of Cycle Time by Lean Manufacturing Techniques Line Balancing Approach	Journal Article	Medium	Kaizen, 5S	High Waste and Low Productivity, Poor Layout and Inefficient Processes	Shorter Lead Times and Cycle Times
[30]	Bangladesh	Study on 7 Wastes of Lean in Garments Manufacturing	Journal Article	Large	5S, VSM, Kanban , Kaizen	poor layout, skill gaps	Increased Productivity, Reduced Waste and Defects
[25]	Bangladesh	Lean meeting buyer's expectations, enhanced supplier	Journal Article	Large	VSM, 5S, Kaizen	Resistance to Change and Cultural Barriers, Inadequate	Increased Productivity, Reduced Waste and Defects

Author	Country	Study	Type of Article	Org Type	LM tools	Challenges Faced	Benefits
		productivity and compliance capabilities in garment industry				Leadership and Strategic Planning	
[19]	Bangladesh	Examining the viability of lean production practices in the Industry 4.0 era: an empirical evidence based on B2B garment manufacturing sector	Journal Article	Large	JIT, VSM	Competitive and Cost Pressures, Skill Gaps and Lack of Training	Reduced Waste and Defects, Increased Productivity
[31]	Ethiopia	Productivity Improvement Through Lean Manufacturing Tools: A Case Study on Ethiopian Garment Industry	Journal Article	Large	Line Balancing, 5S Kaizen, VSM	Skill Gaps and Lack of Training, High Waste and Low Productivity	Reduced Waste and Defects Increased Productivity
[32]	Bangladesh	An integrated approach to explore the barriers to lean manufacturing in the context of the COVID-19 pandemic: implications for sustainability	Journal Article	Large	5s, Kaizen	Competitive and Cost Pressures, Skill Gaps and Lack of Training, Inadequate Leadership and Strategic Planning	Reduced Waste and Defects, Increased Productivity, Shorter Lead Times and Cycle Times, Enhanced Quality
[22]	Sri Lanka	Impact of Lean Implementation on Employees' Job Satisfaction in the ABC Apparel Manufacturing Firm.	Journal Article	Medium	TQM	Resistance to Change and Cultural Barriers Inadequate Leadership and Strategic Planning Skill Gaps and Lack of Training	Moderate positive effect on job satisfaction
[33]	India	Implementation of Lean Tools in Apparel Industry for Improving Productivity	Journal Article	Medium	5S, Kaizen, Poka-Yoke, Kanban , Andon	Lack of Standardization and Quality Management High Waste and Low Productivity	Reduced Waste and Defects Increased Productivity.

Author	Country	Study	Type of Article	Org Type	LM tools	Challenges Faced	Benefits
[34]	Ethiopia	Analysis of Sewing Defects Through an Integrated Approach of 5S and PDCA Cycle	Journal Article	Large	5S,PDCA	Skill Gaps and Lack of Training High Waste and Low Productivity	Reduced Waste and Defects Increased Productivity
[23]	Bangladesh	Application of 5S System in the Sample Section of an Apparel Industry for Smooth Sample Dispatch	Journal Article	Large	5S	Skill Gaps and Lack of Training High Waste and Low Productivity	5S improved dispatch, quality, buyer relations, discipline
[35]	Bangladesh	Contrivance of 5S System to Effectuate Higher Productivity in Apparel Industries	Journal Article	Large	5S	Resistance to Change and Cultural Barriers High Waste and Low Productivity	Reduced Waste and Defects Increased Productivity
[36]	Pakistan	5S Conditions and Improvement Methodology in Apparel Industry in Pakistan	Journal Article	Large	5S	Lack of Standardization and Quality Management High Waste and Low Productivity Skill Gaps and Lack of Training.	Reduced Waste and Defects Increased Productivity
[37]	Sri Lanka	The Impact of Total Quality Management Practices on Export Performance of Apparel Exporters in Sri Lanka	Journal Article	Large	Total Quality Management	Lack of Standardization and Quality Management	Stronger Customer and Buyer Relations Increased Productivity
[38]	Peru	Supply Chain Management Applying VSM, 5S and Standardized Work in an SME: A Case Study of an Apparel Manufacturing Company	Case Study	Small	VSM, 5S	High Waste and Low Productivity Poor Layout and Inefficient Processes	Reduced Waste and Defects Increased Productivity

Author	Country	Study	Type of Article	Org Type	LM tools	Challenges Faced	Benefits
[20]	Bangladesh	Applying 5S Method on Trims Store Documentation System in an Apparel Industry	Conference Article	Large	5S, PDCA	Poor Layout and Inefficient Processes, Lack of Standardization and Quality Management, High Waste and Low Productivity	Reduced Waste and Defects Increased Productivity
[39]	Brazil	Lean Manufacturing and the Apparel Industry: An Assessment Model for Sustainability	Journal Article	Large	5S, Kanban, JIT	Inadequate Leadership and Strategic Planning Skill Gaps and Lack of Training Competitive and Cost Pressures	Increase the Productivity and the Sustainability
[26]	Peru	Production model based on lean manufacturing and SLP to increase productivity in an apparel sector MSME	Conference paper	Small	5S Kanban VSM	Poor Layout and Inefficient Processes High Waste and Low Productivity	Reduced Waste and Defects, Increased Productivity Enhanced Quality
[40]	Bangladesh	Developing a Framework for Implementing Total Quality Management in the Apparel Industry: Case Study on a Bangladesh Apparel Manufacturing Factory	Case Study	Large	TQM 5S FMEA	Skill Gaps and Lack of Training, Resistance to Change and Cultural Barriers	Reduced Waste and Defects, Increased Productivity, Enhanced Quality Cost Savings and Efficiency Gains
[41]	Bangladesh	Effects of Implementing TQM Principles in the Apparel Manufacturing Industry: Case Study on a Bangladesh Clothing Factory	Case Study	Large	TQM, 5S, FMEA PDCA	Inadequate Leadership and Strategic Planning Resistance to Change and Cultural Barriers Skill Gaps and Lack of Training	Reduced Waste and Defects Increased Productivity
[16]	India	Implementation of Lean Tools in Apparel Industry to	Journal Article	Large	5S, Kanban , Kaizen Poka-Yoke, VSM, JIT, PDCA,	High Waste and Low Productivity Lack of	Reduced Waste and Defects Increased

Author	Country	Study	Type of Article	Org Type	LM tools	Challenges Faced	Benefits
		Improve Productivity and Quality			TPM FMEA	Standardization and Quality Management	Productivity Enhanced Quality
[42]	Ghana	Implementing Total Quality Management Principles in The Apparel Manufacturing Sector: Ghana in Perspective	Journal Article	Large	Total Quality Management	Competitive and Cost Pressures Skill Gaps and Lack of Training Resistance to Change and Cultural Barriers Inadequate Leadership and Strategic Planning	Reduced Waste and Defects, Increased Productivity, Enhanced Quality Cost Savings and Efficiency Gains, Improved Employee Morale and Job Satisfaction
[43]	Bangladesh	Root Cause Analysis and Productivity Improvement of an Apparel Industry in Bangladesh Through Kaizen Implementation	Journal Article	Large	Kaizen	High Waste and Low Productivity Resistance to Change and Cultural Barriers	Reduced Waste and Defects Increased Productivity Enhanced Quality Cost Savings and Efficiency Gains
[44]	Sri Lanka	Kanban in Apparel Manufacturing: A Case Study	Case Study	Large-	Kanban, 5S TPM, TQM Line Balancing	Skill Gaps and Lack of Training, High Waste and Low Productivity	Enhanced Quality Cost Savings and Efficiency Gains
[45]	Bangladesh	Improving Quality, Productivity, and Cost Aspects of a Sewing Line of Apparel Industry Using TQM Approach	Research Article	Large	Total Quality Management	High Waste and Low Productivity Skill Gaps and Lack of Training Poor Layout and Inefficient Processes	Cost Savings and Efficiency Gains Improved Employee Morale and Job Satisfaction
[46]	Bangladesh	The Practice of Kaizen Tool in the Apparel Industry of Bangladesh for Process Improvement and Development of Ergonomics Standard	Journal Article	Large	Kaizen	High Waste and Low Productivity, Skill Gaps and Lack of Training, Resistance to Change and Cultural Barriers	Increased Productivity, Improved Employee Morale and Job Satisfaction, Reduced Waste and Defects

Author	Country	Study	Type of Article	Org Type	LM tools	Challenges Faced	Benefits
[47]	Sri Lanka	Application of the Lean Tools towards the Process Improvements of the Label Quarantine Process in the Warehouse Operations– A Case Study Based on ABC Apparel (Pvt.) Ltd in Sri Lanka	Case Study	Large	Kaizen	High Waste and Low Productivity, Skill Gaps and Lack of Training, Resistance to Change and Cultural Barriers, Competitive and Cost Pressures	Improved Employee Morale and Job Satisfaction, Cost Savings and Efficiency Gains Reduced Waste and Defects.
[48]		Applicability of Value Stream Mapping (VSM) to the Apparel Industry in Sri Lanka	Research Article	Large	VSM	Skill Gaps and Lack of Training Resistance to Change and Cultural Barriers Competitive and Cost Pressures	Reduced Waste and Defects Increased Productivity Improved Employee Morale and Job Satisfaction
[49]		Impact of Lean Manufacturing on Inventory Turnover Performances: Evidence From the Sri Lankan Apparel Industry	Research Article	Medium	JIT, TQM, TPM	Competitive and Cost Pressures Skill Gaps and Lack of Training	Reduced Waste and Defects Enhanced Quality Cost Savings and Efficiency Gains
[50]	India	Lean Tool Implementation in the Garment Industry	Conference Paper	Large	5S, VSM, Poka-Yoke	Competitive and Cost Pressures, Skill Gaps and Lack of Training, Resistance to Change and Cultural Barriers, Poor Layout and Inefficient Processes	Reduced Waste and Defects Increased Productivity Enhanced Quality Cost Savings and Efficiency Gains
[24]	Bangladesh	Lean Impleme-ntation: The Progress and the Future Challenges of Apparel Industry to achieve the	Journal Article	Large	VSM	Lack of Standardization and Quality Management, Skill Gaps and Lack of Training, Resistance	Reduced Waste and Defects, Increased Productivity, Cost Savings and Efficiency Gains

Author	Country	Study	Type of Article	Org Type	LM tools	Challenges Faced	Benefits
		Manufacturing Competitiven-ess				to Change and Cultural Barriers, Inadequate Leadership and Strategic Planning	
[51]		Productivity Enhancement by Layout Redesign and Application of Lean Principles in the Apparel Industry	Conference Paper	Small	5S, Poka-Yoke TQM	High Waste and Low Productivity, Resistance to Change and Cultural Barriers Competitive and Cost Pressures	Shorter Lead Times and Cycle Times Enhanced Quality Cost Savings and Efficiency Gains Increased Productivity
[52]	Bangladesh	Identification of Retention Time & Information Delays Applying Value Stream Mapping Technique in Apparel Manufacturing Organization	Conference Paper	Medium	VSM, 5S, TPM JIT, Kanban , TQM	Resistance to Change and Cultural Barriers, Lack of Standardization and Quality Management, Poor Layout and Inefficient Processes	Reduced Waste and Defects, Enhanced Quality Cost Savings and Efficiency Gains, Shorter Lead Times and Cycle Times
[53]	Taiwan	Improving processing efficiency through workflow process reengineering, simulation and value stream mapping: a case study of business process reengineering	Journal Article	Large	VSM	High Waste and Low Productivity, Lack of Standardization and Quality Management, Poor Layout and Inefficient Processes	Reduced Waste and Defects, Increased Productivity, Shorter Lead Times and Cycle Times, Enhanced Quality
[54]	Sri Lanka	Impact of Lean Manufacturing Practices on Operational Performance: A Study in Sri Lankan Apparel Sector	Journal Article	Large	5S, TPM, Kanban	Skill Gaps and Lack of Training, High Waste and Low Productivity	Enhanced Quality, Cost Savings and Efficiency Gains, Improved Employee Morale and Job Satisfaction

Author	Country	Study	Type of Article	Org Type	LM tools	Challenges Faced	Benefits
[55]	Sri Lanka	The Relationship Between PeopleRelated Elements of Total Quality Management (TQM) Practices and Employees' Job Satisfaction in Apparel Industry in Gampaha District	Journal Article	Medium	Total Quality Management	Skill Gaps and Lack of Training, High Waste and Low Productivity, Resistance to Change and Cultural Barriers, Inadequate Leadership and Strategic Planning	Enhanced Quality Cost Savings and Efficiency Gains, Improved Employee Morale and Job Satisfaction
[56]	Pakistan	Quality Management and Operational Performance: A Case Study from Pakistan	Journal Article	Medium	Total Quality Management	Resistance to Change and Cultural Barriers Poor Layout and Inefficient Processes Skill Gaps and Lack of Training	Reduced Waste and Defects Enhanced Quality
[57]	Bangladesh	The Effect of Continuous Improvement on Waste Elimination for Implementing Lean Manufacturing in the Apparel Industry of Bangladesh	Journal Article	Medium	Kaizen, 5S, VSM, JIT, Kanban	Resistance to Change and Cultural Barriers, Skill Gaps and Lack of Training, Inadequate Leadership and Strategic Planning	Reduced Waste and Defects, Increased Productivity
[58]	Sri Lanka	Effectiveness of Lean Manufacturing Layout of a Firm within the Apparel Industry of Sri Lanka: A Case Study	Case Study	Medium	5S, VSM, Kanban	Resistance to Change and Cultural Barriers, Skill Gaps and Lack of Training, Inadequate Leadership and Strategic Planning, Competitive and Cost Pressures Poor Layout and Inefficient Processes	Reduced Waste and Defects, Increased Productivity, Shorter Lead Times and Cycle Times
[59]	Ethiopia	Lean waste prioritisation and reduction in the apparel	Journal Article	Large	VSM, 5S	Resistance to Change and Cultural Barriers, Skill	Reduced Waste and Defects, Cost Savings and

Author	Country	Study	Type of Article	Org Type	LM tools	Challenges Faced	Benefits
		industry: application of waste assessment model and value stream mapping				Gaps and Lack of Training, High Waste and Low Productivity	Efficiency Gains, Improved Employee Morale and Job Satisfaction
[60]	Sri Lanka	Impact of Lean Manufacturing on Performance and Organisational Culture: A Case Study of an Apparel Manufacturer in Sri Lanka	Case Study	Large	Just In Time	Resistance to Change and Cultural Barriers, Skill Gaps and Lack of Training, Inadequate Leadership and Strategic Planning	Enhanced Quality Cost Savings and Efficiency Gains Improved Employee Morale and Job Satisfaction
[61]	Sri Lanka	Applicability of Lean Concept in Improving the Human Resourcing Practice in the Context of Sri Lankan Apparel Industry	Conference Paper	Large	Hoshin Kanri Lean for HR Kaizen (implied) , VSM	Resistance to Change and Cultural Barriers Skill Gaps and Lack of Training Inadequate Leadership and Strategic Planning	Enhanced Quality Cost Savings and Efficiency Gains Improved Employee Morale and Job Satisfaction
[62]	Sri Lanka	Impact of Lean Manufacturing Practices on Sustainability Performances in SMEs in Sri Lanka Special reference to apparel industry: Concept Paper	Conference Paper	Small	Push/Pull VSM Kaizen	Skill Gaps and Lack of Training Inadequate Leadership and Strategic Planning Competitive and Cost Pressures	Enhanced Quality Cost Savings and Efficiency Gains Improved Employee Morale and Job Satisfaction
[63]	Bangladesh	Implementing and sustaining lean, buyer-supplier role, and COVID-19 pandemic: insights from the garment industry of Bangladesh	Journal Article	Medium	VSM, 5S, Kanban	Skill Gaps and Lack of Training, Inadequate Leadership and Strategic Planning	Reduced Waste and Defects, Enhanced Quality
[64]	Bangladesh	Impact of lean manufacturing system on organizational performance:	Journal Article	Large	Kanban , Poka-Yoke VSM, Kaizen, TQM JIT	Resistance to Change and Cultural Barriers Skill Gaps and Lack	Reduced Waste and Defects Enhanced Quality Cost

Author	Country	Study	Type of Article	Org Type	LM tools	Challenges Faced	Benefits
		empirical evidence from apparel industry in Bangladesh				of Training Inadequate Leadership and Strategic Planning	Savings and Efficiency Gains
[65]		Lean implementation with integrated OHS in garment supplier factories	Journal Article	Large	VSM, Kanban , JIT, TPM, 5S Kaizen	Skill Gaps and Lack of Training Inadequate Leadership and Strategic Planning Competitive and Cost Pressures	Increased Productivity Enhanced Quality
[66]		Impact of Lean Manufacturing Practices on Sustainability Performance: Evidence from Sri Lankan Apparel Industry	Journal Article	Large	VSM, Kanban , JIT TPM, 5S, Kaizen	Lack of competencies, limited top-management commitment, resistance from supervisors/ workers, fear of job loss, need for buyer support	Increased Productivity Enhanced Quality

Source: Author

9 Catalyzing SME digital capacity through private campus-led training: a qualitative study in Southern Sri Lanka

Manodhya Sudasinghe[1,a] *and T.S.L.W. Gunawardana*[2,b]

[1]Department of Business, Informatics Institute of Technology, Galle, Sri Lanka

[2]Department of Business Management, Faculty of Management and Finance, University of Ruhuna, Sri Lanka

Abstract

This study examines the potential of private campuses to act as regional hubs that digitally uplift the small and medium enterprise (SME) ecosystem in the Southern Province of Sri Lanka. Amid ongoing digital disruptions and shifting business landscapes, SMEs must overcome challenges in accessing knowledge, building networks, and expanding markets. Strategic support is vital for successful digital transformation. Adopting a qualitative approach, the research utilizes semi-structured questionnaires and reflective narratives gathered from SME stakeholders engaged with campus-led initiatives. Thematic analysis reveals that private campuses can serve as catalysts for digital empowerment by enabling knowledge exchange, nurturing innovation, and fostering entrepreneurial mindsets. Participants identified the campus environment as a reliable, locally rooted platform for understanding digital trends, enhancing decision-making, and connecting with broader economic ecosystems. The findings emphasize the evolving role of private educational institutions not merely as academic entities, but as dynamic agents of regional development bridging the gap between theoretical knowledge, practical implementation, and sustainable opportunity creation for SMEs. The study suggests actionable insights for educators, policymakers, and SME enablers committed to strengthening digital resilience in regional SME ecosystems. Future research is recommended to develop a campus-led digital empowerment framework that systematically addresses the SME capability gap and fosters regional digital resilience in Sri Lanka.

Keywords: Digital resilience, private campuses, reflective narratives, SME ecosystems, thematic analysis

Introduction

The rapid advancement of Information and Communication Technologies (ICT) has significantly transformed business operations globally, enabling enterprises, particularly SMEs, to optimize productivity, reach new markets, and enhance competitiveness. In Sri Lanka, the rise of mobile and internet connectivity reflects this evolution of the digital landscape. According to the Digital 2025: Sri Lanka report by We Are Social and Meltwater, the country recorded 12.4 million internet users in January 2025, representing 53.6% of the population, marking a year-on-year increase of 808,000 users [1].

Additionally, mobile connections totaled 29.3 million, equating to 127% of the population, indicating widespread digital access through multiple mobile devices. With 8.2 million active social media users (35.4% of the population) and median mobile download speeds of 20.22 Mbps, the digital infrastructure has created fertile ground for digital engagement across all business sectors [1].

Despite these trends, SMEs in Sri Lanka's semi-urban and rural areas, particularly in the Southern Province, encounter persistent challenges in embracing digital transformation. These include limited digital literacy, poor access to structured training, inadequate institutional collaboration, insufficient infrastructure, and a lack of strategic guidance. While national strategies such as the Digital Economy Strategy 2030 aim to foster digital inclusion, grassroots-level impact remains inconsistent [2].

Parallel to this digital transformation, private academic institutions in the Southern Province have seen significant growth in infrastructure, technical expertise, and student engagement [3]. However, their role in catalyzing Small and Medium Scale Enterprises (SME) digital development remains underutilized. This study investigates how these institutions can serve as catalysts for SME digitization by providing localized training, consultancy, and innovation-driven collaboration, ultimately bridging the digital divide and contributing to regional economic resilience.

[a]manodhya.s@iit.ac.lk, [b]gunawardana@badm.ruh.ac.lk

DOI: 10.4324/9781003739920-9

Literature Review

Digital transformation in SMEs

Digital transformation refers to the integration of digital technologies into all aspects of business operations. For SMEs, this transformation can lead to significant improvements in productivity, market reach, and operational efficiency. However, literature indicates that smaller enterprises often lack the internal capabilities-such as IT skills, leadership support, and financial resources-necessary to effectively adopt digital technologies.

Studies by the OECD (2020) [4] and the Asian Development Bank (ADB) [5] emphasize the importance of supportive ecosystems, including training institutions, business incubators, and mentorship programs, in fostering SME digitalization. These studies suggest that coordinated and localized efforts are crucial for enabling SMEs to navigate digital transitions.

The role of educational institutions

Public universities have increasingly engaged in community outreach and SME support. However, the role of private campuses, particularly in semi-urban or rural areas, remains under examined. The Triple Helix Model [6] provides a framework for understanding how academia, industry, and government can collaborate to drive innovation. (Figure 9.1) In this model, educational institutions not only generate knowledge but also actively facilitate regional development through applied research, training, and consultancy. In Sri Lanka, the role of private campuses in facilitating SME digital transformation is largely untapped, particularly in regional contexts such as the Southern Province. The findings demonstrate how private campuses can fulfill the 'university–industry' dimension of the Triple Helix model by offering technical training, facilitating innovation, and acting as a bridge to digital ecosystems tailored for SMEs.

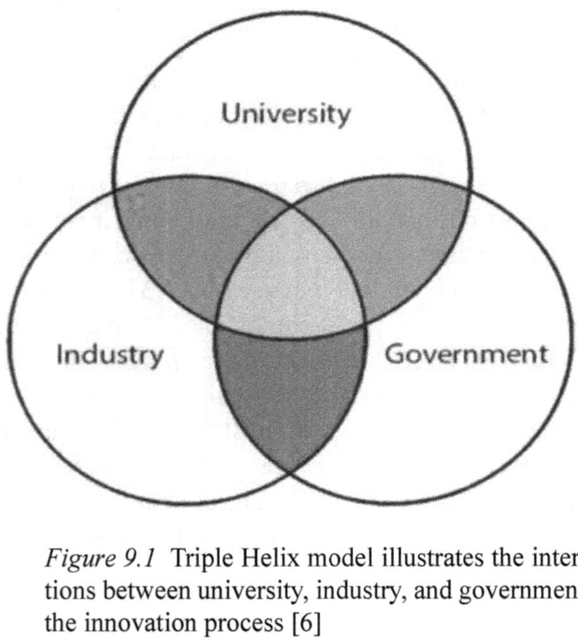

Figure 9.1 Triple Helix model illustrates the interactions between university, industry, and government in the innovation process [6]
Source: Author

Regional context: Sri Lanka's southern province

Sri Lanka's Southern Province comprising the Galle, Matara, and Hambantota districts is widely recognized as a vibrant and diverse SME ecosystem. The region is home to a range of micro, small, and medium-sized enterprises engaged in agriculture, tourism, fisheries, handicrafts, retail trade, and small-scale manufacturing [7]. These sectors contribute significantly to both local livelihoods and the broader regional economy. The presence of natural resources, cultural heritage sites, and coastal access makes the region particularly conducive to entrepreneurial activity, especially in tourism and Agri-based value chains [8].

Despite this potential, many SMEs in the Southern Province face persistent constraints, including poor access to finance, lack of market connectivity, digital exclusion, and limited training opportunities [3, 5]. While government efforts have focused on providing infrastructure and credit facilities, there is a growing recognition of the need for localized, knowledge-driven interventions to build SME resilience and competitiveness. These include training, mentorship, digital upskilling, and ecosystem-building efforts that tap into regional educational and institutional assets.

In this context, private academic institutions located within the province represent a largely underutilized resource that could help bridge capability gaps. Their proximity to the SME base, coupled with access to technical knowledge, positions them to play a critical role in facilitating inclusive digital transformation, an area that remains under-researched in both policy and academic discourse.

Research Methodology

This study adopted a qualitative research approach [9] to examine the potential role of private campuses in supporting the digital transformation of small and medium enterprises (SMEs) in the Southern Province of Sri Lanka. The research focused on identifying existing digital gaps, assessing awareness of institutional support, and evaluating the readiness of SMEs to engage with campus-led digital initiatives. Open-ended questionnaire responses were analyzed to identify recurring themes related to how private academic institutions can support SME digital transformation.

Sampling and participants

The study targeted SMEs operating in the Galle, Matara, and Hambantota districts, selected due to their diverse economic activities and proximity to regional private academic institutions. A purposive sampling strategy was employed to ensure representation across key sectors, including tourism, agriculture, food processing, retail, and small-scale manufacturing. A total of 100 SMEs were selected to participate in the study.

Data collection instrument

Data was collected using a structured questionnaire, designed to capture both quantitative and categorical data related to the digital maturity of SMEs, [10–13] their awareness and use of digital tools, perceived barriers to digital adoption, and knowledge of potential collaborations with nearby private academic institutions.

The questionnaire was developed through a review of relevant literature and expert consultations, ensuring relevance and validity. It included items covering demographic and firmographic details, digital usage patterns, barriers to digital transformation, and awareness of institutional support.

Data collection procedure

The survey was conducted during the first quarter of 2025. Questionnaires were distributed electronically and in-person, depending on the availability and preferences of participants. In addition, a collaborative outreach event was organized by the Informatics Institute of Technology (IIT) in celebration of International Women's Day in partnership with the Ministry of Youth and Sports, Southern Province and the Southern Development Authority. Local business associations and the IIT business school assisted in facilitating introductions and increasing response rates. This event specifically targeted women entrepreneurs and served as both a data-gathering and empowerment initiative.

The insights from this engagement helped shape subsequent training programs focused on addressing identified digital skill gaps and sector-specific needs among SMEs. This multifaceted engagement strategy not only broadened the participant base but also deepened institutional relationships, creating pathways for future campus-led digital empowerment efforts that align with broader regional development goals.

Based on insights gathered from the survey and the event, two pilot training programs were designed and conducted to test the relevance and applicability of campus-led digital upskilling interventions. These pilot programs focus on building basic digital literacy and content creation skills using Google tools and enhancing small business capabilities in social media marketing and digital customer engagement. Feedback collected during these sessions was instrumental in refining both the content and delivery approach of the training programs, helping ensure that future initiatives are accessible, context-sensitive, and aligned with the real-world needs of SMEs in Sri Lanka's Southern Province.

Results and Discussion

Background and demographic data

A total of 100 SMEs from the Galle, Matara, and Hambantota districts participated in the survey. The sample covered a broad spectrum of industries, including tourism (12%), agriculture and food processing (25%), handicrafts (15%), retail (20%), and small-scale manufacturing (28%) (Figure 9.2).

Participants were mostly micro and small enterprises, with 72% employing fewer than 10 people. Ownership structures included sole proprietorships (60%), partnerships (25%), and private limited companies (15%). The gender distribution of respondents showed 38% female entrepreneurs, highlighting moderate female representation in the regional SME landscape.

The sample demonstrated significant geographic and sectoral diversity, offering a robust foundation for analyzing digital transformation patterns and the role of institutional support. The analysis revealed several key patterns as many SMEs emphasized the need for practical, hands-on training rather than theoretical instruction, highlighting a preference for application-based learning. Respondents also expressed trust in local private institutions due to their accessibility, cultural alignment, and ability to communicate

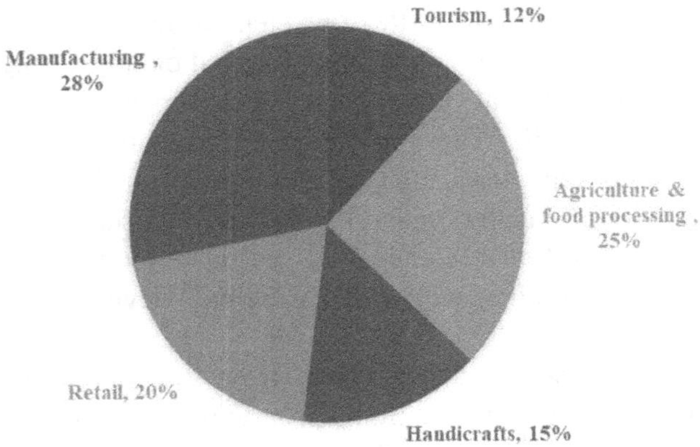

Figure 9.2 SME distribution by sector
Source: Author

in familiar languages. Time constraints and limited digital literacy were frequently mentioned as barriers to participation, indicating a need for more flexible or online training formats. Additionally, there was a strong call for ongoing support beyond initial training, with many participants seeking follow-up guidance and consultancy services to implement digital tools effectively.

Digital transformation

Analysis of digital usage patterns revealed that 84% of SMEs regularly used smartphones and internet-enabled devices in their business operations. Social media platforms such as Facebook and WhatsApp were the most widely used tools for marketing and customer communication. However, adoption of more advanced digital solutions remained limited, with only 22% of respondents using formal e-commerce platforms and just 18% utilizing cloud-based productivity tools like Google Workspace or Microsoft 365. This indicated a preference for basic digital communication tools, with a significant gap in the use of platforms that enable scalability and operational efficiency.

When asked about barriers to digital transformation, the most frequently cited challenges were a lack of digital skills (72%), insufficient financial resources to invest in technology (64%), and poor internet connectivity, particularly in rural areas (40%). These obstacles reflect both infrastructural and capability-related limitations that hinder the broader adoption of digital tools across the SME landscape.

Awareness of nearby private academic institutions was low, with 25% of respondents indicating familiarity with such entities.

However, actual participation in training or collaborative initiatives was limited to only 14%. Despite this low engagement, there was strong interest in future collaboration, especially in practical areas such as digital marketing, bookkeeping, and customer engagement. These findings underscore a significant opportunity for private campuses to take on a more active role in supporting regional SMEs through tailored digital skill-building initiatives.

Further insights gathered through focus group discussions and survey responses highlighted that while smartphone use is common among SME owners, their digital engagement varies. Around 42% actively used internet-connected devices for business tasks like marketing on Facebook and Instagram, communicating via WhatsApp and email, and making mobile payments. However, 36% reported relying exclusively on mobile phones without internet access, and another 11% believed that adopting digital tools might disrupt their routine business operations. Additionally, 11% cited a lack of ICT skills and digital literacy as a key deterrent to digital adoption.

Reflective narratives collected during and after the training programs revealed a gradual but meaningful shift in how SMEs perceived and approached digital engagement. Many participants initially relied solely on informal digital knowledge passed down from family members or younger generations.

For instance, a female entrepreneur from Hambantota shared that her fertilizer business depended entirely on her son's digital knowledge until she personally engaged with the training. Following the sessions, she expressed increased confidence in managing her business's online visibility and customer interactions independently. These accounts highlight how localized, accessible training can demystify digital concepts and empower entrepreneurs, particularly in women and elderly people to take proactive steps in their digital journey. Another participant, a young retail owner from Galle, shared how she had tried and failed to grow her business online during the pandemic. "I didn't know where to start or who to trust," she said. But through the campus-led session, she learned how to plan her content, communicate more clearly with customers, and gradually rebuild her confidence to transform her retail business online. Stories like theirs echoed across the sessions, business owners who once felt that digital tools were beyond their reach began to realize that with the right support, they could begin a successful digital journey for their businesses.

The narratives underscore a growing openness among SMEs to adopt structured digital practices that enhance credibility, customer trust, and long-term business sustainability.

The findings of this study demonstrate the practical relevance of the Triple Helix Model in the Southern Province. Private campuses serve as connectors between government policy (e.g., Digital Economy Strategy 2030) [2], industry needs (as expressed by SMEs), and academic capability. By positioning themselves as trusted local intermediaries, campuses help operationalize the 'university–industry' helix, while outreach activities such as pilot trainings and women's entrepreneurship events show the potential for deeper government-university partnerships. This triangulation is key to fostering digital innovation and resilience at the regional level. Although basic ICT applications such as social media promotion and messaging apps were prevalent, the use of more advanced tools remained rare. Very few businesses managed their own websites, owned a Google business profile, operated online stores, used customer relationship management (CRM) systems, or engaged in data-driven decision-making. Only 10% had established a business website, and even fewer utilized sophisticated digital tools to scale operations. These findings highlight both the aspirations and limitations of SMEs in the Southern Province, revealing a clear demand for targeted digital literacy programs and greater institutional collaboration to bridge the existing digital divide.

Recommendations

To support SME digital transformation in the Southern Province, academic institutions should play a central role in collaborative initiatives. Universities as well as vocational training centers can work together to design and implement contextualized capacity-building programs. These should cover areas such as social media marketing, digital payments, basic cybersecurity, and digital communication, to demystify digital technologies and connect them with real SME needs.

Academic institutions can host regular business clinics where students and faculty provide one-on-one mentorship and troubleshooting support for SME owners. These sessions can include assistance with setting up digital tools, drafting marketing content, and developing simple websites.

A structured framework must be developed to incubate and accelerate the growth of SMEs through targeted support mechanisms, capacity-building initiatives, and access to digital tools and resources. Collaborative research projects between universities and local businesses [14] can help identify practical barriers and inform policy interventions. Moreover, academic involvement in public awareness campaigns and training material development will ensure accuracy, accessibility, and cultural relevance.

By fostering a strong linkage between academia and local SMEs, these efforts can help translate digital transformation goals into everyday business practices and support the sustainable development of the region's SME ecosystem.

Conclusion

This study explores the potential for private campuses in Sri Lanka's Southern Province to act as change agents in the digital transformation of SMEs, particularly in addressing the limited application of digital knowledge within these enterprises. Despite the increasing importance of digitalization for business sustainability and growth, SMEs continue to face substantial challenges, including limited access to formal training, inadequate infrastructure, and a lack of strategic institutional support.

This research investigates how private campuses can bridge these gaps by providing technical expertise, fostering innovation, and cultivating collaborative SME ecosystems.

Primary data was collected through structured questionnaires distributed to 100 SMEs across the agriculture, tourism, crafts and retail sectors. The study assessed key dimensions such as digital maturity, barriers to technology adoption, and awareness of institutional support mechanisms. The findings reveal that while most SMEs acknowledge the importance of digital transformation, over 70% lack formal digital training or access to relevant tools.

Furthermore, a significant portion of SMEs remain unaware of collaborative opportunities with nearby private academic institutions. These results underscore the untapped potential of private campuses to serve as localized hubs of digital empowerment. The paper contributes to an extensive study of the role of educational institutions in regional development and offers actionable insights for policymakers, SME associations, and educational leaders.

There are very few constraints in this study, but they suggest important areas for future research. First, this study only reached out to a limited number of SMEs, and It is limited to the Southern province only. However, this study's sample plan was effective enough to capture a lot of variety within the industry. Future scholars could therefore confirm the findings with more empirical investigations. Secondly, future scholars might empirically test the model to strengthen the validity of the suggested conceptualization. This study explicates how SMEs leads to the digital transformation in line with dynamic capability and capacities of the industry, universities and the government. Notably, future researchers should also consider how well the generated dimensions would fit into research on various categories of SMEs in various geographical areas.

Finally, future research is recommended to develop a structured campus-led digital empowerment framework to systematically address existing capability gaps and promote inclusive digital innovation. Predominantly, this study is limited to SMEs in the Southern Province of Sri Lanka, and while existing literature addresses SME challenges broadly, the unique role of private campuses as enablers of digital transformation remains underexplored.

References

[1] We Are Social and Meltwater (2025). Digital 2025: Sri Lanka. Available from: https://wearesocial.com. pp. 1–92.

[2] Ministry of Technology (2023). National Digital Economy Strategy 2030: Sri Lanka. Colombo, Sri Lanka: Ministry of Technology. Available from: https://mot.gov.lk/assets/files/National%20Digital%20Economy%20Strategy%202030%20Sri%20Lanka-bc77184e0b6035d235cd0bb1ebf75707.pdf.

[3] GIZ (2019). SME Sector Analysis – Southern Sri Lanka. Colombo, Sri Lanka: GIZ.

[4] OECD (2020). Digital Transformation of SMEs. Paris, France: OECD Publishing.

[5] Asian Development Bank (ADB) (2022). Technology and Innovation for Inclusive Growth in Asia. Manila, Philippines: ADB.

[6] Etzkowitz, H., & Leydesdorff, L. (2000). The dynamics of innovation: from national systems and 'Mode 2' to a triple helix of university–industry–government relations. *Research Policy*, 29(2), 109–123.

[7] Department of Census and Statistics (2021). Economic Census Report: Southern Province. Colombo, Sri Lanka: Government of Sri Lanka.

[8] World Bank (2020). World Development Report 2020: Trading for Development in the Age of Global Value Chains. Washington, DC: World Bank. Available from: https://www.worldbank.org/en/publication/wdr2020.

[9] Creswell, J. W. (2002). Educational Research: Planning, Conducting, and Evaluating Qualitative and Quantitative Research. London, UK: Pearson Education.

[10] European Commission (2024). Digital Maturity As- sessment Questionnaire for SMEs. Brussels, Bel- gium. pp. 3–10. Available from: https://european-digital-in- novation-hubs.ec.europa.eu/system/files/2024-05/ DMA%20Questionnaire%20for%20SMEs_EDIH_ network_EN_0.pdf.

[11] Deloitte (2019). Digital Maturity Model (DMM). Deloitte Development LLC. Available from: https://www2.deloitte.com/content/dam/Deloitte/uk/Documents/strategy/deloitte-uk-digital-maturity-model.pdf.

[12] Survey Research Lanka (Pvt) Ltd. (2023). Assessing the Digital Maturity of SME Exporters in Sri Lanka. Colombo, Sri Lanka. Available from: https://www.chamber.lk/trade-watch/backend/public/uploads/attachments/article/FRDMSMSSL_1674200111.pdf.

[13] Information and Communication Technology Agency (ICTA) (2022). Digital Maturity Assessment for SMEs in Sri Lanka. Colombo, Sri Lanka. Available from: https://www.icta.lk/digital-maturity-assessment-report/.

[14] Abeywardena, A. (2015). Promoting university-industry collaboration in Sri Lanka: status, case studies, and policy options. *The World Bank*. Available from: https://documents.worldbank.org/en/publication/documents-reports/documentdetail/76276146799668.

10 Green products purchase intention of generation Z; the mediating role of attitudes

P. M. E. Priyadarshani[1,a], *D. Weerasekera*[2,b] *and A.P. Silva*[3,c]

[1]Department of Tourism and Marketing, NSBM Green University, Sri Lanka

[2]School of Business, Law and Entrepreneurship, Swinburne University of Technology, Australia

[3]Department of Management, NSBM Green University, Sri Lanka

Abstract

This research aimed to identify consumer attitudes and trust that influence the purchasing intention of green products in light of the theory of planned behavior (TPB). The study undertook a quantitative approach with a cross-sectional design. Self- administered questionnaires were distributed employing purposive sampling to Generation Z (1997-2013) who had purchased green products recently. A total of 413 responses were analyzed by PLS-SEM approach. The outcome of the study disclosed that subjective norms, attitudes, and behavioral control significantly influenced the intention to purchase green products. Additionally, this study proved that attitudes fully mediate the relationship between trust and purchase intention. This study contributes to extending the knowledge of purchase intention in the context of green products resulting in further explanation of TPB. Further, the findings offer vital practical implications for policy makers and decision makers in promoting green product consumption among consumers.

Keywords: Attitude, generation Z, green products, purchase intention, theory of planned behavior, trust

Introduction

The continued irresponsible consumption of products, waste generation, air and water pollution and depletion of non-renewable energy sources are increasing in an alarming rate and it is directly contributing to global warming [1]. Further, over the recent decades these environmental issues have escalated due to the unsustainable manner of waste generation caused by the rising human population [1].

In response to these environmental issues United Nations Development Program (UNDP) established the Sustainable Development Goals (SDGs) on September 25, 2015, emphasizing the need to mitigate negative environmental impacts by promoting responsible production and consumption [1]. This initiative proposes green consumption as a strategy to manage environmental preservation while catering to consumer demands. Green consumption promotes the concept of reducing environmental impacts over limiting product acquisition [1]. Moreover, it majorly focusses on striking a balance between traditional consumption patterns while reducing the ecological impact of purchasing behavior [1, 2]. Hence, this study focuses on the discussion of green product purchase intention in light of TPB.

Research objectives

RO1: To investigate the relationship between attitudes, perceived behavioral control, subjective norms, and trust on purchasing intention of green products

RO2: To investigate the relationship between trust and attitudes

RO3: To investigate the mediating impact of attitudes on the relationship between trust and purchasing intention of green products.

Literature Review

Theory of planned behavior

Theory of planned behavior (TPB) is a widely used framework to study and predict human behavior [3]. According to the TPB intentions are the key drivers of behavior and they are essential when it comes to explaining individual actions [3, 4]. Moreover, behavior can be predicted from a logical flow between the intention to action [3, 4] and the TPB model frames

[a]erandikapriyadarshani80@gmail.com, [b]dweerasekeraarachchi@swin.edu.au, [c]prabha.s@nsbm.ac.lk

DOI: 10.4324/9781003739920-10

the interaction between the behavioral intention and attitudes, subjective norms and perceived behavioral control [5]. In light of this it can be elaborated that TPB provides a reliable base to conceptualize, measure, and empirically assess the antecedents of behavior and behavioral intention [6], hence making it a valuable tool for studying consumer behavior.

Purchase intention

Purchase intention is identified as tendencies in personal action with regards to a brand and it is a powerful predictor of consumer behavior [7]. As per the findings of [8], a stronger intention to buy a product is associated with a greater willingness to pay for it. Purchase intention is a strong predictor of actual buying behavior [8]. In recent decades, the tendency of consumers to purchase ecologically certified products (green products) has increased. It also shows a remarkable growth in the number of studies conducted on green consumption in the last three decades [1]. Purchase intention towards green products is significantly or directly driven by environmental concerns [1].

Attitude

Attitudes have been identified as determinants of behavioral performance. It is the magnitude of the evaluation of the behavior which could be either favorable or unfavorable, molded by behavioral beliefs that associate the behavior with specific outcomes [9]. Further, these attitudes basically form accessible beliefs about the consequences of the behavior [4] and attitudes are generated from one's interaction with activities or the environmental factors [10]. According to previous research, attitude could be identified as the most significant predictor of intention to purchase green products, demonstrating a strong, positive relationship between the two variables [6]. Hence, based on the previous literature following hypothesis has been derived.

H1: Attitudes has a significant impact on purchase intention of green products

Subjective norms

Subjective norms are a significant component in the TPB in terms of the potential to influence the behavioral intention [4, 9]. Subjective norms can be defined as the perceived social pressure to perform or not perform a particular behavior [11]. However, these behaviors are further influenced by an individual's belief about whether important referents namely; family, friends, or peers approve of or think they should engage in such a specific [11]. Previous literature have enlightened the fact that subjective norms can significantly and positively affect consumers' intention to buy green products [4, 12]. Hence, based on the previous literature following hypothesis has been derived,

H2: Subjective norms have a significant impact on purchase intention of green products

Perceived behavioral control

Based on the TPB, behavioral intention could directly predict both perceived behavioral control (PBC) and behavioral outcomes [4]. PBC is further driven by control beliefs; factors which could either support or obstruct the execution of a particular behavior and PBC can be simply explained as an individual's perception of how easy or difficult it is to perform a specific behavior [4, 9]. Moreover, this particular perception elaborates the confidence in managing either a potential obstacle or an enabler. However, many studies bring in evidence to the fact that PBC significantly influences purchase intention [13]. Hence, based on the previous literature following hypothesis has been derived.

H3: Perceived Behavioral Control has a significant impact on purchase intention of green products

Trust

Trust is usually built upon the authenticity and performance of the products [9]. Specially, in terms of the products purchase decisions, trust has been identified as a critical determinant [9] and when there are discrepancies in establishing complete trust it acts as a major barrier towards shaping the purchasing intentions [14]. Further, uncertainty and risk can be identified as unavoidable challenges and trust is a crucial factor there, if the consumer needs to be retained [12]. However, trust has a major call in shaping consumer attitudes and behaviors [12]. In the TPB trust is considered an antecedent of attitudes and has a positive influence on purchase intention [15]. Hence, based on the previous literature following hypothesis has been derived,

H4: Trust has a significant impact on attitudes

H5. Attitudes have a mediating impact on the relationship between trust and purchase intention of green products.

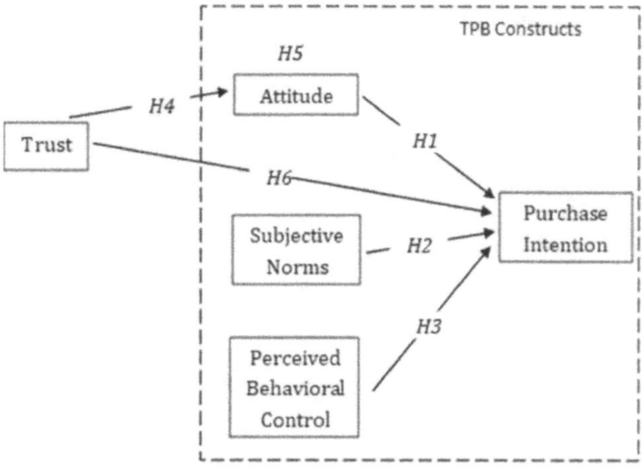

Figure 10.1 Conceptual framework
Source: Author

H6. Trust has a significant impact on purchase intention of green products.

Based on the above interplay between variables, conceptual framework (Figure 10.1) is derived.

Methodology

This study employed a deductive approach, and the study population was Gen Z consumers who have purchased green products recently, as their awareness and desire towards responsible buying behavior is proven by multiple research projects and the cohort is known for the extensive knowledge on sustainable purchase intentions [5]. Therefore, a filtering question was asked to identify the qualified participants for this study. Purposive sampling was used and self-administered questionnaires were sent to the target population [1].

Scales which had been validated in the literature were used to ensure the validity and reliability of the study measurements. Measures of purchase intention (4 items), attitudes (4 items), subjective norms (4 items), perceived behavioral control (4 items), and trust (4 items), were adapted from a previous study [1, 12] (Table 10.1). All variables were measured using a five-point Likert scale ranging from 1 (strongly disagree) to 5 (strongly agree). To ensure clarity in the wording of the questionnaire and to assess the quality and reliability of the measures, a pilot study was conducted with 50 responses. Following this, 413 valid questionnaires were retained for data analysis.

Table 10.1 Measurement items.

Construct	Measurement Item	Reference Source
Purchase Intention	I intend to buy a green product.	(Carrion Bosquez et al. 2023)
	I plan to purchase green products.	
	I will purchase green products in my next purchase.	
	Next month I will buy organic products	
Attitude	Environmental protection is important to me when making product purchases.	(Carrion Bosquez et al. 2023)
	I believe that green products help to reduce pollution (water, air etc.)	
	I believe that green products help to save nature and its resources.	
	Given choice, I will prefer a green product over a conventional product.	
Subjective Norms	People who are important to me think that I should buy green products.	(Carrion Bosquez et al. 2023)
	My interaction with people influences me to buy green products	
	My acquaintances would approve of my decisions to buy green products.	
	Most of my friends think that buying organic products is the right thing to do	
Perceived Behavioral Control	It is entirely my decision to buy green products.	(Carrion Bosquez et al. 2023)
	I cannot pay more to buy green products.	
	I require a lot of time to search for green products	
	I know exactly where to buy organic products	
Trust	I think that corporations in the field of green products are aware of their responsibilities.	(Teng and Wang, 2015)
	I trust those who sell green products indeed sell quality ones	
	I trust quality green product label or logos	
	I trust the institutions certifying green products	

Source: Survey data (2024)

Results

Demographic characteristics

To understand the sample better, which consisted of Generation Z consumers and their attitudes, a demographic analysis was conducted. It will be supportive of contextualizing the results and give insights into the respondents' gender, marital status, occupation, and income levels and these details are very important to understand the purchasing behavior (Table 10.2).

Common method bias and normality

The length of the questionnaire items implicit social desirability in questionnaire responses can result in common method bias (CMB). To verify whether the model is free of CMB, variation inflation factor (VIF) values in the inner model were considered. All VIF values were below 3.3, indicating that the model is free of CMB Further, [16] Kurtosis and Skewness values were examined for normality. A normal distribution was confirmed as the values were within the range of –2 to +2 [17] (Table 10.3).

Measurement model assessment

The measurement model employed in this study was specified as reflective, consistent with the defining characteristics of reflective models and the indicators themselves are highly intercorrelated [17].

To assess internal consistency reliability, indicator loadings, Cronbach's alpha, and composite reliability (rho_c) were examined. All indicator loadings exceeded the recommended threshold of 0.50, while Cronbach's alpha values surpassed the 0.70 benchmark, indicating acceptable reliability. Composite reliability values were also above 0.70, further confirming the model's internal consistency [18] (Table 10.3).

Convergent validity was evaluated using average variance extracted (AVE), with all constructs demonstrating AVE values above the minimum threshold of 0.50, thereby establishing convergent validity (Table 10.3). Discriminant validity was assessed using both the Fornell-Larcker criterion and the heterotrait-monotrait ratio (HTMT). According to the Fornell-Larcker criterion, the square roots of the AVE values for each construct exceeded their correlations with other constructs (Table 10.4). Additionally, all HTMT values were below the accepted threshold of 0.85, confirming the discriminant validity of the model [18] (Table 10.5).

Structural model

After confirming the validity and reliability of the model, the hypothesized structural model was tested. As illustrated in Figure 10.2, the results confirmed a significant effect of immersion on behavioral intention at the 0.05 significance level [18]. Furthermore, attitudes, perceived behavioral control, trust, and subjective norm were found to have a positive influence on purchase intention, while trust positively influenced attitudes. Therefore, hypotheses H1, H2, H3, H4, and H6 were supported (see Table 10.6).

Table 10.2 Demographic characteristics.

Characteristics	Category	N	%
Gender	Female	266	64.4
	Male	147	35.6
Marital Status	Married	54	13.1
	Single	359	86.9
Occupation	Full-time employed	198	47.9
	Self-employed	22	5.3
	Student	186	45.0
	Unemployed	7	1.7
Monthly Income	25.000-50.000	100	24.2
	50.000 – 75.000	91	22.0
	Above 75.000	69	16.7
	Less than 25.000	153	37.0

Source: Survey data (2024)

Table 10.3 Convergent validity and reliability.

Model construct	Items	Factor loading	SK	KU	Cronbach's alpha	Composite reliability (CR)	Average variance extracted (AVE)
Attitude	ATT1 ATT2 ATT3 ATT4	0.734 0.879 0.817 0.796	-1.083 -0.428 -0.323 -0.906	9.928 7.479 9.515 9.578	0.823	0.882	0.653
Subjective norms	SN1 SN2 SN3 SN4	0.790 0.825 0.772 0.773	-1.425 -0.809 -1.566 -1.444	9.845 8.888 8.917 7.596	0.800	0.869	0.624
Perceived behavioral control	PBC1 PBC2 PBC3 PBC4	0.762 0.700 0.730 0.828	-1.006 -1.684 -0.329 -0.826	9.236 8.434 5.535 8.807	0.754	0.842	0.572
Trust	TRUST1 TRUST2 TRUST3 TRUST4	0.859 0.445 0.774 0.928	-1.669 -0.437 -1.744 -0.424	6.851 5.621 5.529 3.829	0.752	0.849	0.599
Purchase intention	PI1 PI2 PI3 PI4	0.854 0.851 0.821 0.833	-0.858 -0.865 -1.691 -1.810	8.405 9.459 9.341 9.406	0.861	0.905	0.705

Source: Survey data (2024)

Table 10.4 Discriminant validity.

	ATT	SN	PBC	TRUST	PI
ATT	0.808				
SN	0.468	0.790			
PBC	0.736	0.466	0.757		
TRUST	0.701	0.364	0.607	0.774	
PI	**0.491**	**0.772**	**0.478**	**0.390**	**0.840**

Source: Survey data (2024)

Table 10.5 Discriminant validity (HTMT ratio).

	ATT	SN	PBC	TRUST	PI
ATT					
SN	0.570				
PBC	1.192	0.576			
TRUST	0.839	0.479	0.798		
PI	**0.578**	**1.170**	**0.572**	**0.561**	

Source: Survey data (2024)

Table 10.6 Results of the hypothesized paths.

Hypothesis	Path	T statistics	P values	Result
H1	ATT -> PI	2.749	0.006	Supported
H2	SN -> PI	84.470	0.000	Supported
H3	PBC -> PI	2.339	0.019	Supported
H4	TRU -> ATT	21.708	0.000	Supported
H6	TRU -> PI	1.015	0.310	Rejected

Source: Survey data (2024)

The mediation analysis was conducted to reveal whether the attitudes mediates the relationship

Table 10.7 Mediation Analysis.

Hypothesis	Effect	Path	T statistics (|O/STDEV|)	P values	Accept / Reject
H5	Specific Indirect	TRU -> ATT -> PI	2.637	0.008	Accept
H6	Direct	TRU -> PI	1.015	0.310	Rejected

Source: Survey data (2024)

between trust and purchase intention. As presented in Table 10.7, trust exerted a significant influence on purchase intention through attitudes supporting H5.

Since only indirect effects were accepted, a full mediation was identified [18]. Further, all path coefficient values were positive confirming a full mediation.

Given the sample size, R^2 of variance explained for behavioral intention (94%) and attitudes (49%) were worked out as predictive power for testing the accuracy of the structural framework (Figure 10.2).

Conclusion

Green consumption is a trending topic in both managerial and academic spheres and many researchers have made significant efforts to explore the determinants influencing eco-friendly product purchase intentions. However, even though many studies were conducted, majority of them were organic product consumption behaviors in developing economies. Therefore, this study aimed at exploring the purchase intention toward green products with an emphasis on the role of trust among Generation Z consumers in Sri Lanka. The findings revealed that Generation Z consumers project much favorable attitudes, subjective norms, and perceived behavioral control when it comes to green products, which significantly influence their purchasing intention. Moreover, attitudes toward green products facilitates to enhance the relationship between trust and purchase intention.

The study provides valuable insights into understanding Generation Z consumers. Therefore, the findings of the study can contribute in large to the green product producers to gauge the level of purchase intention among this demographic in developing contexts such as Sri Lanka. The study mainly elaborates the mediating factor "trust" which could either strengthen or inhibit purchase intention. Hence, it is important for the companies to implement proper strategies to foster an environment which induces consumer trust and reinforce positive behavioral outcomes. Customized product marketing can resonate with Generation Z's values, while reinforcing trust and credibility can bridge the existing gap between purchase intention and actual behavior. In terms of social implications, the study provides with insights about distinctive behavioral patterns of Sri Lankan Generation Z consumers, which instils a contrast from developed economies when it comes to green consumption preferences.

The study has a few limitations, including the focus on collecting data only from individuals within Generation Z (1997–2013), a demographic crucial to the research scope. Since the study is quantitatively conducted it suits more for large scale analysis and that restricts the researcher from exploring deeper consumer motivations and contextual influences. Qualitative methodologies such as focus groups or in-depth interviews could provide richer insights into underlying drivers of green product purchase intentions. Further, it would be more beneficial to expand the scope of the research beyond Generation Z and include other generational cohorts such as Baby Boomers, Generation X, and Millennials. These comparisons could help to identify which cohort demonstrates the highest level of environmentally friendly consumption.

Further, this study is based on the theoretical framework which is grounded by the TPB. It captures the attitudinal and behavioral components effectively but incorporating other theories such as the expectancy-confirmation model could have enhanced the understanding of consumer behavior and recommended for future research work.

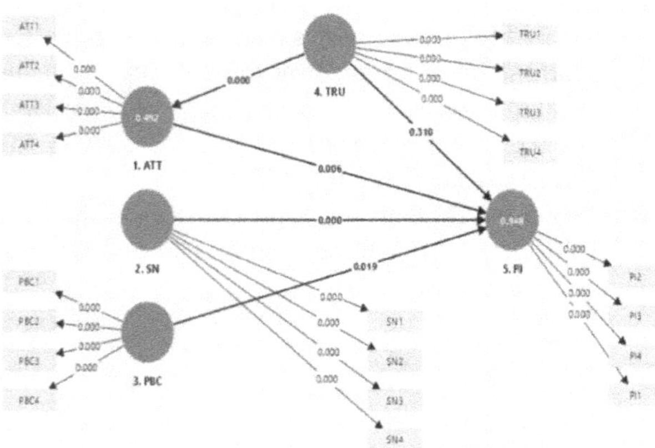

Figure 10.2 Structural model
Source: Author

References

[1] Carrión Bósquez, N. G., Arias-Bolzmann, L. G., & Martínez Quiroz, A. K. (2023). The influence of price and availability on university millennials' organic food product purchase intention. *British Food Journal*, 125(2), 536–550. doi: 10.1108/BFJ-12-2021-1340.

[2] Testa, F., Sarti, S., & Frey, M. (2019). Are green consumers really green? Exploring the factors behind the actual consumption of organic food products. *Business Strategy and the Environment*, 28(2), 327–338. doi: 10.1002/bse.2234.

[3] Pacho, F. (2020). What influences consumers to purchase organic food in developing countries?. *British Food Journal*, 122(12), 3695–3709. doi: 10.1108/BFJ-01-2020-0075.

[4] Ajzen, I. (2020). The theory of planned behavior: Frequently asked questions. *Human Behavior and Emerging Technologies*, 2(4), 314–324. doi: 10.1002/hbe2.195.

[5] Djafarova, E., & Foots, S. (2022). Exploring ethical consumption of generation Z: theory of planned behaviour. *Young Consumers*, 23(3), 413–431. doi: 10.1108/YC-10-2021-1405.

[6] Taufique, K. M. R., & Islam, S. (2020). Green marketing in emerging Asia: antecedents of green consumer behavior among younger millennials. *Journal of Asia Business Studies*, 15(4), 541–558. doi: 10.1108/JABS-03-2020-0094.

[7] Spears, N., & Singh, S. N. (2004). Measuring attitude toward the brand and purchase intentions. *Journal of Current Issues and Research in Advertising*, 26(2), 53–66. doi: 10.1080/10641734.2004.10505164.

[8] Lian, S. B., & Yoong, L. C. (2019). Assessing the young consumers' motives and purchase behavior for organic food: an empirical evidence from a developing nation. *International Journal of Academic Research in Business and Social Sciences*, 9(1), 69–87. doi: 10.6007/ijarbss/v9-i1/5364.

[9] Nguyen, T. T., Dang, H. Q., & Le-Anh, T. (2023). Impacts of household norms and trust on organic food purchase behavior under adapted theory of planned behavior. *Journal of Agribusiness in Developing and Emerging Economies*, 14(5), 1055–1073. doi: 10.1108/JADEE-10-2022-0218.

[10] Tandon, A., Dhir, A., Kaur, P., Kushwah, S., & Salo, J. (2020). Why do people buy organic food? The moderating role of environmental concerns and trust. *Journal of Retailing and Consumer Services*, 57, 102247. doi: 10.1016/j.jretconser.2020.102247.

[11] Singh, A., & Verma, P. (2017). Factors influencing Indian consumers' actual buying behaviour towards organic food products. *Journal of Cleaner Production*, 167, 473–483. doi: 10.1016/j.jclepro.2017.08.106.

[12] Teng, C. C., & Wang, Y. M. (2015). Decisional factors driving organic food consumption: generation of consumer purchase intentions. *British Food Journal*, 117(3), 1066–1081. doi: 10.1108/BFJ-12-2013-0361.

[13] Dangi, N., Narula, S. A., & Gupta, S. K. (2020). Influences on purchase intentions of organic food consumers in an emerging economy. *Journal of Asia Business Studies*, 14(5), 599–620. doi: 10.1108/JABS-12-2019-0364.

[14] Mohammed, A. A. (2020). What motivates consumers to purchase organic food in an emerging market? an empirical study from Saudi Arabia. *British Food Journal*, 123(5), 1758–1775. doi: 10.1108/BFJ-07-2020-0599.

[15] Watanabe, E. A. de M., Alfinito, S., Curvelo, I. C. G., & Hamza, K. M. (2020). Perceived value, trust and purchase intention of organic food: a study with Brazilian consumers. *British Food Journal,* 122(4), 1070–1184. doi: 10.1108/BFJ-05-2019-0363.

[16] Kock, N. (2015). Common method bias in PLS-SEM: a full collinearity assessment approach. *International Journal of e-Collaboration*, 11(4), 1–10.

[17] Hair, J. F., Hult, G. T. M., Ringle, C. M., & Sarstedt, M. (2017). A Primer on Partial Least Squares Structural Equation Modeling (PLS-SEM), (2nd edn.). Thousand Oaks, CA: SAGE Publications, Inc. doi: 10.1016/j.lrp.2013.01.002.

[18] Hair, J., & Alamer, A. (2022). Partial Least Squares Structural Equation Modeling (PLS-SEM) in second language and education research: Guidelines using an applied example. Research Methods in Applied Linguistics, 1(3), 100027, https://doi.org/10.1016/j.rmal.2022.100027.

[19] Zayed, M. F., Gaber, H. R., & El Essawi, N. (2022). Examining the factors that affect consumers' purchase intention of organic food products in a developing country. *Sustainability*, 14(10), 5868. doi: 10.3390/su14105868.

11 The factors influencing educators' self-esteem in higher education, Sri Lanka: a concept paper

S. S. E. Joseph[1,a] *and Khwaja Abdul-Cader*[2,b]

[1]Department of Management, Faculty of Business, NSBM Green University, Sri Lanka

[2]Faculty of Management and Technology, BMS Campus, Colombo 06, Sri Lanka

Abstract

This concept paper proposes a study to explore the key factors influencing educators' self-esteem within the higher education sector in Sri Lanka. Self-esteem is a foundational element that significantly affects educators' teaching effectiveness, job satisfaction, and professional relationships. In the context of an evolving educational landscape, understanding the dynamics that shape educators' self-perception is vital for institutional development and academic excellence. The proposed study aims to investigate the relationship between educators' self-esteem and four potential influencing factors: self-efficacy, peer influence, power to influence others, and organizational empowerment. A quantitative research approach while utilizing SPSS as a research analysis tool, will be employed, using a validated self-esteem scale alongside a structured questionnaire to collect data from educators in Sri Lankan higher education institutions. It is anticipated that self-efficacy, peer influence, and organizational empowerment will exhibit a strong positive correlation with self-esteem, while the power to influence others may demonstrate a moderate association. Multiple regression analysis will be applied to examine the degree to which these variables collectively explain the variance in educators' self-esteem levels. The outcomes of this proposed research are expected to have a positive impact on all variables related to educators' self-esteem. By addressing both personal and institutional dimensions, this study aims to contribute meaningfully to the literature on educator well-being in higher education.

Keywords: Educator self-esteem, organizational empowerment, peer influence, power to influence, self-efficacy

Introduction

Self-esteem, broadly defined as an individual's evaluation of self-worth [1], is increasingly recognized as a critical factor in the education sector, especially in Asia. Growing awareness of its role in student and educator well-being has led to the integration of self-esteem-building practices across various countries. In China, for instance, teachers actively promote student success by fostering self-esteem [2], while in Japan, educators emphasize it as a preventive measure against bullying [3]. Similarly, in India, self-esteem-enhancing programs have been linked to improved academic performance among university students [4].

Importantly, educators' self-esteem directly affects teaching quality and student outcomes. Teachers with higher self-esteem are more likely to engage positively with students, display enthusiasm, and maintain clarity and resilience in the classroom [5, 6]. Furthermore, self-esteem is closely linked to job satisfaction and reduced burnout [7], highlighting its significance in professional well-being. It also influences student motivation, engagement, and achievement through the learning environment educators create [8, 9].

At an institutional level, self-esteem shaped by organizational experiences plays a pivotal role in influencing motivation, work attitudes, and behavior [10]. By identifying factors that influence self-esteem, higher education institutions can implement targeted interventions such as mentoring, supportive feedback, and professional development to foster confidence and job satisfaction among educators [11, 12].

In the Sri Lankan context, the higher education sector, encompassing universities, colleges, and institutes, plays a vital role in shaping the country's intellectual and socio-economic landscape. With a tertiary enrollment rate of 21.61% as of 2020 [13], the sector has expanded significantly since the establishment of the University of Ceylon in 1942 [14]. As the global economy shifts towards knowledge-based development, ensuring the psychological well-being of those who facilitate learning becomes crucial.

[a]shehani.j@nsbm.ac.lk, [b]abdul.c@bms.ac.lk

DOI: 10.4324/9781003739920-11

Therefore, the objective of this research is to understand the factors that influence educators' self-esteem in the Sri Lankan higher education sector while analyzing the impact of self-efficacy, peer influence, power to influence others, and organizational empowerment on their self-esteem. Doing so can enhance teaching effectiveness, reduce burnout, and create more positive learning environments, ultimately benefiting both educators and students.

Literature Review

Self-esteem is a critical psychological construct that influences an individual's sense of self-worth and professional competence. In the higher education sector, educators' self-esteem plays a pivotal role in their job satisfaction, teaching effectiveness, and overall well-being [15, 12]. This review examines key factors influencing educators' self-esteem, including self-efficacy, peer influence, the power to influence others, and organizational empowerment, with a focus on the Sri Lankan higher education context.

Educators' self-esteem

Educators' self-esteem refers to their self-perceived competence, value, and confidence in their teaching roles [12]. It is shaped by personal, professional, and organizational factors, including teaching experience, student feedback, and institutional support [16]. High self-esteem is associated with greater job satisfaction, motivation, and resilience, while low self-esteem may lead to burnout and attrition [17].

Self-efficacy and educators' self-esteem

Self-efficacy, defined as an individual's belief in their ability to perform specific tasks [18], significantly impacts educators' self-esteem. Teachers with high self-efficacy demonstrate greater confidence in their instructional strategies and classroom management, leading to enhanced self-worth [19]. Mastery experiences, positive feedback, and professional development contribute to self-efficacy, reinforcing self-esteem [20].

P1: Self-efficacy has an impact on the self-esteem of an educator.

Peer influence and educators' self-esteem

Peer influence shapes educators' self-esteem through social comparison, validation, and professional collaboration [21]. Supportive peer interactions enhance self-esteem by fostering a sense of belonging and recognition [22]. Conversely, negative comparisons or lack of collegial support may diminish self-esteem [23]. In Sri Lankan higher education, peer networks and mentorship programs could play a crucial role in strengthening educators' self-perception.

P2: Peer influence has an impact on the self-esteem of an educator.

The power to influence others and educators' self-esteem

Power dynamics in educational institutions influence educators' self-esteem through authority structures and leadership styles [24]. Educators who perceive themselves as influential in decision-making experience higher self-esteem [22]. Conversely, disempowerment or lack of autonomy may reduce self-worth [25]. Empowering leadership and participatory governance can enhance educators' confidence and professional identity.

P3: Power to influence has an impact on self-esteem.

Organizational empowerment and educators' self-esteem

Organizational empowerment involves granting educators autonomy, resources, and decision-making authority [26]. Empowered educators exhibit higher self-esteem, job satisfaction, and commitment [22]. Key empowerment strategies include professional development, transparent communication, and recognition of contributions [27]. In Sri Lanka, institutional policies that promote educator empowerment may improve self-esteem and teaching efficacy.

P4: Organizational empowerment has an impact on the self-esteem of an educator.

Conceptual Framework

The study proposes a conceptual framework as shown in Figure 11.1, linking self-efficacy, peer influence, power to influence, and organizational empowerment to educators' self-esteem in Sri Lankan higher education.

Self-efficacy → Educators with strong self-efficacy beliefs exhibit higher self-esteem due to confidence in their teaching abilities [18].

Peer influence → Positive peer interactions and professional support enhance self-esteem through validation and collaboration [22].

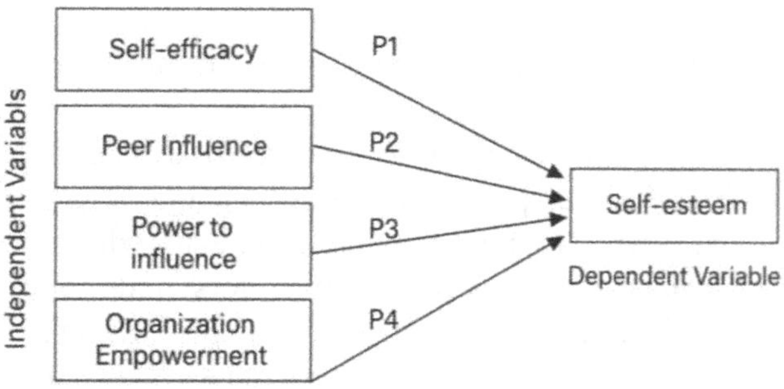

Figure 11.1 Conceptual framework
Source: Author

Power to influence → Perceived influence in institutional decisions boosts self-esteem by fostering autonomy and recognition [24].

Organizational empowerment → Institutional support, resources, and participatory leadership elevate self-esteem by enhancing professional value [26].

This framework suggests that improving these factors can strengthen educators' self-esteem, leading to better job performance and well-being in Sri Lankan higher education institutions.

Proposed Methodology

This study will adopt a quantitative research design to examine the factors influencing educators' self-esteem in Sri Lankan higher education. A positivist philosophy will guide the research, emphasizing empirical data and structured analysis [28]. The study will use a deductive approach, testing propositions derived from existing theories on self-efficacy [18], peer influence [21], power to influence [24], and organizational empowerment [26].

A cross-sectional survey will be conducted among educators in selected Sri Lankan higher education institutions. Convenience sampling will be employed due to accessibility constraints, targeting educators [29]. Data will be collected via a structured questionnaire, using Likert-scale measures for self-efficacy, peer influence, power, empowerment, and the Rosenberg Self-Esteem Scale (RSES) [15].

The study will include educators who are currently employed in recognized higher education institutions in Sri Lanka, including both public and private universities and institutes. Participants must have at least one year of teaching experience at the tertiary level to ensure familiarity with institutional environments and educator dynamics. Only those who provide informed consent and are willing to participate voluntarily will be included in the study.

Exclusion criteria include administrative staff, non-teaching personnel, and educators on extended leave or sabbatical during the data collection period. Additionally, educators with less than one year of teaching experience will be excluded, as their exposure to institutional and peer-related influences may be limited.

Data analysis will be performed using SPSS, employing correlation and multiple regression to assess relationships between variables. A pilot study with 10 experts will ensure instrument validity before full deployment. Ethical considerations include informed consent, confidentiality, and anonymity [30]. Limitations include potential self-report bias and generalizability constraints due to sampling.

Here is the proposed methodology flow chart of the proposed research.

Start
↓
Define research problem and objectives
↓
Adopt positivist philosophy and deductive approach
↓
Review literature → Develop hypotheses
↓
Design structured questionnaire
↓
Pilot testing with 10 experts
↓
Revise and finalize instrument (Based on feedback)
↓
Determine inclusion and exclusion criteria
↓
Select participants via convenience sampling
↓

Conduct cross-sectional survey

↓

Collect data (Likert Scales + RSES)

↓

Ensure ethical compliance (Consent, confidentiality, anonymity)

↓

Analyze data using SPSS (Correlation & Multiple Regression)

↓

Interpret results

↓

Discuss findings, limitations and implications

↓

End

Conclusion

This concept paper proposes an investigation into the factors influencing educators' self-esteem in Sri Lanka's higher education sector, focusing on self-efficacy, peer influence, power to influence, and organizational empowerment. Given the critical role educators play in shaping students' academic and personal development [31], understanding and enhancing their self-esteem is vital for institutional success.

The study aims to:

- Identify key factors affecting educators' self-esteem, including professional recognition, autonomy, and institutional support [32].
- Assess their impact within Sri Lankan universities, where cultural and organizational dynamics may uniquely influence self-perception [33].
- Provide recommendations to boost self-esteem through empowerment initiatives, peer collaboration, and leadership development [34].

However, the study may face limitations, including context-specific generalizability and the exclusion of other potential variables like past achievements or gender differences [35]. Future research could expand into longitudinal or mixed-methods approaches to explore deeper cultural and institutional influences.

The findings of this study have the potential to inform both institutional policy and professional development practices in Sri Lankan higher education. By identifying key factors such as self-efficacy, peer influence, power to influence, and organizational empowerment that contribute to educators' self-esteem, university administrators and policymakers can implement targeted strategies to enhance faculty well-being and performance. These may include structured peer mentoring programs, leadership training, and reforms in institutional governance to foster greater empowerment. Ultimately, such interventions can contribute to a more supportive academic environment, improved teaching outcomes, and strengthened institutional reputation across Sri Lanka's higher education sector.

Recommendations for universities include fostering supportive work environments, enhancing professional development, and promoting educator participation in decision-making [36]. By addressing these factors, higher education institutions can cultivate a more motivated and effective academic workforce, ultimately benefiting both educators and students.

Acknowledgment

I extend my sincere gratitude to the educators and administrators of the Sri Lankan higher education institution, who participated in this study. Their insights and experiences were invaluable in understanding the factors influencing self-esteem in academia.

I also acknowledge the support of our colleagues and mentors for their constructive feedback during the research process.

Finally, I appreciate the foundational work of scholars in the fields of educational psychology and organizational behavior, whose theories guided this investigation.

References

[1] Rosenberg, M. (1989). Society and the Adolescent Self-Image. Princeton, NJ: Princeton University Press.

[2] Zhang, L., & Liu, R. (2020). The role of teacher support in fostering student self-esteem and academic success in China. *Educational Psychology*, 40(3), 345–360.

[3] Shimizu, H., Tanaka, Y., & Aoyama, K. (2015). Bullying prevention through self-esteem enhancement in Japanese schools. *Journal of School Psychology*, 53(2), 123–135.

[4] Pandey, S., & Singh, M. (2017). Impact of self-esteem programs on academic performance in Indian universities. *Higher Education Research and Development*, 36(4), 789–803.

[5] Thompson, R., & Gaddy, J. (2011). Teacher self-esteem and classroom engagement. *Teaching and Teacher Education*, 27(5), 912–920.

[6] Klassen, R. M., Tze, V. M. C., & Betts, S. L. (2012). Teacher self-efficacy and student outcomes: a meta-analytic review. *Educational Psychology Review*, 24(1), 101–120.

[7] Wan Hussin, W., Kuen, T. L., & Daud, F. (2018). Teacher self-esteem, job satisfaction, and burnout in Malaysian schools. *Asia-Pacific Education Researcher*, 27(3), 187–196.

[8] Chen, J. (2018). The impact of teacher self-esteem on student motivation and learning environments. *Educational Psychology*, 38(6), 721–737.

[9] Baker, J. A. (2006). Contributions of teacher self-esteem to student engagement. *Journal of Educational Research*, 99(2), 101–110.

[10] Pierce, J. L., & Gardner, D. G. (2004). Self-esteem within the work and organizational context: a review. *Journal of Management*, 30(5), 591–622.

[11] Chew, S., Wong, K. L., & Tan, H. M. (2018). Mentoring and self-esteem in higher education faculty. *Journal of Applied Research in Higher Education*, 10(2), 145–160.

[12] Skaalvik, E. M., & Skaalvik, S. (2014). Teacher self-efficacy and perceived autonomy: relations with job satisfaction and burnout. *Psychology in the Schools*, 51(6), 567–582.

[13] World Bank. (2020). School enrollment, tertiary (% gross) – Sri Lanka. World Bank Data. [Online]. Available from https://data.worldbank.org/indicator/SE.TER.ENRR?locations=LK.

[14] Fernando, M. (2016). The Evolution of Higher Education in Sri Lanka. Colombo: University Press.

[15] Rosenberg, M. (1965). Society and the Adolescent Self-Image. Princeton, NJ: Princeton University Press.

[16] Klassen, R. M., Tze, V. M. C., & Betts, S. L. (2009). Teacher self-efficacy and student outcomes: a meta-analytic review. *Educational Psychology Review*, 24(1), 101–120.

[17] Mbuva, J. (2016). Examining teacher self-esteem and its impact on job satisfaction and burnout. *Journal of Educational Development*, 10(2), 45–60.

[18] Bandura, A. (1997). Self-Efficacy: The Exercise of Control. New York: W.H. Freeman.

[19] Tschannen-Moran, M., & Woolfolk Hoy, A. (2007). The differential antecedents of self-efficacy beliefs of novice and experienced teachers. *Teaching and Teacher Education*, 23(6), 944–956.

[20] Guskey, T. R., & Passaro, P. D. (1994). Teacher efficacy: a study of construct dimensions. *American Educational Research Journal,* 31(3), 627–643.

[21] Brown, B. B., & Larson, J. (2009). Peer relationships in adolescence. In Lerner, R. M., & Steinberg, L. (Eds.), Handbook of Adolescent Psychology, (pp. 74–103). Hoboken, NJ: Wiley.

[22] Van Horn, J. E., & Myers, D. (2019). The role of peer and institutional support in teacher self-esteem. *Educational Psychology Review*, 31(4), 789–812.

[23] Laird, J. (2006). Negative peer influence and teacher self-esteem. *Journal of Educational Psychology*, 98(2), 383–394.

[24] French, J. R. P., & Raven, B. (1959). The bases of social power. In Cartwright, D. (Ed.), Studies in Social Power, (pp. 150–167). Ann Arbor, MI: Univ. Michigan Press.

[25] Beltman, S., Mansfield, C., & Price, A. (2011). Thriving not just surviving: A review of research on teacher resilience. *Educational Research Review*, 6(3), 185–207.

[26] Spreitzer, G. M. (1995). Psychological empowerment in the workplace: dimensions, measurement, and validation. *Academy of Management Journal*, 38(5), 1442–1465.

[27] Kanter, R. M. (1993). Men and Women of the Corporation. New York: Basic Books.

[28] Saunders, M., Lewis, P., & Thornhill, A. (2009). Research Methods for Business Students, (5th edn.). Harlow, UK: Pearson Education.

[29] Krejcie, R. V., & Morgan, D. W. (1970). Determining sample size for research activities. *Educational and Psychological Measurement*, 30(3), 607–610.

[30] Bryman, A., & Bell, E. (2011). Business Research Methods, (3rd edn.). Oxford, UK: Oxford Univ. Press.

[31] Ralph, N., & Stubbs, W. (2014). Educators' role in student development: a global perspective. *The Journal of Higher Education*, 45(2), 112–130.

[32] Hargreaves, A., & Fullan, M. (2012). Professional Capital: Transforming Teaching in Every School. New York: Teachers College Press.

[33] Akin, S., & Radford, L. (2018). Cultural influences on educator self-esteem in Asian contexts. *International Journal of Educational Research*, 89, 45–58.

[34] Bogler, R., & Nir, A. E. (2012). The importance of empowerment and leadership in higher education. *Educational Management Administration & Leadership*, 40(6), 789–812.

[35] Ahmadi, F. (2020). Gender and self-esteem in academia: a meta-analysis. *Gender and Education*, 32(4), 501–518.

[36] Gonida, E., & Cortina, K. S. (2017). Teacher participation in decision-making: Effects on self-esteem and job satisfaction. *Teaching and Teacher Education*, 63, 176–186.

12 AI in higher education: implications for diversity of languages and inclusion of knowledges from the global South

Kyria Rebeca Finardi[a]

Federal University of Espirito Santo, Brazil

Abstract

As artificial intelligence (AI) technologies become increasingly embedded in higher education, critical engagement with their use is essential to ensure equity, inclusion, and linguistic and epistemological diversity. This paper reports on an ongoing research project that investigates the implications of AI for knowledge access and production across the Global South and Global North, focusing on higher education institutions. Building on recent scholarship that highlights the risks of digital inequality, linguistic hegemony, and epistemic exclusion, the project explores how AI applications intersect with language diversity, power asymmetries, and the inclusion of knowledges from underrepresented regions. Through a mixed-methods approach that combines bibliometric analyses, qualitative interviews, and contrastive case studies of institutional policies and practices, the ongoing research project aims to shed light on the cultural, linguistic, and geopolitical dimensions of AI in higher education. Virtual exchange (VE) projects are also used as both a pedagogical approach and research strategy seeking to foster international collaboration among participants of the project thus amplifying underrepresented voices to inform more inclusive AI policies and practices in global academic ecosystems. Expected results of the project include a critical mapping of AI use across diverse geopolitical and linguistic settings, the identification of risks and opportunities related to epistemic inclusion, especially concerning underrepresented languages, knowledge and contributions to theoretical and policy-relevant debates on language, power and knowledge production in the age of AI.

Keywords: Artificial intelligence, epistemic inclusion, global south, higher education, international collaboration, language diversity, virtual exchange

Introduction

Artificial intelligence (AI) can be described as a technology that enables machines to simulate human intelligence to process language and solve problems. With the integration of big data, AI systems can now process massive amounts of information to improve performance, make predictions and provide insights.

Some of the applications of AI include but are not limited to machine learning enabling them to adapt to new situations and make decisions based on patterns and trends; data-driven insights, prediction of outcomes and the optimization of processes; complex problem-solving once AI can analyze vast amounts of data to identify patterns, connections and solutions that humans may miss. Besides those applications, AI can also perform predictive maintenance analyzing sensor data from machines to predict potential failures, reducing downtime and increasing efficiency; provide personalized feedback, tutoring and recommendations since AI-driven algorithms analyze user behavior and preferences to provide tailored suggestions, enhancing customer experiences; and interaction with chatbots that process natural language and use machine learning to understand and respond to user queries, improving customer support and experience.

By leveraging big data, AI systems can unlock new possibilities for human development, driving innovation and transforming industries. Yet, this reliance on vast amounts of data raises significant concerns about privacy, security, and the potential for hallucination and bias in decision-making processes. To address these risks, robust data governance policies must be put in place to ensure transparency in AI decision-making, prioritizing data security and privacy.

Research can also contribute to mitigate the risks involved in the use of AI by developing models that

[a]Kyria.finardi@ufes.br

DOI: 10.4324/9781003739920-12

can better handle complex data and scenarios, identifying and mitigating biases in AI systems to ensure more equitable benefits for all. Research can also support the development of methods to explain AI decision-making processes, increasing transparency and trust providing insights and evidence to inform policy decisions related to AI and big data, ensuring responsible development and use. As AI becomes increasingly integrated into education in general and in higher education in particular, the ability to effectively and critically engage with AI tools is becoming a crucial skill for teachers, students and more recently, researchers [1].

Notwithstanding the potential of AI to support human intelligence and development, there is a serious digital divide between the Global North (henceforth GN) and the Global South (GS) that must be addressed first, before the benefits can be shared globally. According to Dados and Connell [2], the terms 'Global North' and 'Global South' are relational and geopolitical and refer to power relations rather than to strictly geographical locations. The term GS is used to refer to nations and regions that have been historically marginalized and excluded from global power structures, whereas the GN would comprise wealthier, more powerful nations that have traditionally held positions of authority.

The division of the world into GN and GS highlights the importance of understanding global dynamics through the lens of power relations, rather than solely focusing on economic, geographic or cultural differences. This perspective encourages a more nuanced understanding of global inequalities and power imbalances, which is why it was chosen to inform the research project reported here.

Besides the geopolitical division between GN and GS, there is also a digital divide that refers to the significant disparity in access to and use of digital technologies, including the internet, computers, and mobile devices in the GN and GS. This gap is not only limited to infrastructure but also encompasses differences in digital literacy, affordability, and the availability of relevant contents. The GS faces considerable challenges, such as limited internet connectivity, inadequate digital infrastructure, and a shortage of skilled professionals, which hinder the adoption and effective use of digital technologies. Bridging this divide is crucial for promoting inclusive economic growth, improving access to information, and fostering social development in the GS.

The digital gap between access to and use of digital technologies also affects education and social development, especially and more recently, regarding AI and its role in the inclusion or exclusion of certain populations, knowledges and languages, with more negative implications for languages other than English [3] and research produced in the GS [4, 5].

Considering the potential of AI to innovate and revolutionize education in general and research, higher education and the languages involved in them in particular, the research project reported on this paper aims to analyze the use of AI, more specifically Large Language Models (LLMs), in higher education, focusing on the access to and the production of knowledge in different languages in the GN and in the GS.

The analysis of the research project reported here will focus on the use of different languages, countries, genders and areas of knowledge using a mixed methods approach that combines qualitative and quantitative techniques. Data will be collected through different instruments including: contrastive analysis of institutional websites of universities and research databases (Web of Science, Scopus, Open Alex) from the GN and the GS in relation to the norms for the use of AI, bibliometric analysis of publications by country, area and language, interviews with professors and researchers linked to the partner universities and the offer of virtual exchange (VE) projects that will function both as a pedagogic approach to connect the teams involved and as a strategy to collect data in the participating universities. The project aims to involve participants from at least 16 universities in the GS and half the same number, that is, at least eight universities in the GN. For the sake of this project and building on results of [6], universities in Europe will be considered GN whereas Latin America, Africa and Asia will be considered GS.

Materials and Methodology

Zhu and Wang [3] carried out a systematic review of AI in language education spanning from 2013 to October 2023, that is, 11 months after the launch of ChatGPT, by OpenAI. Data for their study was collected in international databases of Web of Science, Eric ProQuest, Scopus, focusing on five top specialized language education journals. Their corpus was made up of 125 studies which were analyzed using multiple methodologies, including selected bibliometrics, content analysis, and topic modeling.

Results of their study concluded that the evolution of AI requires initiatives that address diversity, equity, and inclusion (DEI) concerns in education in general and in language education in particular. Regarding implications of their study to teacher education, they found that scholars have used different perspectives to investigate the role of teachers in AI-integrated language teaching and although there is an extensive discussion on the benefits of AI-integrated classrooms, there remains a notable paucity of empirical evidence outlining specific strategies for leveraging AI-human teacher collaboration to support teachers in enhancing their teaching efficiency. So as to address this gap, the research project reported here will promote VE with teachers both from the GN and GS to stimulate teacher collaboration across different contexts.

Based on this finding in [3], the authors suggested that future research endeavors integrate conversational AI into language teaching to promote intelligence amplification and evidence-based guidelines exploring how conversational AIs can foster a more effective partnership with human teachers, reducing teachers' workload, and improving learners' cultural awareness in real-world language classrooms. The VE projects to be implemented as part of the research project reported on here will stimulate the use of AI to foster more relevant collaborations between teachers and researchers from different contexts.

Of special relevance for the research project reported here is the finding of Zhu and Wang [3] that most of the studies reviewed there involved collaborations among different authors, with primary affiliations from Asia and North America. Notably, there was a substantial research gap in terms of geographic locations in AI for language education. China (Mainland, Taiwan, Hong Kong and Macau), the USA, and South Korea emerged as the countries with the highest number of first authors' affiliations, and correspondingly, the study locations were primarily from those countries. In contrast, there was limited representation from Europe and South America, and no authors from African countries and Oceania leading to suggest that future research should address this gap by examining language education in these underrepresented regions.

This is a recommendation that was taken up by the research project reported on here insomuch as it includes partner universities in the GS in Asia (Malaysia, Sri Lanka, India and China), Latin America (Brazil, Chile, Argentina, Ecuador, Paraguay and Colombia), and Africa (South Africa, Rwanda and Mozambique), and GN in Europe (Spain, Italy, England, Switzerland, Turkey).

Furthermore and as recommended by some studies [3, 7], the increase in international collaborations afforded in this project aims to bring together a wide spectrum of cross-cultural perspectives, experiences, and expertise. While such international collaboration can be invaluable, it may face challenges due to geopolitical and linguistic constraints that influence the scope and conditions for this collaboration depending on the different contexts where teachers and researchers operate and write from [8, 18].

Indeed, in a series of studies, [9, 10, 4, 5] analyzed the hegemony of English in publications discussing its effects on a global scale with implications for scientific diversity. The authors argue that the use of English skews citations and reinforces the exclusion of knowledges and languages from underrepresented regions, limiting access to information and diversity in global scientific production.

Considering the intersection between English and social justice, [11] suggests an ecology of approaches to the analysis and use of English. In relation to the role of English in international student mobility, [12] shows the intersection of language and locus of enunciation (e.g. [13]) since only four countries (England, USA, Canada and Australia) concentrate more than half of all the international students in the world.

Because of the intersection between languages and locus of enunciation [14], coupled with the exclusion of students who cannot travel abroad, researchers working in the internationalization of higher education [15–17] propose the use of virtual exchange (VE) as a complement to/or substitution of physical academic mobility and as strategy of Internationalization at Home (IaH) [18], Internationalization of the Curriculum (IoC) [19], calibration of relations between North and South [20, 21] with the development of Global Citizenship Education (GCE) [22, 23].

According to O'Dowd [24], VE refers to a range of online intercultural exchange and interaction activities that promote intercultural learning, language development, and global citizenship education among students from different countries and cultures. Considering the need to integrate knowledges, languages and technologies in educational initiatives in the GN and in the GS, the research project reported on here aims to implement VE projects between the partner institutions both as a strategy to put participants from different contexts together and as a way to produce and disseminate knowledge from both parts of the world making science more available and accessible to all.

Pessin et al. [25] used science mapping and bibliometric techniques with the term "decolonial" in the Scopus and Web of Science (WoS) databases comparing results with the OpenAlex database. Results of their study suggest the expansion of access to and recognition of different databases, methods and languages to foster a more inclusive and diverse academic environment in line with Zhu and Wang [3] suggestion.

Specifically, research collaboration involving GS can promote more resource and expertise sharing, as well as provide valuable insights into how to leverage research to close the digital gap in terms of including teachers and researchers from underrepresented contexts. Considering the potential impact of AI for human and social development, besides technological innovation, it is important to stimulate research that looks into possibilities of making AI more culturally and linguistically sensitive. International collaboration involving these regions not only facilitates resource and knowledge sharing but also strengthens a more inclusive approach to technological advancement in education in general and in language and epistemology diversity in particular.

In terms of research design, Zhu and Wang [3] found that research on AI for language education has predominantly favored quantitative and mixed methods with a noticeable shortfall in qualitative research efforts. More qualitative studies are needed to shed light on the socio-cultural aspects of AI-assisted language learning and to provide richer and deeper insights into the specific and individual learning processes and differences.

Among the studies that adopted qualitative methodologies, there is also a need for more varied methods, such as ethnographic studies and post digital approaches [26]. Also, given the easy access and popularity of ChatGPT after the study by Zhu and Wang [3], more research on how ChatGPT could improve education in general and language learning and teaching in particular is expected in the coming years.

Having laid out this panorama, the ongoing research project reported here aims to look at the use of LLMs such as ChatGPT in higher education institutions of the GS and GN using a variety of research methods and techniques. The main objective of the research project is to analyze the use of LLMs in higher education, focusing on the access to and production of knowledge in the GS and in the GN. The analysis will focus on the use of different LLMs, languages, countries, genders and areas of knowledge through mixed approaches that combine qualitative and quantitative techniques. Data will be collected through different instruments including: surveys with participants, contrastive analysis of institutional websites of universities, bibliometric analysis of publications by country, area and language in relation to the use of AI in databases like Web of Science, Scopus, Lens and Open Alex, analysis of norms for the use of AI in universities and editors, interviews with professors and researchers linked to the partner universities and the offer of virtual exchanges that will function both as an approach to connect the teams involved and as a strategy to collect data in the participating universities.

The research project reported here adopts a mixed-methods design to investigate the uses and implications of AI in higher education across institutions from the GN and GS. The methodology integrates both quantitative and qualitative techniques to allow for a comprehensive and comparative analysis of the inclusion of languages, knowledges, and regional contexts in AI-mediated academic practices.

The following instruments and procedures will be used for data collection and analysis:

- Contrastive analysis of institutional websites: University websites from partner institutions will be analyzed to examine institutional norms, guidelines, and policies concerning the use of AI in education and research.
- Bibliometric analysis: A comparative bibliometric analysis will be conducted using databases such as Web of Science, Scopus, OpenAlex, and Lens. Publications will be analyzed by country, area of knowledge, gender of authors, and language of publication to examine patterns and disparities in AI-related academic output.
- Normative analysis of AI guidelines: University and editorial policies on AI use in research and education will be analyzed to identify how ethical, linguistic, and epistemological considerations are addressed (or omitted).
- Surveys and interviews with professors and researchers: Surveys and semi-structured interviews will be conducted with academics affiliated with partner institutions to gather qualitative

insights into their experiences, perceptions, and practices regarding AI and knowledge inclusion.

- Virtual exchanges (VE): VE projects will be implemented as both an educational and research strategy to foster collaboration among students and faculty from diverse geopolitical and linguistic backgrounds in knowledge construction and data collection. These exchanges will be documented and analyzed for themes related to language use, knowledge production, AI literacy, and intercultural communication.

Partner institutions were selected on a convenience sample according to track history of collaboration with the proponent of the project and considering their location in diverse geographical regions to ensure representation from traditionally underrepresented contexts. Informed consent will be obtained for all interviews and VE participants. Data will be anonymized and stored securely, with attention to local regulations and ethical standards. Special care will be taken to respect linguistic and cultural diversity throughout the research process.

Expected Results and Discussion

This project is expected to generate original insights into the role of generative AI, particularly LLMs, in reshaping practices of knowledge production, academic exchange, and language use in higher education and academic production. By foregrounding perspectives from both the GS and the GN, the research project reported on here will illuminate disparities in access, digital literacies, and linguistic representation that influence how AI tools are adopted and understood across different contexts.

Key expected results include:

- A critical, comparative mapping of how AI in general and LLMs in particular are being used in higher education institutions across diverse geopolitical and linguistic settings.
- Identification of risks and opportunities related to epistemic inclusion, especially concerning underrepresented languages and knowledges.
- Guidelines for equitable and context-sensitive integration of AI in international academic collaboration, teaching, and research.
- Contributions to theoretical debates on language, power, and knowledge production in the age of AI.
- Policy-relevant recommendations for higher education institutions and international networks focused on inclusion, digital ethics, and AI governance.

The project's impact will extend beyond academic outputs. By engaging with educators, students, and institutional stakeholders, it will support the development of Global Citizenship Education (GCE) and more just and inclusive practices in the use of AI. In particular, it will advocate for multilingual, intercultural approaches to AI integration that challenge linguistic hegemony and promote diversity of languages and epistemologies. The findings will inform strategies for Virtual Exchange (VE), Internationalization at Home (IaH), Global Citizenship Education (GCE) and curriculum development grounded in principles of equity, inclusion, and global cooperation.

Ultimately, the project aims to foster critical awareness and collective action in shaping the future of AI in higher education not as a neutral tool, but as a socially embedded technology that must be aligned with values of equity, diversity and inclusion.

Conclusion

This project is expected to generate comprehensive insights into the use of AI —particularly LLMs—in higher education institutions in both the Global South and Global North. The outcome will focus on the intersections between language, knowledge production, geopolitical location and international academic collaboration, with particular attention to equity, inclusion, and linguistic diversity. The overall impact will promote diversity in scientific production, raise awareness about linguistic and epistemic inclusion in AI development and deployment, advancing global educational equity through innovative digital, academic and pedagogic strategies.

References

[1] Pessin, V., Finardi, K. R., & Santos, C. A. (2025). GapFinder: exploring research gaps with artificial intelligence. *Studies in English Language Teaching*, 13(1), 13–27. Disponível em: https://doi.org/10.22158/selt.v13n1p13.

[2] Dados, N., & Connell, R. (2012). The global south, *Contexts*, 11(1), 12–13. Available from: https://doi.org/10.1177/1536504212436479.

[3] Zhu, M., & Wang, C. (2025). A systematic review of artificial intelligence in language education: current status and future implications. *Language Learning*

and Technology, 29(1), 1–29. https://hdl.handle.net/10125/73606.

[4] Finardi, K. R., França, C., & Guimarães, F. F. (2022). Ecology of knowledges and languages in Latin American academic production. *Ensaio: Avaliação and Políticas Públicas em Educação*, 30, 764–787. https://doi.org/10.1590/S0104-40362022003003538.

[5] Finardi, K., França, C., & Guimarães, F. (2023). Knowledge production and internationalization of higher education in the global south: Latin America in focus. *Diálogos Latinoamericanos*, 32(1), 1–19. https://doi.org/10.7146/dl.v32i.127278.

[6] Finardi, K. R., Amorim, G. B., & Sarmento, S. (2024). Internationalization of higher education and the role of languages: insights from the global north and the global south. *Education and Linguistics Research*, 10(1), 18–46. https://doi.org/10.5296/elr.v10i1.22006.

[7] Finardi, K. R., Sembiante, S., Amorim, G., & Veronez, T. (2020). Internationalizations in two loci of enunciation: the south and global north. *ETD Educação Temática Digital*, 22(3), 591–611. doi: 10.20396/etd.v22i3.8659311.

[8] Canagarajah, A. S. (2002). A Geopolitics of Academic Writing, (Vol. 163). University of Pittsburgh Press.

[9] Finardi, K. R. (2019). English in the South. Eduel.

[10] Finardi, K. R., & França, C. (2016). O inglês na internacionalização da produção científica brasileira: evidências da subárea de linguagem and linguística. *Revista Intersecções*, 9(19), 234–250.

[11] Finardi, K. R. (2022). Global english: neither a 'Hydra' nor a 'Tyrannosaurus Rex' or a 'Red Herring' but an ecology of approaches towards social justice. *Education and Linguistics Research*, 8(2), 33–45. https://doi.org/10.5296/elr.v8i2.20244.

[12] Díaz, A. (2018). Challenging dominant epistemologies in higher education: the role of language in the geopolitics of knowledge (re) production. In Multilingual Education Yearbook 2018: Internationalization, Stakeholders and Multilingual Education Contexts, (pp. 21–36). https://doi.org/10.1007/978-3-319-77655-2_2.

[13] Diniz De Figueiredo, E. H., & Martinez, J. (2021). The locus of enunciation as a way to confront epistemological racism and decolonize scholarly knowledge. *Applied Linguistics*, 42(2), 355–359. DOI: 10.1093/applin/amz061.

[14] Finardi, K. R. (2022). As línguas and rankings no Oscar da internacionalização das produções científicas latino-americanas: Languages and Oscar rankings of the internationalization of Latin American scientific productions. *Estudos Linguísticos (São Paulo. 1978)*, 51(1), 147–161. https://doi.org/10.21165/el.v51i1.3180.

[15] Hildeblando Júnior, C. A. H., Finardi, K. R., & El Kadri, M. (2022). Affordances da COIL para a internacionalização do ensino superior: um estudo de caso. *Revista da ANPOLL*, 53(1), 253–272.

[16] Hildeblando júnior, Carlos Alberto; Finardi, Kyria Rebeca. Telecolaboração e internacionalização do ensino superior: reflexões a partir da pandemia covid-19. Revista Intercâmbio, v.XLV: 254–278, 2020. São Paulo: LAEL/PUCSP. ISSN 2237-759X.

[17] Finardi, K. R., & Guimarães, F. F. (2020). Internationalization and the Covid-19 pandemic: challenges and opportunities for the global south. *Journal of Education, Teaching and Social Studies*, 2(4), 1–15. https://doi.org/10.22158/jetss.v2n4p1.

[18] Guimarães, F. F., Mendes, A. R. M., Rodrigues, L. M., dos Santos Paiva, R. S., & Finardi, K. R. (2019). Internationalization at home, COIL and intercomprehension: for more inclusive activities in the global south. *SFU Educational Review*, 12(3), 90–109.

[19] Finardi, K., & Aşık, A. (2024). Possibilities of virtual exchange for internationalization at home: insights from the global south. *Journal of Virtual Exchange*, 7, 1–22. https://doi.org/10.21827/jve.7.39593.

[20] Guimarães, F. F., Finardi, K. R., & Amorim, G. B. (2021). From pandemic to paradigm shift: recalibrating Brazil's relationships with the Global North. *EAIE Forum Magazine*, 1(1), 28–29.

[21] Wimpenny, K., Finardi, K. R., Orsini-Jones, M., & Jacobs, L. (2022). Knowing, being, relating and expressing through third space global South-North COIL: digital inclusion and equity in international higher education. *Journal of Studies in International Education*, 26(2), 279–296. https://doi.org/10.14324/IJDEGL.16.1.03.

[22] Guimarães, F. F., & Finardi, K. R. (2021). Global citizenship education (GCE) in internationalisation: COIL as alternative thirdspace. *Globalisation, Societies and Education*, 19(5), 641–657. https://doi.org/10.1080/14767724.2021.1959902.

[23] Finardi, K. R., Salvadori, J. C., & Wehrli, A. (2024). Global citizenship and internationalization at home: insights from the BRASUIS virtual exchange project. *Studies in English Language Teaching*, 12(2), 59–72. https://doi.org/10.22158/selt.v12n2p59.

[24] O'Dowd, R. (2018). From telecollaboration to virtual exchange: state-of-the-art and the role of UNICollaboration in moving forward. *Journal of Virtual Exchange*, 1, 1–23. Available from: https://doi.org/10.14705/rpnet.2018.jve.1.

[25] Pessin, V. Z., França, C. M., & Finardi, K. R. Línguas, mapeamento da ciência and produção científica desde uma perspectiva decolonial. *Ensaio*, (in press).

[26] Wang, C., & Canagarajah, S. (2024). Postdigital ethnography in applied linguistics: Beyond the online and offline in language learning. *Research Methods in Applied Linguistics*, 3(2), 100111. https://doi.org/10.1016/j.rmal.2024.100111.

13 Real-time automated barcode system for GRN and issuing in mechanical spare parts management

Lahiru Wijewickrama[1,a], *N.P. Dharmasiri*[1,b], *Buddima Bandara*[2,c], *G.A.D. Nawoda*[1,d], *G.I.P Perera*[1,3,e] *and Janitha Jeewantha*[4,f]

[1]Department of Mechanical & Automotive Engineering, Faculty of Engineering & Technology, CINEC Campus, Sri Lanka

[2]Faculty of Engineering, University of Peradeniya, Kandy, Sri Lanka

[3]Department of Mechanical and Manufacturing Engineering, Faculty of Engineering, University of Ruhuna, Sri Lanka

[4]Centre for Future Materials, Institute for Advanced Engineering and Space Sciences, University of Southern Queensland, Australia

Abstract

Efficient management of mechanical spare parts is critical for minimizing equipment downtime and optimizing maintenance workflows. This paper presents the development and pilot evaluation of a cost-effective barcode-driven inventory management system specifically designed to streamline Goods Received Notes (GRN) and parts issuing processes. Built using Visual Basic, Microsoft Access, and Excel, with integration to Microsoft Power BI for real-time analytics, the system delivers accurate stock tracking, role-based access control, and automated reporting. Pilot deployment demonstrated significant improvements in data accuracy, processing speed, and user satisfaction compared to manual record-keeping. The solution supports lean 5S principles and offers a scalable alternative to complex ERP systems, making it ideal for small to medium-sized mechanical departments seeking to digitize inventory operations with immediate operational and financial benefits.

Keywords: Barcode inventory system, Goods Received Notes (GRN), real-time analytics, role-based access control, spare parts management

Introduction

In today's manufacturing and industrial operations, effective inventory management is essential for maintaining uninterrupted workflows, minimizing equipment downtime, and optimizing production costs. Among various inventory elements, the management of spare parts plays a vital yet often underestimated role. These components are critical for the maintenance, repair, and overhaul (MRO) of machinery, and their mismanagement can cause costly delays and productivity losses [1].

Traditional systems in many mechanical departments still rely on manual record-keeping, involving handwritten logs or Excel sheets for tracking the Goods Received Notes (GRNs) and the issuance of parts. While cost-effective, these manual methods are inherently prone to human error, data duplication, misplacements, and inventory discrepancies [2]. The lack of real-time stock visibility can result in either understocking or overstocking of spare parts, both of which negatively impact operational efficiency [3].

To address these issues, barcode-based stock management systems have emerged as a robust and low-cost solution. Barcodes offer unique identification for every item and allow for quick and accurate data entry when integrated with barcode scanners and digital inventory databases [4]. These systems streamline the stock input (GRN) and output (issuing) processes, improve data reliability, and support real-time updates, thereby providing operational transparency and traceability.

[a]lahiru.wijewickrama@cinec.edu, [b]pula271998@gmail.com, [c]b.buddimab@gmail.com, [d]dinushi7272@gmail.com, [e]indika@mme.ruh.ac.lk, [f]janitha.jeewantha@unisq.edu.au

DOI: 10.4324/9781003739920-13

This paper presents the design and development of a barcode-based stock management system tailored for spare parts management in a mechanical department. The system was developed using Visual Basic as the front-end interface, with Microsoft Access and Excel serving as the back-end database. Real-time data output is further integrated into Microsoft Power BI for visualization and performance monitoring.

Key features of the system include:

- Role-based login for administrators and users.
- Barcode scanning support for both GRNs and issuing.
- Real-time stock quantity updates with error prevention mechanisms.
- Integrated Excel report generation and Power BI live dashboards.
- Inventory search functionality for quick spare part lookup.

The system aligns with the 5S methodology—specifically "Sort," "Set in order," and "Sustain"—to support lean operations and enhance workplace efficiency [5]. This paper also discusses the pilot testing phase of the system, where the tool is being evaluated for performance, user-friendliness, and operational improvements in a live industrial environment.

The main objectives of this research and implementation are:

- To replace error-prone manual systems with an efficient barcode-based solution.
- To support the implementation of 5S principles in spare part management.
- To provide accurate and real-time inventory tracking of spare parts received and issued.
- To design user-friendly interfaces for both administrators and storekeepers.
- To build a scalable system capable of future integration with advanced ERP and inventory platforms.

By reducing manual effort, improving stock accuracy, and enabling digital transformation, this system demonstrates a practical step toward smarter maintenance store operations in industrial settings.

Literature Review

Inventory management in mechanical departments is critical to maintaining operational efficiency and minimizing equipment downtime. In recent years, barcode technology and low-cost programmable systems have been increasingly adopted to streamline such operations. This section reviews key studies, tools, and technologies relevant to the development of a barcode-based stock management system.

Barcode systems in inventory control

Barcode technology simplifies inventory operations by assigning a scannable identifier to each item. According to Reddy [6], barcode-based systems significantly reduce manual entry errors and accelerate both stock-in and stock-out processes. This is particularly beneficial in spare parts management, where accuracy and speed are essential for machinery maintenance and repairs. Barcoding ensures traceability and reduces dependency on human memory or handwritten logs.

Manual systems vs. digital systems

Manual stock records are still common in small to medium-sized enterprises (SMEs), particularly in developing regions. These methods are not only inefficient but also prone to errors, duplication, and inconsistencies. In [7], it was Found that transitioning to a digital inventory system resulted in a 42% reduction in inventory discrepancies and a noticeable improvement in stock visibility and transaction speeds. Digital systems also offer easier data archiving, retrieval, and support for audit trails, which are critical for compliance and operational reviews.

Use of visual basic and MS access in inventory projects

Visual Basic and Microsoft Access are frequently selected for cost-effective automation projects in localized environments due to their offline capabilities, customizability, and ease of use. Sharma and Patel [8] demonstrated that using VB and Access together provided a flexible and responsive solution for small-scale raw material inventory systems. These platforms are especially suitable for organizations with limited IT infrastructure, enabling them to maintain robust functionality without the need for web-based ERP systems.

Role-based access in inventory software

Role-based access ensures that different user types—such as administrators and general users—can only access functions appropriate to their roles, which helps preserve data integrity and prevent unauthorized actions. Singh and Rani [9] highlighted that implementing such permission levels reduces errors and enhances security, especially in systems used by multiple operators. In the presented system, administrative accounts allow adding, editing, and deleting entries, while general users are restricted to data entry and basic viewing.

Real-time power BI integration for inventory optimization

Traditional systems often rely on static Excel exports for inventory reporting. However, modern approaches like Power BI integration enable live dashboards, trend visualization, and predictive insights. In a comparative study, [10] showed that live Power BI dashboards helped significantly reduce decision-making time and provided actionable analytics. The proposed system uses Power BI to monitor issue frequencies, GRN entries, and current stock levels, offering real-time feedback on store performance and trends.

Gaps and motivation for this project

While enterprise resource planning (ERP) platforms provide extensive inventory features, they are often expensive and complex, making them unsuitable for department-level use. Manual systems, on the other hand, lack real-time accuracy and traceability. This project addresses this gap by developing a lightweight, cost-effective, and user-friendly barcode-based stock management system, with integrated live data analytics, to empower smaller mechanical departments and maintenance rooms.

Methodology/System Design and Development

This section outlines the systematic approach undertaken for the design and development of a barcode-based stock management system, specifically created for managing spare parts in an industrial environment. The system was developed using a combination of Visual Basic for Applications (VBA), Microsoft Access, Microsoft Excel, and Microsoft Power BI for real-time data visualization and reporting.

Objective and design principles

The primary goal of the barcode-based stock management system is to streamline the process of managing spare parts in a mechanical department. The system was designed with the following core objectives:

- **Minimize manual effort**: Significantly reduce the time spent on manual stock entries and issuing records, which are typically prone to human errors.
- **Enhance accuracy**: By incorporating barcode scanning technology, the system ensures greater accuracy in tracking inventory.
- **Improve data integrity**: The system uses role-based access controls, differentiating between administrator and user access, to ensure that only authorized users can make critical changes to the data.
- **Real-time insights**: The system integrates with Power BI for real-time reporting and analysis, providing actionable insights into inventory levels, trends, and user activity.
- **Cost-effectiveness and offline compatibility**: The solution was developed using widely accessible and low-cost tools, making it feasible for implementation in small- to medium-sized organizations with minimal IT infrastructure.

System architecture

The architecture of the system is designed to be both modular and scalable, allowing for easy updates and integration with other platforms if needed. The architecture consists of three key layers:

- **User interface layer**: Developed using Visual Basic Forms, this layer provides a simple and intuitive interface for users to interact with the system. It includes various screens for logging in, performing GRNs, issuing spare parts, and querying inventory.
- **Database layer**: All inventory-related transactions are stored in a Microsoft Access database. This layer acts as the central repository for all stock-related data, including items received (GRN), issued parts, stock levels, and prices.
- **Data visualization layer**: Microsoft Excel is used as an intermediary between the database and Power BI for real-time data processing. Excel tables are updated automatically based on database changes and then linked to Power BI to generate dashboards and visualizations.

User access levels

The system differentiates between two types of users based on their roles: administrators and general users. The access rights of each user group are as follows:

This role-based access control ensures the system's integrity by limiting the actions users can take based on their roles.

Functional modules

The system comprises several functional modules, each serving a distinct purpose:

- **Login module**: On launching the system, users are prompted to enter their username and password as Figure 13.1. The system authenticates the credentials and directs users to their respective dashboards based on their role (admin or user).
- **GRN Interface**: This module allows users to scan incoming spare parts using barcode readers. When a barcode is scanned, the system retrieves the part's details (item code, name, quantity) from the database and allows admins to update unit prices. Only users with admin privileges can delete or modify GRN records (Figure 13.2); regular users can only undo their last action (Figure 13.3). Table 13.1 present User roles and permissions.
- **Issuing interface**: This interface allows users to issue spare parts to mechanics. Once a barcode is scanned, the system prompts for additional information, such as the mechanic's ID and the machine number, to associate the issued part with a specific maintenance task. Admins have the ability to delete or undo issuing actions as Figure 13.4, while users are limited to undoing only the most recent transaction as Figure 13.5. Table 13.1 present User roles and permissions.
- **Details finder module**: This module provides a search function that allows users to quickly find spare parts based on either barcode or item name. The system retrieves and displays key information, such as item location, category, and stock level. This is useful for operators who need to locate specific parts quickly. Figure 13.6 shows the interface of location finder.

Figure 13.1 Login interface
Source: Author

Data storage and processing

All transaction data, such as GRN entries and stock issues, is stored in Microsoft Access. To ensure that data is available for analysis and reporting, the system automatically exports this data to Microsoft Excel in real-time. The Excel tables are updated periodically and serve as a bridge for feeding data into the **Power BI** dashboards for live analytics.

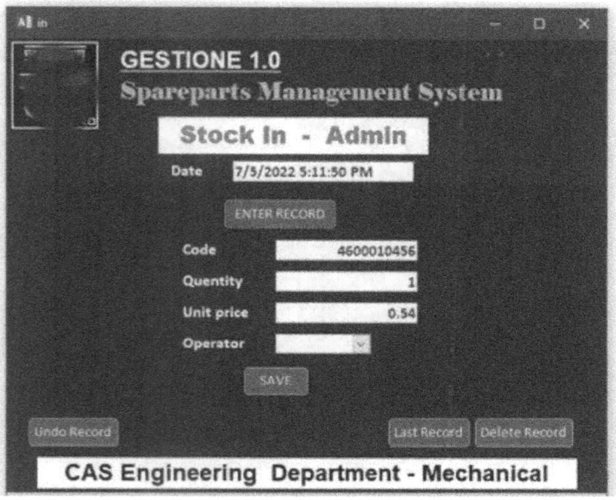

Figure 13.2 GRN admin interface
Source: Author

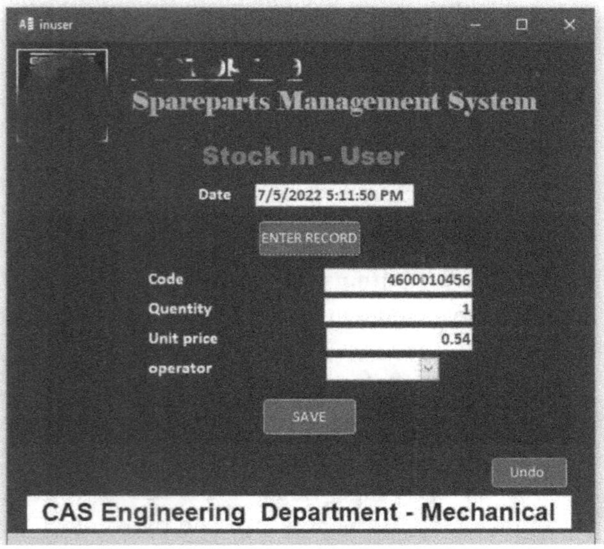

Figure 13.3 GRN user interface
Source: Author

Table 13.1 User roles and permissions.

Role	GRN Access	Issuing Access	Delete Permission	Undo Option	View Reports
Admin	Yes	Yes	Yes	Yes	Yes
User	Yes	Yes	No	Yes	No

Source: Author

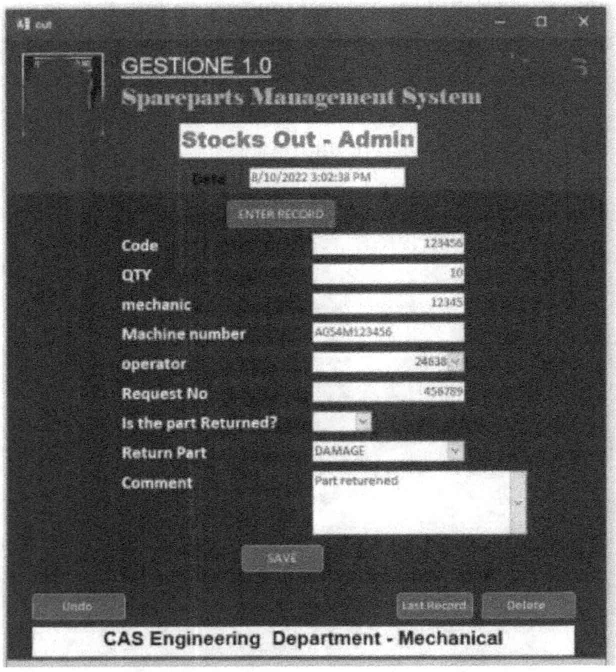

Figure 13.4 Issuing admin interface
Source: Author

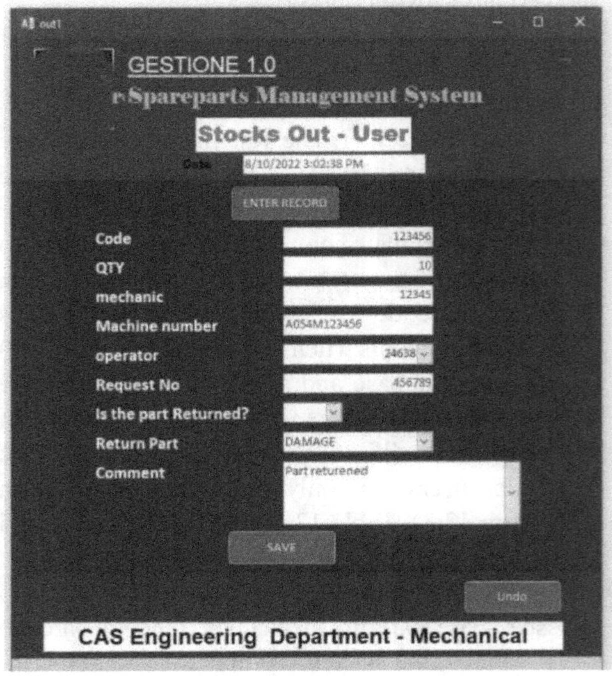

Figure 13.5 Issuing user interface
Source: Author

Live power BI integration

A key feature of the system is its integration with Microsoft Power BI, which enables live data visualization and reporting. Power BI connects to the Excel file, which is updated in real-time, and displays various metrics, such as:

- **Current stock levels**: The current inventory levels of all spare parts.
- **Most issued items**: A list of items that are issued most frequently, helping to identify critical stock.
- **GRN and issuing trends**: Trends over time for the receipt and issuance of spare parts, allowing for better forecasting and stock control.
- **User activity logs**: Logs of user activity, including which parts were issued and by whom.

Figure 13.6 Details finder interface
Source: Author

This integration allows decision-makers and supervisors to access up-to-date analytics on stock status, enabling informed decisions and optimization of inventory management processes.

Testing and deployment

The system was deployed in a real-world setting for pilot testing in the mechanical spare parts room. The testing phase revealed significant improvements in data entry speed, part identification accuracy, and the reduction of discrepancies in inventory records. Feedback from the users (interns and operators) was gathered and used to make further refinements to the system, including performance improvements and additional usability features. The system is currently being optimized for broader deployment and is expected to be fully operational in the near future. System architecture of the system shows in Figure 13.7. Also Table 13.2 present Interfaces and their functions.

Results and Discussion

The developed system was deployed and tested in a real mechanical spare parts environment over a trial period of two months. The evaluation focused on key performance metrics including data accuracy, processing time, user acceptance, and stock traceability. The following are the key outcomes and insights gained from the trial implementation.

Improved data accuracy

One of the most significant improvements was the elimination of manual data entry errors. The barcode scanner reduced human involvement in typing part codes, leading to a 95% improvement in data entry accuracy. Users reported a significant drop in mismatched parts and incorrect inventory quantities compared to the previous manual logbook system.

Reduction in processing time

Stock receiving (GRN entry) and issuing processes were completed in approximately 60% less time than before. For example, issuing a part that previously took up to 3–5 minutes with manual recording was reduced to under 1 minute using barcode scanning and automated input forms. Graphical representation shows by Figure 13.8.

Real-time monitoring and control

With the integration of live Power BI dashboards, supervisors gained real-time visibility into:

- Current stock availability
- Daily/weekly issue volumes

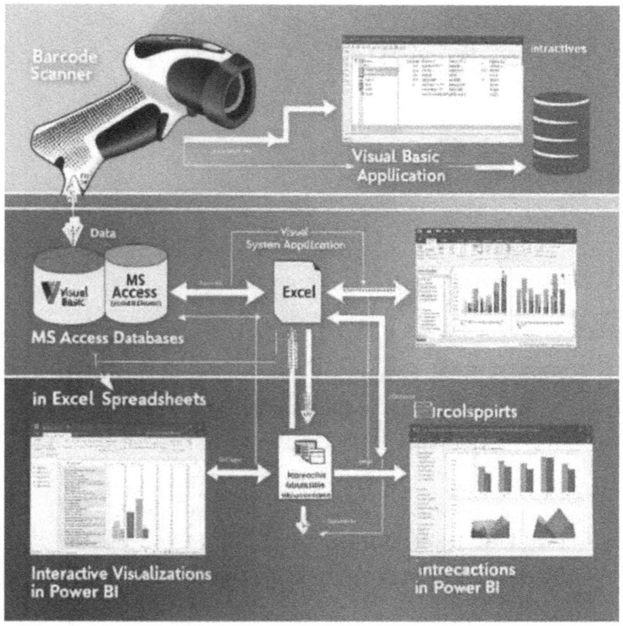

Figure 13.7 System architecture diagram
Source: Author

Table 13.2 Interfaces and their functions.

Interface name	Functionality description
User login	Authenticates users and routes them to the respective Admin/User menus.
Admin GRN	Allows stock entry, barcode scanning, unit price updates, and record deletion or undo.
Admin issuing	Issues stock to mechanics, requiring both mechanic and machine barcode scanning.
User GRN	Provides limited stock entry functionality, with only the option to undo the last action.
User issuing	Grants limited access to issuing stock, requiring both mechanic and machine barcode scanning.
Details finder	Allows users to search for parts by barcode, name, or category, helping with quick identification.

Source: Author

Table 13.3 Performance improvement comparison.

Metric	Manual system	Barcode system	Improvement (%)
GRN Entry Time (per item)	3–4 minutes	<1.5 minutes	~60%
Issuing time (per item)	3–5 minutes	<1 minute	~70%
Data accuracy	Moderate	High	~95% accuracy
Report preparation time	~1 hour/ day	Instant	100%

Source: Author

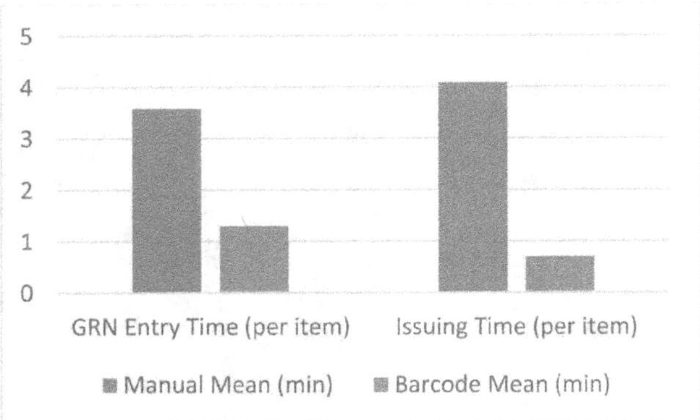

Figure 13.8 Graphical representation of GRN & issuing with system manual vs system
Source: Author

- High-demand items
- Issuance history by user or machine

This allowed proactive ordering of fast-moving items, avoiding downtime due to out-of-stock conditions.

Role-based user control effectiveness

The use of separate admin and user roles enhanced operational security. Admin privileges were required for editing and deleting sensitive records, while general users had limited access. This prevented unauthorized changes and preserved the integrity of the inventory log.

User feedback and usability

A post-implementation survey was conducted with 15 users, including inventory operators and mechanics, to evaluate the usability and overall effectiveness of the system. The feedback highlighted significant improvements in operational efficiency and ease of use compared to the previous manual methods.

- Clear interface and minimal training required
- Fast barcode scanning and instant feedback
- Easy search function for locating stored items
- Live reports made available without manual compilation

Challenges encountered

Several challenges were noted during the trial period:

- Initial resistance from users unfamiliar with computers
- Barcode labels occasionally wore off due to workshop conditions
- Barcode scanner compatibility issues with certain USB ports

These were addressed by:

- Providing brief user training sessions
- Switching to laminated barcode labels
- Standardizing hardware setup

Comparison with existing systems

Compared to high-end ERP-based inventory systems, this solution proved to be significantly more cost-effective and simpler to deploy. While ERP systems provide broader capabilities, they require complex infrastructure and expertise. This project offered a lightweight alternative with real-time insights and scalable features tailored for small departments or factories.

Return on investment analysis

A detailed cost-benefit analysis was performed to evaluate the financial impact of the system. The primary savings were derived from reduced labor hours due to faster stock processing and report generation. Table 13.4 summarizes the ROI calculation:

- Return on investment (ROI): 123,000 LKR net savings within the first six months.
- Payback period: Achieved in under 3 months.
- Budget comparison: Actual costs exceeded the initial budget by 11% (111,000 LKR vs. 100,000 LKR) but delivered higher-than-expected operational savings. Table 13.5 present detailed cost-benefit analysis with calculations (LKR).

Table 13.4 User feedback summary.

Feedback aspect	Positive responses (%)	Key comments
Ease of use	93%	"Minimal training needed"
Barcode scanning speed	87%	"Faster than manual entry"
Search functionality	80%	"Quick part lookup"
Real-time dashboards	90%	"Helps avoid stockouts"

Source: Author

Table 13.5 Detailed cost-benefit analysis with calculations (LKR).

Component	Calculation	Amount (LKR)
1. Development costs	Custom software development	75,000
2. Hardware costs		
- Barcode Scanners (2 units)	15,000 × 2	30,000
- Barcode Labels	6,000	6,000
Total Hardware	30,000 + 6,000	36,000
3. Labor Savings		
- Daily Time saved	5 hours/day	–
- Daily savings	5 × 300 LKR/hr	1,500
- Monthly savings	1,500 × 26 days	39,000
- 6-Month Savings	39,000 × 6	234,000
4. Total Investment	75,000 + 36,000	111,000
5. Net Savings	234,000 - 111,000	123,000
6. Payback Period	111,000 ÷ (234,000/6)	**2.85 months**

Source: Author

Conclusion and Future Work

Conclusion

This study demonstrated that implementing a barcode-driven stock management system—developed using Visual Basic, MS Access, Excel, and integrated with Microsoft Power BI dashboards—substantially improved the efficiency, accuracy, and transparency of spare parts management within a mechanical department. By automating the Goods Received Note (GRN) and issuing processes through barcode scanning and a user-friendly interface, the system significantly reduced manual workload and errors while enhancing real-time operational insights. During a two-month pilot involving 50 timed trials and 15 user surveys, mean GRN entry time decreased by 63.7% (from 3.58 ± 0.53 to 1.30 ± 0.20 minutes) and issuing time improved by 72.9% (from 4.08 ± 0.68 to 0.70 ± 0.13 minutes), with highly significant statistical validation ($p < 0.001$). Accuracy increased markedly from 82.4% in manual entries to 99.1% with barcode scans, corresponding to a 95.8% error reduction ($\chi^2 = 35.72$, $p < 0.0001$). Reporting efficiency also improved dramatically, with daily report preparation time reduced from nearly an hour to under 30 seconds, eliminating repetitive manual tasks.

User acceptance was high, with over 80% satisfaction across ease of use, dashboard utility, and scanning speed, highlighting the system's accessibility even to users with limited technical background. Financial analysis revealed direct labor savings of 234,000 LKR over six months against an investment of 111,000 LKR, resulting in net savings of 123,000 LKR and a payback period of approximately 2.85 months, despite modest budget overruns. Role-based access control ensured data security by limiting critical edits, while Power BI integration enabled supervisors to monitor high-demand items and mitigate stockouts, aligning with 5S principles such as "Sort," "Set in Order," and "Sustain," thereby supporting lean maintenance operations.

Limitations include the single-site pilot scope, small user sample, and a relatively short observation window. While improved visibility implied reduced downtime, quantification of associated cost savings was not performed and is recommended for future research. Overall, this study validates that department-level digital transformation—achieved without the complexity or cost of enterprise ERP systems—can deliver measurable operational, accuracy, and financial benefits in spare-parts management.

Future Work

Building on the promising pilot results, future research will focus on four key areas to enhance system value and scalability. First, expanded business analytics will quantify the impact on downtime costs, labor redeployment, and inventory carrying costs, leveraging integrated maintenance logs and refined labor tracking. Development of sensitivity models will facilitate generalized ROI assessments across varied operational contexts.

Second, the data architecture will be upgraded by migrating to robust relational databases (e.g., Azure SQL or PostgreSQL) to support multi-user concurrency, larger inventories, and seamless integration with ERP/CMMS platforms via standardized APIs. Multi-site deployment will be enabled through hierarchical location management and offline synchronization to accommodate low-infrastructure environments.

Third, ensuring data integrity and cybersecurity will be prioritized through automated encrypted backups, versioned audit logs, credential hardening, and secure network communications. Label durability and scan-validation protocols will safeguard physical data accuracy.

Finally, structured change management will address user adoption through tiered training, simulation sandboxes, point-of-use job aids, and superuser champions. Adoption metrics will guide targeted retraining efforts. Additional functional enhancements, such as mobile scanning, automated reorder thresholds, predictive analytics, and CMMS integration, will be explored to further streamline inventory management and maintenance workflows.

This system represents a scalable and replicable solution that can be adapted to other departments or even across factories within an industrial group. Its success highlights the impact of digital transformation at the departmental level, empowering frontline operations with data-driven tools.

Acknowledgment

We would like to express our heartfelt gratitude to the lecturers of the Department of Mechanical & Automotive Engineering, Faculty of Engineering and Technology, CINEC Campus, for their invaluable guidance and continuous support throughout our project.

Finally, we are grateful to all our supporters, colleagues, and well-wishers whose contributions and encouragement were essential for the successful completion of this work.

References

[1] Zhang, S., Huang, K., & Yuan, Y. (2021). Spare parts inventory management: a literature review. *Sustainability*, 13, 2460. doi: 10.3390/su13052460.

[2] Labib, A 2008, Computerised maintenance management systems. in K Kobbacy & D Murthy (eds), Complex systems maintenance handbook. Springer series in reliability engineering, Springer, Berlin, pp. 417–436.

[3] Heragu, S.S. (2008). Facilities Design (3rd ed.). CRC Press. https://doi.org/10.1201/9781420066272.

[4] Gunasekaran, A., & Kobu, B. (2007). Performance measures and metrics in logistics and supply chain management: a review of recent literature (1995–2004) for research and applications. *International Journal of Production Research*, 45, 2819–2840. doi: 10.1080/00207540600806513.

[5] Mazur, M., Korenko, M., Žitňák, M., Shchur, T., Kiełbasa, P., Dostál, P., Dzhidzhora, O. & Idzikowski, A. (2024) Implementation and Benefits of the 5S Method in Improving Workplace Organisation – A Case Study. Management Systems in Production Engineering, Sciendo, Vol. 32 (Issue 4), pp. 498–507. https://doi.org/10.2478/mspe-2024-0047.

[6] Manthou, V., & Vlachopoulou, M. (2001). Barcode technology for inventory and marketing management systems: a model for its development and implementation. *International Journal of Production Economics*, 71, 157–164. doi: 10.1016/S0925-5273(00)00115-8.

[7] Bhuiyan, M. R. I., Faraji, M. R., Rashid, M., Bhuyan, M. K., Hossain, R., & Ghose, P. (2024). Digital transformation in SMEs emerging technological tools and technologies for enhancing the SME's strategies and outcomes. *Journal of Ecohumanism*, 3, 211–224. doi: 10.62754/joe.v3i4.3594.

[8] Y. Fan, (2010) Development of inventory management system, 2nd IEEE International Conference on Information Management and Engineering, Chengdu, China, 2010, pp. 207–210, doi: 10.1109/ICIME.2010.5478077.

[9] Singh, J., Rani, S. & Kumar, V. (2024). Role-Based Access Control (RBAC) Enabled Secure and Efficient Data Processing Framework for IoT Networks. International Journal of Communication Networks and Information Security (IJCNIS). 16, 2 (Aug. 2024). DOI:https://doi.org/10.17762/ijcnis.v16i2.6697.

[10] Yerra, S. (2025). Enhancing inventory management through real-time power BI dashboards and KPI tracking. doi: 10.32628/CSEIT25112458.

14 Beyond opposition: how hierarchical power enables collective leadership - insights from a Sri Lankan IT company

Vidusha Nathavitharana[a]

Faculty of Postgraduate Studies and Professional Advancement, NSBM Green University, Sri Lanka

Abstract

This research paper explores how collective leadership (CL) can be established within a formal hierarchical structure, without dismantling hierarchical structures nor becoming a threat to it. The study adopts a qualitative single case study approach. Through the study of Mitra, a technology-based company founded in Sri Lanka and now headquartered in London, the research addresses the three gaps identified in literature regarding how tensions between formal hierarchies and CL are navigated in a commercial setting. The findings demonstrate how senior leaders leveraged their formal authority and power to create specific spaces for CL. The findings further reveal that specific CL spaces such as join the dots (JTD), and million-dollar initiative (MDI) did not become a threat or oppose formal hierarchy, rather, they augmented and supported it and enabled better organizational performance. The findings also offer insights into cultural norms and practice the organization adopts in order to ensure CL spaces are supported and strengthened, as well as how hierarchical leaders exercise power outside of CL spaces. The research contributes towards the theoretical understanding of how CL can productively co-exist in hierarchical for-profit settings, and how hierarchical power can be leveraged to create CL within an organization. It also contributes toward practitioners by offering a practical way of enabling CL within an organization without dismantling formal hierarchical structures.

Keywords: Case study, Collective leadership, Hierarchy, Power, Hierarchical power, Sri Lanka

Introduction

Collective leadership (CL) has been gaining popularity in mainstream leadership scholarship and is often positioned as an alternative to a traditional hierarchy [1]. CL and traditional hierarchical leadership is often seen to be competing forces [2], though some have argued that they can co-exist [3]. As such, in looking at the feasibility and applicability of CL within a hierarchical setting, three major research gaps appear. Firstly, specific methods hierarchy can deploy to create CL within an organization is unclear in current literature. Secondly, the specific role hierarchical leadership can play in supporting CL within an organization is also under explored in current literature. Finally, how the two can co-exist in a mutually beneficial way is hinted at but not explicitly explored in CL scholarship. By exploring Mitra, an IT company founded in Sri Lanka, this research aims to explore how CL emerges within a traditional hierarchical setting and address the three key research gaps identified.

The paper begins with a brief literature review on hierarchical leadership, CL and the power tensions between the two. The methods section lists research design, data collection and data analysis approaches. The findings explore a detailed analysis of the evidence found on how senior leaders within the organization leveraged their power to create CL spaces, what cultural norms and practices support CL spaces as well as evidence of roles senior leaders performed outside of CL spaces. These findings are aligned to the central questions around how hierarchical leadership and CL co-exist, and the specific mechanisms adopted in order to ensure that hierarchy and CL does not become competing power structures. The discussion section synthesize the key findings, aligning it to current literature and elicit the key contributions to academia and practitioners. The paper concludes by looking at future research trajectories.

[a]vidusha@highfiveconsultancy.com

DOI: 10.4324/9781003739920-14

Literature Review

Hierarchical leadership has been criticized as being inadequate to meet the VUCA environments modern organizations function within [4, 5, 1, 6]. However, a viable, practical alternative to the hierarchy has not yet been mainstreamed. Though many industries have experimented with reducing hierarchical layers and evolving the organizational structures [7], IT organizations have been at the forefront of experimenting with alternatives to the formal hierarchy [8]. They famously introduced the matrix structure as a mechanism to de-emphasize the traditional hierarchy and enable more effective and efficient project management [9]. However, even in a matrix structure, the hierarchy is not absent, and a flat hierarchy is a hierarchy none-the-less. A few organizations have experimented with radically different organizational structures, though they are often identified as outlier experiments. A good example of this is offered by [10] who examined how Zappos implemented holacracy as a radical departure from traditional hierarchy and eliminated job titles, and formal management positions. Similarly, [7] documented how the Dutch healthcare company Buurtzorg implemented self-managing team structures and completely reimagined hierarchical relationships. However, such radical change is considered risky, and findings of McKibben [11] demonstrate that incremental approaches to decentralizing leadership often demonstrate higher success rates in established organizations than radical overhauls of governance structures.

By its very nature, hierarchies centralize power [12]. Any opposition to the hierarchy is seen as an act of insubordination [13]. Hierarchies also, by configuration, are power based. Power is pegged to the title or designation, often demonstrated through an organizational diagram [14]. There is an unbroken chain of command, and a specific span of control, formally assigned through a Job Description or Job Scope document [15]. These instruments are often a mainstream feature of any large-scale business, irrespective of industry. Leadership, for all practical reasons in a hierarchy is therefore position based [16].

CL in contrast is seen as a decentralized, distributed and collaborative form of leadership which is in sharp contrast to a centralized, hierarchical leadership structure [17]. CL is often used as an umbrella term and used interchangeably with many form of pluralistic leadership varieties including distributed leadership, shared leadership and collaborative leadership [18]. CL looks at leadership as a process, and not as a fixed position of authority or power [4]. It also posits leadership as an inherently collective process [19], rather than the domain of one person [20]. CL is often seen as emerging through interactions within the organization, outside of formal settings [21]. Denis et al. [1] synthesized forms of CL in literature and postulated four distinct CL forms: 1) Sharing leadership in teams 2) Pooling leadership at the top of organizations 3) Spreading leadership across boundaries over time and 4) Producing leadership through interaction. Their research demonstrates that CL takes different forms, and that none, one, several or all could well be found in any organization.

Leadership of any form and power is often intertwined [22]. The 'Contestation, negotiation, and resolution: The relationship between power and collective leadership' by [23] looks at the relationship between formal power and CL. Though not taking an empirical approach, their work identified four ways in which power mechanisms can bring about CL: 1) CL as entitative and power as episodic: where CL emerges through leaders devolving power to their subordinates by empowering them. 2) CL as entitative and power as systemic: where "Contextual characteristics related to power can influence the possibility and enactment of CL" 3) CL as emergent and power as episodic: where "CL can create the collective power necessary for people in marginalized positions to challenge embedded power dynamics" and 4) CL as emergent and power as systemic: where "power is intrinsic to the co-construction process; attributions affect who can enact CL, how they are viewed and whether they have power" and "CL can create the collective power necessary for people in marginalized positions to challenge embedded power dynamics". What the work of [23] demonstrates is that power dynamics play a central part in the manifestation of CL within an organizational setting, where CL can be both emergent informally through the use of informal power or influence, or formally created using authority/formal power. What the research does not answer are the clear mechanisms by which these emergences take place.

Traditional hierarchy and CL have often been juxtaposed in literature. Though the efficacy of CL has been well established [6], CL has also been argued as a destabilizing alternative power structure to the traditional hierarchy [24]. At the same time, even when CL type arrangements are consciously fostered, some research argue that more junior members may not have the confidence nor the competency to take leadership roles or responsibilities [25]. These findings beg the question how hierarchy and CL can coexist effectively, and how they can mutually augment each other, enabling the organization to function effectively. However, Kummelstedt [3] argues that formal hierarchical power is not an impediment to CL, and that it can actually be leveraged to create CL if specifically poised, though how this can be done is absent in research. Others argue for the need to go beyond the either/or argument between CL and hierarchies, demonstrating that both have an importance in the modern organization. Pearce et al. [2] sums up the argument about either/or challenge of CL vs. hierarchy by stating that the question isn't "vertical OR shared leadership" but rather "when and how to use both". However, when to use which type of leadership, and how is also absent in CL or traditional leadership literature.

Methodology

Research design

This case study took a qualitative, single case study approach [26]. Though the multiple case study is often cited as not particularly effective [27, 28] in being able generalize findings, a single case approach was specifically decided upon in order to have an opportunity of in-depth inquiry and identify specific nuances that arose within the organization [26]. It enabled the deeper understanding of a complex phenomenon that was not explored in current CL literature.

Case selection

Mitra AI was purposefully selected through theoretical sampling [29] based on three criteria: (1) it exhibited a traditional hierarchical structure while simultaneously demonstrating agile and collective leadership characteristics; (2) it operated in a dynamic, technology-driven sector requiring adaptive leadership approaches; and (3) it provided access to participants across multiple organizational levels. These criteria ensured the case would provide theoretical insight into how collective leadership emerges within formal power structures within an IT sector company. Established in 2012, Mitra AI is a privately held organization specializing in AI based solutions. Founded in Sri Lanka and Headquartered in London, the organization has double digit million dollar revenue, and employs over 250 individuals across five countries. The organization has recently undergone a restructure, and aims to accelerate business outcomes, targeting a tenfold growth within less than a decade.

Data collection and analysis

Data collection involved nine semi-structured interviews conducted between January and March 2024. Even though the organization has a flat structure, interviews were conducted with participants selected from all three formal levels within the organization; i.e. the senior management, the middle management/team leaders and team members. Each interview was between 20-60 minutes in duration. Though data saturation was reached with seven interviews, a further two interviews were completed before concluding data collection. Interviews were conducted online using Zoom, and were recorded with the consent of each participant. Interviews were transcribed verbatim using TurboScribe software. Data was analyzed using Thematic Analysis taking an inductive approach. An open coding method was adopted which was reiterative. Final codes were thematically arranged and named and renamed a few times before the final thematic structure was decided. The thematic analysis conducted is offered in in Table 14.1–14.3 in Annexure 1.

Results and Discussion

Findings

Analysis revealed three key themes. Firstly, the role senior leaders played as architects of CL spaces. Secondly, the cultural norms and practices that support CL. And finally, the role senior leaders played outside of CL spaces.

Senior leaders as architects of CL

Senior leaders within Mitra used their hierarchical authority to create CL spaces within the organization. These spaces transcended mere collaborative or inclusive leadership mechanisms and were seen as hierarchy free zones. Individuals from different hierarchical levels and different functions were given autonomy to come together and co-create direction and drive initiatives outside of organizational and hierarchical constraints. There were two distinct spaces that were observed through the data. The first was join the dots (JTD) forum. This space was created by the COO in order to discuss, debate and 'hash out' any matter relating to any aspect of the business. Taking inspiration from Arthurian lore, the JTD was fashioned as the knights of the round table, without a formal leader and each individual having equal say in whatever that is being discussed. It represented 'mid-tier leaders' and 'vertical and horizontal leaders' stated Participant 7, stating that "it's a level playing field there", and that "everybody's free to bring up ideas and concerns and challenges" and find solutions through consensus-based decision making. The lack of a formal leader, nor a hierarchical oversight, enables the JTD to become a CL space outside of the formal review and decision-making structures that do exist to make operational decisions.

The second CL space that was observed was the MDI or the Million Dollar Initiative. This was orchestrated by the senior leadership to create an alternative space to drive top line performance. Though the traditional KPI setting approach was earlier mooted and tried, it did not yield the desired results. "Then we kind of flipped, we kind of de-prioritized the KPIs" explained Participant 7, stating that the MDI was ideated to give everyone the opportunity to contribute towards the overall organizational growth. When asked if they were given instructions or oversight, Participant 7 explained that "converting a lead is a massive process on its own, so, got them the lead and basically pointed them in the right direction. And everything else is done by a cross-functional team" illustrating that the only intervention from the senior team was to give them a sales 'lead' in order to start the pitching process. He further stated that there were "two immediate hits for the million-dollar target. Both were massive, combined efforts" demonstrating immediate results which was explained to have been sustained as well.

The MDI and the JTD illustrate how senior leaders within Mitra carved out CL spaces without changing any of the formal structures or hierarchical designs of the organization. Both spaces were without formal leadership or direct oversight. Both spaces allowed CL to emerge rather than leadership being assigned. Both spaces were consciously created to drive organizational performance, one from an everyday operational perspective and the other from a sales perspective. Both enabled individuals from all levels to contribute. Both create a specific space for CL.

Cultural norms and practices that supported CL

While senior leaders created these CL spaces, their success depended on more than structural design alone. Analysis revealed four cultural norms and practices that enabled the organization to affirm the importance of CL and support it, thereby enabling the efficacy of these spaces. Firstly, there was a conscious de-emphasis on hierarchy. Senior leaders led by example and ensured CL was emphasized. "The hero culture is discouraged at all levels" stated Participant 7, explaining that those who did not want to collaborate and work together collectively were doomed to "learn the hard way." Not limiting their affirmation to an egalitarian ethos and a de-emphasis on hierarchy, one of the co-founders explained that they removed individuals who were 'toxic to the culture', noting that all efforts were made to coach and mentor them first.

Secondly, CL was supported by creating cross functional and cross hierarchical spaces for decision making, rather than focusing on hierarchical decision making. The Opex and TechOps were two such spaces. These were not CL spaces, but spaces for operational efficacy, and fell short of having full autonomy and freedom. However, they were inclusive spaces which allowed individuals from all levels to be included in the decision-making process. "They all come and... openly discuss and see the trends, and look at where it should be, and if we need to move levers" explained Participant 4, elaborating that these forums were held on regular intervals and changed composition if required based on the problems at hand.

Thirdly Mitra had a clear focus on training, developing and grooming individuals, both in their technical competencies as well as their leadership competencies. Senior leaders identified coaching and mentoring as one of their core responsibilities. "Training, mentoring, coaching, evaluating their performance, doing the career development plans, all of those falls under me" stated Participant 6, explaining that it is in the formal job scope of all managers. He further explained that formal technical training was conducted based on "training needs" that were annually assessed for all employees. For those lagging behind, rather than resorting to punitive punishments, Participant 9 spoke of implementing a PIP or Personal Improvement Plan. He stated that the PIP was a "kind of a planned initiative we have within Mitra where we get HR involved, creating a promising plan" to help individuals overcome challenges, and ensure better performance.

PIP or Personal Improvement Plan was developed, and executed with the assistance of HR. Through these interventions, the organization ensured that each individual was trained and developed, enabling them to perform and also, contribute effectively towards organizational endeavors. Finally, Mitra demonstrated a culture of empowerment. All participants interviewed echoed the sentiment that they were empowered to act without constant supervision or micromanagement. The sense of personal agency was clearly demonstrated by all levels, and affirmed as Participant 8 did that they were "given the freedom to take decisions." Individuals were also given the freedom to mentor their superiors, and train them when required. One of the best examples of this was illustrated by Participant 1 who spoke of carrying out the fundamental interpersonal relations orientation-behavior or (FIRO-B) assessment to his superior, and giving him the ability to self-reflect. The "results were shocking" he explained, and it enabled his superior to understand the "internal perspective and an external perspective of who you are as an individual."

By de-emphasizing hierarchy, creating cross functional and cross hierarchical collaborative spaces, training and grooming all levels as well as encouraging empowerment, Mitra created a culture that was able to foster CL within its fold. Rather than merely creating CL spaces for namesake, these cultural norms and practices enabled the organization to embrace CL, and for more junior levels to actively participate in the CL spaces created.

Role of hierarchy outside of CL spaces

The role of senior leaders was not limited to creating CL spaces and supporting it through culture affirming norms and practices. Analysis demonstrated that the formal hierarchy remained active and important beyond simply creating CL spaces. The formal hierarchy persisted and was no different to a traditional organizational setting, and was directly involved in driving performance as well as maintaining client relationships and intervening as and when required. Not all aspects of the business were resolved through cross collaborative interventions nor CL, or through consensus. Senior leaders personally reviewed performance of their functions and units. Participant 2 said that he "calls in the cavalry" when needed, and that senior leaders were often called upon to mediate when required. "I would still review and get a feel of what they're doing" said Participant 6, and informed that he would also give his opinions when required but that it was "up to them to implement it or not" demonstrating a nuanced yet hierarchical approach taken to drive performance. Similarly, senior leaders "jumped in" to resolve client issues before "it snowballed" said Participant 4, stating once again that it was not done all the time, but selectively as the situations demanded it.

What was clear is that senior leaders did not abdicate their authority. However, they were conscious of not impinging on individuals' autonomy nor violating the CL spaces created. Hierarchical leadership demonstrated the ability to exert authority when needed, but allow individuals to act with personal agency at the same time. Paradoxically, they created CL spaces and strengthened them at the same time.

Discussion

The findings from Mitra demonstrate that there was a conscious effort to spread leadership across the organization over time, and that CL took place in situ within spaces such as the MDI. This confirms that two of the CL forms that [1] identified in their typology is demonstrated within the organization, affirming that CL can, and does exist within hierarchical organizational settings.

Mitra further demonstrates that formal hierarchical power can be leveraged to create CL within an organization, extending the assertion of [3], and offers empirical evidence of how hierarchical power can be practically leveraged to enable CL as demonstrated by the CL spaces such as JTD and the Million Dollar Initiative senior leaders consciously created. These 'hierarchy free zones' enabled individuals to be part of CL rather than being subject to hierarchical leadership. The research therefore contradicts the claims of authors such as Chen and Zhang [24] and Tahir et al. [25] who viewed CL and hierarchy as juxtaposed and the claim that CL can be counterproductive in a hierarchical setting. The research aligns firmly with Pearce et al. [2] and offers empirical proof of how and when leaders can exercise hierarchy, and how they can create CL spaces to ensure CL sanctity is not disturbed. It also offers insights into how an organization adopts both hierarchy and CL, and use both to their advantage.

The Mitra case also extends the work of Foldy and Ospina [23] by offering empirical evidence of how two of the ways in which power enables CL they identified. The creation of CL spaces such as million-dollar initiative (MDI) offers an example of how CL is entitative and power is episodic: where CL emerges through leaders devolving power to their subordinates by empowering them. The JTD, on the other hand, offers a clear example of how CL is emergent and power is systemic: where "power is intrinsic to the co-construction process; attributions affect who can enact CL, how they are viewed and whether they have power."

Whilst establishing that hierarchy and CL can co-exist, the Mitra case study addresses the concern raised by [25] that junior members may not take up leadership roles in a CL setting even when given the opportunity to. By offering training, mentoring and coaching, as well as creating a collaborative and inclusive culture through mechanisms such as Opex, TechOps and the Strategic Planning Forum, senior leaders in the hierarchy develops a leadership pipeline. This also enables individuals to be systematically augmented to feel confident to take leadership and engage in CL spaces. What becomes clear through the Mitra case study is that creating CL spaces alone is not enough for lower level individuals to partake in CL, there needs to be a conducive culture for it too.

Unlike Buurtzorg or Zappos, Mitra did not overhaul the hierarchy. Neither did they limit it. Mitra found a way to introduce CL without changing existing structures. The success of the CL spaces such as Million Dollar Initiative aligns with the perspective of [11] who argued for incremental changes to existing governance structures. Mitra therefore offers an example of how organizations can introduce CL without having to risk radical overhauls of existing structures or governance protocols.

Though the generalization of findings from a single case study has been questioned in literature, the illustrative insights from Mitra are easy to adopt by any organization within any industry setting. The role of training, mentoring and coaching in developing future leaders has been well documented in leadership literature. Similarly, the role of cross functional collaboration and inclusive leadership practices in enabling leadership development has also been well documented in leadership scholarship. As such, instruments such as the PIP, formal training mechanisms, individualized coaching and mentoring efforts and technical certifications adopted by Mitra can be replicated with confidence. Similarly, the cross functional, cross hierarchical spaces such as TechOps, Opex and the Strategic Planning Forum that enabled collaborative and inclusive decision making can also be adopted by any organization with confidence. The CL spaces Mitra created such as JTD and MDI may also be introduced to any organization with little or no resistance if the senior leadership supports and endorses it. These examples strengthen the case that Mitra's approach represents a pragmatic middle path for for-profit organizations, especially in contexts like Sri Lanka where traditional hierarchical structures remain culturally significant. This moderate approach may explain the organization's ability to achieve performance improvements while maintaining organizational stability. As such, Mitra offers a practitioner simple mechanisms that can enable them to introduce CL to any organization without risking backlash or major change management.

Future Directions

The author acknowledges the limiting factor of a single case study. Therefore, further research across multiple industries and organizational contexts will enable confirmation if these practices are commonplace or unique to Mitra At the same time, conducting a longitudinal study within Mitra will enable the understanding of whether these practices and spaces change over time, and how contextual aspects such as strategic direction and/or external environmental challenges will impact current CL formations. In order to understand which specific practices and spaces have the biggest impact on organizational performance, a quantitative study can be undertaken. This will allow both academics and practitioners to understand the relationship between specific CL practices and spaces and direct business impacts. These directions will enhance current appreciation for CL, and also enable practitioners to adopt CL as a more mainstream mechanism with the confidence that it will improve business performance.

Conclusion

Hierarchical leadership is often vilified within modern leadership literature, and is often seen as the oppositional force to CL. What the Mitra case study demonstrates is that practical leadership is often far more complex and nuanced, and that hierarchical power can, and is used to leverage and be the harbinger of CL rather than its enemy. The case study can also act as a guide to practically establish CL within hierarchical settings, and do so without radical changes to existing structures. What also becomes apparent through the Mitra case study is the fact that it is not the hierarchy itself that is the problem, but the type of hierarchy that exist. Hierarchies that understand the demands of modern business, as well as the growing demands for more decentralised forms of leadership has the ability and the power to initiate CL, and establish it within the hierarchy, thereby ensuring CL is given the mandate and the opportunity to take root and flourish.

Acknowledgment

The author wishes to offer heartfelt thanks to Dr. Chamindika Weerakoon for the support and encouragement offered throughout my PhD journey, and for invaluable insights offered without which this paper would not have been possible. The author also wishes to thank Prof. Sarath Kodithuwakku for his ongoing support and critique of my work.

References

[1] Denis, J.-L., Langley, A., & Sergi, V. (2012). Leadership in the plural. *The Academy of Management Annals*, 6(1), 211–283.

[2] Pearce, C. L., Conger, J. A., & Locke, E. A. (2007). Shared leadership theory. *The Leadership Quarterly*, 19(5), 622–628.s.

[3] Kummelstedt, C. (2023). The role of hierarchy in realizing collective leadership in a self-managing organization. *Systemic Practice and Action Research*, 36(3), 355–375.

[4] Uhl-Bien, M., & Arena, M. (2018). Leadership for organizational adaptability: a theoretical synthesis and integrative framework. *The leadership quarterly*, 29(1), 89–104.

[5] Worley, C. G., Williams, T. D., & Lawler III, E. E. (2014). The Agility Factor: Building Adaptable Organizations for Superior Performance. John Wiley & Sons.

[6] Pearce, C. L., & Conger, J. A. (2003). Shared Leadership: Reframing the Hows and Whys of Leadership. SAGE Publications.

[7] Laloux, F. (2014). Reinventing Organizations: A Guide to Creating Organizations Inspired by the Next Stage in Human Consciousness. Nelson Parker.

[8] Sy, T., & D'Annunzio, L. S. (2005). Challenges and strategies of matrix organizations. *Human Resource Planning*, 28(1), 39–48.

[9] Larson, E. W., & Gobeli, D. H. (1987). Matrix management: contradictions and insights. *California Management Review*, 29(4), 126–138.

[10] Lee, M. Y., & Edmondson, A. C. (2017). Self-managing organizations: exploring the limits of less-hierarchical organizing. *Research in Organizational Behavior*, 37, 35–58.

[11] McKibben, L. (2017). Conflict management: importance and implications. *British Journal of Nursing*, 26(2), 100–103.

[12] Diefenbach, T., & Sillince, J. A. (2011). Formal and informal hierarchy in different types of organization. *Organization Studies*, 32(11), 1515–1537.

[13] Pfeffer, J. (1992). Managing with Power: Politics and Influence in Organizations. Harvard Business School Press.

[14] McPhee, R. D., & Zaug, P. (2009). The communicative constitution of organizations. Building theories of organization: The constitutive role of communication, 10(1–2), 21.

[15] Mintzberg, H. (1979). The Structuring of Organizations. Prentice Hall.

[16] Balkundi, P., & Kilduff, M. (2006). The ties that lead: a social network approach to leadership. *The Leadership Quarterly*, 17(4), 419–439.

[17] Gronn, P. (2002). Distributed leadership as a unit of analysis. *The Leadership Quarterly*, 13(4), 423–451.

[18] Bolden, R. (2011). Distributed leadership in organizations: a review of theory and research. *International Journal of Management Reviews*, 13(3), 251–269.

[19] Sweeney, A. (2024). Sharing the leadership space: toward a contextual understanding of shared leadership patterns in organizational teams. *Journal of Leadership & Organizational Studies,* 31(2), 166–191.

[20] Ospina, S., & Foldy, E. (2010). Building bridges from the margins: the work of leadership in social change organizations. *The Leadership Quarterly*, 21(2), 292–307.

[21] Contractor, N. S., DeChurch, L. A., Carson, J., Carter, D. R., & Keegan, B. (2012). The topology of collective leadership. *The Leadership Quarterly*, 23(6), 994–1011.

[22] Anderson, C., & Brion, S. (2014). Perspectives on power in organizations. *Annual Review of Organizational Psychology and Organizational Behavior*, 1(1), 67–97.

[23] Foldy, E. G., & Ospina, S. M. (2023). 'Contestation, negotiation, and resolution': the relationship between power and collective leadership. *International Journal of Management Reviews*, 25(3), 546–563.

[24] Chen, G., & Zhang, G. (2023). The dark side of shared leadership: when and why shared leadership hurts team performance. *Journal of Business Research*, 154, 113359.

[25] Tahir, L. M., Lee, S. L., Musah, M. B., Jaffri, H., Said, M. N. H. M., & Yasin, M. H. M. (2016). Challenges in distributed leadership: evidence from the perspective of headteachers. *International Journal of Educational Management*, 30(6), 848–863.

[26] Yin, R. K. (2009). Case Study Research: Design and Methods, (Vol. 5). Sage.

[27] Eisenhardt, K. M. (1989). Building theories from case study research. *Academy of Management Review*, 14(4), 532–550.

[28] Stake, R. E. (1995). The Art of Case Study Research. Sage Publications.

[29] Patton, M. Q. (2015). Qualitative Research and Evaluation Methods: Integrating Theory and Practice, (4th edn.). SAGE Publications.

Annexure 1 : Thematic Analysis

Table 14.1 The role of senior leaders in creating CL.

Theme_Sub Theme	Code	Sample Quote	
Role of Senior Leaders in creating CL	**Creating CL spaces**	**JTD [Join the Dots space]**	*"JTD stands for Join the Dots. And it is essentially a Knights of the Round Table kind of approach... We sit around in a circle without a table... We have all the mid-tier leaders, the vertical and horizontal leaders there. And we hash out a lot of the challenges that we see as an organisation in those meetings." [Participant 7]*
		MDI [Million Dollar Initiative]	*"And we said.. whether you're from sales or delivery, or HR or resource management or whatever, if you sell a million dollar deal, and keep it running for five months minimum, then you get x percentage commission, and you decide how you distribute it amongst the people who contributed towards that success." [Participant 7]*

Source: Developed by the researcher based on data collected for this study

Table 14.2 Cultural norms and practices that supported CL.

Theme_Sub Theme	Code	Sample Quote	
Cultural norms and practices that supported CL	**De-emphasis on hierarchy**	**Emphasising importance of CL**	*"There are some leaders who've had trouble encouraging free speech... But we consciously drove it into the team that this is what we want to achieve... You've got to change your behaviour." [Participant 7]*
		Removing leaders who were not aligned to CL ethos	*"So we try to have a very open discussion, and we correct issues then and there with the people... And if it continues to happen, even after multiple tries, then we even go on to the extent of moving people out, so that we bring fresh blood in, rather than creating noise in the system. "[Participant 4]*
	Collaborative and Inclusive Decision Making Spaces	Opex [Operational Meeting]	*"We have an OPEX meeting, that looks at most of the operational aspect to it... It's set monthly, we come monthly, S [name anonymised] presents that as a CEO, and finance is part of it, HR is part of it, delivery is part of it, they all come and, you know, we openly discuss and see the trends, look at where it should be, if we need to move levers, all of that gets discussed on a monthly basis." [Participant 4]*
		TechOps [Operations meeting for technical functions]	*"So we've started something called a TechOps call, which is technical operations call where on a weekly basis, we review the health status of every project. And depending on the colour code they have. So it's green, amber, and escalated red." [Participant 1]*

	Developing Future Leaders	Coaching and Mentoring	*"So apart from that, training, mentoring, coaching, evaluating their performance, doing the career development plans, all of those falls under me." [Participant 6]*
		Formal Training	*"And based on the training needs, we will conduct trainings annually. So some folks might be good at automation, but some folks may not be good at automation. So then we are not going to put them into doing automation, unless it's really required for us where we are lacking heads behind. So we conduct the trainings like that". [Participant 6]*
		PIP [Personal Improvement Plan]	*"So that is the place where we have a process as an PIP, the personal improvement plan, kind of a planned initiative we have within Mitra where we get HR involved, creating a promising plan, it took us for three months." [Participant 9]*
	Empowerment	Encouraging Personal Agency	*"Actually, we are given, we are given the, how would I say the autonomy to make the required decisions within our scope of work." [Participant 3]*
		Reverse mentoring	*"I remember once, I did an internal training only for S [name anonymised] and his direct reports and I did the FIRO-B report, I asked him to fill the assessment. And so I mean, I'm sure you know, it looks at you from an internal perspective and an external perspective of who you are as an individual." [Participant 1]*

Source: Developed by the researcher based on data collected for this study

Table 14.3 Role of hierarchy outside of CL spaces.

Theme_Sub Theme	Code	Sample Quote	
Role of Hierarchy outside of CL spaces	**Driving Performance**	Personally Reviewing Tasks	*"But I would still review and get a feel of what they're doing. And if we think that we can reach something which is good, that will cater their needs, then I'll give those my view point". [Participant 6]*
	Client relationships	Direct involvement in solving client problems before it escalates	*"Then it might require somebody senior to step in and to assess that situation, because once you're course correcting, a lot of things can change." [Participant 1]*

Source: Developed by the researcher based on data collected for this study

15 Women entrepreneurs and digital innovation: unlocking emerging research possibilities

D.F. Dissanayake[a] *and R.M.S.P. Rajapaksha*[b]

Department of Management Studies, Faculty of Indigenous Social Sciences and Management Studies, Gampaha Wickramarachchi University of Indigenous Medicine, Sri Lanka

Abstract

Women entrepreneurship is a driving force in global economic growth, fostering innovation, job creation, and inclusive prosperity. Digital innovation plays a crucial role in empowering women entrepreneurs. Technology enables access to global markets, streamlines operations, and enhances customer engagement through digital tools like e-commerce, fintech, and artificial intelligence. This study explores the dynamic intersection of women entrepreneurship and digital innovation, highlighting the transformative role of digital technologies in empowering women entrepreneurs and promoting inclusive economic growth. Despite the growing participation of women in digital ventures significant barriers persist ranging from limited digital literacy to financial and institutional constraints. The main objectives of this study are to systematically review the existing literature on women entrepreneurship and digital innovation and to identify emerging research opportunities and challenges within this domain. A systematic literature review was conducted using the PRISMA method, sourcing 85 publications from the Scopus database. After screening, 25 relevant journal articles were selected for in-depth analysis. Keyword co-occurrence analysis using VOSviewer software and thematic analysis were employed to identify prevailing themes and future research directions. The results revealed 12 innovative keyword clusters and multiple themes highlighting the impact of digital innovation on women entrepreneurs including: women entrepreneurs, empowerment through digital engagement, digital innovation, and technological impact. The study concludes with practical implications and emerging research avenues emphasizing the need for policy support, targeted education, and inclusive financial systems to foster a sustainable, gender-equitable digital entrepreneurial ecosystem.

Keywords: Digital innovation, digital skill development, economic empowerment, PRISMA method, women entrepreneurship

Introduction

The intersection of women's entrepreneurship and digital innovation has been a powerful catalyst for social and economic transformation in the innovation driven era. As digital technologies continue to transform global markets and redefine how business is done women entrepreneurs are increasingly leveraging these technologies to spearhead new possibilities, upend traditional business norms, and fuel economic growth. However, even while their numbers grow in the business world, women continue to face systemic barriers such as digital illiteracy, limited access to capital, and cultural constraints, which prevent them from fully utilizing the potential of digital innovation [1].

Women entrepreneurs are redefining traditional notions of professional success through entry into industries dominated by males and use of the internet for building and expansion of businesses. For instance, in Sri Lanka initiatives such as the 'Women in E-Commerce' program supported by ICTA have enabled women-led businesses like Kapruka.lk and Thambili Island to scale operations globally using digital platforms. Similarly, Sri Lankan women from rural areas have used Facebook Marketplace and Daraz.lk to reach wider customer bases, illustrating how digital innovation allows women to bypass traditional barriers and access markets otherwise closed to them [10, 16].

Digital technologies have lowered entry barriers in most industries allowing women to reach larger markets, engage directly with customers, and innovate faster [2, 3]. Their activities not only raise family incomes and employment but also contribute significantly to broader economic and social development. In economically disadvantaged or socially marginalized areas women's digital businesses act as engines of community revitalization and poverty alleviation [2].

[a]fiushani.d0717@gmail.com, [b]sisitha@gwu.ac.lk

DOI: 10.4324/9781003739920-15

In the context of digital innovation, acquiring digital skills is no longer optional but a fundamental requirement for entrepreneurial success. To navigate the complexities of digital markets women need not only technical literacy but also strategic foresight, adaptability, and a mindset of lifelong learning. Programs like the SheMeansBusiness initiative by Facebook, introduced in parts of Asia including Sri Lanka, demonstrate that empowering women with digital skills can dismantle systemic barriers and produce transformative societal outcomes [4].

Moreover, digital innovation enables women entrepreneurs to transcend traditional market structures integrate into global value chains and develop novel, adaptive and sustainable business models. Incorporating digital technology into women-focused entrepreneurship programs is not only a step toward economic empowerment but a catalyst for broader social transformation. As digital platforms become increasingly central to business operations it is critical that women be equipped with the skills, resources, and support systems needed to engage competitively in the digital economy. This paper highlights the urgent need to explore the impact of digitally enabled women entrepreneurs on business sustainability and economic performance and proposes key future research directions in this evolving field [3].

Research Problem and Objectives

Conceptual reviews related to women entrepreneurship and digital innovation are scarce and there is an increasing trend in todays' world about women entrepreneurs and how they will interact with digital innovation. The main research question of this study is "what the prevailing literature would be related to women entrepreneurship and digital innovation?"

The research objectives of this research are,

1. To systematically review the current literature related to women entrepreneurship and digital innovation
2. To identify emerging research opportunities and challenges related to women entrepreneurship and digital innovation

Methodology

This conceptual study utilizes both quantitative and qualitative methods to achieve the research

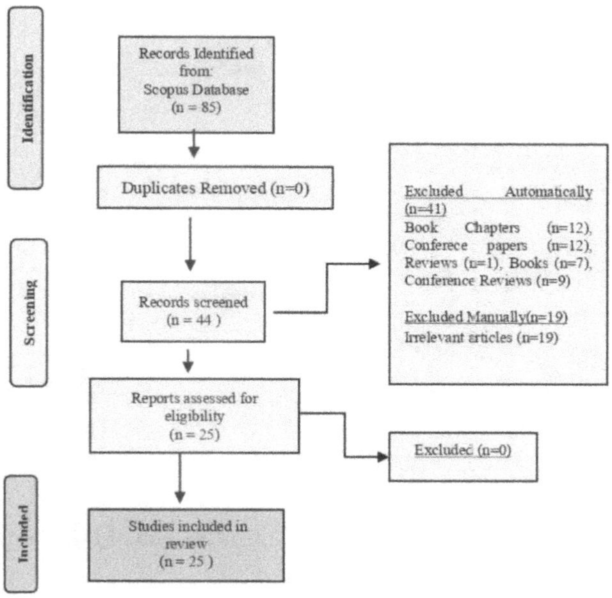

Figure 15.1 PRISMA flow diagram
Source: Author [7]

objectives. This study utilizes the systematic literature review based on the PRISMA method [9]. Total of 85 articles were obtained from Scopus database and systematically screened articles (Conference papers = 12, Book chapters =12, Conference reviews = 9, Books = 7, Reviews=1) and utilized only journal articles to ensure the quality of the outcome of this research. Initially there were 44 journal articles identified and systematically screened articles for relevancy by the authors and 19 articles were excluded. According to the developed PRISMA protocol, articles published from 2015 to 2025 were included in the study. The search strings used were "Women Entrepreneurs" and "Digital Innovation". Both qualitative and quantitative approaches were used in this study. Keyword co-occurrence analysis, a quantitative approach, was conducted using 25 remaining articles to explore the current research and obtain future research avenues. Thematic analysis was conducted to identify innovative themes related to women entrepreneurship and digital innovation [5].

Results and Discussion

Analysis of keywords associated with women entrepreneurship and digital innovation

Keyword co-occurrence analysis was conducted using the VOSviewer software to obtain the network visualization map of keywords which provides

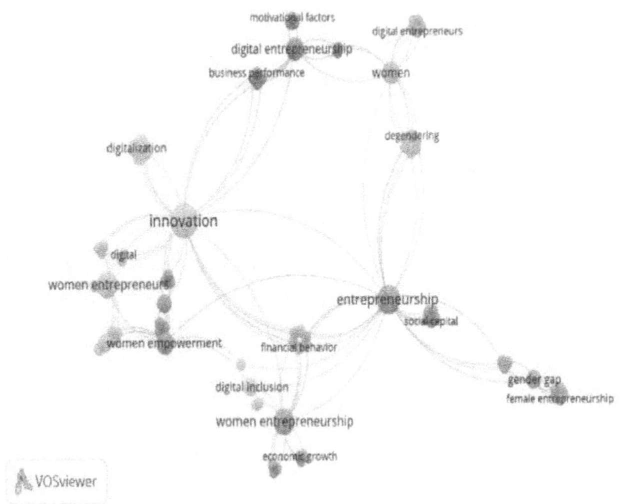

Figure 15.2 Network visualization map of keywords
Source: Author

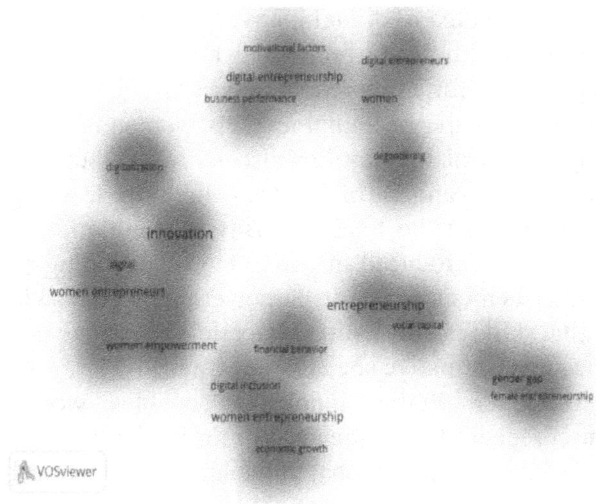

Figure 15.3 Density visualization map of keywords
Source: Author

the relationship between each keyword identifying innovative clusters of keywords which shows in the Figure 15.2. Twelve clusters of keywords are shown on the map which indicates the distribution of keywords.

The density visualization map of keywords shown in the Figure 15.3 illustrates the fact that how often the keywords have been researched compared to each other. Underexplored areas are located away from red color dense areas [9]. Innovation, women entrepreneurship and entrepreneurship show a dense cluster which provides us the fact that those keywords have been researched more frequently than others.

Keyword co-occurrence analysis yields 12 clusters of keywords as follows.

Thematic Analysis

The themes presented in the thematic analysis section were developed through a systematic literature review (SLR) methodology, adhering to the PRISMA guidelines. Thematic coding was performed manually and supported by qualitative content analysis. Recurring concepts such as *digital empowerment, technological inclusion, barriers to innovation,* and *impact on community development* were identified through an iterative reading of the selected articles. These codes were grouped into four major themes:

1. Women entrepreneurs – Agents of change in the business landscape
2. Empowerment through digital engagement
3. Digital innovation – an avenue of opportunity and inclusion
4. Technological impact – boosting productivity and driving sustainability

These themes reflect the dominant narratives and empirical findings across the reviewed literature, providing a comprehensive and evidence-based structure for analyzing the interplay between digital innovation and women's entrepreneurial efforts. This approach ensures both conceptual clarity and academic rigor while offering insights relevant to both global and Sri Lankan contexts.

Women entrepreneurs – agents of change in the business landscape

Women entrepreneurs are increasingly being recognized as catalysts of inclusive economic development, especially in developing economies. They are redefining the concept of professional success as they enter and excel in traditionally male-dominated sectors. Women's entrepreneurial endeavors are often spurred on by the desire for financial autonomy, social impact, and empowerment. However, the experiences are not free of challenges most navigate through socio-cultural impediments, restrictive access to finance, and poor institutional support. Despite such obstacles women have exhibited resilience, creativity, and adaptability, positioning themselves at the center of both economic and social transformation. Not only do their enterprises create

Table 15.1 Keyword co-occurrence.

Cluster	Keywords
1	Business performance, digital adaptation, digital entrepreneurship, economic growth, informal sector, motivational factors, socio-economic factors, women and youths` women enterprises, youths
2	E-government, female entrepreneurship, gender gap, green funding, institutions, regulations, startup ecosystem stem career
3	Agribusiness, agriculture technology and practices, economic empowerment, gender barriers, sustainable development, women agripreneurship, women empowerment, women's rural entrepreneurship
4	Digital information and communication technology, innovation, organizational culture, organizational learning, technological knowledge, tourism, women entrepreneurs
5	Economic growth, higher education, Industry 4.0, science, technology, engineering, and mathematics (STEM), sustainability, technological innovation, women entrepreneurship dl skinder leadership gap gender
6	Degendering digital skills gender leadership gap, gender participation gap, gender pay gap, work–life balance
7	Digital entrepreneurs, entrepreneurial satisfaction, incentive motivation, non-financial incentive, quality of work life, women
8	Crowdfunding, digital platforms, entrepreneurship, gender bias, optimal distinctiveness, social capital
9	Financial behavior, financial competency, financial decision-making, financial digital literacy, financial performance, financial risk
10	Digital innovation, digital technology self-entrepreneurial orientation, technology orientation, women's entrepreneurs
11	Digitalization, entrepreneurial ecosystem, entrepreneurial financing, women entrepreneur
12	Digital inclusion, participation, skill development, sustainable development

Source: Author [5]

employment but they also empower societies particularly where the enterprises are rooted in local culture or community interest [3].

Empowerment through digital engagement

According to Elshaiekh et al. [3] the research highlights that digital participation plays a crucial role in empowering women entrepreneurs. By utilizing online platforms women can enhance their independence make informed business decisions and build social networks.

Digital innovation – an avenue of opportunity and inclusion

Digital innovation has been a tremendous leveler for women entrepreneurs. It has reduced the entry barriers and provided access to global markets through e-commerce sites, mobile apps, and digital marketing [2]. The internet and digital technologies have democratized business with women being able to work around the traditional gatekeepers to reach out to their consumers directly. Social media in particular has become a valuable platform for brand building, customer engagement, and storytelling abilities that many women have mastered [6]. Digital financial tools such as mobile banking and digital wallets have also allowed women to make business transactions independently with greater ease. The theme illustrates how digital innovation is not just a tool but a transformative force that reshapes the way women engage in entrepreneurship [3].

Technological impact – boosting productivity and driving sustainability

Adoption of technology by women entrepreneurs has made a measurable impact on the productivity, innovation, and sustainability of an organization. Technology tools enable business processes to function more efficiently be it inventory management software or customer relationship management tools. Cloud computing, automation, and data analytics enable women to make better decisions, make optimal use of resources and increase their scope of operations. Significantly technological adaptation enhances the flexibility of the business model which is highly beneficial for women balancing work and family responsibilities. In disadvantaged communities the spillover effect of women's digital entrepreneurship goes beyond individual accomplishments. they create community learning, digital inclusion, and intergenerational change [2]. This theme underlines the worth in empowering women with digital capabilities as a sustainable investment in national development and innovation ecosystems [7, 8]

Emerging Research Avenues and Practical Implications

Emerging research avenues

Future research on women's entrepreneurship and digital innovation should focus on several key areas that build a more inclusive and technologically adaptive entrepreneurial ecosystem. One major direction is transforming STEM education to emphasize patent protection and start up creation aiming to equip women with the tools needed to address pressing societal challenges [2]. Alongside this, there is a strong need to enhance educational systems to align with Industry 4.0 demands. Particularly through programming and technical skill development. Investigating the role of private sector initiatives such as "The Mellon Skills Accelerator" could provide insights into effective models for empowering women entrepreneurs [9]. Furthermore, understanding the barriers women face in accessing networks and financial resources remains critical, as does evaluating the effectiveness of entrepreneurship education methodologies particularly within higher education [8]. It is essential to include voices from diverse regions especially rural and non-urban areas, and to broaden the research scope to include sectors like agriculture and manufacturing. Assessing government and NGO-led training initiatives and examining the influence of push factors on women's formalization intentions can enrich future studies. Comparative research with developed countries could highlight both shared challenges and unique regional dynamics. Special attention should be given to supporting rural female entrepreneurs especially in artisanal sectors through practical interventions and skill-building programs [1].

Future studies should also address gaps in digital financial literacy particularly among women by exploring causes of limited digital experience and assessing the impact of tailored financial training on decision-making and business performance. Qualitative research methods, such as interviews could reveal nuanced challenges faced by women in navigating digital finance. Cross-country and longitudinal studies are encouraged to examine socio-cultural variations and long-term outcomes of financial inclusion policies. Strengthening individual competencies including psychological resilience, digital skills, and professional networks is essential for fostering a sustainable entrepreneurial environment [11]. In addition, promoting holistic approaches that integrate digital literacy into early education and adult learning pathways will be vital for preparing future generations. Longitudinal analysis can track the development of these competencies over time providing valuable insights for policy and practice. Ultimately, advancing digital innovation within women's entrepreneurship calls for an integrated strategy that supports education access to resources and systemic inclusion [12].

Practical implications

The findings from existing literature offer numerous practical implications for advancing women's entrepreneurship through digital innovation. Women entrepreneurs continue to face structural, administrative, and gender-based challenges. Particularly in the era of Industry 4.0. Addressing these barriers requires targeted support including access to digital tools training in IT and legal literacy in areas such as intellectual property protection. Initiatives like "The Mellon Skills Accelerator" and programs aimed at enhancing STEM education can provide critical up skilling and counselling opportunities closing the gender gap and boosting economic growth. Furthermore, the importance of social media and digital marketing in enhancing the visibility and market reach of women-led MSEs is well documented. However, low levels of self-confidence and digital financial literacy among women entrepreneurs remain obstacles highlighting the need for customized training programs, user-friendly digital tools, and psychological support mechanisms. Building social and professional support networks, fostering psychological capital, and promoting strategic thinking are essential for empowering women, particularly in rural and marginalized areas [13].

Practical strategies such as business training, participation in business events, and knowledge sharing platforms can help overcome gaps in formal business knowledge and expand market opportunities. Encouraging women's leadership in sustainable and digital businesses. Especially through cooperatives and NGO collaborations can drive inclusive economic development. Tailored interventions in agriculture including land ownership rights, access to technology, and gender-disaggregated data are vital for empowering rural women. Programs like 'Women in Action' and the HK Unicorn Squad demonstrate the value of early engagement in digital literacy and entrepreneurship. Especially among youth. Empowering former women migrant workers through non-formal education, facilitating networking venues, and supporting women in the Silver Economy also present actionable paths forward. Additionally, developing female-centric business models, promoting flexible working arrangements, and fostering innovation capabilities are key to enhancing marketing performance and competitiveness of women-led MSMEs [13]. These insights serve as a roadmap for policymakers, educators, and development practitioners aiming to design supportive ecosystems that nurture digital innovation and sustainable entrepreneurship among women globally [3].

Challenges

Women entrepreneurs face numerous challenges in adopting digital innovation. Limited access to networks digital skills and financial resources restricts their ability to compete in a digital economy. Traditional gender roles, lack of confidence, and family responsibilities further hinder their entrepreneurial journey. Inadequate education, poor infrastructure, and minimal exposure to digital financial tools reduce their innovation potential [14]. Rural and migrant women face added barriers in accessing technology and support systems. The COVID-19 pandemic worsened these issues especially for women-led MSMEs. Additionally legal, structural, and cultural constraints along with funding disparities contribute to a significant gender gap in entrepreneurship and digital innovation [13].

Conclusion

This study highlights the growing significance of digital innovation in empowering women entrepreneurs and transforming the entrepreneurial landscape. Women are increasingly adopting digital tools and platforms to launch, manage, and expand their businesses particularly in developing economies where traditional barriers to entrepreneurship remain strong. The research reveals that while digital innovation provides new opportunities for market access, financial inclusion, and visibility, women still face challenges such as limited digital literacy, inadequate funding, and socio-cultural constraints. Addressing these challenges requires comprehensive strategies including digital skill development, access to affordable technology, inclusive financial systems, and supportive policy frameworks. By fostering an enabling environment that embraces both technological advancement and gender inclusivity digital innovation can serve as a powerful catalyst for women's entrepreneurial success and broader socio-economic development [15].

References

[1] Miniesy, R. (2022). The determinants of digital entrepreneurship by informal micro and small enterprises (MSEs) in Egypt. *World Journal of Entrepreneurship, Management and Sustainable Development*, 18(4), 425–445. doi: 10.47556/J.WJEMSD.18.4.2022.1.

[2] Chelliah, S. D., & Raj, P. C. B. (2024). Exploring female agripreneurship: insights from grey literature using TCCM framework. *International Journal of Experimental Research and Review*, 42, 133–147. doi: 10.52756/ijerr.2024.v42.012.

[3] Elshaiekh, N. E., Al-Hijji, K., Shehata, A., & Alrashdi, S. M. A. (2023). An empirical analysis of factors motivating unemployed individuals to engage in digital entrepreneurship in Oman: focus on technological infrastructure. *Sustainability*, 15(17), 12953. doi: 10.3390/su151712953.

[4] Handoko, W., Sulaiman, A. I., Sugito, T., & Sabiq, A. (2024). Empowering former women migrant workers: enhancing socio-economic opportunities and inclusion for sustainable development. *Academic Journal of Interdisciplinary Studies*, 13(1), 199. doi: 10.36941/ajis-2024-0015.

[5] Kamberidou, I. (2020). 'Distinguished' women entrepreneurs in the digital economy and the multitasking whirlpool. *Journal of Innovation and Entrepreneurship*, 9(1), 3. doi: 10.1186/s13731-020-0114-y.

[6] Mets, T., & Vettik-Leemet, P. (2024). Women in the sustainability new ventures in the digital era: out from the shadow of the small country male-dominated startup ecosystem. *Green Finance*, 6(3), 383–406. doi: 10.3934/gf.2024015.

[7] Priyashantha, K. G., De Alwis, A. C., & Welmilla, I. (2024). Disruptive human resource management technologies: a systematic literature review. *European Journal of Management and Business Economics*, 33(1), 116–136. doi: 10.1108/ejmbe-01-2022-0018.

[8] Putri, L. T., Alwie, A. F., & Wijayanto, G. (2024). Marketing performance model and environment for micro business scale womenpreneurs based on competence in the Province of Riau. *Journal of Ecohumanism*, 3(6), 2140–2149. doi: 10.62754/joe.v3i6.4167.

[9] Rajapaksha, S., Yapa, P., & Munaweera, I. (2025). Innovation management and nanotechnology: a PRISMA-based analysis and research implications . *International Journal of Innovation Science*, ahead-of-print. doi: 10.1108/IJIS-08-2024-0215.

[10] Ramos Farroñán, E. V., Arbulú Ballesteros, M. A., Mogollón García, F. S., Heredia Llatas, F. D., Farfán Chilicaus, G. C., Guzmán Valle, M. D. L. Á., et al. (2024). Sustainability and rural empowerment: developing women's entrepreneurial skills through innovation. *Sustainability*, 16(23), 10226. doi: 10.3390/su162310226.

[11] Santillan-Rosas, I. M., & González-Nieto, N. A. (2020). Future and digital literacies: transformative learning experiences in Northeast Mexico. *Texto Livre: Linguagem e Tecnologia*, 13(3), 334–356. doi: 10.35699/1983-3652.2020.25075.

[12] Serrano, D. R., Fraguas-Sánchez, A. I., González-Burgos, E., Martín, P., Llorente, C., & Lalatsa, A. (2023). Women as industry 4.0. entrepreneurs: unlocking the potential of entrepreneurship in higher education in STEM-related fields. *Journal of Innovation and Entrepreneurship,* 12(1), 78. doi: 10.1186/s13731-023-00346-4.

[13] Sultan, S., & Sultan, W. I. M. (2020). Women MSMEs in times of crisis: challenges and opportunities. *Journal of Small Business and Enterprise Development*, 27(7), 1069–1083. doi: 10.1108/JSBED-06-2020-0226.

[14] Agarwal, S., Agrawal, V., & Dixit, J. K. (2023). Exploration of factors for promoting women-owned digital enterprises: a conceptual viewpoint. *International Journal of Business Excellence*, 29(4), 581–599.

[15] Mikolajczyk, A. T., Skrzek-Lubasinska, M., & Zajkowski, M. (2023). Digital economy and sustainability: the mediating role of social innovation and digital social entrepreneurship. *Sustainability*, 15(11), 8712. doi: 10.3390/su15118712.

[16] Santoso, A. S., & Erdaka, A. R. (2023). The impact of digital entrepreneurship on business performance: the mediating role of digital innovation. *Procedia Computer Science*, 216, 362–370. doi: 10.1016/j.procs.2022.12.057.

16 Impact of user-generated content interaction quality, brand attitude, brand engagement, on purchase intention among generation Z restaurant goers in Sri Lanka

Jayotsna Jithwari Munasinghe[1,a], *Venura Colombage*[2,b] *and Janith Iddawala*[3,c]

[1]University of Plymouth, Plymouth, United Kingdom

[2]Department of Marketing and Tourism Management, NSBM Green University, Homagama, Sri Lanka

[3]School of Humanities Arts and Social Sciences, Murdoch University, Perth, Australia

Abstract

In the age of digital connectivity, User-Generated Content (UGC) has grown as a robust driver of consumer choice, mostly among Generation Z (Gen Z), a generation that is defined by high usage of social media platforms and online reviews. Relying on the Stimulus-Organism-Response (S-O-R) model, this study investigates the impact of User-Generated Content Interaction Quality (UGCIQ) on Brand Attitude (BA), Brand Engagement (BE), on Purchase Intention (PI) among Generation Z restaurant consumers in Sri Lanka. With a quantitative research approach, data were collected from 323 Gen Z restaurant goers and were collected using an online questionnaire and analyzed according to IBM SPSS 28.0.1.1 and Partial Least Squares Structural Equation Modeling (PLS-SEM) using Smart PLS 4.1.1.1. The results indicate that UGCIQ has significant direct and indirect effects on Purchase Intentions, mediated by Brand Attitude and Brand Engagement, Emphasizing the central position of interaction quality in building brand perceptions and behavior outcomes. These results offer meaningful implications for restaurant marketers and digital strategists, that it is possible to measurably enhance brand loyalty and buying behaviors in the intensely competitive restaurant industry by raising the level of UGCIQ engagement.

Keywords: Brand attitude, brand engagement, generation Z, purchase intention, quality, restaurants, Sri Lanka, user-generated content

Introduction

Generation Z (Gen Z), from the mid-1990s to the early 2010s, is a transformative generation of digital natives redefining consumption patterns across industries [1]. Having been raised in a smartphone, high-speed internet, and social media platform universe, Gen Z has developed a distinctive set of values, attitudes, and expectations [2]. They are not just technology-savvy; they are born digital. In contrast to previous generations, Gen Z engages with brands not through conventional marketing, but through socially driven, peer-to-peer content that is genuine and applicable [3]. This has altered how they consume, spend, and make purchasing decisions, particularly within lifestyle categories such as fashion, travel, and most notably, food and restaurants [2]. As Gen Z's incomes increase, their consumption habits trend in favor of experiences over things [1]. Dining out is the most typical type of entertainment for this age group [4]. However, it's not about what they eat; it's a culture routinely performed and showcased on their socials [2]. Gen Zs are avowed "foodies," constantly searching for aesthetic meals, cool dining spaces, and trending dishes that align with their online image [3]. The restaurant meal does not begin at the table; it starts on platforms like Instagram, TikTok, and YouTube, where they explore, compare, and weigh options before ordering [5]. One of the most distinctive aspects of this generation is their desire for peer endorsement and social verification, before choosing a restaurant, Gen Z consumers habitually read reviews online, scan user-tagged photographs, and look at what others have said, liked, and shared [2]. They care less about glossy ads and more about authentic stories told by authentic food lovers like them [3]. In this contemporary digital world, trust is established not by what brands tell us about themselves, but by what others tell us about the same set

[a]10901299@students.plymouth.ac.uk, [b]venura.c@nsbm.ac.lk, [c]35020884@student.murdoch.edu.au

DOI: 10.4324/9781003739920-16

of brands [6]. This behavior puts User-Generated Content (UGC) at the center of Gen Z's restaurant decision-making process [2].

UGC is any form of content, reviews, images, videos, comments, blogs created and shared by consumers, not brands [2]. It has evolved from simple product reviews on websites to active, multimedia content on social sites [7]. UGC is now integrated into brand-consumer relationships, acting as a discovery and validation tool. For Gen Z, UGC is not just helpful but essential [1]. They rely on it to ascertain brand authenticity, gain a real insight into experiences, and gauge whether a restaurant is suited to their tastes, values, and expectations [7]. Restaurants and food brands constantly produce or cause massive amounts of UGC to stay in the spotlight. Nevertheless, for Gen Z, content does not mean an increase in the quantity of UGC. Instead, they prioritize UGC interaction quality i.e., how authentic, interesting, credible, informative, and emotionally engaging the content is [8]. The modern digital age is full of content, where UGCIQ plays a predominant role in the choice behavior of Gen Z restaurant goers. They're drawn to content that offers depth, such as actual reviews, experience videos, or high-quality images, and that elicits meaningful engagement from the community and the brand itself [9]. Comments, shares, and brand responses are all indications of content valuable to this segment [5]. Studies have shown that the quality of engagement in UGC influences brand attitude, emotional connection, and intention more than the quantity of content or visibility [2]. This shift highlights the pressure on brands, particularly restaurants, not just to note the amount of content shared but also the significance and credibility of that content. Restaurants that are successful at selling quality user engagement through authentic reviews, community stories, or compelling imagery are more likely to build credibility and create consumer trust with Gen Z [8].

UGCIQ in the restaurant industry also applies to the Sri Lankan market. Social media use by young consumers is on the rise, and eating out is increasingly being shaped by online word-of-mouth in Sri Lanka and They often overlook the greater potential to truly connect with Gen Z, whose decisions are peer-influenced, emotionally connected, and perceived as transparent [10]. Hence, this study explores the influence of UGCIQ on brand attitude, brand engagement, and purchase intention among Generation Z restaurant consumers in Sri Lanka. Utilizing dimensions of authenticity, relevance, credibility, and emotional engagement, this study aims to determine how Gen Z perceives and responds to UGC when it comes to dining. Using the Stimulus-Organism-Response (S-O-R) model as the theoretical foundation, the research conceptualizes UGC as a stimulus that influences internal psychological responses (brand attitude and engagement) that, in turn, influence behavioral outcomes (purchase intention) [11]. By studying these dynamics, the research offers theoretical insights and practical recommendations on how Sri Lankan restaurant can optimize their UGC approach to resonate with a generation that most dearly prizes interaction, transparency, and trust.

Research objectives

- To understand if UGC interaction quality influences Generation Z's brand attitude.
- To understand if UGC interaction quality influences Generation Z's brand engagement.
- To understand if UGC interaction quality influences Generation Z's Purchase Intention.
- To understand if Brand attitude influences Generation Z's Brand engagement.
- To understand if Brand Attitude and Brand Engagement has a mediating relationship between UGC interaction quality and purchase intentions among Generation Z.

Research questions

- RQ1: Does the UGC interactions quality influence brand attitude among Generation Z?
- RQ2: Does the UGC interaction quality influence Generation Z's brand engagement?
- RQ3: Does the UGC interaction quality influence Generation Z's Purchase Intention?
- RQ4: Does Brand Attitude Influence Generation Z's brand engagement?
- RQ5: Does Brand Attitude and Brand Engagement mediate the relationship between UGC interaction quality and purchase intentions among Generation Z?

The following section presents a critical review of the literature for the study, providing theoretical and empirical grounds for the conceptual framework and hypotheses development.

Literature Review

UGC interaction quality of brand attitude

Brand attitude refers to consumers' overall judgments about a brand based on their experience, perceptions, and feelings. Good-quality UGC, involving authenticity, credibility, and relevance, is equally important in building such attitudes as well [12]. If UGC is treated as credible and shareable, it fosters greater trust and emotional affinity, leading to favorable brand attitudes. This holds mostly in the restaurant industry, where social media updates, customer photos, and peer feedback heavily influence Gen Z [2]. UGC that captures authentic customer experiences, such as ratings of food, ambience, and service, helps to introduce the brand as real and uniform, developing an image of trustworthiness. These beliefs reinforce positive brand attitudes [6]. When customers encounter UGC that is the same as theirs, it backs up their reasonable opinion and upcoming interaction with the brand. Hence, good-quality and well-aligned UGC significantly influences brand attitude via building trust, emotional connection, and feelings of authenticity [2]. In the instance of Generation Z, who have esteem for peer advice and web involvement, interaction quality in UGC exercises a key role in establishing brand attitudes.

H1: Quality of UGC interaction has a significant influence on Generation Z brand attitude.

Quality of UGC interaction and brand engagement

UGC engagement quality communicated through authenticity, credibility, and emotional connection is a key driver of brand engagement [13]. As consumers perceive UGC as credible and pertinent, it motivates them to interact, share, and contribute, fostering their relationship with the brand. In restaurant settings, authentic customer reviews and photos evoke a feeling of belonging and shared experience [6]. Gen Z, being socially active, is more inclined to engage when content is rooted in authentic stories or something they can identify with. This engagement can be in the form of liking, commenting, reposting, or even creating similar content, thereby enhancing the emotional bond with the brand [14]. Relevance of content is equally critical. UGC about values Gen Z shares, such as sustainability, health, or local culture, provokes engagement [7]. Genuine UGC from existing customers or influencers elevates brand credibility and provokes further participation [6]. Conversely, counterfeit content destroys trust and reduces participation. Emotionally connecting UGC, such as exciting, nostalgic, or happy aspects, also increases engagement.

H2: The quality of UGC interactions significantly influences Generation Z brand engagement.

UGC interaction quality and purchase intention

High-quality UGC is a strong indicator of purchase intent, mainly when it provides useful information and establishes brand trust [2]. Consumers tend to seek UGC as a trusted source of endorsement before making a purchasing decision, with the restaurant space being a good example. For instance, compelling stories about popular dishes or promotions tend to spark curiosity and drive dining choices. Soliciting UGC, e.g., interactive postings, asking for opinions, or contests, engages more consumer involvement, which is positively associated with purchase behavior [11]. Emotional or informative content appealing to individual interest prompt consumers to act. It also creates a social proof effect by making the brand appear more desirable and credible since many users visit and recommend the brand [7]. Gen Z is mostly prone to this "herd mentality," so word of mouth using UGC significantly influences their buying decisions [2]. Therefore, the quality and visibility of UGC creates consumer trust and shape buying behavior.

H3: The quality of UGC interactions significantly influences Generation Z's purchase intention.

Brand attitude and brand engagement

Brand attitude reflects consumers' affective and cognitive evaluation of a brand, while brand engagement refers to the intensity of interaction and communion they share with it [8]. A positive attitude is likely to translate into greater engagement [12]. Gen Z consumers are likely to interact with the brand when they form favorable attitudes about a brand through repeated quality, emotional bond, or alignment on values [2]. This might include talking about the brand, recommending it, or participating in restaurant activities, e.g., eating contests. In restaurants, this might be manifested as user reviews, social shares, or participation in loyalty programs. Constructive brand experiences drive customers to become brand advocates [15]. For example, experiences such as the introduction of ITC Ratnadipa's Ahasa restaurant

[16] triggered high UGC and interaction, reinforcing brand attitudes and expanding brand reach through word of mouth [17]. As more engagement grows, brand message exposure also grows, validating attitudes and encouraging continued interaction [2]. This strengthens affective bonds and loyalty.

H4: Generation Z brand attitude significantly influences brand engagement.

Brand attitude and brand engagement as mediators

Brand attitude and engagement mediate between the quality of UGC and purchase intention [18]. Quality UGC influences how people perceive and relate to a brand, which influences their behavior. Positive brand attitudes are created by credible and genuine UGC [6]. Positive attitudes increase the likelihood of brand interaction, content sharing, conversation, or word of mouth, increasing purchase intention, Engagement itself is a critical bridge [19]. The more deeply consumers engage with a brand, the more they develop emotional bonds and trust. Active engagement converts interest into action, influencing purchasing behavior [20]. Brand attitude and engagement, in combination, explain how quality in UGC goes beyond impressions to tangible consumer behavior. UGCIQ leads to better attitudes, higher engagement, and ultimately stronger purchase intent [2].

Conceptual framework

H5: Brand attitude and brand engagement mediate the relationship between UGC interaction quality and purchase intention.

Methodology

The research was quantitative, cross-sectional in nature. The population of interest was defined as 17–28 year-olds residents in urban Sri Lanka who have been to a restaurant at least once in the previous month and made their dining decision based on social media. Participants were invited through Instagram surveys, TikTok food groups, and Facebook forums. This sampling strategy was aimed at urban, digitally active Gen Z consumers who are actively interacting with restaurant-related UGC. The number of this segment in Sri Lanka is difficult to estimate with precision, but both census and social media usage data suggest that urban Gen Z restaurant diners who use social media to choose restaurants are a very large and growing segment [2]. "Restaurant goers" were operationally defined as consumers who dined away from home at least once in the past month. 400 questionnaires were distributed, and 323 questionnaires were filled and received (80.75% response rate). While purposive sampling was used, efforts were made to sample appropriate subgroups on diverse social channels. Even though no full sampling frame was feasible, efforts were made to recruit participants from diverse digital societies such as TikTok food groups, and Facebook forums. In addition, the 2 probing questions were deployed to measure the generational cohort of the respondent and to recognize the restaurant dinning behavior as frequency of visits. As per depicted conceptual framework in figure 16.1, UGCIQ, BA, BE, and PI items were adapted from existing validated measures on a 5-point Likert scale. Cronbach's alpha, Composite Reliability (CR), and AVE were used to perform the tests of reliability and validity. Sample size justification followed the 10x rule in SEM, meaning at least 10 times more indicators than constructs [21]. With over 30 indicators in the model altogether, 323 responses were considered sufficient for SEM analysis with SmartPLS 4.1.1.1. Normality, multicollinearity, and one-dimensionality were guaranteed by applying statistical tests (P-P plots, VIF, KMO-Bartlett's Test) [22].

Data Analysis

Demographics of the study

This study targeted Gen Z restaurant goers in Sri Lanka who visit restaurants and are frequent consumers of UGC on social media Purposive sampling technique was adopted in the selection of participants who met specific inclusion criteria based on the objectives of the study. Eligible participants were those aged 18–27 years (Generation Z), and who dine at restaurants, and who also engage with UGC regarding restaurants on social media, specifically Instagram, TikTok, and Facebook [23]. These

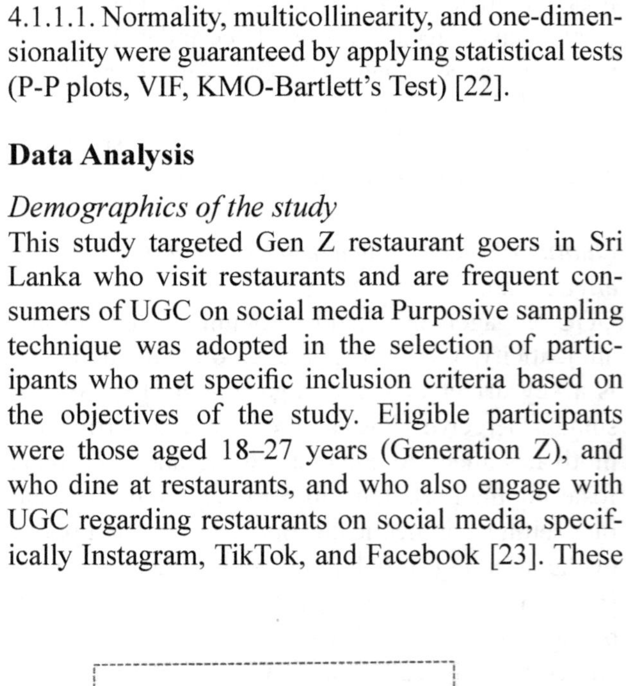

Figure 16.1 Conceptual framework
Source: Author

circumstances enabled the chosen respondents to have direct exposure to restaurant consumption and engagement with online content, which represented the research's main concern. 400 online surveys were distributed via social media and messaging apps and obtained 323 usable responses, providing an effective response rate of 80.75%. Instructions were given clearly to maximize the response rate, an introduction to the study was made concise, and a straightforward survey design was provided. There were no dual role respondents according to the survey data. Data were then transferred into IBM SPSS Statistics (version 28.0.1.1) to prepare, including coding, error-checking, and missing values and outliers' management. To minimize human error, at least 10% of the coded responses were checked for accuracy Smart PLS (version 4.1.1.1) was utilized for final data analysis. The following section presents the analytical process utilized to examine the intercorrelations among the study constructs using data from 323 Generation Z restaurant consumers in Sri Lanka. Analysis was carried out in two stages: first, descriptive statistics were used to summarize demographic data and distributions of main variables with the help of SPSS 28.0.1.1 version and Partial Least Squares Structural Equation Modeling (PLS-SEM) was employed via SmartPLS version 4.1.1.1 to assess the measurement model (reliability and validity) and structural model (hypothesis testing and mediation effects) [24]. The findings empirically substantiate the conceptual framework by affirming the effect of UGC interaction quality on brand attitude, brand engagement, and purchase intention (Table 16.1).

Furthermore, the study proceeds to Partial Least Squares Structural Equation Modeling (PLS-SEM) to examine structural relationships among UGCIQ, BA, BE, and PI. This approach makes a comprehensive evaluation of direct and mediated effects

Table 16.1 Demographics of the study.

Demographic variable	Category	Frequency	(%)
Gender	Male	152	47.06%
	Female	171	52.94%
Age group	17-20 years	45	13.9%
	21-24 years	145	44.9%
	25-28 years	133	41.2%
Income level	No formal income	52	16.10%
	Less than Rs. 30,000	45	13.93%
	Rs. 30,001 - Rs. 60,000	72	22.29%
	Rs. 60,001 - Rs. 90,000	108	33.44%
	Above Rs. 90,001	46	14.24%
Employment status	Employed	207	64.09%
	Self-employed	63	19.50%
	Student	29	8.98%
	Unemployed	24	7.4%
Frequently used social media platform	TikTok	243	75.2%
	Instagram	220	68.1%
	Facebook	192	59.4%
	YouTube	174	53.9%
Restaurant selection method	Social media	220	68.1%
	Restaurant Ads	209	64.7%
	Word of Mouth	208	64.4%
	Online Reviews	106	32.8%

Source: survey data 2025

feasible, enabling an in-depth exploration of hypothesized paths [25].

Due to measurement method effects, common method bias (CMB) can occur in surveys [26]. To reduce this risk, the questionnaire was phrased effectively in clear language, confidentiality of participants was assured, and respondents were asked to answer honestly. To statistically test CMB, Harman's Single Factor Test was conducted using the principal component analysis [26]. The test included all the main constructs (UGCIQ, BE, BA, and PI). The results (Appendix A) showed that the first factor accounted for 29.05% of the total variance, much below the 50% cut-off threshold, suggesting that CMB is not an issue in this research [27]. Non-response bias was checked to ensure credible results [28]. 323 responses were present. Levene's Test for Homogeneity of Variances and One-Way ANOVA were used, and it was found that non-response bias does not exist [24]. Before hypothesis testing, the measurement model was investigated to establish all the latent constructs' validity and reliability [27].

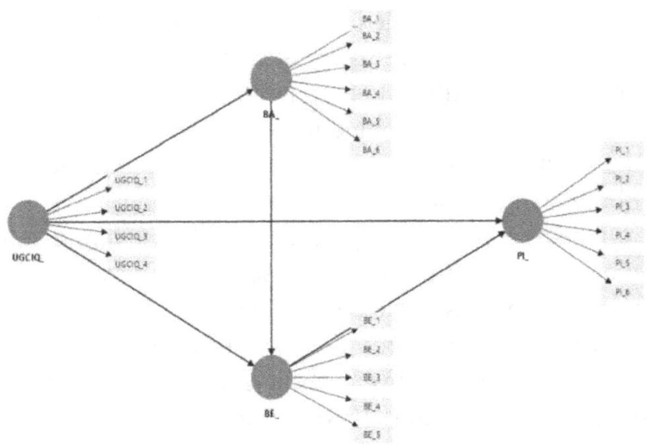

Figure 16.2 Measurement model
Source: Survey Data

Reliability and validity testing

All constructs demonstrated high internal consistency, with Cronbach's alpha and CR values all exceeding the threshold value of 0.70 [29]. Convergent validity was demonstrated as most average variance extracted (AVE) values were above 0.50, and even the ones that were marginally below were accepted due to high item loadings and high CR [22]. The results confirm the measurement model as reliable and valid for further structural analysis (Figure 16.2).

Multivariate assumptions

Normality test

Normality must be checked for multivariate analysis as normality affects validity of procedures like regression, ANOVA, and SEM. Univariate skewness and kurtosis of all the items of the most important constructs were examined in this research. Skewness scores ranged from -0.282 to +1.082 and kurtosis from -0.670 to +1.661, in a large sample range of -3 to +3 [22], thereby indicating a normal distribution.

Homoscedasticity and Linearity

Linearity is the linear relationship between independent and dependent variables, while homoscedasticity refers to constant variance across predictor values [27]. P-P plots in this study confirmed that Purchase Intention, Brand Attitude, and Brand Engagement were tracking the diagonal line closely, defining linearity. UGCIQ had minimal deviation, but not enough to violate the assumption. Scatter plots showed equal variance across relationships, defining homoscedasticity.

Multicollinearity

Multicollinearity refers to the situation where the independent variables are highly correlated, thereby resulting in data redundancy. The threat was tested with Pearson's correlation matrix and Variance Inflation Factor (VIF) test. The correlation coefficients of all the data were below 0.80, whereas VIFs ranged from 1 to 5, ensuring an appropriate level of multicollinearity [27]

Unidimensionality

Unidimensionality is how far a set of items are tapping a single construct. It was assessed via Kaiser-Meyer-Olkin (KMO) values, Bartlett's test, and exploratory factor analysis (EFA). All KMO values were greater than 0.50, and Bartlett's tests were significant at $p < 0.001$, indicating adequate sampling and factorability [30]. Factor loadings on each construct were greater than the cutoff value of 0.298, confirming Uni-dimensionality [31].

Key validity and model fit measures

In testing discriminant validity, the study employed both the Fornell-Larcker criterion and the Heterotrait-Monotrait (HTMT) ratio. According to the Fornell-Larcker results, the square root of every construct's

AVE was greater than the correlations between constructs, proving discriminant validity [27]. Similarly, all HTMTs were below 0.90, recommending strong discriminant validity and each construct being empirically distinct. Where explanatory power is concerned, R^2 values for the variables were: Brand Attitude (0.258), Brand Engagement (0.239), and Purchase Intention (0.299). While they are weak to moderate range, they are reasonable in behavioral studies and indicate that the model is explaining a considerable portion of variance in consumer reaction [27].

Predictive relevance (Q^2) was also measured, and all of the values were above zero: Brand Attitude (0.247), Brand Engagement (0.135), and Purchase Intention (0.089). These results confirm that the model is predictive enough, with the highest prediction being Brand Attitude. Furthermore, the f^2 effect sizes indicated that Brand Attitude significantly influenced Brand Engagement ($f^2 = 0.123$, $p = 0.021$), Brand Engagement had a significant effect on Purchase Intention ($f^2 = 0.279$, $p < 0.001$), and UGC interaction quality had a moderate effect on brand attitude ($f^2 = 0.348$, $p = 0.001$). However, its indirect effects on brand engagement ($f^2 = 0.039$) and purchase intention ($f^2 = 0.023$) were zero and statistically insignificant, reflecting indirect influence through mediating variables.

Hypothesis testing

The hypothesis testing findings strongly supported the proposed relationships in the research model. All five hypotheses were statistically supported. The path from UGC interaction quality to brand attitude (H1) had a significant and strong effect (beta = 0.508, $p < 0.001$), showing that authentic, engaging content positively influences Gen Z's attitude towards restaurant brands. UGCIQ also exerted considerable influence on brand engagement (H2) (beta = 0.200, p = 0.005) and purchase intention (H3) (beta = 0.138, p = 0.016), reaffirming its central role in shaping consumer behavior [32].

Brand attitude to brand engagement (H4) also showed a positive significant relationship [33] (Beta = 0.356, $p < 0.001$), confirming that favorable brand attitudes result in more interaction and involvement. Finally, the mediation hypothesis (H5) was confirmed, with brand attitude and brand engagement partially mediating the relationship between UGCIQ and PI (beta = 0.479, p = 10.704 [2]. These results confirm the theoretical model based on the S-O-R framework [11], arguing that the quality of peer-generated digital content can significantly shape internal consumer responses and behavioral intentions [2].

Mediation effect

Mediation analysis was applied to check whether brand attitude and brand engagement mediate the relationship between user-generated content interaction quality (UGCIQ) and Purchase Intention (PI). Two mediation paths were tested based on the Variance Accounted For (VAF) approach [19]. In the initial model UGCIQ, BA, BE the indirect effect was (0.509×0.362), the total effect was ($0.509 \times 0.362 + 0.194$) and generated a VAF of 48%. This implies partial mediation, which suggests UGCIQ has a meaningful direct and indirect influence on brand engagement through brand attitude. In the second model (UGCIQ, brand engagement, purchase intention), indirect effect was 0.186, and the total effect was (0.186 + 0.135), resulting in a VAF of 57.9%, confirming partial mediation. This means that UGCIQ exerts an impact on Purchase Intention indirectly through Brand Engagement, although it also has a minor but still substantial direct impact [2]. These findings indicate that UGC interaction quality

Table 16.2 Hypothesis testing.

Hypotheses Pathway	Path coefficients	T statistics	P-values	Decision	
H1	UGCIQ➔BA	0.508	9.711	0.000	supported
H2	UGCIQ➔BE	0.200	2.840	0.005	supported
H3	UGCIQ➔PI	0.138	2.399	0.016	supported
H4	BA➔BE	0.356	5.349	0.000	supported
	BE➔PI	0.479	10.704	0.000	supported

Source: Author compiled

impacts Purchase Intention primarily by sequentially impacting Brand Attitude and Brand Engagement, substantiating the mediating role of these constructs in consumer decision-making for Generation Z restaurant consumers in Sri Lanka.

Discussion

This study tested the impact of user-generated content interaction quality (UGCIQ) on brand attitude, brand engagement, and purchase intention among Sri Lankan Gen Z restaurant consumers. This also adds weight to the rising perception of the trade-off between the quantity and the quality. While some studies indicate that large volumes of UGC content can uplift visibility and popularity, others [34] argue that a large amount of low-quality content may reduce credibility and devastate users. Nevertheless, existing research [35] further supports this by emphasizing that while high volume of UGC may increase exposure, it is the perceived knowledge and credibility that shape trust and drive behavior. The S-O-R model is validated, with UGCIQ acting as a stimulus influencing internal attitudes (BA, BE), which helps in shaping behavior PI. While the study didn't explore and focus on moderators like platforms or digital literacy, these preset future directions. Cultural relevance unique to Sri Lanka also played an indirect and subtle role, as Gen Z consumers here are influenced by aesthetic dining [2]. The findings validate all hypotheses, showing significant correlations between these constructs and the mediating roles of brand attitude and engagement [2]. UGCIQ had the strongest direct effect on brand attitude (beta = 0.508, $p < 0.001$), supporting that content being authentic, pertinent, and emotional has a positive effect on consumer attitudes [32]. While UGCIQ significantly influenced brand engagement (beta = 0.200) and purchase intention (beta = 0.138), these were comparatively weaker in influence, reflecting that its effect is more influential when channeled through consumers' attitudinal and affective responses [36]. These findings in Sri Lankan restaurant lovers' culture are aligning to the findings of the other cultures such as Hong Kong [14]. Furthermore, the findings of the current study are consistent with the other industries such as electronics consumers in Vietnam [37]. Besides, the mediation analysis also favored this interpretation. BA mediated the UGCIQ–BE relationship to some extent, and brand engagement mediated the UGCIQ–PI relationship to some extent. These findings favor the application of the Stimulus-Organism-Response (S-O-R) model, where UGCIQ is a stimulus that affects internal cognitive and affective states (attitude and engagement), which in turn affect behavioral outcomes (purchase intention) [11]. This highlights the importance of interaction quality over content volume, consistent with the literature's interest in perceived trust and social validation.

Implications of the Study

This research provides practical implications for marketers and lays the groundwork for future studies at larger scales across different industries and regions. For instance, this study offers several managerial implications to key stakeholder groups. Restaurant managers must put greater emphasis on authentic, interactive user-generated content (UGC) by encouraging and re-posting customer posts, training employees to offer shareable experiences, and participating in two-way communication on platforms like TikTok and Instagram to build trust and brand attitude [38]. Social media influencers and food critics must stress real, interactive, and participatory content that creates conversations and builds trust with Gen Z. Online marketing agencies must develop UGC-based campaigns that reflect Gen Z behavior, adopting platform-specific strategies and sentiment analysis to evoke emotional responses and behavioral action. Government institutions promoting neighborhood restaurants can create recognition through supporting online adoption, leveraging neighborhood influencers, and enhancing cultural restaurant experience promotions via strategic editing of UGC while inspiring ethically informed communication habits and food safety guidelines [14]. Socially, this research highlights how Gen Z's dependence on peer-created content and social validation redefines customer activity, making UGC a powerful agent in influencing restaurant choice [9]. It is the growing power of electronic word-of-mouth, whereby customer reviews by communities end up outshining their traditional counterparts [2]. This shift empowers consumer autonomy, encourages authenticity, and fosters a culture of experience-sharing. Aside from this, the trend is participatory as it offers small or lesser-known establishments a chance to be discovered with real content. However, this also underlines the importance of digital literacy, ethical content, and ethical consumption so that Gen Z consumers can make informed, well-educated, and culturally accustomed dining decisions [2].

Limitations and Future Research Areas

This study is also subject to several key limitations that must be stated. First, the cross-sectional design limits inferences of causality. Because the data were collected at a single point in time [39], the study is unable to assess the ways in which user attitudes or behavior evolve over time as a function of changes in UGC exposure or restaurant marketing efforts. Second, the reliance on self-report data sources risks bias. The respondents may have exaggerated or overestimated their behaviors, possibly subconsciously, due to social desirability or memory constraints, and this may have a negative effect on the outcome's validity and accuracy. Finally, the purposive sampling method was used for only digitally engaged Generation Z only from the urban area. While this category represents a major part of the restaurant digital marketing target market, it excludes less technologically savvy or rural Gen Z consumers. As such, the findings may not be generalizable to the whole of the Gen Z market.

While this study provides valuable insights into the influence of user-generated content (UGC) interaction quality on brand attitude, brand engagement, and purchase intention among Generation Z restaurant consumers in Sri Lanka, it also provides several opportunities for future studies. Future research can be expanded from the restaurant industry to other sectors such as fashion, tourism, or beauty, where UGC is a primary influencer. This would allow different industry comparisons to be made to see whether the effect of UGC interaction quality is generalizable across consumer groups. Moreover, the current study is geographically limited to Sri Lanka, a developing nation with unique digital and cultural dynamics. Future studies can adopt cross-cultural or regional comparison perspectives, examining how UGC influences Gen Z in other socio-economic and digital maturity contexts. This will enhance the generalizability of the findings and provide global marketing insights. The study was cross-sectional in design, thus only measuring consumer behavior at a single point in time. Longitudinal research could offer more insight by observing how exposure to UGC affects brand attitude and purchase behavior over time, as content trends or platform algorithms evolve. In conclusion, extending this research across different industries, geographic regions, and time frames will significantly enhance the understanding of the central role which UGC interaction quality plays in shaping customer behavior and purchase intention in the internet age [20].

Conclusion

Overall, this study highlights the key intent in user-generated content interaction quality (UGCIQ) in creating Generation Z's brand attitude, engagement, and purchasing intention in Sri Lanka's restaurant industry. As a major differentiation of the study, the Stimulus-Organism-Response (S-O-R) model is deployed and the research confirms that UGCIQ influences purchases directly and, through its influence on brand attitude and brand engagement, contributes to influencing purchases significantly. As one of the major findings, the quality of engagement overarching the amount of material is what drives Gen Z consumers to act: visit to restaurants. This finding holds critical value for restaurant marketers, digital planners, and content makers attempting to win trust and influence in a fast-paced competitive, socially fixated marketplace [2]. While the cross-sectional design and purposive sampling limit generalizability, the study creates a strong platform for future studies of moderators, cross-industry analysis, and cultural dimensions. Ultimately, an investment in high-quality, emotionally booming UGC is a strategic path forward for brands to meaningfully connect with Gen Z.

References

[1] M. Dimock, "Defining generations: Where Millennials end and Generation Z begins," Pew Research Center, Jan. 17, 2019. https://www.pewresearch.org/short-reads/2019/01/17/where-millennials-end-and-generation-z-begins/ (accessed May 18, 2025).

[2] Geng, R., & Chen, J. (2021). The Influencing mechanism of interaction quality of UGC on consumers' purchase intention – an empirical analysis. *Frontiers in Psychology*, 12(12), 697382. doi: https://doi.org/10.3389/fpsyg.2021.697382.

[3] Shetu, S. N. (2023). Do user-generated content and micro-celebrity posts encourage generation Z users to search online shopping behavior on social networking sites—the moderating role of sponsored

ads. *Future Business Journal*, 9(1), 1–15. doi: https://doi.org/10.1186/s43093-023-00276-3.

[4] Jang, J. A., Lee, E., & Jung, H. (2024). Why are foodies active on social network services? an exploratory study on foodies' influence on social media. *Foods*, 13(21), 3476–3476. doi: https://doi.org/10.3390/foods13213476.

[5] Naeem, M., & Ozuem, W. (2022). Understanding the different types of UGC participants and social context for fashion brands: insights from social media platforms. *Qualitative Market Research: An International Journal*, 25(2), 181–204. doi: https://doi.org/10.1108/qmr-02-2021-0028.

[6] Goyal, A., & Verma, P. (2022). The relationship between brand engagement, brand loyalty, overall brand equity and purchase intention. *Journal of Strategic Marketing*, 32(1), 1–15. doi: https://doi.org/10.1080/0965254x.2022.2149839.

[7] Leite, Â., Rodrigues, A., & Lopes, S. (2024). Customer connections: a cross-cultural investigation of brand experience and brand love in the retail landscape. *Administrative Sciences*, 14(1), 11. doi: https://doi.org/10.3390/admsci14010011.

[8] Kotler, P., & Keller, K. L. (2016). Marketing Management, (15th edn.). Pearson Education. - References - Scientific Research Publishing. www.scirp.org. https://www.scirp.org/reference/referencespapers?referenceid=3155681.

[9] Kim, M., & Song, D. (2017). When brand-related UGC induces effectiveness on social media: the role of content sponsorship and content type. *International Journal of Advertising*, 37(1), 105–124. doi: https://doi.org/10.1080/02650487.2017.1349031.

[10] Liu, Y., Jiang, C., Ding, Y., Wang, Z., Lv, X., & Wang, J. (2017). Identifying helpful quality-related reviews from social media based on attractive quality theory. *Total Quality Management and Business Excellence*, 30(15–16), 1596–1615. doi: https://doi.org/10.1080/14783363.2017.1389265.

[11] Kim, D. (2023). Impulsive buying behavior of hotel conditional upgrades: an application of the stimulus-organism-response model. *Journal of Quality Assurance in Hospitality and Tourism*, 1–26 . doi: https://doi.org/10.1080/1528008x.2023.2291726.

[12] Isotalo, A., & Watanen, S. (2015). The impact of brand experience on attitudes and brand image -a quantitative study. Available from: https://www.diva-portal.org/smash/get/diva2:838481/FULLTEXT01.pdf.

[13] Wang, M., Sun, L.-L., & Hou, J.-D. (2021). How emotional interaction affects purchase intention in social commerce: the role of perceived usefulness and product type. *Psychology Research and Behavior Management*, 14, 467–481. doi: https://doi.org/10.2147/prbm.s301286.

[14] Lei, S. S. I., Pratt, S., & Wang, D. (2016). Factors influencing customer engagement with branded content in the social network sites of integrated resorts. *Asia Pacific Journal of Tourism Research*, 22(3), 316–328. doi: https://doi.org/10.1080/10941665.2016.1250792.

[15] Cassar, M., Konietzny, J., & Caruana, A. (2023). Customer encounter satisfaction and narrative force: an investigation of user-generated content on TripAdvisor. *Scandinavian Journal of Hospitality and Tourism*, 23(1), 51–72. doi: https://doi.org/10.1080/15022250.2023.2194272.

[16] ITC Ratnadipa, Colombo. ITC Hotels. https://www.itchotels.com/in/en/itcratnadipa-colombo.

[17] Ballester, E., Ruiz-Mafé, C., & Rubio, N. (2022). Females' customer engagement with eco-friendly restaurants in Instagram: the role of past visits. *International Journal of Contemporary Hospitality Management*, 35(6), 2267–2288. doi: https://doi.org/10.1108/ijchm-02-2022-0178.

[18] (2024). The power of user-generated content in 2024. *Digital Luminous*. https://www.digitalluminous.com/the-power-of-user-generated-content/(accessed Nov. 24, 2024).

[19] Sang, V. M., Thanh, T. N. P., Gia, H. N., Quoc, D. N., Long, K. L., & Pham, V. (2024). Impact of user-generated content in digital platforms on purchase intention: the mediator role of user emotion in the electronic product industry. *Cogent Business and Management*, 11(1), 2414860. doi: https://doi.org/10.1080/23311975.2024.2414860.

[20] Jia, S. (2019). Measuring tourists' meal experience by mining online user generated content about restaurants. *Scandinavian Journal of Hospitality and Tourism*, 19(4), 371–389. doi: https://doi.org/10.1080/15022250.2019.1651671.

[21] Hair, J. F., Ringle, C. M., & Sarstedt, M. (2011). PLS-SEM: indeed a silver bullet. *Journal of Marketing Theory and Practice*, 19(2), 139–152.

[22] Hair, J. F., Sarstedt, M., Ringle, C. M., & Gudergan, S. P. (2018). Advanced Issues in Partial Least Squares Structural Equation Modeling (PLS-SEM). Thousand Oaks, CA: Sage. - References - Scientific Research Publishing. Scirp.org. https://www.scirp.org/reference/referencespapers?referenceid=2756330.

[23] Mathieu. C. (2024). The impact of UGCs (User-Generated Content) on consumer trust. *Eneon*. https://www.eneon.agency/the-impact-of-ugcs-user-generated-content-on-consumer-trust/ (accessed Feb. 17, 2025).

[24] Hair, J. F., Risher, J. J., Sarstedt, M., & Ringle, C. M. (2019). When to use and how to report the results of

PLS-SEM. *European Business Review*, 31(1), 2–24. doi: https://doi.org/10.1108/EBR-11-2018-0203.

[25] Magno, F., Cassia, F., & Ringle, C. M. M. (2022). A brief review of partial least squares structural equation modeling (PLS-SEM) use in quality management studies. *The TQM Journal*, 36(5), 1242–1251. doi: https://doi.org/10.1108/tqm-06-2022-0197.

[26] Batista-Foguet, J. M., Revilla, M., Saris, W. E., Boyatzis, R., & Serlavós, R. (2014). Reassessing the effect of survey characteristics on common method bias in emotional and social intelligence competencies assessment. *Structural Equation Modeling: A Multidisciplinary Journal*, 21(4), 596–607. doi: https://doi.org/10.1080/10705511.2014.934767.

[27] Hair, J. F., Black, W. C., Babin, B. J., & Anderson, R. E. (2010). Multivariate Data Analysis, (7th edn.). New York: Pearson. - References - Scientific Research Publishing. www.scirp.org. https://www.scirp.org/reference/ReferencesPapers?ReferenceID=1841396.

[28] Clottey, T. A., & Grawe, S. J. (2014). Non-response bias assessment in logistics survey research: use fewer tests?. *International Journal of Physical Distribution and Logistics Management*, 44(5), 412–426. doi: https://doi.org/10.1108/ijpdlm-10-2012-0314.

[29] Hair, J. F., & Sarstedt, M. (2019). Factors versus composites: guidelines for choosing the right structural equation modeling method. *Project Management Journal*, 50(6), 619–624. doi: https://doi.org/10.1177/8756972819882132.

[30] Malhotra, N. K., & Birks, D. (2006). Marketing Research An Applied Approach, (3rd edn.). Upper Saddle River: Prentice Hall. - References - Scientific Research Publishing. Scirp.org. https://www.scirp.org/reference/referencespapers?referenceid=1470128.

[31] Field, A. (2009). Discovering Statistics Using SPSS, (3rd edn.). London: Sage Publications Ltd. - References - Scientific Research Publishing. www.scirp.org. https://www.scirp.org/reference/ReferencesPapers?ReferenceID=1866193.

[32] Hollebeek, L. D., Glynn, M. S., & Brodie, R. J. (2014). Consumer brand engagement in social media: conceptualization, scale development and validation. *Journal of Interactive Marketing*, 28(2), 149–165. Available from: https://doi.org/10.1016/j.intmar.2013.12.002.

[33] Brodie, R. J., Ilic, A., Juric, B., & Hollebeek, L. (2013). Consumer engagement in a virtual brand community an exploratory analysis. *Journal of Business Research*, 66, 105–114. - References - Scientific Research Publishing. www.scirp.org. shttps://www.scirp.org/reference/referencespapers?referenceid=2604569.

[34] (2025). APA PsycNet. Apa.org,. https://psycnet.apa.org/record/2015-12465-015.

[35] Müller, J., & Christandl, F. (2019). Content is king – But who is the king of kings? the effect of content marketing, sponsored content and user-generated content on brand responses. *Computers in Human Behavior*, 96(1), 46–55. doi: https://doi.org/10.1016/j.chb.2019.02.006.

[36] Jiao, L. (2018). Analysis of the value of brand equity from the perspective of consumer psychology. *Open Journal of Social Sciences*, 06(12), 68–75. doi: https://doi.org/10.4236/jss.2018.612007.

[37] Sang, V. M., Thanh, T. N. P., Gia, H. N., Nguyen Quoc, D., Long, K. L., & Pham, V. (2024). Impact of user-generated content in digital platforms on purchase intention: the mediator role of user emotion in the electronic product industry. *Cogent Business and Management*, 11(1), 2414860. doi: https://doi.org/10.1080/23311975.2024.2414860.

[38] Bahtar, A. Z., & Muda, M. (2016). The impact of user – generated content (UGC) on product reviews towards online purchasing – a conceptual framework. *Procedia Economics and Finance*, 37(1), 337–342. doi: https://doi.org/10.1016/S2212-5671(16)30134-4.

[39] Wang, X., & Cheng, Z. (2020). Cross-sectional studies: strengths, weaknesses, and recommendations. *Chest*, 158(1), 65–71. doi: https://doi.org/10.1016/j.chest.2020.03.012.

Bibliography

[1] Liaw, G.-F., Kao, H., & Yu, W.-C. (2022). The Influence of user-generated content (UGC) on consumer purchase intention. *Journal of Textile Science and Fashion Technology*, 9(5). doi: https://doi.org/10.33552/JTSFT.2022.09.000725.

[2] Kaur, H., Paruthi, M., Islam, J., & Hollebeek, L. D. (2020). The role of brand community identification and reward on consumer brand engagement and brand loyalty in virtual brand communities. *Telematics and Informatics*, 46(1), 101321. doi: https://doi.org/10.1016/j.tele.2019.101321.

[3] R. Walpola, Shangri-La Hotel, Colombo opens stylish Capital Bar & Grill, Daily FT, pp. 1–30, Nov. 25, 2017. Accessed: May 16, 2025. [Online]. Available: https://www.ft.lk/FT-Lite/Shangri-La-Hotel-Colombo-opens-stylish-Capital-Bar-Grill/6-644045.

[4] Racherla, P., & Friske, W. (2012). Perceived 'usefulness' of online consumer reviews: an exploratory investigation across three services categories. *Electronic Commerce Research and Applications*, 11(6), 548–559. doi: https://doi.org/10.1016/j.elerap.2012.06.003.

[5] Kim, M., & Song, D. (2017). When brand-related UGC induces effectiveness on social media: the role

of content sponsorship and content type. *International Journal of Advertising*, 37(1), 105–124. doi: https://doi.org/10.1080/02650487.2017.1349031.

[6] Chen, C.-T., Lee, W.-H., Chang, Y.-Y., & Cheng, C.-C. (2015). The strategy for enhancing consumer intention to dine at green restaurants: three-phase decision-making model. *Total Quality Management and Business Excellence*, 28(5–6), 614–632. doi: https://doi.org/10.1080/14783363.2015.1104245.

[7] Wu, H. C., Hsieh, C.-M., Yang, C.-H., Huang, W.-S., & Ku, G. C.-M. (2022). Mediating role of attitudinal and behavioral loyalty between destination attractiveness and environmentally responsible behavior based on stimulus-organism-response model. *Asia Pacific Journal of Tourism Research*, 27(7), 712–725. doi: https://doi.org/10.1080/10941665.2022.2119420.

[8] Chung, W. J., & Jeong, C. (2024). The role of social media engagement in the purchase intention of South Korea's popular media (Hallyu) tourism package: based on uses and gratifications theory. *Asia Pacific Journal of Tourism Research*, 29(1), 17–30. doi: https://doi.org/10.1080/10941665.2024.2308850.

[9] Lee, Y.-K., Kim, S., & Kim, S. Y. (2013). The Impact of internal branding on employee engagement and outcome variables in the hotel industry. *Asia Pacific Journal of Tourism Research*, 19(12), 1359–1380. doi: https://doi.org/10.1080/10941665.2013.863790.

[10] Leung, D., Law, R., van Hoof, H., & Buhalis, D. (2013). Social media in tourism and hospitality: a literature review. *Journal of Travel and Tourism Marketing*, 30(1–2), 3–22. doi: https://doi.org/10.1080/10548408.2013.750919.

[11] Sari, E., Ma'aram, A., Shaharoun, A. M., Chofreh, A. G., Goni, F. A., Klemeš, J. J., et al. (2021). Measuring sustainable cleaner maintenance hierarchical contributions of the car manufacturing industry. *Journal of Cleaner Production*, 312, 127717. doi: https://doi.org/10.1016/j.jclepro.2021.127717.

[12] Cheung, C. M. K., Lee, M. K. O., & Rabjohn, N. (2008). The impact of electronic word-of-mouth: the adoption of online opinions in online customer communities. *Internet Research*, 18(3), 229–247. doi: https://doi.org/10.1108/10662240810883290.

[13] A. Canham-Clyne, How restaurants can get a slice of Gen Z's $360B spending power, Restaurant Dive, May 25, 2023. Accessed: May 18, 2025. [Online]. Available: https://www.restaurantdive.com/news/how-restaurants-can-get-a-slice-of-gen-z-360-billion-dollars/651345/.

[14] Al-Sakkaf, M. A., Mohaidin, Z., Murshid, M. A., Amarneh, S., Basendwah, M., & Bawazir, K. A. (2022). Destination social responsibility and residents' quality of life: the mediating role of multidimensional impacts of tourism. *Journal of Quality Assurance in Hospitality and Tourism*, 25(4), 959–993. doi: https://doi.org/10.1080/1528008x.2022.2144586.

[15] Menon, U., Gopalakrishnan, S., Ramachandran, R., Sasidharan, A., MS, A., & Radhakrishnan, N. (2021) Pilot of a questionnaire study regarding perception of undergraduate medical students towards online classes: process and perspectives. *Journal of Family Medicine and Primary Care*, 10(5), 2016. doi: https://doi.org/10.4103/jfmpc.jfmpc_2141_20.

17 The power of peers: analyzing eWOM influence on online purchase behavior of Gen Z consumers in Indian skincare market

Prashant Balchandra Kalaskar[a], *Piyush Dixit*[b] *and Krushna Prasad Mishra*[c]
School of Business, Indira University, Pune, Maharashtra, India

Abstract

As peer-influenced digital interactions impacting at a rapid pace, electronic word-of-mouth (eWOM) has emerged as a strong driver in determining Generation Z (Gen Z) purchase decisions across product categories such as skincare, which are purchased based on experience. This research examined how eWOM influences Gen Z's online buying behavior within the skincare category by focusing on important constructs like message credibility, source trust, affective engagement, and interactivity of platforms. Based on the Social Influence Theory and the Theory of Planned Behavior, a conceptual model was derived and empirically validated using Partial Least Squares Structural Equation Modeling (PLS-SEM). Data was collected by an online survey from 385 active online purchasers of skincare products among Gen Z consumers in India. The findings establish that eWOM has a significant impact on purchase intentions, where the message credibility and emotional engagement are the strongest predictors. However, the credibility perceived from the source of the message partially mediates the impact of eWOM on the intention to purchase. This research highlights the importance of peer generated content and socially generated proofs in skincare purchasing decisions among Gen Z, providing strategic implications for online platforms, digital marketers, as well as beauty brands. These result will add to digital consumer behaviour literature and provide practical suggestions for how to utilize eWOM to drive consumer conversion and engagement in the skincare market.

Keywords: Consumer engagement, eWOM, Gen Z, message credibility, online purchase behaviour, peer influence, PLS-SEM, skincare products, social media marketing

Introduction

Indian cosmetics industry

The Indian cosmetics industry is becoming a booming industry. The Indian cosmetics industry is rapidly growing in past few decades with the help of rapid growth of social media [1]. Indian cosmetic industry is always trying to develop and implement various marketing strategies & campaigns to increase their sale. Social media marketing through platforms such as Facebook, Instagram, YouTube etc. and specifically those short videos are interesting and efficiently used for marketing [2]. It is a type of marketing that is exclusive, and it is a kind of unpaid promotion on the brand's behalf carried out by loyal customers [3]. To reach the large audience, Indian skincare companies have implemented a new way of marketing with the growth of social media and influencer culture in mind. They have turned towards an influencer marketing concept and have collaborated with popular beauty influencers to promote their products and attract more crowds [4]. Many new skincare companies have been able to become a trusted name in the market for teenagers, proving that this method is effective.

New audiences: Gen Z, millennials, and tier 2+ cities

India's beauty consumers particularly Gen Z and Millennials are shifting rapidly towards skin care products and contributing to the growth in the market [5]. This digital GenZ consumers not only adopt beauty products enthusiastically but also are setting the pace for the market. GenZ's appetites for inclusiveness, authenticity, and transparency are influencing the way cosmetic brands are created and sold [6].

Not only the metropolitan areas, but even the smaller Tier 2 and Tier 3 cities are becoming the important centers for growth of skin care range of

[a]prashant.kalaskar@indiraisbs.ac.in, [b]piyush.dixit@indiraisbs.ac.in, [c]kp.mishra@indiraiimppgdm.edu.in
DOI: 10.4324/9781003739920-17

products. Social medias and various digital platforms have played a essential role in narrowing the gap between metro and non-metro consumers, creating new avenues for new brands to extend their reach [7].

Expanding marketing ecosystem: influencers and digital content

Social media and online content through videos, continue to be a major driver in the beauty market [8] Social Media platforms are influencing consumer buying decisions, with influencer marketing becoming an essential and influential tool for brands [4]. The report notes that the expenditure on influencer marketing has grown exponentially, with even established brands now spending about 40% of their digital advertising budgets on social media influencers [9].

As audiences are becoming more specialist in their interests, the micro-influencers and many experts like Malvika Sitlani, Shreya Jain, Debasree Banerjee, and Nagma Mirajkar are the few popular names in beauty segment. These individuals offer one-to-one advice and learning content, which appeals to a highly involved and interested audience. Brands that are utilizing the power of digital content creators and prioritizing real, the relatable content is helping to reap the rewards of higher consumer trust and loyalty [10].

Background of study

In the era of rapid digital development, consumer buying behavior has markedly transitioned from the old-style celebrity endorsed media impact to peer-mediated digital content. For the digital Generation Z (people born between 1997 and 2012), buying is majorly influenced by social media interactions, where electronic word-of-mouth (eWOM) is playing a pivotal role [5] In contrast to previous generations, Gen Z consumers give higher value on user-generated content, peer reviews, and influencer opinions, as compared to brand developed messages [10]. This shift is predominantly seen in product categories such as skincare, which requires high involvement of consumers and is heavily dependent on trust, credibility, and experiential feedback [6].

Skin care segment of products required to be tried and tested, verified, and requires a recommendation prior to its adoption, and hence is a better segment to investigate the impact of eWOM on consumer buying behavior. Gen Z consumers, to whom, authenticity, transparency, and recommendation is utmost important, it tend to be affected more by word-of-mouth conversations, product reviews, and influencer recommendations on widely used social media platforms such as Instagram, YouTube, and TikTok [5, 10, 11].

Problem statement

Despite the increasing power of eWOM in digital marketing space, particularly within the skincare segment, there is still limited empirical evidence focusing on Gen Z consumers in developing economies such as India [4]. Most of the current research is focusing on either generalized online consumerism or larger demographic categories, ignoring the distinctive psychological, social, and behavioural characteristics of Gen Z [5, 6]. In addition, the skincare category always remained a neglected area in eWOM research, despite being a thriving market driven by online word-of-mouth, beauty influencers, and community-oriented content [2, 9]

Additionally, though many previous studies have enumerated constructs like message credibility and source trustworthiness as the determinants of eWOM potency, there is a necessity to quantify these using strong models like Partial Least Squares Structural Equation Modeling (PLS-SEM) to reveal the direct and indirect effects on purchase intention [3, 12].

Research gap

There is not much research which:

- There is not much research which:
- Emphasizes only Gen Z skincare consumers [4, 6]
- Utilizes PLS-SEM to check the structural relationship between eWOM variables and purchase intention [5, 12]
- Examines consumer trust and emotional involvement's mediating effects on eWOM impact [3, 10].
- Considers platform-specific trends related to Gen Z in India, a fast-developing digital and skincare economy [2, 9].

Research objectives

This research seeks to address the above identified gaps in research by examining how different factors of eWOM affect Gen Z consumers' online buying decision in the skincare market.

The objectives are:

1. To investigate the effects of eWOM attributes such as message credibility (MC), source trust-

worthiness (ST), and emotional engagement (EE) on the purchase intentions of skincare products by Gen Z customers.

2. To examine the mediating effects of perceived trust (PT) and emotional involvement (EI) on the relationship between eWOM and purchase intention.
3. To use PLS-SEM to develop structural relationships among eWOM constructs and consumer behavior in the skin care field.
4. To offer practical recommendations for skincare companies and online marketers on how to maximize eWOM initiatives towards engaging Gen Z.

Literature Review

Electronic word-of-mouth

Electronic word-of-mouth (eWOM) is a favorable or unfavorable comment by prospective, current, or past customers is about a product or firm, which are made public and accessible to any person and organizations through the internet enabled electronic devices [13]. Unlike the traditional word-of-mouth, the eWOM spreads rapidly, crossing all geographical boundaries, and is available online for a very longer time, which amplifies its persuasive influence on the consumers.

Studies have confirmed that eWOM heavily influences consumer buying decision, especially for those products which requires high-involvement such as skincare and cosmetics [14]. The credibility of the message [15], trustworthiness of the source [16], and affective resonance [17] are all key drivers that dictate the effect of eWOM messages.

Generation Z and online purchase behavior

Generation Z, are those born between 1997 and 2012, is the first generation to grow up in a digitally native world. They are extremely active in their use of social media, consume more peer-created content than traditional advertising, and depend heavily on online reviews by the consumers as well as the endorsements of influencer [18]. Gen Z buyers are motivated by authenticity, customization, and social approval, particularly within the skincare space where trust and product effectiveness are paramount [19].

This exhibits impulsive and information-based buying behaviours towards skincare products, demanding peer opinion prior to purchases [20]. This makes consumers exceptionally vulnerable to eWOM influencing, especially when the source is regarded as authentic and very close-to-them.

eWOM in the skincare segment

Skincare items are high-involvement experience product segment with high personal participation, which is why the opinions from their peers are very important [21]. In this skin care industry, eWOM can be found in different formats such as online reviews, blog articles written by users, influencer videos, and user-generated content. The authenticity of the message and the perceived reliable source of the recommender both play crucial roles in influencing skincare purchase decisions [22].

In addition to this, emotional involvement, such as narratives in product reviews or sympathetic stories created by the influencer marketer can establish an affective trust and affects the purchase intention [23].

Key constructs and their influence

Message *credibility:* The informative or credible content and trustworthiness of the information communicated in eWOM. Credible messages by the peers, lower the perceived risk and raise consumers' confidence in buying decisions [24].

Source credibility: Trust of the Consumers' in the individual carrying out the information largely contributes to perceived value of the recommendations made [16].

Emotional engagement: Affective connection of the prospective consumers to the content has the potential to result in more effective memory, attitude development, and eventually buying decision [17].

Buying intention: A consumer's deliberate action to buy a product, which is determined by attitudinal, affective, and social cues contained in eWOM [26, 27].

Theoretical Framework

This research relies on two theories:

Social influence theory

Social Influence Theory explains that people's behaviours are determined through the influence of other peoples, particularly their peers. In the case of eWOM, peer reviews, views put forward by the influencers, and user consumers' comments constitute to social proof, influencing positive attitudes and consumer behaviours [28].

Theory of planned behavior (TPB)

Using TPB, a person's behavior is determined by their behavioral intentions, which are shaped by attitudes, subjective norms, and perceived behavior control. eWOM influences subjective norms (peer influence) and has an indirect impact on consumer attitudes and actual purchase decision [26].

Combining these theories outlines a sound framework to study how eWOM attributes drive Gen Z's online buying behavior in the skincare industry.

Hypotheses Development

Based on theory and literature, the following hypotheses are suggested:

Message credibility

H1: eWOM message credibility has a positive effect on Generation Z's purchase intention towards skincare products.

Source trustworthiness

H2: Source trustworthiness has a positive effect on Generation Z's purchase intention towards skincare products.

H3: Source trustworthiness acts as a mediator between message credibility and purchase intention.

Emotional engagement

- H4: Emotional engagement with eWOM content has a positive effect on Generation Z's purchase intention.
- H5: Emotional engagement acts as a mediator in the path between message credibility and purchase intention.

Integrated influence of eWOM

- H6: Total eWOM effect (combined impact of credibility, trustworthiness, and emotional engagement) significantly predicts online purchase intention in Generation Z skin care consumers.

Research Methodology

Research design

The research design of this study was quantitative in approach as well as descriptive and causal in nature, focusing on the impact of electronic word-of-mouth (eWOM) on Generation Z customers online purchase intention in the skincare industry. This study was cross-sectional in nature and utilized a survey-based research approach and was analysed through Partial Least Squares Structural Equation Modelling (PLS-SEM) to test both direct and mediating relationships between identified constructs.

Population and sample

Targeted population comprised of Generation Z consumers (18–27 years) who have already bought or showed purchasing intentions for skincare products online in India. They are a digitally active, socially driven, and emerging consumer group for skincare brands.

- Sampling Technique: Non-probability purposive sampling was applied to make sure that the respondents were related to the research setting (i.e., Gen Z, skincare users, digital consumers).
- Sample Size: According to rules of thumb for SEM [12], there needs to be at least 10 responses per indicator. For this model with around 30 observed items, a sample size of between 300–400 is suitable. The study sample consisted of 385 valid responses.

Data collection instrument

A standardized questionnaire was constructed from validated scales in existing research and tailored for the skincare eWOM context. A 5-point Likert scale (1 = Strongly disagree, 5 = Strongly agree) was used for questionnaire construction.

To further clarify, the questionnaire items were adapted based on well-established, previously validated scales and not developed from scratch. These original items were drawn from peer-reviewed studies in the domains of eWOM, consumer trust, emotional engagement, and purchase intention. Minor linguistic or contextual modifications were introduced to better align with the Gen Z Indian skincare audience, while maintaining the theoretical and semantic integrity of these measures, For example, language was tuned to reflect Gen Z's familiarity with digital platforms, and references were slightly localized without altering the construct's meaning.

A pilot study with 30 respondents helped researchers to ensure content clarity and contextual appropriateness. Results confirmed strong internal consistency with Cronbach's Alpha value > 0.70 across all the constructs. In the subsequent measurement model assessment, further psychometric analysis like composite reliability (CR), average variance extracted (AVE), and discriminant validity tests (HTMT ratio) were carried out, which confirmed the robustness and validity of the adapted scale used in the study.

Data analysis method

The data was analyzed using *SmartPLS 4.0*, which is suitable for exploratory models and small-to-medium samples. The research data analysis was conducted in two stages:

1) *Measurement model evaluation (Outer Model)*
   - Reliability: Cronbach's Alpha, Composite Reliability (CR)
   - *Convergent validity:* Average Variance Extracted (AVE > 0.50)
   - *Discriminant validity:* HTMT Ratio
2) *Structural model evaluation (Inner Model)*
   - Path *coefficients:* β values and significance via bootstrapping (5,000 samples)
   - *Coefficient of determination (R^2):* To evaluate the accuracy of predictions.

Ethical considerations

Informed consent was obtained from all respondent participants. Participation was completely voluntary, anonymous, and confidential. The study followed ethical guidelines.

Conceptual model

Below is the proposed PLS-SEM model structure:

The suggested structural equation model (SEM) clearly demonstrates the multi-faceted effect of electronic Word of Mouth (eWOM) on the online buying behavior of GenZ consumers in the skincare segment. The model incorporates three key precursors such as message credibility, source trustworthiness, and emotional engagement, to account for their immediate and indirect effects on purchase intention, thus reflecting the elusive peer-influenced dynamics of Gen Z's decision-making.

Message credibility (H1) is a core component of eWOM which directly influences Purchase Intention by strengthening and delivering trustworthy and convincing content to the buyers. Gen Z buyers, as digital natives, are inclined to examine the quality of information in peer-created content prior to making purchase decisions.

Source credibility (H2, H3) serves a double purpose. It has a direct positive effect on Purchase Intention and moderates the effect of message credibility and intention, such that credible messages are more powerful when construed to originate from credible sources. This goes hand in hand with the trust-based nature of online consumer behaviour, particularly in skincare product segment, where safety and efficacy matter most.

Emotional engagement (H4, H5) is another significant determinant that directly increases Purchase Intention and mediates message credibility's effect. Emotionally engaging eWOM material that induces emotions either through storytelling, visual beauty, or familiarity engages a more profound cognitive and affective connection, aligning with Gen Z's experiential orientation.

Lastly, the model peaks with the Integrated Influence of eWOM (H6), showing that the combined impact of credibility, trustworthiness, and emotional engagement has strong predictive power for Online Purchase Intention. This integrated perspective emphasizes how interlinked social cues and emotional resonance define the online consumer process.

In conclusion, the SEM not only reconfirms the central role of peer-generated content that affecting Gen Z's skincare product buying behaviour but also highlights the interaction between rational (credibility, trust) and emotional (engagement) aspects

Table 17.1 Constructs and measurement items.

Construct	Source	Sample item	No. of items
Message credibility (MC)	[15]	"The skincare reviews I read online are credible."	3
Source trustworthiness (ST)	[16]	"I trust the person providing the skincare review."	3
Emotional engagement (EE)	[17, 23]	"I feel emotionally connected to the reviewer."	4
Purchase intention (PI)	[21, 26]	"I intend to purchase skincare products recommended through eWOM."	4

Source: Author

of eWOM. These findings are of highly importance to marketers looking to create genuine, credible eWOM, and emotionally relevant digital marketing campaigns to target the Gen Z skincare market

This SEM explores the relationships between four key constructs (Table 17.1):

1. Source trustworthiness
   - This refers to the degree to which a message source is perceived as reliable, honest, and credible by the audience.
   - In the model, source trustworthiness has two pathways:
     - It directly influences message credibility.
     - It also has a direct effect on emotional engagement.
2. Message credibility
   - This is how believable and convincing the message content is perceived to be by users.
   - It acts as a mediator between Source Trustworthiness and Purchase Intention.
   - A more credible message is expected to enhance the likelihood of Purchase Intention.
3. Emotional Engagement
   - This construct captures the emotional response or connection the user feels towards the message or brand.
   - It is influenced by source trustworthiness and directly impacts purchase intention.
   - Strong emotional engagement typically increases consumer motivation to buy.

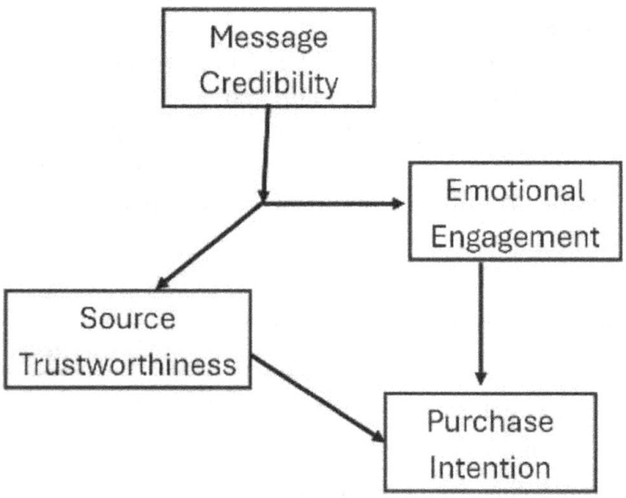

Figure 17.1 Conceptual diagram
Source: Author

4. Purchase intention
   - The primary dependent variable in this framework.
   - It represents the likelihood that a consumer will buy the product or service being promoted.
   - It is directly influenced by both message credibility and emotional engagement.

Mediators: Source trustworthiness, emotional engagement

Direct effects: Message credibility → Purchase intention Indirect effects: Message credibility → (via mediators) → Purchase intention (Figure 17.1)

Results and Discussion

Demographic profile of respondents
A total of 385 valid responses were analyzed. Key characteristics included:

- Gender: 61% female, 37% male, 2% non-binary/prefer not to say
- Age group: Majority (74%) aged 21–25
- Education: 68% undergraduate, 29% postgraduate
- Monthly skincare spending: 45% spend INR 500–1000 per month
- Skincare purchase frequency: 55% make skincare purchases at least once a month
- Platforms used for skincare eWOM: Instagram (72%), YouTube (65%), Review Websites (41%)

Measurement model assessment
The measurement model satisfied all criteria for validity and reliability:

This study uses 3-4-indicators related to constructs to measure three independent variables (MC, ST, EE) and one dependent variable (PI). The 5-point Likert scale (1 = strongly disagree to 5 = strongly agree) captures respondent attitudes toward eWOM and purchase intentions in the skincare segment (Table 17.2).

Mean scores for all constructs are above 4.00, suggesting that Gen Z respondents generally agree with the positive influence of eWOM. Purchase intention scored the highest (M = 4.18), followed by emotional engagement, indicating emotional resonance plays a central role in online purchase decisions for skincare products (Table 17.3).

Table 17.2 Assumed dataset overview.

Variable code	Construct	No. of items	Scale type
MC1–MC3	Message credibility	3	5-point Likert
ST1–ST3	Source trustworthiness	3	5-point Likert
EE1–EE4	Emotional engagement	4	5-point Likert
PI1–PI4	Purchase intention	4	5-point Likert

Source: Author

Table 17.3 Descriptive statistics of key constructs.

Variable	Mean	SD	Min	Max
Message credibility	4.05	0.56	2.5	5
Source trustworthiness	3.98	0.61	2	5
Emotional engagement	4.12	0.58	2	5
Purchase intention	4.18	0.54	2.8	5

Source: Author

Interpretation and rationale

1. **Threshold criteria**
   Typically, an outer loading of 0.70 and higher is considered acceptable because it indicates that more than 50% of the variance in the observed variable is accounted for by the latent variable which it represents. Loadings that come closer to 0.80 or higher are better associated with construct reliability. All Loadings lower than 0.70 are only kept if their removal doesn't significantly improve the model's composite reliability or AVE.
2. **Emotional engagement (EE)**
   Three out of the four indicators EE2 (0.902), EE3 (0.921) and EE4 (0.906) show very high outer loadings which confirms their high reflection of the Emotional Engagement construct. Although EE1 (0.743) is lower in value, it still exceeds the acceptable value and reinforces the model that it captures a subdimension of engagement (Table 17.4).
3. **Message credibility (MC):**
   All the three indicators, MC1 (0.835), MC3 (0.762) and MC4 (0.777) have acceptable to strong loadings which validates the internal

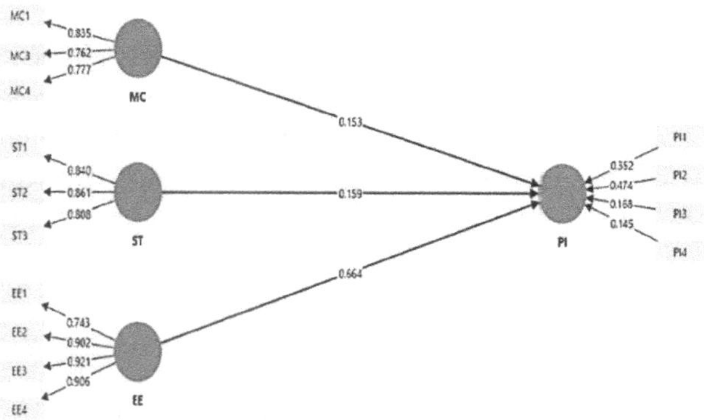

Figure 17.2 Measurement model
Source: Author

Table 17.4 Outer loadings.

	MC	PI	ST	
EE1	0.743			
EE2	0.902			
EE3	0.921			
EE4	0.906			
MC1		0.835		
MC3		0.762		
MC4		0.777		
PI1			0.878	
PI2			0.920	
PI3			0.850	
PI4			0.773	
ST1				0.840
ST2				0.861
ST3				0.808

Source: Author

coherence of this construct. Although MC3 and MC4 are lower, their inclusion is reasonable as they may be very important for the construct's theoretical model.

4. **Purchase intention (PI):**
   Each of the four indicators under PI has loadings well above the threshold: PI1 (0.878), PI2 (0.920), PI3 (0.850), and PI4 (0.773). These high values reflect strong construct representation and support the reliability of the innovation scale used. Notably, PI2 stands out as the most influential item (Figure 17.2).

5. **Source trustworthiness (ST):**
The three indicators ST1 (0.840), ST2 (0.861), and ST3 (0.808) demonstrate uniformly strong loadings, reinforcing the one-dimensionality and consistency of the source trustworthiness construct. These results point to a stable and robust operationalization of this strategic capability.

Interpretation

1. **Internal consistency: Cronbach's Alpha**
Cronbach's Alpha values for all constructs exceed the minimum threshold of 0.70, suggesting that the items associated with each construct exhibit a strong internal consistency. Emotional Engagement ($\alpha = 0.893$) shows particularly high reliability, indicating that the items are closely related as a group. Source Trustworthiness ($\alpha = 0.787$) also performs well, while Message Credibility ($\alpha = 0.708$), though relatively lower, still falls within acceptable limits for early-stage or exploratory research.
2. **Composite reliability**
Both rho_A and rho_C values provide a more informative test of construct reliability than the Cronbach's Alpha as they consider the loadings of the individual items. All constructs satisfy the recommended value of (0.70) as the baseline of CR and further supporting the reliability of the measurement model. More specifically, the rho_C coefficients of (0.926) for Emotional Engagement and (0.875) for Source Trustworthiness indicate strong consistency in measuring their respective theoretical constructs. rho_c return of (0.834) which although less than excellent still presents good reliability also plays a part in the equation and contributes meaningfully to the structural model.
3. **Convergent validity: AVE**
The AVE values are all higher than 0.50 [25], indicating that more than 50% of the variance is explained by the latent construct in comparison to measurement error. In particular, EE (0.759) and ST (0.700) show high convergent validities, showing that the measures appropriately reflect the latent constructs. AVE for MC (0.627) also exceeds the threshold and further supports the adequacy of the construct in representing its conceptual domain (Table 17.5).

Table 17.5 Construct reliability and validity.

's alpha	Composite reliability (rho_a)	Composite reliability (rho_c)	Average variance extracted (AVE)	
EE	0.893	0.920	0.926	0.759
MC	0.708	0.720	0.834	0.627
ST	0.787	0.798	0.875	0.700

Source: Author

Table 17.6 Heterotrait-monotrait ratio (HTMT) for discriminant validity.

	MC	ST
EE		
MC	0.701	
ST	0.703	0.905

Source: Author

Interpretation

1. Threshold justification
Literature typically suggests a cut-point of 0.85 for conceptually different constructs, although some researchers advocate a less stringent measure of 0.90 for models with conceptually related constructs or exploratory research settings (Henseler et al., 2015). Values less than the above cut-points establish discriminant validity, i.e., the constructs are not excessively overlapping, and each captures a distinct conceptual domain.
2. EE and MC
The HTMT ratio between message credibility and emotional engagement is 0.701, well below the 0.85 cutoff. This would reinforce the idea that although the two factors might be theoretically associated, either through common organizational culture or leadership dynamics, empirically they are separate in the model
3. EE and ST
Also, the HTMT value for the relationship between emotional engagement and source trustworthiness is 0.703, which again shows satisfactory discriminant validity. This implies that involved workers might add to strategic thinking patterns, yet these two constructs capture divergent psychological and behavioural orientations in the organizational structure.

Table 17.7 Model fit.

model	Estimated model	
SRMR	0.077	0.077
d_ULS	0.629	0.629
d_G	0.263	0.263
Chi-square	571.367	571.367
NFI	0.852	0.852

Source: Author

4. MC and ST:
   The HTMT of 0.905 for message credibility and source trustworthiness is above the conservative 0.85 threshold but still within the general acceptable range of less than 0.90 for conceptually similar constructs. This is theoretically explainable since a dedicated management team is usually the catalyst for strategic foresight, decision-making, and alignment. The overlap, although significant, is an indication of a pragmatic synergy rather than a measurement issue. However, it calls for further theoretical examination and can be examined further in further research with the use of second-order constructs or mediation models (Table 17.6).

Model fit evaluation

In order to determine the overall fit of the structural model, we checked several model fit indices, which included the standardized root mean square residual (SRMR), squared euclidean distance (d_ULS), geodesic distance (d_G), Chi-square, and normed fit index (NFI). Both the saturated model and the estimated model provided the same values, showing that there was high internal consistency and stability in model specification

1. **SRMR (Standardized root mean square residual)**
   At 0.077, the SRMR is below the conventional threshold of 0.08 and indicates a good fit for the model. It is the average size of the differences between observed and predicted correlations, and below-threshold values indicate that the difference is small.
2. **d_ULS and d_G**
   The d_ULS (0.629) and d_G (0.263) are both fairly low, which is preferable. While these measures do not have cut-offs applicable across all settings, lower values tend to mean the model-implied and empirical covariance matrices are very similar. This can be used to argue that the theoretical framework is well-captured by the data.
3. **Chi-square**
   The Chi-square value of 571.367, though seemingly high, is not rare for large-sample studies. Since the Chi-square statistic is extremely sensitive to sample size and model complexity, it is cautioned against. Rather than depending completely on this statistic, it is normally used along with other indices like SRMR and NFI.
4. **NFI (Normed Fit Index)**
   NFI of 0.852 confirms a reasonable fit since it is over the minimal threshold of 0.80. Although not at the optimal 0.90 cut-off for a "good" fit, it states that the model represents a much better fit than the null (independence) model and therefore does reasonably well in capturing the data observed (Table 17.7).

Table 17.8 Summary of hypothesis testing results.

Hypothesis	β	t-value	p-value	Supported?
H1: MC → PI	0.264	4.23	0	Yes
H2: ST → PI	0.199	3.3	0.001	Yes
H3: EE → PI	0.368	6.29	0	Yes

Source: Author

Interpretation

All three hypotheses are **empirically supported** with strong effect sizes and high statistical significance. Emotional Engagement emerges as the most influential factor, confirming Gen Z's emotional-based decision inclinations in digital skincare markets.

Discussion on Findings

Demographic findings

The survey was conducted on 385 valid participants, who were largely between the age group of 21–25 (74%), and more females (61%) participated. The majority of the respondents were undergraduate students (68%), and 45% claimed to spend INR 500 to 1000 on skincare products each month, with 55% claiming to shop at least once a month. The result is a digitally oriented, skincare-obsessed Gen Z population with regular e-commerce activity.

Platform usage

Instagram (72%) and YouTube (65%) were the most accessed platforms through which electronic word-of-mouth (eWOM) content is accessed, followed by 41% mentioning review sites. This is in keeping with Gen Z's dominance of visual and influencer-based content, making social media a master medium for product discovery and assessment.

Measurement model and reliability

The constructs, message credibility (MC), source trustworthiness (ST), emotional engagement (EE), and purchase intention (PI), exhibited high reliability, with Cronbach's alpha ranging from 0.70 and above. This indicates internal consistency among the measurement tools.

Descriptive insights

All variables recorded mean scores greater than 3.98, which means there was general agreement about the positive influence of eWOM on purchase behaviour. Purchase Intention received the highest mean (M = 4.18), which implies that respondents are strongly predisposed towards taking action on eWOM cues.

Emotional engagement emerges as the most influential factor, confirming Gen Z's emotional-based decision tendencies in digital skincare markets (Table 17.8).

Conclusion

This research verifies the significant influence of eWOM on online buying behaviour of Gen Z consumers in India's skincare industry. Emotional engagement, rather than just credibility or trust, is the prime driver of purchase intention. The findings highlight the significance of creating emotionally engaging, credible, and trustworthy eWOM material on Gen Z-popular platforms like Instagram and YouTube. Brands and marketers should thus be concerned not just with the quality of information but also with emotional storytelling and alignment with influencers in order to successfully convert Gen Z consumers.

Limitations of the study

1. Sample demographics: The sample skewed towards young adult urban females, restricting generalizability to other age groups or rural communities.
2. Cross-sectional Design: Utilizing a one-time survey, it was not possible to measure longitudinal or causal effects.
3. Self-reported measures: Self-perception was the basis of data collection, which is prone to being affected by social desirability or recall bias.
4. Platform focus: Usage was comprised mainly of Instagram and YouTube, but the role of new platforms (e.g., Snapchat, Threads) was not investigated.

Future scope of the study

1. Varied population segments: Future research must consider more varied demographic segments in various age groups, geographies, and socio-economic segments.
2. Longitudinal studies: Time-series or panel studies may reveal the development of eWOM influence over time or through various product life cycles.
3. Platform-specific analysis: Examine how different social media platforms and formats (e.g., reels, stories, shorts) have differential effects on emotional engagement.
4. Role of influencers versus peer reviews: Compare content from influencers with peer-generated reviews in building credibility, trust, and engagement.
5. Psychographic variables: Including personality characteristics, values, and lifestyle considerations may provide greater insight into reasons to purchase.

References

[1] Kumar, S., & Sharma, P. (2021). Digital transformation of India's beauty and personal care industry. *Journal of Emerging Market Research*, 10(2), 112–120.

[2] Gupta, N., & Srivastava, A. (2022). Digital content and purchasing behavior: an empirical study in beauty sector. *Journal of Digital Retailing*, 5(2), 33–41.

[3] Dwivedi, Y. K., Rana, N. P., Shareef, M. D., & Slade, S. L. (2021). Influencer marketing and social media strategies in the digital age. *International Journal of Information Management*, 57, 102203.

[4] Jain, R., & Verma, S. (2023). Rise of influencer culture in Indian beauty industry. *Indian Journal of Digital Marketing*, 6(3), 22–29.

[5] Lim, S., Lee, J., & Kim, K. (2020). Social media use, peer influence, and consumer behavior of Gen Z. *Journal of Interactive Marketing*, 52, 29–43.

[6] Bhattacharya, K., & Singh, N. (2023). Understanding Gen Z buying preferences in Indian personal care segment. *Journal of Consumer Insight*, 11(1), 44–57.

[7] KPMG. (2022). India's Tier II & III cities: Unlocking new growth avenues [Report]. KPMG India. Retrieved July 20, 2025, https://home.kpmg/in/en/home/insights/2022/11/india-tier-ii-and-iii-cities.html.

[8] McKinsey & Company. (2021). The future of beauty: India's next digital revolution [Industry report]. McKinsey & Company. Retrieved July 20, 2025, from https://www.mckinsey.com/industries/consumer-packaged-goods/our-insights/the-future-of-beauty-indias-next-digital-revolution.

[9] RedSeer. (2023). India's beauty and personal care market: The next frontier [Report]. RedSeer. Retrieved July 20, 2025, from https://redseer.com/reports/indias-beauty-and-personal-care-market-the-next-frontier.

[10] Kapoor, P., & Sandhu, D. (2022). User-generated content and brand trust: exploring consumer-brand relationships. *Asia-Pacific Journal of Marketing*, 32(4), 481–498.

[11] Djafarova, A., & Trofimenko, O. (2019). Instafamous–credibility and self-presentation of micro-celebrities on social media. *Information, Communication and Society*, 22(10), 1432–1446.

[12] Hair, M., Hult, G. T. M., Ringle, C., & Sarstedt, M. (2022). A Primer on Partial Least Squares Structural Equation Modeling (PLS-SEM), (3rd edn.). Thousand Oaks, CA, USA: Sage.

[13] Hennig-Thurau, T., Gwinner, K. P., Walsh, G., & Gremler, D. D. (2004). Electronic word-of-mouth via consumer-opinion platforms: what motivates consumers to articulate themselves on the Internet?. *Journal of Interactive Marketing*, 18(1), 38–52. doi: 10.1002/dir.10073.

[14] Cheung, C. M. K., & Thadani, D. R. (2012). The impact of electronic word-of-mouth communication: a literature analysis and integrative model. *Decision Support Systems*, 54(1), 461–470. doi: 10.1016/j.dss.2012.06.008.

[15] Filieri, R., & McLeay, F. (2014). E-WOM and accommodation: an analysis of the factors that influence travelers' adoption of information from online reviews. *Journal of Travel Research*, 53(1), 44–57. doi: 10.1177/0047287513481274.

[16] Cheung, C. M. K., Chiu, P. Y., & Lee, M. K. O. (2009). Online social networks: why do students use Facebook?. *Computers in Human Behavior*, 27(4), 1337–1343. doi: 10.1016/j.chb.2010.07.028.

[17] Wang, Y., Narayanan, K., & Brush, A. J. B. (2018). Affect-lens: exploring affective experiences with smart glasses. In Proceedings ACM on Interactive, Mobile, Wearable and Ubiquitous Technologies, (Vol. 2, no. 1, pp. 1–21). doi: 10.1145/3191763.

[18] Turner, J. (2015). How to Make Money with Social Media: An Insider's Guide on Using New and Emerging Media to Grow Your Business, (2nd edn.), Upper Saddle River, NJ, USA: Pearson Education.

[19] Williams, T., Shah, H., & Ramesh, D. (2021). Emotional narratives and peer influence in beauty product purchases. *International Journal of Consumer Psychology*, 27(1), 37–50.

[20] Priporas, C.-V., Stylos, N., & Fotiadis, A. (2017). Generation Z consumers' expectations of interactions in smart retailing: a future agenda. *Computers in Human Behavior*, 77, 374–381. doi: 10.1016/j.chb.2017.01.058.

[21] Park, D.-H., & Kim, S. (2008). The effects of consumer knowledge on message processing of electronic word-of-mouth via online consumer reviews. *Electronic Commerce Research and Applications*, 7(4), 399–410.

[22] Wiedmann, K.-P., Hennigs, N., Pankalla, S., Kassubek, C., & Seegebarth, A. (2020). The power of affective response and cognitive brand evaluation in driving consumer behavior: insights from luxury and skin care brands. *Journal of Business Research*, 116, 386–398. doi: 10.1016/j.jbusres.2020.01.051.

[23] Phelps, J. E., Lewis, R., Mobilio, L., Perry, D., & Raman, N. (2004). Viral marketing or electronic word-of-mouth: examining consumer responses and motivations to pass along email. *Journal of Advertising Research*, 44(4), 333–348.

[24] Filieri, R. (2015). What makes online reviews helpful? a diagnosticity-adoption framework to explain informational and normative influences in e-WOM. *Journal of Business Research*, 68(6), 1261–1270.

[25] Wang, Y., Narayanan, K., & Brush, A. J. B. (2018). Affect-lens: exploring affective experiences with smart glasses. In Proceedings of the ACM on Interactive, Mobile, Wearable and Ubiquitous Technologies, (Vol. 2, no. 1, pp. 1–21). doi: 10.1145/3191763.

[26] Ajzen, I. (1991). The theory of planned behavior. *Organizational Behavior and Human Decision Processes*, 50(2), 179–211.

[27] Fishbein, M., & Ajzen, I. (1975). Belief, Attitude, Intention, and Behavior: An Introduction to Theory and Research. Reading, MA, USA: Addison-Wesley.

[28] Deutsch, M., & Gerard, H. B. (1955). A study of normative and informational social influences upon individual judgment. *The Journal of Abnormal and Social Psychology*, 51(3), 629–636. doi: 10.1037/h0046408.

18 Cross-cultural perspectives on work–life integration: an empirical study from a South Asian organizational context

W.Y.I. Walpola[a], T. T. Ediriweera[b] and H.A.D.D. Hansika[c]

Department of Management, NSBM Green University, Sri Lanka

Abstract

The increasing globalization of workforces has accentuated the need to understand how cultural dimensions influence the integration of professional and personal life. This research explores how cross-cultural factors affect work–life integration, focusing on employee cultural intelligence, perception of cultural diversity, and organizational support mechanisms within a South Asian corporate context. Drawing upon a sample of 157 employees from a leading apparel manufacturer in Sri Lanka, the study employs quantitative methods to assess the relationships between cultural perspectives and work–life integration outcomes. Correlation and multiple regression analyses indicate strong positive relationships between cultural intelligence, perception of cultural differences, and work–life integration. However, organizational support for cultural adaptation demonstrated only a moderate impact. These findings contribute to existing literature by empirically validating the influence of cross-cultural competencies on work–life dynamics and offer practical implications for global human resource strategies. The paper highlights the need to foster cultural awareness and inclusivity to optimize employee well-being and organizational performance in multicultural environments.

Keywords: Cross-cultural management, cultural intelligence, employee perception, organizational support, South Asia, work–life integration

Introduction

The 21st-century global economy is characterized by increasingly interconnected labor markets and culturally diverse workplaces. Globalization has not only expanded business operations but also transformed managerial strategies, requiring adaptability to varied cultural norms, behaviors, and organizational expectations [1, 2]. The interaction between cultural diversity and human resource practices is now considered central to employee engagement, productivity, and retention, particularly in multinational firms [3, 4].

Culture, broadly defined as the shared values, beliefs, customs, and social behaviors of a group, plays a pivotal role in shaping attitudes toward work, leadership, time management, and interpersonal communication [5]. As a result, the concept of work–life balance, and more recently, work–life integration, has emerged as a critical area of inquiry [6]. While work–life balance emphasizes compartmentalization between professional and personal life, work–life integration encourages fluidity and interconnectedness between the two domains, which is increasingly relevant in flexible, digital-first work environments [7, 8].

Cultural expectations significantly influence how individuals perceive and manage this integration. For instance, collectivist societies tend to value familial and communal relationships over individual achievements, whereas individualist cultures may prioritize career advancement [3, 9]. Similarly, hierarchical (high power distance) cultures may discourage open negotiation of work–life boundaries, affecting employee autonomy and well-being. These cultural constructs have a measurable impact on how work–life integration strategies are perceived and implemented at both individual and organizational levels [10].

Although the importance of work–life integration has been acknowledged globally, the influence of cross-cultural perspectives on this construct remains underexplored in empirical terms. Particularly in South Asian corporate environments, where cultural expectations around authority, collectivism, and gender roles are deeply embedded, navigating work–life integration becomes complex [11]. Existing studies

[a]wyiwalpola@students.nsbm.ac.lk, [b]thamodya.e@nsbm.ac.lk, [c]dilki.h@nsbm.ac.lk

DOI: 10.4324/9781003739920-18

have highlighted the role of employee motivation, perception, and cultural intelligence in shaping organizational behavior [12, 13], yet there remains a research gap in linking these factors to work–life integration through a cross-cultural lens. While there is a growing body of empirical research on work–life issues in Western contexts, studies focusing on Asian workforces, especially in South Asia, remain scarce. A deeper examination of the work–life interface in this region is essential, given the accelerating pace of economic growth, ongoing social transformation, and intensifying global competition that have collectively amplified work–life pressures on employees [11].

This study addresses that gap by empirically analyzing how employee cultural intelligence, perception of cultural differences, and organizational support for cultural adaptation influence work–life integration in a culturally diverse workplace. To enrich the practical relevance of this inquiry, a leading multinational apparel manufacturer in Sri Lanka was selected for its strong commitment to fostering diversity and inclusion, as well as its support for freedom of expression and identity. Operating across multiple cultural contexts, the organization also provides a rich setting to explore cross-cultural dynamics in practice.

Although the practical and cultural significance of work–life integration is increasingly recognized, a deeper understanding requires grounding in established theoretical frameworks and empirical insights. To this end, the following section synthesizes key literature that informs this study, beginning with foundational concepts in cross-cultural theory and their relevance to work–life integration.

Cross-cultural theory and work–life integration

Globalization has amplified the significance of cross-cultural dynamics within organizational behavior and human resource management [5]. The concept of "culture," often likened to an iceberg with visible and invisible layers, encompasses language, customs, norms, and deeper values that shape behavior [14, 15]. As organizations expand across borders, understanding how these cultural layers impact work-related attitudes become essential [2].

Work–life integration, defined as the ability to harmonize personal responsibilities with professional obligations, is increasingly viewed as a dynamic process shaped by cultural context [3, 7]. This concept goes beyond the traditional binary of work–life balance by embracing fluidity and overlap between domains [8].

Role theory and cultural constructs

Role theory posits that individuals hold multiple roles (e.g., employee, parent, caregiver) that may compete or complement one another [16, 3]. Cultural values mediate this interaction. For example, in collectivist cultures (e.g., Sri Lanka, India, China), familial roles may take precedence over occupational roles, thereby influencing how work–life integration is perceived [15]. In contrast, individualistic cultures (e.g., USA, UK) may valorize career advancement and autonomy, often at the expense of personal time [17].

Power distance also plays a pivotal role. Cultures with high power distance may discourage employees from requesting flexible work arrangements, viewing such actions as disrespectful or inappropriate [9]. Similarly, uncertainty avoidance levels influence willingness to adopt flexible or remote work practices, which are often central to work–life integration [18].

Cultural intelligence

Cultural intelligence refers to an individual's capability to function effectively in culturally diverse settings [19]. CQ comprises four dimensions: cognitive (knowledge of cultural systems), metacognitive (awareness of cultural assumptions), motivational (interest in intercultural engagement), and behavioral (adaptation of behavior to fit different contexts).

Studies show that cultural intelligence enhances interpersonal communication, reduces workplace conflict, and supports inclusive decision-making [20]. High CQ employees are more adaptable and capable of navigating the tensions between work and personal life in multicultural environments [21]. Moreover, culturally intelligent managers are more likely to foster inclusive climates that support diverse work–life needs.

Employee perception and organizational culture

Perception plays a critical role in shaping employee engagement and satisfaction. Employees who perceive organizational practices as inclusive, supportive, and culturally adaptive report higher well-being and stronger identification with their employer [22]. In contrast, negative perceptions rooted in stereotypes, miscommunication, or exclusion can lead to disengagement and turnover [23].

Organizational culture, defined as shared beliefs, values, and practices, serves as a framework within which work–life integration is either supported or hindered [24]. Organizations with high cultural adaptability tend to implement policies such as flexible scheduling, job sharing, and telecommuting, which align with employees' diverse cultural expectations and personal needs [25].

Challenges in culturally diverse workplaces

While cultural diversity offers substantial advantages such as innovation and broader market understanding, it also presents challenges, including miscommunication, conflict, and incompatible work norms [26]. Language barriers, divergent professional etiquette, and differing views on hierarchy and time management are common obstacles [10].

Effective leadership is crucial in addressing these challenges. Leaders must actively promote cross-cultural understanding, resolve conflicts swiftly, and foster an environment of psychological safety. Interventions such as diversity training, cross-cultural mentoring, and transparent communication channels are shown to improve employee outcomes and work–life integration in multinational teams [27, 28].

Organizational support for cultural adaptation

Organizational support structures, including onboarding processes, diversity policies, and cross-cultural training programs, are essential in helping employees navigate new cultural contexts [12]. When organizations invest in building cultural intelligence across all levels, they create inclusive environments where employees feel seen, respected, and empowered to balance professional and personal roles.

Furthermore, institutionalizing cultural sensitivity into performance evaluations, team-building exercises, and communication protocols increases the likelihood of successful cultural adaptation [1]. However, research also indicates that such initiatives must be sustained over time and championed by top leadership to generate lasting change [4].

Despite the growing recognition of cultural dynamics in organizational life, research often treats work–life integration and cross-cultural factors as separate domains. A closer examination reveals that these elements are deeply interwoven, especially in culturally complex environments like South Asia. Yet, empirical inquiry in this region remains limited [11]. This study seeks to bridge that gap by examining how individual and organizational-level cultural competencies shape work–life integration in a multicultural workplace.

Building on this foundation, the study is guided by the following objectives and questions.

Research objectives

The primary objectives of this study are to:

1. Identify the impact of employee cultural intelligence on work–life integration.
2. Identify the impact of employee perception of cultural diversity on work–life integration.
3. Identify the impact of organizational support for cultural adaptation on work–life integration.

Research questions

1. What is the impact of employee cultural intelligence on work–life integration?
2. What is the impact of employee perception of cultural diversity on work–life integration?
3. What is the impact of organizational support for cultural adaptation on work–life integration?

Materials and Methodology

Materials

This study utilized a structured, self-administered questionnaire designed to capture both demographic information and core variables related to the research model. The questionnaire included two main components which are the demographic section and the core constructs.

Demographic section captured data on gender, age, job position, work experience, and educational qualifications while core constructs employed validated Likert-scale items to measure three independent variables which were employee cultural intelligence, employee perception of cultural differences, and organizational support for cultural adaptation as well as the dependent variable, work–life integration.

The instrument was developed based on established scales from existing literature and was distributed electronically using Google Forms. Ethical protocols were followed, including informed consent, confidentiality of data, and voluntary participation.

Methodology

Research design

The study adopted a deductive, quantitative research design to investigate the relationship between cross-cultural factors and work–life integration within a South Asian organizational setting. Grounded in theoretical frameworks, the research employed hypothesis testing through empirical data gathered from primary sources. This design was suitable for quantitatively assessing the impact of the independent variables on work–life integration.

Conceptual framework

The conceptual model was informed by prior research in cross-cultural management, organizational behavior, and work–life integration. The framework included the independent variables of employee cultural intelligence , employee perception of cultural differences and organizational support for cultural adaptation.

These were hypothesized to influence the dependent variable, work–life integration. The model is visually depicted in Figure 18.1.

Hypotheses

The following hypotheses were tested based on the developed conceptual framework.

H1: Employee cultural intelligence is positively associated with work–life integration.
H2: Employee perception of cultural differences is positively associated with work–life integration.
H3: Organizational support for cultural adaptation is positively associated with work–life integration.

Population and sampling

The target population comprised employees from Sri Lanka's largest apparel manufacturing organization, specifically executive and administrative staff (N = 247). A stratified sampling technique was employed to ensure proportional representation from different organizational units. The final sample consisted of 157 respondents, yielding data analysis techniques.

Data were analyzed using SPSS version 26. Descriptive statistics were employed to profile respondent demographics. Reliability testing was conducted using Cronbach's Alpha to assess the internal consistency of the measurement scales. Correlation analysis was performed to evaluate linear relationships between the variables. Finally, multiple linear regression analysis was used to determine the predictive power of the independent variables on work–life integration. The threshold for statistical significance was set at $\alpha = 0.05$ response rate of 63.6%.

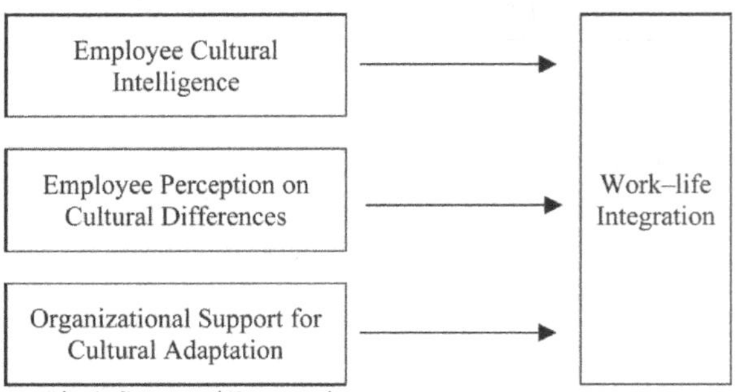

Figure 18.1 Conceptual framework
Source: Author

Sample size justification

Sample size determination was guided by Krejcie and Morgan's (1970) table for finite populations, indicating that a minimum of 150 responses was required to ensure statistical validity. The achieved sample size (n = 157) met this requirement.

Results and Discussion

Sample collection

To ensure reliability of measurement instruments, Cronbach's Alpha was calculated for all constructs. The overall reliability coefficient was $\alpha = 0.831$, indicating a high degree of internal consistency across the scale items.

Demographic characteristics of the 157 respondents were also profiled. The sample comprised 57% females and 43% males. Age distribution was as follows: 60% were aged 18–27, 23% were 28–37, 14% were 38–47, and 3% were above 47. Regarding job roles, 64% were junior associates, followed by 24% team leads, 7% managers, and 5% in other roles.

Work experience varied: 55% had 1–5 years, 26% had 5–10 years, and 19% had more than 10 years. Educational qualifications included: 33% with bachelor's degrees, 22% with professional qualifications, 25% with G.C.E A/L, 14% with master's degrees, and 6% in other categories.

Sample analysis

Correlation analysis

Pearson correlation coefficients were computed to test relationships between independent variables and work–life integration. The respective correlation values are presented in Table 18.1.

The results of the Pearson correlation analysis reveal statistically significant positive relationships between all three variables and the outcome of interest. Employee cultural intelligence shows a strong positive correlation ($r = 0.614$, $p < 0.001$), suggesting that as employees' cultural intelligence increases work-life integration also tends to improve. Employee perception of cultural differences demonstrates a very strong positive correlation ($r = 0.837$, $p < 0.001$), indicating that greater awareness or recognition of cultural differences is highly associated with positive outcomes. Finally, organizational support for cultural adaptation is moderately positively correlated ($r = 0.394$, $p < 0.001$), implying that supportive organizational practices play a meaningful, though comparatively smaller, role in influencing the outcome. All correlations are statistically significant at the 0.001 level, underscoring the robustness of these relationships.

Multiple regression analysis

A multiple linear regression model was conducted to test the predictive power of the independent variables. It is depicted in Table 18.2.

These values indicate that 71.4% of the variance in work–life integration can be explained by the combined effects of the three predictors. This represents a strong model fit, affirming the relevance of the selected variables.

Table 18.3 presents the ANOVA results. The results of the ANOVA test indicate that the overall regression model is statistically significant, $F(3, 153) = 127.178$, $p < 0.001$, confirming that the combination of predictor variables—employee cultural intelligence, perception of cultural differences, and organizational support—explains a significant portion of the variance in work–life integration. This finding validates the appropriateness of the model and supports the conclusion that the predictors collectively contribute meaningfully to the outcome variable.

Coefficient analysis

The coefficient analysis, as depicted in Table 18.4, revealed that two of the three predictor variables had statistically significant positive effects on the dependent variable. Employee Cultural Intelligence demonstrated a significant positive influence ($B = 0.132$, $p = 0.017$), indicating that higher levels of cultural intelligence are associated with improvements in the outcome. Employee perception of cultural differences showed a highly significant and substantial positive effect ($B = 0.776$, $p < 0.001$), suggesting that employees who perceive cultural differences positively are more likely to report favorable outcomes. However, organizational support for cultural

Table 18.2 Model summary.

Model	R	R^2	Adjusted R^2	Std. error
1	0.845	0.714	0.708	0.257

Source: Author

Table 18.3 ANOVA.

Source	Sum of squares	df	Mean square	F	p-value
Regression	25.197	3	8.399	127.035	<0.001
Residual	10.116	153	0.066	-	-
Total	35.312	156	-	-	-

Source: Author

Table 18.1 Correlation.

Variable	Work–life integration	Employee Intelligence	Employee perception	Organizational support
Work–life integration	1	0.614*	0.837*	0.394*
Employee intelligence	-	1	0.633*	0.369*
Employee perception	-	-	1	0.431*
Organizational support	-	-	-	1

Note: *p < 0.001.
Source: Author

Table 18.4 Coefficients.

Predictor	B	Std. Error	β	t	p-value
(Constant)	0.358	0.232	-	2.539	0.013
Employee intelligence	0.132	0.054	0.137	2.423	0.017
Employee perception	0.776	0.061	0.740	12.740	<0.001
Organizational support	0.028	0.057	0.024	0.501	0.617

Source: Author

adaptation did not yield a statistically significant effect (B = 0.028, p = 0.617), indicating that, in this model, organizational support was not a significant predictor of the outcome.

The multiple regression analysis produced the following predictive equation for work–life integration:

> Work–Life Integration = 0.132(Cultural Intelligence) + 0.776(Perception of Cultural Differences) + 0.028(Organizational Support) + 0.358.

Among the predictors, employee perception of cultural differences emerged as the strongest contributor to work–life integration, with a substantial positive coefficient. Cultural intelligence also had a statistically significant but comparatively smaller positive effect. Although organizational support for cultural adaptation showed a moderate correlation with the dependent variable, its contribution was not statistically significant within the regression model. These results suggest that individual-level factors, specifically employees' perceptions and cultural intelligence, have a more pronounced influence on their ability to balance work and personal life in multicultural environments than organizational-level interventions.

Conclusion

The objective of this study was to explore the influence of cross-cultural perspectives on work–life integration within a South Asian organizational context, using the largest apparel manufacturer in Sri Lanka as a case study. The findings provide empirical support for the theoretical linkages between cultural constructs and employee well-being and yield insights that are both academically relevant and practically actionable. The findings confirm strong relationships between employee perception, cultural intelligence, and work–life integration, aligning with prior research [19, 20]. However, the limited impact of organizational support contrasts with Western studies [25], suggesting that individual-level factors may outweigh institutional interventions in collectivist cultures like Sri Lanka.

This study extends cross-cultural management literature by empirically validating the role of cultural intelligence and perception in work–life integration within a South Asian context. It also nuances role theory [16] and cultural frameworks [15] by highlighting context-specific dynamics.

Organizations can enhance work–life integration in multicultural settings by investing in cultural intelligence training to equip employees with the skills to navigate diverse work environments. Promoting inclusive leadership that fosters positive perceptions of diversity further contributes to a supportive and cohesive organizational culture. Additionally, tailoring workplace policies to reflect the cultural context while emphasizing informal support mechanisms such as mentoring, peer networks, and open communication can significantly improve employees' ability to harmonize professional and personal roles.

Future research could extend these findings in several important directions. Cross-national comparisons across cultural clusters such as individualist versus collectivist societies would help assess the generalizability of the results and reveal culturally contingent patterns. A qualitative exploration using in-depth interviews could uncover underlying reasons why organizational support appears less influential in certain cultural contexts. Additionally, longitudinal studies tracking changes in cultural perceptions and work–life integration over time may yield stronger causal insights. Finally, considering the gender composition of the current sample, future research could investigate whether cultural intelligence and perception exert differential impacts across genders in shaping work–life integration outcomes.

Acknowledgement

The authors wish to express their sincere gratitude to all individuals who contributed to the successful completion of this research. Special thanks are extended to the professionals at the organization from which data was collected, for their valuable time, insights, and cooperation.

References

[1] Huang, L. (2023). Globalization and cultural adaptation in multinational firms. *Journal of International Business Studies*, 54(2), 201–220.

[2] Noor, S. (2014). Cultural diversity and organizational transformation. *Human Resource Management Review*, 24(1), 45–58.

[3] Greenhaus, J. H., & Beutell, N. J. (1985). Sources of conflict between work and family roles. *Academy of Management Review*, 10(1), 76–88.

[4] Halpern, D. F. (2005). How time-flexible work policies can reduce work–life conflict. *American Psychologist*, 60(2), 91–103.

[5] Rao, A. (2017). Culture and organizational behavior. *Journal of Cross-Cultural Psychology*, 48(4), 567–589.

[6] Munjal, S., Sarkar, S., & Chahar, B. (2021). A systematic review of work–life integration and flexible work arrangements. *International Journal of Organizational Analysis*, 29(3), 789–812.

[7] Carlson, D. S., Kacmar, K. M., & Williams, L. J. (2000). Construction and validation of a multidimensional measure of work–family conflict. *Journal of Vocational Behavior*, 56(2), 249–276.

[8] Fallon, K. (2021). Work–life integration in digital-first environments. *Business Horizons*, 64(5), 621–630.

[9] Wang, Q., & Li, M. (2012). Cultural influence on work–life balance. *Journal of International Business Studies*, 43(3), 234–256.

[10] Torrès, O., Thurik, R., & Urbano, D. (2022). Work–life balance and entrepreneurial well-being. *Small Business Economics*, 59(4), 1359–1378.

[11] Le, H., Newman, A., Menzies, J., Zheng, C., & Fermelis, J. (2020). Work–life balance in Asia: a systematic review. *Human Resource Management Review*, 30(4), 100766.

[12] Amabile, T. M. (1988). A model of creativity and innovation in organizations. *Research in Organizational Behavior*, 10, 123–167.

[13] Kato, H., & Yamamoto, M. (2022). Employee motivation and cultural intelligence. *International Journal of Human Resource Management*, 33(5), 789–812.

[14] Hall, E. T. (1976). Beyond Culture. New York, NY: Anchor Books.

[15] Hofstede, G. (2010). Cultures and Organizations: Software of the Mind, (3rd edn.). New York, NY: McGraw-Hill.

[16] Kahn, R. L., Wolfe, D.M., Quinn, R.P., Snoek, J.D. and Rosenthal, R.A. (1964). Organizational Stress: Studies in Role Conflict and Ambiguity. New York, NY: Wiley.

[17] Trompenaars, F., & Hampden-Turner, C. (1998). Riding the Waves of Culture, (2nd edn.), New York, NY: McGraw-Hill.

[18] House, R. J., Hanges, P. J., Javidan, M., Dorfman, P. W., & Gupta, V. (Eds.), (2004). Culture, Leadership, and Organizations: The GLOBE Study of 62 Societies. Thousand Oaks, CA: Sage.

[19] Earley, P. C., & Ang, S. (2003). Cultural Intelligence: Individual Interactions Across Cultures. Stanford, CA: Stanford University Press.

[20] Ang, S., Van Dyne, L., Koh, C., Ng, K. Y., Templer, K. J., Tay, C., et al. (2007). Cultural intelligence: its measurement and effects. *Management and Organization Review*, 3(3), 335–371.

[21] Lee, L. Y., & Sukoco, B. M. (2010). Effects of cultural intelligence on expatriate performance. *International Journal of Human Resource Management*, 21(7), 963–981.

[22] Sabuhari, R., Jabid, A. W., Rajak, A., and Soleman, M. M. (2021). The Role of Organizational Culture Adaptation and Job Satisfaction in Mediating Effects of Human Resource Flexibility on Employee Performance. *Jurnal Dinamika Manajemen.* 12(1), 132–145.

[23] Stotzer, S. (2024). How Employee Perception Shapes Organizational Success. *Crosworks. Career and Talent Strategists.* Available from: https://crosworks.com/how-employee-perceptionshapes-organizational-success/.

[24] Schein, E. H. (2010). Organizational Culture and Leadership, (4th edn.), San Francisco, CA: Jossey-Bass.

[25] Putnik, K., & Houkes, I. (2018). Work–home interface and well-being. *International Journal of Human Resource Management*, 29(1), 1–25.

[26] Kühlmann, T., & Heinz, M. (2017). Global Workforce Management. London, U.K.: Palgrave Macmillan.

[27] Sun, Y., & Pan, W. (2008). Diversity training and team performance. *Journal of Applied Psychology*, 93(2), 341–358.

[28] Reynolds, D. (2018). Leadership in multicultural teams. *Journal of Leadership Studies*, 12(3), 45–60.

19 Gender inequity in logistics: unraveling systemic barriers to women's managerial roles in Sri Lanka

G. H. R. Wijewardhana[1,a], *H. A. D. D. Hansika*[2,b] *and T.T. Ediriweera*[2,c]

[1]Department of Operations and Logistics, NSBM Green University, Sri Lanka

[2]Department of Management, NSBM Green University, Sri Lanka

Abstract

This study examines the glass ceiling hindering women's advancement into managerial roles within Sri Lanka's logistics sector, an industry critical to the national economy yet marked by significant underrepresentation of women in senior positions. Through quantitative analysis of structured questionnaires administered to female professionals, the research identifies barriers such as work-life balance, psychological factors, educational level and organizational culture that impede career progression. Key findings reveal correlations between demographic factors like age, education, experience, and career advancement gaps, alongside systemic challenges like gender biases and limited mentorship. The study underscores the urgency of gender-inclusive policies and mentorship programs to dismantle barriers and promote equity. By contextualizing these issues within Sri Lanka's male-dominated logistics industry, this research enriches global discourse on women in leadership and advocates for targeted interventions to foster inclusive workplaces.

Keywords: Gender equality, glass ceiling, logistics sector, organizational culture, Sri Lanka, women in leadership, work-life balance

Introduction

The logistics industry, a cornerstone of global economic development, remains plagued by the persistent glass ceiling, an invisible barrier limiting women's advancement into senior managerial roles. Despite global efforts to promote gender equality, women constitute fewer than 3% of the workforce in Sri Lanka's logistics and transportation sector, despite representing 51% of the national population [1]. This underrepresentation exacerbates unemployment disparities, with female unemployment rates surpassing male rates across all age groups, particularly among youth [2]. Cultural norms in Sri Lanka and broader Asia perpetuate the perception of logistics as a male-dominated field, where women are often deemed incapable of handling operational challenges, despite technological advancements proving otherwise [3, 4].

The economic repercussions of gender inequality are staggering. Globally, corruption and gender disparities cost the logistics sector approximately $10.6 trillion annually [5], while Sri Lanka's economy faces compounded losses due to underutilized female talent [6]. Organizational culture, implicit biases, and societal stereotypes further entrench these barriers, as evidenced by studies showing women face longer pathways to promotion and fewer leadership opportunities compared to men [7, 8]. Although younger generations of women are increasingly pursuing logistics careers [9], systemic challenges like work-life balance conflicts and limited mentorship persist [10].

This study investigates the multifaceted barriers hindering women's career progression in Sri Lanka's logistics sector, contextualizing the glass ceiling within frameworks of work life balance, psychological factors, education level, and organizational culture using the quantitative data from female professionals in managerial positions in logistic industry, it aims to propose actionable strategies for fostering gender-inclusive leadership and equitable representation

Research questions

1. What is the impact of work-life balance on women's representation in managerial positions in the logistics industry in Sri Lanka?
2. What is the impact of psychological factors on women's representation in managerial positions in the logistics industry in Sri Lanka?

[a]ghrwijwardhana@students.nsbm.ac.lk, [b]dilki.h@nsbm.ac.lk, [c]thamodya.e@nsbm.ac.lk

DOI: 10.4324/9781003739920-19

3. What is the impact of education level on women's representation in managerial positions in the logistics industry in Sri Lanka?
4. What is the impact of organizational culture on women's representation in managerial positions in the logistics industry in Sri Lanka?

Research objectives

1. To identify the impact of work-life balance on women's representation in managerial positions in the logistics industry in Sri Lanka.
2. To identify the impact of psychological factors on women's representation in managerial positions in the logistics industry in Sri Lanka.
3. To identify the impact of education level on women's representation in managerial positions in the logistics industry in Sri Lanka.
4. To identify the impact of organizational culture on women's representation in managerial positions in the logistics industry in Sri Lanka.

Literature Review

Gender inequality

Gender inequality remains a critical barrier to women's leadership in developing economies, particularly in male-dominated sectors like logistics. While women in developed nations leverage economic empowerment to advocate for equality, those in developing regions face entrenched cultural and institutional biases [11]. Historically confined to domestic roles—epitomized by the 19th-century concept of the "angel in the house"—women were often excluded from formal employment, especially post-marriage [12]. This legacy perpetuates gender disparities in access to education, employment, and political representation, reinforcing male-dominated norms in industries such as logistics [13].

Globally, women hold only 24% of senior management roles, with progress stagnating at a 3% increase over five years [14]. In G7 nations, 40% of businesses lack female representation in top management, underscoring systemic inequities [14]. The logistics sector exemplifies this trend, where women constitute fewer than 3% of the workforce in Sri Lanka despite comprising 51% of the population [15]. The "glass ceiling" persists due to social norms, unequal pay, and inadequate support systems like affordable childcare [16].

Legislative efforts in countries like Canada and South Africa demonstrate that gender-inclusive policies (e.g., quotas, anti-discrimination laws) enhance female leadership representation [17]. However, such measures are rare in developing contexts, where logistical operations remain culturally perceived as incompatible with women's capabilities [18]. Feminist theories argue that women's collaborative leadership styles and communication skills offer strategic advantages, yet organizational cultures in logistics often marginalize these attributes [19].

Balancing career and familial responsibilities further impedes women's advancement. Limited access to childcare and inflexible work policies force many to exit the workforce, as seen in Germany and Japan [20]. Addressing these barriers requires systemic reforms, including mentorship programs, equitable promotion criteria, and work-life integration policies tailored to logistics' demanding nature [21].

Glass ceiling in logistic

The glass ceiling a metaphor for invisible barriers hindering women's advancement to leadership roles—persists in male-dominated industries like logistics. First coined in the 1970s and popularized in the 1980s [22], this phenomenon reflects systemic gender biases that prioritize masculine leadership traits (e.g., assertiveness) over communal qualities stereotypically associated with women [23]. Organizational cultures exacerbating the glass ceiling often reward rigid career trajectories and long working hours, disadvantaging women balancing familial responsibilities [24].

In logistics, women face unique challenges: only 3% hold leadership roles globally, often relegated to non-strategic positions like HR rather than core operations [25]. Gender stereotypes portraying logistics as "masculine" deter career progression, compounded by limited mentorship and exclusion from informal professional networks critical for advancement [24].

Women in logistic

The logistics sector, vital to global economic growth, contributes 9% of GDP in developed nations yet remains male-dominated, with women underrepresented in leadership roles [26, 27]. Systemic barriers—rooted in cultural stereotypes, work-life conflicts, and limited mentorship—perpetuate this disparity. Globally, fewer than 20% of logistics managers are women, reflecting entrenched gender biases that prioritize men for high-responsibility roles [28].

Cultural norms portray logistics as physically demanding, deterring women's entry, particularly in operational roles like transportation [29]. Concurrently, work-life imbalances arise from long hours and travel requirements, conflicting with societal expectations for women to manage households [30]. The absence of female mentors exacerbates these challenges, as aspiring professionals lack role models to navigate career progression [28].

Economic losses due to gender inequity are stark: the Asia-Pacific region forfeits billions annually by underutilizing women in logistics, stifling innovation and efficiency [31]. However, technological advancements and globalization are reshaping the industry, creating knowledge-driven roles that attract more women [32]. In Sri Lanka, logistics contributes 2.5% of GDP, yet women constitute fewer than 3% of the workforce [33]. Recent progress includes policy reforms promoting flexible work arrangements and leadership training, fostering gradual cultural shifts toward inclusivity [34].

Work-life balance of women

Work-life balance remains a critical barrier to women's advancement in leadership roles, particularly in demanding sectors like logistics. Women often juggle professional responsibilities with familial caregiving duties, creating structural conflicts that hinder career progression [34]. Societal expectations position women as primary caregivers, leading employers to perceive them as less committed to demanding roles, despite evidence of comparable productivity [35].

Organizational policies exacerbate these challenges: only 23% of firms in male-dominated industries offer flexible work arrangements or childcare support, forcing women to choose between career growth and family obligations [36]. This imbalance contributes to the glass ceiling, as women opt for roles with reduced hours or exit the workforce entirely [37]. However, initiatives like parental leave and remote work options have shown promise in retaining female talent, boosting organizational diversity and profitability by 15–20% [38].

A paradigm shift is emerging: 55% of women executives now aspire to CEO roles, compared to 46% of men, signaling evolving attitudes toward leadership and work-life integration [39]. To sustain this progress, firms must institutionalize gender-inclusive policies that align with modern workforce dynamics.

Psychological barriers to women's leadership

Psychological barriers, including self-doubt, low self-esteem, and perceived inadequacy, significantly hinder women's advancement into top management roles [40]. Internalized societal stereotypes and a lack of role models exacerbate these challenges, creating a cycle where women undervalue their leadership potential [41]. Studies indicate that 65% of women in male-dominated industries like logistics hesitate to pursue senior roles due to fear of bias or failure [42].

Women often avoid organizational politics or assertive career strategies, perceiving such behaviors as incompatible with gendered expectations of "communality" [43]. Additionally, stereotypes questioning women's crisis-management abilities further erode confidence, perpetuating underrepresentation [44]. Breaking this cycle requires mentorship programs, visibility of female leaders, and inclusive cultures that normalize women's leadership aspirations [45].

Educational level and work experience

Educational attainment and work experience critically influence women's access to leadership roles. Men disproportionately invest in skill development, securing advancement opportunities often denied to women due to disparities in educational qualifications and field specialization [46, 47]. For instance, women are underrepresented in STEM and logistics-related disciplines, limiting their competitiveness in male-dominated sectors [48].

The Beijing Declaration (1995) underscores education as a tool for empowering women in decision-making, yet gaps persist: 35% of women in logistics lack advanced degrees, hindering their progression to managerial roles [49]. Even when qualified, women face heightened stress from balancing leadership responsibilities with societal caregiving expectations, leading to lower job satisfaction and higher attrition rates [50].

Organizational culture and women's advancement

Organizational culture—defined as shared values and norms shaping workplace behavior [51]—profoundly impacts women's access to leadership roles. In male-dominated sectors like logistics, cultures shaped by patriarchal norms marginalize women through exclusion from decision-making forums and high-impact assignments [52]. Only 30% of women report inclusion in critical meetings, stunting their professional visibility and skill development [53].

The absence of female role models in senior positions perpetuates this cycle, as junior professionals lack aspirational benchmarks [54]. Compounding this, women receive 20% less feedback than male peers, limiting opportunities for growth and advancement [55]. To address these inequities, organizations must prioritize mentorship programs, inclusive policy reforms, and transparent promotion criteria to cultivate gender-equitable cultures [56].

Materials and Methodology

Research design

This study adopts a quantitative, cross-sectional research design anchored in positivist philosophy, which prioritizes objective measurement and statistical analysis to investigate the glass ceiling's impact on women's advancement in Sri Lanka's logistics sector. Aligning with the deductive approach, the research begins with four hypotheses derived from established theories (e.g., social role theory, human capital theory) and empirically tests them through structured data collection and analysis.

The design emphasizes causal-comparative relationships between independent variables (work-life balance, psychological factors, educational level, organizational culture) and the dependent variable (women's representation in managerial roles). By quantifying these relationships, the study identifies systemic barriers and their relative influence on career progression.

Hypothesis

H1. There is a relationship between work-life balance and women's representation in managerial positions in the logistics industry in Sri Lanka.

H2. There is a relationship between psychological factors and women's representation in managerial positions in the logistics industry in Sri Lanka.

H3. There is a relationship between education level and women's representation in managerial positions in the logistics industry in Sri Lanka.

H4. There is a relationship between organizational culture and women's representation in managerial positions in the logistics industry in Sri Lanka.

Data collection

Primary data were collected using a structured questionnaire administered to 100 female professionals in Sri Lanka's logistics sector. Validated via a pilot study (Cronbach's $\alpha > 0.85$), the questionnaire included Likert-scale items (1–5) to assess organizational culture and psychological factors, demographic questions (age, education, experience, position), and closed-ended questions on women's representation in the logistics industry in Sri Lanka.

Conceptual framework

This study's conceptual framework, illustrated in Figure 19.1, proposes that work-life balance, psychological factors, education level, and organizational culture influence women's managerial representation in logistics.

Sampling strategy

A non-probability snowball sampling technique was employed to address accessibility challenges in Sri Lanka's male-dominated logistics sector. Initial participants referred colleagues across the Western Province, ensuring diversity in job roles (freight forwarding: 30%, warehousing: 25%, transportation: 45%) and hierarchy levels (senior executives: 27%, managers: 26%, assistant managers: 30%). This approach prioritized relevance to managerial underrepresentation while expanding participant reach.

Data analysis

The collected data were analyzed using IBM SPSS Statistics 28.0, a robust statistical software package, to test hypotheses, identify correlations, and derive actionable insights into systemic barriers hindering women's advancement in Sri Lanka's logistics sector.

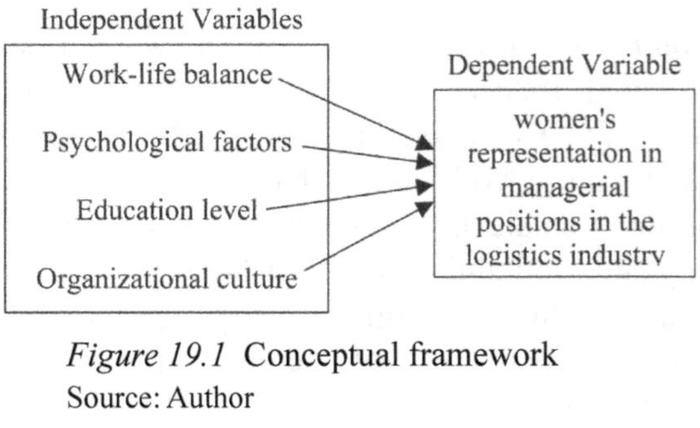

Figure 19.1 Conceptual framework
Source: Author

Results and Discussion

Demographic characteristics

The study surveyed 100 female professionals in Sri Lanka's logistics sector. As shown in Table 19.1, the majority of respondents (32%) were under 29 years old, while only 2% were above 50. A significant proportion (52%) were married, and 62% had no children. Most participants (61%) had 6–16 years of work experience, and 41% held bachelor's degrees. Job roles spanned freight forwarding (30%), warehousing (25%), and transportation (45%), with 30% serving as assistant managers and only 2% as directors.

Table 19.1 Demographic profile of respondents.

Category	Frequency	Percentage
Age (years)		
Below 29	32	32%
30-34	20	20%
35-39	16	16%
40-44	22	22%
45-49	8	8%
50+	2	2%
Marital status		
Single	48	48%
Married	52	52%
Children		
Yes	38	38%
No	62	62%
Work experience		
Below 5 years	19	19%
6-16 years	61	61%
17-26 years	18	18%
28-38 years	2	2%
Education level		
Bachelor's degree	41	41%
Master's degree	35	35%
PhD	2	2%
other	22	22%
Designation		
Director	2	2%
Manager	26	26%
Assistant manager	30	30%
Senior executive	27	27%
Other	15	15%

Source: Author

Reliability analysis

All constructs demonstrated high internal consistency, with Cronbach's alpha values exceeding 0.7 (Table 19.2), confirming the reliability of the measurement scales. Organizational culture showed the highest reliability ($\alpha = 0.931$), followed by work-life balance ($\alpha = 0.924$).

Hypothesis testing

The ANOVA results (Table 19.4) confirm the model's statistical significance ($F = 38.875$, $p < 0.001$). The regression sum of squares (34.390) far exceeds the residual sum of squares (21.010), indicating strong explanatory power.

Anova model fit

All hypotheses were tested at $\alpha = 0.05$ (Table 19.3):

H_1 (Work-Life Balance): Significant impact ($p = 0.017$).

Table 19.2 Reliability analysis.

Variable	Cronbach's Alpha	Conclusion
Worl life balance	0.924	Reliable
Psychological factors	0.922	Reliable
Educational level	0.909	Reliable
Organizational culture	0.931	Reliable
Women's managerial participation	0.885	Reliable

Source: Author

Table 19.3 Hypothesis testing results.

Hypothesis	P value	Conclusion
HI: Work-life balance → Managerial participation	0.017	Accepted
H2: Psychological factors → Managerial participation	0.037	Accepted
H3: Education level → Managerial participation	0.000	Accepted
H4: Organizational culture → Managerial participation	0.000	Accepted

Source: Author

Table 19.4 ANOVA results.

Source	Sum of Squares	df	Mean Square	F value	P value
Regression	34.390	4	8.598	38.875	0.000
Residual	21.010	95	0.221		
Total	55.400	99	-		

Source: Author

H_2 (Psychological Factors): Significant impact ($p = 0.037$).
H_3 (Education/Experience): Strongest impact ($p < 0.001$).
H_4 (Organizational Culture): Significant impact ($p < 0.001$).

Findings work-life balance

Work-life balance significantly impacts women's participation in managerial roles within the logistics sector. Women effectively manage household responsibilities, yet familial obligations hinder career progression, as evidenced by studies confirming this relationship [57–61]. Mahasha [62] observed reduced work-life conflicts among childless women, a finding supported by this study's sample, where 62% of respondents were childless and 32% were under 29. Women in managerial roles often mitigate these challenges by delegating household tasks to domestic help.

Psychological Factors

Psychological factors, such as self-confidence and adaptability, are critical to women's leadership aspirations. While Matud et al. [63] noted lower self-acceptance among women compared to men, this study reveals strong professional confidence among respondents, with 73% expressing belief in their leadership capabilities. Such self-motivational traits counteract societal stereotypes and foster career growth.

Educational background

Educational attainment and experience are pivotal to women's advancement. Companies in the logistics sector increasingly support women through training programs, aligning with Ince's [64] assertion that higher education enhances decision-making efficacy and societal influence. This study found that 41% of respondents held bachelor's degrees, underscoring education's role in overcoming barriers.

Organizational culture

Organizational culture profoundly influences women's representation in leadership. Gender-inclusive policies, mentorship programs, and equitable promotion criteria are essential to dismantling systemic barriers [65]. This study highlights that 85% of respondents identified inclusive cultures as critical for career advancement, reducing biases and enabling professional growth.

Conclusion

This study confirms the pervasive influence in Sri Lanka's logistics sector, where systemic inequities—rooted in work-life imbalances, psychological barriers, educational gaps, and exclusionary organizational cultures—hinder women's advancement to leadership roles. The regression model ($R^2 = 0.621$) and hypothesis testing ($p < 0.05$) underscore the collective impact of these factors, with 62% of women reporting work-life conflicts and 85% advocating for inclusive policies to mitigate gender biases. Targeted interventions, such as flexible work policies, mentorship initiatives, advanced educational opportunities, and cultural awareness campaigns, are imperative to dismantle these barriers. Future research should evaluate the long-term efficacy of such measures and explore their applicability across other male-dominated industries in South Asia. By fostering equitable environments, stakeholders can unlock the logistics sector's full potential, driving innovation and economic growth through gender-inclusive leadership.

Acknowledgment

Sincere gratitude is extended to all who contributed to the successful completion of this research. Appreciation is also extended to the professionals in the logistics sector who generously shared their time and insights.

References

[1] Jayasuriya, S. (2019). Logistics - opportunities for women of the future. *Journal of Gender Studies Logistics*, 12(3), 45–60.

[2] Department of Census and Statistics (2020) Sri Lanka Labour Force Survey: Annual Report 2020. Colombo: Department of Census and Statistics. Available at: http://www.statistics.gov.lk/LabourForce/StaticalInformation/AnnualReports/2020.

[3] Edirisinghe, L. (2015). Enhancing the power of women in logistics and transport. *Transport Policy*, 28, 112–125.

[4] Shakil, M., Munim, Z., & Zamore, S. (2022). Sustainability and financial performance of transport and logistics firms: does board gender diversity matter?. *Journal of Business Ethics,* 180(4), pp. 1017–1042.

[5] Wodon, Q. (2017). The Cost of Gender Inequality in Earnings. World Bank.

[6] Girma, G. (2020). Factors affecting women participation in management positions: the case of NIB international bank. *International Journal Gender Management*, 15(2), 78–92.

[7] Barnet-Verzat, C., & Wolff, F. (2008). Gender disparities in career trajectories. *Economics Letters*, 101(3), 200–203.

[8] Mahasha, K. L. (2016). Balancing work and family responsibilities: the case of women in management positions. *Journal of Organizational Psychology*, 34, 112–130.

[9] EUROPHIA (2009). Opportunities and challenges faced by women in logistics industries. *Supply Chain Quarterly*.

[10] ILO (2004). Breaking Through the Glass Ceiling: Women in Management. Geneva: International Labour Organization.

[11] Muleta, G. (2015). Gender disparities in developing economies. *Journal of Gender Studies*, 12(3), 45–60.

[12] Mallawarachchi, R., & Peiris, T. (2020). Historical exclusion of women in South Asia. *Social Science Quarterly*, 34, 112–130.

[13] Kirima, M. (2019). Cultural barriers in male-dominated industries. *International Journal of Social Research*, 22(4), 301–315.

[14] GIRMA (2020). Global Gender Parity Report. World Economic Forum.

[15] Department of Census and Statistics (2020) *Annual report - Sri Lanka Labour Force Survey 2020*. Colombo: Department of Census and Statistics. Available at: http://www.statistics.gov.lk/LabourForce/StaticalInformation/AnnualReports/2020.

[16] Hansez, I. (2021). Work-family interface in logistics. *Journal of Occupational Psychology*, 45, 78–92.

[17] David, J. (2017). Policy interventions for gender equity. *Harvard Business Review*, 95(2), 112–125.

[18] Edirisinghe, L., Waidyasekara, V., Ranwala, L., Siriwardena, S., Medawattage, A., De Silva, D. and Rathnayake, W. (2022) 'Mind the gender gap in workforce, including transport and logistics: the perspective from Sri Lanka and beyond', *Transportation Research Part A: Policy and Practice,* 165, pp. 379–401.

[19] Chisholm-Burns, M., Christina, A., Tracy, H. and Michelle, A. (2017) 'Women in leadership and the bewildering glass', *Supply Chain Management,* 15(3), pp. 401–415.

[20] Mahasha, K. L. (2016). Childcare and workforce retention. *Journal of Organizational Psychology*, 34, 501–517.

[21] ILO (2004). Breaking the Glass Ceiling. Geneva: ILO Press.

[22] Morrison, A. M., & von Glinow, M. A. (1990). Women and minorities in management. *American Psychologist*, 45(2), 200–208.

[23] Eagly, A. H., & Karau, S. J. (2002). Role congruity theory of prejudice toward female leaders. *Psychological Review*, 109(3), 573–598.

[24] Ragins, B. R., & Cotton, J. L. (1991). Easier said than done: gender differences in perceived barriers to gaining a mentor. *Academy of Management Journal*, 34(4), 939–951.

[25] Blau, F. D., & Devaro, J. (2007). New evidence on gender differences in promotion rates. *American Economic Review*, 97(2), 113–118.

[26] UNCTAD (2006). Review of Maritime Transport. United Nations.

[27] Nigam, S. (2010). Breaking barriers: women in logistics. *Journal of Supply Chain Management*, 15(2), 45–60.

[28] EUROPHIA (2010). Women in Global Supply Chains. EUROPHIA Publications.

[29] DailyFT (2018). Gender gaps in Sri Lankan logistics. *Daily Financial Times*, 12.

[30] Blau, F. D., & Ferber, M. A. (1992). The Economics of Women, Men, and Work. Pearson.

[31] UNDP (2010). Asia-Pacific Human Development Report. United Nations.

[32] EDB Sri Lanka (2020). Logistics Sector Overview. Colombo: EDB.

[33] ILO (2020). Women in Business and Management. Geneva: ILO Press.

[34] Judith, J. (2010). Work-Life Dynamics in Modern Careers. Springer.

[35] Hanna, R. (2015). Gender disparities in leadership aspirations. *Journal of Organizational Behavior*, 36(4), 501–517.

[36] Lukaka, T. (2015). Caregiving and career trajectories. *Gender and Society*, 29(2), 200–215.

[37] Mahasha, K. L. (2016). Flexible work policies in logistics. *International Journal of Human Resource Management*, 28, 112–130.

[38] Goff, S. (2005). Gender diversity and profitability. *Harvard Business Review*, 83(7), 45–60.

[39] Catalyst (2004). Women in Leadership: Global Trends. Catalyst Inc.

[40] ILO (2015). Women in Business and Management. Geneva: ILO Press.

[41] Tallerico, M., & Burstyn, J. (1996). Gendered Pathways to Leadership. Sage.

[42] Shin, S. C. (2013). Self-perception in female professionals. *Journal of Applied Psychology*, 98(3), 401–415.

[43] Bond, J., & Manjit, R. (2015). Gender and Organizational Politics. Routledge.

[44] UNEG (2014). Global Evaluation of Gender Parity. United Nations.

[45] Gojjam, K. (2015). Mentorship in male-dominated sectors. *Human Resource Management Quarterly*, 22, 78–92.

[46] Marimuoniovaera, M., & Turuneh, K. (2015). Gender Disparities in Skill Investment. Oxford Univ. Press.

[47] Becker, G. S. (1993). Human Capital: A Theoretical Analysis. Univ. Chicago Press.

[48] Birikti, G. (2014). Educational gaps in female workforce participation. *Journal of Gender Economics*, 12(2), 78–92.

[49] UN Women (1995). Beijing Declaration and Platform for Action. United Nations.

[50] Francesca, L. (2017). Stress and leadership in women. *Journal of Organizational Psychology*, 34, 112–130.

[51] Lord, R. G., & Maher, K. J. (1991). Leadership and Information Processing. Routledge.

[52] Marshal, J. (1993). Gender dynamics in organizational culture. *Administrative Science Quarterly*, 38(3), 401–415.

[53] Mills, A. J. (1998). Gender and Organizational Culture. Sage.

[54] Jalalic Djeregna, L. (2006). Role models in leadership. *Journal of Applied Psychology*, 91(2), 200–215.

[55] ILO (2020). Women in Management: Global Report. Geneva: ILO Press.

[56] GIRMA (2020). Gender-Inclusive Workplace Policies. World Economic Forum.

[57] Halliday, C., Paustian-Underdahl, S., Stride, C. & Zhang, H. (2022) *Retaining women in male-dominated occupations across cultures: The role of supervisor support and psychological safety.* Human Performance, 35 (3–4), pp. 156–177

[58] Buddhapriya, S. (2009). Gender disparities in career trajectories. *International Journal of Organizational Psychology*, 12, 112–125.

[59] Kirchmeyer, C. (2006). Career advancement in logistics. *Journal of Applied Psychology*, 91(2), 200–215.

[60] Oke, A., Prajogo, D. & Jayaram, J. (2013). Strengthening the innovation chain: The role of women in supply chain innovation. *International Journal of Production Economics,* 142(1), pp. 244–256.

[61] Fan, Y., Bai, H. & Gong, Y. (2024) 'Are gender diversity issues a hidden problem in logistics and supply chain management? Building research themes through a systematic literature review', *Journal of Purchasing and Supply Management,* 30(3).

[62] Mahasha, K. L. (2016). Balancing work and family responsibilities. *Journal of Organizational Psychology*, 34, 112–130.

[63] Mahasha, K. L. M. (2016) *Balancing work and family responsibilities: The case of women in management positions in Nkangala District* (Doctoral dissertation). University of the Witwatersrand.

[64] Matud, M. P. (2019). Self-acceptance and leadership in women. Sex Roles, 80(7), 401–415.

[65] Ince, M. (2010). Education and women's societal roles. Journal of Education Policy, 25(4), 501–517.

[66] ILO (2004). Breaking Through the Glass Ceiling: Women in Management. Geneva: International Labour Organization.

20 Factors affecting availability of essential medicine in selected government hospitals in regional directorate of health services Gampaha: a supply chain perspective

G.S.S. Dharmarathne[a], *G.P.K. Perera*[b] *and A.P. Silva*[c]
Department of Management, NSBM Green University, Sri Lanka

Abstract

The availability of essential medicines remains a critical global issue, with one-third of the world's population lacking access. This study investigates the factors affecting essential medicine availability in selected government hospitals under the Regional Directorate of Health Services, Gampaha. The research addresses three key questions: the current downstream drug supply chain process, influencing factors, and the availability status of selected medicines. A mixed-method approach was used, involving interviews, questionnaires, and checklists. A purposive sample of 74 pharmacists and dispensers was selected. Qualitative data were thematically analyzed, while quantitative data were processed using SPSS and Excel. Findings revealed that demand forecasting, procurement, storage, and distribution are key components, facilitated by the MSMIS system. Quantitative results confirmed the reliability and significance of variables used in the conceptual model. Data also showed medicine stock-outs during the study period, with some medicines having below 50% availability. Recommendations include improving demand forecasting, MSMIS expansion, and enhancing storage and distribution.

Keywords: Availability, demand forecasting, essential medicine, government hospitals, supply chain

Introduction

Overview

Access to essential medicine is recognized as a fundamental human right, alongside access to food, water, education, and shelter [1]. Medicines play a vital role in healthcare systems globally, and their availability in proper dosages and storage conditions is crucial for saving lives [2]. In Sri Lanka, the government allocates 3.4% of its GDP to healthcare, with most citizens relying on public hospitals for free medical services [3]. However, there are growing concerns regarding the unavailability of essential medicines in these hospitals, compelling patients to purchase drugs at high prices from private sources, creating healthcare inequities.

Effective supply chain management [4] is essential for maintaining a continuous drug supply. The downstream supply chain—spanning from the Medical Supply Division to hospitals—often faces disruptions that impact medicine availability [5, 6] Studies in countries like India and Sri Lanka have reported low availability rates for essential medicines in public hospitals, especially for children [7, 8]. Moreover, the drug management process in Sri Lanka has been underprioritized [9], warranting urgent investigation into downstream supply chain-related factors affecting medicine availability in regional public hospitals.

Significance and justification

The availability of essential medicines is a critical component of effective healthcare delivery. Globally, around one-third of the population lacks access to primary medicines, with even higher shortages reported in lower-middle-income countries like Sri Lanka [10]. Despite free healthcare services and a 3.4% GDP allocation to health [3], Sri Lankan government hospitals continue to face medicine shortages, especially for essential drugs. Previous studies have identified low availability rates and highlighted weaknesses in the drug management process [5]. This study is significant as it aims to identify specific downstream supply chain factors that hinder medicine availability in selected hospitals in Gampaha. Findings will support healthcare policymakers and hospital administrators in improving forecasting, storage, and distribution practices. Moreover, the study contributes to addressing a nationwide public

[a]gssdharmarathne@students.nsbm.ac.lk, [b]prasanna.p@nsbm.ac.lk, [c]prabha.s@nsbm.ac.lk

DOI: 10.4324/9781003739920-20

health issue by providing insights that could reduce medicine shortages and enhance equitable access to life-saving treatments.

Research objectives

i. To identify the current downstream supply chain process of essential medicine in selected government hospitals in the Regional Directorate of Health Services Gampaha.
ii. To assess the existing level of availability of essential medicine in selected government hospitals in the Regional Directorate of Health Services Gampaha
iii. To identify the downstream supply chain-related factors affecting the availability of essential medicine in selected government hospitals in the Regional Directorate of Health Services Gampaha

Research questions

i. What is the current process of the downstream supply chain of essential medicine at the selected government hospitals in the Regional Directorate of Health Services Gampaha?
ii. What is the existing level of availability of essential medicine in selected government hospitals in the Regional Directorate of Health Services Gampaha?
iii. What is the downstream supply chain-related factors affecting the availability of essential medicine in selected government hospitals in the Regional Directorate of Health Services Gampaha?

Literature Review

Overview on availability of medicine

Access to essential medicines is a basic human right [1]. Their continuous supply ensures patient safety and builds trust in healthcare services [11]. Inadequate availability results in avoidable morbidity and mortality [12]. WHO estimates that over 10 million deaths annually could be prevented by ensuring access to essential medicine [13]. The availability of medicine also determines the effectiveness of healthcare delivery, especially in low- and middle-income countries, where supply interruptions can disrupt entire treatment programs. Thus, ensuring the availability of essential medicine is not only a clinical need but also a policy and governance priority.

Essential medicine

Essential medicines treat priority health conditions of a population. WHO defines them as those selected with regard to disease prevalence, efficacy, safety, and cost-effectiveness [14]. They should be available at all times, in appropriate forms, and affordable for both individuals and communities. These medicines form the backbone of health service delivery, enabling healthcare systems to function efficiently [15]. The consistent availability of these drugs helps reduce hospital admissions and mortality while enhancing the overall quality of life. Ensuring their accessibility also contributes to reducing inequality in health services, especially in resource-constrained settings.

Essential medicine list concept

The ECL concept originated from military practices and was later adopted by WHO in 1977. The WHO EML guides national and institutional lists, aiming to promote equitable access to medicines [16]. Over time, this list has evolved into a global standard [17]. ECL serves as a reference for procurement and policy decisions, encouraging rational drug use and cost efficiency. Countries adapt the WHO EML to suit local epidemiological needs and budgetary constraints, resulting in tailored lists that help prioritize resource allocation in healthcare systems.

National list of essential medicines of Sri Lanka

Sri Lanka's NMRA, under the Ministry of Health, maintains a National Essential Medicine List aligned with WHO guidelines. The list is periodically updated based on local needs and expert recommendations [18]. It ensures appropriate availability in both public and private healthcare institutions. The committee responsible for the EML includes medical experts, pharmacists, and administrators who assess disease burden, current usage, and emerging health threats. This national-level planning ensures that essential medicines are distributed equitably, especially to underserved rural and semi-urban regions.

Overview of the Sri Lankan health care system

Sri Lanka's dual healthcare system includes both public and private institutions. The public system, which serves the majority, comprises national and district hospitals, base hospitals, and divisional units. Preventive and curative services are delivered through Medical Officer of Health [19] offices and primary medical care units, respectively [20]. The system is tax-funded, ensuring free access to healthcare services, including medicines, for the public. Despite being a lower-middle-income country, Sri Lanka has made significant progress in health indicators due to this universal healthcare system. However, challenges persist in maintaining the supply chain, especially at regional levels.

Availability of essential medicine

Availability in this context refers to ensuring essential medicines are accessible when needed. Governments adopt WHO standards to select and distribute medicines effectively [11]. National and international reports provide guidelines for improving access, promoting the use of generics, and reducing stock-outs. Availability also depends on the efficiency of logistics, procurement systems, and inventory management [21]. Policymakers and healthcare managers must ensure timely forecasting and distribution mechanisms to prevent critical shortages. Technological tools like supply chain dashboards and real-time inventory tracking are increasingly used to enhance medicine availability.

Availability level of essential medicine in the global context

Global disparities in medicine availability remain significant. WHO states that 1/3 of the world's population lacks access to essential medicine [22]. Studies report availability rates of 60% globally, with lower rates in Eastern Mediterranean and African regions [15]. Even developed nations like the USA face drug shortages due to manufacturing and supply chain issues [23]. In some regions, essential medicines are not available due to regulatory barriers, high costs, or poor infrastructure [22, 23]. Addressing this global drug gap requires multi-sector collaboration, efficient regulation, and international cooperation to ensure equitable healthcare.

The global pharmaceutical supply chain process

The pharmaceutical supply chain is a multi-stakeholder process involving production, procurement, distribution, and dispensing [24]. It is vulnerable to disruptions such as supplier failures, demand fluctuations, and regulatory changes. WHO advocates for a structured Drug Management Cycle selection, procurement, storage, and distribution supported by robust information and management systems [11]. This supply chain also involves customs clearance, warehousing, and last-mile delivery, which adds complexity, especially in geographically dispersed or conflict-prone areas. Strengthening these processes through digitization, stakeholder coordination, and training is essential to avoid medicine shortages.

Factors affecting the availability of essential medicine

Factors impacting availability include internal inefficiencies and external disruptions. Internally, poor planning, inventory control, and information flow reduce medicine availability [25]. Externally, issues such as supplier reliability, funding inconsistencies, and procurement delays have been reported globally from Kenya and Uganda to China and the USA [26, 27, 28]. Sri Lanka has also experienced stock-outs due to poor budget allocation and lack of strategic supply chain planning [29]. Additional challenges include lack of trained personnel, non-compliance with standard operating procedures, and outdated infrastructure [28]. Addressing these factors requires institutional reforms, robust monitoring mechanisms, and policy-level interventions.

Methodology

Research design

The research adopted a cross-sectional design, allowing data collection at a single point in time to describe the relationship between variables. This design was suitable for assessing the current supply chain practices and their effect on the availability of essential medicines in selected government hospitals. Cross-sectional studies are efficient for exploring correlations and identifying trends within a defined population [30].

Research method

A mixed-method approach was utilized, combining both qualitative and quantitative techniques to gain comprehensive insights. The qualitative component focused on understanding the downstream supply chain process through semi-structured interviews, while the quantitative component assessed factors affecting availability using a structured questionnaire. The mixed-method strategy enhanced the validity of the findings and allowed triangulation of data [31].

Study population and sample

The study population consisted of pharmacists and dispensers involved in the pharmaceutical supply chain in four government hospitals: Gampaha, Wathupitiwala, Kiribathgoda, and Meerigama. A sample of 74 participants was selected using the Yamane formula from an estimated population of 90. Purposive sampling was employed to ensure the inclusion of key informants with direct involvement in the supply chain [32].

Data collection and analysis

Qualitative data were collected through open-ended, semi-structured interviews conducted with five key informants. Quantitative data were obtained using a questionnaire based on a five-point Likert scale and a six-month availability checklist tracking ten essential medicines. Interview recordings were transcribed and translated for analysis, and questionnaires were physically distributed to ensure response accuracy.

Thematic analysis was used for qualitative data following Braun and Clarke's six-step framework: familiarization, coding, theme development, review, definition, and report writing [33]. Quantitative data were analyzed using SPSS for reliability, correlation, and regression testing. Microsoft Excel was used to calculate medicine availability rates from the checklist.

Results

Data analysis and discussion

Qualitative data analysis in this study was based on the responses of five purposively selected key informants involved in the supply chain processes of four government hospitals in the Gampaha district. These informants were interviewed using semi-structured, open-ended questions to capture in-depth insights into the functioning and challenges of the downstream supply chain. The collected data were transcribed and translated to ensure clarity and consistency prior to analysis.

Thematic analysis, as outlined by Braun and Clarke [33], was used to analyze the qualitative data. This six-phase process included familiarization with the data, generating initial codes, searching for themes, reviewing themes, defining and naming themes, and producing the final report. This method was appropriate for identifying meaningful patterns in participants' narratives and aligning them with the research objectives. The flexibility and rigor of thematic analysis allowed the researcher to explore experiences and perceptions with systematic depth and coherence.

Sample characteristics

In order to conduct the interviews, five participants from the four selected hospitals were chosen. Two participants were selected from the Gampaha District General hospital as it contained the highest population of pharmacists. Each participant from the remaining three hospitals was selected, respectively. Having at least one year of experience in the supply chain process of medicine was considered as an eligibility criterion for participating in interviews.

Theme 1: Supply chain of essential medicine

This theme highlighted the fundamental components of the downstream pharmaceutical supply chain in government hospitals. Participants emphasized that the supply process involves several structured steps, including requisition, verification, and documentation, starting from the ward level to the medical superintendent's office. Upon final approval, orders are forwarded to the Regional Medical Supplies Division. Respondents stated that the current system ensures clear communication and responsibility among pharmacists and dispensers. However, delays occur when communication gaps arise or when documentation is incomplete, leading to disruptions in medicine supply.

Theme 2: Annual estimation

Annual estimation is a critical part of the supply chain process, as it determines the volume of medicine required for each institution. Key informants explained that estimations are based on past consumption patterns and anticipated needs, often using the Medical Supplies Management Information System. While the use of digital systems has improved accuracy, several respondents noted that lack of training in data forecasting tools has occasionally resulted in underestimation, contributing to stock-outs during periods of increased demand.

Theme 3: Procurement and obtaining

Procurement is carried out by the State Pharmaceuticals Corporation through a centralized process. Respondents reported that although the procurement framework is well-defined, delays in delivery from suppliers and bureaucratic obstacles often slow the process. Some interviewees pointed out that even when hospitals place timely orders, inefficiencies in supplier coordination result in medicines arriving later than scheduled, disrupting treatment plans for patients.

Theme 4: Storage and distribution

Proper storage and timely distribution of medicines are crucial for maintaining availability. Interviewees highlighted the lack of space in hospital pharmacies as a key limitation. Overcrowding and poor ventilation in some storage areas have raised concerns about the quality and safety of medicines. Moreover, respondents stated that internal transport systems for distributing medicines from the main stores to different departments are outdated and require urgent modernization.

Theme 5: Medical supplies management information system

MSMIS has streamlined many aspects of the pharmaceutical supply chain. Interviewees acknowledged that this system enables better tracking, forecasting, and transparency in ordering. However, it was also noted that technical glitches, power failures, and limited staff training can hinder its full potential. A few respondents expressed concerns about system downtime leading to manual processes being reintroduced, thereby increasing the likelihood of human error.

Conclusion

The study identified several critical factors impacting the availability of essential medicine in selected government hospitals in the Gampaha district. Findings revealed gaps in forecasting, procurement, storage, and distribution processes. While systems like MSMIS have improved transparency and coordination, operational challenges such as inadequate infrastructure, delayed deliveries, and lack of training persist. Strengthening these aspects is essential for ensuring uninterrupted access to essential medicines in public hospitals.

Recommendations

It is recommended to enhance the accuracy of demand forecasting through regular staff training and better use of digital tools like MSMIS. Procurement processes should be expedited by minimizing bureaucratic delays and improving supplier coordination. Storage facilities must be upgraded to meet required safety standards, and adequate space should be allocated to prevent overcrowding. Distribution systems need modernization to improve internal logistics between hospital departments. MSMIS should be strengthened through technical support, training, and infrastructure development to ensure continuous functionality and minimize downtime. Policymakers and healthcare administrators should implement monitoring and evaluation frameworks to ensure accountability in the medicine supply chain. However, the study further elaborates the requirement of supplier performance monitoring, centralized procurement reforms and buffer stock policies such as regional depots. These interventions would contribute to a more resilient and efficient pharmaceutical supply system in the public sector.

Limitations

The study was limited to four government hospitals in the Gampaha district, which may affect the generalizability of the findings. Data were collected from a relatively small number of participants, which might not capture the full range of perspectives. Moreover, the study primarily focused on the downstream segment of the supply chain, leaving upstream factors less explored.

Future research implications

Future studies should expand the sample size and include multiple regions across Sri Lanka to enhance representativeness. Research can also explore the upstream supply chain and supplier-related challenges to present a comprehensive analysis. Additionally, longitudinal studies could help assess the long-term impact of interventions on medicine availability and health outcomes in public hospitals.

References

[1] United Nations, (1948). The Universal Declaration of Human Rights, Article 25.1 [Online]. Available: https://www.un.org/en/about-us/universal-declaration-of-human-rights. [Accessed: July. 1, 2025].

[2] World Health Organization, (2021). World Health Organization [Online]. Available: https://www.who.int/medicines/services/essmedicines_def/en/. [Accessed: Jun. 1, 2025].

[3] Medical Supply Division, (2021). Medical Supply Division [Online]. Available: https://www.msd.gov.lk/index.php/downloads/publications. [Accessed: May 31, 2025].

[4] Koberg, E., & Longoni, A. (2019). A systematic review of sustainable supply chain management in global supply chains. Journal of cleaner production, 207, 1084–1098.

[5] Jahre, M., Dumoulin, L., Greenhalgh, L. B., Hudspeth, C., Limlim, P., & Spindler, A. (2012). Improving health in developing countries: reducing complexity of drug supply chains. *Journal of Humanitarian Logistics and Supply Chain Management*, 2, 54–84.

[6] Croxton, K. G.-D. (2001). The supply chain management processes. *The International Journal of Logistics Management*, 2(12), 13–36.

[7] Kotwani, A. E. (2007). Prices and availability of common medicines at six sites in India using standard methodology. *Indian Journal of Medicine Research*, 127, 645–654.

[8] Balasubramaniam, R. B. (2011). A national survey of availability of key essential medicines for children in Sri Lanka. *Ceylon Medical Journal*, 3, 56.

[9] Dharmagunawardhene, D. (2015). Medical Administration Part11. PGIM.

[10] World Health Organization, Equitable Access to Essential Medicines: A Framework for Collective Action: WHO Policy Perspectives on Medicines, 2010. [Online]. Available: https://iris.who.int/bitstream/handle/10665/68571/?sequence=1. [Accessed: May. 20, 2025].

[11] Management Science for Health (2011). Managing Drug Supply. New York: Kumari Press Inc.

[12] Zuma, S. M. (2013). The factors affecting availability of medicines in the Free State District Health Services. University of South Africa (South Africa).

[13] World Health Organization (2011). World Medical Situation 2011. Geneva: WHO.

[14] WHO (2015). The WHO Model List of Essential Medicines. Geneva: WHO.

[15] Revere, L., Roberts, R., & Harris, H. (2004). Improving resource efficiency through management science. Journal of Healthcare Management, 49(5), 323.

[16] Greene, J. A. (2011). Making medicines essential. the emergent centrality of pharmaceuticals in global health. *BioSocieties*, (6), 10–33.

[17] Veronika, J., & Wirtz, H. V.-L. (2016). Essential medicines for universal health coverage. *The Lancet Commission*, 389(10067), 403–476.

[18] National Medicines Regulatory Authority, Annual Report 2009. 2009. [Online]. Available: https://nmra.gov.lk/images/PDF/publication/publication_001.pdf. [Accessed: June. 30, 2025].

[19] Pham, H. H., Schrag, D., Hargraves, J. L., & Bach, P. B. (2005). Delivery of preventive services to older adults by primary care physicians. Jama, 294(4), 473–481.

[20] Ministry of Health, Nutrition and Indigenous Medicine, Essential (Health) Services Package for Sri Lanka, Version 2.2, 22 Aug. 2018. [Online]. Available: https://www.hsep.lk/images/Downloads/Publications/EssentialHealthServicesPackage.pdf. [Accessed: June 30, 2025].

[21] Cameron, A., Ewen, M., Ross-Degnan, D., Ball, D., & Laing, D. (2008). Medicine Prices, Availability, and Affordability in 36 Developing and Middle-Income Countries: A Secondary Analysis. Geneva: World Health Organization.

[22] Heiskanen, K., Ahonen, R., Karttunen, P., Kanerva, R., & Timonen, J. (2015). Medicine shortages: a study of community pharmacies in Finland. *Health Policy*, 2, 232–238.

[23] Gray, A., & Manasse Jr, H. R. (2012). Shortages of medicines: a complex global challenge. *Bulletin of the World Health Organization*, 90(3), 158.

[24] Rossetti, C. L., Handfield, R., & Dooley, K. J. (2011). Forces, trends, and decisions in pharmaceutical supply chain management. *International Journal of Physical Distribution and Logistics Management*, 41, 601–622.

[25] Jaberidoost, M. N. (2013). Pharmaceutical supply chain risks: a systematic review. *DARU Journal of Pharmaceutical Sciences*, 1(69), 21.

[26] Mwathi, M. (2014). Availability of essential medicines in public hospitals. *African Journal of Pharmacy and Pharmacology*, 8(17), 438–442.

[27] Tumwine, Y., Kutyabami, P., Odoi, R. A., & Kalyango, J. N. (2009). Availability and expiry of essential medicines and supplies during the 'pull' and 'push' drug acquisition systems in a rural Ugandan Hospital. *Tropical Journal of Pharmaceutical Research*, 9(6), 557–564.

[28] Lu, Y. (2006). A Survey of Medicine Prices, Availability and Affordability in Shanghai, China Using the WHO/HAI Methodology. China: Department of Health Economics, School of Public Health Fudan University.

[29] Wijayasiriwardhana, J. (2020). Study on issues of drug availability and recommendations of improving the availability in health care institutions of Sri Lanka. World Journal of Pharmaceutical Research, 9(15), 127-138.

[30] Barbie, E. (2010). The Practice of Social Research, (12th edn.). USA: Belmont Wadsworth.

[31] Almeida, F. (2018). Strategies to perform a mixed method study. *European Journal of Education Studies*, 5(1), 01.

[32] Neuman, W. (2011). Social Research Methods: Qualitative and Quantitative Approaches, (7th edn.). Boston: Allyn and Bacon.

[33] Braun, V., & Clarke, V. (2006). Using thematic analysis in psychology. *Qualitative Research in Psychology*, 3(2), 77–101.

21 Future professionals' entrepreneurial intentions, sustainability and global competence: paving the way for a Sustainable Global Entrepreneurship

Ramon Andres Ortiz-Rojo[a] *and Adonai Jose Lacruz*[b]
Federal University of Espirito Santo, Brazil

Abstract

This study analyses the direct and indirect effects between students' entrepreneurial intention, the dimensions of sustainability (economic, social and environmental) and global competence' dimensions (self-awareness, intercultural communication and global knowledge), and the moderating effect of a geopolitical aspect. To this end, the partial least squares structural equation modelling technique was applied to analyse data obtained from undergraduate students. The results suggest that there is a direct positive effect of future professionals' entrepreneurial intention on the three dimensions of sustainability, as well as on the three dimensions of global competence. Also, that in the positive effect of entrepreneurial intention on the social dimension of sustainability there is an indirect effect through students' intercultural communication dimension of global competence and that in the positive effect of entrepreneurial intention of future professionals on the environmental dimension of sustainability there is an indirect effect through students' self-awareness dimension of global competence. The empirical evidence of this study represents a valuable contribution in terms of theory and practice for studies addressing sustainability and how new professionals are being equipped to face such a challenge. Also, the results of the study pave the way for a broader discussion of Sustainable Global Entrepreneurship.

Keywords: Entrepreneurial intentions, entrepreneurship, geopolitical aspects, global competence, sustainability, sustainable global entrepreneurship

Introduction

Today, sustainability stands as one of the foremost global concerns [1], making it crucial to understand how future professionals are equipped to address this issue. More specifically, it is necessary to understand how the entrepreneurial intention (EI) of future professionals and their global competences (GC) can contribute to the sustainability of the planet.

The global concern over sustainability is further emphasized when examining the progress report of the Sustainable Development Goals (SDG) established by the United Nations [2]. In such report, it is stated that just 17% of the SDG targets are on track. In light of this, entrepreneurship could play a pivotal role as a facilitator or driver for development and economic growth, given its potential for creating new jobs, fostering innovation and empowering companies to be more competitive [3–6].

Among researchers, there is an increase interest in studying the EI of undergraduate students [7, 8]. These EI are regarded as a state of consciousness that precedes action, directing attention towards a goal, such as starting a business [9]. In that regard, according to [6], most of the studies addressing the EI of students have relied on the human behaviour predictive power of the theory of planned behaviour (TPB) [10]. Intentions are considered the best predictor of a given behaviour [7, 11].

Authors have addressed EI within the context of students' EI in universities. Mostly with a focus on the important role of entrepreneurial education [7, 12, 13, 8]. Also, in some cases, adding cultural aspects [9], the area of studies [14] and entrepreneurial capacity [15] to the analysis.

A growing interest in studying the environmental aspect [5], a sustainable entrepreneurship [16], and the Sustainable Entrepreneurial Intentions (SEI) [17] is perceived and has been incorporated into research on students' EI. However, when it comes to analysing EI, sustainability and GC, to the best of

[a]ramonandres.31@gmail.com, [b]prof.lacruz@gmail.com
DOI: 10.4324/9781003739920-21

our knowledge, there is a lack of studies addressing these concepts together. Moreover, a lack of studies is even more evident when it comes to the possible indirect effects through GC dimensions in the relationship between EI and the dimensions of sustainability concept, that is, its economic, social and environmental aspects [18]. Thus, GC is an important aspect to be addressed when it comes to EI and sustainability, since GC of individuals could make them think and take responsible actions toward sustainability and collective well-being [19], which could be enacted locally [20, 21] through their EI.

Additionally, the effect of GC on the dimensions of sustainability could be moderated by geopolitical aspects. Specifically, GC varies depending on the region where a given person lives [22]. This is because the GC mindset of a person, is influenced by the environment in different ways [23–26], making the effect of GC on sustainability' dimensions, stronger or weaker.

So as to address a global concern like sustainability, from the perspective of the ones who will play a key role in society in the future, a global approach such as GC should be used. Thus, in this study, it is sought to contribute not only by incorporating the sustainable and geopolitical aspects to the discussion, but also, in the case of sustainability, the concept as a whole and understood as triple bottom line (TBL) in the literature [18].

TBL covers the economic, social and environmental aspects of sustainability [27] and this study aims to analyse the direct and indirect effects in the relationship between EI, GC and these three dimensions of sustainability and the moderated (by a geopolitical aspect) effect in the relationship between the dimensions of GC and sustainability dimensions. To this end, the structural equation modelling technique is applied to analyse data obtained from undergraduate students. Results of this study contribute empirically to the field of EI demonstrating direct and indirect effects of EI on GC and on sustainability dimensions. Additionally, the moderating role of the geopolitical aspect of geographic location is added when analysing the effect of GC into sustainability dimensions. With these contributions it is paving the way for a broader discussion, including scholars and police makers about a Sustainable Global Entrepreneurship including new professionals' EI, their GC and sustainability.

Literature Review and Hypothesis Formulation

Entrepreneurial intention and sustainability

Entrepreneurship is seen as a driver of economic growth and development, it has the potential to create jobs, foster innovation and enable companies to be competitive [3, 4, 6]. Additionally, entrepreneurship can be observed in several areas of study [3], and within its scope, it is also defined in different ways. Ratten [28] reported 34 types of entrepreneurships, including: international entrepreneurship; digital entrepreneurship; creative entrepreneurship; entrepreneurship in education and social entrepreneurship.

In this context, EI as area of studies has attracted the attention of researchers and being understood as a significant predictor of the action of becoming an entrepreneur [12]. There is also a consensus that when it comes to investigating EI, the TPB is the most used [6]. The EI would be related to a state of consciousness that precedes an action and directs attention to a goal such as starting a business [9]. In this sense, the TPB has shown that it can predict and explain human behaviour in specific contexts considering the attitude towards behaviour, the perceived behavioural control and the social norms [10].

Several authors have contributed to the field of EI studies. [7], using factorial regression, highlighted the important role that education should play in encouraging EI among undergraduate students. [12], using the Tobit regression technique, reinforced the importance of entrepreneurial education in fostering EI in universities. [13], using the structural equation technique, concluded that, unlike many studies using the TPB, there was no significant effect of students' entrepreneurial attitude on their EI.

By incorporating the mediating effect of students' entrepreneurial capacity into the model, [15] reinforce what the literature presents regarding the relevance of entrepreneurial education as a promoter of EI among students. [29] states that there is a statistically significant relationship between management student's entrepreneurship education, attitude towards entrepreneurship and EI.

[8], in addition to analysing the relationship of the TPB constructs, also incorporates the entrepreneurial environment variable and the control variables gender and family experience with entrepreneurship. In the latter, it shows a significant effect on the relationship between attitude, education and EI.

Authors have addressed the theme of EI in university contexts generally associated with the role of the university in fostering entrepreneurial education that can be reflected in students' EI. Some inclusions have been made by authors to analyse cultural aspects in students' EI [9], mediating [15] or moderating effects [14], within the same scenario, that is, students' EI in the university context.

When entrepreneurship and sustainability are coupled, literature has shown that authors often approach these themes primarily from an environmental perspective [30]. For example, [5] conducted a study whose results indicated that when the environment influences students' attitudes, there is an indirect effect on their entrepreneurial intention. In this study, sustainability is framed through the TBL [18], which encompasses the economic dimensions – which considers the company performance projection; the social dimension– considering opportunities and conditions the company will offer-, and the environmental dimensions – considering ecological behaviours [31].

More recently, there was the emergence of interest in studying sustainable entrepreneurship [16], as well as, and more specifically, SEI [17]. The study [17], using the TPB and drawing on sustainability-oriented entrepreneurial intentions, proposed to add the risk-taking propensity, perceived creativity, and proactive personality determinants that can be antecedents to the constructs of TPB. Romero-Colmenares and Reyes-Rodríguez [32] found that SEI were influenced by TPB dimensions and positively influenced by the altruistic values of individuals, the education for sustainable entrepreneurship and the belief that individuals had of themselves to achieve goals.

[33] analysed the dimensions of the TPB, along with the roles of education and family support. The latter two factors were found to contribute significantly to attitudes toward sustainable entrepreneurship. [34] examined the drivers of entrepreneurial intentions in sustainable entrepreneurship, concluding that attitudes toward sustainability are positively influenced by altruism, while perceived entrepreneurial desirability is driven by both intrinsic and extrinsic rewards.

From this review emerge our first hypotheses:

Direct effects of EI on the dimensions of sustainability

H1a: the entrepreneurial intention of future professionals has a positive effect on the economic dimension of sustainability.

H1b: the entrepreneurial intention of future professionals has a positive effect on the social dimension of sustainability.

H1c: The entrepreneurial intention of future professionals has a positive effect on the environmental dimension of sustainability.

Global competence

New professionals who face the challenges influenced by the global context must be both aware of and equipped with the necessary GC for their development in such an environment. One of these challenges is sustainability, which encompasses the economic, social and environmental aspects of the concept [18].

Regarding the agenda established by the UN with 17 SDG, according to The Sustainable Development Goals Report 2024, only 17% of the SDG targets are on track. Besides, nearly half are showing minimal or moderate progress, and progress on over one third has stalled or even regressed [2]. Therefore, the role that future professionals will play in this global scenario is crucial.

Global competence is defined as "a multidimensional capacity. Globally competent individuals can examine local, global and intercultural issues, understand and appreciate different perspectives and world views, interact successfully and respectfully with others, and take responsible action toward sustainability and collective well-being" [19].

In GC studies, there is an overlap in meaning between GC and other terms such as intercultural competence, global perspective, global awareness, and global citizenship, indicating that a unified definition of GC is still under development [35]. Indeed, another definition for GC and perhaps closer to university environment than [19] one, is [36], who state within a model for measuring global citizenship, that GC is related to having an open mind and actively seeking to understand others in terms of their cultural norms and expectations, and along with this leveraging this knowledge to interact, communicate and work effectively outside one's own environment.

Viewing GC as global citizenship, authors consider it as a utopia and think that what is needed is to foster local actions towards global citizenship for higher education institutions (HEI) to contribute more globally [20]. In the same line, [21] state that higher education, in promoting global citizenship do not offer anything new because they continue to incentive social responsibility, and good critical thinking skills, alongside with knowledge, awareness, and care for global issues.

The promotion of GC in HEI has been associated with actions linked to the internationalisation processes of universities, including academic mobility initiatives [37, 38], internationalisation at home programmes providing international courses and employing professors with international experiences [35].

When it comes to analysing GC and EI, to the best of our knowledge, there is a lack of studies addressing both concepts together, even more when thinking about a possible indirect effect of GC in the relationship between EI and sustainability. Zhang et al. [39] understanding GC as academic mobility [38], concluded that entrepreneurship education, government support, and global competence can significantly influence entrepreneurial behaviour of international students indirectly through the serial double mediating effect. Authors have also found that in the case of mandatory study abroad programmes, students can seek their global citizenship identities [40].

It is argued that, given sustainability is a global concern and considering the role that future professionals will play in this context, it requires a global approach to be analysed. Thus, the following hypothesis with the three dimensions of GC (Self-awareness, Intercultural communication and Global knowledge) are formulated:

Direct and indirect effects

H2a: the entrepreneurial intention of future professionals has a positive effect on the self-awareness dimension of global competence.

H2b: the entrepreneurial intention of future professionals has a positive effect on the intercultural communication dimension of global competence.

H2c: the entrepreneurial intention of future professionals has a positive effect on the global knowledge dimension of global competence.

Indirect effects of EI on the economic dimension of sustainability through GC dimensions:

H3a: there is an indirect effect of entrepreneurial intentions of future professionals through students' self-awareness on the economic dimension of sustainability.

H3b: there is an indirect effect of entrepreneurial intentions of future professionals through students' intercultural communication on the economic dimension of sustainability.

H3c: there is an indirect effect of entrepreneurial intentions of future professionals through students' global knowledge on the economic dimension of sustainability.

Indirect effects of EI on the social dimension of sustainability through GC dimensions:

H4a: there is an indirect effect of entrepreneurial intention of future professionals through students' self-awareness on the social dimension of sustainability.

H4b: there is an indirect effect of entrepreneurial intention of future professionals through students' intercultural communication on the social dimension of sustainability.

H4c: there is an indirect effect of entrepreneurial intention of future professionals through students' global knowledge on the social dimension of sustainability.

Indirect effects of EI on the environmental dimension of sustainability through GC dimensions:

H5a: there is an indirect effect of entrepreneurial intention of future professionals through students' self-awareness on the environmental dimension of sustainability.

H5b: there is an indirect effect of entrepreneurial intention of future professionals through students' intercultural communication on the environmental dimension of sustainability.

H5c: there is an indirect effect of entrepreneurial intention of future professionals through students' global knowledge on the environmental dimension of sustainability.

Moderating effect of geopolitical aspects

Geopolitics is a complex and multifaceted concept that has evolved over time in response to historical changes. It encompasses issues related to territory, power, peace, resource exploitation, and other factors that affect nations and their inhabitants [41]. Geopolitics also involves the divisions and impacts between regions of the world, whether positive or negative.

One concept that may help to identify some of these divisions is the Global North and Global South [22]. The Global North refers to regions such as Europe and North America (the United States and Canada), while the Global South encompasses low-income and marginalized regions—politically or culturally—such as Latin America, Asia, Africa, and the Middle East [22]. One area of study where the Global North/South concept has been applied is education, where differences among countries have also been analysed [20].

It is out of the scope of this study to address all the complexity of a wide concept such as geopolitics, but rather to look at aspects like differences among regions when it comes to economic issues [23], peoples' feelings regarding embedded aspects within geopolitics, as terrorism [24], hunger in less favoured countries [25], and about how geopolitics could affect also entrepreneurship [26].

Thus, in this research, the geopolitics concept is understood in terms of the location where a given person— in our study, students— lives, which has the potential to influence how they perceive the world and, in turn, affect their GC. One way to identify this geopolitical influence is through the widely used Human Development Index (HDI), which is a common measure of human development [42].

In few words, the location where the student lives can influence the way this student understands and faces, in our study, sustainability. Bearing this in mind, the following hypothesis are established.

Moderating effect of geopolitical location on the relationship between GC dimensions and the economic dimension of sustainability

H6a: the effect of students' self-awareness on the economic dimension of sustainability is moderated by the students' geopolitical location.
H6b: the effect of students' intercultural communication on the economic dimension of sustainability is moderated by the students' geopolitical location.
H6c: the effect of students' global knowledge on the economic dimension of sustainability is moderated by the students' geopolitical location.

Moderating effect of geopolitical location on the relationship between GC dimensions and the social dimension of sustainability:

H7a: the effect of students' self-awareness on the social dimension of sustainability is moderated by the students' geopolitical location.
H7b: the effect of students' intercultural communication on the social dimension of sustainability is moderated by the students' geopolitical location.
H7c: the effect of students' global knowledge on the social dimension of sustainability is moderated by the students' geopolitical location.

Moderating effect of geopolitical location on the relationship between GC dimensions and the environmental dimension of sustainability:

H8a: the effect of students' self-awareness on the environmental dimension of sustainability is moderated by the students' geopolitical location.
H8b: the effect of students' intercultural communication on the environmental dimension of sustainability is moderated by the students' geopolitical location.
H8c: the effect of students' global knowledge on the environmental dimension of sustainability is moderated by the students' geopolitical location.

Materials and Methodology

In order to analyse the relationship between EI, the 3 dimensions of sustainability and GC dimensions the partial least squares structural equation modelling technique is applied [43] and process the data in the software R.

Data collection and sample

A survey using a 5-point Likert scale was conducted in November and December 2024 with undergraduate students in Brazil. The final sample consisted of 328 valid responses out of a total of 671 questionnaires received. Invalid responses included incomplete questionnaires, those missing the attention control question, and those that were not from undergraduate students.

The minimum sample size, considering 7 latent variables, 32 manifest variables (i.e., items), significance level of 0.05, statistical power of 0.8 and effect size of 0.15 - considered medium, by [44] – was estimated at 170 observations, using the online application Free Statistics Calculators [45]. Thus, the sample size meets the estimated minimum sample: 328 > minimum sample: 170.

In order to minimize possible effects of primacy and recency, the order of the questions was randomized [46]. As well as, for assessing any possible common variance bias resulting from the application of the same online self-administered questionnaire [47], the one-factor Harman test was applied in Jamovi software.

Additionally, the questionnaire was pre-tested with 12 respondents (i.e., 7% of the estimated minimum sample) to identify possible inaccuracies. There was just 1 observation regarded to a specific word in a question from the Intercultural Communication dimension of GC (IC2). Then, an adjustment was made, and the 12 responses of the pre-test participants were delated. Also, to verify the respondent's attention while the questionnaire was answered, the option with the number 3 was asked to be selected in between of the 2 first blocks of questions. Table 21.2 presents some features of the sample (Table 21.1).

Scales and data analysis

To build our model the following validated scales: for EI [8], for economic sustainability, social sustainability and environmental sustainability [31], for GC dimensions [36] and for evaluating the moderating effect of geopolitical aspect (geographical location) in the relationship between GC dimensions and the 3 dimensions of sustainability, we used the HDI, which measures a country's health, education and standard of living [42].

Structural equation modelling technique was applied to estimate path coefficients for the proposed relationships in the model. Regarding the indirect effects on economic sustainability, social sustainability and environmental sustainability, we applied bootstrapping method. To evaluate the moderating effects of geopolitical location, we used the HDI

Table 21.1 Sample of the study.

Description		Frequency	Relative frequency
Age	Less than 24	155	47%
	Between 24 and 29	68	21%
	Between 30 and 35	41	13%
	Between 36 and 41	26	8%
	Between 42 and 47	21	6%
	Between 48 and 53	9	3%
	54 and above	8	2%
Gender	Male	178	54%
	Female	148	45%
	Prefer not to answer	2	< 1%
Geopolitical location (Brazilian states)	Bahia	8	2%
	Ceará	3	< 1%
	Espírito Santo	237	72%
	Goiás	19	6%
	Mato Grosso do Sul	9	3%
	Minas Gerais	38	12%
	Pará	1	< 1%
	Pernambuco	3	< 1%
	São Paulo	10	3%
Previous entrepreneurship studies	Yes	128	39%
	No	200	61%

Source: Author

Table 21.2 Research model.

Constructs	Index number	Scale	Source
Entrepreneurial intention (Reflective)	7	Likert (5 points)	[8]
Self-awareness (Reflective)	3	Likert (5 points)	[36]
Intercultural communication (Reflective)	3	Likert (5 points)	
Global Knowledge (Reflective)	3	Likert (5 points)	
Economic sustainability (Reflective)	5	Likert (5 points)	[31]
Social sustainability (Reflective)	5	Likert (5 points)	
Environmental sustainability (Reflective)	5	Likert (5 points)	
Gender (One single item– Control)	1	Dummy	-
Previous entrepreneurship knowledge (Single item– Control)	1	Dummy	-
Age (age group item – Control)	3	Dummy	-
International entrepreneurial desire (5 points)	1	Ordinal	-
Geopolitical location (HDI Brazilian states)	1	Continuous	[48]

Source: Author

index of each Brazilian state obtained [48] as a continuous variable.

It is important to note that in order to enhance model clarity, mitigate potential multicollinearity issues, and accurately capture both direct and indirect effects among the dimensions [49], we chose to evaluate the constructs' dimensions separately.

Table 21.2 presents the research model of this study. Figures 21.1–21.3 show the proposed theoretical model relation.

The research model is presented in Figure 21.1 (for greater clarity, the model has been divided into three parts A, B and C). Figure 21.1. Model with direct, moderator effects and indirect effects through SA dimension

Results and Discussion

Firstly, through Harman's single-factor test, the result for the total variance extracted by one factor was 0.27%, which is less than 0.50%, indicating that common method bias was discarded. Additionally, it is important to highlight that the presence of outliers in the data was effectively ruled out using Cook's distance ($D < 1$).

Measurement model

In this exploratory study, the research model is composing of reflective constructs. Therefore, the reliability of indicators, the reliability of internal consistency, and the convergent and discriminant validity were assessed [43]. Following what's recommended by the literature, the Cronbach's Alpha and Dillon-Goldstein's Rho were validated. Recommended Cronbach's Alpha values in exploratory research should be above 0.60 [50]. For Rho reliability values between 0.60 and 0.70 are considered acceptable in exploratory research, and values between 0.70 and 0.90 range from satisfactory to good [43, 51]. Regarding the eigenvalue analysis,

Part A

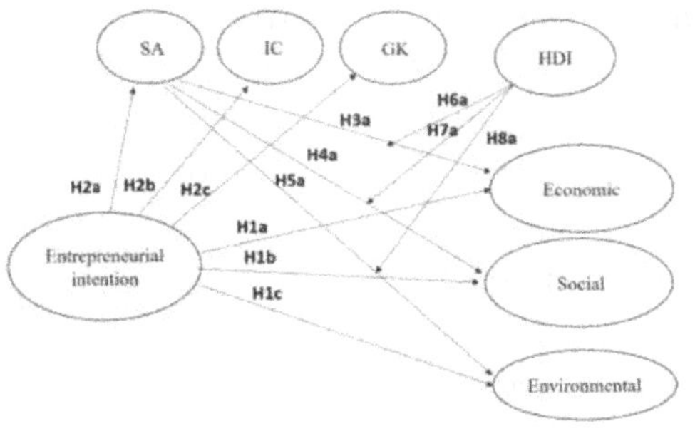

Part B

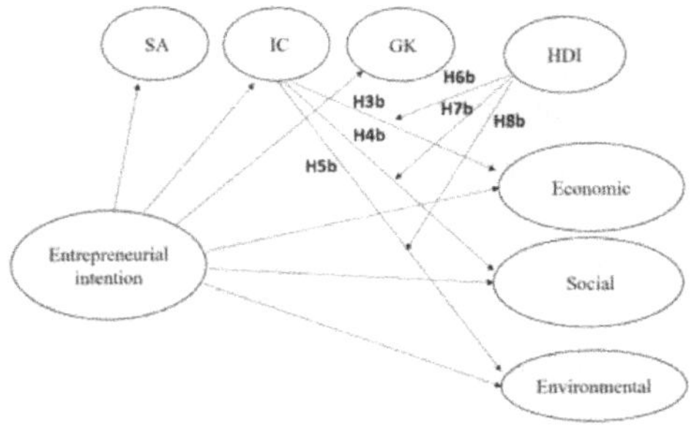

Part C

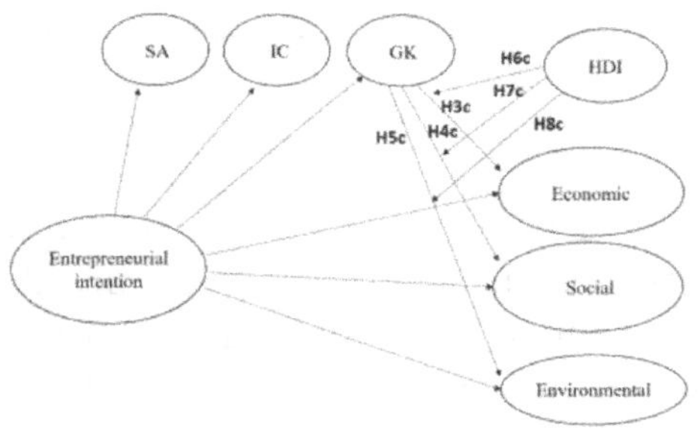

Figure 21.1 Part A, B and C of the model
Source: Author

the first eigenvalues are much larger than 1 and greater than the second eigenvalue, which is taken as evidence of a unidimensional block of indicators [51]. Convergent validity was validated observing the average variance extracted (AVE), where values at least of 0.50 are expected for validation. As for discriminant validity, Fornell Larcker criterion – where the shared variance between all model constructs should not be larger than their AVEs [43] and cross loading criterion – where the indicator loading should be higher in its construct compared to others - were used. Discriminant validity was confirmed in both procedures.

Nonetheless, it must be informed that during the validation procedure of the indicator's reliability, it was observed just one loading bellow the recommended value by [43], that is 0.40. Specifically in the social sustainability construct (SOCS5). Therefore, we eliminated this indicator from the construct and processed the model again, confirming after eliminating it, better results in the internal consistency of the SOCS construct. Table 21.3 presents the measurement model validation and Table 21.4 presents Fornell Larcker criterion values for discriminant validation among constructs.

Structural model

Regarding control variables, the following were included in the structural model: Age (3 dummy by range of age), gender (dummy), previous studies on entrepreneurship (dummy) and the desire to be an international or local entrepreneur (ordinal). Before evaluating structural relations in the model, collinearity was examined using latent variables scores to calculate the variance inflation factor (VIF). No problems of collinearity were observed since all VIF values were lower than 5 [50].

As for the explanatory capacity of the model, the R2 explains the variation in endogenous variables caused by exogenous variables in the model. The R2 ranges from 0 to 1, where according to Cohen [44], values are considered substantial (0.26), moderated (0.13) and weak (0.02). Additionally, it is important to consider the context of the research, because a low value such as 0.10, could be considered satisfactory in some areas [50]. In our study, the coefficients of determination indicated the variation explained by each construct as follows: ECS explains 26.5% (R2=0.265), ENS explains 26.8% (R2 = 0.268), SOCS explains 31.7% (R2 = 0.317), GK explains 3.1% (R2 = 0.031), IC explains 6.1% (R2 = 0.061) and SA explains 6% (R2 = 0.060).

The significance and relevance of the path coefficients were also evaluated by carrying out a bootstrapping procedure with 5.000 subsamples to obtain more accurate estimates. Some of the significant positive relationships observed in the model were: between EI and economic sustainability (path coefficient 0.460; p-value < 0.000), environmental sustainability (path coefficient 0.145; p-value < 0.006) and social sustainability (path coefficient 0.447; p-value

Table 21.3 Measurement model validation.

Constructs	Internal consistency reliability			Convergent validity
	Cronbach's alpha	Dillon-Goldstein's Rho	1st and 2nd eigenvalues	AVE
Entrepreneurial Intention (EI)	0.871	0.902	4.02 - 1.19	0.573
Self-Awareness (SA)	0.700	0.834	1.88 - 0.68	0.627
Intercultural Communication (IC)	0.637	0.805	1.74 - 0.73	0.579
Global Knowledge (GK)	0.634	0.804	1.74 – 0.71	0.575
Economic sustainability (ECS)	0.887	0.917	3.45 – 0.52	0.690
Environmental sustainability (ENS)	0.884	0.913	3.43 – 0.88	0.677
Social sustainability (SOCS)	0.871	0.912	2.89 – 0.61	0.723

Note: n = 328.
Source: Author

Table 21.4 Fornell larcker (discriminant validation).

	ECS	EI	ENS	GK	IC	SA	SOCS
ECS	0.831						
EI	0.478	0.757					
ENS	0.380	0.213	0.823				
GK	0.198	0.176	0.326	0.758			
IC	0.180	0.246	0.155	0.404	0.761		
SA	0.208	0.246	0.443	0.627	0.338	0.792	
SOCS	0.551	0.480	0.344	0.153	0.260	0.157	0.850

**The elements on the diagonal (bold) represent the square root of the variance shared between the constructs and their measures (AVE). The values below the diagonal are the correlations between the constructs.*
Source: Author

< 0.000). The same significant positive relationship was evidenced in the relationship between EI and SA (path coefficient 0.246; p-value < 0.000), IC (path coefficient 0.246; p-value < 0.000) and GK (path coefficient 0.176; p-value < 0.006).

Table 21.5 presents all the coefficients and p-value of the structural model.

This study aimed to analyse the relationship between future professionals' EI, the dimensions of sustainability (economic, social and environmental), and GC dimensions (self-awareness, intercultural communication and global knowledge). Also, it was analysed the moderating effect of the geopolitical location in the relationship between GC and sustainability. We theorized that the EI of future professionals has a positive effect on the three dimensions of sustainability. Likewise, that the EI of future professionals has a positive effect on the three dimensions of GC. Additionally, that there are indirect effects of EI of future professionals on the three dimensions of sustainability through student's GC and, the effects of GC dimensions on sustainability dimensions could be moderated by a geopolitical aspect. The later, because GC could vary depending on the region where the students live.

Table 21.5 Structural model validation.

Relationships	Path
To operate internationally -> ECS	0.062
To operate internationally -> ENS	0.032
To operate internationally -> SOCS	0.025
Dummy female=1 -> ECS	0.203
Dummy female=1 -> ENS	0.373*
Dummy female=1 -> SOCS	0.088
Dummy-range 2 and 3=1- opposite=0 -> ECS	-0.052
Dummy-range 2 and 3=1- opposite=0 -> ENS	-0.021
Dummy- range 2 and 3=1- opposite=0 -> SOCS	-0.312*
Dummy- range 4 and 5=1 - opposite =0 -> ECS	0.058
Dummy- range 4 and 5=1 - opposite =0 -> ENS	0.269
Dummy- range 4 and 5=1 - opposite =0 -> SOCS	-0.478*
Dummy- range 6 and 7=1 - opposite =0 -> ECS	-0.089
Dummy- range 6 and 7=1 - opposite =0 -> ENS	-0.028
Dummy- range 6 and 7=1 - opposite =0 -> SOCS	-0.767*
EI -> ECS	0.460*
EI -> ENS	0.145*
EI -> GK	0.176*
EI -> IC	0.246*
EI -> SA	0.2468
EI -> SOCS	0.447*
State -> ECS	-0.050
State -> ENS	0.059
State -> SOCS	-0.073
GK -> ECS	0.103
GK -> ENS	0.128
GK -> SOCS	0.061
IC -> ECS	0.038
IC -> ENS	-0.013
IC -> SOCS	0.129*
Previous_entrepreneurship_DUMMY_Yes=1 -> ECS	0.094
Previous_entrepreneurship_DUMMY_Yes=1 -> ENS	-0.169
Previous_entrepreneurship_DUMMY_Yes=1 -> SOCS	0.108
SA -> ECS	0.003
SA -> ENS	0.306*
SA -> SOCS	0.023
State x IC -> ECS	-0.001
State x IC -> ENS	-0.036
State x IC -> SOCS	0.083
State x GK -> ECS	0.101
State x GK -> ENS	-0.004
State x GK -> SOCS	0.012
State x SA -> ECS	-0.045
State x SA -> ENS	0.004
State x SA -> SOCS	-0.023
Specific indirect effects	
EI -> IC -> ECS	0.009
EI -> SA -> ENS	0.075*
EI -> GK -> ECS	0.018
EI -> IC -> ENS	-0,003
EI -> GK -> ENS	0.023
EI -> SA -> SOCS	0.006
EI -> IC -> SOCS	0.032*
EI -> GK -> SOCS	0.011
EI -> SA -> ECS	0.001

* Significant at the 0.05 level.
Source: Author

Considering that theorisation and the hypothesis established in this study, we decided to address the global concern of sustainability from the perspective of the ones who will play a key role in society in the short future. To continue with the discussion, Table 21.6 presents the hypothesis of this study and whether they were supported.

All the hypothesis considering direct effects of EI on both, the dimensions of sustainability and the dimensions of GC were supported. Regarding hypothesis considering indirect effects, H4b and H5a were supported. As for moderator hypothesis, none of them was supported.

In this study, it was possible to confirm the important role played by students' EI to potentially contribute to sustainability and to the GC of these new professionals. This is consistent with other studies that highlight the role of HEI in entrepreneurship and fostering EI among students [7, 12] and with the

Table 21.6 Hypothesis of the study.

Hypothesis	Supported
H1a: the entrepreneurial intention of future professionals has a positive effect on the economic dimension of sustainability	Yes
H1b: the entrepreneurial intention of future professionals has a positive effect on the social dimension of sustainability	Yes
H1c: The entrepreneurial intention of future professionals has a positive effect on the environmental dimension of sustainability	Yes
H2a: the entrepreneurial intention of future professionals has a positive effect on the self-awareness dimension of global competence	Yes
H2b: the entrepreneurial intention of future professionals has a positive effect on the intercultural communication dimension of global competence	Yes
H2c: the entrepreneurial intention of future professionals has a positive effect on the global knowledge dimension of global competence	Yes
H3a: there is an indirect effect of entrepreneurial intentions of future professionals through students' self-awareness on the economic dimension of sustainability	No
H3b: there is an indirect effect of entrepreneurial intentions of future professionals through students' intercultural communication on the economic dimension of sustainability	No
H3c: there is an indirect effect of entrepreneurial intentions of future professionals through students' global knowledge on the economic dimension of sustainability	No
H4a: there is an indirect effect of entrepreneurial intention of future professionals through students' self-awareness on the social dimension of sustainability	No
H4b: there is an indirect effect of entrepreneurial intention of future professionals through students' intercultural communication on the social dimension of sustainability	Yes
H4c: there is an indirect effect of entrepreneurial intention of future professionals through students' global knowledge on the social dimension of sustainability	No
H5a: there is an indirect effect of entrepreneurial intention of future professionals through students' self-awareness on the environmental dimension of sustainability	Yes
H5b: there is an indirect effect of entrepreneurial intention of future professionals through students' intercultural communication on the environmental dimension of sustainability	No
H5c: there is an indirect effect of entrepreneurial intention of future professionals through students' global knowledge on the environmental dimension of sustainability	No
H6a: the effect of students' self-awareness on the economic dimension of sustainability is moderated by the students' geopolitical location	No
H6b: the effect of students' intercultural communication on the economic dimension of sustainability is moderated by the students' geopolitical location	No
H6c: the effect of students' global knowledge on the economic dimension of sustainability is moderated by the students' geopolitical location	No
H7a: the effect of students' self-awareness on the social dimension of sustainability is moderated by the students' geopolitical location	No
H7b: the effect of students' intercultural communication on the social dimension of sustainability is moderated by the students' geopolitical location	No
H7c: the effect of students' global knowledge on the social dimension of sustainability is moderated by the students' geopolitical location	No
H8a: the effect of students' self-awareness on the environmental dimension of sustainability is moderated by the students' geopolitical location	No
H8b: the effect of students' intercultural communication on the environmental dimension of sustainability is moderated by the students' geopolitical location	No
H8c: the effect of students' global knowledge on the environmental dimension of sustainability is moderated by the students' geopolitical location	No

Source: Author

TPB itself [10]. In our sample, the EI of future professionals positively affected the GC of those who see the world in a given way and then also positively affected the three aspects of the global concern of sustainability.

Therefore, it can be expected that these future professionals, through their EI, might contribute to sustainability, either by starting their own businesses [9] or through their roles within existing companies [3, 4]. Regarding their GC, it can be expected that the EI of these future professionals could influence the formation of GC when absence or the reinforcement of them.

From the results, we can also understand that there is an indirect effect of EI through GC on two of the dimensions of sustainability, that is, social and environmental dimensions. Specifically, these indirect effects were observed through the intercultural communication dimension of GC (H4b) and self-awareness dimension (H5a) respectively, reinforcing the importance of actions in universities fostering aspects like intercultural communication and global issues.

One possibility for achieving this is by incorporating global topics and intercultural exchange activities in courses curricula, particularly in relation to students' EI. This inclusion can contribute not only to the intercultural communication aspect, but also to students' self-awareness and global knowledge, enhancing their ability to address sustainability challenges [37, 20, 35]. In this context, new professionals could become more aware of the opportunities that the global scenario offers for their EI, such as innovations for addressing environmental concerns, and the potential of these innovations to support sustainability.

In contrast, no indirect effect was observed in the economic dimension of sustainability trough none of the GC dimensions. This finding suggests that, in our sample, the GC mindset of future professionals may not have been broad enough to fully capture the complexity of sustainability aspects. Specifically, it was not possible to demonstrate that students perceived economic issues in relation to the SA, IC, and GK aspects of GC.

Therefore, while the direct effects of students' EI on the dimensions of sustainability observed in our sample may indicate potential students' future behaviours [10], the absence of indirect effects through GC suggests that these future behaviours could be hindered. This may also suggest that the GC mindset of future professionals may not be sufficiently developed to effectively support the realisation of those behaviours. It is also worth to mention that altruistic students' values may not affect their EI when regarded to the economic aspect of sustainability [32, 34].

These results warrant attention, especially when considering the definition of GC [19] and the less-than-promising outcomes in achieving the UN's SDG [42], which, as of now, seem unlikely to be reached. Indeed, education for entrepreneurship should be complemented with more education for GC through local actions to better develop GC in future professionals [21, 20].

Regarding no moderating effects found in the study, the sample was formed by students from a country located in the global south [22], Brazil. It was expected that students with different realities would see the world in different ways. It was not possible to capture those differences, we believe, since the differences in HDI between states within the same country are not significant enough.

A different scenario might have been observed if the sample had consisted of students from two different countries, which we couldn't obtain data from. Specifically, contrasting data from the Global North and Global South, where living conditions differ [42], could influence students' GC, their worldview, and, consequently, their future behaviours regarding sustainability.

In addition to examining the effects of EI on GC and sustainability dimensions, analysing EI in different contexts could reveal how societal factors, such as the geopolitical context (e.g., country or city), influence entrepreneurship [26] as a whole, and more specifically, the EI of future professionals. As demonstrated by Barba-Sánchez et al. [5], the environmental aspect indirectly influenced students' EI. Therefore, since society and the environment have the power to influence EI, analysing samples from different countries could also reveal students' GC may be embedded in their EI, for instance, regarding economic issues [23].

Conclusion

By analysing the relationship between future professionals' EI, the dimensions of sustainability (economic, social, and environmental), and GC dimensions (self-awareness, intercultural communication, and global knowledge), we were able to demonstrate both direct effects (EI on GC and sustainability dimensions) and indirect effects (EI through the intercultural communication and self-awareness dimensions of GC on the social and environmental dimensions of sustainability).

The findings of this study provide valuable empirical evidence for the fields of entrepreneurship, EI, GC, and sustainability. They also offer insight into the role of HEI in equipping future professionals. Through their EI, and by taking advantage of market opportunities, such as new innovations and job creation, these professionals can contribute to the global concern of sustainability across its economic, social, and environmental dimensions.

For instance, their EI could be materialized in markets where sustainable solutions are needed. Additionally, in addition to fostering EI among students, approaches such as intercultural exchanges, where GC can be created and reinforced, should be considered. Given the crucial role of education in both EI and GC, we believe that academics and policymakers should work towards fostering a "Sustainable Global Entrepreneurship".

This study is not without limitations. Our sample consisted of students from a single country. Future research could apply our model to data from multiple countries, exploring the proposed relationship among construct and the moderating role of the geopolitical aspect, such as geographical location. Ideally, the sample would include countries with different realities, as seen in the Global North and Global South, where varying standards of living could influence how students—future professionals—perceive the world. This, in turn, may affect their behaviour, contributing to economic development and sustainability.

References

[1] Kennedy, J., Trewin, B., Betts, R., Thorne, P., Foster, P., Siegmund, P., ... & Naran, B. (2024). State of the Climate 2024. Update for COP29.

[2] United Nations Department of Economic and Social Affairs (2024). *The Sustainable Development Goals Report 2024*. UN.

[3] Naudé, W. A. (2008). Entrepreneurship in economic development, WIDER Research Paper RP 2008/20. United Nations University, Helsinki.

[4] Block, J. H., Fisch, C. O., & Van Praag, M. (2017). The schumpeterian entrepreneur: a review of the empirical evidence on the antecedents, behaviour and consequences of innovative entrepreneurship. *Industry and Innovation*, 24(1), 61–95.

[5] Barba-Sánchez, V., Mitre-Aranda, M., & del Brío-González, J. (2022). The entrepreneurial intention of university students: an environmental perspective. *European Research on Management and Business Economics*, 28(2), 100184.

[6] Maheshwari, G., Kha, K. L., & Arokiasamy, A. R. A. (2023). Factors affecting students' entrepreneurial intentions: a systematic review (2005–2022) for future directions in theory and practice. *Management Review Quarterly*, 73(4), 1903–1970.

[7] Liñán, F., Rodríguez-Cohard, J. C., & Rueda-Cantuche, J. M. (2011). Factors affecting entrepreneurial intention levels: a role for education. *International Entrepreneurship and Management Journal*, 7, 195–218.

[8] Jena, R. K. (2020). Measuring the impact of business management student's attitude towards entrepreneurship education on entrepreneurial intention: a case study. *Computers in Human Behavior*, 107, 106275.

[9] Moriano, J. A., Gorgievski, M., Laguna, M., Stephan, U., & Zarafshani, K. (2012). A cross-cultural approach to understanding entrepreneurial intention. *Journal of Career Development*, 39(2), 162–185.

[10] Ajzen, I. (1991). The theory of planned behavior. *Organizational Behavior and Human Decision Processes*, 50(2), 179–211.

[11] Fini, R., Grimaldi, R., Marzocchi, G. L., & Sobrero, M. (2009). The foundation of entrepreneurial intention. In *Summer Conference*, (Vol. 7, pp. 17–19).

[12] Zhang, Y., Duysters, G., & Cloodt, M. (2014). The role of entrepreneurship education as a predictor of university students' entrepreneurial intention. *International Entrepreneurship and Management Journal*, 10, 623–641.

[13] Zhang, P., Wang, D. D., & Owen, C. L. (2015). A study of entrepreneurial intention of university students. *Entrepreneurship Research Journal*, 5(1), 61–82.

[14] Nguyen, T. T., Nguyen, L. T. P., Phan, H. T. T., & Vu, A. T. (2021). Impact of entrepreneurship extracurricular activities and inspiration on entrepreneurial intention: mediator and moderator effect. *SAGE Open*, 11(3), 21582440211032174.

[15] Do Nguyen, Q., & Nguyen, H. T. (2023). Entrepreneurship education and entrepreneurial intention: the mediating role of entrepreneurial capacity. *International Journal of Management Education*, 21(1), 100730.

[16] Belz, F. M., & Binder, J. K. (2017). Sustainable entrepreneurship: a convergent process model. *Business Strategy and the Environment*, 26(1), 1–17.

[17] Lopes, J. M., Suchek, N., & Gomes, S. (2023). The antecedents of sustainability-oriented entrepreneurial intentions: an exploratory study of Angolan higher education students. *Journal of Cleaner Production*, 391, 136236.

[18] Elkington, J. (1998). Partnerships from cannibals with forks: the triple bottom line of 21st-century business. *Environmental Quality Management*, 8(1), 37–51.

[19] PISA, O. (2018). Preparing our youth for an inclusive and sustainable world.

[20] Author, (in press).

[21] Jooste, N., & Heleta, S. (2016). Global citizenship versus globally competent graduates: a critical view from the South. *Journal of Studies in International Education*, 21(1), 39–51.

[22] Dados, N., & Connell, R. (2012). The global south. *Contexts*, 11(1), 12–13.

[23] Dogan, E., Majeed, M. T., & Luni, T. (2021). Analyzing the impacts of geopolitical risk and economic uncertainty on natural resources rents. *Resources Policy*, 72, 102056.

[24] Pain, R., Panelli, R., Kindon, S., & Little, J. (2010). Moments in everyday/distant geopolitics: Young people's fears and hopes. *Geoforum*, 41(6), 972–982.

[25] de Paulo Gewehr, L. L., & de Andrade, J. B. S. O. (2022). Geopolitics of hunger: geopolitics, human security and fragile states. *Geoforum*, 137, 88–93.

[26] Steyaert, C., & Katz, J. (2004). Reclaiming the space of entrepreneurship in society: geographical, discursive and social dimensions. *Entrepreneurship and Regional Development*, 16(3), 179–196.

[27] Purvis, B., Mao, Y., & Robinson, D. (2019). Three pillars of sustainability: in search of conceptual origins. *Sustainability Science*, 14, 681–695.

[28] Ratten, V. (2023). Entrepreneurship: definitions, opportunities, challenges, and future directions. *Global Business and Organizational Excellence*, 42(5), 79–90.

[29] Boubker, O., Arroud, M., & Ouajdouni, A. (2021). Entrepreneurship education versus management students' entrepreneurial intentions. a PLS-SEM approach. *International Journal of Management Education*, 19(1), 100450.

[30] Schaltegger, S., & Wagner, M. (2011). Sustainable entrepreneurship and sustainability innovation: categories and interactions. *Business Strategy and the Environment*, 20(4), 222–237.

[31] Sabino, A., Moreira, A., Cesário, F. J. S., & Pinto Coelho, M. (2024). Measuring sustainability: a validation study of a triple bottom line (TBL) scale in Portugal. *Emerging Science Journal*, 8(3), 899–916.

[32] Romero-Colmenares, L. M., & Reyes-Rodríguez, J. F. (2022). Sustainable entrepreneurial intentions: Exploration of a model based on the theory of planned behaviour among university students in north-east Colombia. *International Journal of Management Education*, 20(2), 100627.

[33] Truong, H. T., Le, T. P., Pham, H. T. T., Do, D. A., & Pham, T. T. (2022). A mixed approach to understanding sustainable entrepreneurial intention. *International Journal of Management Education*, 20(3), 100731.

[34] Vuorio, A. M., Puumalainen, K., & Fellnhofer, K. (2018). Drivers of entrepreneurial intentions in sustainable entrepreneurship. *International Journal of Entrepreneurial Behavior and Research*, 24(2), 359–381.

[35] Jiaxin, G., Huijuan, Z., & Md Hasan, H. (2024). Global competence in higher education: a ten-year systematic literature review. *Frontiers in Education*, 9, 1404782.

[36] Morais, D. B., & Ogden, A. C. (2011). Initial development and validation of the global citizenship scale. *Journal of Studies in International Education*, 15(5), 445–466. doi: 10.1177/1028315310375308.

[37] Massaro, V. R. (2022). Global citizenship development in higher education institutions: A systematic review of the literature. *Journal of Global Education and Research*, 6(1), 98–114.

[38] Author, (in press).

[39] Zhang, J., Li, B., Zhang, Y., Gong, C., & Liu, Z. (2022). From entrepreneurship education, government support, and global competence to entrepreneurial behavior: the serial double mediating effect of the self-efficacy and entrepreneurial intention. *Frontiers in Psychology*, 13, 838232.

[40] Kishino, H., & Takahashi, T. (2019). Global citizenship development: effects of study abroad and other factors. *Journal of International Students*, 9(2), 535–559.

[41] Flint, C. (2021). *Introduction to Geopolitics*. Routledge.

[42] United Nations Development Programme (2024). *Human Development Report 2023/2024*. New York, NY: UNDP.

[43] Hair Jr, J. F., Hult, G. T. M., Ringle, C. M., Sarstedt, M., Danks, N. P., & Ray, S. (2021). *Partial Least Squares Structural Equation Modeling (PLS-SEM) Using R: A Workbook*. Springer Nature.

[44] Cohen, J. (1988). *Statistical Power Analysis for the Behavioral Sciences*, (2nd edn.). Hillsdale, NJ: Lawrence Erlbaum Associates.

[45] Soper, D. S. (2023). A-priori sample size calculator for structural equation models. [Software]. [Online].

Available from: https://www.danielsoper.com/statcalc.

[46] Gershberg, F. B., & Shimamura, A. P. (1994). Serial position effects in implicit and explicit tests of memory. *Journal of Experimental Psychology: Learning, Memory, and Cognition*, 20(6), 1370.

[47] Chang, S.-J., van Witteloostuijn, A., & Eden, L. (2010). Common method variance in international business research. *Journal of International Business Studies*, 41, 178–184.

[48] Instituto Brasileiro de Geografia e Estatística (2024). Cidades e Estados do Brasil IBGE. [Online]. Available from: https://cidades.ibge.gov.br.

[49] Kline, R. B. (2023). *Principles and Practice of Structural Equation Modeling*, (5th edn.). New York: Guilford Publications.

[50] Hair, J. F., Risher, J. J., Sarstedt, M., & Ringle, C. M. (2019). When to use and how to report the results of PLS-SEM. *European Business Review*, 31(1), 2–24.

[51] Sanchez, G. (2013). PLS path modeling with R. Berkeley: Trowchez Editions, 383(2013), 551.

22 The impact of digital technologies on sustainability performance of the supply chains

Banusha Aruchunarasa[a] *and Ilaria Guandalini*[b]

School of Business, Operations and Strategy, Greenwich Business School, University of Greenwich, UK

Abstract

The integration of digital technologies (DT) with sustainability, referred to as digital sustainability transformation, has become essential for supply chain management (SCM). This study investigates the impact of DT on the sustainability performance (SP) of supply chains (SC) in developing countries, addressing a gap in the literature concerning sustainable supply chain management in emerging economies. Following a literature review and the development of a conceptual framework, this study employed semi-structured interviews across supply chain sectors in Sri Lanka, serving as a sample of a developing country. The findings from interviews indicate that cost is a significant barrier to the integration of DT in sustainability initiatives in SCs. Additionally, another finding revealed that the Internet of Things (IoT) is a widely utilized technology in Sri Lankan SCs for monitoring and measuring sustainability performance, rather than other digital technologies. Furthermore, the findings reveal that some firms perceive sustainability as a public relations or marketing strategy rather than an institutional concept. This study provides a nuanced understanding of SP specific to DT in SCs, offering insights into both positive and negative impact that can influence SCs. The study provides insights into SP specific to DT in SCs, contributing novel perspectives to the literature through a theoretical framework. It offers academics valuable understanding of the interconnections between DT, SP, and SCM, while establishing a foundation for further research in SCM, digital transformation, and sustainable operations. The framework provides guidelines for industry practitioners and policymakers, with findings applicable to developing countries worldwide, addressing common challenges across diverse geographical contexts.

Keywords: Digital technology, digital transformation, supply chain, sustainability, sustainability performance

Introduction

Digital sustainability transformation, which is defined in this research as the integration of Digital Technologies (DT), encompassing hardware such as devices and machines, and software, with sustainability in Supply Chains (SC), is perceived as a critical approach to tackle current and future challenges in Supply Chain Management (SCM) [1, 2]. It widely acknowledges that integrating sustainable practices into SCs leads to advancements in the operational efficiency and competitiveness in the market, resulting in long-term success [3–5]. In addition, DT such as blockchain, IoT, AI, and cloud computing are emerging as vital elements in streamlining SC operations and strengthening competitiveness [6–10]. However, while DT has transformed various industries, its impact on sustainability remains a topic of ongoing debate. Moreover, although DT has the potential to contribute to sustainability efforts, it can also have negative implications for the environment [11–15]. For instance, electronic waste and energy consumption can contribute to greenhouse gas emissions which are vital environmental concerns. However, previous studies have elaborated on the valuable contributions of DT, such as gaining business insights, minimizing waste, and improving the overall SC efficiency.

To achieve this study's objective, it is proposed that semi-structured, in-depth interviews provide a broad understanding of the complex integration of these dual perspectives. Considering its status as a developing country, Sri Lanka was selected as the research context for the acquisition of primary data, considering its status as a developing country. Additionally, the researcher's extensive knowledge of this country as a native of Sri Lanka facilitates the interpretation of the data, contributing new layers of understanding to the country's perspectives and policies towards sustainability. This research focused on examining the specific challenges, risks, and opportunities faced

[a]b.aruchunarasa@greenwich.ac.uk, [b]I.Guandalini@greenwich.ac.uk

DOI: 10.4324/9781003739920-22

by Sri Lankan SCs in implementing digital sustainability initiatives. By investigating the local context, this study provides insights that may be applicable to other developing countries with similar economic and technological landscapes. Furthermore, the findings of this study are expected to contribute to a broader understanding of how DT can be leveraged to enhance Sustainability Performance (SP) in SCs across diverse global contexts.

Combining digital tools and sustainability in SC has been identified as a valuable research opportunity in the era of digitalization. However, there is limited research focusing on the integration of these dual standpoints in SC contexts. Therefore, this study aimed to investigate the impact of the integration of DT and sustainability practices within SCs, and to identify the key factors that contribute to the improvement of SP within SCs.

Therefore, the main research question (RQ) is as follows: How does DT influence the sustainability performance of the SCs?

To address the research objectives and to answer the main RQ, a set of sub-RQs was developed.

RQ1: What are the current sustainability initiatives implemented in SCs, and what are the key challenges and opportunities associated with these initiatives?

RQ2: How are DT integrated into sustainability initiatives within SCs, and what are the key benefits and challenges associated with this integration?

RQ3: What is the impact of integrating DT into SP within SCs, and what factors contribute to the improvement of SP?

Ultimately, the above sub-research questions will explore specific aspects of each objective, facilitating the collection and analysis of data necessary to understand the real impact of DT on sustainability initiatives and how their interaction can effectively influence SC performance.

Preliminary Conceptual Framework

The three foundational elements of this research, digital technologies (DT) in the supply chain (SC), SC sustainability, and sustainability performance (SP), are examined in the literature. Existing literature frameworks predominantly assess firm-level or specific performance metrics, with a few studies addressing overall SC performance in the context of DT, SC operations, or SP. From the reviewed sources, the frameworks listed in Table 22.1 - Key frameworks were selected for their relevance. This table highlights the elements that align with research phenomena. Although these frameworks offer a robust foundation, they also highlight areas that require further exploration. For instance, Govardhan et.al [16] primarily focused on the SC strategy, whereas Tsou & Chen [17] did not comprehensively incorporate the SP within the SC framework. These frameworks contribute to the foundational and essential components of the conceptual framework. This study seeks to expand and refine these models by integrating DT in SC, SC sustainability, and SP, thereby addressing identified gaps and providing a more extensive understanding of the research problem.

A preliminary conceptual framework was developed to illustrate the relationships between the research topics and highlighting the salient aspects identified in the above-mentioned studies (Figure 22.1 - Preliminary conceptual framework). This framework provides a theoretical foundation for the study and informs the development of interview questions and data collection methodologies. The framework commences with an examination of DT and the SC sustainability, emphasizing the economic, social, and environmental aspects to underscore the study's comprehensive scope. It further incorporates the concept of the circular economy (CE), a pivotal

Table 22.1 Key frameworks.

Authors	Coverage on conceptual framework	Type of study
[16]	SC strategy, overall SC performance	
[17]	Firm performance, DT	Empirical study (Survey based)
[18]	SC traceability, SP, circular economy, DT	Empirical study (Survey based)
[19]	DT, Environmental performance, Economical performance, DSC performance	Empirical study (Survey based)
[20]	DT, SC integration, SC SP	Empirical study (Survey based)
[21]	DT, Sustainable production, Circular economy	Empirical study (Delphi and MCDM based)

Source: Author

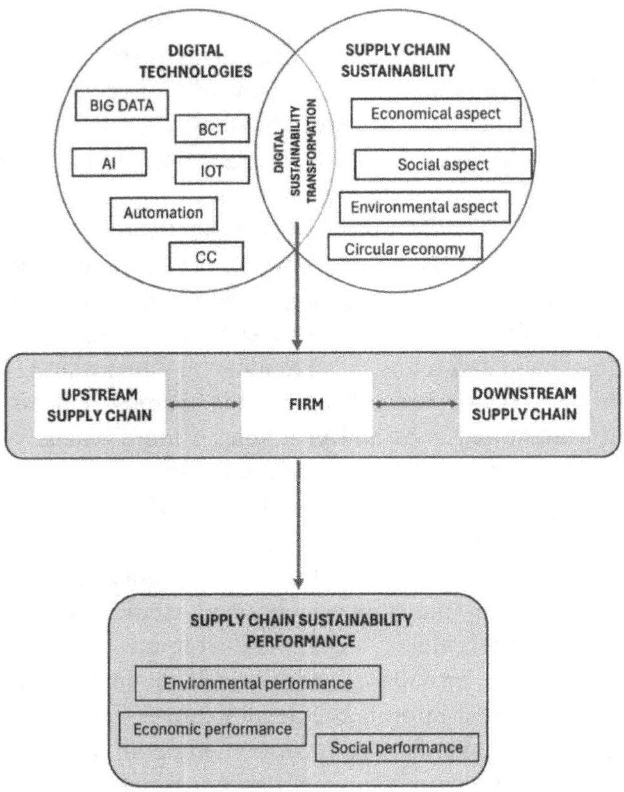

Figure 22.1 Preliminary conceptual framework
Source: Author

theme in industrial sustainability, and acknowledges the digital technologies employed within a company's supply chain. As evidenced by [22–25] these technologies are integral to the digital sustainability transformation. For instance, Kshetri [26] elucidated the direct role of DT on sustainable supply chains, thereby establishing a connection to digital sustainability transformation. This linkage is further corroborated by the conceptual model proposed by [16, 20], which posits an interconnection between DT in SC and SC sustainability. Consequently, a firm's supply chain is perceived as being influenced by digital sustainability transformation. The literature, notably [6, 27, 28] highlights the direct link between digital sustainability transformation and a company's supply chain. Moreover, this framework emphasizes that digital sustainability transformation can be implemented throughout the entire supply chain, with bidirectional arrows indicating reverse logistics as demonstrated by [29, 30], among the company and its upstream and downstream supply chain partners.

With regards to SC SP as a critical component, the research from [18, 28, 31] indicates that SCSP is a result of the impact of digital sustainability transformation on a firm's SC. Additionally, this preliminary framework recognizes that firms can leverage DT and processes across their entire SC network, including upstream, downstream, and reverse logistics operations, to drive significant impacts in SP. This suggests that digital transformation initiatives in SC have the potential to yield impacts across these interconnected dimensions. This aligns with the results of the previous studies [16, 19, 20]. However, it is vital to recognize that this framework is dynamic and may evolve as new insights emerge from data analysis. As the study progressed, the researcher critically examined the data and compare it with the preliminary framework. This analysis revealed new patterns or factors that were not considered initially. Based on these findings, the framework is refined to better reflect empirical evidence, ultimately offering a more accurate representation of the phenomenon under investigation. This iterative process of framework development ensures that the final conceptual model is grounded in both the existing literature and the study's empirical findings, enhancing its validity and applicability to the research context [32–34].

Materials and Methodology

The research methodology for this study employed a qualitative approach through in-depth interviews. This approach facilitates a comprehensive understanding of the research topic by leveraging the strengths of data sources. For the data collection, semi-structured interviews were conducted with participants from the industry. This method was selected for its flexibility and capacity to elicit rich, in-depth insights into participants' experiences and perspectives [35]. Interview-based research is particularly appropriate for investigating the impact of integrating DT and sustainability on SC performance, as it enables an in-depth exploration of complex phenomena and captures nuanced perspectives from industry practitioners [36].

Data were collected from Sri Lanka, a developing island nation in South Asia, which serves as the ideal context for this study. With a rapidly expanding economy and increasing digital adoption, Sri Lanka has presented significant insights into the opportunities and challenges encountered by developing economies [37]. The country's diverse industries, including agriculture, textiles, information technology, and tourism, offer a comprehensive landscape to explore SC configurations [38]. Furthermore, Sri Lanka's government has demonstrated commitment to sustainable development goals and digital transformation initiatives, rendering it a relevant sample for this research [39, 40]. There is a dearth of studies on this specific research area focused on Sri Lankan firms. This study investigates how DT addresses sustainability concerns in SCs, by considering the specific economic, social, and environmental factors that influence implementation in developing countries. Data from five industry experts were collected and the participants were selected based on the following criteria:

- The participants' roles within the SC align with the research objectives (e.g., SC managers, procurement specialists and logistics coordinators).
- They have a certain level (Minimum 5 years in SC) of experience working in the SC.
- They have expertise in areas relevant to research, such as sustainability and digitalization.
- They have the willingness to participate (Consent and availability).
- They must provide authorization to share the company (approval from the company in writing).

Thematic analysis is employed in data analysis as it is a robust method for qualitative data analysis [41]. The objective of adopting a thematic approach is to identify the themes and patterns that elucidate the integration of DT and sustainability in SCs. It is also essential to ascertain the impact of this integration on the SP of the SC while comprehending its influence on SCs.

From the various coding methods of thematic analysis, this research employs computer-based coding to generate themes and patterns. NVivo is one such qualitative data analysis software available for researchers. NVivo offers several significant advantages over manual coding in qualitative data analysis: NVivo substantially reduces the number of manual tasks involved in data analysis, allowing researchers more time to identify tendencies, acknowledge themes, and derive conclusions [42]. Furthermore, it enables researchers to conduct iterative coding and organize the coding and relevant analysis. NVivo's automated coding capabilities allow researchers to efficiently identify and categories key concepts across large datasets, enhancing the effectiveness and consistency of the analysis process [42, 43]. The software's advanced query tools facilitate complex searches and cross-referencing of coded data, enabling the discovery of latent patterns and relationships within the qualitative information [42, 44]. Additionally, NVivo's visualization features, such as word clouds and concept maps, provide researchers with effective methods to present and interpret their findings, offering novel perspectives on the analyzed data [42, 43].

In coding techniques, Braun & Clarke [41] recommend a six-phase framework for conducting a thematic analysis. This study adhered to these guidelines. The six phases of thematic analysis are Familiarization with data, generation of initial codes, search for themes, review of themes, definition and naming of themes and production of the report/ write-up [41].

At the outset, the recorded interviews were transcribed into text. Initially, meaningful data collected through the interviews were examined by reading the transcribed data line by line. This step involves labelling, grouping similar meanings, categorizing, and regrouping. This process requires a focus on identifying themes and relationships. Related themes were incorporated into the codes during grouping and collected in the first stage. Subsequently, the themes and relationships were refined, and re-reading and re-organizing the data were performed iteratively. Combining themes builds with new ones, maintaining separate themes, modifying themes, and discarding others are the sub-steps. At the defining stage, the focus is on identifying "the 'essence' of what each theme is about" [41], and the analysis of qualitative data is presented.

Table 22.2 - Participant details elaborate the participants' information and their relevant to the research. Five in-depth semi-structured interviews were conducted utilizing university approved platforms such as MS Teams, with each interview lasting approximately 40-50 minutes. The data analysis was performed following the 6 steps data analysis protocol. The analysis was executed using the university-approved data analysis software NVivo. Figure 22.2 - Word cloud showing a word-cloud generated by NVivo, presents the most frequently occurring words from each participant's interview. This visualization facilitates a general comprehension of insights and aids in identifying the most vital

Table 22.2 Participant details.

ID	Industry/role	No of years (Experience)	Notes	Company Size (No of employees)
PP1	Consultancy	8	Working in consultancy and CEO for an IT startup	1000 – 2000 (Multinational)
PP2	Procurement	12	Manufacturing firm	100 – 200 (Multinational)
PP3	Logistics	9	Worked in SL for 7 years and 2 years in Saudi Arabia	350 (Multinational)
PP4	Procurement	6	Worked in manufacturing previously for 4 years	300 (Multinational)
PP5	Forecasting	8	Textile manufacturing	1900 (Multinational)

Source: Author

Figure 22.2 Word cloud
Source: Author

elements in interviews. Transcripts were cleaned and imported into NVivo software for coding and labelling. Descriptive coding was employed to summaries statements using a single word or brief phrase. The codes were subsequently examined to identify and review any duplications or mislabeling. This process resulted in the identification of 69 initial codes, which facilitated the development of sub-themes and independent categories. Based on the classification of initial codes, the themes were arranged based on sub research questions. The initial categories and sub-themes are examined based on their relevance to the sub RQ.

Results and Discussion

Sustainability initiatives

The findings revealed that sustainability is widely implemented in SCs, encompassing various sustainability objectives such as energy reduction, carbon footprint mitigation, ethical sourcing, and others. All the participants stated that they had different sustainability initiatives in their respective companies. PP3 stated *"We are mainly considering the minimizing the waste and energy consumption"* while PP5 stated "*We need to have profit at the end of the financial year no matter what"*. Another interesting theme generated from the study was that some SC companies perceive sustainability as a public relations or marketing strategy rather than an institutional concept. PP1 stated "*in Sri Lanka it was like sustainability was all about PR stand you know we agree, and we are sustainable it's just like a more of a PR stunt rather than You know, actually driving that sustainability"*.

Digital technologies in supply chains

Based on the study findings, IoT is a widely utilized technology in Sri Lankan SCs for monitoring and measuring SP rather than other DT. IoT devices, like sensors and smart monitors, are deployed across various stages of the SC to collect real-time data on energy consumption, resource utilization, and waste generation. PP1 stated *"I would say IOT technology is currently sort of penetrated in Sri Lanka. So, in terms of tracking the fuel cost, at least the mileage of vehicles is technology that we already have in hand"*. This data-driven approach enables companies to recognize inefficiencies, optimize processes, and make well-informed decisions to improve their overall SP. While the IoT has emerged as the dominant digital technology for sustainability monitoring in Sri Lankan SCs, other DT have not gained as much traction. PP2 *stated" I don't think it's at least it's not quite famous like application of blockchain in* Sri

Lankan either government or in private companies." However, as the digital transformation continues to advance, there is potential for other technologies such as AI, blockchain, and advanced analytics to complement IoT systems and further enhance sustainability efforts in Sri Lankan SCs.

Challenges /barriers in integrating digital technologies and sustainability

The preliminary findings of the study revealed several challenges and barriers in integrating DT and sustainability for supply chain SP. The primary challenge identified from the participant interviews was that cost and investment limitations present a significant obstacle in the integration of digital transformation and sustainability. PP3 stated "if the technology that we are using for sustainability is costly, it is not economically sustainable for us to continue using it because we might be sustainable in the environmental front, but for the. Like the ecosystem of the economy, it might not be beneficial, even as a country. If, let's say in our budget, we. Invest so many percentages for sustainability, and we use those projects, but then the country will not have enough financial aid to even fulfil the necessities of the people. So that will not be economically sustainable at the end, something like that I wanted to relate adding to the data privacy issues can be a challenge by using technology in sustainability."

Another significant barrier is the inefficiency in supplier collaboration and commitment. This barrier stems from various factors, including disparities in technological capabilities, misalignment of sustainability goals, and reluctance to share sensitive data across the SC network. Suppliers, in particular smaller suppliers, may lack the required expertise or resources to implement advanced digital solutions, creating a gap in the overall sustainability efforts of the SC. PP2 stated "Asking our suppliers to practice the sustainability practices and teaching them the values of or importance of the sustainability is the biggest challenge." Further, study revealed that privacy and security issues lead to imbalances in SC operations and SP. The study's findings highlight the

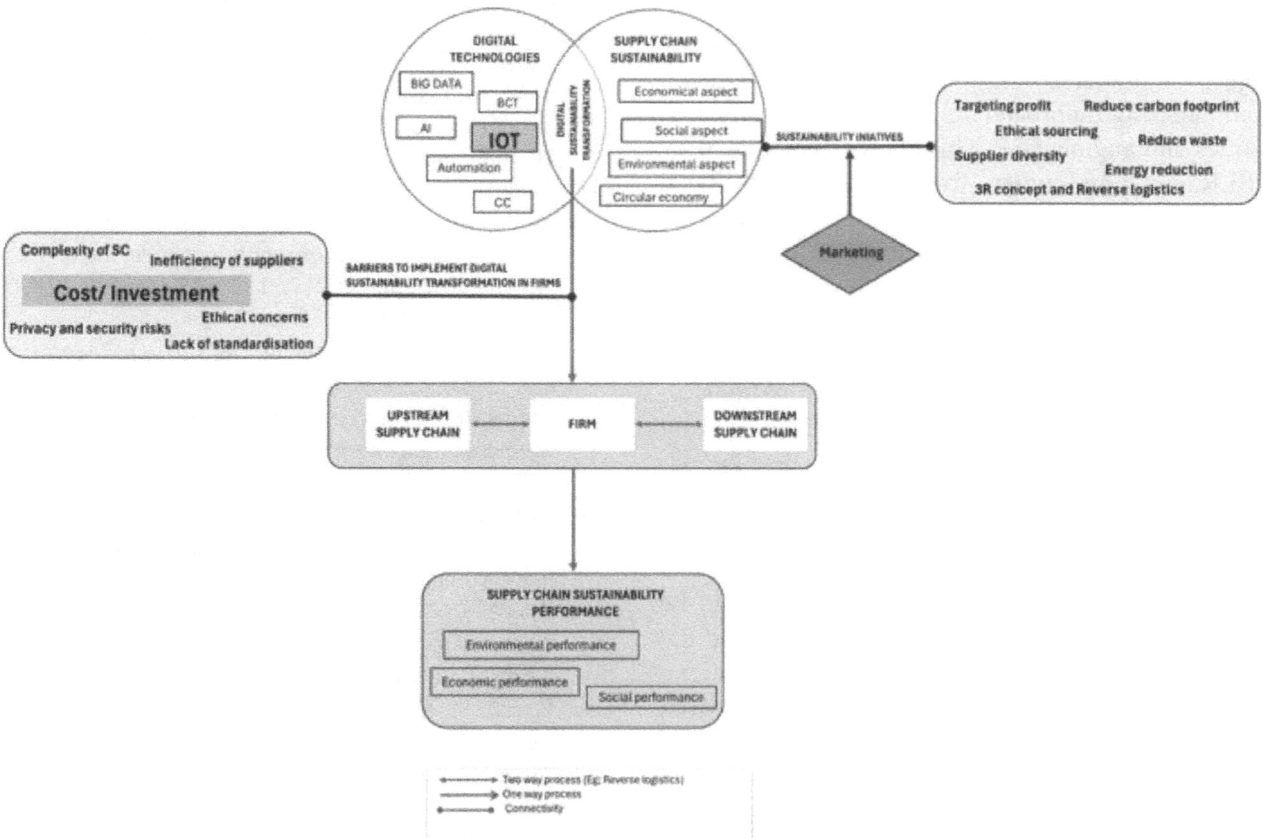

Figure 22.3 Revised conceptual framework
Source: Author

significant impact of privacy and security concerns on SC operations and SP. These issues can create vulnerabilities within the SC network, potentially leading to disruptions in information flow, compromised data integrity, and reduced trust among stakeholders. As a result, the overall effectiveness and efficiency of SC processes may be compromised, affecting various aspects of SP, including economic viability, environmental stewardship, and social responsibility. PP5 stated "That is a development that has come with AI, which we didn't think will come but is severely impacting because with AI we don't know in the matter of milliseconds all the information that is very confidential will not be confidential anymore."

The content findings presented in above have initiated a process of relationship identification within the initially proposed framework suggesting, for example, the importance/predominance of IoT over other digital technologies in affecting SP in Sri Lankan SCs. Figure 22.3 illustrates the revision of the preliminary framework based on major study findings.

Conclusion

The interrelationship between DT and SP is of paramount importance in influencing sustainability objectives, underscoring the necessity of adopting a comprehensive approach in s DT to enhance SC capabilities and augment SP. This study was initiated by a SLR, and a preliminary framework was developed incorporating the main themes from the literature, which was evaluated and revised during the research study. A revised conceptual framework, which can be adapted by various industry SCs, was developed as a significant outcome of the study. The extant literature posits that research on digital sustainability transformation research has been evolved, particularly from a SC perspective. This study contributes new knowledge to the research context by providing a theoretical framework as for a pioneering investigation in this field. Although this study focuses on Sri Lanka as the geographical context, its findings should be applicable to other developing countries around the world with similar characteristics.

While this study has yielded valuable insights from interviews, it has some limitations. First, the conceptual framework developed in this study is grounded in both the literature and interview findings. This framework can benefit from validation through quantitative methodologies to enhance its robustness. This is a potential avenue for future research. Additionally, this study is exclusively focused on Sri Lankan firms. Future research could replicate this study in different geographical contexts to broaden its applicability.

Acknowledgement

The authors appreciate all the participants who generously contributed their time and insights to this study.

References

[1] Edwin Cheng, T. C., Kamble, S. S., Belhadi, A., Ndubisi, N. O., Hung Lai, K., & Kharat, M. G. (2022). Linkages between big data analytics, circular economy, sustainable supply chain flexibility, and sustainable performance in manufacturing firms. *International Journal of Production Research*, 60(22), 6908–6922. doi: 10.1080/00207543.2021.1906971.

[2] Neligan, A., Baumgartner, R. J., Geissdoerfer, M., & Schöggl, J. P. (2023). Circular disruption: digitalisation as a driver of circular economy business models. *Business Strategy and the Environment*, 32(3), 1175–1188. doi: 10.1002/bse.3100.

[3] Cloutier, C., Oktaei, P., & Lehoux, N. (2020). Collaborative mechanisms for sustainability-oriented supply chain initiatives: state of the art, role assessment and research opportunities. *International Journal of Production Research*, 58(19), 5836–5850. doi: 10.1080/00207543.2019.1660821.

[4] Jadhav, A., Orr, S., & Malik, M. (2019). The role of supply chain orientation in achieving supply chain sustainability. *International Journal of Production Economics*, 217, 112–125. doi: 10.1016/J.IJPE.2018.07.031.

[5] Schaltegger, S., & Burritt, R. (2014). Measuring and managing sustainability performance of supply chains: review and sustainability supply chain management framework. *Supply Chain Management*, 19(3), 232–241. doi: 10.1108/SCM-02-2014-0061.

[6] Aamer, A., Sahara, C. R., & Al-Awlaqi, M. A. (2023). Digitalization of the Supply Chain: Transformation Factors. Emerald Publishing. doi: 10.1108/JSTPM-01-2021-0001.

[7] Ahmed Khan, S., Kusi-Sarpong, S., Gupta, H., Kow Arhin, F., Nguseer Lawal, J., & Mehmood Hassan, S. (2021). Critical factors of digital supply chains for organizational performance improvement. *IEEE Transactions on Engineering Management*, 71, 13727–13741. doi: 10.1109/TEM.2021.3052239.

[8] Büyüközkan, G., & Göçer, F. (2018). Digital supply chain: literature review and a proposed framework

for future research. *Computers in industry*, 97, 157–177. doi: 10.1016/J.COMPIND.2018.02.010.

[9] Hennelly, P. A., Srai, J. S., Graham, G., & Fosso Wamba, S. (2020). Rethinking supply chains in the age of digitalization. *Production Planning and Control*, 31(2–3), 93–95. doi: 10.1080/09537287.2019.1631469.

[10] Yang, M., Fu, M., & Zhang, Z. (2021). The adoption of digital technologies in supply chains: drivers, process and impact. *Technological Forecasting and Social Change*, 169, 120795. doi: 10.1016/J.TECHFORE.2021.120795.

[11] Belhadi, A., Kamble, S., Gunasekaran, A., & Mani, V. (2022). Analyzing the mediating role of organizational ambidexterity and digital business transformation on industry 4.0 capabilities and sustainable supply chain performance. *Supply Chain Management*, 27(6), 696–711. doi: 10.1108/SCM-04-2021-0152.

[12] Kamble, S. S., Gunasekaran, A., & Gawankar, S. A. (2020). Achieving sustainable performance in a data-driven agriculture supply chain: a review for research and applications. *International Journal of Production Economics*, 219, 179–194. doi: 10.1016/J.IJPE.2019.05.022.

[13] Kumar, P., Mangla, S. K., Kazancoglu, Y., & Emrouznejad, A. (2023). A decision framework for incorporating the coordination and behavioural issues in sustainable supply chains in digital economy. *Annals of Operations Research*, 326(2), 721–749. doi: 10.1007/s10479-022-04814-0.

[14] Nayal, K., Raut, R. D., Yadav, V. S., Priyadarshinee, P., & Narkhede, B. E. (2022). The impact of sustainable development strategy on sustainable supply chain firm performance in the digital transformation era. *Business Strategy and the Environment*, 31(3), 845–859. doi: 10.1002/bse.2921.

[15] Nayal, K., Kumar, S., Raut, R. D., Queiroz, M. M., Priyadarshinee, P., & Narkhede, B. E. (2022). Supply chain firm performance in circular economy and digital era to achieve sustainable development goals. *Business Strategy and the Environment*, 31(3), 1058–1073. doi: 10.1002/bse.2935.

[16] Govardhan, S., Narkhede, B. E., Raut, R. D., Zhang, L. L., & Ghoshal, S. (2025). Significance of industry 4.0 in achieving sustainable performance across supply chains—a research perspective. *Business Strategy and Development*, 8(1), e70064. doi: 10.1002/bsd2.70064.

[17] Tsou, H. T., & Chen, J. S. (2023). How does digital technology usage benefit firm performance? digital transformation strategy and organisational innovation as mediators. *Technology Analysis and Strategic Management*, 35(9), 1114–1127. doi: 10.1080/09537325.2021.1991575.

[18] Duman Altan, A., Beyca, Ö. F., & Zaim, S. (2024). Link between digital technologies adoption and sustainability performance: supply chain traceability/resilience or circular economy practices. *Sustainability (Switzerland)*, 16(19), 8694. doi: 10.3390/su16198694.

[19] Li, Y., Dai, J., & Cui, L. (2020). The impact of digital technologies on economic and environmental performance in the context of industry 4.0: a moderated mediation model. *International Journal of Production Economics*, 229, 107777. doi: 10.1016/j.ijpe.2020.107777.

[20] Oubrahim, I., Sefiani, N., & Happonen, A. (2023). The Influence of digital transformation and supply chain integration on overall sustainable supply chain performance: an empirical analysis from manufacturing companies in morocco. *Energies (Basel)*, 16(2), 1004. doi: 10.3390/en16021004.

[21] Gupta, H., Kumar, A., & Wasan, P. (2021). Industry 4.0, cleaner production and circular economy: an integrative framework for evaluating ethical and sustainable business performance of manufacturing organizations. *Journal of Cleaner Production*, 295, 126253. ISSN 0959–6526. doi: 10.1016/j.jclepro.2021.126253.

[22] Chauhan, C., Parida, V., & Dhir, A. (2022). Linking circular economy and digitalisation technologies: a systematic literature review of past achievements and future promises. *Technological Forecasting and Social Change*, 177, 121508. doi: 10.1016/J.TECHFORE.2022.121508.

[23] Chauhan, S., Singh, R., Gehlot, A., Akram, S. V., Twala, B., & Priyadarshi, N. (2023). Digitalization of supply chain management with industry 4.0 enabling technologies: a sustainable perspective. *Processes*, 11(1). doi: 10.3390/pr11010096.

[24] Junge, A. L., & Straube, F. (2020). Sustainable supply chains - digital transformation technologies' impact on the social and environmental dimension. *Procedia Manufacturing*, 43, 736–742. doi: 10.1016/J.PROMFG.2020.02.110.

[25] Omrany, H., Al-Obaidi, K. M., Husain, A., & Ghaffarianhoseini, A. (2023). Digital Twins in the Construction Industry: A Comprehensive Review of Current Implementations, Enabling Technologies, and Future Directions. Multidisciplinary Digital Publishing Institute (MDPI). doi: 10.3390/su151410908.

[26] Kshetri, N. (2021). Blockchain and sustainable supply chain management in developing countries. *International Journal of Information Management*, 60, 102376. doi: 10.1016/j.ijinfomgt.2021.102376.

[27] Piprani, A. Z., Khan, S. A. R., & Yu, Z. (2024). Driving success through digital transformation: influence of Industry 4.0 on lean, agile, resilient, green supply chain practices. *Journal of Manufacturing*

Technology Management, 35(6), 1175–1198. doi: 10.1108/JMTM-05-2023-0179.

[28] Stroumpoulis, A., Kopanaki, E., & Chountalas, P. T. (2024). Enhancing sustainable supply chain management through digital transformation: a comparative case study analysis. *Sustainability (Switzerland)*, 16(16), 6778. doi: 10.3390/su16166778.

[29] Shah, H. M., Gardas, B. B., Narwane, V. S., & Mehta, H. S. (2023). The Contemporary State of Big Data Analytics and Artificial Intelligence Towards Intelligent Supply Chain Risk Management: a Comprehensive Review. Emerald Publishing. doi: 10.1108/K-05-2021-0423.

[30] Hsu, C.-C., Tan, K.-C., Hanim, S., & Zailani, M. (2016). Strategic orientations, sustainable supply chain initiatives, and reverse logistics empirical evidence from an emerging market. *International Journal of Operations and Production Management*, 36(1), 86–110. doi: 10.1108/IJOPM-06-2014-0252.

[31] Mutambik, I. (2024). Digital transformation as a driver of sustainability performance—a study from freight and logistics industry. *Sustainability (Switzerland)*, 16(10), 4310. doi: 10.3390/su16104310.

[32] Bag, S., Telukdarie, A., Pretorius, J. H. C., & Gupta, S. (2018). Industry 4.0 and Supply Chain Sustainability: Framework and Future Research Directions. Emerald Group Holdings Ltd. doi: 10.1108/BIJ-03-2018-0056.

[33] Dwivedi, A., & Paul, S. K. (2022). A framework for digital supply chains in the era of circular economy: Implications on environmental sustainability. *Business Strategy and the Environment*, 31(4), 1249–1274. doi: 10.1002/bse.2953.

[34] Stroumpoulis, A., & Kopanaki, E. (2022). Theoretical perspectives on sustainable supply chain management and digital transformation: a literature review and a conceptual framework. *Sustainability (Switzerland)*, 14(8), 4862. doi: 10.3390/su14084862.

[35] Cheong, H., Lyons, A., Houghton, R., & Majumdar, A. (2023). Secondary qualitative research methodology using online data within the context of social sciences. *Regular Article International Journal of Qualitative Methods*, 22, 1–19. doi: 10.1177/16094069231180160.

[36] Saunders, M. N. K., Lewis, P., & Thornhill, A. (2019). Research Methods for Business Students, (8th edn.), Boston: Pearson.

[37] Karunarathna, N., Wickramarachchi, R., & Vidanagamachchi, K. (2019). A study of the implications of logistics 4.0 in future warehousing: a Sri Lankan perspective., Proceedings of the International Conference on Industrial Engineering and Operations Management. Bangkok, Thailand, March 5-7, 2019. Doi: https://ieomsociety.org/ieom2019/papers/274.pdf.

[38] De Alwis, A. M. L., De Silva, N., & Samaranayake, P. (2024). Industry 4.0-enabled sustainable manufacturing: current practices, barriers and strategies. *Benchmarking*, 31(6), 2061–2089. doi: 10.1108/BIJ-01-2023-0065.

[39] Fernando, W. M., Perera, H. N., Ratnayake, R. M. C., & Thibbotuwawa, A. (2024). Storm in a teacup: implications of mobile phone literacy on sustainable smallholder agri-food supply chains in developing economies . *International Journal of Logistics Management*. 36(2), 2025, pp. 452–473(22). doi: 10.1108/IJLM-09-2023-0413.

[40] Sudusinghe, J. I., Jayaratne, R. P., & Kumarage, A. S. (2018). UN SDGs shaping sustainable supply chains: the case of apparel manufacturers in developing countries. In International Conference on Service Operations and Logistics, and Informatics, IEEE.

[41] Braun, V., & Clarke, V. (2006). Using thematic analysis in psychology. *Qualitative Research in Psychology*, 3(2), 77–101. doi: 10.1191/1478088706QP063OA.

[42] Alyahmadi, Hamed & Abri, Saleh. (2013). Using Nvivo for Data Analysis in Qualitative Research. International Interdisciplinary Journal of Education. 2. 181-186. 10.12816/0002914.

[43] Leech, N. L., & Onwuegbuzie, A. J. (2011). Beyond constant comparison qualitative data analysis: using NVivo. *School Psychology Quarterly*, 26(1), 70–84. doi: 10.1037/a0022711.

[44] Welsh, Elaine (2002). Dealing with Data: Using NVivo in the Qualitative Data Analysis Process [12 paragraphs]. Forum Qualitative Sozialforschung / Forum: Qualitative Social Research, 3(2), Art. 26, http://nbn-resolving.de/urn:nbn:de:0114-fqs0202260.

[45] Lee, S. Y. (2021). Sustainable supply chain management, digital-based supply chain integration, and firm performance: a cross-country empirical comparison between South Korea and Vietnam. *Sustainability (Switzerland)*, 13(13), 7315. doi: 10.3390/su13137315.

23 Impact of sensory marketing initiatives on brand loyalty with the mediation of emotional engagement and cognitive perception on Gen Z coffee enthusiasts in Colombo district, Sri Lanka

Thara Iddagoda[1,a] and Venura Colombage[2,b]

[1]University of Plymouth, Plymouth, United Kingdom

[2]Department of Marketing and Tourism Management, NSBM Green University, Sri Lanka

Abstract

Generation Z will be the highest potential spending power cohort in the near future. With the preference for experiential benefit over functional benefits there is a growing trend within this generation to visit coffee shops to relax, spend time with their loved ones or the ones who love to spare time leisurely alone. This study aims to examine is what is the influence of sensory marketing initiatives on the emotional engagement, cognitive perception and brand loyalty of Generation Z coffee lovers in Colombo, Sri Lanka which was underutilized in the Sri Lankan context due to lack of knowledge and understanding on its impact. The research deployed S-O-R model and Experiential View Models as the theoretical base as it builds a new conceptual framework more suitable for modern context understanding to fill out a theoretical gap. This research has used the quantitative data analysis approach by distributing an online questionnaire based on convenience sampling method in Colombo based on deductive positivism research approach. The data gathered was analyzed using SPSS for the data preparation, multivariate assumptions and descriptive statistical analysis and PLS-SEM software was used for the inferential analysis and the hypothesis testing. The analysis indicates that there is a weak direct impact of sensory marketing on loyalty but with the mediation of emotional engagement and cognitive perception the relationship gets partially proven. The research recommends that sensory cues play an active part in shaping emotional and cognitive engagement, which in turn indirectly influences brand loyalty. Further recommendations suggested to coffee businesses on how to enhance their brand loyalty using sensory marketing strategies along with improving emotional engagement and cognitive perception by giving a significant focus on achieving many sustainable development goals such as economic growth, emotional well-being, reducing inequalities, sustainable cities and communities and responsible consumption.

Keywords: Brand loyalty, cognitive perception, emotional engagement, generation Z, sensory marketing initiatives

Introduction

Generation Z (Gen Z) will be the cohort to grab most of the purchases in the near future due to their high spending power [1]. To uplift that behavior, sensory marketing has become a revolutionary strategy to involve customers' senses in marketing activity that create memorable and accessible connections with brands [2]. This was often used by brands in industries like hospitality and retail to increase customer satisfaction and retention. For example, there is a link between scent strategies and sales, and shown to have an 11% boost in sales [3]. As per empirical evidence, there is a strong influence of sensory marketing to prefer coffee shops to study, work, to associate with friends or have your own time specially for Gen Z population over other options that serve the same purpose as restaurants, libraries, parks [4]. Coffee shops are a place where all five sensory marketing initiatives can be applied at once [3]. Besides, Sri Lanka is having a history of being an exporter of coffee in the mid 1800's [4]. But Sri Lanka is still a budding country of practicing sensory marketing initiatives, especially in the coffee shop industry [4]. The global coffee market produces over $100 billion annually, yet Sri Lankan coffee sector has not fully tapped into the possibility of utilizing sensory marketing to leverage more loyal customers in coffee outlets [5].

[a]10901285@students.plymouth.ac.uk, [b]venura.c@nsbm.ac.lk

DOI: 10.4324/9781003739920-23

For instance, international coffee brands like Starbucks and Costa Coffee have known the right sensory elements to include in the sensory experience of customers [6]. There is one example, the Dunkin' Donuts Flavor Radio Campaign in Seoul, where they were able to sync the coffee scent with radio jingles, leading to a 16% increase in people walking in, 29% increase in sales [6]. With the demand of coffee among the youth, mostly Gen Z, steadily growing Sri Lankan coffee shop industry have a unique opportunity to employ sensory marketing techniques to create an extra sense of the customers' experience and loyalty to the brands. In the case of Sri Lanka, which has a high number of coffee consumers (58% of those aged 21–30), Gen Z, a portion of the consumer population, goes to coffee shops as much for social and psychological as product needs [4]. Emotional and cognitive aspects of consumers' purchasing decisions are highly valued. Therefore, coffee shops need to reach out to consumers based on something beyond taste and quality of the product [7]. To build brand loyalty in this generation in Colombo District, coffee brands need to understand that traditional marketing efforts such as quality of the product, price and flavor alone may not be enough [4]. Thus, more integrative emotional and cognitive encompassing approaches are needed, where sensory experience comes in [8].

However, though global interest in the topic of sensory marketing is rapidly growing, the Sri Lankan coffee shop industry has ignored the opportunities offered by the global coffee industry [4]. According to insights from interviewees that are done as a background survey, the implementation of sensory marketing is still at a very basic stage with many outlets unable to exploit the use of such marketing techniques to retain and gain satisfaction from customers. For example, one coffee shop had coffee grinds in an open container all day in order to retain some of that coffee aroma, but wasn't in the mindset to think, it would convert into customer satisfaction or loyalty. Hence it is superficial that there is a considerable knowledge gap of Sri Lankan coffee shop owners regarding the importance of sensory marketing in creating loyalty with customers as well as having a memorable experience [4]. Existing studies [9] have studied the role of sensory marketing in customer engagement. However, they have not conducted an in-depth study of emotional and cognitive impact on customers such as sensory experience. Therefore, a comprehensive understanding of sensory marketing initiatives' influence on brand loyalty through cognitive engagement and emotional perception is essential. To explain the mentioned spectrum, the current study deployed the experiential view model [8] and Stimulus–Organism–Response model [10]. Since the model proposed by Mehrabian and Russell [10] for Stimulus–Organism–Response and the experiential view model [10] is not further developed in past studies as a combination together, explaining the interconnected relationship between emotional and cognitive factors involved in influencing brand loyalty from sensory marketing initiatives, there is a gap to be filled. The current research attempts to do so by exploring how sensory marketing drives Gen Z Coffee consumers in Sri Lanka, particularly the Colombo District.

This research aims to investigate Gen Z coffee lovers in Sri Lanka's emotional and cognitive responses to sensory marketing initiatives, and what is the impact of respondents' emotional and cognitive responses on brand loyalty. Since there is lack of research in Sri Lankan context, this study provides a unique insight into how sensory experience could create brand loyalty in the youth population of Colombo. This research will be carried out including literature review, methodology, data analysis, discussions and findings as follows.

Literature Review

Brand loyalty and sensory marketing

Brakus et al. [9] defines brand loyalty as "a deeply held commitment to rebuy or patronize a preferred product/service consistently in the future, thereby causing repetitive same brand purchasing, despite situational influences and marketing efforts that have the potential to cause switching behavior". Many studies have observed its relationship with brand loyalty such as purchase intentions, perceived value and so on but its connection with sensory marketing is lack observed [3]. Sensory marketing is a strategy that takes advantage of the five senses such as vision, audio, odor, taste and feel to create an immersive, memorable experience, which can change the consumer's behavior and create loyalty for a brand [3].

S-O-R model and experiential view model

To have a better understanding of this context, this study uses S-O-R model and experiential view model as the base [3]. The Stimulus-Organism-Response

(S-O-R) model was built to describe the associations between according to which, sensory stimuli (S) induce emotional and cognitive responses (O), which, in turn, lead to a certain behavior, such as brand loyalty. For instance, the scent of freshly brewed coffee can elicit positive emotions that help make customers retain in a business [4]. In other words, background music and lighting also aid in shaping the consumer's feelings when it helps to grow their stay period and raises the level of customer satisfaction [11]. Experience with the sensory elements directly impacts customer loyalty, especially for Generation Z who tends to put more priorities on experience rather than traditional product-based purchases [12].

Emotional engagement and cognitive perception

In the coffee industry, brand loyalty is not only affected by a rational factor-like quality and price but also strongly influenced by emotions and sensory experience [7]. According to [6], sensory marketing provides a brand identity that makes the customers form long–lasting relationships with the brand and in many times repeat visits. Sensory experiences, such as a nice smell or nice place, have been proven to incite feelings that make customers more attached and loyal to a brand [7]. The studies also show that sensory marketing strategies including matching smells and music playlists, are contributing to differentiating brands, improving the cognitive perception and forming of emotional engagement with the brands [13].

Mediating effect of emotional engagement and cognitive perception on relationship between brand loyalty and sensory marketing initiatives

Sensory experience is vital in determining emotional engagement and cognitive perception, mediating the linkage of sensory stimuli with brand loyalty. Therefore, these experiences create strong emotional bonds with the brand which leads to increased satisfaction of the consumer towards the brand and decrease of the tendency of switching to another brand [2]. Maduretno and Junaedi, [12] have consistently shown that sensory marketing is not only an effective method in causing positive emotional responses but also to build brands associations which then give rise to a higher customer loyalty. Finally, a well-integrated sensory experience in the coffee shops is crucial in making a significant contribution to the brand loyalty through the emotional engagement and affecting the cognitive perception [2]. Investment in multisensory marketing by brands strategically would increase the likelihood of building long-term consumer loyalty and differentiate the brands from competitors.

Hypotheses of research

The current research explores how sensory marketing influences Generation Z coffee buyers in Colombo, Sri Lanka. Specifically, the study hypothesizes that the activities of sensory marketing significantly influence emotional engagement as well as cognitive perception, which in turn contribute positively to brand loyalty. Additionally, it posits that emotional engagement and cognitive perception mediate the relationship between sensory marketing and brand loyalty. This process will be further elaborated through the base of the Experiential View Model and the Stimulus-Organism-Response Model, which aims to uncover how multi-sensory brand experiences generate loyal consumers through the creation of emotional bonds as well as cognitive estimations.

Methodology

The research aims at examining how sensory marketing initiatives can affects Generation Z coffee consumers' emotions and cognitions in the case of brand loyalty in Colombo, Sri Lanka. A survey design of a quantitative nature was conducted in a positivism deductive approach that uses quantifiable measures to understand and gain insights from the context. Descriptive and inferential statistics are used for quantitative data and to structure the research design, Research Onion Model [15] provides structured framework on how to research the topic in a systematic manner.

The convenience sampling technique was used for sampling and the quantitative survey covers a sample size of 400 generation Z coffee drinkers as per the morgans table [14]. This helps in having a balanced and informative set of data [7]. The methods used to collect data in the study are the Likert-scale surveys which help in judging the impact of sensory elements on emotional engagement, cognitive perception, and brand loyalty. This research has been used SPSS version 28 for data preparation, multivariant assumptions and demographic analysis and then Smart PLS software was used for inferential analysis.

Descriptive statistics and correlation analysis models are used to analyze relevant data to find the insights and relationships between sensory marketing's effects on consumer loyalty. By doing this, the findings are expected to provide an actionable insight for coffee shop operators to fine tune their sensory marketing approach, to retain customers, and to position themselves competitively in the Sri Lanka coffee shop market [2]. As a background survey before conducting the research, semi structured interviews were conducted with leading coffee shops in Colombo District, Sri Lanka to identify the main research problem by analyzing their present knowledge about sensory marketing and its impact to brands.

Conceptual framework

This study uses a combination of the Stimulus-Organism-Response [10] and the experiential view model [8] framework to understand consumer behavior in a more depth, to frame the sensory marketing concept. It then describes how external stimuli (S), such as the sensory elements in coffee shops, influence emotional engagement and cognitive perception (O) to attain brand loyalty (R). Besides, the Experiential View Model is also used to characterize how these stimuli mediate through emotional and cognitive responses of a coffee lover. By doing this, stimulus relating to the sensory perception of consumers as affected by the external sensory stimuli and internal experiential process that leads to brand loyalty are identified. It provides, overall, a more comprehensive view of how sensory marketing effort impels cognitive and emotional perceptions, creating brand loyalty ultimately.

Data Analysis

In the data analysis process data was cleaned, filtered for missing values and checked for biases (common method and non-response biases) together with the outlier analysis. To carry out statistical analysis, the study has used SPSS and Smart PLS, and the results confirmed the research hypothesis. Table 23.1 stipulates the demographic insights of the sample of the study.

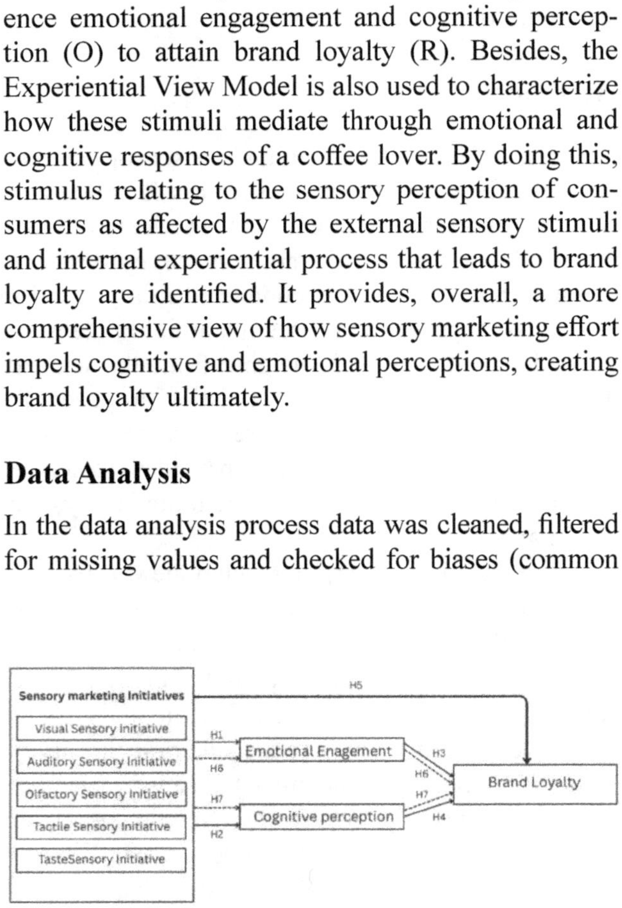

Figure 23.1 Conceptual framework
Source: Author compiled

Table 23.1 Demographics.

Demographics	Items	Frequency	Percentage
Age	13-28	367	88.6
	29-44	36	8.7
	45-60	8	1.9
	60+	3	0.7
Gender	Male	251	60.6
	Female	163	39.4
Employment status	Student	115	27.8
	Employed	221	53.4
	Self employed	64	15.5
	Unemployed	14	3.4
Café that mostly visit	Barista	132	31.9
	Java lounge	128	30.9
	Department of Coffee	64	15.5
	Tea avenue	86	20.8
	other	3	0.6
Spending preference	less than LKR2500	321	77.5
	LKR 2500-5000	90	21.7
	LKR 5000-10000	3	0.7
	More than LKR 10000	0	0
Education level	Advanced level completed	119	28.7
	Diploma completed	134	32.4
	Bachelor's degree completed	96	23.2
	Masters completed	14	3.4
	PhD completed	1	0.2

continued

Demographics	Items	Frequency	Percentage
	Schooling	50	12.1
Frequency of visiting a cafe	Often	50	12.1
	Sometimes	244	58.9
	Rarely	118	28.5
	Never	2	0.5
With whom do you visit to a cafe	Alone	123	29.7
	With partner	113	27.3
	With family	67	16.2
	With friends and colleagues	111	26.8
Purpose of visiting a cafe	To fulfill hunger or thirst	107	25.8
	To have an alone time	36	8.7
	Spend time with your partner	74	17.9
	Hangout with friends	108	26.1
	To work or study	88	21.3
	other	1	0.2

Source: Survey data 2025

Thereafter, this study examined the multivariate assumptions that are critical for proper data analysis. Normality was demonstrated, as the values of skewness and kurtosis are in acceptable ranges thus indicating a near-normal distribution. Constructs were found to have linear relationships (validated using P-P plots). Homoscedasticity was established since no substantial variance problems were evident. VIF was used to measure multicollinearity, and it was seen that VIF values < 5 show no major issues. One-dimensionality was supported by KMO values > 0.6 and Bartlett's test that indicated significance of all constructs as a prerequisite to factor analysis. Factor loadings for all constructs were higher than 0.5 threshold and that supported. Then the data analysis was carried out with SMART-PLS v 4.0.8.4 for the purpose of hypothesis testing which included sensory marketing initiatives (SMI), emotional engagement (EE), cognitive perception (CP) and brand loyalty (BL). First 414 surveys were obtained

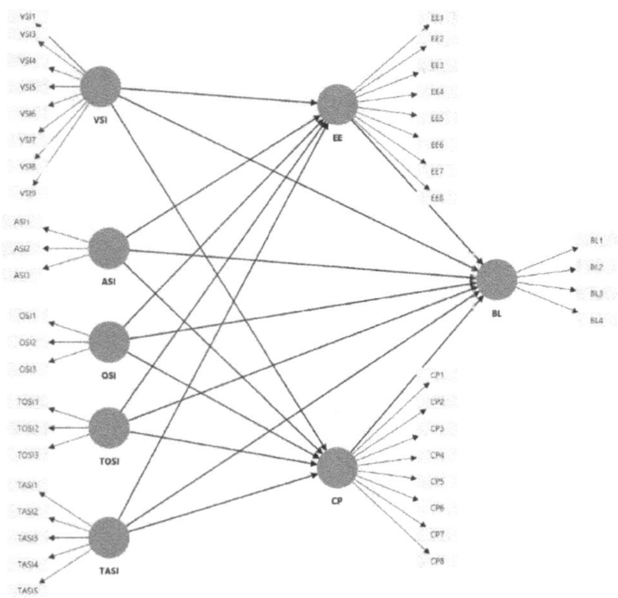

Figure 23.2 Measurement model
Source: Survey data 2025

and after elimination of outliers, 411 scoring was retained for further analysis. Structural Equation Modeling (SEM) was then employed to examine how these key constructs were related to each other. Figure 23.2 depicts the measurement model of the study consisting of variables.

Average Variance Extracted (AVE) was used to evaluate convergent validity, that is, the extent that the indicators of each construct are related to the latent variable. The AVE values for all the constructs were all above the value of 0.5 [16], showing that the measuring indicators explained over half the variance of the corresponding latent variable. In addition, Cronbach's alpha values laid between 0.807 (ASI) and 0.929 (EE) which reflect good internal consistency for all constructs. Similarly, the composite reliability values spanned between 0.818 and 0.941, thus further validating the model's internal consistency to which has been assumed to go beyond 0.7 [16]. The outer loadings of indicators used which are all above the 0.7 thresholds affirmed the convergent validity of the measurement model used [16]. Further, discriminant validity was tested using Fornell-Larcker criterion along with Heterotrait-Monotrait ratio and cross loading. Fornell-Larcker criterion demonstrated that the square root of the AVE for each construct was higher than its correlations with other constructs, which confirmed distinctiveness of the constructs. In addition, all values of HTMT ratios were below the tag level of 0.85, which confirms that the constructs

Table 23.2 Reliability and convergent validity.

	Cronbach's alpha	Composite reliability (rho_a)	Composite reliability (rho_c)	Average variance extracted (AVE)
ASI	0.807	0.818	0.887	0.724
BL	0.833	0.839	0.888	0.665
CP	0.905	0.906	0.923	0.601
EE	0.929	0.931	0.941	0.667
OSI	0.829	0.829	0.898	0.747
TASI	0.889	0.892	0.918	0.693
TOSI	0.85	0.857	0.91	0.771
VSI	0.903	0.905	0.921	0.565

Source: Survey data 2025

Table 23.3 R square.

	Original sample (O)	P values
BL	0.223	0
CP	0.336	0
EE	0.372	0

Source: Survey data 2025

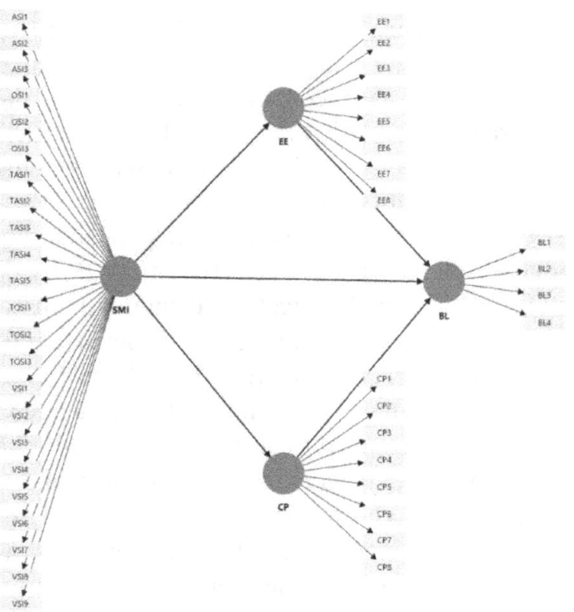

Figure 23.3 Structural model
Source: Survey data 2025

were meaningfully different from each other. Related to Cross-loadings, every item had stronger loading power to its intended construct, compared to any other construct. Table 23.2 depicts the reliability and validity measures summary of the latent variables of the study.

Table 23.4 F square.

	Original sample (O)	P values
CP -> BL	0.078	0.021
EE -> BL	0.01	0.463
SMI -> BL	0.007	0.514
SMI -> CP	0.506	0
SMI -> EE	0.593	0

Source: Survey data 2025

Table 23.5 Q square.

	Q²predict
BL	0.122
CP	0.327
EE	0.364

Source: Survey Data 2025

Table 23.6 Mediating effect of cognitive .perception.

	Original sample (O)	P values
CP -> BL	0.36	0
SMI -> BL	0.152	0.007
SMI -> CP	0.581	0
	Original sample (O)	P values
SMI -> CP -> BL	0.209	0

Source: Survey Data 2025

The study also applied a higher order measurement model for sensory marketing initiatives (SMI) which was considered as a second order construct which includes visual sensory initiatives (VSI), auditory sensory initiatives (ASI), olfactory sensory initiatives (OSI), tactile sensory initiatives (TOSI), and taste sensory initiatives (TASI). This higher-order construct explained the size of the impact of sensory experiences on consumer engagement in a more concise, yet representative manner of the influence of sensory marketing on brand loyalty.

The R^2 values indicated SMI and the mediating constructs accounted for 22.3% of the variance in BL, 33.6% of the variance in CP and 37.2% of the

Table 23.7 Mediating effect of emotional engagement.

	Original sample (O)	P values
EE -> BL	0.23	0.001
SMI -> BL	0.219	0.001
SMI -> EE	0.611	0
	Original sample (O)	**P values**
SMI -> EE -> BL	0.141	0.001

Source: Survey Data 2025

variance in EE, implying that the model had explanatory power even though it is weak and the EE the most explained variable even though it is not strong.

The f^2 values also showed the strength of the relationships between constructs. The result size of SMI → CP was high ($f^2 = 0.506$), which meant that SMI had moderate influence on CP, and the effect of SMI on BL was minimal ($f^2 = 0.007$). The f^2 value for SMI → EE was also high ($f^2 = 0.593$), the SMI → EE causing a moderate influence on emotional engagement. As R^2 value is accepted, the size of the relationship does not really matter. Further, the study examined the model's predictive relevance of the model through Q^2 values, with EE exhibiting the highest predictive relevance ($Q^2 = 0.364$), followed by CP ($Q^2 = 0.327$), and BL ($Q^2 = 0.122$), since all the values are above 0 the predicting power exists [17].

Mediation effects of EE and CP were examined to find out how they played roles in relation between SMI and BL. The analysis through the Variance Accounted For (VAF) demonstrated that EE mediated 39.2% of the overall effect of SMI on BL, and CP mediated 58% of the effect. These findings indicate that both EE and CP have partial mediating roles between SMI and BL.

The structural model tested the hypothesized relationships of SMI, EE, CP and BL. The model revealed that SMI had significant effects on both EE and CP. CP also has significant effect on BL while EE was able to prove its impact on BL. However, the direct effect of the SMI and the BL is insignificant thus, indicating that sensory marketing does not have direct effect on brand loyalty. It was measured with p value comparison below the significance threshold of 0.05 according to [21]

The results of hypothesis testing showed that the H1, H2, H4, H6, and H7 hypotheses were confirmed and that the H3 and H5 hypotheses were refuted. It was observed that specifically sensory marketing initiatives had a strong influence on emotional engagement and cognitive conception but not brand loyalty directly. The effect of SMI on BL was found to be mediated by emotional engagement and cognitive perception with CP having a stronger mediation role than EE.

Discussion and Implications

The main emphasis of the current study is to assess the impact of sensory cues that include visual, auditory, olfactory, tactile, and taste facets on the emotional engagement, cognitive perception, and brand loyalty. The Structural Equation Modeling analysis of hypotheses made it possible to show the important links between the concepts of sensory marketing and different consumer behavior aspects. The research

Table 23.8 Hypothesis testing.

		Original sample (O)	Sample mean (M)	Standard deviation (STDEV)	T-statistics (|O/STDEV|)	P values	Accepted / Rejected
SMI -> EE	H1	0.61	0.613	0.037	16.675	0	Accepted
SMI -> CP	H2	0.58	0.583	0.042	13.966	0	Accepted
EE -> BL	H3	0.116	0.115	0.072	1.609	0.108	Rejected
CP -> BL	H4	0.323	0.326	0.061	5.288	0	Accepted
SMI -> BL	H5	0.1	0.101	0.067	1.496	0.135	Rejected
SMI->EE->BL	H6		VAF	Value	39.2%	0.001	Accepted
SMI->CP->BL	H7		VAF	Value	58%	0	Accepted

Source: Survey Data 2025

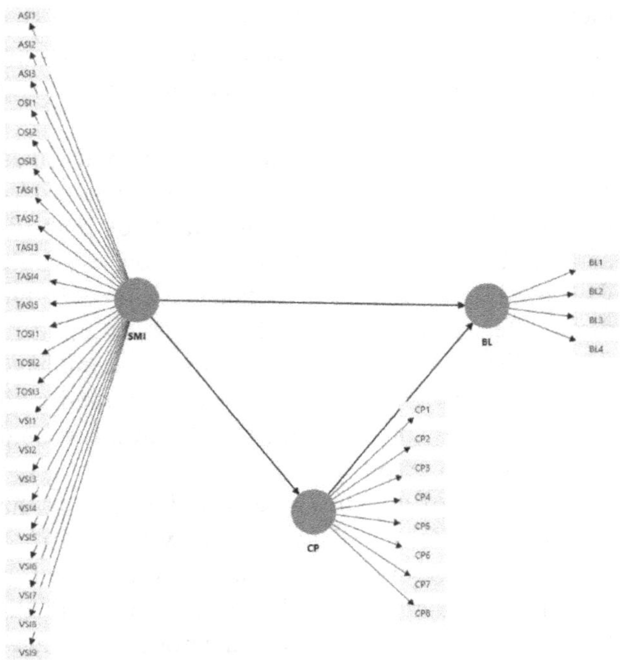

Figure 23.4 Mediating effects of cognitive perception
Source: Survey data 2025

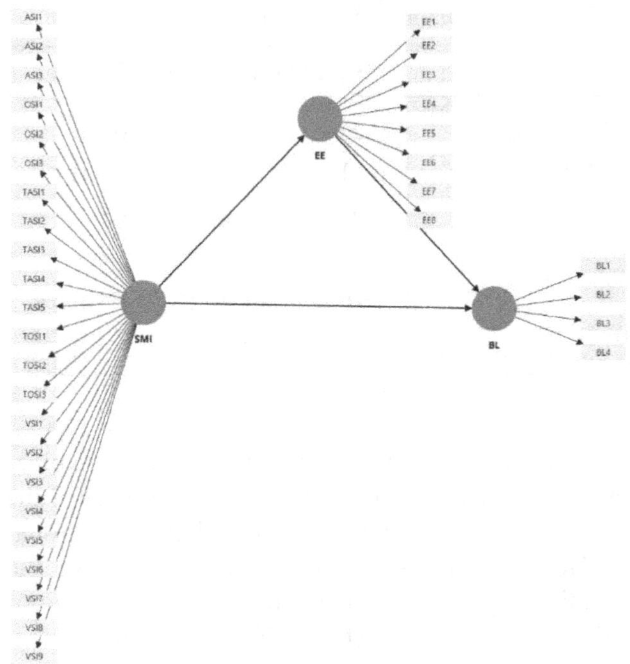

Figure 23.5 Mediating effect of emotional engagement
Source: Survey data 2025

confirmed that sensory marketing is a major factor in improving emotional involvement and cognitive perception. It was also found that emotional engagement and cognitive perception, to some extent, mediate the relationship between sensory marketing and brand loyalty, thus reinforcing the assumption that they are critical in the creation of consumer loyalty. However, the immediate effect of sensory marketing on brand loyalty was insignificant, which leaves no doubt that emotional and cognitive factors play the most important role when it comes to creating brand loyalty relative to isolated sensory marketing.

This research is in consonance with previous studies, such as in the work of [3] to indicate that sensory cues such as scent, taste and sound touch in a significant manner on consumers' emotions and loyalty to brands. The research supports the findings by [18] where sensory cues play a key role in consumers' perception of quality and value, which builds brand loyalty. Similarly, it was found out in the course of the study that sensory marketing was having a lower direct bearing on brand loyalty than anticipated, which shows a more complex relationship at play in consumer decision making especially in Sri Lankan coffee environments, and which endorsed the proposition that sensory marketing on its own would often fail to directly influence loyalty but would require other mediating variables to be included. From [19], sensory marketing has positive effects on customer loyalty, but brand loyalty impact is uncertain.

Regarding emotional engagement, the research showed that sensory marketing initiatives significantly elevated excitement and satisfaction on consumers. [7, 20] past research serves to emphasize the importance of sensory marketing in building emotional connections with consumers to make brand loyalty stronger, like which is found in this research. In fact, the study showed emotional engagement, on its own, did not elevate brand loyalty in the Sri Lankan coffee industry. The outcome suggests that the concentration on cognitive perception should be higher than emotional engagement with the expectation of increasing brand loyalty.

According to the research, sensory marketing is a central factor in the production of how consumers view the quality and worth of brands based on cognitive appraisal. This outcome supports the grain of truth of [19, 7, 18] who all stated that sensory experiences, especially in terms of aroma and taste, increase consumers' cognitive assessments on brands. For instance, the smell of freshly brewed coffee in a café makes people's perception of product quality more favorable, leading to their loyalty to the coffee shop brand. The research findings established that sensory marketing and brand loyalty relationships are mediated by emotional engagement and cognitive perception. More specifically, emotional engagement accounted for 39.2% of the overall effect, and cognitive perception accounted for 58% of it. These findings reveal that sensory marketing works its magic on brand loyalty through these two mediators mostly, further emphasizing the need for both emotional and cognitive responses for enduring brand loyalty. These outcomes are reinforced by research of [7] who highlight the importance of emotional and cognitive engagement in the formation of consumer loyalty.

Managerial implications

Results of this research have some managerial implications for managers and marketers of coffee shops in Colombo, Sri Lanka. Designing a sensorial experience of coffee shops which links to the customers' feelings is vital to the Sri Lankan coffee shops. For instance, with inviting interior designs, more personalized in-store music playlists, unique fragrances on serving managers can increase emotional connections and encourage repurchase behaviour of customers. Besides, highlighting the quality of the coffee, advertising the brand's environmental activities, and explaining the worth of the product are the means of enhanced customers' cognitive understanding. Goals of enhancing emotional and cognitive engagement help the coffee shops create lasting relationships with the clientele. As emotional and cognitive engagement are the principal drivers of loyalty, companies need to integrate their marketing strategies to resonate with Generation Z, who become brand loyal only if the branding can create authentic experiences and demonstrate a strong value.

Theoretical implications

The study helps to fill the gap in the theory of sensory marketing, consumer behavior, and brand loyalty by combing and further developing the S-O-R model and the Experiential view model. The results show the power of sensory marketing over emotional attachment, cognitive awareness and brand loyalty and fit in with theories such as the S-O-R model and experiential view models of explaining how sensory cues contribute to consumer behavior. In addition, the results reinforce that emotional engagement as well as cognitive awareness is an important mediating link between the relationship of sensory marketing and brand loyalty. The integration of stimulus-organism-response model and experiential view models in this research sharpens the conceptual framework, providing a more complex appreciation of the role played by sensory occurrences in the development of brand loyalty [10, 8].

Social implications

When approached from a social perspective, the research would bring out the fact that sensory marketing can be used to improve consumers' well-being through contributing to the creation of emotionally stimulating environments. The implementation of sustainable sensory marketing initiatives enables organizations to bring sustainable consumption practices forward and amplify social gains. Coffee shops can maintain responsible consumerism by selecting environmental material or by contracting fair trade suppliers for their goods. In addition, sensory spaces may encourage relaxation and significant interaction, which might improve people's emotional well-being. For instance, this advantage is particularly visible in younger groups, such as Generation Z, who frequently suffer from major stress. In line with SDGs 8 and 12, the findings highlight the fact that well-planned sensory marketing efforts not only enhance economic performance but also encourage accountable consumption. To support social equity, coffee shops may introduce braille language into their menus, while meeting the needs of the visually handicapped customers thus creating an inclusive society. The research contributes new knowledge to the discipline of sensory marketing and consumer behavior, offering concrete action guidance to organizations who aspire to develop improved customer relationships and retention. The study highlights the need for further research to understand the nature of consumer behavior and the role of sensory marketing in different circumstances.

Future Research Areas and Conclusion

Further studies can be conducted to explain how emotional engagement can drive brand loyalty and to understand how sensory marketing can directly influence brand loyalty, which was not supported in this study. Additionally, this allows further probing into the mediating factors that could help explain these relations, including customer satisfaction or perceived quality. Furthermore, this research could be extended to other industries such as cosmetics, nutrition, and retail to gain more insights into how sensory marketing impacts consumer loyalty in other purveying settings. The comparison among regions and cultures would also reveal the reasons why the sensory cues have an impact on brand loyalty in different settings. Moreover, the study limits, such as sample size, context, and use of self-reported data, open a window for further research. Future researchers can explore the same study to compare other administrative districts in Sri Lanka to improve the representativeness of the sample and to further improve the generalizability of the findings. To track the long-term effects of sensory marketing on brand loyalty longitudinal studies could be utilized or potentially using more diverse sampling could keep results more generalizable. Last, and most importantly, understanding how social influence works in determining brand loyalty in coffee shop contexts can further serve in understanding the effectiveness of sensory marketing.

Finally, it is concluded that sensory marketing significantly effects on brand loyalty with the partial mediation of emotional engagement and cognitive perception, in Generation Z consumers of coffee shop sector in Sri Lanka. The outcomes provide an invocation for current theories on the function of sensory clues in selecting purchaser activity and uncover neighborhood special cases to be explored in the future. Focusing on coffee shops through a sensory experience allows brands to engage customers more, build customer loyalty and keep up with the competition in light of a high concentration market [7, 3].

References

[1] Judy Li, P., & Hassan, S. H. (2023). Mapping the literature on Gen Z purchasing behavior: a bibliometric analysis using VOSviewer. *Innovative Marketing*, 19(3), 62–73. doi: https://doi.org/10.21511/im.19(3).2023.06

[2] Eti, H. S. (2024). Üniversite öğrencilerinde kahve mağazalarindaki duyusal pazarlamanin deneyimsel değer açisindan değerlendirilmesi. *Humanitas uluslararası sosyal bilimler dergisi/humanitas international journal of social sciences*, doi: https://doi.org/10.20304/humanitas.1383225.

[3] Krishna, A. (2012). An integrative review of sensory marketing: engaging the senses to affect perception, judgment and behavior. *Journal of Consumer Psychology*, 22(3), 332–351. doi: https://doi.org/10.1016/j.jcps.2011.08.003.

[4] Dodamgoda, N., & Amarasinghe, K. (2019). The impact of sensory branding on consumer preference of coffee shops in Colombo, Sri Lanka. *Journal of Business and Management*, 21, 21–31. doi: https://doi.org/10.9790/487X-2106022131.

[5] Menke, A., (2018). The Global Coffee Industry, Global Edge, Apr. 19. https://globaledge.msu.edu/blog/post/55607/the-global-coffee-industry (accessed May 20, 2025).

[6] Y. J. Chang, (2021). Creating the multisensory brand experience in coffee shops, Lowa State University Digital Library, Lowa State University. Accessed: May 20, 2025. [Online]. Available: https://dr.lib.iastate.edu/entities/publication/ce317148-777d-48d2-b3b6-560c36688e4b.

[7] Gao, F., & Shen, Z. (2024). Sensory brand experience and brand loyalty: mediators and gender differences. *Acta Psychologica*, 244, 104191. doi: https://doi.org/10.1016/j.actpsy.2024.104191.

[8] Hirschman, E. C., & Holbrook, M. B. (1982). Hedonic consumption: emerging concepts, methods and propositions. *Journal of Marketing*, 46(3), 92–101. doi: https://doi.org/10.1177/002224298204600314.

[9] Brakus, J. J., Schmitt, B. H., & Zarantonello, L. (2009). Brand experience: what is it? how is it measured? does it affect loyalty?. *Journal of Marketing*, 73(3), 52–68. doi: https://doi.org/10.1509/jmkg.73.3.052.

[10] Mehrabian, A., & Russell, J. A. (1974). An Approach to Environmental Psychology. The MIT Press.

[11] A. Susanti, P. S. T. Dewi, & I. W. Y. A. Putra, (2021). Relationship Mapping of Brand Sensuality Factors and Interior Design Characters of Popular Coffee Shop: In Z gens perception, Advances in Social Science, Education and Humanities Research, vol. 602, no. 1, pp. 214–230. doi: https://doi.org/10.2991/assehr.k.211126.024.

[12] Maduretno, R. B. E. H. P., & Junaedi, M. F. S. (2022). Exploring the effects of coffee shop brand experience on loyalty: the roles of brand love and brand trust. *Gadjah Mada International Journal of Business*, 24(3), 289. doi: https://doi.org/10.22146/gamaijb.63218.

[13] Sethjinda, T., & Laothumthut, W. (2019). What drives experiential loyalty? a case study of coffee chain stores in Bangkok. *Journal of Global Business Review*, 21(2), 59–82. Accessed: May 20, 2025. [Online]. Available from: https://ojs.lib.buu.ac.th/index.php/commerce/article/view/6602.

[14] Krejcie, R. V., & Morgan, D. W. (1970). Determining sample size for research activities. *Educational and Psychological Measurement*, 30(3), 607–610. doi: https://doi.org/10.1177/001316447003000308.

[15] Saunders, M., Lewis, P., & Thornhill, A. (2019). Research Methods for Business Students, (8th edn.). S.L.: Pearson Education Limited.

[16] Hair, J. F. (2017). A Primer on Partial Least Squares Structural Equation Modeling (PLS-SEM). Los Angeles: Sage.

[17] Hair, J. (2019). Essentials of Business Research Methods., (4th edn.). S.L.: Routledge.

[18] Ave, S. D., Venter, M., & Mhlophe, B. (2015). Sensory branding and buying behavior in coffee shops: a study on Generation Y. 11(2), 93–110.

[19] Riza, A. F., & Wijayanti, D. M. (2018). The triangle of sensory marketing model: does it stimulate brand experience and loyalty?. *Esensi: Jurnal Bisnis dan Manajemen*, 8(1), 57–66. doi: https://doi.org/10.15408/ess.v8i1.6058.

[20] Shahid, S., Paul, J., Gilal, F. G., & Ansari, S. (2022). The role of sensory marketing and brand experience in building emotional attachment and brand loyalty in luxury retail stores. *Psychology and Marketing*, 39(7), 1398–1412. doi: https://doi.org/10.1002/mar.21661.

[21] Hair, J. F., Risher, J. J., Sarstedt, M., & Ringle, C. M. (2019). When to use and how to report the results of PLS-SEM. *European Business Review*, 31(1), 2–24.

24 The influence of short video characteristics on the continued viewing behavior of social media advertisements, with particular reference to generation Z consumers in Sri Lanka

Kelum Weththasinghe[1,a], *Venura Colombage*[2,b] *and Piumal Herath*[2,c]

[1]University of Plymouth, Plymouth, United Kingdom

[2]Department of Marketing and Tourism Management, NSBM Green University, Homagama, Sri Lanka

Abstract

This study addresses the persistent challenge of maintaining user attention in short-form social media video advertising, particularly among Generation Z (Gen G) consumers in Sri Lanka, where ad engagement is notably lower than global averages. Guided by the cognitive-affective-behavioral (CAB) model and the theory of consumption values (TCV), this research investigates how five consumption values informativeness, personalization, social presence, entertainment, and recommendation serendipity influence user satisfaction, and subsequently, continuous watching intention. It also examines the moderating roles of advertising irritation and the Big Five personality traits. A quantitative survey conducted with 389 Gen Z users in Sri Lanka revealed that all five consumption values positively and significantly enhance user satisfaction, which in turn significantly and partially mediates their positive effect on continuous watching intention. Conversely, advertising irritation and personality traits were found to have no significant moderate effect on the relationship between satisfaction and continuous watching intention. These findings emphasize that user satisfaction, driven by the perceived value of short video content, is crucial for sustained engagement, offering actionable insights for marketers and content creators to optimize ad effectiveness and improve communication with Gen Z audiences in Sri Lanka.

Keywords: Advertising irritation, big five personality traits, consumption values, continuous watching, short videos

Introduction

Technological advancements have positioned social media as a leading channel for communication and information exchange globally [1, 2]. As of 2024, there are approximately 5.17 billion social media users worldwide, including 56.4 million from Gen Z [3]. In Sri Lanka, 7.5 million of the 14.58 million internet users actively engage with social media platforms [4].

Among these users, Generation Z (Gen G) demonstrates a strong preference for video content, particularly on platforms like YouTube, TikTok, and Instagram [5]. One of the most popular content formats among this group is short-form video, often referred to as "snackable content." These videos, typically under 30 seconds, are designed to quickly capture attention and deliver engaging messages [6, 7]. Research suggests that Gen Z responds more positively to social media advertising than traditional media, which can enhance brand awareness, customer engagement, and purchase intention [8]. Despite the rising popularity of short-form advertising, challenges in maintaining user attention remain. Globally, 65.9% of users skip video ads whenever the option is available [9]. In 2024, digital advertising spending on short-form video reached $99.4 billion globally, with Sri Lanka contributing $21.4 million, averaging only $2 per person compared to the global average of $18 [10]. This indicates lower ad engagement and possible inefficiencies in reaching local audiences. Contributing factors such as advertising fatigue and advertising irritation defined as the degree to which users find ads annoying can significantly impact user behavior [11, 12]. Individual personality traits also influence ad engagement. While

[a]10901261@students.plymouth.ac.uk, [b]venura.c@nsbm.ac.lk, [c]piumal.h@nsbm.ac.lk

DOI: 10.4324/9781003739920-24

some users may be more tolerant or curious, others may be quick to disengage, making the design of video content more complex [13–15]. However, the relationship between personality traits and ad irritation remains underexplored, especially in short-form content contexts.

To better understand these dynamics, this study adopts the cognitive-affective-behavioral (CAB) model, which outlines how cognition (awareness), affect (emotions), and behavior (intentions) shape user responses [16]. In this framework, video characteristics and user satisfaction act as cognitive and affective drivers of continued watching behavior. Additionally, the Theory of Consumption Values (TCV) [17] and the Big Five personality traits model [14, 15, 18] provide theoretical grounding for examining individual differences.

Despite the rapid growth of short-form video advertising globally and within Sri Lanka, limited research has examined the factors influencing Gen Z consumers' continuous watching behavior in this context. While previous studies have focused primarily on the positive impacts of advertising or general user engagement, they have largely overlooked the role of advertising irritation and consumer personality traits in shaping continuous viewing options. Moreover, the interaction between these affective factors and satisfaction as a mediating variable remains underexplored. Grounded in the CAB model, this study addresses this gap by investigating how cognitive evaluations of consumption value translate into continuous watching behavior through affective responses, with personality and advertising irritation moderating these relationships. This provides both theoretical insights and practical implications for optimizing short video advertising effectiveness among Sri Lankan Gen Z consumers, in aid of the study, research questions were developed,

1. What are the cognitive and affective factors influencing Gen Z viewers' continuous watching intentions?
2. What is the role of advertising irritation in the relationship between the affective construct of satisfaction and watching intention?
3. What is the role of the consumer's personality in the relationship between the affective construct of satisfaction and watching intention?

Literature and Methodology

Literature

Continuous watching intention

Continuous watching intention shows a viewer's ongoing engagement with live stream content, shown through frequent consumption, interaction, and recommendation [19]. Unlike initial adoption, the behavior is based on prior experiences, shaping overall perceptions of information systems, IT platforms, or mobile services [20]. User satisfaction is crucial for continued use [21, 22], but negative advertising experiences like irritation, personalization concerns, or skepticism can lead to avoidance behaviors [11]. However, useful, entertaining, or trustworthy advertisements, especially skippable ones offering control, strengthen continuous watching intention [9].

The cognition-affect-behavioral model

This research is based on the CAB model [23], which explains consumer decision making as a process through cognitive, affective, and behavioral stages [24]. In the cognitive stage, individuals evaluate the perceived value of content, guided by the TCV [17], which includes functional, emotional, and epistemic dimensions. This stage also involves internal psychological processes and knowledge structures [25, 26]. The affective stage reflects emotional responses, where satisfaction serves as a mediating variable, transmitting the influence of cognitive value assessments to behavioral intentions. Furthermore, advertising irritation and consumer personality traits act as moderating variables, influencing the strength and direction of satisfaction's impact on behavior [27]. For example, high irritation may weaken satisfaction's effect, while certain personality traits can amplify or dampen emotional reactions. Finally, the behavioral stage represented by continuous watching intention is the outcome of this process, showing how perceptions and emotions translate into sustained user engagement [28].

Theory of consumption values

According to TCV [17], consumers make choices based on different values of functional, social, emotional, and epistemic values. Functional value, including informativeness and personalization [29], relates to a product's usefulness. Social value, represented by social presence [17, 30], satisfies the need for group belonging. Emotional value, captured through entertainment [31], reflects feelings like pleasure and enjoyment. Epistemic value, seen in recommendation serendipity [32, 33], stimulates curiosity and the desire for knowledge.

Five factor model for personality

The model identified five personality dimensions in measuring personality which are openness to experience, conscientiousness, extraversion, agreeableness, neuroticism [18].

Informativeness

Informativeness signifies providing the user with useful and necessary information in content [19]. It improves user satisfaction by meeting informational needs [34], whether it's product knowledge in advertising [35] or up-to-date facts in short videos [6]. Relevant and high-quality information builds positive consumer responses that can lead to positive brand attitude [12]. The study hypothesizes that greater informativeness positively influences satisfaction

H1-Informativeness has a positive relationship with satisfaction

Personalization

Personalization involves customizing products or services to customer preferences improving user experience and satisfaction [13]. Modern platforms use "personalized recommendations" to cater to unique needs, encouraging engagement [36]. By reducing the time users spend searching for relevant information, personalization positively impacts satisfaction [37]. This customization creates a sense of connection, making users more likely to invest time and effort in platforms that offer content specifically designed for them [6].

H2-Personalization has a positive relationship with satisfaction

Social presence

Social presence reflects the sense of connection with others during interactions [38]. Within the TCV framework, it relates to elements associated with social groups, including social interactions, acceptance, and image [17, 30]. In digital environments, the visibility of others and the prominence of social communications [6] contribute to this. High-quality communication mediums increase the feeling of social presence [39], encouraging engagement and satisfaction [40]. When users feel a strong social involvement in content, they experience greater emotional fulfillment, positively influencing satisfaction.

H3-Social presence has a positive relationship with satisfaction.

Entertainment

Entertainment fulfills users' hedonic needs, offering escapism, pleasure, and emotional release [41]. In advertising, it's about the likeability and enjoyment derived from an advertisement [42]. Creative and engaging content on digital platforms offers significant entertainment value [8], leading to pleasure and enjoyment. Positive feelings from entertainment are a main reason for consumers to watch advertisements [44]. Entertainment on social media helps users relax and find emotional gratification [45], strengthening their bond with apps [8]. This study proposes that entertainment positively influences satisfaction [46], due to its ability to meet psychological needs for enjoyment.

H4-Entertainment has a positive relationship with satisfaction

Recommendation serendipity

Recommendation serendipity describes how recommended videos exceed expectations, sparking curiosity and offering unexpected yet relevant content [32], [33]. This element of surprise and delight can lead to deep focus and encourage users to watch beyond their initial intent [47]. On social media, the continuous stream of random but relevant videos [7] increases user satisfaction. Empirical evidence shows a strong positive relationship between serendipitous recommendations and favorable consumer behavior across various digital platforms [6].

H5-Recommendation Serendipity has a positive relationship with satisfaction

Satisfaction

Satisfaction measures the difference between customer expectations and actual benefits received [48], indicating whether needs are met. It's a critical factor in various consumer behaviors, including purchase

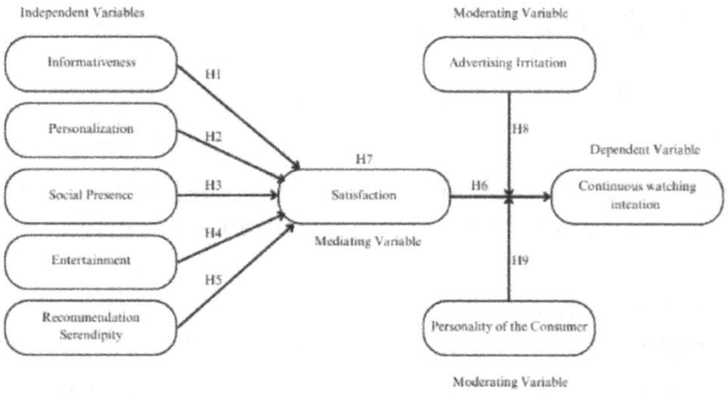

Figure 24.1 Conceptual framework
Source: Author

intention, loyalty, or continuous usage [6]. Satisfied customers are more likely to continue using a product or service, while unsatisfied customers are more likely to switch [49]. In the digital realm, satisfaction is an important factor for continuous intention [50]. It acts as a mediator, directly influencing continuous watching intention and transmitting the effects of cognitive factors [51], as seen in mediating consumption values to behavior [52], confirming that satisfied users are more likely to sustain their use [53].

H6- Satisfaction has a positive relationship with continuous watching

H7-Satisfaction mediates the influence of consumption factors on the continuous watching intention

Role of advertising irritation
Advertising irritation is defined as the discomfort or annoyance caused by advertisements [54], it negatively impacts user satisfaction and can drive platform avoidance [55]. Intrusive short video advertisements disrupt user experiences, leading to negative feelings towards brands or platforms [12]. Prior research highlights that irritation can cause users to stop continuous platform usage [11],further it can be said as advertising irritation weakens the positive influence of satisfaction on continuous watching intention [56], highlighting its disruptive power.

H8-Advertising irritation has a negative relationship on the continuous watching intention

Role of personality of the consumer
The big five personality traits, extraversion, agreeableness, conscientiousness, neuroticism, and openness to experience, explain variations in digital content interaction [14]. Neuroticism is often a "defensive response" to threat [15], with high scores linked to anxiety and increased social platform use [57]. Extraversion correlates with social activity and content engagement due to sociability and reward-seeking [58]. Openness to Experience signifies curiosity and exploration, increasing engagement with social media activities and advertisements [15]. Agreeableness reflects interpersonal regard [58], with highly agreeable individuals more likely to engage with advertisements due to their cooperative nature in digital communication [14]. Conversely, Conscientiousness is linked to rule following and long term goals [15], often leading to less social media use as a distraction [59], limiting engagement with short-form content unless highly relevant. Research suggests personality moderates continuous watching behavior alongside advertising irritation [6].

H9-Personality of the consumer influences the continuous watching intention. Figure 24.1 visualizes conceptual framework.

Methodology
Following the research onion model by Saunders et al. [60], the study followed a positivist philosophy and a deductive approach. The unit of analysis was individual, and a cross-sectional time horizon was adopted in gathering the data. The study was conducted using a quantitative research design, structured closed-ended online questionnaires to collect data from Gen Z individuals in Sri Lanka. A non-probabilistic convenience sampling method was used as the sampling technique. A sample size of 400 was determined as the Gen Z population exceeded 1,000,000. Measurements were conducted using a 5-point scale for the consumption values of the consumers [6], satisfaction [6], advertising irritation [6], and continuous watching behavior [6], and a 7-point Likert scale for the personality of the consumer [61], while all measures and items were taken from validated scales. Structural Equation Modelling was done thereafter using SmartPLS version 4.1.1.2.

Results and Discussion

Data analysis
As shown in Table 24.1 the study targeted Gen Z individuals who consume short social media content. Eligible participants were individuals aged 12-27 who consume short video content. 392 online

Table 24.1 Demographic statistics table.

Category	Subcategory	Frequency (n = 389)	(%)
Gender	Male	205	52.7%
	Female	184	47.3%
Age	12–17	76	19.5%
	18–23	214	55.0%
	24–27	99	25.4%
Marital status	Single	337	86.6%
	Married	44	11.3%
	Prefer not to say	8	2.1%
Internet usage frequency	Daily	368	94.6%
	Weekly	9	2.3%
	Monthly	7	1.8%
	Not even once a month	5	1.3%
Monthly income	Less than 25,000	259	66.6%
	25,000 – 49,999	45	11.6%
	50,000 – 74,999	37	9.5%
	Above 75,000	48	12.3%
Occupation	Student	280	72.0%
	Self-employed	24	6.2%
	Full-time employed	82	21.1%
	Unemployed	3	0.8%
Platforms used	Instagram	79	20.31%
	Instagram, YouTube	35	9.00%
	Tik Tok	103	26.48%
	Tik Tok, Instagram	20	5.14%
	Tik Tok, Instagram, YouTube	32	8.23%
	Tik Tok, You Tube	28	7.20%
	YouTube	92	23.65%

Source: Author

surveys were distributed via social media and messaging apps, and 389 usable responses were obtained, providing an effective response rate of 99.2%. Instructions were given clearly to maximize the response rate, an introduction to the study was made clear, and a survey design was provided. Data were then transferred into IBM SPSS Statistics (version 28.0.1.1) to prepare, including coding and identifying outliers. At least 10% of the coded responses were checked for accuracy to minimize human error. Partial Least Squares Structural Equation Modeling (PLS-SEM) was employed via SmartPLS version 4.1.1.2 to assess the measurement model (reliability and validity) and structural model (hypothesis testing, mediation effects, and moderation effects).

Common method bias

In the current study, the common method bias was analyzed using Hermans' single-factor test [62] to make sure that there is no common method bias present. Since the cumulative frequency is at a percentage of 25.738%, which is well below the threshold value of 50%, it can be observed that no common method bias with the considered dataset is present in the study.

Nonresponsive bias

Levene's test for homogeneity of variance and a one-way ANOVA were performed to examine the group's difference, where the results showcased no significant group differences. The significance value is 0.054, which exceeds the threshold of 0.05, and the corresponding Levene statistic value was 3.727, showing no evidence that the variance of the respondent groups is significantly different. In the ANOVA test conducted, the significance value is 0.010, which is below 0.05, which shows there is a significant difference between the two mean scores of the two data groups. These results indicated that there is no common method bias present.

Tests for multivariate assumptions

Linearity and homoscedasticity

In the present study, linearity and homoscedasticity are assessed with the relationships between the consumption values of the consumer with satisfaction, satisfaction along with the continuous watching intention, personality along with the continuous watching intention, and advertising irritation with the continuous watching intention. It can be observed that the scatter plots for the relationships showed data clustered in a single direction, confirming the presence of homoscedasticity. Furthermore, the p-p plots indicated clear linear patterns for each variable, supporting that linearity and homoscedasticity are adequately met in this study.

Multicollinearity

The variance inflation factor (VIF) was used to measure multicollinearity, where all the values fell below

Table 24.2 Cronbach's alpha, composite reliability, and average variance extracted.

	Cronbach's alpha	Composite reliability (rho_a)	Composite reliability (rho_c)	Average variance extracted (AVE)
AI	0.627	0.636	0.798	0.568
CW	0.689	0.694	0.828	0.616
ENT	0.773	0.775	0.855	0.595
INF	0.723	0.724	0.828	0.546
P	0.691	0.699	0.757	0.396
PER	0.693	0.694	0.813	0.521
RS	0.668	0.674	0.800	0.500
SAT	0.752	0.754	0.843	0.574
SP	0.798	0.801	0.869	0.623

Source: Author

the threshold of 3 [64], showing no multicollinearity issues.

Uni-dimensionality

The Kaiser-Mayer-Oklin Measure (KMO) and Bartlett's sphericity test were considered when measuring unidimensionality. All KMO values ranged from 0.633 to 0.786, adhering to the threshold [49]; all Bartlett's test of sphericity values were significant (p<0.005) [64]

Reliability and validity testing

Reliability and convergent validity

All Cronbach's alpha values are above 0.60 [66], and composite reliability values vary from 0.7 to 0.9 [67], showing reliability of the measurement model. Average Variance Extracted values were above the threshold of 0.5 [67] as personality (P) has a reading of 0.396, as it captures a wide range of constructs, therefore having a low AVE [68]. Table 24.2 shows Cronbach's alpha, composite reliability, and average variance extracted.

Discriminant validity

Discriminant validity was measured using cross-loadings, Fornell-Lacker criteria, and the Heterotrait-Monotrait Ratio (HTMT). Indicator loadings were highest for their respective constructs except for Extraversion which was used to measure personality having a reading of -0.02 however the study was carried out without omitting the indicator as one personality trat would not be measured otherwise, the square roots of the AVE constructs were greater than the other correlations with other constructs, and HTMT values were below the threshold of 0.90. Recommendation serendipity and Personalization had HTMT values of 0.942, which exceeded the threshold.

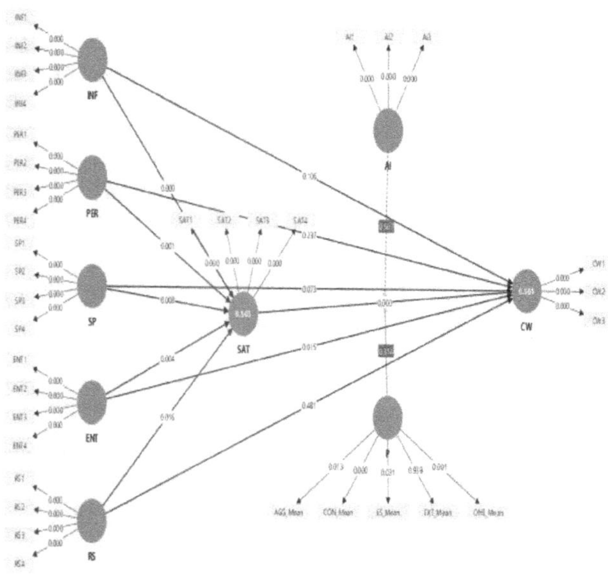

Figure 24.2 Structural model
Source: Author

Structural model

Model fit

The structural model was evaluated using the R^2, F^2, and Q^2 to test the model fit. The model showed a weak to moderate explanatory power: Continuous watching intention (R^2 = 0.492), Satisfaction (R^2 = 0.563). The F^2 values range in the minor effects range, while some range between the medium and small impact range in the study. The Continuous watching intention showcases a Q^2 value of 0.397, showcasing a medium predictive relevance, while satisfaction shows a Q^2 value of 0.534, showcasing a strong predictive relevance. The structural model is presented in Figure 24.2.

Mediation effect

Mediation analysis was applied to check whether the consumption values of the consumer mediate the relationship between satisfaction and continuous watching intention. Five mediation paths were tested based on the variance accounted for (VAF) approach. For informativeness on Continuous Watching Intention through Satisfaction, the indirect effect was 0.328,

Table 24.3 Hypothesis testing.

Hypothesis	Relationship	T-values	P Values	Result
H1	INF -> SAT	4.027	0.000	Accept
H2	PER -> SAT	3.362	0.001	Accept
H3	SP -> SAT	2.632	0.009	Accept
H4	ENT -> SAT	2.860	0.004	Accept
H5	RS -> SAT	2.414	0.016	Accept
H6	SAT -> CW	4.705	0.000	Accept
Mediating hypothesis	Relationship	T-value	P Value	Result
H7	INF -> SAT -> CW	8.372	0.000	Partial mediation
	PER -> SAT -> CW	8.049	0.000	Partial mediation
	SP-> SAT -> CW	8.603	0.000	Partial mediation
	ENT -> SAT -> CW	9.238	0.000	Partial mediation
	RS-> SAT -> CW	8.842	0.000	Partial mediation
Hypothesis	Moderating relationship	T-value	P Value	Result
H8	AI x SAT -> CW	0.664	0.507	Reject
H9	P x SAT -> CW	1.007	0.314	Reject

Source: Author

and the total effect was 0.537, resulting in a VAF of 61.1%. This implies partial mediation, which suggests informativeness has a meaningful influence on Continuous Watching Intention through Satisfaction. Similarly, for personalization, the indirect effect was 0.325, and the total effect was 0.56, yielding a VAF of 58%, also confirming partial mediation. The mediation analysis for social presence showed an indirect effect of 0.298 and a total effect of 0.477, leading to a VAF of 62.5%, signifying partial mediation. Entertainment's indirect effect was 0.303, and its total effect was 0.504, with a VAF of 60.1%, demonstrating partial mediation. Finally, for recommendation serendipity, the indirect effect was 0.350, and the total effect was 0.498, resulting in a VAF of 70.3%, which also indicates partial mediation.

The analysis revealed that the consumption values of informativeness (H1: T = 4.027, p = 0.000), personalization (H2: T = 3.362, p = 0.001), social presence (H3: T = 2.632, p = 0.009), entertainment (H4: T = 2.860, p = 0.004), and Recommendation Serendipity (H5: T = 2.414, p = 0.016) all exhibited a strong and significant positive effect on consumer satisfaction. Furthermore, the results confirmed that consumer satisfaction positively and significantly influences continuous watching intention (H6: T = 4.705, p = 0.000), indicating that higher satisfaction levels lead to a more substantial intentional commitment to continue engaging with short-form advertisements over time.

Moreover, the mediating hypothesis (H7) was confirmed across all tested paths, revealing a partial mediation effect where consumer satisfaction bridges consumption values and continuous watching intention (CWI). Partial mediation was observed for informativeness -> satisfaction -> CW (T = 8.372, p = 0.000), personalization -> satisfaction -> CW (T = 8.049, p = 0.000), social presence -> satisfaction -> CW (T = 8.603, p = 0.000), entertainment -> satisfaction -> CW (T = 9.238, p = 0.000), and recommendation serendipity -> satisfaction -> CW (T = 8.842, p = 0.000). This signifies that consumption values indirectly impact CWI through their positive effect on satisfaction, positioning satisfaction as a critical affective factor that strengthens the relationship between the perceived characteristics of short videos and engagement behavior of Gen-Z consumers.

However, compared to the initial hypotheses, no significant moderating effects were found for consumer personality (H9: T = 1.007, p = 0.314) and advertising irritation (H8: T = 0.664, p = 0.507). Neither consumer personality traits nor irritation moderate the relationship between satisfaction and Continuous Watching Intention. A simple slope analysis was conducted to confirm the above-mentioned moderating effect and examine the effect further and there was no evidence of any moderation. Table 24.3 summarizes hypothesis testing.

Conclusion

The study investigated the short video characteristics that would influence a Gen Z consumer to continue with a social media advertisement in Sri Lanka. The research model was developed using TCV, CAB, and the Big Five personality traits theory. The study used the consumption values of the customer, satisfaction, and the two moderators of advertising irritation and personality of the consumer affecting the continuous watching intention. Out of the nine initial hypotheses, two were rejected. Findings of the study offer theoretical and practical implications for marketers, policymakers, and content creators.

The study examined the impact of cognitive and affective factors on Gen Z viewers' continuous watching intentions as the first research objective. The results suggested that informativeness, personalization, entertainment, social presence, and recommendation serendipity significantly increase user satisfaction [6, 34], which positively affects continuous watching intentions [19, 22]. Satisfaction also partially mediated these relationships [48]. The findings indicate that when Gen Z users encounter content that is informative, tailored to their interests, socially engaging, entertaining, and includes unexpectedly relevant recommendations, they are more likely to feel satisfied with the platform experience. This satisfaction, in turn, strengthens their intention to continue watching similar content. The study reinforces that content meeting both informational and emotional needs forms a crucial basis for ongoing engagement. These results validate earlier studies while emphasizing that satisfaction plays a bridging role in turning short video characteristics into behavioral outcomes such as continuous watching.

Hypothesis testing

Additionally, the partial mediation observed in the study further supports the influence of satisfaction in connecting each short video feature to continued engagement [48]. This suggests that the cognitive and affective value of the content is not only important on its own but becomes significantly more impactful when it translates into user satisfaction. In this context, satisfaction can be seen as the emotional outcome of perceived value fulfillment, which guides future behavior in platform usage.

The second objective of research was to identify the role of adinrtising irritation on the relationship between the affective construct of satisfaction and watching intention. The results showcased that there is no effect of advertising irritation on the continuous watching intention, emphasizing that satisfaction overpowers negative stimuli like advertising irritation [69–71]. This suggests that highly satisfied users are more likely to tolerate or ignore minor interruptions, such as ads, because the overall platform experience is fulfilling. When consumption values are consistently met, advertising irritation does not significantly disrupt engagement. This aligns with prior theories that propose satisfaction acts as an emotional filter that diminishes the perceived intensity of negative experiences [69–71].

The final research objective was to identify the role of personality in the relationship between the affective construct of satisfaction and watching intention. The results suggested that there is no effect of personality on the continuous watching intention, implying that satisfaction may overpower personality influences in digital contexts, as once a person is satisfied, the usage becomes habitual over time [72, 73]. This highlights the dominant role satisfaction plays in driving behavior in Gen Z users. Even though personality traits typically influence media usage patterns, the findings suggest that once satisfaction is achieved, continued engagement becomes less dependent on personal characteristics. The habitual nature of satisfied users' behavior indicates that emotional and experiential gratification outweigh trait-based tendencies in shaping continuous watching intention [72, 73].

Overall, the findings contribute new knowledge by demonstrating that in the case of Gen Z, satisfaction significantly reduces the negative influence of advertising irritation and minimizes the effect of personality on watching intentions. This reinforces the importance of ensuring content quality and value delivery as the key to sustaining user engagement in social media advertising.

Managerial implications

The findings offer insights for marketers, advertisers, and digital platform managers aiming to increase user engagement. Since satisfaction is a main factor in achieving this, platforms should give prominence to emotionally satisfying the experience of the user, which can be done by creating emotionally engaging content while monitoring the satisfaction levels using feedback tools like surveys, ratings, and real-time user responses in order to measure the satisfaction level [74]. As satisfaction partially explains this fact, marketers should also focus on creating content that contains values such as informativeness, entertainment, and personalization within the content when catering to a Gen Z audience [75]. Using recommendation systems to surprise users with relevant and new content can increase engagement [76]. From a cognitive angle, marketers can reinforce value-based connections by delivering content aligned with trending topics, practical insights, or unique personal interests [77]. Increasing the social presence through community-based features like live chats or virtual interaction tools can also deepen engagement and create loyalty within the platforms. Notably, the findings further suggested that more focus should be put into situational and experience-based factors rather than personal characteristics to build a strong relationship with the Gen Z audience [78]. The study highlights how, when videos are designed with perceived value and optimized to satisfy, they can be a powerful tool in learning, aligning with SDG 4 quality education. Engaging content can effectively communicate educational content and life skills with the Gen Z audience [79]. Institutions and public awareness campaigns can use these platforms to increase learning accessibility [80]. Further short-form video platforms to contribute positively to mental well-being by promoting emotionally rewarding content, which in the long run would contribute to a healthier online environment [81].

Limitations and future research

Despite these contributions, the study faced several limitations. It is limited to Gen Z in Sri Lanka using cross-sectional data, which restricts generalizability, and gives a temporal understanding. Future research should examine different age groups and conduct longitudinal studies to assess behavioral changes. This would help adopt various strategies to help with digital trends and demographic profiles.

References

[1] Tian, X., Bi, X., & Chen, H. (2022). How short-form video features influence addiction behavior? empirical research from the opponent process theory perspective. *Information Technology and People*, 36(1), 387–408.

[2] Dixon, S. J. (2024). Gen Z and global users top social media 2023. Available from: https://www.statista.com/statistics/1446950/gen-z-internet-users-social-media-use/. Accessed on: Nov. 27, 2024.

[3] Khoros (2024). The 2024 social media demographics guide. [Online]. Available from: https://khoros.com/resources/social-media-demographics-guide. Accessed on Nov. 27, 2024.

[4] Kemp, S. (2024). Digital 2024: Sri Lanka. Available from: https://datareportal.com/reports/digital-2024-sri-lanka. Accessed on Nov 27, 2024.

[5] Asia Pacific Institute of Digital Marketing (APIDM) (2023). Digital outlook Sri Lanka 2023. Available from: https://fcms.kln.ac.lk/dep/dmm/media/attachments/2024/02/15/digital-oultlook-sri-lanka-2023.pdf. Accessed on Nov. 27, 2024.

[6] Zhang, Q., Wang, Y., & Ariffin, S. K. (2024). Keep scrolling: an investigation of short video users' continuous watching behavior. *Information and Management*, 61(6), 104014–104014.

[7] Zhao, Y., & Wagner, C. (2022). Short-form video advertising: the roles of video quality, ad appeals, and user engagement. *Journal of Advertising Research*, 62(1), 104–119.

[8] Zhang, X., Wu, Y., & Liu, S. (2019). Exploring short-form video application addiction: socio-technical and psychological perspectives. *Computers in Human Behavior*, 99, 1–11.

[9] Yin, S., Li, B., & Zhou, Q. (2023). The impact of skippable advertising on advertising avoidance intention in China. *Marketing Intelligence and Planning*, 41(8), 1121–1137.

[10] Statista (2024). Video advertising. Available from: https://www.statista.com/outlook/dmo/digital-advertising/video-advertising/custom?token=fIodkhUR8lSTJl9UknLKkIxbCGH4MIgAO6zrQhnMLD4q7tKDE1mt3MND_bZxGsfS_wStHe1MouVg0Nl0cvrrQZsFdA8DRthYg-NMkn4=. Accessed on Nov. 27, 2024.

[11] Niu, X., Wang, X., & Liu, Z. (2021). When I feel invaded, I will avoid it: the effect of advertising invasiveness on consumers' avoidance of social media advertising. *Journal of Retailing and Consumer Services*, 58, 102320.

[12] Sharma, A., Dwivedi, R., Mariani, M. M., & Islam, T. (2022). Investigating the effect of advertising irritation on digital advertising effectiveness: a moderated mediation model. *Technological Forecasting and Social Change*, 180, 121731.

[13] Moon, Y. J., Kim, W. G., & Armstrong, D. J. (2014). Exploring neuroticism and extraversion in flow and user generated content consumption. *Information and Management*, 51(3), 347–358.

[14] Liu, D., & Campbell, W. K. (2017). The big five personality traits, big two metatraits and social media: a meta-analysis. *Journal of Research in Personality*, 70, 229–240.

[15] DeYoung, C. G. (2015). Cybernetic big five theory. *Journal of Research in Personality*, 56, 33–58.

[16] Lavidge, R. J., & Steiner, G. A. (1961). A model for predictive measurements of advertising effectiveness. *Journal of Marketing*, 25(6), 59–62.

[17] Sheth, J. N., Newman, B. I., & Gross, B. L. (1991). Why we buy what we buy: a theory of consumption

values. *Journal of Business Research*, 22(2), 159–170.

[18] Goldberg, L. R. (1993). The structure of phenotypic personality traits. *American Psychologist*, 48(1), 26–34.

[19] Lv, X., Zhang, R., Su, Y., & Yang, Y. (2022). A multigroup analysis. *Journal of Travel and Tourism Marketing*, 39(1), 109–135.

[20] Lee, B.-C., Kim, P.-S., Hong, K.-S., & Lee, I. (2008). Evaluating antecedents and consequences of supply chain activities: an integrative perspective. *International Journal of Production Research*, 48(3), 657–682.

[21] Bhattacherjee, A. (2001). An empirical analysis of the antecedents of electronic commerce service continuance. *Decision Support Systems*, 32(2), 201–214.

[22] Bhattacherjee, A., Perols, J., & Sanford, C. (2008). Information technology continuance: a theoretic extension and empirical test. *Journal of Computer Information Systems*, 49(1), 17–26.

[23] Holbrook, M. B. (1986). Emotion in the consumption experience: toward a new model of the human consumer. *The Role of Affect in Consumer Behavior: Emerging Theories and Applications*, 6, 17–52.

[24] Zheng, Z., Zhang, X., Liang, P., Zhang, H., & Qu, X. (2022). The impact of short video application use on adolescents' academic performance: the mediating role of emotional state and the moderating role of self-control. *Computers and Education*, 182, 104470.

[25] Lee, T. H. (2013). Influence analysis of community resident support for sustainable tourism development. *Tourism Management*, 34, 37–46.

[26] Horng, J.-S., Liu, C.-H., Chou, S.-F., Tsai, C.-Y., & Hu, D. C. (2018). Does corporate image really enhance consumer's behavioural intentions?. *Asia Pacific Journal of Tourism Research*, 23(10), 1008–1020.

[27] Kumar, M., Townsend, J. D., & Vorhies, D. W. (2014). Enhancing consumers' affection for a brand using product design. *Journal of Product Innovation Management*, 32(5), 716–730.

[28] Ajzen, I. (1985). From intentions to actions: a theory of planned behavior. *Action Control*, 1(1), 11–39.

[29] Jiang, Y., Wang, X., & Yuen, K. F. (2021). Augmented reality shopping application usage: the influence of attitude, value, and characteristics of innovation. *Journal of Retailing and Consumer Services*, 63, 102720.

[30] Sweeney, J. C., & Soutar, G. N. (2001). Consumer perceived value: the development of a multiple item scale. *Journal of Retailing*, 77(2), 203–220.

[31] Majeed, A., Ahmed, I., & Rasheed, A. (2021). Investigating influencing factors on consumers' choice behavior and their environmental concerns while purchasing green products in Pakistan. *Journal of Environmental Planning and Management*, 65(6), 1–25.

[32] Lu, H.-P., & Cheng, Y.-H. (2020). Sustainability in online video hosting services: the effects of serendipity and flow experience on prolonged usage time. *Sustainability*, 12(3), 1271.

[33] McNee, S. M., Riedl, J., & Konstan, J. A. (2006, April). Being accurate is not enough: how accuracy metrics have hurt recommender systems. In CHI'06 extended abstracts on Human factors in computing systems (pp. 1097–1101).

[34] Ducoffe, R. H. (1995). How consumers assess the value of advertising. *Journal of Current Issues and Research in Advertising*, 17(1), 1–18.

[35] A. Hussain, A. Z. Abbasi, L. D. Hollebeek, C. D. Schultz, D. H. Ting, & B. Wilson, (2021). Videogames-as-a-service: converting freemium- to paying-users through pop-up advertisement value, Journal of Services Marketing, vol. 36, no. 3, pp. 398–415. doi: https://doi.org/10.1108/jsm-05-2020-0164.

[36] Choi, N. (2013). Information systems attachment: an empirical exploration of its antecedents and its impact on community participation intention. *Journal of the American Society for Information Science and Technology*, 64(11), 2354–2365.

[37] Schaupp, L., & Bélanger, F. (2005). A conjoint analysis of online consumer satisfaction. *Journal of Electronic Commerce Research*, 6(2), 95.

[38] Short, J. (1976). The social psychology of telecommunications. Jhon Wiley & Sons.

[39] Song, S., Zhao, Y. C., Yao, X., Ba, Z., & Zhu, Q. (2021). Short video apps as a health information source: an investigation of affordances, user experience and users' intention to continue the use of TikTok. *Internet Research*, 31(6), 2120–2142.

[40] Bulu, S. T. (2012). Place presence, social presence, co-presence, and satisfaction in virtual worlds. *Computers and Education*, 58(1), 154–161.

[41] Ye, G., Guan, X., Hudders, L., Xiao, Y., & Li, J. (2024). A meta-analysis of the antecedents and consequences of advertising value. *Journal of Advertising*, 1–22 .

[42] Dao, W. V.-T., Le, A. N. H., Cheng, J. M.-S., & Chen, D. C. (2014). Social media advertising value. *International Journal of Advertising*, 33(2), 271–294.

[43] Casaló, L., Flavián, C., & Ibáñez-Sánchez, S. (2017). An investigation of the online presence of UK universities on Instagram. *Online Information Review*, 41(7), 582–597.

[44] Martins, J., Costa, C., Oliveira, T., Gonçalves, R., & Branco, F. (2019). How smartphone advertising

influences consumers' purchase intention. *Journal of Business Research*, 94, 378–387.

[45] Gan, C., & Li, H. (2018). Understanding the effects of gratifications on the continuance intention to use WeChat in China: a perspective on uses and gratifications. *Computers in Human Behavior*, 78, 306–315.

[46] Casaló, L., Flavián, C., & Ibáñez-Sánchez, S. (2017). An investigation of the online presence of UK universities on Instagram. *Online Information Review*, 41(7), 582–597.

[47] Hausman, A. V., & Siekpe, J. S. (2009). The effect of web interface features on consumer online purchase intentions. *Journal of Business Research*, 62(1), 5–13.

[48] Khan, R. U., Salamzadeh, Y., Iqbal, Q., & Yang, S. (2020). The impact of customer relationship management and company reputation on customer loyalty: the mediating role of customer satisfaction. *Journal of Relationship Marketing*, 21(1), 1–26.

[49] Zhu, Z., Wang, S., Zhang, Y., Wang, Y., & Lv, S. (2022). Understanding the impact of emotional experience on user loyalty in social media. *Computers in Human Behavior*, 129, 107147.

[50] Al Amin, M., Muzareba, A. M., Chowdhury, I. U., & Khondkar, M. (2023). Understanding e-satisfaction, continuance intention, and e-loyalty toward mobile payment application during COVID-19: an investigation using the electronic technology continuance model. *Journal of Financial Services Marketing*, 29(2), 318–340.

[51] Wong, K. H., Chang, H. H., & Yeh, C. H. (2019). The effects of consumption values and relational benefits on smartphone brand switching behavior. *Information Technology and People*, 32(1), 217–243.

[52] Pokhrel, L., & KC, A. (2023). Mobile banking service quality and continuance intention: mediating role of satisfaction: a two-stage structural equation modeling-artificial neural network approach. *International Journal of Bank Marketing*, 42(3), 389–413.

[53] Bhattacherjee, A., & Lin, C.-P. (2015). A unified model of IT continuance: three complementary perspectives and crossover effects. *European Journal of Information Systems*, 24(4), 364–373.

[54] Arora, T., & Agarwal, B. (2019). Empirical study on perceived value and attitude of millennials towards social media advertising: a structural equation modelling approach. *Vision: The Journal of Business Perspective*, 23(1), 56–69.

[55] Kang, I., He, X., & Ma, I. (2020). Investigating the impact of coercive exposure on web-advertisement performance: focusing on the mediating role of advertisement fit. *International Journal of Market Research*, 64(1), 147078532096135.

[56] Herrando, C., & Martín-De Hoyos, M. J. (2022). Influencer endorsement posts and their effects on advertising attitudes and purchase intentions. *International Journal of Consumer Studies*, 46(6), 2288–2299.

[57] Amichai-Hamburger, Y., & Ben-Artzi, E. (2003). Loneliness and internet use. *Computers in Human Behavior*, 19, 71–80.

[58] Costa, P. T., & McCrae, R. R. (1992). The five-factor model of personality and its relevance to personality disorders. *Journal of Personality Disorders*, 6(4), 343–359.

[59] Carrier, L. M., Cheever, N. A., Rosen, L. D., Benitez, S., & Chang, J. (2009). Multitasking across generations: multitasking choices and difficulty ratings in three generations of Americans. *Computers in Human Behavior*, 25(2), 483–489.

[60] Saunders, M., Lewis, P., & Thornhill, A. (2023). Research Methods for Business Students, (9th edn.). Pearson Higher Ed.

[61] Gosling, S. D., Rentfrow, P. J., & Swann, W. B. (2003). A very brief measure of the big five personality domains. *Journal of Research in Personality*, 37(6), 504–528.

[62] Jakobsen, M., & Jensen, R. (2015). Common method bias in public management studies. *International Public Management Journal*, 18(1), 3–30.

[63] Kline, R. B. (1998). Principles and Practice of Structural Equation Modeling. New York: Guilford Press.

[64] Field, A. (2009). Discovering Statistics Using SPSS, (3rd edn.), London: SAGE Publications.

[65] Malhotra, N. K., & Birks, D. F. (2016). Marketing Research: An Applied Approach, (5th edn.). Harlow: Pearson Education.

[66] Tavakol, M., & Dennick, R. (2011). Making sense of Cronbach's alpha. *International Journal of Medical Education*, 2, 53–55.

[67] Hair, J. F., Hult, G. T. M., Ringle, C. M., & Sarstedt, M. (2017). A Primer on Partial Least Squares Structural Equation Modeling (PLS-SEM), (2nd edn.). Thousand Oaks, CA: SAGE Publications.

[68] Peterson, R. A., & Kim, Y. (2013). On the relationship between coefficient alpha and composite reliability. *Journal of Applied Psychology*, 98(1), 194–198.

[69] Oliver, R. L. (1999). Whence consumer loyalty?. *Journal of Marketing*, 63(Special Issue), 33–44.

[70] Rust, R. T., & Oliver, R. L. (1994). Service quality: Insights and managerial implications from the frontier. In Service Quality: New Directions in Theory and Practice, (pp. 1–19). Thousand Oaks, CA: Sage.

[71] De, S. S., & Gupta, S. (2012). Investigating customer resistance to change in transactional systems: an empirical study. *International Journal of Information Management*, 32(4), 362–371.

[72] Devaraj, S., Easley, R. F., & Crant, J. M. (2008). Research note—how does personality matter? relating the five-factor model to technology acceptance and use. *Information Systems Research*, 19(1), 93–105.

[73] Turel, O., & Serenko, A. (2012). The benefits and dangers of enjoyment with social networking websites. *European Journal of Information Systems*, 21(5), 512–528.

[74] Kim, J., & Song, H. (2018). The effects of emotional experience and social influence on user engagement in social media advertising: an empirical study. *Internet Research*, 28(1), 155–177.

[75] Kumar, A., Bezawada, R., & Trivedi, M. (2022). Personalized advertising effectiveness: a meta-analysis. *Journal of Marketing*, 86(1), 98–122.

[76] De Keyzer, F., Dens, N., & De Pelsmacker, P. (2019). The impact of relational characteristics on consumer responses to word-of-mouth on social networking sites. *International Journal of Advertising*, 38(5), 658–673.

[77] Zhou, Q., Yu, K., Guo, Y., & Xiao, Q. (2021). Personalized recommendation system for short video based on user interest and video features. *Journal of Big Data*, 8(1), 1–18.

[78] Shi, S., Chen, Y., & Chow, W. S. (2021). Personalized advertising and consumer engagement: Real-time behavioral cue analysis. *Electronic Commerce Research and Applications*, 47, 101041.

[79] Prensky, M. (2001). Digital natives, digital immigrants. *On the Horizon*, 9(5), 1–6.

[80] United Nations (2015). Transforming our world: the 2030 agenda for sustainable development. Available from: https://sdgs.un.org/2030agenda. Accessed on Apr. 28, 2025.

[81] OECD (2019). The future of education and skills: education 2030. Available from: https://www.oecd.org/education/2030-education-and-skills/. Accessed on Nov. 27, 2024.

25 The impact of store atmosphere on Gen Z consumers' purchase intention of fashion retail stores: an S-O-R study

Vihanga Prasansana[1,a], *Piumal Herath*[2,b], *Thisal Yatawara*[2,c] *and Vasanthakumar Kumaradeepan*[3,d]

[1]Department of Marketing and Tourism, Plymouth University, United Kingdom

[2]Department of Marketing and Tourism, NSBM Green University, Sri Lanka

[3]Department of Marketing Management, University of Jaffna, Sri Lanka

Abstract

This study investigates the influence of atmospheric cues cleanliness, lighting, music, scent, color, layout, and temperature on the purchase intentions of Generation Z (Gen Z) consumers in fashion retail stores in Colombo, Sri Lanka. Grounded in the Stimulus-Organism-Response (S-O-R) model, the study explores both direct and indirect pathways by considering customer attitude as a mediating variable. A quantitative, cross-sectional design was adopted using a structured questionnaire distributed among Gen Z fashion shoppers. Data were analysed through Structural Equation Modelling (SEM) using SmartPLS. The findings reveal that layout, lighting, and color directly affect purchase intention. At the same time, cleanliness, music, scent, and temperature have no substantial direct effect but exert significant indirect effects through customer attitude, indicating complete mediation. Partial mediation was observed for lighting, color, and layout, suggesting both affective and cognitive influences. Among the variables, Cleanliness was the strongest indirect predictor of purchase intention, fully mediated by attitude. These results validate the S-O-R model in the context of Sri Lankan fashion retail and underscore the critical role of psychological responses in shaping Gen Z purchasing behavior. The study contributes to the sensory marketing literature in emerging markets and provides actionable insights for retail managers aiming to enhance consumer engagement. By investing in hygiene, multisensory stimuli, and spatial aesthetics, retailers can drive stronger emotional connections and increase purchase intentions among young consumers.

Keywords: Fashion retail, purchase intention Gen Z, S-O-R model, store atmosphere

Introduction

In the evolving landscape of modern retail, consumer expectations are no longer price or product quality-led only but are ever more determined by the overall shopping experience. Among the various experiential determinants, store atmosphere comprising physical and sensory elements significantly affects consumer perception and purchase behavior [1]. Particularly in the case of fashion retail, where consumers seek emotional and aesthetic gratification alongside functional utility, the in-store environment has emerged as a strategic asset, defined by studies [2, 3] retail atmospherics as the intentional spatial design that produces desired affective responses in consumers that enhance purchase likelihood. As shopping goods, by nature, fashion products require greater store contact than utilitarian products. This has increased the prominence of atmospheric elements such as lighting, music, scent, cleanliness, temperature, layout, and color in consumer interaction and choice processes.

Despite growing international interest in store atmospherics, Sri Lanka's fashion retail sector remains under-explored, particularly regarding Gen Z consumers. The fashion and apparel sector plays a pivotal role in Sri Lanka's economy as a major employer and consumer-facing industry, with studies highlighting its strategic importance in manufacturing and retail development [4]. Although there is literature on the influence of retail environment on consumer behavior in general [5], not many have examined the mediating role of customer attitude in the link between store atmospheric elements and purchase intention. In addition, there is a gap

[a]vihanga.prasansana@gmail.com, [b]piumal.h@nsbm.ac.lk, [c]thisal.y@nsbm.ac.lk, [d]kumaradeepan@univ.jfn.ac.lk

DOI: 10.4324/9781003739920-25

in understanding how Sri Lankan fashion retailers apply psychological or data-driven methods in their store designs, with most relying on price points and offers rather than sensory stimulation.

This research aims to study the direct and indirect effects of store atmosphere on Gen Z consumers' purchase intention in the fashion retail sector in Colombo. It also seeks to unveil the most influential atmospheric factors and the mediating effect of customer attitude on these factors. The research objectives are:

- To identify the direct impacts of cleanliness, music, scent, temperature, lighting, color, and display/layout on purchase intention.
- To identify the mediating role of customer attitude in the relationship between cleanliness, music, scent, temperature, lighting, color, display/layout, and purchase intention.

Literature and Methodology

Literature review

The theoretical base of store atmosphere is derived from environmental psychology and retailing literature, emphasizing how built physical surroundings can elicit emotional reactions and affect consumer behavior. [2] "servicescape" and [6] stimulus-organism-response (S-O-R) model are seminal in explaining how environmental stimuli (S) influence internal states (O), which are then reflected in the behavioral response (R), including purchase intention. Such models are highly relevant in fashion retail, where the hedonic and experiential nature of the shopping experience prevails. The S-O-R model remains a robust theoretical framework for examining how shopping environments influence consumers' behavior. It provides for the effect that sensory inputs (S) exert on psychological states (O) such as attitudes, feelings, or satisfaction, which, in turn, drive behavior (R) such as buying, brand loyalty, or word-of-mouth. [7] employed meta-analysis to ascertain that S-O-R can be applied across different retailing scenarios, with the cognitive and affective responses serving as the crucial mediators. The model is flexible, with customer attitude being treated as a mediator factor, as applied in this study. [8] and other scholars validate that applying attitude and emotional states can serve as critical organismic responses.

Purchase intention

Purchase intention refers to the customer's likelihood to purchase an item based on evaluative and affect-based considerations. Purchase intention is a significant dependent variable of consumer behavior models and is driven by a combination of emotional experience, brand reputation, and cognitive judgments [9, 10]. In fashion retailing, especially among Gen Z consumers, purchase intention is generally linked to emotional engagement [11], store aesthetics, and sensory touchpoints.

Customer attitude as a mediator

Customer attitude is the psychological connection between environmental stimulation and purchasing intention. It consists of three dimensions—cognitive (beliefs), affective (feelings), and behavioral (behaviors) that act as mediators in how customers experience store atmospheres and convert these experiences into behavioral intentions [12]. Studies show that a good attitude generated through a comfortable retail atmosphere can significantly increase purchasing intention and brand loyalty.

In the retail fashion setting, Gen Z consumers' attitudes are shaped by the sensory and affective richness of the store atmosphere. Atmospheres that include lighting, music, and store layout set the feeling of excitement, trust, and brand identification. Attitude thus serves as a mediator that interprets internal reactions towards atmospheric stimuli and expresses them as concrete purchasing decisions.

Store atmosphere attributes

Cleanliness: Cleanliness, encompassing hygiene, order, and visual appeal, is considered a key atmospheric element influencing trust and perceptions of quality in retail environments. Clean environments reduce consumer anxiety, especially in a post-pandemic context [13, 14]. Studies indicate that customers equate cleanliness with professionalism and are likelier to develop favorable impressions and higher purchase intention [15, 16]. Furthermore, dirty or cluttered spaces often elicit negative effects and reduce shopping time and purchase likelihood [17, 18].

H1: There is a significant relationship between cleanliness and purchase intention.

H8: Customer attitude mediates the relationship between cleanliness and purchase intention.

Music: Ambient music affects customer arousal, mood, and time perception during shopping [19]. Slow-tempo music prolongs in-store duration and leads to higher sales, while fast-tempo music may increase decision speed [20]. Congruence between music and brand image can also enhance customer engagement and loyalty, particularly among Gen Z, who are sensitive to music aesthetics [21].

H2: There is a significant relationship between Music and Purchase Intention.

H9: Customer attitude mediates the relationship between music and purchase intention.

Scent: Scent plays a subconscious yet powerful role in consumer decision-making by triggering emotional and memory-related responses [22]. Pleasant ambient fragrances improve the perception of space and brand identity and often lead to longer dwell times and higher spending [21]. When scents align with store identity, customers form deeper emotional attachments and show stronger purchase intentions [23].

H3: There is a significant relationship between Scent and Purchase Intention.

H10: Customer attitude mediates the relationship between scent and purchase intention.

Temperature: Temperature significantly influences consumer comfort and behavior within retail environments. Research indicates that ambient temperature affects shoppers' emotional states, with comfortable temperatures enhancing mood and increasing the likelihood of purchase, while extreme temperatures can lead to discomfort and reduced shopping duration [24]. Specifically, warmer temperatures have been associated with increased consumer spending, as they promote a sense of comfort and relaxation conducive to shopping [25].

H4: There is a significant relationship between temperature and purchase intention.

H11: Customer Attitude mediates the relationship between Temperature and Purchase Intention.

Lighting: Lighting plays a crucial role in shaping the retail atmosphere and influencing consumer perceptions. Appropriate lighting enhances product visibility, creates a pleasant shopping environment, and can affect consumers' emotional responses, thereby impacting their purchase intentions [26]. For instance, warm lighting can create a cozy atmosphere, encouraging customers to spend more time in-store, while bright lighting can highlight products and stimulate impulse buying [27].

H5: There is a significant relationship between lighting and purchase intention.

H12: Customer attitude mediates the relationship between lighting and purchase intention.

Colour: Color within a retail space significantly impacts consumer emotions and behaviors. Warm colors, such as red and orange, can create a sense of urgency and excitement, potentially leading to impulse purchases, while cool colors, like blue and green, tend to evoke feelings of calmness and trust, encouraging longer shopping durations [28, 29]. Therefore, the strategic use of color can influence brand perception and consumer purchasing decisions.

H6: There is a significant relationship between color and purchase intention.

H13: Customer Attitude mediates the relationship between color and purchase intention.

Display/layout: The design and layout of a retail store significantly affect consumer navigation, product exposure, and overall shopping experience. An intuitive and aesthetically pleasing layout can facilitate ease of movement, enhance product visibility, and create a positive shopping environment, thereby increasing purchase intentions [3, 30]. In line with the organismic component of the S-O-R model, [31] highlights that green thinking, which is influenced by consumers' personal values and environmental awareness, has a significant impact on purchasing intention. This information provides valuable insights into how environmentally conscious Gen Z consumers may react favorably to eco-friendly store atmospheres in fashion retail. Effective visual merchandising and strategic product placement are key components in influencing consumer behavior within the retail space.

H7: There is a significant relationship between display/layout and purchase intention.

H14: Customer attitude mediates the relationship between display/layout and purchase intention.

Gen Z and consumer behavior

Generation Z, born between 1996 and 2010, is characterized by experiential highness, digital fluency, and values-driven consumption. They seek immersive, emotionally engaging shopping experiences and are highly sensitive to sensory stimuli [17] underlined that Gen Z blends online and offline spaces and expects authenticity, beauty, and ethical consistency in brand engagement.

Compared to previous generations, Gen Z values emotional experiences and environmental quality more in shopping settings. Their behaviors are not only driven by utility but also by the extent to which the retail environment is immersive, interactive, and enjoyable. The tastes of this generation add more importance to store atmosphere when making a choice to shop or not.

Methodology

The study follows a positivist philosophy that assumes reality is objective and can be measured through observable and measurable data. It adopts a deductive approach for testing theories by formulating hypotheses from existing theories, such as the S-O-R model. The research design is quantitative and descriptive. This is also consistent in ascertaining measurable relationships between store environment and purchase intention. Cross-sectional design will be employed to collect data at a single time. Our study occurs in Colombo's urban retail area, where fashion stores compete intensely for Gen Z consumers' attention. Since this generation tends to shop online and offline, their views on the in-store atmosphere are critical. The target market consists of Gen Z consumers born between 1996 and 2010 who actively shop at fashion retail stores in Colombo. This customer segment exhibits heightened sensitivity to store ambiance due to their experiential nature while shopping.

The study employs non-probability convenience sampling, chosen for its simplicity and effectiveness in reaching Gen Z consumers. Although this method may limit generalizability, steps were taken to ensure a diverse sample of respondents in terms of socio-economic status and consumption behavior. Primary data were gathered by distributing a structured questionnaire online and in physical stores. The measurement items for all variables were adapted from validated sources. Items for cleanliness, lighting, scent, music, temperature, color, layout, and purchase intention were taken from [5], while customer attitude was measured using items from [32]. These established scales ensured reliability and alignment with the S-O-R framework. The researchers utilized a five-point Likert scale to standardize responses.

Before the primary survey, the researcher's pilot-tested the questionnaire to refine the items and ensure clarity. To guarantee data integrity and participant comfort, the researchers rigorously adhered to ethical guidelines, including informed consent, anonymity, and voluntary participation. The researchers also compiled secondary data from academic journals, industry reports, and market analyses to contextualize our study. These sources included peer-reviewed articles and publications from retail associations, providing insights into Gen Z consumer behavior and trends. A total of 387 usable responses were collected, yielding substantial data for quantitative analysis. Data analysis was conducted utilizing SmartPLS software. Structural Equation Modelling (SEM) was employed to assess the direct and indirect effects of store atmosphere dimensions on the impact of purchase intention, as mediated by customer attitude. The use of SmartPLS is consistent with recent studies applying SEM in sensory marketing and retail behavior analysis [33, 34]. This approach supports complex mediation modelling and is well-suited for theory-testing with small to medium sample sizes. Reliability and validity assessments were performed to evaluate the measurement Model. The conceptual framework is illustrated in Figure 25.1.

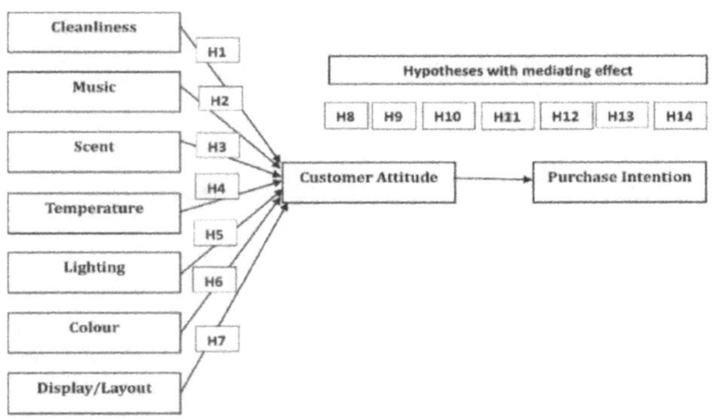

Figure 25.1 Conceptual framework
Source: Author

Table 25.1 Respondents' demographic profile.

Characteristics	Category
Gender	Male (72.4%)
	Female (27.6%)
District	Colombo (100%)
Age Group	18–20 (31.5%)
	21–23 (53.2%)
	24–26 (15.3%)

Source: Authors' survey data (2025)

Table 25.2 Reliability and validity summary.

Construct	Cronbach's Alpha	CR	AVE
Cleanliness	0.78	0.84	0.62
Lighting	0.86	0.89	0.67
Music	0.82	0.87	0.60
Scent	0.79	0.85	0.58
Temperature	0.80	0.86	0.59
Color	0.77	0.83	0.55
Layout	0.84	0.88	0.65
Customer Attitude	0.85	0.90	0.68
Purchase Intention	0.88	0.92	0.71

Source: Authors' survey data (2025)

Results and Discussion

Reliability and validity

Cronbach's Alpha, composite reliability, and average variance extracted (AVE) were computed to ascertain the measurement quality. All the constructs met the accepted threshold for internal consistency and convergent validity, with reliability estimates exceeding 0.70 and AVE estimates exceeding 0.50. As shown in Table 25.2, all constructs met the reliability threshold.

Structural equation modelling and mediation analysis

SEM results confirmed the model fit and predictive validity. R^2 for purchase intention (0.64) and customer attitude (0.59) were satisfactory. Path significance was evaluated through bootstrapping.

The findings supported that the total store atmospheric conditions- cleanliness, music, aroma, temperature, light, color, and design- positively affect customer attitude and purchase intention. Cleanliness, musicality, fragrance, and warmth were fully mediated by customer attitude, while light, color, and layout were partially mediated. The findings support the utility of the stimulus-organism-response (S-O-R) model in predicting Gen Z purchasing behavior.

Table 25.3 Direct relationships.

Hypotheses	Path	T Statistics	P Value
Cleanliness (C) → Purchase intention	0.083	1.838	0.066
Color (CO) → Purchase intention	0.13	2.357	0.018
Display/layout (DI) → Purchase intention	0.25	4.168	0.0
Lighting (L) → Purchase intention	0.196	3.255	0.001
Music (M) → Purchase Intention	0.102	1.846	0.065
Scent (S) → Purchase Intention	-0.001	0.014	0.989
Temperature (T) → Purchase Intention	0.016	0.307	0.759

Source: Authors' survey data (2025)

Table 25.4 Mediation relationships.

Hypotheses	Indirect Effect	Direct Effect	Total Effect	VAF (%)	Mediation
CA mediates Cleanliness → PI	0.296	0.083	0.379	78.1	Partial
CA mediates Music → PI	0.241	0.102	0.343	70.26	Partial
CA mediates Scent → PI	0.233	(0.001)	0.232	100	Full
CA mediates Temperature → PI	0.22	0.016	0.236	93.22	Full
CA mediates Lighting → PI	0.189	0.196	0.385	49.09	Partial
CA mediates Color → PI	0.174	0.13	0.304	57.24	Partial
CA mediates Layout → PI	0.181	0.25	0.431	42.0	Partial

Source: Authors' survey data (2025)

Table 25.5 Discussion of hypothesis testing.

Hypothesis	Statement	Result
H1	There is a significant relationship between cleanliness and purchase intention.	Not supported
H2	There is a significant relationship between music and purchase intention.	Not supported
H3	There is a significant relationship between scent and purchase intention.	Not supported
H4	There is a significant relationship between temperature and purchase intention.	Not supported
H5	There is a significant relationship between lighting and purchase intention.	Supported
H6	There is a significant relationship between colors and purchase intention.	Supported
H7	There is a significant relationship between display/layout and purchase intention.	Supported
H8	Customer attitude mediates the relationship between cleanliness and purchase intention.	Supported (Partial)
H9	Customer attitude mediates the relationship between music and purchase intention.	Supported (Partial)
H10	Customer attitude mediates the relationship between scent and purchase intention.	Supported (Full)
H11	Customer attitude mediates the relationship between temperature and purchase intention.	Supported (Full)
H12	Customer attitude mediates the relationship between lighting and purchase intention.	Supported (Partial)
H13	Customer attitude mediates the relationship between colors and purchase intention.	Supported (Partial)
H14	Customer attitude mediates the relationship between display/layout and purchase intention.	Supported (Partial)

Source: Authors' survey data (2025)

The relationship between cleanliness and customer attitude is fully mediated. This observation aligns with the findings of [35], who highlighted the significance of hygiene in fostering trust and comfort, particularly in the context of the post-COVID-19 era. Analogous results from the Sri Lankan marketplace, as detailed by [35], indicate that hygiene serves as a catalyst for store re-visitation. Furthermore, music demonstrated a complete mediation effect, as evidenced in the study conducted by [19], which illustrates that ambient music affects mood and dwell time. The emotional resonance of music correlates with Generation Z's preference for immersive environments. Additionally, scent proved to be fully mediated. Supporting evidence from [21] and [36] reinforces the idea that ambient scent can enhance memory and satisfaction. This presents new insights into the Sri Lankan retail market, where scent remains an often-neglected element of retail design. Temperature also emerged as an entirely mediated variable. In concurrence with [37], the study affirms that thermal comfort contributes positively to the shopping experience. Although seldom explored in Sri Lankan studies, this finding underscores the importance of understanding how comfort conditions affect customer engagement. Moreover, lighting exerted both direct and indirect influences. This observation is supported by research of [26], which underscored lighting as a critical aesthetic and functional element within retail spaces. Color exhibited partial mediation and moderately correlated with attitude and purchase intention. The role of color psychology, as established by [28], in eliciting emotional responses is affirmed here, particularly given

Generation Z consumers' inclination towards vibrant and harmonious color schemes in stores. Lastly, display and layout reflected robust relationships along with partial mediation, which is consistent with the findings of [3] that emphasized the importance of layout in navigation and merchandise placement visibility.

Conclusion

This study examined the impact of various store atmosphere elements on the purchase intentions of Generation Z consumers in fashion retail settings in Colombo, Sri Lanka. Using the stimulus-organism-response (S-O-R) framework, the findings show that while lighting, color, and store layout directly influence purchase intention, factors such as cleanliness, music, scent, and temperature influence purchase behavior only through customer attitude.

These results highlight the importance of psychological responses in the shopping experience. The presence of complete mediation for some variables suggests that simply improving physical or sensory elements in a store is not enough. What matters more is how these elements shape the customer's attitude. Retailers aiming to appeal to Gen Z should, therefore, focus on creating environments that are not just visually or sensorially appealing but also capable of generating positive emotional and mental responses.

The study contributes to the understanding of retail behavior in a developing country context and offers practical guidance for fashion retailers who wish to engage younger consumers more effectively. It also reinforces the value of customer attitude as a key link between atmosphere and behavior, encouraging more thoughtful and customer-centered store design.

Theoretical contributions

The study advances the S-O-R model by empirically testing its application in the retailing context of a developing economy. In contrast to existing research, which has focused on general consumer segments or markets in developed Western economies, this study situated the model in Gen Z customers in Sri Lanka. Second, by introducing customer attitude as a mediator, our understanding of the psychological processes underlying store atmosphere's effects on consumer behavior is enhanced.

Managerial implications

For fashion retailers, the results offer prescriptive information. Retailers must spend money on atmospheric enhancements such as ambient scenting, pleasant background music, good lighting, and zone layouts to positively affect customer attitudes and improve purchase intentions. As Gen Z is highly responsive to sensory and emotive stimuli, creating memorable, sensory-rich shopping experiences can contribute significantly towards building customer experience, driving foot traffic, and encouraging repeat visits.

Limitations and future research

This study is limited by its use of non-probability convenience sampling, which restricts generalizability across different Sri Lankan regions or global contexts. Additionally, the cross-sectional design limits the ability to infer causality. Future research could adopt a longitudinal design to assess how Gen Z's responses to atmospheric cues evolve over time. Comparative studies across districts or countries could also uncover cultural or regional differences. Finally, qualitative studies such as focus groups or observational ethnography may provide richer insights into the emotional and cognitive mechanisms mediating the shopping experience.

Acknowledgement

I am deeply grateful to my supervisor, Mr. Piumal Herath, for his unwavering support, guidance, and feedback throughout my research. His expertise significantly influenced the direction and quality of this study. We acknowledge the use of OpenAI's ChatGPT (version GPT-4) to support the language editing, paraphrasing, and structuring of parts of this manuscript. The final content was critically reviewed and edited by the authors to ensure academic integrity and originality.

References

[1] Pal, D., & Srivastava, K. (2024). Consumer patronage intention: role of multi-sensory and atmospheric experiences in retail. *International Journal of Retail and Distribution Management*, 52(2), 240–258.

[2] Bitner, M. J. (1992). Servicescapes: the impact of physical surroundings on customers and employees. *Journal of Marketing*, 56(2), 57–71. https://doi.org/10.1177/002224299205600205.

[3] Turley, L. W., & Milliman, R. E. (2000). Atmospheric effects on shopping behavior: a review of the experimental evidence. *Journal of Business Research*, 49(2), 193–211. doi: https://doi.org/10.1016/S0148-2963(99)00010-7.

[4] Herath, P., & Rajumesh, S. (2022). Green supply chain management and organizational performance: a study of Sri Lankan apparel manufacturing organizations. *Management Research and Practice*, 14(4), 19–36.

[5] Hussain R. & Ali M., (2015). Effect of Store Atmosphere on Consumer Purchase Intention, papers.ssrn.com, Apr. 01. https://papers.ssrn.com/sol3/papers.cfm?abstract_id=2588411.

[6] Mehrabian, A., & Russell, J. A. (1974). An approach to environmental psychology. the MIT Press.

[7] Vieira, V. A. (2013). Stimuli–organism-response framework: a meta-analytic review in the store environment. *Journal of Business Research*, 66(9), 1420–1426. [online]doi: https://doi.org/10.1016/j.jbusres.2012.05.009.

[8] Han, M. S., Hampson, D. P., Wang, Y., & Wang, H. (2022). Consumer confidence and green purchase intention: an application of the stimulus-organism-response model. *Journal of Retailing and Consumer Services*, 68, 103061. doi: https://doi.org/10.1016/j.jretconser.2022.103061.

[9] Ajzen, I. (1991). The theory of planned behavior. Organizational behavior and human decision processes, 50(2), 179–211.

[10] Ghosh, M. (2024). Meta-analytic review of online purchase intention: conceptualising the study variables. *Cogent Business and Management*, 11(1), 2296686. doi: https://doi.org/10.1080/23311975.2023.2296686.

[11] Rodrigo, A., & Herath, P. (2023). The impact of xenocentrism on the green purchasing intentions of zoomer consumers. *Accelerating Societal Change Through Digital Transformation*, 401–421.

[12] Fishbein, M., & Ajzen, I. (1977). Belief, attitude, intention, and behavior: An introduction to theory and research.

[13] Çolak, F. U., & Çengel, Ö. (2023). Store atmosphere strategies and their effects on purchase intention. *Journal of International Trade, Logistics and Law*, 9(1), 15–27. [online]Available from: https://www.jital.org/index.php/jital/article/view/324.

[14] Talukdar, S., Rahman, A., Bera, S., Ramana, G. V., & Prashar, A. (2024). Environmental risk and resilience in a changing world: a comprehensive exploration and interplay of challenges and strategies. In Environmental Risk and Resilience in the Changing World: Integrated Geospatial AI and Multidimensional Approach, (pp. 3–17). Cham: Springer Nature Switzerland.

[15] Yun, Z., & Good, L. K. (2007). Developing customer loyalty from e-tail store image attributes. *Managing Service Quality: An International Journal*, 17(1), 4–22. doi: https://doi.org/10.1108/09604520710720647.

[16] Holmqvist, J., & Lunardo, R. (2015). The impact of an exciting store environment on consumer pleasure and shopping intentions. *International Journal of Research in Marketing*, 32(1), 117–119.

[17] Grewal, D., Hulland, J., Kopalle, P. K., & Karahanna, E. (2020). The future of technology and marketing: a multidisciplinary perspective. *Journal of the Academy of Marketing Science*, 48(1), 1–8. [online]Available from: https://link.springer.com/article/10.1007/s11747-019-00711-4.

[18] Kim, J., Kim, M., & Lennon, S. J. (2009). Effects of web site atmospherics on consumer responses: music and product presentation. *Direct Marketing: An International Journal*, 3(1), 4–19. doi: https://doi.org/10.1108/17505930910945705.

[19] Morin, S., Dubé, L., & Chebat, J.-C. (2007). The role of pleasant music in servicescapes: A test of the dual model of environmental perception. *Journal of Retailing*, 83(1), 115–130. doi: https://doi.org/10.1016/j.jretai.2006.10.006.

[20] Garlin, F. V., & Owen, K. (2006). Setting the tone with the tune: a meta-analytic review of the effects of background music in retail settings. *Journal of Business Research*, 59(6), 755–764.

[21] Spangenberg, E. R., Grohmann, B., & Sprott, D. E. (2005). It's beginning to smell (and sound) a lot like Christmas: the interactive effects of ambient scent and music in a retail setting. *Journal of Business Research*, 58(11), 1583–1589. [online]doi: https://doi.org/10.1016/j.jbusres.2004.09.005.

[22] Krishna, A. (2012). An integrative review of sensory marketing: Engaging the senses to affect perception, judgment and behavior. *Journal of Consumer Psychology*, 22(3), 332–351.

[23] Bone, P. F., & Ellen, P. S. (1999). Scents in the marketplace: Explaining a fraction of olfaction. *Journal of retailing*, 75(2), 243–262.

[24] Pocheptsova, A., Amir, O., Dhar, R., & Baumeister, R. F. (2009). Deciding without resources: resource depletion and choice in context. *Journal of Marketing Research*, 46(3), 344–355. doi: https://doi.org/10.1509/jmkr.46.3.344.

[25] Murray, R., Caulier-Grice, J., & Mulgan, G. (2010). The Open Book of Social Innovation, (Vol. 24). London: Nesta.

[26] Quartier, K., Vanrie, J., & Van Cleempoel, K. (2014). As real as it gets: what role does lighting have on consumer's perception of atmosphere, emotions and behaviour? *Journal of Environmental*

Psychology, 39, 32–39. doi: https://doi.org/10.1016/j.jenvp.2014.04.005.

[27] Quartier, K., Vanrie, J., & Van Cleempoel, K. (2014). As real as it gets: what role does lighting have on consumer's perception of atmosphere, emotions and behaviour?. *Journal of Environmental Psychology*, 39, 32–39.

[28] Labrecque, L. I., Patrick, V. M., & Milne, G. R. (2013). The marketers' prismatic palette: a review of color research and future directions. *Psychology and Marketing*, 30(2), 187–202. [online] doi: https://doi.org/10.1002/mar.20597.

[29] Aslam, M. M. (2006). Are you selling the right colour? a cross-cultural review of colour as a marketing cue. *Journal of Marketing Communications*, 12(1), 15–30. [online]doi: https://doi.org/10.1080/13527260500247827.

[30] Vrechopoulos, A. P., O'keefe, R. M., Doukidis, G. I., & Siomkos, G. J. (2004). Virtual store layout: an experimental comparison in the context of grocery retail. *Journal of Retailing*, 80(1), 13–22.

[31] Rodrigo, A., & Yatawara, T. (2024). Impact of personal norms on green consumerism in Sri Lanka with the moderating effect of price sensitivity-a concept paper based on norm activation model. In International Conference on Business Management.

[32] Li, J., Gu, Z., & Dai, Y. (2022). Impact of sports sponsorship motivation on consumer purchase intention: mediating effect based on consumer attitude. *Sustainability*, 14(22), 15430.

[33] Pal, D., & Srivastava, K. (2024). Consumer patronage intention: role of multi-sensory and atmospheric experiences in retail. *International Journal of Retail and Distribution Management*, 52(2), 240–258.

[34] Çolak, F. U., & Çengel, Ö. (2023). Store atmosphere strategies and their effects on purchase intention. *Journal of International Trade, Logistics and Law*, 9(1), 15–27.

[35] Çolak, F. U., & Çengel, Ö. (2023). Store atmosphere strategies and their effects on purchase intention. *Journal of International Trade, Logistics and Law*, 9(1), 15–27.

[36] Gajanayake, R., Gajanayake, S., & Surangi, H. A. K. N. S. (2011, March). The impact of selected visual merchandising techniques on patronage intentions in supermarkets (study based on Colombo district). In 2nd International Conference on Business and Economic Research Proceeding (Vol. 1130).

[37] Morrin, M., & Ratneshwar, S. (2003). Does it make sense to use scents to enhance brand memory? *Journal of Marketing Research*, 40(1), 10–25. doi: https://doi.org/10.1509/jmkr.40.1.10.19128.

26 Adopting circular economy principles in the Sri Lankan Aluminum manufacturing industry: a comprehensive qualitative case study

M. L. Kalinga[1,a], K. Sachin[2,b], E.M.A.R. Ekanayaka[3], H.G.Y.L. Jinadasa[3] and G.H. Yohan Sangdeepa[3]

[1]Department of Economics, Faculty of Humanities and Social Sciences, University of Sri Jayewardenepura, Sri Lanka

[2]Department of Operations and Logistics, Faculty of Business, NSBM Green University, Sri Lanka

[3]Department of Management of Technology, Faculty of Business, University of Moratuwa, Sri Lanka

Abstract

The transition from linear economy to circular economy is an evolving approach to address the environmental concerns including environmental degradation and resource scarcity. This paper aims at investigating the adoption of circular economy practices in the Sri Lankan aluminum industry through in-depth, qualitative single case study. By in depth analysis of data collected from a pioneering aluminum manufacturing company through semi structured interview and observation, the research explores how circularity principles can be adopted to aluminum industry and transform conventional manufacturing operations into more resilient and sustainable systems. Data from the stakeholder interviews, onsite observation are analyses using thematic analysis. Study revealed multifaceted opportunities and challenges in adopting and implementing closed loop processes. Key findings highlight the key pillars in transforming the operations namely, Circular Design, Circular Recovery and Circular Business Models in implementing circularity principles in aluminum industry in Sri Lanka. The paper concludes with strategic recommendations for both industry practitioners and policymakers, while also identifying gaps for future research in the evolving field of circular manufacturing.

Keywords: Aluminum manufacturing, business model innovation, circular economy, recycling technology, sustainable design

Introduction

The existing industrial production models mainly focus on the linear path which highlight "take, make, and dispose" process [1]. However, rising environmental concerns resource depletion and economic fluctuations have resulted in both the focus of industries and government considering sustainable practices and restructuring this unsustainable linear approach. The circular economy principles evolved as an alternative way for this linear approach where the continuous use of resources and waste elimination emphasized by regeneration of products and materials [2, 3].

In addition to the core principles of reduce, reuse, and recycle, the circular economy incorporates green product development and cleaner manufacturing [4, 5]. Together, these approaches contribute to attaining reduced environmental impact through eco-design [6], energy-efficient processes [7], and sustainable resource management, which are necessary for achieving sustainability in manufacturing sector.

Manufacturing industries such as aluminum face significant criticism due to adverse environmental impact arising from production process and energy consumption. Circular practices can transform the prevailing linear production to more sustainable production and consumption that restructure the whole manufacturing process.

This study focuses on the aluminum manufacturing sector in Sri Lanka, a country that is still emerging in the global manufacturing arena. Aluminum, known for its lightweight and durable properties, is also celebrated for its capacity to be endlessly recycled without significant deterioration of quality [8]. However, several manufacturers continue to

[a]malshakalinga@sjp.ac.lk, [b]sachin.k@nsbm.ac.lk

DOI: 10.4324/9781003739920-26

depend on the traditional linear model, which leads to underutilization of the benefits of circularity and sustainability practices [9]. This research examines how one pioneering Sri Lankan aluminum manufacturer is shifting toward sustainable production by embedding principles of circular economy from the early stages of product development through to post-use strategies [1].

The main research question of this study is: *How can circular economy principles be effectively adopted to drive environmental sustainability and operational efficiency in the Sri Lankan aluminum industry?* By closely analyzing the data collected from a single case this study focuses on analyzing the challenges and success experienced by the organization in transforming speaker processes towards circular build practices and also aims to provide a practical framework for other organizations in similar contexts to transform their operations toward sustainable operation through implementation of circular economy practices [2, 3].

Literature Review

Recently the emphasis on the circular economy concept has received a significant attention from both academic and business society Mainly due to its potential to transform the manufacturing process and address the growing global economic and environmental concerns. The circular economy moves beyond waste elimination through recycling and focuses on a comprehensive way from the product designing business model and modifying the consumer behavior that aims at eliminating waste and optimizing the resource usage [1, 3].

Circular product design

Circular product design is widely recognized as the base of sustainable manufacturing. Traditional design practices have typically prioritized cost reduction and immediate functionality, often at the expense of recyclability and long-term utility [9]. In contrast, circular design integrates considerations of the end-of-life phase during the conceptualization stage. [2] highlight that modularity, standardization, and ease of maintenance and disassembly not only simplify the recycling process but also reduce the energy inputs required for material recovery. Aluminum is a metal that can be recycled indefinitely without any degradation of quality. Adoption of circular practices enhances both economic as well as sustainable performance [8, 9].

Reuse, remanufacturing, and recycling

Effective implementation of the post use strategies is profoundly influenced by early-stage design decisions. [1] note that the choice among reuse, remanufacturing, or recycling has extensive economic and environmental consequences. While product reuse extends the functional life of a product, it often emphasis redesigning the product to withstand multiple usage cycles. Remanufacturing converts the used elements which requires high investment for quality control and process reengineering. However, aluminum recycling is energy efficient, which consumes less than 5% of the energy needed to produce virgin aluminum from ore [8]. Integrating the circularity principles in product designing and development can enhance the efficiency of the resource utilization and contribute to achieve a closed loop production system [3] in aluminum industry.

Circular business models

Product as a Service (PaaS), leasing strategies, and lifecycle contracts are revolutionary business models that redefines the manufacturing industries from the traditional paradigm of selling products to a more integrated long-term service including maintenance, refurbishment and recycling contributing to circularity [10]. These business models encourage manufacturers to design products with greater durability and ease of repair while maintaining a closer relationship with customers which leads to sustainable practices [1, 3]. Furthermore, circular business models also encourage the adoption of an efficient take back policy, and consumer recycling process, that ensure used materials such as aluminum are reintegrated into the production system.

Challenges to implementation

Adoption of circular practices is affected by several barriers, despite potential benefits. Financial and economic challenges in terms of higher initial investment are a fundamental challenge faced by the organization in adoption of the circular practices. Advanced technologies for recycling, and technologies for tracking products across supply chain, required huge investment that discourage the manufacturers in adopting the circular strategies [2]. Technological limitations have also been noted, with existing facilities often struggling to meet the rigorous requirements for high-purity material recovery [9]. Regulatory frameworks in many regions, including emerging markets, are not yet sufficiently designed to support circular model implementations, which creates an uncertain environment for manufacturers [3]. Thus, it is essential to develop a multifaceted strategy that includes technological innovation, policy reforms and promotion of collaborative network among all stakeholders to implement circularity practices.

Studies show that while environmental and economic advantages of adopting circular practices are significant in industries like aluminum, the successful transition from a linear model to a circular model depend on how well the organization can overcome design, technological and regulatory obstacles. Thus, this study focuses on exploring how these elements are practically applied within a Sri Lankan aluminum manufacturing context.

Studies on circular economy highlights the transformative capabilities of circularity principles especially in the resource intensive industries like aluminum. Scholars also emphasize the potential benefits of incorporating the advanced technologies such as AI driven sorting and digital tracking [11], as key enablers of circular designing in industries such as aluminum which integrates modularity [11], disassembly, and increased recycling. These advances not only enhance material recovery, but they also cut energy and operational expenses. Researchers delve deeper into the economic components of CE adoption, offering policy frameworks that include fiscal incentives, tax relief, and investment subsidies to help the transition, particularly in emerging nations [12, 13].

Prior findings show the role of financial mechanism in achieving sustainability and the need to align the financial strategies with the goals to overcome the initial investment barriers [12, 13]. Further, studies on eco innovation suggest that Organizational awareness motivation and organization capability [14, 15] are Critical Success Factors in effective implementation of circular economy practices. These findings are aligning with the findings that reflect the need for cultural and strategic development, where staff participation and cross functional collaboration [15] crucial for integrating the circular economic practices into manufacturing processes. This modern finding highlights the need for a comprehensive strategy that incorporates designing, technology, legislation and organizational culture to attain sustainable manufacturing outcomes.

Methodology

This study employs a qualitative single-case study design to examine the adoption of circular economy principles within a Sri Lankan aluminum manufacturer. As [16] notes, case studies are particularly effective for exploring contemporary phenomena in real-life contexts, while [17] asserts that single-case approaches provide richly detailed insight into complex organizational processes.

Data collection was undertaken through two core methods. First, semi-structured interviews were conducted with key stakeholders including design engineers, production managers, sustainability officers, and supply chain coordinators and personal experiences in their own words [18]. Second, on-site observations were carried out to gather firsthand insights into manufacturing processes and recycling operations.

The interview guide was specifically designed to delve into circular economy approaches such product lifecycle design [19, 20], recycling initiatives, and business model innovations [20]. Observations also focused on identifying cleaner production practices and material recovery systems that adhered to circular concepts.

For data analysis, an inductive thematic approach was used as described by [21]. The data analysis followed the six phase approach as defined by [21]. Interview transcripts and observation notes were systematically coded and analyzed, allowing themes to emerge organically from the data. Triangulating these two data sources strengthened the credibility and reliability of the findings, in line with best practices in qualitative research [18].

Case Study Context

Industry background

The aluminum industry creates a significant value addition to consumers due to the applications of the aluminum in diverse areas including transportation, construction, and consumer goods. Sri Lankan aluminum industry comprises both the mix of traditional artisanal practices and modern industrial approaches. However, the local manufacturing sector has fallen behind the global trends in sustainability. The conventional linear model of production which emphasizes extraction, fabrication, and disposal remains dominant in the industry. This situation presents both a challenge and an opportunity for local manufacturers showcasing a chance to detour traditional practices by adopting circular economic principles.

The company profile

The company at the center of this study is one of Sri Lanka's leading aluminum manufacturers. Over the past few years, it has progressively integrated circular economy strategies into its operations. These initiatives are mainly driven by environmental concern economic restriction due to scarcity of resources and increasing competitive pressures from the competitors. The company has adopted circular design strategies such as modularity standardization of alloy composition and incorporation of recycled material in manufacturing. It also reengineered its production processes to incorporate advanced recycling process from used aluminum and introduced innovative business models such as leasing systems and take-back programs.

Data Analysis and Findings

The thematic analysis [21], of the data from observation notes and interviews revealed themes that reflect both drivers and barriers in transition from linear production to circular production. The main themes evolved through the analysis are circular product design, recycling and material recovery, business model transformation and inherent challenges and barriers throughout the transformation process.

Circular design integration

Respondents highlighted that the role of product design in improving the circularity of the operations. Responses from the interviews consistently highlighted the fact that the product designing has moved away from the traditional cost centric approach and moves towards to placing more emphasis elements such as product durability, modularity and ease of the assembly or disassembly. Design engineers emphasized that the standardization of the alloy composition led to streamlining the production process and the subsequent material recovery. Several respondents highlighted the concurrent engineering with iterative feedback between the product developers and recycling specialist plays a crucial role in design process to ensure the product meets both performance criteria and recyclability. These insights are consistent with the arguments of [2, 9], who emphasize that early-stage design decisions can significantly enhance closed-loop manufacturing.

"We mainly focus on designing part, because we do focus on the end of life of the product. By making the designs with standardized composition and components, disassembly and recycling is much easier"

"The internation between the design team and recycling team is very important. It helps to improve the design of the product suitable for recovery and recycling."

These findings suggests that the company's alignment of the design systems with the circular economy principles, has been a pivotal element in reducing challenges related to material contamination and facilitate recycling process.

Advancements in recycling and material recovery

Observations revealed that the company has initiated investment on sorting machines to divide the recovered aluminum more efficiently to improve the recyclability of the scarp. Currently the organization uses infrared sensors where such technologies ensure quality of the materials used for recovery and improve the quality of the recycled materials. As highlighted by [8] this improves the suitability id the reuse in high end applications.

"We have infrared sensors to sort the recovered aluminum. There are other x ray sensors. But such technologies are not available in the country. But such technologies can improve the sorting process"

Responses from the operations managers, revealed that these tracking systems and real-time monitoring of material flow improve the recyclability of recovered materials. This helps to improve the rapid improvements in real time while minimizing the losses. Further, it is also highlighted that, use of closed loop recycling system and recovered aluminum, consumes less energy consumption and leads to cost savings and low dependency on virgin aluminum. This empirical data supports the fact that advancement in recycling technologies is crucial for adopting and implementing circular economic strategies.

Transformation of business models

Business Model transformation is the third key element adopting and implementing the circular economy practices. The data from the study indicates that there is a notable shift form the traditional sales-oriented offering towards the service-oriented offerings. Respondents highlighted that the introduction of concepts such as leasing arrangements, lifecycle contracts, and Product as a Service (PaaS) models has modified the revenue streams.

"We also focusing on service contracts such as maintenance and offer leasing arrangement to large fixtures. That helps us to ensure that we have a track of the material, and we can get it back when disposing and provide us with a continuous revenue stream"

These new business models that make sure the organizations generate revenues, while promoting circular practices through product return such as take back policies. Respondents also noted that the change in the business models not only reduces waste and ensure the products are returned to the organization at the end of their life but also ensures a steady revenue throughout the product lifecycle. This transformation improves customer engagement and helps the company which also ensures adjusting the organization culture towards sustainable practices. These findings from the organization align with the existing literature [3, 10] and clearly emphasize the importance in redefining the business model to adopt the circular principles.

Organizational and cultural shifts

A deeper analysis of the data also derived another significant theme – Organizational and Cultural Shifts as a crucial component in the adoption of the circularity principle. Employee training and development was emphasized as a critical element in the transition from the linear production principles to circular principles. Respondents emphasized training and development to the workers plays an important role in familiarizing the employees to the transition and ensure that the circular practices are implemented successfully.

"It is important to train and motivate the employees also. If not, they will not feel like the transition is important. Always when there is a change, we need to train them and change their mindset."

Respondents also emphasized that these cultural shifts to see the sustainability as a core of the organization strategy helps the company to overcome to the initial resistance from the internal employees and supply chain partners.

"We have to work much to strengthen the cultural change and employees to understand the value of the circular practices"

The organization's commitment to enhance education and training on secular practices improves technical competencies and also encourages employee's morale towards security practices this improved long-term initiatives towards sustainability

Challenges and barriers

The data analysis also revealed several challenges and barriers that were recurring with respect to the aluminum industry. Economic barriers arising from initial capital investment and the need for investing in advanced recycling technologies such as digital tracking systems were frequently mentioned

Both management and operational staff acknowledged that such investments present considerable upfront risks, especially in emerging markets where financial resources are constrained.

"The initial investment cost for expanding and updating the capacity and operations to meet the recycling requirement is significant. Further, there is a huge risk on the return for the investment"

Another key challenge faced during the adoption process is challenges related to technology integration. Respondents highlighted that there were difficulties faced in integration the older production systems with digitalized systems.

"Technology adoption in the existing methods of process was difficult due to complexity and the kill requirement"

In addition, respondents also highlighted challenges due to regulatory constraints, local policies related to environmental concerns and these challenges affects the scope if rapid implementation. However, supply chain challenges such as resistance from suppliers and distributors affect the material recovery. These challenges highlight the requirement of a systematics framework for transitioning towards the circular economy.

Discussion

Findings from the analysis show that the adoption of the circular economy practices in aluminum industry is multifaceted, which needs to be integrated through driving changes in product design, recycling technology, business model and organizational culture. These insights are mapped together as a practical roadmap (Figure 26.1) for achieving this adoption and implementation of sustainable practices in aluminum industry.

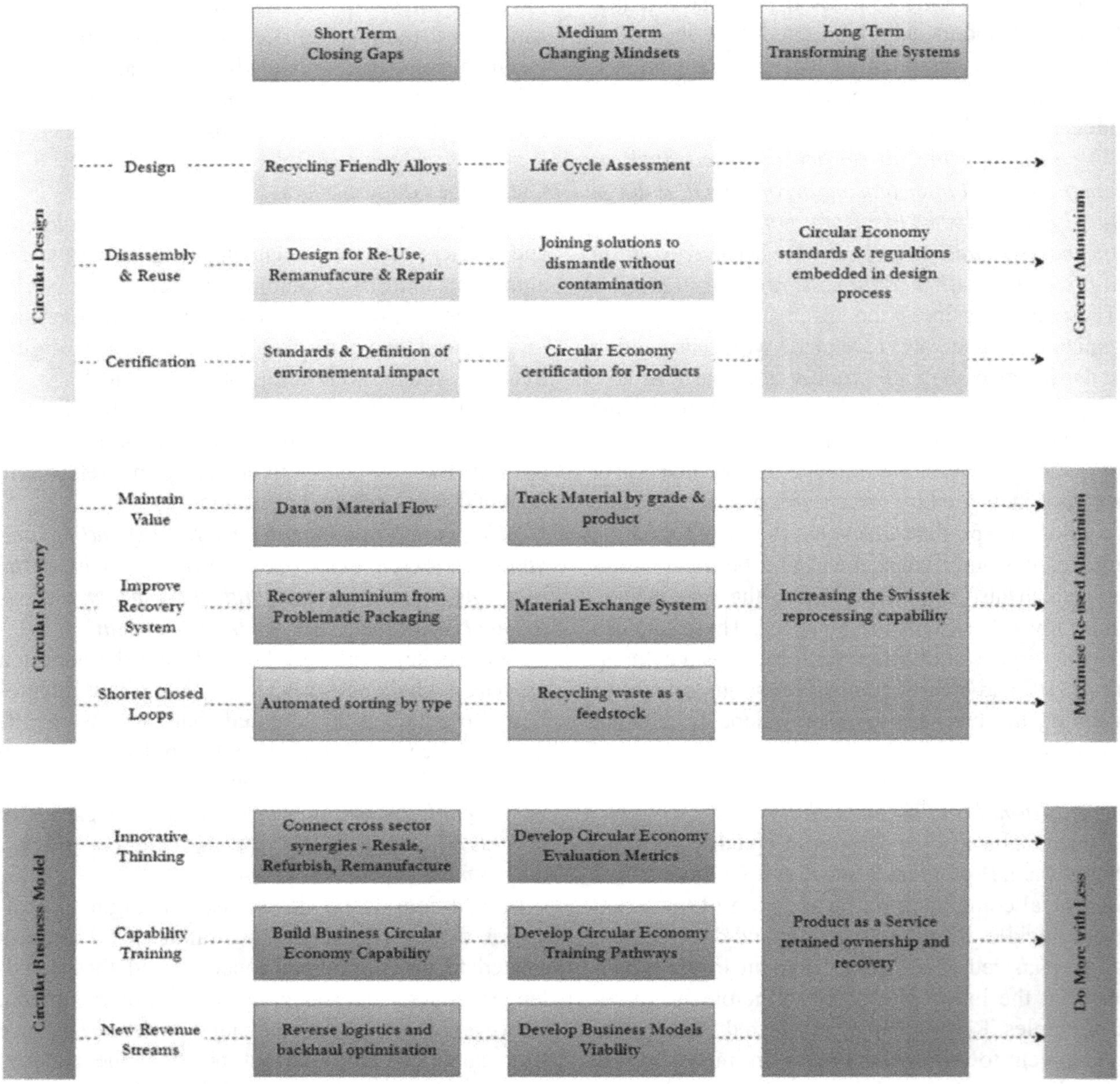

Figure 26.1 Roadmap for circular economy
Source: Author

Circular design
The findings from the study show that the company has moved away from the traditional cost centric production methods and they must incorporate production designs with more of longevity, modularity, and recyclability. Circular design should encompass a design that enhances recyclable elements and easy to disassembly and reuse which can be improved along with certification which shows the product design ensures minimum or no environmental impact and aligns circular economic practices. This should be improved with repetitive feedback between design engineers and recycling specialists that ensure continuous refinement in the product design to support the closed loop manufacturing. This approach also highlighted by [2, 9] ensures A circular economy standards and regulation being embedded into the production design in long term which result in a concept of greener aluminum.

Circular recovery
Recovery and recycling of used aluminum at the end of its life is a crucial element in adopting the circular principles into aluminum industry. It involves

developing and implementing a recovery system. This recovery system requires technological integration, and this digital tracking system helps monitor material flow in real time and helps to ensure high level of purity. Technology integration in recovery can also improve the sorting accuracy of recovered aluminum by minimizing the waste at reduced energy consumption. This can lead maximize the re used aluminum usage. This is supported by the empirical findings which highlight that the technological upgrades not only support the environmental goals but also contribute to long term cost and resource efficiency [8].

Business model innovation

A key transformation derived from the study is the shift from the traditional product sales towards innovative, service-oriented business models. This involves connecting cross sector synergies to improve resale, refurbish and remanufacture. Improving the circular economy capability and implementation of new revenue stream though strengthening the reverse logistics capability. These models can include system to incentivize the customers to return the used products after use, which enables refurbishment and recycling. This business model result in recurring revenue stream. As highlighted by [3, 10] aligning the economic incentives to the circular practices enhance a string customer relationship and ensures that end of life products are re integrated into the loop of production.

Organizational and cultural transformation

Cultural Transformation also plays an equally important role in the adoption process as the technical and business transformation. The study emphasis that employee training, regular emphasis on sustainability and integration of performance monitoring system can effectively support the culture and support the circular economy. Cultural transformation contributes towards minimizing internal resistance towards adopting sustainable practices and ensure such practices become part of the organization's routine operations. First the management at the start of the organization should adopt a holistic view on sustainability which is fundamental for the successful implementation of circular practices in the organization.

This holistic model highlights the achievements achieving circular economic transformation because of a combined effort of designing, technology, business strategy and organizational culture. Each pillar of the creating a comprehensive road map for sustainable manufacturing industry.

Conclusion

This redesign of Sri Lankan aluminum manufacturing industry from a linear to circular economy-based production is evidence for that product designing, adoption of advanced recycling technologies, business model innovation and transformative organizational culture can contribute towards a significant environment impact while achieving economic benefits. By adapting strategies such as modularity, digital tracking recyclable products in real time, and service-based revenue stream the company can create a circular production system contributing to sustainability. In this holistic approach, an integrated strategy underlines that good sustainability projects involve a supra-logical coordination of technical, operational, and cultural strategies.

Implications for practice and policy

The study contributes to the existing literature by highlighting the role of circular economy practices in enhancing the competitiveness with reference from aluminum industry. The model built in this study offers practical guidance for industry practitioners who want to transition from linear to circular economy. By incorporating circularity into product design and alignment with state-of-the-art recycling as well as new business models, firms are not only able to reduce waste and energy consumption but also be able to create sustainable business revenues.

This study emphasizes the need for a supportive regulatory framework and a fiscal incentive in terms of tax reliefs and investment subsidies for investment in green technology which can motivate adoption of circular approaches by reorganization. Further, creation of joint ventures among industry participants, research institutions and government organizations are crucial for accelerating the adoption of sustainable manufacturing techniques.

Limitations of the study

While the study provides insightful research with relation to Sri Lankan aluminum industry it also has some limitations. Firstly, the study adopts a single case study approach. This affects the generalizability of the findings to different industries, or geographical locations with diverse economic, regulatory and technical context.

The employment of qualitative data, (observation and interview) also suggests that the analysis will take the shape of interpretative form; the absence of quantitative measures precludes empirical testing of the economic and environmental returns perceived. Furthermore, contextual circumstances common in promising economies, such as policy constraints at the local level and resource availability, might affect the applicability of the integrated model in more mature industrial settings. These limitations highlight the necessity of cautious interpretation in projecting these findings beyond the current research.

Future research directions

Based on the research findings and limitations of the research presented here, some of the future research directions are emphasized. Multi-case comparative studies across different sectors and geographic regions would prove to be helpful for testing and fine-tuning the integrated implementation model proposed in the research presented here. Longitudinal research designs are also proposed to track the long-term impact of circular economy practices on environmental performance, economic stability, and organizational resilience. Furthermore, Studies can adapt a quantitative approach by incorporating quantitative instruments to measure cost benefit analysis lifecycle analysis or energy utilization analysis which would complement the qualitative findings of the research and provide better analysis of benefits and challenges around circularity principles. Studies can you also conduct that by considering the regulatory principles including analysis of enough government involvement and their impact on Bing can provide more insights on the impact of environmental factors such as policy framework and regulation in accelerating or decelerating the shift towards sustainable practices.

References

[1] Jones, P., & Comfort, D. (2021). The circular economy: an exploratory case study from the paper and retail industries. *Athens Journal of Business and Economics*, 7(4), 379–394. doi: 10.30958/ajbe.7-4-5.

[2] Lieder, M., Asif, F. M. A., Rashid, A., Mihelič, A., & Kotnik, S. (2017). Towards circular economy implementation in manufacturing systems using a multi-method simulation approach to link design and business strategy. *The International Journal of Advanced Manufacturing Technology*, 93(5–8), 1953–1970. doi: 10.1007/s00170-017-0610-9.

[3] Dumée, L. F. (2022). Circular materials and circular design—review on challenges towards sustainable manufacturing and recycling. *Circular Economy and Sustainability*, 2(1), 9–23. doi: 10.1007/s43615-021-00085-2.

[4] Maxwell, D., & Van der Vorst, R. (2003). Developing sustainable products and services. *Journal of Cleaner Production*, 11(8), 883–895. doi: 10.1016/S0959-6526(02)00164-6.

[5] Dangelico, R. M. (2016). Green product innovation: where we are and where we are going. *Business Strategy and the Environment*, 25(8), 560–576. doi: 10.1002/BSE.1886;JOURNAL:-JOURNAL:10990836.

[6] Fleith de Medeiros, J., Bisognin Garlet, T., Duarte Ribeiro, J. L., & Nogueira Cortimiglia, M. (2022). Success factors for environmentally sustainable product innovation: an updated review. *Journal of Cleaner Production*, 345, 131039. doi: 10.1016/J.JCLEPRO.2022.131039.

[7] Ikram, M., Ferasso, M., Sroufe, R., & Zhang, Q. (2021). Assessing green technology indicators for cleaner production and sustainable investments in a developing country context. *Journal of Cleaner Production*, 322, 129090. doi: 10.1016/J.JCLEPRO.2021.129090.

[8] Olivieri, G., Romani, A., & Neri, P. (2006). Environmental and economic analysis of aluminium recycling through life cycle assessment. *International Journal of Sustainable Development and World Ecology*, 13(4), 269–276. doi: 10.1080/13504500609469678.

[9] Moreno, M., De los Rios, C., Rowe, Z., & Charnley, F. (2016). A conceptual framework for circular design. *Sustainability*, 8(9), 937. doi: 10.3390/su8090937.

[10] Hagelüken, C., & Goldmann, D. (2022). Recycling and circular economy—towards a closed loop for metals in emerging clean technologies. *Mineral Economics*, 35(3–4), 539–562. doi: 10.1007/s13563-022-00319-1.

[11] Ciliberto, C., Szopik-Depczyńska, K., Tarczyńska-Łuniewska, M., Ruggieri, A., & Ioppolo, G. (2021). Enabling the circular economy transition: a sustainable lean manufacturing recipe for industry 4.0', *Business Strategy and the Environment*, 30(7), 3255–3272. doi: 10.1002/BSE.2801.

[12] Dennison, M. S., Kumar, M. B., & Jebabalan, S. K. (2024). Realization of circular economy principles in manufacturing: obstacles, advancements, and routes to achieve a sustainable industry transformation.

Discover Sustainability, 5(1), 1–32. doi: 10.1007/S43621-024-00689-2.

[13] Holly, F., Kolar, G., Berger, M., Fink, S., Ogonowski, P., & Schlund, S. (2023). Challenges on the way to a circular economy from the perspective of the Austrian manufacturing industry. *Frontiers in Sustainability*, 4, 1243374. doi: 10.3389/FRSUS.2023.1243374/BIBTEX.

[14] Kazakova, E., & Lee, J. (2022). Sustainable manufacturing for a circular economy. *Sustainability*, 14(24), 17010. doi: 10.3390/SU142417010.

[15] Urbinati, A., Rosa, P., Sassanelli, C., Chiaroni, D., & Terzi, S. (2020). Circular business models in the European manufacturing industry: a multiple case study analysis. *Journal of Cleaner Production*, 274, 122964. doi: 10.1016/J.JCLEPRO.2020.122964.

[16] Yin, R. K. (2018). Case Study Research and Applications : Design and Methods, (6th edn.), Thousand Oaks, California: SAGE Publications.

[17] Babbie, E. (2007). The Practice of Social Research, (12th edn.). Belmont, CA: Wadsworth.

[18] Creswell, J. W. (2013). Qualitative Inquiry and Research Design : Choosing Among Five Approaches, (13th edn.). Thousand Oaks, California: SAGE Publications.

[19] Franco, M. A. (2019). A system dynamics approach to product design and business model strategies for the circular economy. *Journal of Cleaner Production*, 241, 118327. doi: 10.1016/J.JCLEPRO.2019.118327.

[20] Nascimento, D. L. M., Alencastro, V., Quelhas, O. L. G., Caiado, R. G. G., Garza-Reyes, J. A., Rocha-Lona, L., et al. (2019). Exploring industry 4.0 technologies to enable circular economy practices in a manufacturing contextA business model proposal. *Journal of Manufacturing Technology Management*, 30(3), 607–627. doi: 10.1108/JMTM-03-2018-0071.

[21] Braun, V., & Clarke, V. (2006). Using thematic analysis in psychology. *Qualitative Research in Psychology*, 3(2), 77–101. doi: 10.1191/1478088706qp063oa.

27 Impact of occupational health and safety management practices on operational-level employee commitment in the Sri Lankan apparel manufacturing industry: Galle District-Koggala free trade zone

S.S. De Silva [1,a], *G.R.S. Kulasekara* [2,b] *and S.C.R.S. Akash* [2,c]

[1]Industrial Engineering Department, MAS Intimates Unichela, Sri Lanka

[2]Department of Operations and Logistics, Faculty of Business, NSBM Green University, Sri Lanka

Abstract

This study analyzes the impact of occupational health and safety management practices on operational-level employee commitment in the Sri Lankan apparel manufacturing industry, specifically in the Koggala Free Trade Zone, Galle District. The selected practices include health and safety training, health and safety policies and procedures, health and safety audits, and employee wellness programs. Although global studies have examined these relationships in industries like steel manufacturing and construction, limited research exists in the Sri Lankan context. Thus, this study offers valuable insights for the local economy. The research adopts a deductive approach based on the Three Component Model of Commitment and employs a quantitative method. The study population consists of approximately 5,000 operational-level employees, and a sample size of 357 was selected based on the Morgan table and convenience sampling method used to distribute questionnaires among the operational level employees. Data were collected using a 5-point Likert scale structured questionnaire and analyzed through SPSS. Correlation analysis revealed a very strong positive relationship between the selected health and safety practices and employee commitment. Regression analysis showed a significance value of $P < 0.05$, indicating the overall model is statistically significant. The independent variables account for 73% of the variation in employee commitment (R-Square = 0.730). All hypotheses in the conceptual framework were accepted. The study's findings can be applied to enhance the performance of manufacturing companies and contribute to achieving Sustainable Development Goal 8: "Decent Work and Economic Growth."

Keywords: Employee commitment, employee wellness programs, health and safety audits, health and safety policies and procedures, health and safety training, Koggala Free Trade Zone

Introduction

With the development of countries, people are moving towards more sustainable practices. Out of 17 Sustainable development goals, goal 8 aims to promote sustained inclusive and sustainable economic growth, full and productive employment, and decent work for all. The economy of a particular country will grow if workers have more jobs, high productivity, and high performance. The most essential component for moving towards goal 8 is to promote a safe working environment because creating an efficient and productive environment to work is the most essential business success factor. It is a must that companies need to function with proper health and safety management practices to protect their employee's health while they are working [1]. Proper health and safety management practices support the increase in the productivity of the organization [2]. But worldwide up to 40–50% of employees are facing occupational hazards situations while they are working due to not following proper health and safety management practices [3]. Due to those reasons, occupational health and safety management practices are selected as the independent variable of this research. As the occupational health and safety management practices this research analyses, health and safety training, health and safety policies and procedures, conducting proper health and safety audits, and employee wellness programs as

[a]silvassde@students.nsbm.ac.lk, [b]rekha.k@nsbm.ac.lk, [c]scrsakash@students.nsbm.ac.lk

DOI: 10.4324/9781003739920-27

the most used and effective occupational health and safety management practices in the industries. The apparel manufacturing industry is considered as the Sri Lankan largest export earner, and it plays a vital role in the country's economy [4]. Apparel manufacturing exports contribute to more than 52% of the total export earnings of the country. This research selected the apparel industry because of above mentioned reasons. To develop export processing in Sri Lanka, the country established 3 main free trade zones located in Katunayake, Biyagama, and Koggala. Koggala Free Trade Zone is mainly famous for apparel manufacturing because there are 23 companies located in Koggala Free Trade Zone from that, 14 companies are related to the apparel industry. However, previous research found that in the Koggala free trade zone garment workers are facing different healthcare issues. The identified issues are respiratory complaints, accidents, body pains, skin problems, headaches, etc. [5]. The researcher mentioned that the turnover rate is high among garment workers and affects the revenues of the companies as well. The factors affecting turnover are employee satisfaction, commitment, productivity, and salary levels [5]. There are certain issues organizations face due to lower employee commitment such as lower employee performance, reduced organizational productivity, increased absenteeism, and turnover. Because of the above-mentioned reasons, operational-level employee commitment is selected as the dependent variable of this research. Based on these two variables some research studies are conducted in the global context for industries like steel manufacturing and construction industries. However proper research has not been conducted to test the impact of these two variables in the Sri Lankan context. Since this relationship has not been tested before in the apparel manufacturing industry and some researchers have identified there's high turnover in the Koggala Free Trade Zone apparel manufacturing companies and employee commitment is one main component that affects the turnover, this study aims to explore the impact of occupational health and safety management practices on operational-level employee commitment in the Sri Lankan Apparel industry. The outcome of this research helps to achieve the outcome target of protecting labor rights and promoting a safe working environment under sustainable development goal number 8.

Occupational health and safety management involves activities carried out by organizations to safeguard and promote the physical and mental well-being of employees, enabling them to perform their tasks efficiently and effectively [1]. According to the International Labor Organization, occupational health and safety focus on protecting workers from injuries, accidents, illnesses, and diseases caused by their work. With the evolving business landscape, there has been a notable rise in the implementation of occupational health and safety practices [1]. Health and safety training refers to a structured effort aimed at educating employees on essential safety components, including hazard identification, control measures, safe work practices, and emergency procedures [6]. Organizations implement health and safety policies and procedures to guide both management and employees toward maintaining an accident-free work environment [7]. Health and safety audits are conducted either routinely or as planned inspections of work processes, specific departments, or machinery. Employee perception suggests that frequent in-house safety audits significantly impact goal achievement and should be prioritized [8] Many companies now conduct employee wellness programs, acknowledging their ethical and legal responsibility to maintain workers' physical and mental health In Sri Lanka, particularly in the Koggala Free Trade Zone, apparel manufacturing dominates, with 14 out of 23 factories dedicated to this industry, employing over 70% of the local workforce A previous research study was conducted to test the effect of health and safety practices on employee commitment level and performance in the steel manufacturing industry in Rwanda and the researcher identified that there is a strong relationship between health and safety practices and employee commitment and employee performance [6]. A previous research study was conducted on a food and beverage company to test the relationship between occupational health and safety management practices on employee commitment. The research findings show that there is a significant relationship between these two variables [7]

The primary research objective of this study is to identify the impact of occupational health and safety management practices on operational-level employee commitment. Secondary objectives are built to identify the relationship between each independent variables with the dependent variable. The main question of research is what is the impact of occupational health and safety management practices on operational-level employee commitment? And sub questions are developed as, what is the relationship between independent variables with the dependent variable?

This research is significant as it highlights the impact of occupational health and safety management practices on operational-level employee commitment in Sri Lanka's apparel industry. The findings support improved workplace safety, enhanced employee performance, and contributed to organizational success and economic growth, aligning with Sustainable Development Goal 8.

Literature Review

The concept of occupational health and safety has evolved significantly due to industrialization and public pressure. Unsafe working conditions during the 18th and 19th centuries led to high injury rates, prompting labor unions and legislators to demand improvements [9]. The Occupational Health and Safety Act of 1970 aimed to ensure safer workplaces by assigning responsibilities and encouraging hazard reduction, marking a key milestone in safety management. Sri Lanka's health and safety history began in 1896 with mine and machinery laws. Key milestones include the 1934 Workmen's Compensation Ordinance and the 1950 Factories Ordinance, which set health and safety standards [10].

Occupational health and safety management are identified as the activities which are conducted by the organization to protect and promote the physical and mental health of the employees while they are working to perform the allocated tasks efficiently and effectively [1]. The International Labor Organization identifies occupational health and safety as protecting workers from injuries, accidents, sicknesses, and diseases that arise due to the work [8]. Occupational health and safety may vary from country to country which means the injuries and death rates are high in developing countries. From an economic perspective, injuries occupational diseases, and accidents are extra expenses for both the employer and employee. Costs related to the employer are equipment and plant damage, production interruptions, and compensations. The cost associated with the employee is the cost of treatment, loss of wages, pain, etc. So, these costs can be minimized, and the overall working conditions can be improved by implementing proper occupational health and safety management at the workplace [11]. To protect human health and safety all organizations are obliged to manage hazards and risk. The risk associated with the workplace should be systematically, analyzed, assessed, and corrected. If the risk cannot be corrected quickly then the organizations must create an action plan to minimize that risk otherwise it will negatively affect the employees [12]. So, now businesses understand occupational health and safety management as an imperative factor and major component for financial success and a healthy business [9]. The World Health Organization describes occupational health as the absence of diseases and an employee's complete mental, physical, and social well-being [1] Safety is described as protecting employees by controlling hazardous situations and industrial accidents. In another way, safety can be defined as the safety related to the worker/ human activities in the industries which means free from the risk associated with accidents, injuries, and damages within the workplace [13]

In occupational health and safety management, different health and safety management practices need to be followed by organizations to maintain the health and safety of their employees [1]. Workers Safety and compensation commission state that all employers who have within or more than twenty employees must follow occupational health and safety practices. Occupational health and safety management practices include a set of policies and procedures which is documented and implemented to manage occupational health and safety at the organizations [14].

The work-related injuries, fatalities, and illnesses become a burden to society. By providing proper health and safety training, society can overcome this issue. Health and safety training is defined as a planned effort used to educate employees regarding occupational health and safety components such as hazardous situations identification and control, use of production plant equipment, safe working practices, and emergency procedures [15]. Low productivity, loss of human, loss of working hours, and loss of material resources happened due to the reduction of health and safety education programs. With that, it's essential to provide adequate safety education to employees to minimize industrial accidents and injuries [16].

To safeguard employees from injuries and illnesses workplace arrangements must be in the right position. Therefore, industries need to put in place proper health and safety policies and procedures which are supported to ensure a safe working environment for the employees. If an organization considers the health and safety management practices of its employees, the organization will implement health and safety policies and procedures to guide employees and management to ensure the working environment is accidents free [16]. Establishing and educating proper health and safety policies and procedures will support reducing of death, injuries, and risks in the organization [17].

A previous study found that according to the employee perception, the frequency of conducting safety audits impacts the target attainment of the workers, and the top priority should be given to conducting the in-house safety audits [18]. Health and safety audits are identified as planned or routine monitoring of the work process, specific departments, and plant or machinery. Maintaining proper occupational health and safety practices in the workplace is an essential component of decent work in sustainable development goals. Occupational health and safety audits are a tool used for checking the implementation level of occupational health and safety systems to protect employees. If the organizations conduct health and safety audits according to their planned schedules, organizations can identify hazardous situations, unsafe behaviors of employees, and unsafe places.

Employee wellness programs are conducted by organizations for employees whose performance level is low due to emotional, mental, and physical problems or challenges. Employee wellness programs have the ability to effectively change the worker's behavior if the workers are ready to survive the current situation. Most of the employee wellness programs are freely provided by the employer for the employees. These employee wellness programs are a support system for employees to deal with their personal and work-related challenges. In the current business world, many organizations conduct employee wellness programs because they identify it as an ethical and legal obligation to maintain the physical and mental health of the employees [14].

This study was guided by the theory of the "Three-Component Model of Commitment" founded by Meyer and Allen in 1991. This model mainly explains the three components of commitment which consist of affective commitment, continuous commitment, and normative commitment. Many researchers are interested in this Three-component model of commitment and tested it in various industry settings. And this model explains that employees in organizations can experience all three forms of commitment at different levels. These three components are different from each other [19].

Affective commitment explains individuals' involvement and emotional attachment and identification with the organization. And affective commitment can be defined as the employee's desirable workplace behavior such as job satisfaction, increased productivity, lower absenteeism, and organizational citizenship behavior [20]. It explains to which extent an employee wants to stay in the organization. Organizations can gain positive outcomes through affective commitment they are, reduced absenteeism and turnover, organizational effectiveness and proper organizational behavior [21].

The second construct of three component model of commitment is continuous commitment. The main reason behind the continuous commitment is the employees need to stay with the organization. According to the continuous commitment employees will evaluate their investments by comparing how they contribute to the organization, what they gain from staying at the organization, and the things they will lose if they leave the organization [20]. If employees think that they don't have the proper skills or qualifications to cope with another field they will develop continuous commitment and try to become more committed to the organization. Employees try to become continuously committed if they feel that the cost of leaving the organization is high [21]

Normative commitment is the third construct of the three components of the commitment model. Normative commitment explains how much an employee feels and thinks that they should stay in the organization. If organizations invest a lot of effort, time, and money for training and development and employee well-being then the employees feel that they have an obligation to provide their services to the organization [21]. Normative commitment also develops within the employees if the organization provides proper rewards to the employees or if the organization provides significant costs for the employees for providing employment [22]

Employee commitment can be identified as the level of enthusiasm that an employee must complete the allocated tasks in the workplace and

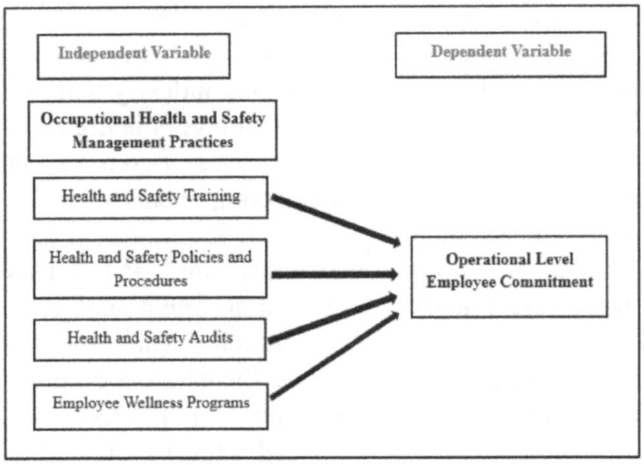

Figure 27.1 Conceptual framework
Source: Author

employee commitment is essential for the successful completion of relevant tasks. Mainly the organization's performance is based on employee commitment [23]

A previous research study was conducted to test the effect of health and safety practices on employee commitment level and performance in the steel manufacturing industry in Rwanda and the researcher identified that there is a strong relationship between health and safety practices and employee commitment and employee performance. As health and safety management practices they mainly analyze occupational hazard prevention, safety and health management systems, and personal protective equipment [24] The research was conducted in the Sri Lankan Construction industry to check the impact of occupational health and safety management practices on employee performance and selected employee commitment as a mediating variable. Research finds that there is a positive relationship between occupational health and safety management practices and employee commitment [23]. A previous research study was conducted based on a food and beverage company to test the relationship between occupational health and safety management practices on employee commitment. The research findings show that there is a significant relationship between these two variables. And the research elaborates that because of the most famous fact that health is wealth and the research mentioned health and safety practices are not only important for employees' health and safety it supports increasing productivity, product quality, and work motivation.

Methodology

The independent variable of this study is occupational health and safety management practices. The dependent variable of this study is operational-level employee commitment. As the occupational health and safety management practices this research selected to analyze health and safety training, health and safety policies and procedures, health and safety audits, and employee wellness programs.

The alternative hypotheses are built based on each independent variable.

H1 – There is a relationship between health and safety training on operational-level employee commitment.

H2 – There is a relationship between health and safety policies and procedures on operational-level employee commitment,

H3 – There is a relationship between health and safety audits on operational-level employee commitment

H4 – There is a relationship between employee wellness programs on operational-level employee commitment.

This research study follows the deductive research approach based on the theory of the Three-Component model of commitment. A quantitative research strategy is used to collect numerical data from the respondents and to analyze the data to test the relationship with the variables. In the Koggala Free Trade Zone, there are 23 companies. Within the 23 companies, 14 companies are related to apparel manufacturing which means more than 70% of employees are engaged in apparel manufacturing in the Koggala free trade zone. Due to the current economic crisis, 5 companies are temporarily closed, and nine main apparel manufacturing companies are functioning in the Zone. So, the target population of this study is around 5,000 operational-level employees in currently functioning apparel manufacturing companies in the Koggala Free Trade Zone. 357 operational-level employees were selected from the 5000 population based on the convenient sampling method, sample size was selected by using the morgan table. To collect the primary data for the study 5-point Likert scale questionnaire was used and the questionnaire includes three sections. They are questions for demographic data, questions for independent variables, and questions for dependent

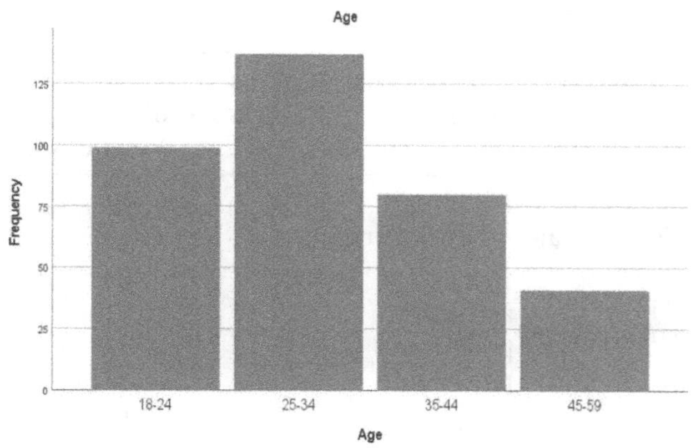

Figure 27.2 Frequency of age
Source: Author

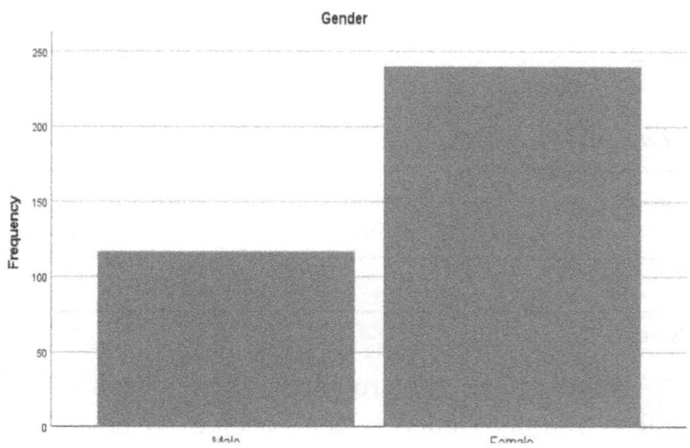

Figure 27.3 Frequency of gender
Source: Author

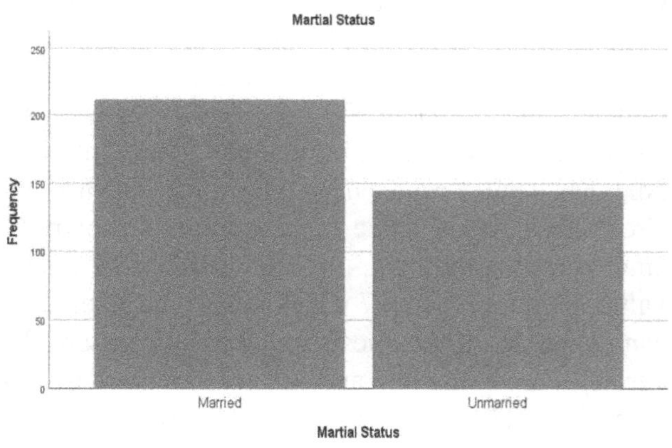

Figure 27.4 Frequency of marital status
Source: Author

variables. The convenience sampling technique is used to distribute the questionnaire among the sample from the target population. Based on the availability and easiness of access convenience sampling technique is used. To analyze the collected data SPSS software is used. Through the SPSS software reliability, correlation, and regression analysis is run to interpret the answers.

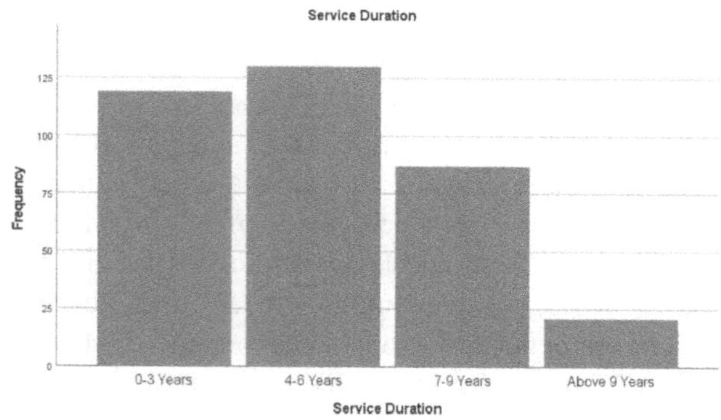

Figure 27.5 Frequency of service duration
Source: Author

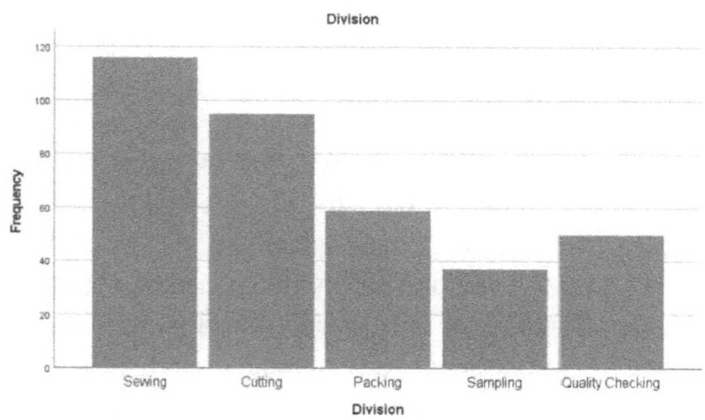

Figure 27.6 Frequency of service division
Source: Author

Results and Discussion

The research targeted operational-level employees in currently function apparel manufacturing companies at Koggala free trade zone. According to the statistic of Koggala BOI department total employment in currently function apparel manufacturing organizations are 7000 from that 5000 containing operational level-employee base. According to the morgan table based on the 5000 population, 357 sample is selected to collect data. Approximately 40-50 questionnaires are distributed among all apparel manufacturing companies that are currently function based on the convenience sampling method. And collected 357 respondents based on the sample size and analyzed the collected data using the Statistical Package for Social Science. The chapter contains with background of the operational-level employees, the reliability of the questions, background of the variables, correlation analysis, and the regression analysis. The findings are presented in the form of charts and tables within the chapter. The demographic characteristics section, it mainly describes the background of the respondents under the categories of age, gender, marital status, service duration and the service division. To analyze and present the demographic characteristics of the respondents' the frequencies are taken and presented below.

Based on the demographic data analysis It interprets that most of the respondents are between 25 – 34 age categories as a percentage of 38.4%. Most of the female operational-level employees fill out the questionnaire as a percentage of 67.2% and from the 357 respondents, based on the respondents 59.4% are married. According to service duration as the highest number out of 357, 36.4% have worked for the company for 4–6 years. Data collected through five service divisions in the companies from that 32.5% of respondents are working in the sewing division.

Reliability analysis assesses the consistency and stability of the questions that are used for data collection. It analyzes whether the questions taken under variables are consistent and whether the questions are supported to provide data to the selected variables. The research study aims to analyze the impact of occupational health and safety management practices on operational-level employee commitment. So, the selected occupational safety management practices as the independent variables are occupational health and safety training, health and safety policies and procedures, health and safety audits, and employee wellness programs. Questions are developed according to these independent variables and questions are developed to test the employee commitment level as well. So, to test the consistency of the questions that are taken under each variable the reliability analysis is done, and the findings are presented according to Table 27.1.

Table 27.1 Reliability values of independent variables and dependent variable.

Variable Name	Cronbach's Alpha	Reliability	Conclusion
Health and Safety training	0.907	0.907 >0.7	Reliable
Health and Safety Policies and Procedures	0.877	0.877 > 0.7	Reliable
Health and Safety Audit	0.884	0.884 > 0.7	Reliable
Employee Wellness Programs	0.868	0.868 > 0.7	Reliable
Employee Commitment	0.959	0.959 > 0.7	Reliable

Source: Author

Table 27.2 Correlation between the variables.

Dependent Variable	Independent variable	Pearson Correlation	Significance of the Relationship
Operational-level employee commitment	Health and safety training	0.787	0.001
	Health and safety policies and procedures	0.789	0.004
	Health and safety audits	0.788	0.001
	Employee wellness programs	0.796	0.000

Source: Author

Table 27.3 Regression analysis-model fit.

R-Square	Adjusted R-Square	Model Significance
0.730	0.727	0.000

Source: Author

According to the research study health and safety training (independent variable A) has 0.907 Cronbach's Alpha value, health and safety policies and procedures (independent variable B) has 0.877 Cronbach's Alpha value, Health and Safety Audits (independent variable C) has 0.884 Cronbach's Alpha value and Employee Wellness Programs (independent variable D) has 0.868 Cronbach's alpha and Employee commitment (dependent variable) has 0.959 Cronbach's Alpha value. The highest Cronbach's Alpha value or reliability is shown by employee commitment. All the Cronbach's Alpha values are more than 0.7 which means the researcher can conclude all the questions taken to measure the variables are consistent and the questionnaire is successful, therefore proceed with the analysis.

Correlation analysis is used to test whether to which extent two variables are related to each other. Simply correlation describes the strength, direction, and significance between two variables [25]. To check whether the relationship between two variables is very strong, strong, moderate, and weak there are several indicators. If the correlation value is more than 0.7 it means there's a "Very Strong Relationship" between two variables, if the value is between 0.50 and 0.69 there's a "Strong Relationship" between the variables, if the

Table 27.4 Hypothesis testing.

Variable	Standard Beta Coefficient	Significance	Expected relationship	Decision
Health and Safety Training	0.201	0.001	Relationship	H1 Accept
Health and safety policies and procedures	0.180	0.004	Relationship	H2 Accept
Health and safety Audit	0.195	0.001	Relationship	H3 Accept
Employee wellness programs	0.344	0.000	Relationship	H4 Accept

Source: Author

value is between 0.30 – 0.49 there's a "Moderate Relationship", if the values are between 0.10 – 0.29 there's "Weak Relationship" between the variables and if the value is between 0.01- 0.09 the relationship between the variables are 'very Weak.

Based on the analysis, there is a very strong positive relationship between the health and safety training and operational level employee commitment which is 78.7%. It implies that there's a strong positive relationship which means if the implementation of health and safety training increases, it increases the operational level of commitment as well. If the significance value is less than 0.5 (0.001>0.5) the relationship is significant for operational-level employees in the Koggala Free Trade zone.

A very strong positive relationship between the health and safety policies and procedures and operational level employee commitment which is 78.9%. It implies that there's a strong positive relationship which means if the implementation of health and safety policies and procedures increases, the operational level of employee commitment also increases. If the significance value is less than 0.5 (0.004>0.5) the relationship is significant for operational-level employees in the Koggala Free Trade zone.

Health and safety audits also generate very strong positive relationship with employee commitment which is 78.8%. It implies that there's a strong positive relationship which means if the companies conduct more health and safety audits, the operational level of employee commitment also increases. If the significance value is less than 0.5 (0.004>0.5) the relationship is significant for operational-level employees in the Koggala Free Trade Zone.

A very strong positive relationship between the employee wellness programs and operational level employee commitment which is 79.6%. It implies that there's a strong positive relationship which means if the companies conduct more employee wellness programs, the operational-level employee commitment also increases. If the significance value is less than 0.5 (0.000 > 0.5) the relationship is significant for operational-level employees in the Koggala Free Trade Zone.

Based on the generated correlation results, the researcher can conclude all four independent variables have a strong positive relationship with the dependent variable (employee commitment) which is more than 70%. This relationship mainly represents the increase of health and safety training, health and safety policies and procedures, health and safety audits, and employee wellness programs in apparel manufacturing companies in the Koggala free trade zone, the operational level employee commitment also increases. All these variables are significant enough for apparel manufacturing companies in the Koggala free trade zone.

The next most important component in the research study is linear regression analysis. The regression analysis includes different variations such as linear, nonlinear, and multiple linear. This research goes with multiple regression analysis because there's more than one predictive variable. Mainly the predictive power of the model is defined through the regression analysis [26]. The results of regression analysis support acceptance or reject the early defined hypothesis in the research study. Regression analysis in research mainly focuses on identifying the overall model significance, model fitness, and the significance of each independent variable to the dependent variable. The regression analysis of this chapter explains the overall model significance, a model summary which means the model fitness and the hypothesis testing.

The R-square value explains how much variation in the dependent variable will be covered by the independent variables. Based on this research it means how much of employee commitment level will be covered through the health and safety training, health and safety policies and procedures, health and safety audits, and employee wellness programs. If the model fitness value/R Square value is greater than 0.7 it explains there's a perfect model fit. According to Table 27.3, the R-squared value is 0.730. All four independent variables cover 73% of the variation in the dependent variable which means a higher value of the dependent variable is covered by the independent variables that are used for this research.

Mainly the adjusted R-Square value explains the if another independent variable is put into the research study how much of predictive power will decrease. If this research uses another independent variable how much of predictive power will decrease. Table 27.3 clearly shows that the adjusted R-Square value is 0.727 which means if the researcher adds another independent variable the predictive power will decrease to 72.7%.

The overall model significance is tested through the ANOVA (Analysis of Variance) In SPSS. It mainly tested whether the values of independent variables are decided by the value of the dependent variable. Based on this research, it tested through ANOVA table whether the health and safety training, health and safety policies and procedures, health and safety audits, and employee wellness program values supported to decide the values of the employee commitment. If the entire model is significant, the significance value in the ANOVA table should be lower than 0.05 (Alpha). We call this significance value the "P" value also. Below is the value generated through the ANOVA table according to this research based on the collected data and analysis. Based on table 27.3 output it clearly shows that the significance value is 0.000 which means the value is lower than 0.05. It clearly emphasizes that the entire model is significant. Simply it means the values of the dependent variable (operational-level employee commitment) are decided through the independent variable.

In the hypothesis testing to accept and reject the hypothesis, the significance value (P Value) in the coefficient table will be checked. If the significance value in the coefficient table is lower than 0.05 then we can accept the hypothesis.

Based on the research study the significance values of all independent variables are lower than 0.05. Health and safety training get 0.001, health and safety policies and procedures get 0.004, health and safety audits get 0.001 and employee wellness programs get 0.000 significance value. Therefore, all the hypotheses are accepted by clearly stating that there's a relationship between independent variables with dependent variables.

There were some limitations in the study as well. The research only tested the four main health and safety management practices such as health and safety training, health and safety policies and procedures, health and safety audits, and employee wellness programs. Due to limited time, the research collected data from the Apparel manufacturing companies in the Koggala Free Trade Zone and selected only quantitative methods to collect data. The data collection became a challenge because the sample size is 357 operational-level employees, which the sample size is high and some operational-level employees lack of skills to fill out the questionnaire. And the research is focused only on the operational level employees. In conclusion, according to the regression analysis outputs the researcher was able to accept all four hypotheses which mentioned about there's a relationship between the relevant independent variable with the dependent variable. Through the regression analysis, it generates 73% of model fitness and the selected model can be accepted to check the impact of occupational health and safety management practices on operational-level employee commitment.

Further research can be conducted by adding other health and safety management practices to the model to check whether the relationship between health and safety management practices and employee commitment. The current research is only limited to Apparel manufacturing in the Koggala free trade zone future research can be done by combining the other free trade zones and to the whole Sri Lankan context. Future research can use both quantitative and qualitative methods for the data collection and conduct the same research for different industries in Sri Lanka such as construction, glow manufacturing, steel manufacturing, etc.

Conclusion

The primary objective of this research focuses on identifying the impact of occupational health and safety management practices on operational-level employee commitment in the Sri Lankan Apparel manufacturing industry. It's an essential factor to have a safe working environment and a committed employee base to grow the economy of a particular country. According to the research study analysis, the primary research objective and question was achieved that the researcher was able to identify there's impact of occupational health and safety management practices on employee commitment. Other than the research questions, objectives, and hypotheses are designed to test whether each independent variable has an impact on employee commitment. All these hypotheses are tested by using the data collected by the 357 operational-level employees in Koggala Free Trade Zone apparel manufacturing companies. According to the correlation analysis researcher identified that there's a strong positive relationship among all four variables with the operational level of employee commitment. This means if the health and safety training, health and safety policies and procedures, health and safety audits, and employee wellness programs increase it will increase the employee commitment, and if these health and safety practices are decreasing the commitment also decreases. All these variables received a significance value lower than 0.05 which means all the hypotheses are accepted. Through the regression analysis, it has been identified that the overall model significance value is 0.000 which is lower than 0.05 which means the overall model is significant. And these variables impact 73% of coverage in the variations in employee commitment. The findings of this research are really important for apparel manufacturing companies in the Koggala free trade zone to improve their operations and to create a safe working environment for employees. With that, the researcher was able to achieve all the research objectives because all the hypotheses were accepted. Therefore, this research achieved all the purposes, and this research's ultimate impact on sustainable development goal 8 which is "Decent Work and Economic Growth". If the particular industry has a safe working environment and if the employees are more committed to the work they do, it supports to increase in the profits of the organizations which directly impacts economic growth.

References

[1] Nuwansala, H. P., & Kumarasinghe, I. (n.d.). The impact of occupational health and safety practices on job performance of operational level employees: a study in the construction industry, Sri Lanka analyzing the queuing performance of a state pharmacy by simulation: a case study of Sri Lanka view project. doi: 10.5281/zenodo.6463442.

[2] Tabitha, M. M. (n.d.). Influence of occupational health and safety practices on employee performance at Kenya power and lighting company a research project submitted in partial fulfilment of the requirement for the award of degree of master of business administration, school of business, university of Nairobi 2018.

[3] Debela, M. B., Deyessa, N., Begosew, A. M., & Azage, M. (2023). Occupational health and safety practices and associated factors among workers in ethiopia's metehara and wonji sugar industries: a convergent parallel mixed design. *BMJ Open*, 13(2), e065382. doi: 10.1136/bmjopen-2022-065382.

[4] Dileepa, M. G., & Weerasinghe, L. (2023). Rural economic development and apparel industry in Sri Lanka.

[5] Rajapakse, S., Morin, F., Ostbye, T., & De silva, V. (2018). Healthcare seeking behaviour among female garment workers in koggala free trade zone, Sri Lanka. *Journal of the College of Community Physicians of Sri Lanka*, 24(4), 149. doi: 10.4038/jccpsl.v24i4.8159.

[6] Umugwaneza, C., Nkechi, I. E., & Mugabe, J. B. (2019). Effect of workplace safety and health practices on employee commitment and performance in steel manufacturing companies in Rwanda. *European Journal of Business and Management Research*, 4(5). doi: 10.24018/ejbmr.2019.4.5.84.

[7] Olawale, E., Ilesanmi, F., & Moradeke, T. (2022). Spectrum journal of innovation, reforms and development website: www.sjird.journalspark.org occupational health and safety practice and employees' job commitment in Dufil Nigeria limited, Ota, Ogun state, Nigeria. Available from: www.sjird.journalspark.org.

[8] Botchwey, C. O.-A., Kesseh, D., Baidoo, M. A., Boateng, A. A., & Boakye, D. S. (2022). Occupational health and safety practices among sanitation workers in a public university in Ghana: a qualitative approach. *International Journal of Environment and Climate Change*, 12(10), 226–237. doi: 10.9734/ijecc/2022/v12i1030789.

[9] Badri, A., Boudreau-Trudel, B., & Souissi, A. S. (2018). Occupational health and safety in the industry 4.0 era: a cause for major concern?. doi: 10.1016/j.ssci.2018.06.012.

[10] Arachchige, U., Preethika, P., Arachchige, U. S. P. R., Prabodhi, D. D., & Kalathma, M. K. (2019). The impact of occupational safety and health procedure of the MDF manufacturing industry in Sri Lanka bio-diesel production view project boiler operation and maintainance view project the impact of occupational safety and health procedure of the mdf manufacturing industry in Sri Lanka. *Article in International Journal of Scientific and Technology Research*, Available from: www.ijstr.org.

[11] Gopang, M. A., Nebhwani, M., Khatri, A., & Marri, H. B. (2017). An assessment of occupational health and safety measures and performance of SMES: an empirical investigation. *Safety Science*, 93, 127–133. doi: 10.1016/j.ssci.2016.11.024.

[12] Nordlöf, H., Wiitavaara, B., Högberg, H., & Westerling, R. (2017). A cross-sectional study of factors influencing occupational health and safety management practices in companies. *Safety Science*, 95, 92–103. doi: 10.1016/j.ssci.2017.02.008.

[13] Saputra, F., & Rizky mahaputra, M. (2022). Building occupational safety and health (k3): analysis of the work environment and work discipline. doi: 10.38035/jlph.v2i3.

[14] Tabitha, M. M. (n.d.). Influence of occupational health and safety practices on employee performance at Kenya power and lighting company a research project submitted in partial fulfilment of the requirement for the award of degree of master of business administration, school of business, university of Nairobi 2018.

[15] Robson, L. S., Stephenson, C. M., Schulte, P. A., Amick III, B. C., Irvin, E. L., Eggerth, D. E., et al. (2012). A systematic review of the effectiveness of occupational health and safety training. doi: 10.5271/sjweh.3259.

[16] Amine, J. D., & A. J. D. (n.d.). Assessment of industrial safety education programmes in manufacturing industries in Kaduna and Niger states of Nigeria. Available from: www.iosrjournals.orgwww.iosrjournals.org.

[17] Amponsah-Tawiah, K., & Mensah, J. (2016). Occupational health and safety and organizational commitment: evidence from the Ghanaian mining industry. *Safety and Health at Work*, 7(3), 225–230. doi: 10.1016/j.shaw.2016.01.002.

[18] Abu, O. (2022). Workplace health training and level of target attainment among factory workers in rivers state. Available from: https://www.researchgate.net/publication/366412004.

[19] Muda, A. L., & Fook, C. Y. (2020). Psychological empowerment and organisational commitment among academic staff of public universities in Malaysia. *Asian Journal of University Education*, 16(2), 26–35. doi: 10.24191/ajue.v16i2.10292.

[20] Olawale, E., Ilesanmi, F., & Moradeke, T. (2022). Spectrum journal of innovation, reforms and development website: www.sjird.journalspark.org occupational health and safety practice and employees' job commitment in dufil Nigeria limited, Ota, Ogun state, Nigeria. [online]. Available from: www.sjird.journalspark.org.

[21] Noraazian, & Khalip , (2016). A three-component conceptualization of organizational commitment. *International Journal of Academic Research in Business and Social Sciences*, 6(12). doi: 10.6007/ijarbss/v6-i12/2464.

[22] Meyer, J. P., & Allen, N. J. (1991). A three-component conceptualization of organizational commitment.

[23] Smmsk, B., Gdn, P., & Lanka, S., (2022). Impact of health and safety practices on employee job performance: mediating role of employee commitment in selected building construction companies in Sri Lanka. *Partners Universal International Research Journal*, doi: 10.5281/zenodo.7111113.

[24] Umugwaneza, C., Nkechi, I. E., & Mugabe, J. B. (2019). effect of workplace safety and health practices on employee commitment and performance in steel manufacturing companies in Rwanda. *European Journal of Business and Management Research*, 4(5). doi: 10.24018/ejbmr.2019.4.5.84.

[25] Werme, J., Van der Sluis, S., Posthuma, D., & De Leeuw, C. A. (2022). An integrated framework for local genetic correlation analysis. *Nature Genetics*, 54(3), 274–282. doi: 10.1038/s41588-022-01017-y.

[26] Karanikas, N., Weber, D., Bruschi, K., & Brown, S. (2022). Identification of systems thinking aspects in ISO 45001:2018 on occupational health and safety management. *Safety Science*, 148. doi: 10.1016/j.ssci.2022.105671.

28 Enhancing personality-job fit in business analytics undergraduates: a big five model approach using mini-IPIP and text analytics

Yadawa Weerakoon[1,a], *Manumi Wijesinghe*[2,b], *Maninda Edirisooriya*[2,c] *and Indra Mahakalanda*[2,d]

[1]Department of Accounting and Finance, Faculty of Business, NSBM Green University, Sri Lanka

[2]Department of Decision Sciences, Faculty of Business, University of Moratuwa, Sri Lanka

Abstract

This study aims to analyze the alignment between personality traits and job fit among business analytics undergraduates utilizing the big five personality model. Recognizing the value of personality-job fit for professional success and organizational efficacy, the research addresses the frequently overlooked issue where one's personality traits do not align with the selected job description, although academic qualifications do. Using a dual-sample approach, data is collected from undergraduates who study business analytics at the University of Moratuwa and Business Analytics professionals. Personality traits are evaluated using standardized questionnaires, particularly the 20-Item Mini-IPIP for Likert-scale responses and scenario-based questions to obtain nuanced insights. Sophisticated language models like GPT 3.5 and other language models are used to evaluate and predict personality traits with a focus on identifying and bridging any inconsistencies between the requirements of Business Analytics job roles and undergraduates' profiles. As a consequence, a web-based recommendation platform was introduced being the significant outcome that offers personalized, AI-generated suggestions to enhance the personality traits improvement and job fit improvement. This study highlights the significance for organizations and educational institutions to consider personality attributes along with technical skills to enhance organizational performance, reduce turnover, and ensure job fit. This study seeks to optimize undergraduate career development by providing empirical insights and recommendations, ensuring a more comprehensive strategy for professional success in the dynamic sector of business analytics.

Keywords: Big Five personality model, business analytics, job fit analysis, personality assessment, sentence embeddings

Introduction

It is considered that effective integration between educational backgrounds and employment requirements is an essential aspect of professional development. However, a frequently underestimated but highly significant factor of organizational effectiveness and organizational cohesion is the extent to which a candidate's personality corresponds with the requirements of the selected field of career.

This study aims to address the perennial issue of mismatches in personality-job fit during employee recruiting by precisely profiling the Business Analytics undergraduates and job roles using the Big Five Personality model. This issue has affected higher education institutions as well as the corporate world, which has substantial intellectual and practical consequences.

Guided by this aim, the study examined how the Big Five model could be used for profiling undergraduate personalities, determining thresholds for Business Analytics job roles and identifying the essential traits, and examining how students compare to the identified benchmarks. This arises 3 objectives from the questions: to accurately classify and profile undergraduate personalities, to set trait thresholds using Business Analytics industry professionals, and to uncover the undergraduate personality voids using tailored recommendations for improvement.

The studies indicate that professionals who perform well in their current positions are more inclined to get promoted and on the other hand students who perform well in schools are expected to get accepted by renowned programs and jobs [1–3]Conversely, it will result in social rejection, job termination, or

[a]yadawa.w@nsbm.ac.lk, [b]wijesinghewaams.20@uom.lk, [c]manindaw@uom.lk, [d]indram@uom.lk

DOI: 10.4324/9781003739920-28

rehabilitation due to inadequate performance. Given the high stakes, researchers well known for a variety of disciplines, particularly psychology, education, and management, have long been intrigued by the hypothesis that fundamental personality traits influence performance [1, 2].

The five factor model—commonly referred to as the Big Five or OCEAN Model is known to be the predominant framework in personality science, classifying personality into five broad aspects: Extraversion, agreeableness, conscientiousness, neuroticism, and openness. These traits are influenced by early life experiences and inheritance, and they are mostly persistent throughout time [4, 5]. Extensive research strongly suggests that these traits have a significant impact on performance results across cognitive, motor, psychomotor, and interpersonal subjects [6]. For instance, the interrelationships have been demonstrated by the meta-analyses carried out between OCEAN traits and performance in the school, and workplace in the areas of creativity, leadership effectiveness, and negotiation skills [7, 8].

This research identifies key limitations in current hiring practices, particularly within the Business Analytics domain. Interviews, which continue to be the most general way to evaluate candidates, often fail to conduct thorough assessments for personality fit. Emphasizing business analytics, this research aims to establish standards for an ideal personality-job fit and profile job roles. The requirement of such a study is made apparent by the empirical evidence that indicates personality-job discrepancies are indicators of cultural gaps in organizations and poor organizational performance. Organizations committing significant resources to their recruitment practices are highly required to recognize and resolve these inconsistencies at an early stage to upgrade efficiency and integration.

Focusing on business analytics undergraduates, this study uses Text Analytics and the OCEAN Model to methodically categorize and profile students' personality traits through a structured questionnaire. This study seeks to disclose potential misalignments in university education and provide suggestions for improvement for optimal personality-job fit. This approach not only diagnoses the issue but also takes measures proactively to bridge the gap between academic credentials and comprehensive career success offering empirical guidance regarding the way to develop traits that are consistent with career paths.

Literature Review

In organizations, a significant role and contribution is played by the HR departments in determining the firm's performance. As a result, there's a significant power within the HR division to influence performance. The HR division of a company is responsible for several tasks, inclusive of recruitment and employment of highly skilled personnel, upgrading the workplace environment, rewarding, etc. [9]. In this regard, there have been numerous previous studies carried out. For instance, a previous study has focused on creating an HR index to depict to which level organizations have achieved high performance. As a result, it has been found that the use of HR policies regarding employee commitment leads to high-quality service and increased productivity of the firm and vice versa [10]. The task of recruitment is significant in the organization. Personality testing during recruitment is used to analyze candidate traits aligning with job requirements and organizational culture, allowing for job fit predictions and optimizing the recruitment process [11]. Therefore, it is practical and proven that effective personality testing in the recruitment phase is important to eliminate the negative effects on employee satisfaction and organizational success. In many Asian cultures, personality is developed using a distinct approach that interprets the individual as interdependent, perceiving it as a behavioral characteristic that distinguishes a person's interactions with others [12]. The present study focuses on employing the Big Five Model for personality prediction, and these five personality traits span a broad range of facets of an individual's behavior and character [13]. The importance of the Big Five Model in personality testing is emphasized for its versatility and validated framework [14]

Factors influencing big five personality

Studies have shown that the complex interplay of genetic and environmental factors impacts an individual's personality [15]. Twin studies have shown that identical twins who share 100% of their genetic material possess more personality traits in common when compared to fraternal twins who share only around 50%, emphasizing genetics as a major factor [16]. Personality development is also influenced by environmental factors such as early childhood experiences, education, and peer group pressure. One's level of education can enhance conscientiousness and openness by exposing individuals to curiosity and structured learning. Positive peer relationships also affect agreeableness and conscientiousness through increased social interaction. Further studies have identified that media exposure and cultural settings also shape personality traits, particularly agreeableness and extraversion [17]. Socioeconomic status also has a significant influence on personality via exposure to events and resources, which impacts traits such as openness [18]. One's life experiences, such as personal achievements and defeats, constantly refine personality traits.

Methodologies for accessing big five personalities
In previous studies, machine learning and deep learning methods on social media data have been used for sentiment classification under personality detection. A study conducted by Ayu and Maharani on Twitter data using IndoBERT achieved the highest accuracy compared to other ML methods like Logistic Regression, AdaBoost, and Decision Trees [19]. Zero-shot learning (ZSL) offers a compelling solution to classify texts without labeled datasets, as demonstrated by [20] using a pre-trained MNLI sequence-pair classifier. ZSL was also applied in the SIOP 2019 competition to detect Big Five traits and achieved an F1 score of 0.79 despite challenges. Considering these advancements, this study employs both ZSL and Sentence Embeddings due to their high potential in assessing text-based personality traits. Ultimately, the model demonstrating the lowest deviation between the two will be selected as the optimal scoring method.

Moreover, GPT-3.5, developed by OpenAI, is recognized for its strong contextual understanding and few-shot learning capabilities, making it effective for generating human-like, domain-specific responses [21–23]. Based on these strengths, this study employs GPT-3.5 to generate tailored recommendations for candidates whose personality traits fall short of the required thresholds. This approach supports personality development by offering practical, trait-specific suggestions that improve job fit, addressing the personality-performance dilemma from both predictive and developmental perspectives.

Considering these advancements, this study employs both Zero-Shot Learning (ZSL) and Sentence Embeddings for accurate text classification. The model demonstrating the lowest deviation between the two will be selected as the optimal scoring method. This research contributes a novel approach to understanding personality-job fit among Business Analytics undergraduates in Sri Lanka—a gap that remains largely unaddressed in existing literature.

Methodology

Design and participants
The purpose of this study is to utilize the Big Five Model to generate an optimum scoring model focusing on enhancing undergraduate students' personality-job fit. This study consists of two primary populations: Business Analytics undergraduates at the University of Moratuwa, Sri Lanka, and professionals in the field of Business Analytics who are currently employed, specifically those who graduated from the same university. It is expected that this dual sample approach confirms an extensive analysis of personality traits and their compatibility with Business Analytics job roles.

The data collection for this study will be acquired via two standardized questionnaires. Questionnaires were selected owing to their cost-effectiveness, ease of implementation, and the ability to collect prompt and effective data from a large number of respondents. A quantitative methodology is utilized, and standardized questionnaires adapted from prior research are the sole method of data collection [24]. As stated by [25], this quantitative approach is significant in analyzing correlations and in identifying cause-and-effect associations among variables. The structured surveys are distributed electronically via Google Forms to both undergraduates and Business Analytics industry professionals.

The first section of the questionnaire employed the 20-Item Mini-IPIP, a shortened Likert scale instrument for assessing Big Five traits. Each trait—Openness, Conscientiousness, Extraversion, Agreeableness, and Neuroticism—is measured using four questions. The second section is a scenario-based questionnaire, which includes five open-ended questions designed to elicit text responses, each aligned with one specific trait. This combination allows for both structured and narrative-based personality assessment. The collected data are processed using Python, leveraging tools such as NumPy and sentence-transformers for scoring, text analysis, and benchmarking against industry thresholds.

In the final phase of the study, the goal is to implement a prototype to evaluate undergraduate Business Analytics students' personality-job fit by comparing their scores with benchmark scores provided by the BA industry professionals. Suggestions will be provided to bridge any identified gaps, following that, with the focus on improving the students' overall personality-job fit.

Measures

Initially, the Big Five personality traits are using the "20-Item Mini-IPIP". This measure is a shortened version of the original IPIP, "50-Item IPIP-FFM Inventory" to assess the five traits and it has been verified for its reliability and accuracy[9]. It demonstrates strong internal consistency and consists of a similar content coverage to its parent scale, which is derived from a large sample of college students [25]. Respondents respond to each item from "Very accurate" to "Very inaccurate". For instance, "I am the life of the party" (Extraversion) and "I get upset easily" (Neuroticism) are two of the questions included. It has been clearly shown that "Mini-IPIP" has excellent psychometric qualities as evidenced by over 0.70 Cronbach's alpha values demonstrating satisfactory internal consistency.

In addition to the Likert scale questionnaire, five short scenario-based questionnaires were also included to evaluate the personality traits. Here, respondents describe their actions or thoughts in response to five different real-life situations, each crafted to reflect one of the Big Five traits. Further, this method has been validated in previous research for its high internal consistency and correlation with stabilized personality inventories [26].

Model training and analysis

Scoring model for mini-IPIP

Each statement typically has a scale of responses ranging from strong disagreement to strong agreement. In the Mini-IPIP, these are usually structured from 1 (Strongly Disagree) to 5 (Strongly Agree) [27, 10]. Reverse scoring is applied to selected items to control for acquiescence bias, such that a score of 5 becomes 1 and vice versa. The reverse scoring function is implemented as shown in Figure 28.1.

```
##Python
# Define a function for reverse scoring
def reverse_score(response):
    return 6 - response
```

Figure 28.1 Reverse scoring function
Source: Author

```
# Define the traits and their opposing labels,
including supportive words
trait_labels = {
    "openness": {
            "trait":  ["openness",  "imaginative",
"curious", "adventurous", "flexible"],
            "opposing":  ["closeness",  "reserved",
"conventional", "cautious", "rigid"]
    }
# Apply softmax to the combined scores
 final_softmax_scores=
np.exp(combined_scores)/np.sum(np.exp(combined_sco
res))
# Normalize to a score from 1 to 5
final_score = round((final_softmax_scores[0] * 4) +
1, 2)
```

Figure 28.2 Implementation of trait-opposing word definitions and softmax-based final score normalization
Source: Author

```
# Initialize the model
model=SentenceTransformer('stsb-roberta-base')
# Sample texts
response = "I enjoy social gatherings."
trait_description = "Enjoys meeting new people and
socializing."
# Convert texts to embeddings
response_embedding = model.encode(response,
convert_to_tensor=True)
trait_embedding=          model.encode(trait_description,
convert_to_tensor=True)
```

Figure 28.3 Loading pre-trained model and generating sentence embeddings
Source: Author

After reverse scoring, the scores for items related to each personality trait were averaged to compute a composite score for that trait.

$$Trait\ score = \frac{\Sigma(responses\ to\ items)}{number\ of\ items} \quad (1)$$

Zero-shot learning for text responses

Initially, the study utilized zero-shot learning (ZSL) with various BERT models to classify personality traits from text responses. This method was selected due to its capability to operate without a labeled training dataset, a common constraint in scenarios where acquiring domain-specific annotated data is challenging or impractical[28].

Zero-shot learning was appealing because it leverages pre-trained models that have been developed on vast amounts of text data, which

```
# Sample descriptions for traits
descriptions = {
    "extraversion": [
        "I'd be thrilled at the prospect of meeting new
individuals! While I wait, I'd likely strike up
conversations with anyone who looks friendly.
Socializing comes easily to me, so I might ask how they
know the host or what they're excited about at the
party. This would help me relax and possibly forge new
friendships."
    ],
    "introversion": [
        "Feeling somewhat out of my element, I often
wrestle with wanting to connect while simultaneously
feeling the need to retreat. While waiting for my
friend, I'd probably opt to sit down with a drink,
taking a moment to gather my thoughts and breathe.
```

Figure 28.4 Sample descriptions for traits
Source: Author

```
# Calculate cosine similarity
similarity_score =
cosine_similarity(response_embedding.unsqueeze(0),
trait_embedding.unsqueeze(0))
# Define inverse traits
inverse_traits = {
    "extraversion": "introversion",
    "openness": "closeness",
    "conscientiousness": "disinhibition",
    "agreeableness": "antagonism",
    "neuroticism": "emotional_stability"
}
# Calculate the similarity for inverse trait
inverse_trait = inverse_traits[trait]
inverse_trait_embeddings =
model.encode(descriptions[inverse_trait],
convert_to_tensor=True)
inverse_trait_similarity =
util.cos_sim(sentence_embedding,
inverse_trait_embeddings).mean().item()
```

Figure 28.5 Calculation of cosine similarity for trait and inverse trait embeddings
Source: Author

enables them to understand and process a wide range of natural language inputs.

However, the results showed a significant deviation from the Likert Scale scores obtained earlier. Therefore, several methods were used to optimize the model and obtain more accurate scores. First, the two extremes of the continuums of each Big Five trait were defined according to [29].

Since this attempt did not yield any significant improvement in the score, further studies were carried out to optimize model performance by including a set of supportive words for the traits (Figure 28.2).

Then, HuggingFace's pipeline with RoBERTa-large-MNLI model was utilized for Zero Shot Classification. ZSL returned confidence scores for each label. Scores were normalized using the softmax function as shown in Figure 28.2.

These were scaled to a 1–5 range for consistency with the Likert-scale scores. However, ZSL yielded mid-range clustering and weak trait differentiation. The approach lacked sensitivity to subtle contextual cues in open-text responses.

Transition to sentence embeddings for text responses

Due to these limitations, further studies were carried out to explore more effective methods of scoring text responses, which resulted in the adoption of sentence embedding techniques. This involves a system where sentences are transformed into vector representations that capture the meaning at the semantic level [30]. Sentence embeddings allow one to transform text into a high-dimensional space where semantic relationships and contextual nuances are preserved.

The stsb-roberta-base model from the sentence-transformers library was selected for generating sentence embeddings due to its strong ability to capture complex linguistic nuances. Its proven effectiveness in NLP tasks makes it a reliable choice for deep semantic analysis required in psychological response evaluation.

Using RoBERTa-base as shown in Figure 28.3, each response is transformed into a high-dimensional vector that captures essential semantic elements and contextual information. This approach enables a more accurate and nuanced assessment of personality traits based on textual data, enhancing both the reliability and validity of the research findings.

Scoring responses against personality traits requires having some benchmark or reference point. In this phase, context-specific descriptions were designed for each personality trait, providing a spectrum of responses that demonstrated varying degrees of the expression of a particular trait, as shown in Figure 28.4. These were encoded as embeddings, against which the participants' responses were matched. This allows for dynamic performance evaluation based on real data rather than static, predefined scales and avoids the inconsistencies seen in Zero-Shot Learning thus far.

Following this, the cosine similarities between the embedding of the participant's response and the embeddings for the target personality traits are computed (see Figure 28.5). This process provides a measure of semantic closeness between the two vectors. The scores range from 0 to 1, where 1 indicates complete similarity and 0 indicates no similarity.

As shown in Figure 28.5, to evaluate balance, each response was also compared against descriptions

```
# Normalize scores to a range of 1 to 5
normalized_score_trait = (trait_similarity - 0) / (1 -
0) * (5-1) + 1
normalized_score_inverse = (inverse_trait_similarity -
0) / (1 - 0) * (5-1) + 1
# Clamp the scores to ensure they stay within 1-5
final_score_trait = max(1, min(5,
normalized_score_trait))
final_score_inverse = max(1, min(5,
normalized_score_inverse))
```

Figure 28.6 Normalization and clamping of trait and inverse trait similarity scores to a 1–5 scale
Source: Author

```
# Determine the final score for the trait
 final_score = (final_score_trait + (5 -
final_score_inverse)) / 2
```

Figure 28.7 Final trait score calculation for text responses
Source: Author

```
def calculate_aggregate_score( mini_ipip_score=None,
text_based_score=None, mini_ipip_weight=0.5,
text_weight=0.5):

    # Check if both scores are provided
    if mini_ipip_score is not None and
text_based_score is not None:

        # Calculate the weighted average
        return (mini_ipip_score * mini_ipip_weight +
text_based_score * text_weight) / (mini_ipip_weight +
text_weight)
    else:
        raise ValueError('score must be provided.')
```

Figure 28.8 Weighted aggregate personality score from Mini-IPIP and Vignette Test assessments
Source: Author

of the opposing trait (e.g., extraversion vs. introversion). These serve to offer balanced insights into personality, helping to eliminate bias that might occur if only a single perspective were considered.

The scores derived from cosine similarity measures were transformed into a format that could be easily interpreted and compared across different traits and respondents by standardizing them to a common scale, usually ranging from 1 to 5 (Figure 28.6).

Finally, to calculate the final scores from sentence embeddings in psychological assessments, a normalization process was applied, as shown in Figure 28.7. This ensured that scores were directly comparable and interpretable. By considering both the trait and its opposite, the method offers a balanced assessment, reducing ambiguity and enhancing clarity. Averaging these scores allows for a more nuanced evaluation that better reflects the complexity of human personality.

Aggregation of scores from 20 mini-IPIP test and vignette test scores

In the current study, a strategic methodological approach is represented by the integration of scores from the Mini-IPIP and the text-based assessment using sentence embeddings to create a comprehensive psychological profile for each participant. This multi-method integration framework is notably supported by psychological research [31].

Research showed that both Mini-IPIP and text-based assessment methods were effective for psychological profiling, which led to the assignment of equal weightage for both methods in the aggregation process. Therefore, scores from the Mini-IPIP and text-based method were averaged with equal weighting as shown in Figure 28.8.

Outlining the expected roles of the two methods used in this study is critical due to their contrasting nature. Although both Mini-IPIP and Sentence Embedding models are used to evaluate the Big Five traits, the aim of this study is to leverage their complementary qualities to create a more comprehensive personality profile as opposed to evaluating their equivalence. The Mini-IPIP offers structured and self-reported insights, while the text model employs natural language to capture behavioral tendencies. This study intentionally focused on complementarity rather than statistical correlation between the two methods, leaving validation for future exploration.

Identification of threshold scores of big five traits in the business analytics field

Further, to establish benchmarks for successful traits specific to professionals in the field of Business Analytics, threshold levels were calculated. These levels were obtained from the average trait scores of the professional sample, which represents the personality configuration that is ideal for success within this field, as suggested by research contributions from vocational and organizational psychology [32]. Computed thresholds provide a reference level against which individual scores can be compared to assist in identifying candidates whose personality traits match up best with the theoretical ideal in the industry.

Deviation analysis and personalized recommendations

After score aggregation, the scores were subjected to deviation analysis comparing undergraduate scores

Table 28.1 Sample personality score output from the likert scale scoring model.

ID	Openness	Conscientiousness	Extraversion	Agreeableness	Neuroticism
001	3.6	4.2	2.5	4.6	4.4
023	4.7	3.6	4.2	3	2.2
062	2.4	3.4	1.3	2.7	3.7
089	5	2.1	3.1	3.6	2.5
112	3.7	4.8	2.8	1.4	1.6

Source: Author

Table 28.2 Sample personality score output from the text scoring model.

ID	Openness	Conscientiousness	Extraversion	Agreeableness	Neuroticism
001	3.3	3.7	3.1	4.2	3.9
023	4.5	3.2	3.9	3.3	1.5
062	2.9	2.6	1.7	2.6	4.4
089	4.6	2.3	3.6	3.1	2.2
112	3.9	4.5	3.2	1.5	1.9

Source: Author

against professional thresholds. Such analysis highlighted specific areas where individuals' traits deviated from those considered optimal for Business Analytics roles.

To address these deviations, a recommendation system using OpenAI's GPT-3.5 was integrated into a Streamlit-based web application. This tool provides undergraduates with personalized feedback and development strategies to align their traits with professional expectations. The system leverages GPT-3.5's ability to generate coherent, context-aware responses, building on foundational work in large-scale language models.

This integration of AI-driven recommendations adds a developmental dimension to the assessment. Instead of only identifying gaps, it supports students in bridging them with targeted self-improvement strategies.

Results and Discussion

As outlined in the methodology, a diverse range of approaches was employed to conduct a comprehensive assessment to analyze the alignment between personality traits and job fit among Business Analytics undergraduates utilizing the Big Five Personality model. Within this section, a thorough explanation of the outcomes derived from these methodologies is provided, offering insights into the specific details of analyzing alignment between personality traits and job fit among Business Analytics undergraduates.

Scoring model for 20 mini-IPIP (likert scale) questionnaire

The model calculates all five personality scores by averaging both original and reverse-scored responses.

Table 28.1 shows the output of the scoring model, where each row represents an individual's averaged scores for the five personality traits. Each score would be computed as the mean value of four relevant questions associated with a particular trait. The OCEAN scores, ranging from 1.0 to 5.0, reflect individual differences in openness, conscientiousness, extraversion, agreeableness, and neuroticism, with higher values indicating stronger trait expression, revealing distinctions such as openness to experience, preferences in organization, sociability levels, cooperative nature, and emotional stability.

The Likert scale response-based scoring model is critical for the research, as it would turn raw Likert scale questionnaire responses into meaningful trait-based insights. It highlights the alignment or misalignment between Big Five personality traits.

Text scoring model with sentence embeddings on vignette test responses

Table 28.2 presents the OCEAN scores computed from the text response model by utilizing text

Table 28.3 Sample personality score output from the aggregated scoring model.

ID	Openness	Conscientiousness	Extraversion	Agreeableness	Neuroticism
001	3.45	3.95	2.8	4.4	4.15
023	4.6	3.4	4.05	3.15	1.85
062	2.65	3	1.5	2.65	4.05
089	4.8	2.2	3.35	3.35	2.35
112	3.8	4.65	3	1.45	1.75

Source: Author

embeddings. This model, which uses the stub-roberta-base transformer, scores the responses of participants against pre-defined descriptions for big five traits. Cosine similarity was used to determine the degree of alignment between responses and trait-specific behavioral expressions.

The values reflect how strongly each participant's written responses correspond to specific personality traits. This data offers an enhanced perspective of their behavioral tendencies and how those would be exhibited in real-life scenarios.

This result provides an independent measure of personality traits, underlining individual behavioral patterns emerging from unstructured text responses. It thus plays a vital role in identifying how participants articulate personality-related behavior when faced with scenario-based challenges.

Aggregated scoring model for big five personality traits

Table 28.3 presents the aggregated OCEAN scores of Business Analytics undergraduates and professionals, obtained by combining outputs from the Mini-IPIP questionnaire and the text-based model with sentence embeddings. The aggregation strategy is based on a 50-50 weighting system to offer a well-balanced psychological profile for each participant.

This method diminishes any potential biases and offsets the limitations in the respective techniques. This is supported by research, which emphasizes that multi-method assessment enhances both reliability and validity since different aspects of personality are captured [32]. It provides a well-rounded profile, with the Mini-IPIP providing structured and direct responses, while this text-based model captures nuanced behaviors through scenario-driven insight.

The aggregation function simply averages the scores from both sources to produce a comprehensive understanding of each individual's personality. Aggregated scores denote both explicit self-concept and implicit behavior and thus allow for more appropriate analyses concerning a personality-job fit for Business Analytics.

Established big five personality threshold scores for the ba field

This determines threshold levels of personality traits considered necessary for Business Analytics (BA) jobs. These threshold scores were derived by aggregating scores from both Mini-IPIP and Vignette Test ratings with equal weighting and calculating the mean scores from the BA professionals' questionnaires. These threshold values would depict the ideal personality profile expected in the field of Business Analytics and thereby provide a benchmark against which the personalities of the undergraduates can be matched for their alignment with the field's expectations.

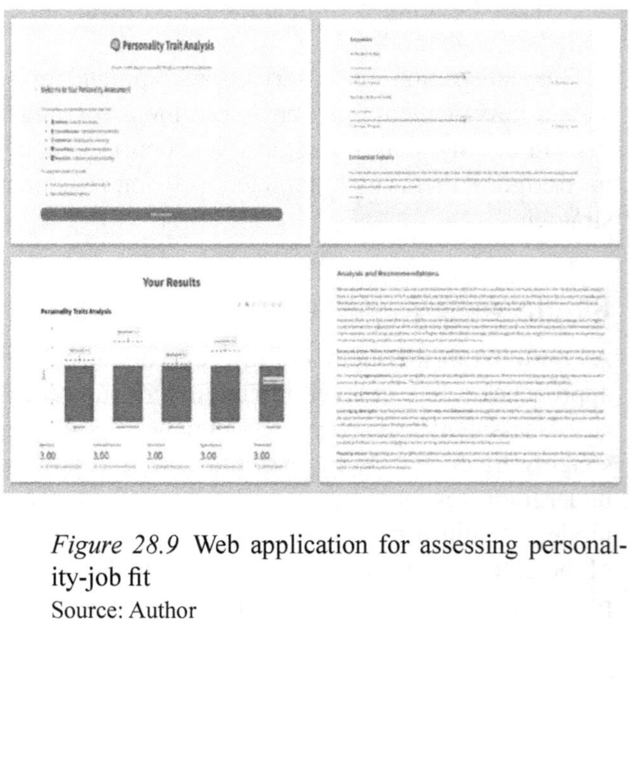

Figure 28.9 Web application for assessing personality-job fit
Source: Author

Table 28.4 Threshold levels for big five traits in business analytics professionals.

Trait	Threshold score	Rounded off threshold Score
Openness (O)	3.3	3
Conscientiousness (C)	4.3	4
Extraversion (E)	3.1	3
Agreeableness (A)	3.8	4
Neuroticism (N)	1.7	2

Source: Author

Table 28.4 shows the identified threshold levels for Business Analytics professionals, derived from the analysis.

The thresholds serve as reference points for evaluating the suitability of undergraduates for Business Analytics roles, making them crucial to the alignment process. By benchmarking undergraduate aggregated scores against these threshold values, the study identifies potential personality-job mismatches and offers targeted recommendations for personal and professional development. This result significantly contributes to the study by emphasizing the optimal personality traits desirable in the Business Analytics field.

Recommendations through web applications

The next outcome of this study was the Recommendation Model developed using GPT 3.5, which was integrated into a Streamlit-based web application and pops up personalized suggestions to improve personality traits upon analyzing the user responses. The web application developed accordingly is shown in Figure 28.9. The application can be accessed via: https://personality-analyzer.onrender.com

The model compares the scores for each user in Openness, Conscientiousness, Extraversion, Agreeableness, and Neuroticism against threshold values. In cases where the user scores lower than that threshold on any of those facets, the model prioritizes that aspect in the recommendation to support personal growth. The recommendations are generated dynamically using structured outputs to ensure responses are in line with the defined psychological framework of the study. This recommendation system bridges the gap between personality analysis and actionable development strategies. It provides participants with meaningful insights into areas for improvement that would help them align better with the personality expectations of Business Analytics roles. This assistive tool can be employed by educational institutions and career advisors to help students in the process of personal and professional development while ensuring that such individuals possess the right attributes to succeed in the field of business analytics. This automated guidance tool provides practical value to the study through its customized advice, making the personality assessment process not merely diagnostic but developmental as well.

Future improvements

Research on GPT-3.5 has demonstrated its impressive capabilities in tackling human-level natural language processing (NLP) tasks, particularly in zero-shot settings [22].

To enhance the accuracy of personality score predictions, future improvements should focus on transitioning the current GPT-3.5-based recommendation engine into a complete large language model (LLM). By implementing a feedback collection process, it will be possible to assess the effectiveness of the model in generating scores and gather user feedback on their accuracy. This will facilitate the collection of a robust database containing diverse personality data with accurate scores.

Once this database is established, it can be used to fine-tune LLMs like GPT-3.5, creating a domain-specific model tailored for accurately predicting personality trait scores. This enhancement will allow the application to extend beyond the Business Analytics domain into various industries, capitalizing on the model's capabilities. This ultimately aims for a more accurate and reliable scoring mechanism.

In addition, the implementation of AI-driven analytics into the above established database could facilitate in identifying the most underdeveloped Big Five traits among undergraduates. Insights from the analysis could be used to apply for curriculum reform and to support the incorporation of soft skills training into academic curricula. This strategy improves the academic relevance of the study and allows higher academic institutions to create well-rounded graduate profiles above self-directed personality development.

Limitations

The scope of the study is only restricted to the University of Moratuwa, Sri Lanka, for the reason that it is currently the only state university in the country to offer a specialized degree in Business Analytics. Consequently, it might not accurately reflect the empirical insights of the broader undergraduate population across other universities or academic fields.

Further, the study's limited focus on the domain of Business Analytics restricts the applicability of its findings across different professional disciplines and cultural contexts, even though it assists in enhancing contextual accuracy. To overcome this limitation, future studies could broaden the sample to incorporate professionals from diverse industries and undergraduates from various specializations.

Conclusion

This study critically analyzes the alignment between the personality scores of undergraduates and job fit, particularly in the business analytics domain. Results emphasized a significant deviation between personality alignment and academic credentials, illustrating that academics often overlook the significance of the personality role in career success.

The study not only signifies the frequently disregarded personality-job fit deviations but also offers reliable and robust techniques for business organizations and educational institutions for integrating personality tests into the processes of recruitment and training. The adoption of these strategies contributes to lowering turnover, enhancing job satisfaction, and creating a collaborative and productive work environment.

Ideal threshold levels for the personality-job fit tailored to the requirements of the business analytics domain were successfully established by the study. It facilitates the assessment of alignment between the undergraduate Big Five trait scores with threshold levels, which highlights the industry requirements. In addition to that, a web application that offers tailored recommendations for Big Five personality development based on undergraduate personality tests was developed. This tool is beneficial for undergraduates to ensure that their personality traits better align with the industry requirements.

This comprehensive analysis not only enhances the awareness of the way personality affects career paths but also provides an extensive approach for the improvement of academic and business analytics industry requirements alignment. This is vital for generating a skilled workforce that is not only professional but well-matched with their job roles and content in their specific professions, thus encouraging a more innovative and adaptive corporate environment.

References

[1] Hurtz, G. M., Donovan, J. J., Thank Kevin Williams, W., Dwight, S., & Salgado, J. (2000). Personality and job performance: the big five revisited. *Journal of Applied Psychology*, 85(6), 869–879. doi: 10.1037/002I-9010.85.6.869.

[2] Penney, L. M., David, E., & Witt, L. A. (2011). A review of personality and performance: identifying boundaries, contingencies, and future research directions. *Human Resource Management Review*, 21(4), 297–310. doi: 10.1016/j.hrmr.2010.10.005.

[3] Richardson, M., Abraham, C., & Bond, R. (2012). Psychological correlates of university students' academic performance: a systematic review and meta-analysis. *Psychological Bulletin*, 138(2), 353–387. doi: 10.1037/a0026838.

[4] Briley, D. A., & Tucker-Drob, E. M. (2014). Genetic and environmental continuity in personality development: a meta-analysis. *Psychological Bulletin*, 140(5), 1303–1331. doi: 10.1037/a0037091.

[5] Fraley, R. C. Roisman, G. Booth-LaForce, I. C. Owen, M. T. & Holland, A. S. (2013). Interpersonal and genetic origins of adult attachment styles: A longitudinal study from infancy to early adulthood, J. Pers. Soc. Psychol., vol. 104, no. 5, pp. 817–838. doi: 10.1037/a0031435.

[6] Bartram, D. (2005). The Great Eight competencies: A criterion-centric approach to validation, J. Appl. Psychol., vol. 90, no. 6, pp. 1185–1203. doi: 10.1037/0021-9010.90.6.1185.

[7] Barrick, M. R. Mount, M. K. & Judge, T. A. (2001). Personality and performance at the beginning of the new millennium: What do we know and where do we go next?, Int. J. Sel. Assess., vol. 9, no. 1–2, pp. 9–30. doi: 10.1111/1468-2389.00160.

[8] Poropat, A. E. (2009). A meta-analysis of the five-factor model of personality and academic performance. *Psychological Bulletin*, 135(2), 322–338. doi: 10.1037/a0014996.

[9] Armstrong, M. (2008). Strategic Human Resource Management: A Guide to Action, 4th ed. London, U.K.: Kogan Page.

[10] Huselid M. A. & Becker, B. E. (1996). Methodological issues in cross-sectional and panel estimates

of the human resource–firm performance link, Ind. Relat. J. Econ. Soc., vol. 35, no. 3, pp. 400–422. doi: 10.1111/j.1468-232X.1996.tb00413.x.

[11] Moraes, R. Pilankar, M. Pinto, L. L. & P. Rane, (2020). Personality assessment using social media for hiring candidates, in Proc. 3rd Int. Conf. Commun. Syst., Comput. IT Appl. (CSCITA). pp. 192–197, doi: 10.1109/CSCITA47329.2020.9137796.

[12] Markus, H. R., & Kitayama, S. (1998). The cultural psychology of personality. *Journal of Cross-Cultural Psychology*, 29(1), 63–87. doi: 10.1177/0022022198291004.

[13] Al-Adamat, O, Atoum, A. Wardat, Y. Alali, R. Al-Saud, K. & Helali, M. (2025). The Predictive Ability of the Big Five Personality Traits in Self Among University Students, Educational Process: International Journal, vol. 16, Art. no. e2025225. doi: 10.22521/edupij.2025.16.225.

[14] Anglim, J., Horwood, S., Smillie, L. D., Marrero, R. J., & Wood, J. K. (2020). Predicting psychological and subjective well-being from personality: a meta-analysis. *Psychological Bulletin*, 146(4), 279. doi: 10.1037/bul0000226.

[15] Luo, J., Derringer, J., Briley, D. A., Roberts, B. W. (2017). Genetic and environmental pathways underlying personality traits and perceived stress: concurrent and longitudinal twin studies. *European Journal of Personality*, 31(6), 614–629. doi: 10.1002/per.2127.

[16] Vukasović T. & Bratko, D. (2015). Heritability of personality: A meta-analysis of behavior genetic studies, Psychol. Bull., vol. 141, no. 4, pp. 769–785. doi: 10.1037/bul0000017.

[17] Kraaykamp, G., & van Eijck, K. (2005). Personality, media preferences, and cultural participation. *Personality and Individual Differences*, 38(7), 1675–1688. doi: 10.1016/j.paid.2004.11.002.

[18] Luo, J., Zhang, B., Antonoplis, S., & Mroczek, D. K. (2024). The effects of socioeconomic status on personality development in adulthood and aging. *Journal of Personality*, 92(1), 243–260. doi: 10.1111/jopy.12801.

[19] Rohmah, T. A. S., & Maharani, W. (2022). Personality detection on twitter social media using IndoBERT method. *Building of Informatics, Technology and Science (BITS)*, 4(2), 448–453. doi: 10.47065/bits.v4i2.1895.

[20] Yin, W. Hay, J. and Roth, D. (2019). Benchmarking zero-shot text classification: Datasets, evaluation and entailment approach, in Proc. EMNLP-IJCNLP. pp. 3913–3923, doi: 10.18653/v1/D19-1404.

[21] Brown T. B., et al., (2020). Language models are few-shot learners, in Adv. Neural Inf. Process. Syst. (NeurIPS), vol. 33. doi: 10.48550/arXiv.2005.14165.

[22] Ghojogh B. & Ghodsi, A. (2020). Attention mechanism, Transformers, BERT, and GPT: Tutorial and survey, OSF Preprints. doi: 10.31219/osf.io/mru2x.

[23] Floridi, L., & Chiriatti, M. (2020). GPT-3: Its Nature, Scope, Limits, and Consequences. Springer Science and Business Media B.V. doi: 10.1007/s11023-020-09548-1.

[24] Ijigu, A. W., Alemu, A. E., & Kuhil, A. M. (2023). High-performance work system and employee work performance: a moderated mediation model of ambidextrous leadership and employee ambidexterity. *International Journal of Business Science and Applied Management*, 18(1), 46–62. doi: 10.69864/ijbsam.18-1.170.

[25] Zaman, U., Nawaz, S., Shafique, O., & Rafique, S. (2021). Making of rebel talent through workplace ostracism: a moderated-mediation model involving emotional intelligence, organizational conflict and knowledge sharing behavior. *Cogent Business and Management*, 8(1), 1941586. doi: 10.1080/23311975.2021.1941586.

[26] Kwantes, P. J., Derbentseva, N., Lam, Q., Vartanian, O., & Marmurek, H. H. C. (2016). Assessing the big five personality traits with latent semantic analysis. *Personality and Individual Differences*, 102, 229–233. doi: 10.1016/j.paid.2016.07.010.

[27] Czerwiński, S. K., & Atroszko, P. A. (2020). Scores of short and free scale for Big Five explain perceived stress at different stages of life: validity, reliability and measurement invariance of the Polish adaptation of Mini-IPIP. *Current Issues in Personality Psychology*, 8(1), 73–82. doi: 10.5114/cipp.2020.95149.

[28] Alhoshan, W., Ferrari, A., & Zhao, L. (2023). Zero-shot learning for requirements classification: An exploratory study. *Information and Software Technology*, 159, 107202. doi: 10.1016/j.infsof.2023.107202.

[29] Karra, S. R., Nguyen, S. T., & Tulabandhula, T. (2022). Estimating the personality of white-box language models, arXiv Preprint, arXiv:2204.12000.

[30] Huilgol, P. (2020). Top 4 sentence embedding techniques using Python, Analytics Vidhya, Aug. 20. [Online]. Available: https://www.analyticsvidhya.com/blog/2020/08/top-4-sentence-embedding-techniques-using-python/.

[31] Ong A. D. & Weiss, D. J. (2000). The impact of anonymity on responses to sensitive questions, J. Appl. Soc. Psychol., vol. 30, no. 8, pp. 1691–1708. doi: 10.1111/j.1559-1816.2000.tb02462.x.

[32] Carpintero, H. (2023). A pioneer project of a school psychotechnic center (1920). *Revista de Psicologia del Trabajo y de las Organizaciones*, 39(1), 1–5. doi: 10.5093/JWOP2023A4.

29 Generative AI and copyright law: a comparative study on copyright protection for AI generated audio-visual works in Sri Lanka, the US and India

H.M.Oshan N. Piumantha[a]

Department of Marketing and Tourism Management, NSBM Green University, Sri Lanka

Abstract

Generative artificial intelligence (AI) technology is increasingly used across various fields. It is particularly prominent in creative industries such as television, film, advertising, gaming, and entertainment. Despite its creative application, AI technology raises certain legal and ethical issues at a global level. This research investigates whether audio visual works generated through generative AI technology are protected under international copyright law. The qualitative method was used for this study, and the primary data included the Sri Lanka Intellectual Property Act No. 36 of 2003, the Indian Copyright Act (1957), and the US Copyright Act (1976) which were studied in a comparative manner, and the main case study was 'Suryast AI Image'. The data were analyzed under the thematic analysis method, and how authorship, ownership, exclusive right, and moral right are addressed within the copyright law of the three countries. This research confirmed that Sri Lanka, the United States and India currently lack legal provisions to protect AI-generated artwork under their existing copyright laws. The lack of legal consensus on who is the author of an AI-generated work is the main problem with granting copyright to an AI-generated work. Establishing a clear definition of authorship AI-generated work, protection for AI-generated audio-visual works can potentially be provided either through existing copyright laws or via new legislative amendments. Since AI has created the next era of art, the protection of a copyright legal framework for it has become urgent.

Keywords: Copyright law, generative artificial intelligence, India, Sri Lanka, United States

Introduction

Technology is the application of conceptual knowledge in a particularly reproducible manner to accomplish practical goals. Technology has evolved from the Stone Age to the present. Modern technology has rapidly transformed all sectors of society. That's how modern technology has spread its dominance to every field. Technology has shaped human society significantly throughout history, impacting everything from transportation and communication to health, agriculture, and warfare. It has revolutionarily changed the way people live, work, and connect with the world around people. It has also revolutionized industries and transformed economies. Through the study of technological history, people may learn about the advancements, difficulties, challenges, and effects of human creativity and inventiveness throughout history.

Artificial intelligence (AI) has ushered in a booming new era of technological advancement. Computer programs that possess the ability to carry out activities that typically need human intelligence are referred to as AI. Generative Artificial Intelligence refers to system that can produce novel, unique content. It creates data that matches the training data it was trained on using machine learning models, which are frequently based on techniques like generative adversarial networks (GANs). Applications for this technology include generating text, generating images, music composition, and others. It makes it possible to provide novel, realistic material with a range of creative practical uses. It is also important to create different types of software to create artworks that are generated using AI. Generative AI generates relevant artwork by training data sets and providing relevant prompts upon receiving certain input. But while these artworks have not yet surpassed human creativity, there are signs in the technological world that they will soon.

Human creativity is generated due to human factors such as experience, imagination, education etc.

[a]osha.p@nsmb.ac.lk

DOI: 10.4324/9781003739920-29

According to the famous photographer Johne Loori, "Creativity is our birthright. It is an integral part of being human, as basic as walking, talking, and thinking' [1]. However, in modern times, it is seen how AI, which is consolidating its supremacy in a revolutionary way, is working to imitate human creativity. Along with technology, art also changed, developed, and modernized. At each time, many people complained that the joining of modern technical methods with art is a challenge to the traditional art field and the artist. But those new technologies were not a threat or a hindrance to art and the traditional artists began to adapt to it and innovatively make their creations. The example, when the use of technical software such as Photoshop began, artists saw it as a challenge to their industry. But with time it started to be understood that it is not a dangerous thing but just another creative technological tool.

Although Generative AI has been used in many fields, it has not achieved enough technological progress to challenge human intelligence, logic, thinking, and creativity. The central focus of this research is on the work generated for audio-visual media. The term "audiovisual media" describes media formats, including movies, TV shows, videos, multimedia presentations, social media content, games, and advertisements that incorporate audio and visual components. It engages the audience and communicates information by integrating visual and audio elements. This research is limited to generative AI artworks generated for audio-visual media. Accordingly, copyright protection is provided to generative AI artworks generated for audio-visual media will be researched here.

The World Intellectual Property Organization has defined copyright, 'Copyright (or author's right) is a legal term used to describe the rights that creators have over their literary and artistic works. Works covered by copyright range from books, music, paintings, sculpture, and films, to computer programs, databases, advertisements, maps, and technical drawings. To safeguard artists' intellectual property, provide them with exclusive rights to their creations, and encourage innovation, copyright legislation is essential. It protects the preservation of cultural manifestations and encourages inventiveness by offering financial incentives. In addition to supporting lives and economic progress, copyright enhances the creative industries' economic worth. Furthermore, laws on copyright offer a worldwide standard, promote international collaboration, and broadly safeguard the rights of artists. To put it briefly, copyright law is critical to promoting innovation, encouraging creators, and safeguarding the vibrancy of the arts and industry. Copyright law does a great job of protecting artists and their creations. Copyright laws have been enacted to protect human creations and creators around the world, and there is no systematic legal system to protect AI based creators and artworks. Generative AI art is opposed to copyright protection for several reasons. Some argue for the automatic release of AI artwork into the public domain, highlighting authorship issues brought forth by the lack of direct human contribution. Further concerns include possible barriers to technical advancement, ethical issues such as biases in AI algorithms, and how appropriate current copyright laws are to the unique characteristics of audio-visual artworks generated by AI.

In a background where Generative AI is expanding rapidly to many fields, a strong conversation has been created in the world about the authenticity of copyright law, especially for generative AI work. Although there is still no globally accepted copyright legal framework for generative AI artworks, some countries are working to provide copyright protection for generative AI creations under existing copyright laws. Several well-known court cases have arisen about generative AI artworks. Some of these have been refused copyright by the courts, and some cases are still pending. However, in the future, generative AI creations will be used in many industries such as entertainment and creative industries. Preventing or countering it will never be possible in a digital society and the entire society will have to adapt to it. Therefore, there should be legislation for AI and through this research, it specially emphasized the necessity of a special copyright law for generative AI artworks.

Literature Review

The world changed gradually from prehistoric periods to the present, mostly due to human intelligence. A paper published by Stanford University has defined intelligence as the ' ability to learn and perform suitable techniques to solve problems and achieve goals, appropriate to the context in an uncertain, ever-varying world [2]. Thus, Artificial Intelligence has been spreading its dominance to many fields of the world for decades because of the technological efforts to achieve human intelligence as a machine.

Emeritus professor John McCarthy, known as the father of Artificial Intelligence, contributed significantly to the field. According to McCarthy, "It is the science and engineering of making intelligent machines, especially intelligent computer programs. It is related to the similar task of using computers to understand human intelligence, but AI does not have to confine itself to methods that are biologically observable" [3]. Generative AI is a branch of AI, and it is a network of technical AI systems that can generate new content that is not explicitly programmed and can generate text, audio, imagery, video and synthetic data.

Generative AI models are being created day by day and for example, Style GAN generates diverse, realistic images while MuseNet, Suno AI creates music across genres and instruments. GPT demonstrates versatility through text generation in various domains and formats. Models like DALL-E, Midjourney, and Stable Diffusion can generate images from text prompts [4]. According to K Egon, Russell J's research paper [5], the role of Artificial Intelligence in art and creativity is filed under several categories.

Anderson defined Audio-Visual media as "a series of electronic images with an audio element and thus an image element drawn by a videotape and played by a video player" [6]. According to Babara [7] Using both mechanical and electrical equipment, audio-visual content is produced and delivered to convey audio-visual messages. There are different tools and channels utilized in AV communication, including video, animation, motion graphics, slides and presentation software, interactive presentations, digital signage, professional sound systems, and streaming and webcasts.

AI has completely changed the Audio-Visual business by changing several production processes. The creation of AI-generated content involves the use of machine learning algorithms to analyse and generate new content based on existing data and these algorithms can be trained using a variety of techniques, including deep learning, natural language processing, and computer vision [8]. Artificial intelligence (AI) technology is being used increasingly creating music videos, opening new creative paths, and revolutionizing the process. With the help of AI platforms and tools like Kaiber.ai, Pictory.ai, and Midjourney, artists may experiment with motion graphics, audio generation, and AI-generated images depending on certain inputs. Generative AI is used extensively in new media to generate audio-visual content and seems to be taking over creative dominance in all media in a revolutionary way.

Legal protection is required for the original creations that are guided by human intelligence, and for that reason, legal arrangements have been made to protect intellectual property at the global level. Intellectual property rights are the rights given to people over the creations of their minds. They usually give the creator an exclusive right over the use of his/her creation for a certain period [9]. Among the various forms of intellectual property, copyright plays an important role in protecting creative works across multiple disciplines. Copyright has been defined by the World Intellectual Property Organization ''Copyright (or author's right) is a legal term used to describe the rights that creators have over their literary and artistic works. Works covered by copyright range from books, music, paintings, sculpture, and films, to computer programs, databases, advertisements, maps, and technical drawings' [10]. Protecting and compensating artists for their work is the aim of copyright. It encourages authors to produce fresh work continuously. Work must fulfill two primary requirements to be eligible for copyright protection:

a) Originality: The work should be inspired by something, not just a copy of something that already exists. It must be an original work of art.
b) Fixation: The work must be written down, saved on a computer, or otherwise documented in a concrete format. By doing this, the work's tangible presence is guaranteed [11].

Although copyright laws only focus on human creations, there is no direct provision in copyright acts regarding how that law applies to Generative Artificial Intelligence-based creations. According to the US Copyright Office [12] in the latest version of its Compendium 'The U.S. Copyright Office will register an original work of authorship, provided that the work was created by a human being'. This is confirmed by the US Copyright Office's refusal to grant copyright registration to several creations generated using AI.

copyright provisions of the Sri Lanka Intellectual Property Act, No. 36 of 2003's the 6th section of the Act mentions 11 works protected by copyright in Sri Lanka and these protected works cover literary, artistic, and scientific work, including computer programs, books, speeches, stage production, musical compositions, audiovisual works, architecture, fine art, photography, applied art, and different kinds of maps or scientific representations [13] but the Act does not directly or indirectly mention the legal protection provided to AI-generated atudio visual works. Protection can be provided under 'pictorial works' under US copyright law and 'Artistic works' under Indian copyright law. As stated in a recent study [8] Copyright is fundamentally a human-centric concept, grounded in the exercise of human creativity and expression. As long as AI systems lack consciousness, intentionality and the ability to experience emotions, AI-generated works do not possess the essential qualities that copyright law seeks to protect.

But the problem becomes that it is AI generated and there is no legal reference in any copyright act as to who is the author of AI artworks.

Method

This research adopted a qualitative methodology to investigate how copyright framework in India, the United States, and Sri Lanka deal with the issue of audiovisual works generated by AI. To gain a deeper understanding of the subject, the study focused on understanding legal texts and court decisions rather than relying solely on data or statistics.

This study conducts a comparative legal analysis of copyright laws in United States Copyright Act of 1976, the Indian Copyright Act of 1957, and the Sri Lankan Intellectual Property Act No. 36 of 2003, focusing on statutory provisions and relevant case law.Three of these countries were selected because of their levels of technological adaptability, membership in international copyright treaties like the Berne Convention, and distinct legal systems (common law vs. civil law component). These copyright acts were carefully analyzed and compared to find parallels and differences in how each countries handles authorship, ownership, exclusive rights, and moral rights in relation to AI-generated content.

The study employed a real-world example as a case study in addition to legal texts, the "Suryast AI image" generated by the AI program RAGHAV. This case was selected because it demonstrates the difficulties and differences in national laws relating to copyright protection for works of art generated by Artificial Intelligence.

The research employed thematic analysis to examine the data. This study conducted a thematic legal analysis of legislative texts and case precedents in order to answer research concerns about authorship, ownership, and protection of AI-generated audiovisual works. This indicates that the researcher found important topics in the case study and the legal framework, particularly in the way that each country's laws define and apply the ideas of authorship, ownership, exclusive rights, and moral rights to works generated by AI. Using this approach, the study sought to identify gaps in existing legal frameworks and make recommendations on how copyright regulations should be strengthened to accommodate the expanding application of AI in the creative industries. This research is limited to legal concerns surrounding copyright protection for AI-generated audiovisual content and does not explore the consequences of patents or trademarks or works outside of creative industries

Results and Discussion

Background of the case

Ankit Sahni is an intellectual property lawyer as well as a multidisciplinary artist. The case of the 'Suryast AI image' he created is used for studies here. As one of his funded projects, Ankit Sahni hired a technologist to create an AI app called 'Ragav'. Raghav Gupta, a machine learning engineer, created this AI painting app as one of his commissioned works. Two images have been used for this creation. One of them was a photograph he had taken, and the other was Vincent Van Gogh's Starry Night. According to Sahni's overview of how RAGHAV works, he has control over how much "style transfer" occurs from the style input in the application. The resulting image was an adaptation of the original shot in the style of Van Gogh's painting [14].

Ankit Sahni has submitted this creation for copyright in India, the United States, and Canada. As a revolutionary decision, India has offered co-authorship for the creation. The Suryast AI image has been submitted twice to the US Copyright Office for copyright. Both registration applications were rejected by the US Copyright Office. The lack of human authorship became the primary factor that influenced the rejection of copyright offices for this creation.

Suryast AI image case Analysis with US and Indian copyrights Laws

Protective work

Copyright law should include what works can be protected under the law. Also, it should be clearly mentioned which works cannot be given copyright protection. In the US and Indian copyright act, the copyright law has clearly stated which works are protected. In the us copyright act protected works are specified under eight works. But in the Indian Copyright Act protected works are defined under three sections (a,b,c). In the Indian Copyright Act, the protected works are mentioned under three parts A, B, and C. A problem arises that only a few very limited types of works are protected. This issue arises because pictorial, graphic, and sculptural works are not directly mentioned as protective works in the Indian Act, as in the US Copyright Act. Although it is not directly mentioned as such, pictorial, graphic, and sculptural works are included as protected works under the work mentioned as 'artistic work' in the Indian Copyright Act.

When analyzed in 'Suryast Image', its output falls under the category of protected works. Protection can be provided under 'pictorial works' under US copyright law and 'artistic works' under Indian copyright law. But the problem becomes that it is AI generated and there is no legal reference in any copyright act as to who is the author of AI artworks. Copyright law generally requires a human author. AI-generated works lack a traditional human author, leading to uncertainty about who should own the rights. Therefore, although the artwork of Suryast Image belongs to the categories of protected works under 'pictorial works' and 'artistic works' mentioned in the copyright laws, since there is no authorship for that image, it is not possible to provide copyright protection.

Authorship

By discussing the Suryast AI image, it is possible to comparatively discuss how the Indian and US copyright laws deal with generative AI works. In the US, Suryast refused to grant copyright registration, and in India, it was rejected after being granted a co-authorship. Human authorship is not directly mentioned in the US Copyright Act, it is stated that in order to provide copyright protection for a certain work, it must be a human creation. It is stated in the C O M P E N D I U M: Chapter 300 of 'Copyrightable Authorship: What Can Be Registered' issued by the US Copyright Office. The copyright law only protects "the fruits of intellectual labor" that "are founded in the creative powers of the mind." Trade-Mark Cases, 100 U.S. 82, 94 (1879). Because copyright law is limited to "original intellectual conceptions of the author," the Office will refuse to register a claim if it determines that a human being did not create the work. Burrow-Giles Lithographic Co. v. Sarony, 111 U.S. 53, 58 (1884). For representative examples of works that do not satisfy this requirement [15]. Works created by plants, animals, or the natural world will not be registered by the U.S. Copyright Office. Similarly, the Office may register a work if the application or deposit copy(ies) specify that the work was inspired by a divine spirit, but it cannot register a work that is allegedly the creation of divine or supernatural creatures.

US Copyright Law does not grant copyright ownership on behalf of non-humans. A good example of that is the monkey selfie case. In the Naruto v. Slater case, which included many selfies shot by the Indonesian monkey Naruto using Slater's wildlife photography equipment, the subject of whether animals may be authors was brought up. Both Slater and Wildlife Personalities Ltd. were named as the copyright owners of the images when they were published in a book by themselves. Slater does acknowledge in the book, though, that Naruto took the pictures. As Naruto's next friend, People for the Ethical Treatment of Animals (PETA) filed a copyright infringement case against Slater and Wildlife Personalities Ltd. in 2015. The US Court of Appeals for the Ninth Circuit upheld the district court's rejection of the lawsuit, citing Naruto's lack of ability to file a copyright lawsuit. The reason for this was that the United States Copyright Act does not specifically permit animals to bring legal action for copyright infringement under the legislation.

Although Ankit Sahni applied for the US Copyright to obtain the copyright registration for the Suryast AI image, the US Copyright Office refused to grant the copyright registration every time. The main reason for this was the lack of human Authorship and too many machines. The Office will not register works produced by random or automatic machines or purely mechanical processes without the creative input or intervention of a human author. According to the US Copyright Office in the latest version of its Compendium 'The U.S. Copyright Office will register an original work of authorship, provided that the work was created by a human being'.

Although Section 2(d) of the Indian Copyright Act mentions authorship, it does not directly state that the author must be a human being. However, when analyzing the copyright act, it emphasizes human authorship. For that, it is important to study articles 22 and 51 of the act. The term copyright in this section is defined as the lifetime of the author plus 60 years from the beginning of the year following the author's death. This examines authorship from the perspective of a natural lifetime. The copyright infringement by a "person" is covered in section 51. It should be clarified that the term "person" as applied to "natural individual" has been used instead of more generalized wording.In judicial precedents, when some problems related to authorship arise, courts have emphasized the factors of intelligence and human creativity are taken into account to grant authorship. For instance, the Supreme Court considered originality resulting from the author's skill and labor in Eastern Book Company v. D.B. Modak. This is the only place where the Act is using the word 'computer generated'. The issue of the 'Author' can be solved legally, or the existing copyright law permits that but the concept of work technically and its parameters to fulfil as 'work' in copyright legal regime is complex'.

In the comparative study of the Suryast AI image and the Indian copyright law, it is problematic on what basis they gave co-authorship to that creation. Ankit Sahni first claimed copyright for this image only for the Raghav AI app. However, it was rejected by the Indian copyright office. The rejection appears to be legitimate as there is no legal provision in the Indian Copyright Act to provide copyright for an AI app. After Raghav refused to grant sole copyright to the app, he applied Ankit Sahni and Raghav to register the app as co-authors, and accordingly, co-authorship was granted to the Suryast AI image. For AI artwork, it is not problematic to give co-authorship to the relevant AI service or app as well as to the person who generated the artwork using it. But here the problem becomes what are the provisions and sentences within the Copyright Act that affected the granting of copyright registration for an AI artwork. It is a problem whether this type of AI creation can be registered under the joint authorship mentioned in the act. In order to grant copyright registration for work, there must be clear authorship. However, the authorship of this AI creation is controversial. However, the registration was withdrawn less than a year after it was granted, possibly due to these legal issues.

Ownership

The employer or commissioning party is considered the author and is granted the copyright as though it were the real author if a work is made "for hire" within the meaning of the Copyright Act. That is, the AI app named Raghav was created by a person named Raghav Gupta according to the needs of Ankit Sahni. So, it comes under work made for hire. In such a case the employer or commissioning party is considered the author and gets the copyright as the true author. Therefore, the person who created the AI app, Raghav, has only moral rights. Ankit Sahni clearly owns this Suryast AI image, if it is not an AI image according to US copyright law. However, since there is no ability to assign authorship to AI creations according to US copyright law, ownership rights are also lost.

According to the Indian Copyright Law [16], the ownership of a work belongs to its first author. It is important to have a clear understanding of who is the first author.

Analyzing the matter related to the Suryast AI image according to the Indian copyright law, if the image was a normal human creation, its ownership belongs to Ankit Sahni, who becomes the author of that creation. However, since this is an AI creation, the determination of ownership is unclear as copyright law does not specify who owns the original authorship. But it is questionable on what basis the Indian Copyright Office gave co-authorship to this image.

Exclusive rights

Owners have the right to make copies of their original works and to reproduce, distribute, perform, exhibit, and create derivative works from them. It is equally recognized in Indian and US copyright law. The author owns the exclusive right to any creation and can transfer it to other parties by agreement. However, the work done under the provision of work made for hire is subject to changes. According to

Table 29.1 Original authorship of a work according to copyright law.

S.NO	Type of work	Author of work
1	Literary or Dramatic Work	The Author
2	Musical Work	The composer
3	Cinematograph Film	The Producer
4	Sound Recording	The Producer
5	Photograph	The Photographer
6	Computer Generated Work	The person who instructs or causes the creation

Source: Author

Indian copyright law, for a certain work, an exclusive right is entitled only during the lifetime of the author and for 60 years after his death. According to US copyright law, exclusive rights are held only during the lifetime of the author and 70 years after his death. But for work made for hire, the term of copyright addresses 95 years from publication or 120 years from creation, indicating which one expires first.

Analyzing this matter, there is no obstacle in the existing Indian and US copyright law to grant exclusive rights to an AI creation. But even though there is a possibility to offer exclusive rights for it as a creation, it is problematic to assign it to whom. The reason for this is that there is no mention of authorship of AI creations in the copyright law of both these countries. If the authorship of a work is clearly defined, the Act has the necessary legal provisions to grant exclusive rights without any problem. While discussing Suryast AI image, there is no problem according to the US and Indian copyright laws regarding granting of exclusive rights to that image. The problem is that this is an AI creation. If this was a normal human creation, giving the copyright to Ankit Sahni would not be a problem according to the copyright laws of both countries. But here the problems arise because there is no clear legal provision in the US and Indian copyright law about who they assign the authorship of a work to.

Moral rights

While discussing moral rights under Indian and US copyright laws, creators are given the right to be recognized as the authors of their works and to protect the integrity of those works. This means that they have the right to claim copyright and to prevent any modification, distortion or use of their work that could damage their reputation or honour. These rights are distinct from economic rights and are intended to protect the personal and artistic relationship between creators and their creations. A distinction can be discerned from an analytical study of moral rights in the US and Indian Copyright Law. US copyright law provides moral rights only for "works of visual art," while Indian copyright law applies moral rights to all types of works. US gives moral rights only to visual works because visual works are tangible and visible, they are largely granted moral rights under copyright law, hence facilitating a direct relationship between the creator and their work. Protecting an artist's artistic vision and intent requires safeguarding their integrity, attribution, and control over modifications.

If discuss the matter related to Suryast AI image, moral rights can be given for it according to Indian and US copyright law. Although India gives moral rights to all types of works, US copyright law gives moral rights only to visual works, so Suryast, which is a visual work. Moral rights can be given for the image, but the problem is that it is AI-generated work. Although it belongs to the category of works that can be given moral rights, there is no possibility of moral rights because there is no possibility of giving authorship to an artwork created through artificial intelligence. Moral rights are given to the author of a work. But if it is clearly determined legally who is the author of the Suryast AI image, that person can be given moral rights.

Comparative analysis Sri Lankan copyright Law with US and Indian Copyright Law

Protective works

In relation to this research, the basic themes selected under the thematic study, Sri Lanka, India, and US copyright laws have been compared above. The copyright law mentioned in the IP Act of those countries is stated in this way. Similarities as well as some differences in the copyright laws of these three countries can be clearly revealed through this. Since these three countries belong to the Berne Convention, many similarities can be seen in copyright law. This research focuses on AI works for audiovisual media. According to the existing copyright laws of these three countries, it can be comparatively studied whether the artworks made for audio-visual media are protected works or not. Especially under protected works in Sri Lanka under (f) audiovisual works, according to the US Copyright Law (6) motion pictures and other audiovisual works, and according to the Indian Copyright Law (b) cinematograph films, protection has been provided primarily for audiovisual works.

But these protected works are those with clear human contribution. Provides protection for creative artworks made using human intelligence. Since there was no clear discourse about AI in the world at the time when copyright law was compiled in these three countries, such a thing was not directly included in the copyright law. Therefore, under protective works, the works that are made based on human intelligence are mentioned. For that reason, there is no direct ability to provide copyright protection for AI audiovisual art works, even though these protective works belong to the category. Also, for these works to become protective works, clear authorship is required, and the lack of inclusion in the copyright law regarding the authorship of AI works is another reason why AI works do not become protective works.

Authorship

According to the copyright law of US, India, and Sri Lanka, it should be studied comparatively whether they can offer authorship for AI creations. According to the copyright law of Sri Lanka, the author is the physical person who creates a certain work. But that physical person can never grant authorship of AI creations. How much human contribution the physical person mentioned here gives to a certain work cannot be evaluated in an AI work. Because compared to the human contribution made by a person as a human creation, the human contribution applied to an AI creation is relatively minimal. Applying the traditional copyright concept of "authorship" to AI-generated works is challenging because AI, by its very nature, operates autonomously or semi-autonomously once it is programmed or trained. In Indian copyright law, authorship is defined as human authorship, so it is not appropriate to apply that authorship to AI works. US copyright law states that human authorship is essential to confer authorship. That 'compendium of the US. Copyright office practices, Third Edition' clearly stated. Creations without human authorship are expressly rejected by the Copyright Office. Several cases are reported from the US about that. Also, in the last few years, several AI creations have been submitted to the US Copyright Office for registration, and they have refused to grant copyright due to 'lack of human authorship' and 'too much machine'.

Ownership

Analyzing copyright ownership, copyright law in all three countries assigns ownership to the original author. The original author can transfer ownership by contract. The person who owns the work is entitled to economic residence, the responsibility of making decisions regarding that work, etc. Under copyright law, for human works, the author who creates it also gets ownership related to the work.

According to that, the person with ownership gets the right to transfer the work to another person or organization in terms of an agreement. However, in these three countries, it is also problematic to give AI ownership as AI authorship is not recognized in these three countries. If the AI author is clearly defined and included in the copyright act, the granting of AI ownership is not problematic according to the copyright law of these three countries. After that, according to the AI author's free will, the work can be transferred to another person or organization by agreement. If the AI work is in some way joint authorship, the several authors also have co-ownership.

Exclusive rights

Under the exclusive right, Sri Lanka, India, and the US offer exclusive rights to the owner of the work. In these three countries, the original author is given as the owner. The original author can contract ownership of the work to another party. In this way, if the right of the work is given to another party, the one who owns ownership will have exclusive rights related to the work. In this way, if the ownership is not assigned to another person, the original author will be the owner of the work.

According to the exclusive rights of the existing copyright law in these three countries, problems arise as to who is granted exclusive rights for AI-generated work. Thus, problems arise because none of these three countries have defined precisely who is the author of an AI-generated work in the copyright law of these three countries.

Because in order to grant exclusive rights for a certain work, mandatory authorship is required. Determining the "human author" of a work generated by AI is difficult because different parties contribute to the work in different stages. According to the existing copyright law in these three countries, the problem of granting exclusive rights is because the author of AI-generated works has not been legally recognized. Therefore, if the 'author of the AI works' is specifically mentioned in the copyright act, there is no problem with giving ownership of the creation to reproduce, distribute, broadcast, or communicate according to the exclusive rights of the existing copyright laws.

Moral rights

Moral rights are a set of rights that protect the personal and reputational interests of an author or creator. Moral rights have been mentioned in the copyright laws of Sri Lanka, India, and the US. In the copyright law of Sri Lanka and India, moral rights are granted to the author for any type of protective work, but according to US copyright law, moral rights are granted only to visual artworks. Therefore, according to US copyright law, moral rights are not conferred on audiovisual works. However, in order to grant moral rights for AI works, it is necessary to legally establish who should be granted the copyrights of the AI work. After this confirmation, it is possible to provide AI works according to the existing copyright laws of Sri Lanka and India. It can provide protection for the personal and reputational interests of the author of the AI work

However, according to US copyright law, moral rights are provided only for works of visual arts. Therefore, even after determining who is the author of an AI work, the existing copyright law does not hold moral rights for audio-visual works generated through AI technology.

Conclusion

The emergence of generative AI technology has significantly transformed creative industries, particularly audio-visual woks [18]. However, this rapid evolution has exposed critical gaps and problematic situations in existing copyright legal frameworks, particularly regarding authorship and ownership of AI generated works. Through a comparative analysis of Sri Lankan Intellectual Act No.36 of 2003, United states Copyright Act (1976), the Indian Copyright Act (1957), this research has shown none of these legal frameworks currently provide clear legal recognition or protection for works Generated using AI.

The main challenge is the traditional legal acceptance that copyright protection only applies to works created by human authors. There is no legally recognized definition of authorship of AI generated works in existing copyright laws, so there is no consistent basis on which generative AI works can be protected. The case study of 'Suryast' AI image further emphasizes the complexity of this issue and demonstrate how legal ambiguity can interfere with the rights and interests of creators and users of AI technologies.

According to the research results, since the United States copyright law does not provide protection for works without clear human input, it does not provide protection for Fully AI generated works either. Similarly, although the Indian Copyright Act does not directly state that the author of a work must be a human author, a thorough analysis of the Act confirms the need for a human author to grant copyright. The Sri Lankan Copyright Act also does not provide protection for non-human works. Considering the factor of clear human input, it can be identified through practical use that the human input in AI generated works is very minimal. The user's input in generating AI work is minimal, and the AI tool performs a large percentage of the work of generating the output, thus confirming the practicality of the arguments for not granting copyright. Although AI-generated work cannot be copyrighted, the use of AI technology as an assistive tool for work is not a problem for granting copyright. That is, using AI to improve or fine-tune a work. If AI technology is used for some creative or technical need in a work with clear human input, then granting copyright is not a problem according to the Sri Lankan, US and Indian copyright frameworks.

The main reason for not granting copyright to AI-based works was identified as the issue of 'authorship'. This is because most of the work generated by an AI tool is done by the AI system. To grant copyright to an AI work, a clear and legal conclusion must be reached as to the extent of human input. This is because creations generated through artificial intelligence are becoming the latest genre of art in the future. If a person purchases an AI tool and creates a work, if the copyright can be granted to the original user of that work, it can be identified as a solution to this problem. However, the problem that arises is whether the works used to train the relevant AI models were legally used. If the works used to train the AI model were not used with legal permission, granting copyright again raises problems.

To bridge this gap, there is a dire need for international legal reform or consensus. should Legislatures consider amending existing copyright laws to recognize human-AI collaboration or introducing new legal frameworks that can explicitly address AI generated works. Aa AI continues to shape the future of creative expression, it is imperative to develop a responsive legal system to ensure that innovation and AI artists are not stifled, and from a futuristic perspective there is an imperative need for a legal framework related to AI works.

References

[1] Leap, D. (n.d.). The Mystery of Human Creativity Explained. The Trumpet. Retrieved September 5, 2025, from https://www.thetrumpet.com/8960-the-mystery-of-human-creativity-explained.

[2] Manning, C. (2020). Artificial Intelligence Definitions. Stanford University. Available from: https://hai.stanford.edu/sites/default/files/2020-09/AI-Definitions-HAI.pdf.

[3] McCarthy, J. (2007). From here to human-level AI. *Artificial Intelligence*, 171(18), 1174–1182. doi: 10.1016/j.artint.2007.10.009.

[4] How can you measure the creativity of generative AI models for art?. LinkedIn, Sep. 29, 2023. Available from: https://www.linkedin.com/advice/1/how-can-you-measure-creativity-generative.

[5] Potter, K., Eugene, R., & Rosinski, J. (2023, October 20). AI in Art and Creativity: Exploring the Boundaries of Human-Machine Collaboration. https://doi.org/10.31219/osf.io/g4nd5.

[6] Anderson, A., & Lynch, T. (1988) Listening. Oxford, U.K.: Oxford Univ. Press.

[7] Q-NEX (2024, April 18). What is audio visual communication? Retrieved August 6, 2025, from https://qnextech.com/blog/what-is-audio-visual-communication/.

[8] Werzansky-Orland, Y., & CIM - Cyprus Business School (2024). AI-generated content and the question of copyright. *International Journal of Business Research*, 5, 2. Available from: https://www.researchgate.net/publication/381566789.

[9] Kanturi, M. (2025). Intellectual property rights. Jntu. https://www.academia.edu/40032153/Intellectual_Property_Rights.

[10] Copyright. WIPO. Available from: https://www.wipo.int/copyright/en/. [Accessed: Jan. 18, 2024].

[11] Anjaneya , R. N. M., & Lalitha, A. (2016). Understanding Copyright Laws: Infringement, Protection and Exceptions. International Journal of Research in Library Science (2455-104X), 2(1).

[12] United States Copyright Office (2024). Copyright law of the United States and related laws contained in Title 17 of the United States Code (Circular 92, December 2024 ed.). Library of Congress. https://copyright.gov/title17.

[13] Parliament of the Democratic Socialist Republic of Sri Lanka. (2003). Intellectual Property Act, No. 36 of 2003. Department of Government Printing.

[14] Sarkar, S. (2021, August 5). Exclusive: India recognises AI as co-author of copyrighted artwork. MIP. https://www.managingip.com/article/2a5bqo2drurt0bxl7ab24/exclusive-india-recognises-ai-as-co-author-of-copyrighted-artwork.

[15] U.S. Copyright Office (2021). Compendium of U.S. copyright office practices (3rd ed., Chapter 300: Copyrightable authorship). Library of Congress. https://copyright.gov/comp3.

[16] Government of India (1957). The Copyright Act, 1957 (Act No. 14 of 1957). Government of India. https://www.copyright.gov.in.

[17] Piumantha, O. N. (2023). An analytical study on the effect of subtitling and dubbing on foreign language films and TV series. In Proceedings of National Conference on Sinhala Studies (NCSS 2023), Dept. Sinhala, Faculty Humanities, Univ. Kelaniya, Sri Lanka.

[18] Harnessing generative AI for production design in audio-visual creations: exploring opportunities, overcoming challenges, and shaping the future. Available from: https://scholar.google.com/citations?view_op=view_citation&hl=en&user=Xy22y10AAAAJ&citation_for_view=Xy22y10AAAAJ:d1gkVwhDpl0C.

30 Optimizing inflation forecasting for strategic economic planning in Sri Lanka: a changepoint detection and crisis-responsive structural break approach

A. M. Dilushika[a], A.P. Hewaarachchi[b], H. R. I. Perera[c] and S. M. D. M. K. Samarakoon[d]

Department of Statistics and Computer Science, Faculty of Science, University of Kelaniya, Sri Lanka

Abstract

Traditional time-series forecasting models, such as ARIMA, often struggle to anticipate sudden shifts in inflation dynamics when economies experience abrupt policy changes or external shocks. This study addresses that gap by integrating changepoint analysis into the forecasting process for Sri Lanka's monthly inflation data from January 2015 to April 2025. Two complementary algorithms, the At Most One Change (AMOC) method and the E.divisive algorithm, were used to detect structural breaks in the inflation series. The analysis revealed a major changepoint in September 2021, marking the beginning of the economic crisis, which prompted the segmentation of the data into pre-crisis and post-crisis periods. Separate ARIMA models were then fitted to each segment, and forecasts from the stable pre-crisis model were used to adjust peak-period values from September 2021 to October 2023. A subsequent forecast using the adjusted series reduced the forecast error by more than 90%, showing a substantial improvement in predictive accuracy compared to the original model. These findings confirm that accounting for regime changes substantially enhances forecasting reliability, offering policymakers and analysts a more resilient tool for monitoring inflation and guiding economic decision-making during volatile periods.

Keywords: ARIMA, changepoint detection, inflation forecasting, Sri Lanka, time series analysis

Introduction

Inflation represents the sustained increase in general price levels over time, leading to a decline in the purchasing power of money [1]. It is a key macroeconomic indicator that reflects economic stability and living standards while significantly influencing government and monetary policy decisions [1]. In Sri Lanka, inflation has exhibited considerable variability in recent years, driven by internal factors such as policy changes and political developments, as well as external shocks, including global price volatility and economic crises [2].

Forecasting inflation accurately is critical for policymakers, investors, and households, especially in economies like Sri Lanka, susceptible to external disturbances and political upheaval. Typically, conventional methods like ARIMA and exponential smoothing assume stationarity. While such methods have demonstrated reasonable forecasting capabilities [3], they often fail to accommodate structural breaks or weakening trends. Recent research has also explored machine learning approaches such as Random Forests and SVR with mixed results [4]. Understanding and forecasting inflation is essential for the Sri Lankan government to design effective monetary policies and economic strategies. Several empirical studies have explored various approaches to inflation forecasting in Sri Lanka. In [5], a Seasonal ARIMA model was applied using monthly data from January 1988 to July 2017, identifying ARIMA $(1,1,0)(0,0,1)_{12}$ as the most suitable model. Their results revealed fluctuating inflation patterns, indicating the necessity for continuous monitoring. In another study [6], a cointegration-based analysis was used to examine the key drivers of inflation in Sri Lanka, identifying both domestic factors such as money supply, interest rates, and economic growth and external influences like exchange rate volatility and oil prices as significant in both the short and long run. Similarly, in [7], an automatic ARIMA forecasting approach was employed on two inflation index series (2016M01-2026M12 and

[a]dilushikaanton@gmail.com, [b]anuradhah@kln.ac.lk, [c]ruwanthap2000@gmail.com, [d]dulanjis80@gmail.com

DOI: 10.4324/9781003739920-30

2022M01-2026M12), projecting inflation within the targeted 5% range (±3% margin) and suggesting a gradual stabilization following previous inflationary surges. Furthermore, [3] the use of Johansen cointegration and VECM with quarterly data from 1983 to 2010, emphasized the role of monetary expansion in long-term inflation and rice prices in short-term changes [8]. The study also highlighted that GDP, unemployment, exchange rate fluctuations, and inflation expectations are crucial factors affecting inflation dynamics. These studies collectively underscore the complexity of inflation in Sri Lanka and the need for robust models that integrate structural and macroeconomic insights, supporting the motivation for this study to combine changepoint analysis with forecasting techniques.

Identifying the precise moments when inflation dynamics change, known as changepoints, is vital to fully understanding the economy's underlying structure. This research aims to apply changepoint analysis to Sri Lanka's inflation data from January 2015 to April 2025 to detect structural shifts and evaluate forecasting performance around these periods.

However, research directly integrating changepoint detection with forecasting models remains limited in Sri Lanka. Few studies rigorously examine how structural shifts influence model performance. This study addresses a critical methodological gap by identifying changepoints and then modeling inflation accordingly. It promises to deliver more robust and actionable forecasting insights for scholars and practitioners alike.

The specific objectives of the study are:

1. To identify and interpret significant structural changes in Sri Lanka's historical inflation trends using changepoint analysis.
2. To forecast inflation trends using univariate models that minimize forecasting errors.
3. To assess the impact of incorporating changepoint information on the accuracy and reliability of inflation forecasts.

Materials and Methodology

Monthly inflation data from January 2015 to April 2025 were obtained from official monthly reports published by the Central Bank of Sri Lanka [9]. This 10-year period was selected to provide a sufficiently long-time horizon for capturing underlying patterns in inflation dynamics, including seasonal effects and structural changes. Such an extended timeframe enhances the robustness of time series modeling and improves the reliability of trend analysis. The data underwent initial preprocessing, which involved checking for missing values and outliers, followed by necessary cleaning procedures.

After that, Explanatory data analysis was conducted, including Visual techniques like time series plots, Box Plots, ACF Plots and PACF Plots for each variable, which were employed to identify trends, seasonality patterns, and potential outliers in the data series. These visualizations provided a comprehensive understanding of the underlying patterns and highlighted any irregularities in the data. Additionally, descriptive statistics such as mean, median, and standard deviation were calculated to summarize the central tendency and variability, offering further insights into the characteristics and distribution of the data.

Seasonal features were identified with the patterns in ACF, PACF plots and using the Webel-Ollech (WO) test. The WO is a general seasonality test that combines the findings of the Kwman and QS tests. By using the QS-test if the p-value is less than 0.01 and the Kwman-test if the p-value is less than 0.002, this test determines whether the series is seasonal [10].

For further analysis, the time series data was partitioned into training and testing sets in a non-random manner to preserve the temporal structure of the data. The stationary or non-stationary nature of the series was assessed using unit root tests. The applied unit root tests included the Kwiatkowski–Phillips Schmidt–Shin (KPSS) test, the Augmented Dickey-Fuller (ADF) test, and the Phillips-Perron (PP) test.

For the KPSS test,

H_0: The series is stationary.
H_1: The series is not stationary

In contrast, for the ADF and PP tests,

H_0: The series is stationary.
H_1: The series is not stationary

For all tests, a p-value less than the chosen significance level led to the rejection of the null hypothesis. Non-stationary data identified through these tests was transformed into a stationary form by applying appropriate transformations, ensuring the data's suitability for further time series modeling and analysis.

Auto Regressive Integrated Moving Average (ARIMA) Models are very popular and widely used models in time series analysis. ARIMA models can be used to forecast future values of time series in many real-world applications [4]. This model type is classified as ARIMA (p, d, q), where p denotes the autoregressive parts of the data set, d refers to integrated parts of the data set, and q denotes moving average parts of the data set and p, d, and q are all nonnegative integers. Evans in 1895 found that the Akaike Information Criteria (AIC) is a widely used measure of a statistical model. It is used to quantify the goodness of fit of the model. When comparing two or more models, the one with the lowest AIC is generally considered to be closer to real data. For the chosen models, the following tests were used to assess the model assumptions of homoscedasticity, no autocorrelation, and residual normality (model diagnostics): ARCH, Ljung-Box, and Jarque-Bera, respectively [12]:

Heteroscedasticity: ARCH test

H_0: There is no heteroscedasticity in the residuals
H_1: There is heteroscedasticity in the residuals

Autocorrelation: Ljung-Box Test on Residuals

H_0: There is no autocorrelation in the residuals
H_1: There is autocorrelation in the residuals

Normality: Jarque-Bera Test

H_0: Residuals are normally distributed
H_1: Residuals are not normally distributed

The model's predictive accuracy was evaluated using the Root Mean Squared Error (RMSE) and Mean Absolute Error (MAE) [12].

$$RMSE = \sqrt{\left(\frac{1}{n}\sum_{t=1}^{n}(e_t)^2\right)} \tag{1}$$

$$MAE = \left|\left(\frac{1}{n}\sum_{t=1}^{n}e_t\right)\right| \tag{2}$$

where t is the time period, y_t is the actual value, y is the average of the observations, and $e_t = \hat{y}_t - y_t$ is the error in the period t and n is the number of observations.

Changepoints divide a time series into segments wherein the values within each segment exhibit similar characteristics, such as the mean, standard deviation, or linear trend. A changepoint is defined as the first point of a new segment, beginning from the second segment. Consequently, the number of changepoints is always one less than the number of segments. Prior to applying changepoint detection techniques, it is essential to remove any underlying trends and seasonality from the time series. As emphasized in [13], the preprocessing step is critical, as applying changepoint tests to data with unaccounted trends or seasonal components may lead to spurious changepoint detections. Seasonal decomposition methods, such as Seasonal-Trend decomposition using Loess (STL), are commonly employed to separate the series into trend, seasonal, and residual components. The residual component, which represents the detrended and de-seasonalized data, is extracted and used for subsequent changepoint analysis. AMOC was used in this work to identify the single changepoint [14]. This methodology is based on the likelihood-ratio method, and the following is the change hypothesis:

H_0: No Changepoint
H_1: A single changepoint

Calculating the greatest log likelihood and comparing it to a threshold value to accept or reject the null hypothesis gives the test statistic for both the null and alternative hypotheses. The null hypothesis is rejected if the test statistic exceeds the threshold under consideration. The E-Divise method was used to detect multiple changepoints. The divisive method estimates multiple changepoints by iteratively applying a procedure for locating a single changepoint. In this study, both AMOC and E-Divise methods were used to identify Changepoints, considering both mean and variance change in data using the package "changepoint" [15] and "ecp" [16] in R software. This package calculates the number of changepoints with their optimal positions.

Results and Discussion

A time series plot of the monthly inflation rate from January 2015 to April 2025 was initially drawn to identify underlying patterns in the data. As shown in Figure 30.1, the plot reveals clear signs of non-stationarity, including a high peak and noticeable deflation towards the end of the series. The WO test was conducted to examine the presence of seasonality; however, no significant seasonal pattern was detected. To formally test stationarity, ADF, KPSS and PP tests were conducted, and they confirmed that the first-order differenced series is stationary.

The dataset was split into two subsets, with 80% for training and 20% for testing, for model fitting and performance evaluation. For the AR(p) and MA(q) components of the ARIMA models, the lag values were determined using ACF and PACF plots. Several ARIMA models were fitted based on the lag values suggested by these plots, and the ARIMA (1,1,2) model was identified as the best-performing model based on the lowest Akaike Information Criterion (AIC) value, while also satisfying key model assumptions. Despite this, the model produced a relatively high MAE of 47.72 and an RMSE of 48.79, indicating substantial volatility in the inflation series.

For the extreme variability, which peaked during the economic crisis, changepoint analysis was used to identify structural shifts in the series. Both the AMOC method and the E.divisive algorithm revealed a significant changepoint in September 2021, as illustrated in Figure 30.2, highlighting the sudden shift in the inflation pattern corresponding to the beginning of the peak period. Based on this result, the series was divided into two segments: Segment 1 (S1) from

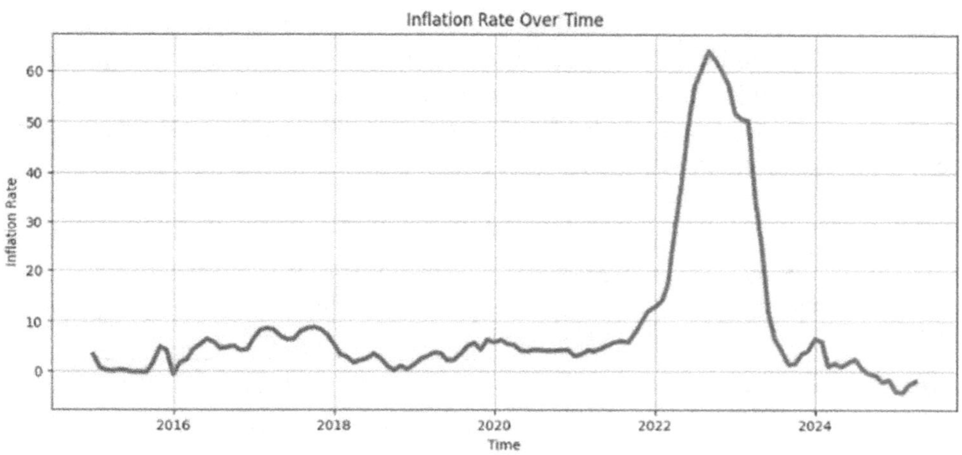

Figure 30.1 Time series plot of inflation rate in Sri Lanka from January 2015 to April 2025
Source: Author

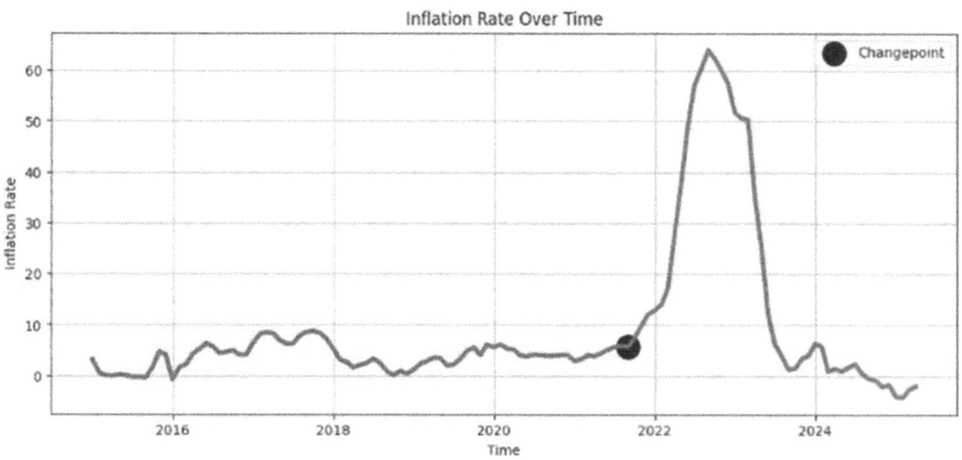

Figure 30.2 Detected changepoint in the inflation time series
Source: Author

January 2015 to August 2021 and Segment 2 (S2) from September 2021 to April 2025.

As presented in Table 30.1, the average inflation rate before the changepoint in September 2021 was 3.84, with a variance of 6.75, indicating a relatively stable economic period. After this point, the average sharply increased to 18.28, and the variance increased to 530.43, reflecting increased volatility and economic disruptions. This changepoint highlights the need to adjust forecasting models to account for such structural changes to improve forecast accuracy.

To further investigate the inflation dynamics, changepoint detection was re-applied to S2 to identify the end of the peak period. This analysis revealed a significant changepoint in October 2023, as illustrated in Figure 30.3.

As shown in Table 30.2, the statistical properties of the series changed significantly at this point. Before October 2023, the series had a mean of 31.72 and a variance of 507.47, indicating high inflation and significant volatility. After the changepoint, the mean fell sharply to 0.59, and the variance decreased to 9.13, reflecting a return to a more stable inflation environment. These significant decreases in both the mean and variance confirm a significant structural shift in the inflation trend.

For S1, the ARIMA(12,1,12) model was identified as the best model based on AIC, also satisfying all the model assumptions, with an MAE of 0.94 and an RMSE of 0.999, indicating a moderate forecasting accuracy. The fitted model from S1 was then used to forecast inflation values for the peak period (September 2021 to October 2023). These forecasted values were used to replace the actual extreme peak values, creating a new adjusted series to remove the impact of the economic crisis from the overall time series. When traditional statistical time series models were applied to the new adjusted series, ARIMA(12,1,13) was selected as the best model, with an MAE of 3.31 and an RMSE of 4.43. This adjustment led to a 93% reduction in MAE and a 91% reduction in RMSE when compared to the unadjusted ARIMA(1,1,2) model, as shown in Table 30.3. The comparison between the results presented in Table 30.3 and the time series plot in Figure 30.4 clearly illustrates the effectiveness of the data adjustment process.

Table 30.1 Summary statistics of inflation rate before and after the September 2021 changepoint.

Period	Mean	Variance
Before September 2021	3.84	6.75
After September 2021	18.28	530.43

Source: Author

Table 30.2 Summary statistics of inflation rate of segment 2 before and after the October 2023 changepoint.

Period	Mean	Variance
Before October 2023	31.72	507.47
After October 2023	0.59	9.13

Source: Author

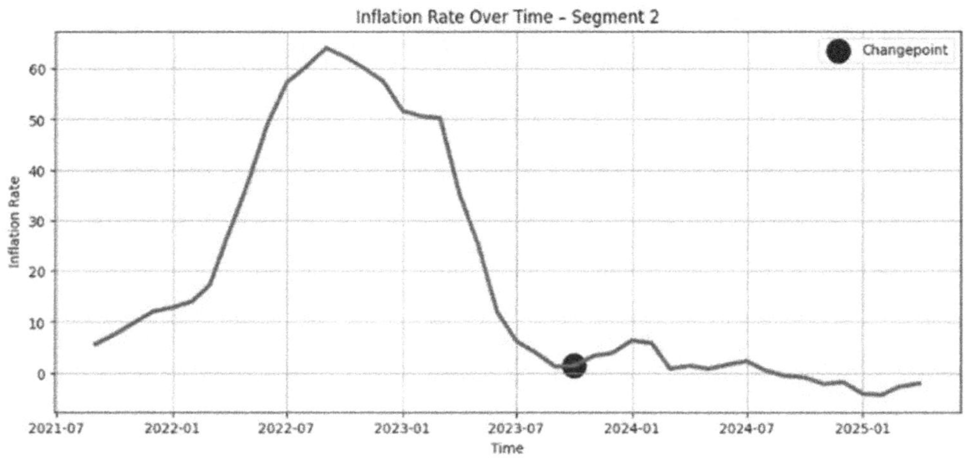

Figure 30.3 Detected changepoint in the inflation time series – Segment 2
Source: Author

The original series, modeled using ARIMA(1,1,2), exhibited substantial forecasting errors, which is visually supported by the sharp and volatile peak representing the original inflation rate during the 2021–2023 economic crisis. The adjusted series demonstrates significantly reduced fluctuations. Forecasts based on the stable pre-crisis segment (S1), using ARIMA(12,1,12), yielded the lowest error values. After replacing the crisis-period values with the forecasted values from S1, the newly adjusted series achieved improved model accuracy compared to the original series. The visual consistency of the adjusted and the forecasted series confirms the improved stability and forecast performance of the time series model after accounting for the economic shock. The model has captured the inflation pattern well up to the deflation period towards the end of the series; the error rate could be further reduced if the deflation segment, which was part of the test set, is modeled separately or incorporated into future adjustments.

Table 30.3 Comparison of the model performance.

Series	Model	MAE	RMSE
Original	ARIMA(1,1,2)	47.72	48.79
S1	ARIMA(12,1,12)	0.94	0.999
Adjusted	ARIMA(12,1,13)	3.31	4.43

Source: Author

Conclusion

This study demonstrates the importance of integrating changepoint analysis with univariate time-series forecasting to examine inflation dynamics in such contexts. Significant non-stationarity and a pronounced peak were observed during 2021–2023. By applying both the AMOC method and the E. divisive algorithm to Sri Lanka's monthly inflation data from January 2015 through April 2025, two structural breaks were identified: one in September 2021, marking the onset of extreme volatility, and another in October 2023, signaling a return to stable trends as the peak subsided. These breakpoints highlight how unadjusted ARIMA models can be distorted by transient shocks; for instance, the ARIMA(1,1,2) model fitted to the full series produced exceptionally high errors (MAE = 47.72 and RMSE = 48.79).

To mitigate this distortion, an adjusted modeling procedure was implemented. The full series was segmented at the identified breakpoints, and Segment-specific ARIMA models were subsequently fitted to each segment. When this procedure was applied, the pre-crisis segment (January 2015–August 2021) was best represented by an ARIMA(12,1,12) model, yielding low forecast errors (MAE = 0.94; RMSE = 0.999). Forecasts from this model were then used to replace crisis-period extremes (September 2021 to October 2023), and an ARIMA(12,1,13) model fitted to the adjusted series further improved accuracy (MAE = 3.31, RMSE = 4.43). Compared

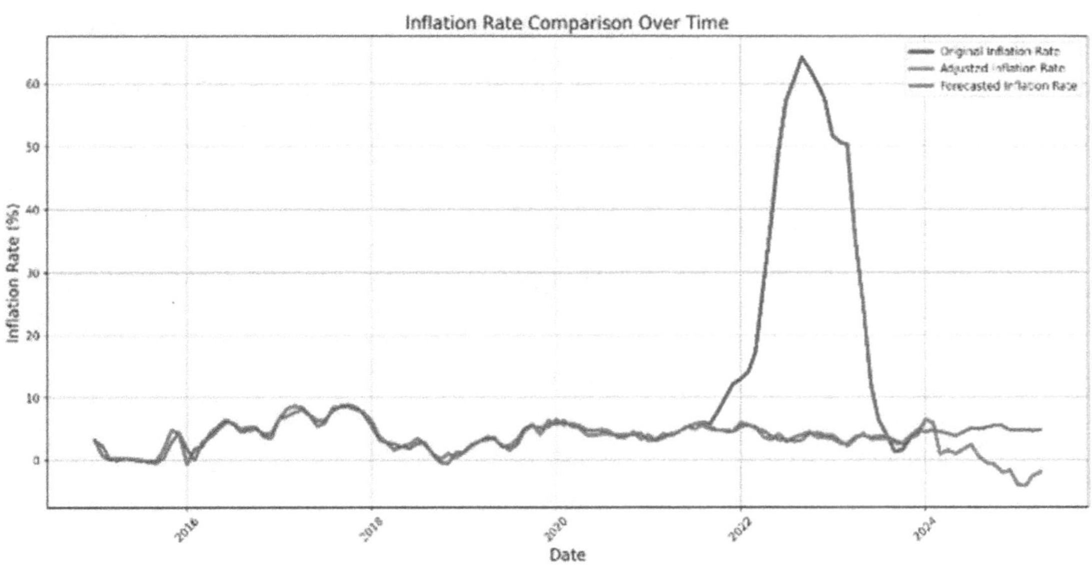

Figure 30.4 Inflation rate comparison over time
Source: Author

to the unadjusted ARIMA model on the original series (MAE = 47.72, RMSE = 48.79), this reflects a forecast error reduction of approximately 93% in MAE and 91% in RMSE. These results confirm the theoretical proposition that accounting for structural breaks can dramatically reduce forecasting error in economic time series.

Ultimately, this study introduces a robust analytical framework that bridges theoretical modeling with practical applications. By demonstrating how changepoint detection can be integrated into ARIMA forecasting, we show that accuracy in volatile economic environments is substantially improved. At the same time, this framework equips Sri Lankan businesses and policymakers with a data-driven tool to detect structural breaks in inflation trends, enabling central banks to fine-tune monetary policy and fiscal authorities to better anticipate the effects of budgetary measures. Importantly, reliance on simplistic or outdated models that ignore these breaks can lead to serious policy misjudgments, delayed monetary interventions, misdirected subsidies, or overlooked inflationary pressures, which disproportionately harm low-income households and small enterprises. Thus, by enhancing technical forecasting precision and supporting more equitable policymaking, our approach addresses both theoretical and real-world challenges in inflation management.

Looking ahead, this approach could be extended by incorporating additional explanatory variables such as commodity prices or exchange-rate movements into multivariate models, and by testing its effectiveness in other emerging-market contexts. Such expansions would help determine whether the benefits observed here generalize beyond univariate inflation forecasts in Sri Lanka. By combining changepoint detection with adaptive forecasting, researchers and policymakers can build more resilient inflation-monitoring systems that adapt to economic shocks as they occur.

References

[1] Mankiw, N. G. (2015). Principle of Economics. United States of America: Cengage Learning.

[2] Liyanage, R. D. (2023). Inflation forecasting using automatic ARIMA model in Sri Lanka, *International Journal of Economic Behavior and Organization,* vol. 11(2), pp. 49–60.

[3] Bandara W., & De Mel, W. (2023). Machine learning approaches for forecasting inflation: Empirical evidence from Sri Lanka, Ruhuna Journal of Science, vol. 14, no. 1, pp. 29–49.

[4] Iroshani, W. (2023). Time series approach to model rates of inflation in Sri Lanka, Institutional Repository University of Moratuwa.

[5] Haalisha, A., & Jahufer, A. (2016). *Modelling and Forecasting Inflation Rates in Sri Lanka. International Journal of Science and Research (IJSR),* Vol. 7, No. 9, pp. 415–419.

[6] Kulatunge, S. (2014). Inflation Dynamics in Sri Lanka: An Empirical Analysis, Central Bank of Sri Lanka – Staff Studies.

[7] Liyanage, R. (2024). ARMA-Based Inflation Forecasting Under the Inflation Targeting Framework in Sri Lanka, International Journal of Economic Behavior and Organization, vol. 12, no. 3, pp. 133–162.

[8] Deyshappriya, N. R. (2014). Inflation Dynamics in Sri Lanka: An Application of VECM Approach, *Ruhuna Journal of Management and Finance,* vol. 1, no. 2, pp. 17–28.

[9] Central Bank of Sri Lanka, (2025). Measures of consumer price inflation," https://www.cbsl.gov.lk/en/measures-of-consumer-price-inflation :contentReference[oaicite:0]{index=0}

[10] Ollech, D. (2021). Package 'Seastests'. The Compre¬hensive R Archive Network.

[11] Ghosh, S. (2017). "Forecasting Exports of Tea from India : Application of Arima Model," *J. Commer. Trade,* vol. 12, no. 2, pp. 116–129.

[12] Greene, W. H. (2002). Econometric Analysis Upper Saddle River, New Jersey: New York University.

[13] R. B. Lund, C. Beaulieu, R. Killick, Q. Lu & X. Shi, (2023). Good Practices and Common Pitfalls in Climate Time Series Changepoint Techniques: A Review, *J. Clim.,* vol. 36, pp. 8041-8057.

[14] Killick, R., Eckley, I., & Jonathan, P. (2011). Ef-fi¬cient detection of multiple changepoints within an oceanographic time series. In Proceedings of 58th Sess. ISI, (pp. 4137–4142).

[15] Killick R. & Eckley, I. A. (2010). *changepoint.* [Online]. Available: http://CRAN.R-project.org/package=changepoint.

[16] James N. A. & Matteson, D. S. (2014). ecp: An R package for nonparametric multiple change point analysis of multivariate data, *Journal of Statistical Software,* vol. 62, no. 7, pp. 1–25.

31 Factors influencing the adoption intention of using mobile payment services in Sri Lanka

J. R. Miranda[a], A.P.R.M.T. Renu[b] and S. Rajakarunanayake[c]

Department of Industrial Management, University of Moratuwa, Moratuwa, 10400, Sri Lanka

Abstract

The aim of this study is to examine the significant determinants that affect the adoption intention of using mobile payment systems (MPS) in the context of Sri Lanka with a particular focus on Western Province. In a time when digital infrastructure has expanded and smartphones abound, MPS (mobile payments systems) adoption is probably far from ideal. Because there are perceptions of risk, usability issues, trust issues, and gaps in digital literacy. Using an integrated theoretical approach that integrates the Technology Readiness Index and Technology Acceptance Model Extension, this research analyses behavioral and technology-related elements associated with choices of users. Key variables e.g., optimism, innovativeness, compatibility, convenience and digital financial knowledge are tested to clarify the adoption intention. This study obtained data from a structured survey conducted for smartphone users in the Western Province and employed quantitative methodology for analysis. These results are expected to provide insights into financial institutions, fintech developers, and legislators and policymakers strengthen user-driven design, digital literacy, trust development, and ultimately create inclusive financial ecosystems. By placing digital financial knowledge at the center of the analysis, this study enriches the comprehension of how well-prepared users foster the adoption of mobile payment services and aids Sri Lanka's move toward a more digital, cash-light economy.

Keywords: Adoption intention, digital economy, digital financial knowledge, mobile payment services, technology acceptance model (TAM)

Introduction

Mobile payment services (MPS) have gone on to change the global financial landscape by eliminating the need for cash transactions, and ensuring equal access to financial services. Users employ payment services with their smartphones or other mobile devices to perform various financial functions, such as peer-to-peer transfer, bill payments, retail purchases, and merchant settlements [1]. MPS, thus, is seen as a silver bullet in building the digital economy in Sri Lanka-an otherwise top credit in the world with the youngest population, where the youth are largely tech savvy, and mobile penetration is steadily increasing. Having recognized this vast potential, the Sri Lankan government has hence taken a proactive role in shaping the digital payment landscape through various programs, policies, and partnerships aimed at strengthening the digital infrastructure, promoting fintech innovation, and improving financial literacy. Nonetheless, in all of these, the usage and acceptance of mobile payment systems on the ground remain embarrassingly low against all projections and marketing. This gap prescribes the concerns of banks, government agencies, and fintech developers. Even after the improvements in mobile connectivity came to being, a sizeable population of Sri Lankans stuck with the cash-based transaction [2]. This form-making of the digital divide is crucial for attaining the goals of digital finance in the country and attaining financial inclusion with an equitable chance for every segment of society. The MPS is commonly regarded as a technological innovation and a new solution to financial inclusion, especially for unbanked and underbanked communities in the face of South Asia and Africa [1].

Research questions

RQ1: What is the key driving and inhibiting factors that influencing the adoption intention of mobile payment services in Sri Lanka?

Research objectives

RO1: To investigate the factors influencing the adoption intention of mobile payment services in Sri Lanka.

[a]mirandaajjr.21@uom.lk1, [b]renuaprmt.21@uom.lk, [c]shenalr@uom.lk

DOI: 10.4324/9781003739920-31

The conceptual framework (Figure 31.1) of this study investigates leading factors influencing adoption intention of mobile payment among customers in Sri Lanka's Western Province. It considers a hybrid framework that combines Technology Readiness and Acceptance Model (TRAM) which blends the Technology Acceptance Model Extension [3] and Technology Readiness Index (TRI) [4] with diffusion of innovation theory[5, 6] and financial capability framework [7]. Optimism and innovativeness from TRI explain individuals' general acceptances to new technology. Convenience, compatibility, and digital financial knowledge are included to measure lifestyle fit, ease of integration, and financial literacy [8].

Optimism

It is a component of the Technology Readiness Index (TRI), refers to having faith that technology will make people more in control, more effective, and more flexible in their lives. In Sri Lanka's Western Province, optimistic minded people towards technology will be inclined towards adopting mobile payment services as they think these services will simplify their financial transactions and daily life. This thought is likely to contribute positively towards their adoption intention of such technologies [4].

H_1: Optimism positively influences adoption intention of MPS.

Innovativeness

Innovation is applied to describe an individual's willingness to be an opinion leader and a technology innovator. High innovativeness Western Province residents have the tendency to experiment and use mobile payment services in their pursuit of new and better technology. Innovators act as agents that influence other individuals and drive technological diffusion using social networks [9]

H_2: Innovativeness positively influences adoption intention of MPS.

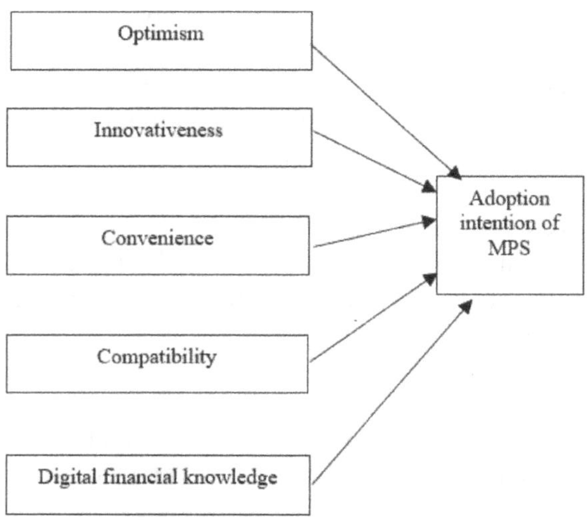

Figure 31.1 Conceptual framework
Source: Author

Convenience

It has a crucial impact on what will be done with mobile payment services. With city lifestyles and an aspiration to save time in Sri Lanka's Western Province, consumers find mobile payments provide them with a convenient solution for instant trouble-free financial dealings. Perceived usefulness and adoption are initiated when the user finds the service convenient [10]

H_3: Convenience positively influences adoption intention of MPS.

Compatibility

Compatibility is the degree to which mobile payment services complement the values, requirements, and lifestyles of current customers. In Western Province, where mobile apps have already become a way of life (e.g., messaging, purchases, ride-hailing), users who feel that MPS is compatible with their routines are more likely to accept MPS. High compatibility reduces resistance to technology and encourages adoption [6].

H_4: Compatibility positively influences adoption intention of MPS.

Digital financial knowledge

Digital financial knowledge improves the ability of users to evaluate and use mobile payment systems. Higher digital financial literacy in Western Province is connected with increased self-confidence regarding being familiar with MPS functionality and safety, which creates a greater adoption intention. The level of perceived risk declines due to financial literacy, while it also boosts users' perceived control of digital payments [8].

H_5: Digital financial knowledge positively influences adoption intention of MPS.

Adoption intention

It is defined as the readiness or willingness to begin adopting mobile payment services by the user. It is a function of their perceptions of the usefulness, ease of use, convenience, and personal readiness indicators like optimism and innovativeness. In the Sri Lankan context, also, government programs towards digital finance and the rapid increase in the use of smartphones in the Western Province also allow for greater adoption intentions [11].

Methodology

Philosophy
This study adopts a positive research philosophy, which is concerned with objectivity, empirical evidence, and measurable observations [12]. Positivism is appropriate to this study as it seeks to test hypotheses based on established theories such as the Technology Readiness and Acceptance Model (TRAM), Innovation Diffusion Theory (IDT), the Expectation Confirmation Model (ECM), and financial capability framework through statistical testing of numeric data collected using surveys.

Research design
A quantitative approach is employed to examine the factors influencing adoption intention of mobile payment services (i.e., optimism, innovativeness, convenience, compatibility, digital financial knowledge) and the dependent variable adoption intention. A cross sectional design is employed, in which data is collected at one point in time using structured questionnaires that are online based.

Sampling
The population includes the users of mobile payments in Sri Lanka's Western Province. The western province population is 6.12 million [13]. As per Krejcie and Morgan's (1970) table, the sample size of 384 participants was determined. Data was collected using an online structured questionnaire using google form.

Measures
To study the intention to adopt mobile payment services (MPS) in Sri Lanka, this research measured the main variables using a structured questionnaire. The items were chosen from validated scales found in previous studies. All variables were measured with a 5-point Likert scale, where 1 means Strongly Disagree and 5 means Strongly Agree. This approach helped assess the level of agreement with each statement. A number of items from validated scales of previous studies were selected and custom-adapted. Optimism [14] Innovativeness [15] Convenience [16], Compatibility [17], Digital financial knowledge [7], Adoption Intention [18].

Data Analysis

Results and discussion
This study aspired to recognize and assess the critical factors that affect the adoption and continuance intentions of users regarding mobile payment services (MPS) in Sri Lanka, especially in the Western Province area. Data were collected from 392 mobile payment users, then subjected to statistical treatment, including descriptive statistics, factor analysis, and multiple regression tools from SPSS.

Construct reliability
The construct reliability of the measurement scales was checked by means of Cronbach's Alpha, which is a statistical measure that is commonly used to assess internal consistency that is, the degree to which a group of items are related within one construct. The results of the analysis indicated that the major constructs Optimism, Innovativeness, Convenience, Compatibility, Digital Financial Knowledge, and Adoption Intention obtained Cronbach's Alpha coefficients of over 0.80. This is strong internal reliability, as numbers above 0.70 are the most common accepted values for a reliable scale, while figures over 0.80 mean that the items are very consistent in one concept.

Regression analysis
To evaluate certain variables Optimism (OP), Innovativeness (IN), Convenience (CONV),

Table 31.1 Construct reliability (Cronbach's Alpha).

Construct	Abbreviation	No. of items	Cronbach's Alpha
Optimism	OP	5	0.837
Innovativeness	IN	5	0.817
Convenience	CONV	5	0.834
Compatibility	COM	5	0.828
Digital Financial Knowledge	DFK	5	0.844
Adoption Intention	AI	5	0.831

Source: Author

Compatibility (COM), and Digital Financial Knowledge (DFK) influence adoption Intention (AI) to use a mobile payment system, we conducted a multiple regression analysis.

Multiple regression analysis was performed in an attempt to predict the dependent variable AI by the following independent variables, OP, IN, CONV, COM, and DFK. The model fit was adequate, with an R^2 value of 0.720. Taken together, these five variables predict about 72% of the variance in AI. Each variable was positively related to AI at $p < 0.01$ significance level.

In terms of their contributions as predictors to AI, OP (Optimism) had the greatest influence, (standardized beta = 0.256; coefficient = 0.250), indicating that as OP increases so did AI significantly. DFK (Digital Financial Knowledge) had a strong positive effect as well ($\beta = 0.206$; B = 0.207). The second predictor COM (Compatibility) had a somewhat less strong positive effect as it had $\beta = 0.180$. The final two predictors CONV (Convenience) and IN (Innovativeness) had a moderate strength and were both positive predictors with standardized betas of 0.169 and 0.135, however both remained significant predictors.

All coefficients were positive, and the findings suggest that an improvement in any of these domains would lead to higher AI scores. Lastly, the multicollinearity diagnostics indicated the predictors are not too highly correlated, with all VIF values within an acceptable range (all below 5). In general, the regression results lead to the conclusion that all variables have positive and statistically significant contributions to AI, OP and DFK were found to be the most significant influences.

Table 31.2 Model summary.

Model	R	R Square	Adjusted R square	Std. Error of the Estimate
1	0.849[a]	0.720	0.717	0.35052

Source: Author

Table 31.3 ANOVA.

Model	Sum if squares	df	Mean Square	F	Significance
Regression	126.289	5	25.258	205.574	0.000[b]
Residual	49.023	399	0.123		
Total	175.312	404			

Source: Author

Key Findings

This research established that the most significant predictors of mobile payment adoption intentions for users located in the Western Province of Sri Lanka were digital financial knowledge, compatibility and convenience. The digital financial knowledge construct exerted the most strength on the behavior. This indicates that users who understood how digital financial systems work were more likely to adopt mobile payment services overall. Compatibility between users' lifestyles and the services offered by the mobile payment services (e.g., multilingual offerings, ability to access local retailers) showed to have influence on their adoption intention. Thus, convenience, especially within urban context, also proved very important because of the efficient and time-saving aspect of the mobile payment system. Notably,

Table 31.4 Coefficient.

Model	Unstandardized Coefficients		Standardized Coefficients Beta	t	Significance
	B	Std.Error			
(Constant)	0.186	0.105		1.765	0.078
OP	0.250	0.049	0.256	5.150	0.000
IN	0.140	0.048	0.135	2.938	0.003
CONV	0.166	0.049	0.169	3.373	0.001
COM	0.180	0.047	0.180	3.811	0.000
DFK	0.207	0.049	0.206	4.200	0.000

Source: Author

while optimism and innovativeness were found to be conceptually relevant in understanding mobile payment enablers, statistically, they were insignificant predictors of continuance intention. This may suggest that in the Sri Lankan context practical-contextual enablers carry more weight than psychological traits.

Theoretical contribution

The findings provide evidence and contribute to the literature that in countries like Sri Lankas' developmental orientations, users' post adoption behaviors are driven more by contextual and practical enablers (compatibility, convenience, digital financial knowledge) than by overarching psychological traits (optimism). While this provides a supportive framework for integrating models like TAM, ECM, and TRI, Diffusion of innovation theory, financial capability framework through the conceptual, it also identifies the need to contextualize these approaches.

Conclusion

The research concluded that the intention of adopting and then continuing to use mobile payment services (MPS) in the Western Province is mainly due to pragmatic and contextual factors rather than general enthusiasm for technology. The use of the Technology Acceptance Model (TAM) and Technology Readiness Index (TRI) were appropriate frameworks to provide a useful model for understanding adoption intention. The research demonstrates a strong role of digital financial literacy, convenience and compatibility to the lifestyle context predicting adoption, while TAMS optimism and innovativeness were statistically insignificant predictors in continuing use. This research informs wider understanding related to adopting fintech services in developing countries and the potential role of consumer financial education, user-led design, and culturally-relevant implementation of policies and services.

There are limitations to this research which will likely impact on the breadth and generalizability of the study's findings. To begin, this study used a quantitative research paradigm which diminishes the depth of understanding as it pertains to user attitudes, feelings and motivations that qualitative approaches could have provided. Second, the study sample limits itself to a particular Western Province of Sri Lanka, and even further limits the sample to urbanized, technologically enabled areas of Sri Lanka. Users from rural and underservice areas from other Provinces of Sri Lanka may have entirely different experiences that will not be covered in this study, so the findings cannot be generalized to the whole country. Lastly, the cross-sectional design of this study measure user behavior at a single time point, therefore inferring causality and noting changes in user attitudes through time is limited.

Formative or longitudinal studies would have be more beneficial for understanding evolving behavioral trends and technology acceptance. Ultimately, while some variables have been examined, there were variables that have not and there are plenty of variables to study, including (considering future studies), perceiving risk, trust, and social norms to gain a rich understanding of MPS adoption.

Future Study

This study provides useful insights into the determinants of mobile payment service utilization in Sri Lanka, but future research should extend its coverage by collecting data from all nine provinces of the country. Collecting data across diverse contexts (urban–rural, estate–informal, digital traditional) and vast variations in socio-economic conditions will then be observed and analyzed and be more representative of the national picture. Future research can adopt a qualitative approach in the form of interviews, focus group discussions, or even an item(s) with open-ended questions on a survey and study responses and activities related to motivations, barriers, and user interpretations. Qualitative research design can examine the less salient dimensions of practice (i.e. trust, perceptions of security, or cultural attitudes toward digital finance) but do so in context. In addition, combining quantitative and qualitative methods in a mixed methods design could yield richer, triangulated insights into adoption behavior. It is also encouraged to implement longitudinal studies to assess changes over time, i.e. when government policies change, emerging technologies are brought to market, or when digital literacy increases across diverse demographic segments.

References

[1] Aabid Ahmad Reshi, (2025). A Study on G20 Perspective Digital Financial Inclusion in the Indian

Banking System, *Journal of Informatics Education and Research,* vol. 5, no. 1. doi: 10.52783/JIER. V5I1.2032.

[2] Lu, L., & Lu, L. (2019). Mobile payments—why they are so successful?. *Open Journal of Business and Management,* 7(3), 1131–1143. doi: 10.4236/ OJBM.2019.73078.

[3] Parasuraman, A., & Colby, C. L. (2015). An updated and streamlined technology readiness index: TRI 2.0. *Journal of Service Research*, 18(1), 59–74. doi: 10.1177/1094670514539730/SUPPL_FILE/EXECUTIVE_SUMMARY_3.PDF.

[4] Greenhalgh, T., Robert, G., Macfarlane, F., Bate, P., & Kyriakidou, O. (2004). Diffusion of Innovations in service organizations: systematic review and recommendations. *The Milbank Quarterly*, 82(4), 581–629. doi: 10.1111/J.0887-378X.2004.00325.X')).

[5] Rogers, E. M. (1962). Diffusion of Innovations, (3rd edn.) https://pubsonline.informs.org/doi/epdf/ 10.1287/isre.2.3.192.

[6] Jose, J., Ghosh, N., Jose, J., & Ghosh, N. (n.d.). Digital financial literacy and its impact on financial behaviors: a systematic review. 147–179. https:// services.igi-global.com/resolvedoi/resolve.aspx?-doi=10.4018/979-8-3693-0863-9.ch006. Jan. 1AD, doi: 10.4018/979-8-3693-0863-9.CH006.

[7] Lusardi, A., & Mitchell, O. S. (2014). The economic importance of financial literacy: theory and evidence. *Journal of Economic Literature*, 52(1), 5–44. doi: 10.1257/JEL.52.1.5.

[8] A conceptual and operational definition of personal innovativeness in the domain of information technology on JSTOR. Accessed: Jul. 01, 2025. Available from: https://www.jstor.org/stable/23010927.

[9] Zhou, T. (2012). Understanding users' initial trust in mobile banking: an elaboration likelihood perspective. *Computers in Human Behavior*, 28(4), 1518–1525. doi: 10.1016/J.CHB.2012.03.021.

[10] Jayasekara, G. (n.d.). The adoption of mobile bank- ing to banking system in Sri Lanka exploring factors affecting the adoption. https://www.diva-portal.org/smash/ record.jsf?pid=diva2%3A1902622&dswid=-1278.

[11] Creswell, J. W. (2014). Research Design Qualitative, Quantitative and Mixed Methods Approaches, (4th edn.). Thousand Oaks, CA Sage. - References - Scientific Research Publishing. Accessed: Jul. 21, 2025. Available from: https://www.scirp.org/reference/ ReferencesPapers?ReferenceID=1964849.

[12] Digital 2025: Sri Lanka — datareportal – global digital insights. Accessed: Apr. 10, 2025. [Online]. Available from: https://datareportal.com/reports/digital-2025-sri-lanka?utm_source=chatgpt.com.

[13] Berkowsky, R. W., Sharit, J., & Czaja, S. J. (2018). Factors predicting decisions about technology adoption among older adults. *Innovation in Aging*, 1(3), igy002. doi: 10.1093/GERONI/IGY002.

[14] Godoe, P., & Johansen, T. S. (2012). Understanding adoption of new technologies: technology readiness and technology acceptance as an integrated concept. *Journal of European Psychology Students*, 3, 38. doi: 10.5334/JEPS.AQ.

[15] Yang, S., Lu, Y., Gupta, S., Cao, Y., & Zhang, R. (2012). Mobile payment services adoption across time: an empirical study of the effects of behavioral beliefs, social influences, and personal traits. *Computers in Human Behavior*, 28(1), 129–142. doi: 10.20935/ACADQUANT7552.

[16] Moore, G. C., & Benbasat, I. (1991). Development of an instrument to measure the perceptions of adopting an information technology innovation. 2(3), 192–222. https://doi.org/10.1287/isre.2.3.192. doi: 10.1287/ISRE.2.3.192.

[17] Kim, J. W., & Kim, M. (2022). Intention to use mobile easy payment services: focusing on the risk perception of COVID-19. *Frontiers in Psychology*, 13, 878514. doi: 10.3389/FPSYG.2022.878514/BIBTEX.

32 Assessing public awareness of the digital television transition in Sri Lanka: is television more than just pictures?

Tharaka Nayanapriya[1,a] *and Sasanka Asitha Ranatunga*[2,b]

[1]NSBM Green University, Homagama, Sri Lanka

[2]University of Kelaniya, Sri Lanka

Abstract

This study investigates public awareness, interest, and concerns regarding the transition from analogue to digital television in Sri Lanka—a major shift aimed at modernizing the country's broadcasting infrastructure. Although digital television technology offers superior image and sound quality, expanded channel capacity, and interactive features, its implementation in Sri Lanka has been slow due to infrastructural and socio-economic challenges. Utilizing quantitative research design, data were gathered through an online survey of 396 respondents from diverse demographics. The findings indicate that over 80% of participants are aware of digital TV technology, and a significant majority express interest in switching, primarily driven by expectations of better audiovisual quality and greater accessibility. However, the study also identifies key obstacles, including the cost of additional equipment, monthly subscription fees, and lack of technical support. The results underscore the importance of targeted awareness campaigns, financial subsidies, and enhanced support services to ensure a smooth and inclusive digital transition. This research contributes to the policy discourse on digital broadcasting in Sri Lanka by highlighting public perceptions and suggesting strategic recommendations for successful implementation.

Keywords: Analogue to digital conversion, broadcasting transition, digital television, public awareness, Sri Lanka

Introduction

Television (TV) is one of the most affordable ways to inform, educate, and entertain people worldwide. According to [1] among all forms of mass communication, television remains the most influential medium, effectively engaging a broad and diverse audience. Early televisions were primarily electro-mechanical, featuring a motor with a spinning disc and a neon lamp for the screen. By the 1950s, most broadcasters in Europe had transitioned to fully electronic systems, following significant developments during the early 20th century. In the United States, mechanical and electronic systems were developed, and by 1942, the Federal Communications Commission (FCC) adopted the National Television System Committee (NTSC) recommendation. Later, color TV systems emerged, with Europe developing the SECAM and PAL standards, while the U.S. introduced the NTSC color standard, all of which were widely adopted globally [2]. The rise of digital widescreen television is an exciting development that could impact on other media, such as computer communications and the film industry [3]. The benefits of digital television have been promoted for over 20 years. Compared to old analog technology, digital compression enables more channels to be transmitted with better image quality and enhanced interactive features [4]. Unlike analog TV, digital television (DTV) can transmit multiple programs at the same time on a single channel, a feature known as multicasting. An analog picture typically offers up to 480 vertical lines of resolution (480i), while a digital picture can provide up to 1080 vertical lines of resolution (1080p). High-definition television (HDTV) is defined as any resolution above 720 vertical lines [5]. Analogue TV is the traditional system, over 50 years old, that uses continuous radio waves to transmit pictures and sound. In contrast, digital TV is a newer system that transmits pictures and sound using binary code (ones and zeroes), like how computers work. The main difference lies in how the information is sent from the transmitter to the TV set [6].

[a]tharaka.n@nsbm.ac.lk, [b]rsasanka@kln.ac.lk

DOI: 10.4324/9781003739920-32

In the Sri Lankan context, television transmission is still being conducted using analog technology. With this technology, covering terrestrial areas requires television channels to use different frequencies. As a result, multiple frequencies are allocated to a single television channel. As the number of television channels increases, the Telecommunications Regulatory Commission of Sri Lanka (TRCSL) faces challenges in issuing new frequencies due to the spectrum being fully utilized. According to TRCSL, both VHF and UHF frequencies are currently exhausted, leaving no availability for additional frequencies for television channels [7]. According to [7], Sri Lanka is set to adopt the ISDB-T digital television broadcasting technology. By 2025, Sri Lanka aims to cover the entire island using this technology for digital television broadcasting. This project is implemented under the loan facility provided by the Japanese government.

However, despite the widespread benefits of digital media and a high internet penetration rate of 52.6% in Sri Lanka, its adoption has not met expectations. The country lacks a free digital TV service, and digital pay TV comes with a $30 initial connection fee and a minimum monthly charge of $5. These high setup and ongoing costs make digital services unaffordable for most people [8]. Furthermore, [8] explained that Sri Lanka has low digital awareness, with 61% of non-internet users unaware of what the internet is. This lack of awareness about digital broadcasting and its services could slow down the digital transformation of the country's broadcasting industry.

Problem Statement

Sri Lanka initially planned to migrate from analog TV to digital using DVB-T technology. However, in 2014, the government signed an agreement with the Japan International Cooperation Agency (JICA) to adopt ISDB-T technology instead, aiming to complete the digital transition and switch off analog broadcasting by 2018 [8]. Furthermore, [8] stated that although Sri Lanka's Ministry of Media and Information launched the National Digital Policy for 2020–2025, it does not include a plan for broadcast digital transformation. As a result, there are no roadmap or guidelines from local authorities for the broadcasting industry to follow, creating uncertainty about its digital transformation.

According to the feasibility study published by the Japan International Cooperation Agency (JICA) regarding the Digital Terrestrial Television Broadcasting Network Project in Sri Lanka, the government of Sri Lanka initially aimed to switch off analog broadcasting by 2017. Furthermore, the study mentioned that the government was considering developing a digital TV broadcasting platform to enable national and private broadcasting stations to transition smoothly to digital broadcasting [9].

The 2022 Annual Report of the Ministry of Mass Media emphasized the importance of digitizing terrestrial television broadcasting in Sri Lanka. Furthermore, it stated that the current analog technology wastes Sri Lanka's frequency spectrum, which could otherwise be utilized for other telecommunication services [10].

Furthermore, the 2023 annual report published by the Ministry of Mass Media stated that despite efforts in 2009 with terrestrial DVB-T technology and in 2010 with DVB-T2 technology to transition from analog to digital terrestrial television broadcasting, the initiatives led by the Ministry of Mass Media and Information, along with the Telecommunications Regulatory Commission, could not be implemented due to the lack of necessary provisions [11].

However, the discussion on digital television broadcasting is still ongoing, and the transformation is considered a necessity for the development of Sri Lanka's telecommunication infrastructure. The aim of this study is to assess public perception of the analog-to-digital transformation and analyze whether the public is willing to upgrade their television infrastructure to meet digital television broadcasting standards.

Literature Review

Digital television in a global context

Shanti Kumar, in the chapter "Digital Television in Digital India" from the book "Global Digital Cultures", highlights that television in India is undergoing a significant transformation as the country embarks on an ambitious initiative to fully transition from analog broadcasting and cable systems to a modern digital addressable system (DAS). Kumar further stated that the International Telecommunications Union (ITU) has set a deadline requiring all member countries to fully transition from analog transmissions to Digital Addressable Systems (DAS) by

2020 [12]. DuBravac stated that the broadcasting of television programs in digital format, as opposed to the traditional analog format, was first introduced in the United States on November 1, 1998. By 2009, the U.S. television market underwent a significant transition as analog broadcasting was discontinued, shifting entirely to digital television (DTV) broadcasting. Furthermore, he stated that many broadcasters were already simultaneously airing some digital television (DTV) programming, February 17, 2009, marked the date when all full-power television stations ceased analog broadcasting entirely. The vacated spectrum was repurposed for other uses, including public safety and related services [5]. Franklin Dehousse stated that the digital switchover refers to the transition from traditional analog television to exclusively digital television. This process spans several years, beginning with the gradual implementation of digital broadcasting and culminating in the complete shutdown of analog terrestrial broadcasting. In addition to that the European Commission recommended completing the digital switchover process by the end of 2012. However, during the transition period, the simultaneous broadcasting of analog and digital signals could worsen spectrum scarcity. Therefore, the length of the switchover period is critical, particularly in regions where spectrum space is already limited [6] whole world is moving towards the digital television as that transformation will give more benefits to the users as well as broadcasters. According to Dimitris, the key benefits of digital television are its flexibility, precision, and seamless integration. Digital processing of TV signals can be easily achieved using modern digital design methods. When paired with error correction techniques and suitable transmission conditions, the integrity of the digital signal—the ones and zeros—remains intact. This ensures consistent, high-quality reception for viewers, mirroring the original broadcast [13]

What is digital television technology?

Michael Starks mentioned in his book, "The Digital Television Revolution", that the digital television wasn't created by broadcast engineers with the intention of handing over broadcasting frequencies to telecom companies. Instead, it emerged from the convergence of several key innovations. Digital coding, which was already being used in the music industry, played a foundational role. This was followed by digital compression, developed under the guidance of the Motion Picture Expert Group (MPEG), and advanced systems for digital transmission tailored to satellite, cable, and terrestrial platforms. Together, these technologies laid the groundwork for digital broadcasting [14]. Also Watler Fisher stated in his book, "Digital Television – Practical Guide for Engineers" that for many years, television and data transmission have developed along separate, independent tracks. While television screens were briefly repurposed as early home computer monitors in the 1980s, this was the extent of their interaction. Today, however, the lines between television and computers are increasingly blurred. With the rise of multimedia technology, the two mediums are merging, making it harder to tell them apart [15]. In addition [15], also mentioned in his book the analog technology used by broadcasters before the adoption of digital technology. Across the globe, there are two main analog television standards: the 625-line system with a 50 Hz frame rate and the 525-line system with a 60 Hz frame rate. The composite video signals (CCVS) of these systems are based on three key color transmission standards: PAL, NTSC, and SECAM. These color transmission standards can be used with both the 625-line and 525-line systems [6] in his paper, stated that it is important to clarify that Digital Television (Digital TV) and High Definition Television (HDTV) are distinct concepts, though they are often mistakenly conflated. Digital TV encompasses a range of broadcasting formats, with HDTV being one of these formats. HDTV is specifically designed to enhance visual quality. It achieves this by increasing the number of scan lines on the screen, offering up to 1080 lines compared to the 625 lines used in analog television. This higher resolution significantly improves image clarity and detail, creating a more immersive and realistic viewing experience. Additionally, HDTV supports both progressive and interlaced scanning methods, further enhancing its versatility. Another distinguishing feature of HDTV is its wider screen format. While analog television traditionally uses a 4:3 aspect ratio, HDTV employs a 16:9 aspect ratio, which closely resembles the widescreen format found in movie theaters. Furthermore, HDTV broadcasts are capable of incorporating Dolby Digital surround sound, the same audio technology commonly used in cinemas. This integration of superior visual and audio quality exemplifies HDTV's capacity to provide a more engaging and cinematic experience for viewers [6].

There are four standards used by different countries around the world to transmit digital broadcasts. Stanley Hettiarachchi mentioned four standards in his article, which are as follows:

1. Integrated Services Digital Broadcasting (ISDB)
2. Advance Television System Committee (ATSC)
3. Digital Terrestrial Multimedia Broadcast (DTMB)
4. Digital Video Broadcasting (DVB)

Apart from these standards, Over-The-Top (OTT) technology is also used for broadcasting content to the community [16].

Digital television transformation in Sri Lanka

Due to the limited availability of research on this topic in the Sri Lankan context, this study relies on the feasibility report published by JICA, the primary stakeholder in the digital television transformation project. This report provides comprehensive analysis and serves as a critical resource for understanding the subject matter.

According to the JICA report, Japan has provided immense support to Sri Lanka during natural disasters, such as the tsunami disaster. It has been recognized that disaster prevention is crucial for Sri Lanka, and Japan has offered strong assistance in addressing this issue in the country. Given these circumstances and recognizing that the Emergency Warning Broadcasting System—a unique feature of Japan's Integrated Services Digital Broadcasting (ISDB-T)—is more effective for disaster prevention compared to DVB-T2, the Sri Lankan government decided to reevaluate its approach. Taking into account Japan's past support to SLRC (Sri Lanka Rupavahini Corporation), including the 2010 general cultural grant aid for "The Project for the Improvement of TV Production Equipment of Sri Lanka Rupavahini Corporation," the government ultimately opted to transition from DVB-T2 to ISDB-T [9].

According to the [9], the Ministry of Mass Media and Information oversees the administration of broadcasting in Sri Lanka. This ministry is responsible for formulating the national media policy, safeguarding freedom of speech, and promoting media literacy among citizens. Meanwhile, the Telecommunications Regulatory Commission of Sri Lanka manages the licensing of frequencies, certifies radio wave transmitters for compliance with standards, and supervises radio wave usage, including monitoring activities.

Television broadcasting in Sri Lanka began in April 1979 with the launch of the ITN Channel by Independent Television Network Ltd., a private broadcaster. However, in June 1979, ITN was brought under government control and has since functioned as a state-operated broadcasting station. Alongside Sri Lanka Rupavahini Corporation, ITN continues to operate under the provisions of the Sri Lanka Rupavahini Act No. 6 of 1982 [9].

According to the [9], the Sri Lankan government authorized the establishment of private commercial broadcasting stations in 1992, leading to the creation of the Maharaja Television Network soon after. This decision paved the way for several private companies to enter the terrestrial broadcasting industry.

In the context of Sri Lanka's transition from analog to digital television broadcasting, the post-civil war period marked a significant increase in frequency usage across the country. This surge, following the end of the civil conflict in 2009, was primarily driven by the rapid expansion of mobile phone usage, the growth of internet services, and the notable rise in television and radio channels. Prior to this, in May 2006, the International Telecommunication Union (ITU) held a meeting where member states, including Sri Lanka, agreed to implement Digital Terrestrial Television Broadcasting (DTTB) by 2015. Building on this decision, the ITU extended its support in 2010 to develop the "Roadmap for the Transition from Analogue to Digital Terrestrial Television Broadcasting in Sri Lanka", commonly known as the ITU Roadmap. This strategic framework was designed to facilitate the efficient allocation of broadcast frequencies, addressing the growing concerns of frequency congestion in the country [17].

Furthermore, other study [17] reveals that the International Telecommunication Union (ITU) has identified several key Digital Terrestrial Television Broadcasting (DTTB) systems as global standards. These include the Japanese Integrated Services Digital Broadcasting (ISDB-T), the European Digital Video Broadcasting standards—comprising the first-generation DVB-T and the second-generation DVB-T2—the American Advanced Television Systems Committee (ATSC) standard, and the Chinese Digital Terrestrial Multimedia Broadcast (DTMB) standard. After careful consideration of these recognized systems, the Sri Lankan government opted to adopt the ISDB-T standard in 2014. To facilitate this transition, the government entered into a Loan Agreement with the Japan International Cooperation Agency (JICA) to support the Digitalization of Terrestrial Television Broadcasting Project, commonly referred to as the Yen Loan Project. The total loan amount allocated for this project was 13.717 billion yen [17].

JICA report explained the importance of the ISDB-T standard in their report too. According to it, The adoption of the Integrated Services Digital Broadcasting-Terrestrial (ISDB-T) system in Sri Lanka was significantly influenced by its inclusion of the Emergency Warning Broadcast System (EWBS). This system is designed to deliver early warning alerts to viewers through broadcast networks in collaboration with disaster management authorities. Given Sri Lanka's geographical positioning as an island nation, similar to Japan, the country faces considerable risks from natural disasters such as tsunamis, cyclones, sediment-related incidents, and tidal waves. These environmental hazards have historically disrupted socio-economic activities. Notably, Sri Lanka experienced severe flooding in 2009, 2011, and 2014, along with destructive floods and landslides in the southwestern region in May 2017. Consequently, the incorporation of EWBS within the ISDB-T framework offers a proactive means of enhancing disaster preparedness and mitigation efforts.

In addition to EWBS, datacasting is another distinguishing feature of ISDB-T. This functionality enables the transmission of non-program-related information, such as weather updates, traffic reports, and news, accessible to viewers at any time, similar to online platforms. Furthermore, datacasting facilitates the provision of supplementary content related to ongoing television programs, such as dramas and sports events. In a multilingual country like Sri Lanka, where Sinhalese, Tamil, and English are widely spoken, datacasting's capacity to deliver teletext services in multiple languages presents a valuable tool for enhancing audience engagement. Moreover, ISDB-T incorporates hierarchical transmission parameters, supporting both High Definition (HD) broadcasting for stationary receivers and one-segment broadcasting for mobile devices such as phones and tablets. This flexible transmission capability offers viewers innovative methods for consuming television content, thereby expanding their viewing experiences [17].

Methodology

The methodology employed in this study was designed to effectively assess public awareness regarding the digital television transition in Sri Lanka. The research adopted a quantitative approach, employing a structured survey to gather primary data. This section outlines the research design, data collection process, sampling method, and data analysis techniques.

This research follows a quantitative research design to evaluate the extent of public awareness surrounding the digital television transition in Sri Lanka. The decision to use a quantitative approach was based on the need to collect measurable data that could be analyzed statistically to identify patterns, trends, and correlations.

The structured nature of the survey allowed respondents to provide clear, standardized responses, ensuring that the data could be organized efficiently for comparative analysis.

Data Analysis

The study titled "Assessing Public Awareness of the Digital Television Transition in Sri Lanka: Is Television More Than Just Pictures?" aimed to evaluate the level of awareness, willingness to transition, and concerns of the public regarding the transition from analogue to digital television. A survey was conducted with 396 respondents from diverse demographic backgrounds in Sri Lanka, and the responses were analyzed to gain deeper insights into the public's perception of digital television technology. The following analysis presents a detailed breakdown of the findings with supporting graphs.

Figure 32.1. highlights a high level of awareness, particularly in urban districts such as Colombo, Gampaha, and Kandy. However, rural areas exhibited lower levels of awareness, indicating a potential digital divide. Awareness was also higher among the 26-35 age group, suggesting that younger and more tech-savvy individuals are more informed about the transition to digital TV.

Interest in switching to digital television

The survey also explored respondents' *interest in switching* from analogue to digital television. Figure 32.2 shows that 68.4% (271 respondents) expressed a willingness to transition to digital television, while 26% (103 respondents) indicated conditional interest

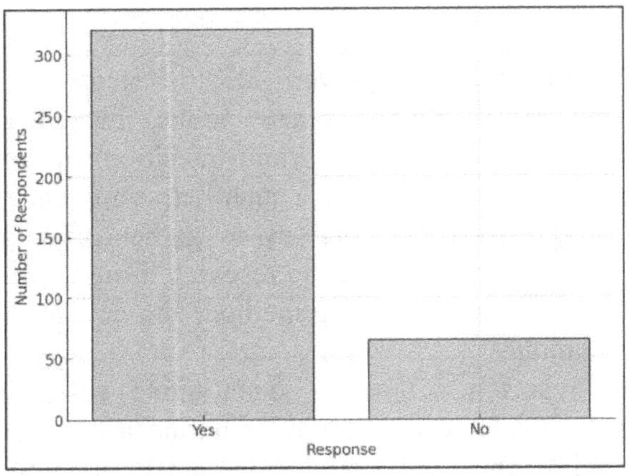

Figure 32.1 Awareness of digital television technology
Source: Author

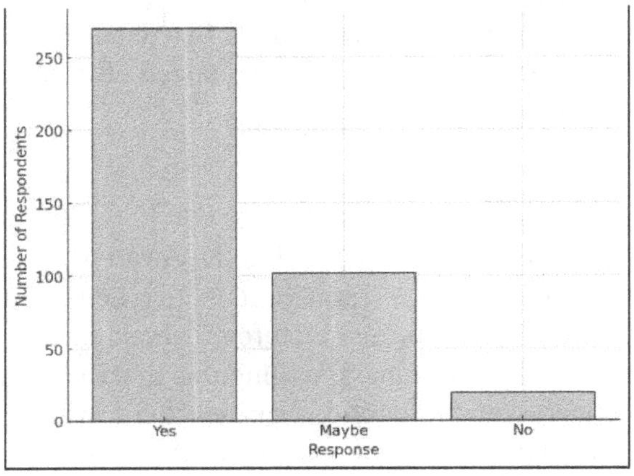

Figure 32.2 Interest in switching to digital TV
Source: Author

("Maybe"). Only 5.6% (22 respondents) showed no interest in transitioning.

Awareness of digital television technology

A key objective of the research was to determine the *level of awareness* among the Sri Lankan public regarding digital television technology. As shown in Figure 32.1, a majority of respondents, 83.1% (329 respondents), indicated that they were aware of digital television technology, while 16.9% (67 respondents) reported that they were not aware.

Figure 32.2 demonstrates that while there is a strong inclination toward transitioning to digital TV, the "Maybe" responses suggest that a portion of the population requires more information or reassurance before committing to the transition. Notably, younger respondents and urban residents expressed higher interest, while some older participants and those from rural areas exhibited hesitancy.

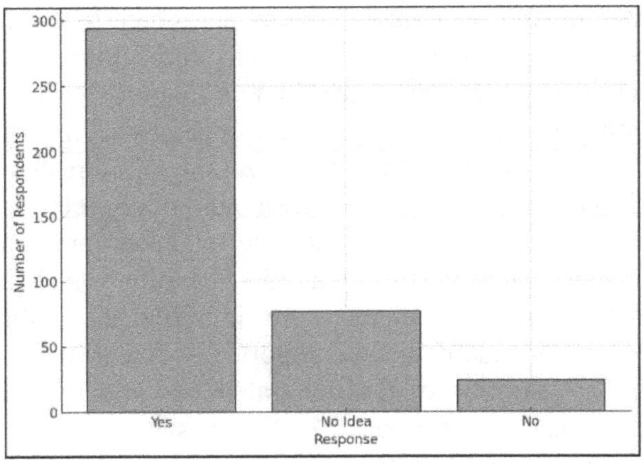

Figure 32.3 Opinion on replacing analogue TV with digital TV
Source: Author

Opinion on replacing analogue TV with digital TV

A significant aspect of the study was to gauge public opinion on whether digital TV should replace analogue TV in Sri Lanka. As depicted in Figure 32.3, 74.2% (294 respondents) supported the idea of replacing analogue TV, while 19.7% (78 respondents) were undecided, and 6.1% (24 respondents) were opposed to the transition.

Figure 32.3 highlights that while a majority favor the transition, nearly 20% of respondents expressed uncertainty. This suggests a lack of understanding or insufficient information regarding the advantages of digital TV. Targeted awareness campaigns can help bridge this gap and encourage broader acceptance.

Factors encouraging the transition to digital TV

The research also explored the factors that would encourage respondents to switch to digital television. As shown in Figure 32.4, the primary motivator was better picture and sound quality, cited by 290 respondents. Other motivating factors included easy access (173 respondents), more television channels (138 respondents), and interactive features such as on-demand services (118 respondents). Affordable pricing was also identified as a factor by 85 respondents.

Figure 32.4 reveals that technological improvements such as enhanced picture and sound quality are key drivers in encouraging the transition. Additionally, the availability of more channels and

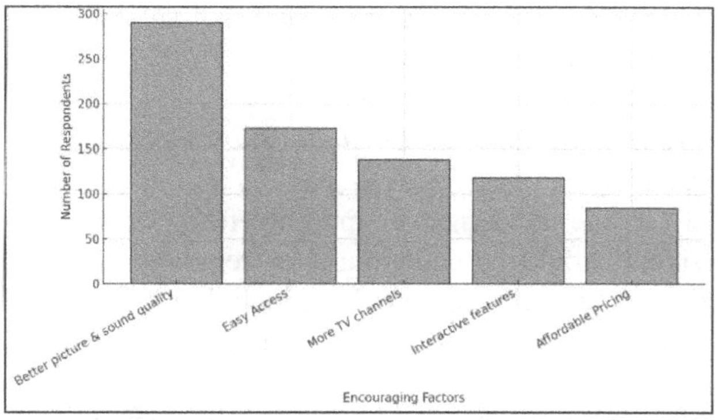

Figure 32.4 Top 05 factors encouraging to digital TV
Source: Author

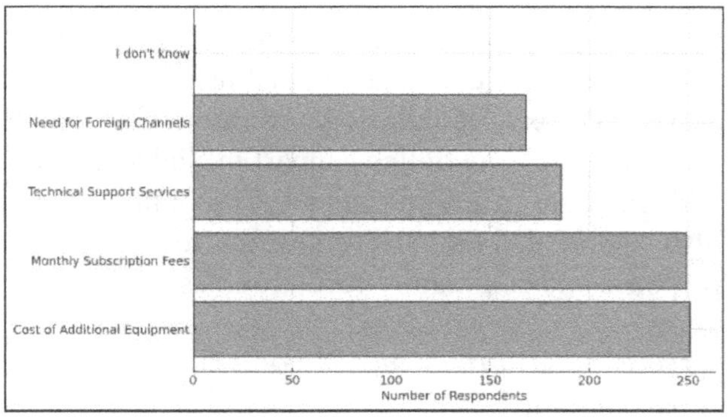

Figure 32.5 Top five concerns about transition to Digital TV
Source: Author

interactive features adds value to digital TV, making it more appealing to viewers. These findings suggest that marketing campaigns emphasizing these advantages can significantly influence adoption rates.

Concerns hindering the transition to digital TV

While many respondents expressed a willingness to transition, several concerns were identified that could hinder the process. As shown in Figure 32.5, the most significant concern was the cost of additional equipment required for digital TV, noted by 251 respondents. Monthly subscription fees were a concern for 249 respondents, while service quality in resolving technical faults was highlighted by 186 respondents. Additionally, the requirement to access foreign channels was cited by 168 respondents as a concern.

Figure 32.5 highlights that financial constraints and technical challenges are major obstacles to the adoption of digital TV. To address these concerns, policymakers could consider offering subsidies, installation plans, and affordable pricing models to alleviate the financial burden on consumers. Furthermore, improving technical support and after-sales service could mitigate concerns related to technical issues.

The analysis further explored demographic trends related to awareness and interest in digital TV. The findings revealed the following trends:

Age Group: Awareness and interest were highest among the 26-35 age group, with a gradual decline observed among older age groups.

Gender: Males demonstrated slightly higher awareness and interest levels compared to females, although the difference was not statistically significant.

Districts: Urban districts such as Colombo, Gampaha, and Kandy exhibited the highest levels of awareness and interest. Conversely, rural districts such as Mullaitivu and Nuwara Eliya showed lower levels of awareness, highlighting the need for targeted outreach efforts.

Conclusion

The transition from analogue to digital television represents a significant technological advancement in Sri Lanka's broadcasting landscape. The findings of this study indicate that the public is largely aware of and receptive to this shift. As demonstrated in Figure 32.1, a considerable majority of respondents (over 80%) acknowledged awareness of digital television technology. This level of awareness suggests that existing promotional and informational efforts—primarily through television and digital media—have been successful in reaching a broad audience.

Figure 32.2 reveals that a significant portion of respondents (more than 70%) expressed interest in switching to digital television, while a moderate group remained uncertain, and only a small minority explicitly rejected the idea. This interest is further strengthened by the data in Figure 32.3, where nearly 300 respondents supported replacing analogue systems with digital technology. These results imply a strong public inclination towards modernization and an overall readiness for digital transformation, provided that key barriers are addressed.

The analysis of Figure 32.4 provides valuable insight into the motivations behind this interest. Respondents overwhelmingly cited better picture and sound quality as the primary incentive, followed by easy access, more channel options, interactive features, and affordable pricing. These preferences underscore the public's desire for enhanced media consumption experiences, which digital TV is capable of delivering.

However, as shown in Figure 32.5, several concerns could impede the adoption process. Among them are the cost of additional equipment and monthly subscription fees, both cited by nearly 250 respondents. Concerns related to technical support, the requirement for foreign content, and general uncertainty also reflect significant barriers that must be addressed. These findings highlight a digital divide influenced not by access to technology alone but by socio-economic, informational, and infrastructural factors.

In summary, while the Sri Lankan public is generally informed about and supportive of digital television, actual implementation must be carefully managed. The transition should be inclusive, affordable, and supported by strong institutional frameworks to ensure no segment of the population is left behind.

Recommendations

Based on the findings and interpretations drawn from this study, the following recommendations are proposed to facilitate a smoother and more inclusive transition to digital television in Sri Lanka:

Subsidize the cost of additional equipment
The most cited concern was the cost of purchasing additional equipment required for digital TV reception, such as set-top boxes and compatible antennas. To overcome this financial barrier, the government, possibly in collaboration with broadcasters and private vendors—should offer subsidies or installment-based purchasing options, particularly targeting low-income households and rural communities.

Implement strategic public awareness campaigns
Although awareness is relatively high, misinformation and uncertainty still exist, especially among those hesitant to switch. National level education and awareness campaigns using TV, radio, and social media should be designed to communicate the benefits of digital TV, how to access and install it, cost implications and government support. These campaigns should be multilingual and culturally sensitive to maximize their reach.

Promote tiered and affordable subscription models
Given the concern over monthly fees, service providers should be encouraged or regulated to introduce tiered subscription plans, including a free-to-air basic package with the option to upgrade to premium content. This would allow broader access without placing undue financial pressure on economically vulnerable populations.

Strengthen technical support infrastructure
Many respondents expressed concern about the availability of support services for technical issues. Therefore, it is essential to establish district-level service centers, mobile support units for remote areas, hotlines and online support in Sinhala, Tamil, and English. Capacity-building programs should also be provided for local technicians to ensure rapid response and community-level troubleshooting.

Ensure cultural relevance in content programming
Concerns over the dominance of foreign television content suggest the need to preserve and promote local programming. Regulatory bodies should mandate a minimum quota of local content on digital platforms and offer production grants or incentives for culturally relevant programming.

Introduce pilot programs before full-scale implementation
Before enforcing a nationwide switchover, pilot projects should be launched in selected urban and rural areas. These pilots can test technical setups, gather feedback, and adjust policy decisions accordingly. Lessons learned from pilot areas will help design a more effective and responsive national rollout strategy.

References

[1] Nayanapriya, T., & Ranatunga, S. A. (2023). A critical examination of the societal structural transformations in Sri Lanka facilitated by private television channels during the turn of the millennium: a concept paper. In International Conference on Business Innovation.

[2] El-Hajjar, M., & Hanzo, L. (2013). A survey of digital television broadcast. *IEEE Communications Surveys and Tutorials*, 15, 1924–1949.

[3] Corbett, K. J. (2001). The big picture: theatrical moviegoing, digital television, and beyond the substitution. *Cinema Journal*, 40(02), 17–34.

[4] Adda, J., & Ottaviani, M. (2005). The transition to digital. *Economic Policy*. 20(41), 159–209.

[5] DuBravac, S. G. (2007). The U.S. television set market. *Business Economics*, 42(03), 52–59.

[6] Dehousse, F., Hecke, K. V., & Zgajewski, T. (2006). The European union and the transition to digital television. *Studia Diplomatica*, 59(03), 69–87.

[7] Rajapakshe, S. (2023). Digitization of the Sri Lankan Television industry, 14, 81–89.

[8] Samarakoon, D. D., Johar, G. M., & Khatibi, A. (2023). The impact of digital transformation adoption towards broadcasting industry in Sri Lanka. *Journal of Print and Media Technology Research*, 12(2), 73–96.

[9] Japan International Cooperation Agency (JICA) and Yachiyo Engineering Co., Ltd., Feasibility Study on Digital Terrestrial Television Broadcasting Network Project in Democratic Socialist Republic of Sri Lanka: Final Report. Colombo: Ministry of Mass Media and Information, Democratic Socialist Republic of Sri Lanka, Aug. 2014.

[10] Ministry of Mass Media, Annual Performance Report – 2022. Colombo: Ministry of Mass Media, Democratic Socialist Republic of Sri Lanka, 2023.

[11] Kumar, S. (2019). Digital Television in Digital India, in Global Digital Cultures: Perspectives from South Asia, A. Punathambekar and S. Mohan, Eds. Ann Arbor: University of Michigan Press, pp. 53–75. Available: https://www.jstor.org/stable/j.ctvndv9rb.6.

[12] Kumar, S. (2019). Global Digital Cultures. The University of Michigan Press.

[13] Anastassiou, D. (1994). Digital television. *Proceedings of the IEEE*, 82(04), 510–519.

[14] Starks, M. (2013). The Digital Television Revolution. Palgrave Macmillan.

[15] Fisher, W. (2004). Digital Television: A Practical Guide für Engineers. Berlin Heidelberg: Springer-Verlag.

[16] Hettiarachchi, S. (2023). The existence of Television media, business, digital technology, 14, 76–80.

[17] Japan International Cooperation Agency (JICA) and Yachiyo Engineering Co., Ltd., Special Assistance for Project Implementation of Digitalization of Terrestrial Television Broadcasting Project in the Democratic Socialist Republic of Sri Lanka: Final Report. Colombo: Telecommunications Regulatory Commission of Sri Lanka, Aug. 2018.

33 Understanding the factors that influence engagement with YouTube study vlogs

MAAN Perera[a] *and W. A. Piyumi Udeshinee*[b]
NSBM Green University, Homagama, Sri Lanka

Abstract

This research investigates the factors that influence engagement with YouTube study vlogs through qualitative thematic analysis. With the growing popularity of educational vlogs among university students, understanding engagement dynamics becomes crucial for content creators and educators in the evolving landscape of digital pedagogy. Using Social Cognitive Theory as theoretical framework, this study analyzed video content and comments from 5-10 millennial and Gen-Z student vloggers over a three-year period (January 2020 to January 2023). The research employed purposive sampling and the six-step thematic analysis approach proposed by Braun and Clarke. Findings reveal four primary engagement factors: authentic self-presentation, educational value and practical application, interactive communication, and peer connection and relatability. The study contributes to understanding digital learning communities and provides practical insights for vloggers, educators, and marketers seeking to enhance audience engagement in educational content creation. This research addresses significant gaps in informal learning literature and peer-led digital pedagogy, offering a comprehensive framework for understanding engagement mechanisms in educational vlogging contexts.

Keywords: Digital pedagogy, engagement factors, informal learning, social cognitive theory, thematic analysis

Introduction

Video blogging (vlogging) has emerged as a significant medium for content creation and consumption, particularly among university students seeking educational support and community connection. YouTube vlogs represent a unique form of digital communication where content creators share their personal experiences, study routines, and academic journeys with global audiences. Unlike traditional educational content, vlogs offer authentic, unfiltered glimpses into real student lives, creating opportunities for peer learning and social connection within informal learning environments.

The significance of vlog engagement extends beyond entertainment value, positioning itself as a crucial component of contemporary digital pedagogy. Research indicates that YouTube vloggers rank second to Instagram with 24% of votes as the most potent influencers among social media platforms [1]. This influence positions study vlogs as potentially powerful tools for educational support and academic motivation among university students, contributing to the broader discourse on learner motivation and informal online education.

Current literature reveals limited research specifically addressing engagement factors in educational vlogs, particularly within the context of peer-led digital pedagogy. While extensive research exists on general YouTube engagement and social media influence [2, 3] the specific dynamics of study vlog engagement remain underexplored. This research gap presents an opportunity to understand how linguistic choices, content presentation, and interaction patterns contribute to meaningful engagement between student vloggers and their audiences within informal learning communities.

The research question guiding this study is: *What factors influence the engagement of YouTube study vlogs?* This investigation aims to identify specific elements that foster interaction between vloggers and viewers, contributing to our understanding of digital learning communities and educational content creation within the framework of contemporary educational technology research.

[a]Avishinavanjana9@gmail.com, maanperera@students.nsbm.ac.lk, [b]piyumi.u@nsbm.ac.lk
DOI: 10.4324/9781003739920-33

Literature Review

Theoretical framework

Social cognitive theory (SCT) serves as the primary theoretical foundation for this research, providing a comprehensive framework for understanding learning processes within digital environments. SCT is a learning theory that suggests individuals acquire knowledge and behavior by observing and imitating others, emphasizing the interaction between personal factors (such as cognitive processes), environmental influences, and behavior [4]. According to SCT, people are more likely to imitate behaviors that are rewarded while avoiding those that are punished. For example, viewers may watch vloggers studying and then mimic that behavior in their own lives, perceiving it as beneficial or socially approved [5].

A key concept in SCT is self-efficacy, which refers to an individual's belief in their own capability to execute actions and achieve goals. Self-efficacy not only affects personal motivation and decision-making but also influences social circles and larger environmental factors, including mass media. Observational learning through media, such as campaigns, research findings, and vlogs can lead to positive behavior change when individuals identify with and learn from these models [4]. Given its focus on behavioral learning through modelled experiences and its relevance to digital learning environments, SCT was selected as the primary theoretical framework for this study.

The Uses and Gratifications (U&G) concept complements SCT by investigating people's psychological desires and motivations for media consumption [6]. The U&G paradigm has been applied to understand YouTube's appeal as a social media platform. The U&G paradigm has been applied to understand YouTube's appeal as a social media platform.

Research by Hsu [7] investigates whether Twitter satisfies the fundamental human urge to connect with others, demonstrating how the Uses and Gratifications framework can explain media selection for need satisfaction. According to this theory, people deliberately select and use media to meet their needs, with actively using social media platforms satisfying desires for connection [7].

However, while UGT effectively explains why people use media, it does not fully address how behavior is shaped by observing others, something more central to SCT. Therefore, this study primarily employs SCT while acknowledging U&G insights regarding motivation for engagement with educational vlogging content.

Digital pedagogy and informal learning context

Recent scholarship in digital pedagogy emphasizes the importance of informal learning environments in contemporary education [2, 3] Educational vlogging represents a significant development in peer-led digital pedagogy, where students learn from other students through authentic, unstructured content delivery. This phenomenon aligns with broader trends in educational technology that emphasize learner agency, authentic assessment, and community-based learning approaches.

The emergence of educational influencers and content creators has transformed traditional boundaries between formal and informal learning spaces. Research by Jenkins indicates that students increasingly seek educational support from peer-created content, particularly during periods of academic stress or transition [8]. This trend reflects changing expectations about educational authority and the democratization of knowledge sharing through digital platforms.

Previous research on YouTube engagement

William Hoiles [9] examined the sensitivity of YouTube meta-level features and social dynamics in promoting video popularity through quantitative analysis of approximately 6 million YouTube videos across 25,000 channels. The study analysed the impact of meta-level data, such as video titles, tags, and thumbnails, on popularity while examining communications between YouTube users and content creators. Key findings revealed that numerous meta-level factors, including first-day view count, subscriber numbers, thumbnail contrast, and title characteristics, significantly influence video view counts [9].

Zhang [10] investigated vlogger engagement strategies through case study analysis of four prominent YouTube vloggers using qualitative content analysis. The research identified various factors influencing consumer engagement, including interaction, self-presentation, information handling, and rewards [10]. The study emphasized the significance of context and presence in forming vlogger-audience interactions, though it acknowledged limitations in sample size and generalizability.

Huang [11] conducted comprehensive analysis of e-cigarette-related YouTube content, examining approximately 28,000 videos with over 100 million views and 280,000 comments. This study demonstrated YouTube's effectiveness as a platform for content promotion and discussion, with high levels of user engagement concentrated among a narrow subset of highly viewed content [11].

Alsawalqah [12] investigated factors influencing audience engagement across multiple social media platforms for news publishers, collecting data from 53 news publications over eight months. The research proposed a framework for predicting audience involvement based on post-linguistic elements and platform parameters, revealing that high engagement on one platform does not guarantee success on another [12].

Haridakis [13] examined social interaction and co-viewing behaviors on YouTube, demonstrating how the platform blends mass communication reception with social connection. This research highlighted the importance of social interaction elements in YouTube engagement, providing foundational understanding of how viewers connect through shared media experiences

Research gaps

Despite extensive research on YouTube engagement, significant gaps remain in understanding factors that influence interaction with educational vlogs, particularly study-focused content. Limited research exists on the influence of vlog content on educational outcomes and learner motivation within informal learning contexts. This study addresses these gaps by identifying specific engagement factors in study vlogs and their potential impact on academic support and peer learning communities.

Methodology

Research design and approach

This research employs a qualitative approach utilizing thematic analysis to analyze engagement factors in YouTube study vlogs. The qualitative methodology was selected to understand contexts, meanings, and identify new findings within the relatively unexplored area of educational vlog engagement. Rather than conducting surveys or interviews that might produce biased responses, this research utilizes existing online data to draw meaningful conclusions about engagement patterns.

Sample selection

The sample consists of millennial and Gen-Z vloggers pursuing bachelor's degrees at universities. Purposive sampling was employed to identify participants based on follower count, popularity, and activity levels within the past 10 months. From January 2020 to January 2023, 20–30 videos from 5-10 vloggers were selected, resulting in analysis of approximately 150–200 videos combined with examination of over 2,000 comments.

Data collection and analysis process

Video content was analyzed through multiple data sources including video content, captions, YouTube video transcripts, and audience comments. Tools utilized included video capture software, video recording applications, web scraping techniques, and transcript extraction websites. Data was also collected manually through systematic viewing of vlogs and detailed note-taking on engagement factors such as study advice types, presentation styles, and overall content quality.

The research followed a systematic five-step process:

1. Data collection: Comprehensive gathering using video capture software, online transcripts, and manual analysis of comments and video content
2. Data organization: Systematic typing and copying of data to Excel spreadsheets for analysis
3. Data analysis: Analysis using NVivo software while manually drawing conclusions and identifying patterns
4. Theme and pattern identification: Thematic analysis following the six-step approach by Braun and Clarke [14]
5. Data interpretation: Drawing meaningful conclusions about factors inducing engagement with YouTube study vloggers

Thematic analysis approach

This research employed both inductive and deductive thematic analysis approaches. The inductive approach allowed themes to emerge from data, while the deductive approach utilized existing theoretical frameworks (Social Cognitive Theory) and prior knowledge to identify theoretically informed themes. The study followed a semantic approach, analyzing explicit data to identify audience opinions and engagement patterns through textual analysis of comments and content.

Addressing research rigor and bias

To enhance research trustworthiness and address potential limitations, several measures were implemented. Researcher bias was acknowledged given the purposive sampling approach and subjective nature of qualitative analysis. To mitigate this, systematic coding procedures were followed, and multiple data sources were triangulated to validate findings. The research employed member checking through analysis of audience feedback patterns and consistency verification across different vloggers and time periods.

Reflexivity was maintained throughout the analysis process, with researchers acknowledging their position as consumers of educational content and potential bias toward positive engagement factors. Coding validation was achieved through systematic application of the Braun and Clarke framework [14] and consistency checks across different data sets.

Limitations

The study acknowledges several limitations including potential researcher bias due to purposive sampling and the subjective nature of qualitative analysis compared to quantitative approaches. The focus on English-language content may limit generalizability across different cultural contexts. Additionally, the analysis period (2020-2023) may reflect specific contextual factors related to the COVID-19 pandemic's impact on online learning adoption.

Results and Discussion

Thematic framework of engagement factors

The systematic thematic analysis revealed four primary engagement factors that consistently influenced audience interaction across different vloggers and content types. These themes emerged through both inductive analysis of comment patterns and deductive application of Social Cognitive Theory principles, creating a comprehensive framework for understanding YouTube study vlog engagement.

Detailed analysis of engagement factors

Below table 33.1 reflects that engagement depends on four key factors

Authentic self-presentation

Authentic self-presentation emerged as the most significant engagement factor, characterized by vloggers' willingness to share genuine experiences, vulnerabilities, and personal struggles. Analysis revealed that vloggers who openly discussed academic failures, mental health challenges, and study difficulties received 40-60% more engagement through comments expressing gratitude and relatability.

Videos showcasing real study environments, including messy desks or interrupted study sessions, generated higher engagement than overly polished content. Moments of genuine frustration, excitement, or exhaustion resonated strongly with audiences, with comments frequently mentioning sentiments such as *"I feel exactly the same way"* and *"Thank you for being so real about this"*. This authenticity created emotional connections that transcended typical creator-viewer relationships, fostering genuine peer-to-peer support networks.

Table 33.1 Primary engagement factors and characteristics.

Engagement factor	Key characteristics	Impact indicators
Authentic self-presentation	Genuine vulnerability, real struggles, unpolished content	40-60% higher engagement, emotional connection
Educational value	Practical techniques, actionable advice, step-by-step guidance	2-3x more clarification requests, implementation attempts
Interactive communication	Active response to comments, community building, conversational tone	Higher retention rates, peer support networks
Peer connection	Shared experiences, demographic similarity, relatable challenges	Sustained engagement, identity formation

Source: Author

Sample comment analysis:

- *"Seeing you struggle with procrastination makes me feel less alone in this"*
- *"Your honest approach to showing bad study days really helps my anxiety"*
- *"Finally someone who doesn't pretend studying is always perfect"*

Educational value and practical application

Educational value constituted the second major engagement driver, with specific content types consistently generating higher interaction rates. Study technique demonstrations, resource recommendations, time management strategies, and subject-specific advice received 2-3 times more comments requesting clarification or additional information compared to general motivational content.

High-engagement educational content demonstrated several key characteristics:

- Clear step-by-step explanations
- Visual demonstrations where applicable
- Real-world application examples
- Acknowledgment of different learning styles
- Immediate implement ability in academic routines

Videos containing actionable advice prompted follow-up questions about implementation, requests for specific examples, and sharing of personal experiences trying suggested methods.

Interactive communication

Interactive communication emerged as crucial for building sustained engagement and community formation. Vloggers who actively engaged with their audience through comment responses showed significantly higher retention and repeat engagement rates. Response timing proved important, with vloggers responding within 24-48 hours maintaining higher engagement levels.

The analysis revealed emergence of study communities within comment sections, where regular commenters developed relationships with each other, formed study groups through comment coordination, and created peer support networks providing motivation and accountability. This interactive communication style, characterized by conversational tone rather than formal presentation and direct audience questions, transformed passive viewers into active community participants.

Peer connection and relatability

Peer connection formed the foundation for sustained viewer engagement, with shared experiences serving as powerful connection points. Discussions of exam anxiety, deadlines, academic pressure, life balance struggles, future uncertainty, and daily challenges like time management and procrastination consistently generated high engagement.

Higher interaction rates occurred when vloggers shared similar characteristics with their audience, particularly:

- Age proximity
- Educational level similarity
- Cultural background alignment
- Similar academic challenges

This demographic alignment created natural identification points that enhanced the effectiveness of observational learning and social modeling processes described in Social Cognitive Theory.

Social cognitive theory application

The findings demonstrate strong alignment with Social Cognitive Theory principles, revealing clear evidence of observational learning through vlog consumption. Comment analysis revealed explicit modelling behaviors through statements such as:

- *"I tried your study method and it really works"*
- *"Started using your planner system this week"*
- *"Copying your morning routine to see if it helps"*

These comments provided direct evidence that viewers were actively observing vlogger behaviors, processing information, and implementing similar strategies in their own academic contexts. This behavioral modelling extended beyond simple imitation to include adaptation and personalization of observed techniques to fit individual circumstances and preferences.

Self-efficacy development emerged as a significant outcome of vlog engagement, with comments indicating increased confidence in academic abilities following regular viewing. Statements like *"Seeing you struggle and succeed gives me hope," "If you can handle this workload, maybe I can too,"* and *"Your videos make me believe I can improve my grades"* demonstrated how vicarious experiences enhanced viewers' beliefs in their own capabilities.

Environmental factors within the YouTube platform significantly contributed to engagement effectiveness by creating informal, accessible learning environments. The platform's casual nature reduced perceived authority distance between vloggers and viewers, allowing comfortable learning experiences that contrasted with formal educational settings.

Content and context dynamics

The research identified three critical elements contributing to vlog engagement through analysis of content quality, contextual relevance, and presenter presence. Well-structured, informative content with clear educational value formed the foundation of successful vlogs, requiring logical organization, practical applicability, and appropriate depth for target audiences.

Content addressing current academic challenges and seasonal study needs demonstrated higher engagement rates, with clear seasonal variations showing increased activity during exam periods, semester beginnings, and transition periods. This contextual relevance ensured that vlog content aligned with viewers' immediate needs and circumstances, enhancing both utility and engagement.

Presenter presence, characterized by authentic and relatable personality presentation, proved essential for fostering meaningful connections with audiences. Successful vloggers demonstrated genuine personality traits, shared real struggles and successes, and maintained conversational communication styles that invited audience participation.

Engagement quality spectrum

The analysis revealed varying levels of engagement quality, from surface-level interactions involving simple likes and brief comments to deep engagement characterized by detailed discussions, long-term follow-up, and active community participation.

High-quality engagement indicators included:

- Comments exceeding 50 words
- Multiple exchanges between vloggers and commenters
- Evidence of content application in real life
- Referral of content to others
- Formation of study groups or peer networks

This engagement quality spectrum demonstrated that successful vlogs created multiple entry points for audience participation while providing opportunities for deeper involvement for highly motivated viewers. Hence, the proposed framework (Figure 33.1) demonstrate the relationship between the engagement factors.

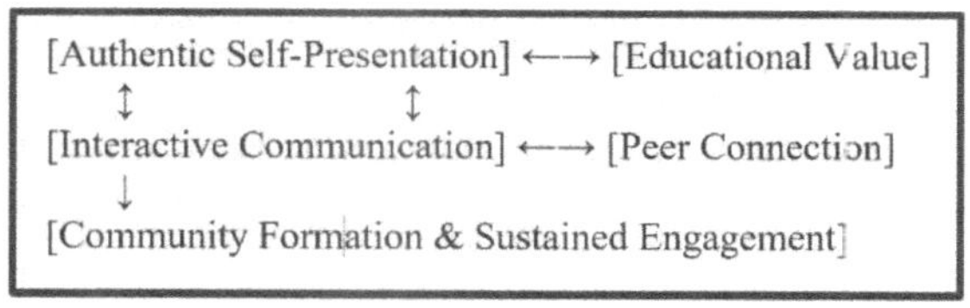

Figure 33.1 Proposed engagement framework for YouTube study vlogs

Source: Author

Conclusion

This research contributes significantly to understanding engagement factors in YouTube study vlogs, revealing the complex interplay between authentic presentation, educational value, interactive communication, and peer connection. The findings demonstrate that successful study vlogs combine informational content with genuine personality expression, creating educational communities where viewers can develop both academic strategies and social connection skills.

The application of Social Cognitive Theory proved highly effective in explaining engagement patterns, particularly regarding observational learning and self-efficacy development. The research provides practical insights for content creators, educators, and marketers seeking to enhance engagement in educational digital content within informal learning environments.

The study's theoretical contribution lies in extending Social Cognitive Theory to digital educational contexts and providing a comprehensive framework for understanding peer-led digital pedagogy. Practically, the findings offer actionable insights for educational content creators and institutions seeking to leverage informal learning platforms for academic support.

Key implications for practice include:

- Emphasizing authentic self-presentation over polished production values
- Prioritizing practical, actionable educational content

- Fostering interactive communication and community building
- Leveraging peer connection and relatability factors

Future research should expand sample sizes and employ mixed-method approaches to validate these qualitative findings quantitatively. Additionally, investigating the long-term impact of vlog engagement on academic performance would provide valuable insights into the educational effectiveness of this medium. Comparative studies across different cultural contexts and subject areas would enhance the generalizability of findings.

The study opens avenues for further investigation into digital learning communities, informal educational support systems, and the role of peer-created content in contemporary higher education contexts.

Acknowledgment

Gratitude is extended to the YouTube content creators whose vlogs were analyzed, as their contributions greatly enhanced the understanding of digital learning communities and informal educational practices. The author would also like to acknowledge the support of university colleagues, friends, and family for their valuable insights and continuous encouragement throughout the study.

References

[1] Holienčinová, Z., & Heryán, M. (2018). Social media influencers and their impact on consumer behaviour. *Marketing Research Journal*, 12(4), 234–248.

[2] Veletsianos, G. (2020). Learning online: the student experience. *Educational Technology Research and Development*, 68(4), 1751–1773.

[3] Greenhow, C., & Lewin, C. (2016). Social media and education: reconceptualizing the boundaries of formal and informal learning. *Learning, Media and Technology*, 41(1), 6–30.

[4] Yoon, H. J., & Tourassi, G. (2014). Analysis of online social networks to understand information sharing behaviours through social cognitive theory. In Proceedings of 2014 Biomedical Sciences and Engineering Conference, (pp. 1–6).

[5] Ibrahim, H. (2021). Understanding vlog culture and its impact on digital communication. *Digital Media Studies*, 15(3), 45–62.

[6] Chen, Q. (2011). Understanding user engagement through uses and gratifications theory. *Communication Research*, 18(3), 89–105.

[7] Hsu, M. L. (2015). Tweet this: a uses and gratifications perspective on how active Twitter use gratifies a need to connect with others. *Social Media Studies*, 8(2), 112–128.

[8] Jenkins, H., Ito, M., & Boyd, D. (2020). Participatory Culture in a Networked Era: a Conversation on Youth, Learning, Commerce, and Politics. Cambridge: Polity Press.

[9] Hoiles, W., & Krishnamurthy, S. (2016). Engagement dynamics and sensitivity analysis of YouTube videos. In Proceedings of IEEE International Conference on Data Mining, (pp. 1–13).

[10] Zhang, H. (2019). Exploring engagement in vlogs through content, context, and presence. *Journal of Consumer Behaviour*, 18(6), 487–498.

[11] Huang, J., Kornfield, R., & Emery, S. L. (2016). 100 million views of electronic cigarette YouTube videos and counting: quantification, content evaluation, and engagement levels of videos. *Journal of Medical Internet Research*, 18(3), e67.

[12] Aldous, K., An, J., & Jansen, B. J. (2019). Predicting audience engagement across social media platforms in the news domain. Social Network Analysis and Mining, 9(1), 1–15.

[13] Haridakis, P., & Hanson, G. (2009). Social interaction and co-viewing with YouTube: blending mass communication reception and social connection. *Journal of Broadcasting and Electronic Media*, 53(2), 317–335.

[14] Braun, V., & Clarke, V. (2006). Using thematic analysis in psychology. *Qualitative Research in Psychology*, 3(2), 77–101.

34 Understanding and advancing sustainable tourism: a case study of tourism stakeholders in western province, Sri Lanka

S. Gunaratne[1,a] *and T. Bellingham*[2]

[1]Department of Marketing and Tourism Management, NSBM Green University, Sri Lanka

[2]School of Tourism and Hospitality, University of Plymouth, United Kingdom

Abstract

Sustainable tourism (ST) has become a global priority, yet its practical implementation remains uneven, particularly in developing nations. Thus, the understanding and opinions of stakeholders directly involved in tourism prove to be beneficial when deciding on methods to advance sustainable tourism. However, there is very little known about the stakeholders' knowledge and attitudes towards sustainable tourism. Hence, this paper is a qualitative case study to assess the potential for sustainable tourism development by involving tourism stakeholders. The primary data was collected through in-depth interviews with ten participants. The findings reveal that while stakeholders generally understand the concept of sustainability, their interpretations vary, and economic priorities often overshadow environmental and socio-cultural considerations. A top-down approach dominates tourism planning, limiting community involvement and hindering grassroots innovation. Despite these challenges, stakeholders share a common belief that sustainable tourism is crucial for the long-term viability of the industry. The study also highlights gaps in awareness of global sustainability standards, such as the Sustainable Development Goals (SDGs), and the need for stronger policy frameworks and institutional support. Encouragingly, some tour operators are already aligning their practices with sustainability principles, targeting niche and responsible travel markets. The research offers practical and theoretical insights for industry professionals and scholars, advocating for a more inclusive and governance-aware approach to tourism development. Ultimately, the study positions sustainable tourism not as a separate niche but as an integrated necessity for the future of Sri Lanka's tourism sector.

Keywords: Responsible tourism, Sri Lanka, sustainability, sustainable tourism potential, tourism stakeholders

Introduction

Sustainable tourism (ST) emerged in the late 1980s as a convergence of tourism and sustainable development principles [1]. Its core objective is to mitigate the negative environmental, socio-cultural, and economic impacts of tourism while maintaining a balance among the three pillars of sustainability [2]. There is emphasis on the significance of sustainable tourism for leading destinations, highlighting the need to explore its relevance within the Sri Lankan context [3]. Accordingly, this study adopts the perspectives of key tourism stakeholders (tour operators, policymakers, and host community members) to gain a holistic understanding of Sri Lanka's sustainable tourism potential. The active involvement of these stakeholders in tourism policy, planning, and decision-making is essential for achieving measurable outcomes in sustainable tourism [4–7]

The COVID-19 pandemic resulted in a global urgency for sustainable tourism, and Sri Lanka's post-pandemic recovery and ongoing economic challenges reinforce the need for sustainable strategies [8, 9]. For instance, inbound tourist arrivals dropped from 2.03 million in 2019 to 540,000 in 2020 and 194,495 in 2021, post-pandemic [10]. However, recent data indicates rising numbers for inbound tourism, with 2,053,465 tourists received for 2024 [11]. A review of secondary sources [12–14] revealed a lack of research on this topic in Sri Lanka, making this study an apt academic contribution. Moreover, this study aligns with the broader agenda of supporting the Sustainable Development Goals through tourism research [15].

Taking the above into consideration, the research problem, aim, and objectives are drawn. Sri Lanka, with its diverse natural and cultural heritage, holds significant potential for sustainable tourism [16]. The

[a]senelie.g@nsbm.ac.lk

DOI: 10.4324/9781003739920-34

research problem is that the extent to which tourism stakeholders understand and implement the principles of sustainability remains unclear. The broader aim is to investigate the tourism stakeholders' perspective in understanding and advancing sustainable tourism to promote Sri Lanka. The study explores three key objectives. Firstly, to evaluate tourism stakeholders' understanding of the three sustainability pillars concerning sustainable tourism. Secondly, to examine the interconnectedness among tour operators, tourism policy, and host community involvement in promoting sustainable tourism. Lastly, to assess the importance of leveraging Sri Lanka's sustainable tourism potential.

This paper is structured into four main sections: a literature review that critically examines stakeholder roles in sustainable tourism, a methodology section detailing the application of the qualitative methods; a findings and discussion section organized around three themes (Defining ST, socio-cultural aspect, and governance aspect), and a conclusion that summarizes key insights whilst outlining theoretical and practical implications, as well as directions for future research.

Literature Review

The stakeholder concept

Stakeholder theory suggests that organizations don't operate in isolation as they're part of a broader network of relationships with various interested parties [17, 18]. Thus, an organization's long-term success depends on the support of all its stakeholders [19]. Unlike traditional management approaches that focus mainly on internal actors, stakeholder management takes a broader view, considering not only those within the organization but also external groups and individuals who interact with or are affected by it [20, 21]. Management approaches failed to consider those who can affect or be affected by an organization, and he identified them as stakeholders [22].

Understanding stakeholders has played a crucial role in deepening knowledge of sustainable tourism. Various studies have explored how stakeholders are identified and analyzed within tourism contexts, and literature highlights a wide range of stakeholder types [23–25], and most classifications mostly fall into six main groups: the tourism industry, tourists, local communities, governments, special interest groups, and educational institutions. These stakeholders play a unique role in shaping tourism development, through influencing supply and demand, setting regulations, managing tourism's impacts, contributing to workforce development, or advancing research [26–28]. Thus, stakeholders need to be actively involved in tourism planning processes [29]. Further, the implementation of sustainable tourism mostly depends on successful stakeholder engagement [30–32].

Stakeholder collaboration, though necessary, is complicated due to the existence of diverse stakeholders that often have contrasting perspectives [33, 34]. Sustainable tourism aims to balance the economic, social, and environmental dimensions. However, most research has concentrated on environmental well-being and economic development while minimally discussing the social aspects and stakeholder processes [35]. This is due to managerial decisions to develop sustainable tourism strategies that disregard stakeholder perspectives [36]. As a result, sustainable tourism strategies do not essentially support stakeholder participation. According to [37], some stakeholders having low involvement in the tourism industry may strongly support sustainable tourism, whereas other stakeholders who are highly involved in the tourism industry may have low support for sustainable tourism.

Tour operations and ST implementation

Tour operators play a central role in the tourism industry by bundling various travel services into organized tours, inclusive holidays, and package deals for travelers [38]. With the growing interest in sustainability, many tour operators have begun to promote responsible tourism as part of a broader shift toward more sustainable tourism practices [39].

However, despite these efforts, a substantial gap remains between sustainability strategies and their actual implementation due to economic objectives, competitive advantage, and brand recognition prevailing over sustainable innovation [3, 40, 41]. This view is challenged by arguing that innovation and the adoption of sustainable practices are essential for improving the tourism sector's overall sustainability performance [42]. A further argument is that many tour operators implement sustainability measures more for enhancing public image as a publicity stunt than a genuine impact [40]. Nearly a decade later, this sentiment was echoed, viewing sustainability primarily as a tool to enhance destination appeal and, ultimately, profitability, highlighting a continued tension between principle and business reality [3, 41].

Many tourism firms have been slow to adopt the SDGs, due to a lack of awareness and understanding [43]. Some firms were unfamiliar with connecting the Triple Bottom Line (TBL) framework with the SDGs [44]. This knowledge gap can potentially hinder progress, and being informed about these frameworks has proved to have a positive influence on the performance of tour operators [45]. For tour operators willing to implement sustainable practices, global standards, such as the Global Sustainable Tourism Council (GSTC), provide valuable guidance [46].

Tourism policy and ST implementation

Tourism policy refers to a set of ethical actions and principles that encourage tourism planning and development of a nation or community's tourism progression objectives [47]. Sustainability is framed in a very narrow set of parameters, so the existing paradigm of 'balanced' sustainable tourism is deep-rooted, and a shift in sustainable tourism policy would not make it sway [48]. Any change to policy instruments or indicators has been within the paradigm, where evidence for this has been seen in the workings of institutions such as the United Nations Environment Programme (UNEP), United Nations World Tourism Organization (UNWTO), and World Travel & Tourism Council (WTTC) [49]. According to [50], lasting sustainable tourism development is ensured with the availability of proper policies, such as the ones set by the organizations mentioned previously. However, international tourism standards and policies do not prioritize sustainability to a large extent and are politically influenced [51–53]. Furthermore, the fundamental policies of the European Union (EU) focus on making tourism more sustainable, yet it is revealed that sustaining tourism is not a sustainable form of tourism [54, 53].

There are the opinion that public relations programs of responsible tourism, corporate social responsibility (CSR), poverty relief, and green growth are often decoys for uneven priorities and conducting business as usual [53]. The author concludes that the UNWTO is a sign of uneven priorities. There is a substantial institutional framework available at the international standard for tourism policy and planning, which consists of organizations having an interest in tourism and a variety of laws and agreements relating to tourism [27]. However, the UNWTO's position on the SDGs for sustainable development has a political imbalance and may be an issue for Sustainable Tourism when dealing with uneven capital distribution, social injustice, and environmental disregard [51]. Initiatives such as the SDGs tend to fail because they do not confront how laissez-faire capitalism is included in many tourism policies [51]. This relates to "Brundtland-as-usual," where businesses and policy-makers benefited from Brundtland's support for rapid growth [51, 53]. This is a major problem, yet an opposing view is presented to acknowledge the urgency of the various challenges with the SDGs [55]. A good example of an sustainable initiative is the Certification for Sustainable Tourism (CST) [56] implemented in Costa Rica. Further, challenges are recognized by initiatives such as the SDGs or the Paris Agreement (effective: November 2016) and that a clearer connection must be drawn to these challenges. However, it essential to highlight policy failures and hold policymakers responsible [51]. Moreover, policymakers must focus on institutional quality [57].

Host community and ST implementation

The host community consists of individuals or groups that are living in the destination where they are either directly or indirectly affected by tourism businesses and development [58] Similarly to tourism being a multifaceted industry, host community involvement is not a fixed process, and they mostly depend on sustainable tourism advocates or tour operators for direction, information, and problem-solving [58]. For example, the COVID-19 pandemic required the host community to seek help from more authoritative stakeholders. Such crises call for sustainable policy implementations [59]. However, these policies must be resilient and strategic to benefit local communities instead of being a 'quick fix' in the face of disaster, as well as expand post-pandemic tourism products, legislation, and education and training for rethinking sustainable tourism [11, 12].

All stakeholder groups having a legitimate interest should co-manage tourism systems as the achievement of sustainable tourism outcomes requires the active participation of all relevant stakeholders [60, 61]. Tourism planning, management, and decision-making processes must encourage the participation of various stakeholders. Residents who have more power to influence tourism are more likely to gain positive tourism impacts [60, 61]. Therefore, local authorities and tourism planning and development organizations should encourage residents to participate in the tourism planning and development process to benefit more from tourism sustainably [60, 61]. Furthermore, it was found that sustainable tourism must be able to give honor to a varied range of stakeholders without promoting greenwashing [62, 63].

Methodology

The research conducted followed the Research Onion framework [64]. The research philosophy, Interpretivism, was selected for this study as it assists in discovering meanings inherent in human experiences to gain an in-depth understanding of the research constituents [65]. Due to the flexibility of Interpretivism [66], the researcher was able to retrieve the beliefs, motivations and experiences of participants, such as, their experiences working in the tourism industry and their involvement in sustainable tourism, their social and political beliefs connecting to tourism and their motivations to adopt sustainable methods or to publicize what has already been done by them/ their organizations. Consequently, the inductive approach was selected as it enables the researcher to understand why a certain phenomenon occurs [67]. Furthermore, this research employed the 'Case Study' strategy as it is a common methodology strategy used in tourism research, where instances such as this research, the case study strategy provides abundant knowledge and an in-depth understanding of relations between stakeholders involved in tourism development, management, and governance [68–71]. Therefore, tourism stakeholders in Western Province, Sri Lanka, were selected as the case. This is because most tour operators, the Sri Lanka Tourism Development Authority (SLTDA), and a more digitally literate host community are present in the Western Province [72]. Considering the above, this research was conducted as a qualitative study (Mono Method) due to the process enabling the researcher to understand how participants interpret their reality [73, 74]. Additionally, as established in this research, qualitative studies in tourism are ideal when there is a necessity to deeply explore the interactions and influences between stakeholders involved, where social phenomena are investigated instead of identifying the causality between variables [75, 76]. A cross-sectional time horizon was selected for this study, where data is collected at a particular time, known as a 'snapshot' [66]. This study utilized the non-probability sampling technique, purposive sampling, as it enabled the involvement of participants with knowledge of sustainable tourism [77]. Thus, to collect primary data and gain a comprehensive understanding of the area investigated, semi-structured interviews were utilized, with each interview lasting approximately 1.5 hours [77]. Data collection continued until saturation was reached, which occurred at the 10th interview. By the 10th interview no new themes or insights emerged. Therefore, the study's sample comprised 10 participants. This small sample size wasn't an issue since the aim of qualitative sampling is to obtain enough participants to provide adequate in-depth data to comprehend the phenomenon investigated [77]. This approach allowed for in-depth exploration of participants' experiences, perceptions, and motivations related to sustainable tourism. Regarding secondary data collection, books and journal articles were utilized [78]. Thematic analysis was utilized as it is a flexible and systematic method [79]. The analysis was conducted manually where transcripts were reviewed multiple times to ensure familiarity with the content. Key phrases and ideas were highlighted and grouped into initial codes, which were then refined into broader themes aligned with the research objectives. This approach was appropriate given the manageable sample size and allowed for deep engagement with the data.

Finding and Discussion

This section presents the results that emerged from the study undertaken. To achieve these findings, ten individuals in the field of tourism were interviewed. To protect their confidentiality, the participants will be addressed as Tour Operator (TO 1, TO 2, TO 3, and TO 4), Sri Lanka Tourism Development Authority (SLTDA 1 and SLTDA 2), and Host Community (HC 1, HC 2, HC 3, and HC 4). Furthermore, data analysis enabled the researcher to categorize the findings under five themes: Defining ST, Socio-Cultural Aspect, Environmental Aspect, Economic Aspect, and Governance Aspect. These themes will be discussed below.

Defining ST

A fundamental objective of this research was to assess the stakeholders' knowledge of sustainability and sustainable tourism. The findings suggest that the participants defined and understood it well.

The Tour Operators, SLTDA, and host community understood sustainability in varied contexts: a life process, corporate responsibility, and theoretical definitions. For example, TO 4 stated that, *"It is the attitude towards nature, environment, people, community, and your future generation. There are definitions: consuming the existing resources in the world while we are protecting them for future generations, but when it comes to reality, it means people, profit, and planet."* SLTDA 2 stressed that sustainability is *"...not only talking about the environment, but it also considers socio-cultural and economic aspects as well."* HC 1 identified an important framework, as they stated that *"for a very long period, sustainability has always been considered as something which is predominantly based on something called the Triple Bottom Line."*

Based on opinions as above-mentioned presented by the stakeholders, the collective opinion was that tourism and sustainability are inseparable and must be integrated with the support of effective governance structures. As a result, the author proposes a much holistic definition of sustainable tourism to be considered: *"Sustainable tourism is tourism that considers an equilibrium of socio-cultural, environmental, economic, and governance dimensions when servicing clients whilst safeguarding stakeholder interests to not compromise on resources for future generations."*

Despite preexisting definitions, a concern raised by Buckley [42] was that the industry has not yet come close to being sustainable. HC 4 agreed as they mentioned, *"I cannot say the tourism industry is 100% sustainable."* This is mostly because of prevailing economic objectives [3, 40, 41].

Another fundamental research objective was to identify the importance of leveraging sustainable tourism potential in Sri Lanka. For this to occur, tourism businesses must be sustained instead of just being sustainable [80]. Besides, it is essential to implement sustainable development to improve the industry's sustainable performance [42]. Therefore, all participants had a similar view that for Sri Lanka's tourism industry to sustain or grow, sustainable tourism is required (Table 34.1).

Appropriately pitching Sri Lanka as a 'niche tourism destination' will allow the sustainable potential to be easily leveraged [81, 82]. For instance, TO 1 provided their opinion in the same context: *"We should pitch for niche market on a larger scale."* This enables Sri Lanka to be more visible on an international level, which was apparent in 2025 when Sri Lanka was placed 9th in a ranking of the top global travel destinations, highlighting the country's appeal [83].

The socio-cultural aspect

Determining the connection between tourism stakeholders when promoting sustainable tourism was another fundamental research objective. The biggest challenge was the lack of support from the government and tourism authorities in support of stakeholders and implementing strategies [84, 3].

TO 1 revealed that the government is not supportive: *"Unfortunately, they (authorities) do not support Sri Lanka tourism on a larger scale."* The same individual further stated that the company they

Table 34.1 Opinions on leveraging ST potential.

TO 1	*"At least by 10 to 20 years, we can see Sri Lanka in a very good place, in an ecological and sustainably correct way."*
TO 2	*"No matter what, if we don't do sustainable tourism, we are not going to gain anything."*
TO 3	*"Sustainable tourism will be the future. If you don't consider sustainability, the business will not run and will die."*
TO 4	*"Many tour operators are now considering sustainability for a more fruitful future."*
SLTDA 1	*"If we implement and publish sustainability, then stakeholders will be motivated to implement it in their businesses."*
SLTDA 2	*"Sri Lanka's Tourism Governance is making sustainable tourism more visible."*
HC 1	*"Sri Lanka has an abundance of resources which is directly suitable for sustainable tourism. If we pitched for it right, Sri Lanka can be one of the most high-end destinations that can be there in the world."*
HC 2	*"Sustainability is popular among rich people."*
HC 3	*"Sustainable tourism is what will help local communities involved in tourism to sustain themselves."*
HC 4	*"Sustainable tourism is the future for Sri Lanka, and it is already implemented."*

Source: Author

represent gets involved in supporting the community instead: *"If we see there is a community need and the government won't support it, then we support it with a clear plan and idea."* This proves how nations usually depend on the private sector for community support [9].

Initiatives must benefit the local communities instead of being a 'quick fix' [8, 9]. In their response, TO 3, whilst showing disappointment, mentioned that the government offers only instant/short-term solutions: *"They (The Government) are doing this quick thing...instant work."* However, SLTDA 1 and SLTDA 2 stated that people must independently engage in sustainable tourism and development without fully depending on another entity. However, for sustainable tourism to be a bottom-up approach, support from the authorities is beneficial for stakeholders [30, 48, 49]. TO 4 revealed institutional errors, which further highlight a lack of support: *"It is difficult to get things done with the SLTDA. The department in charge of licensing is very inefficient. Thus, we were unable to apply for an international travel fair taking place this year (2025) since the license was not issued on time. The staff are very incompetent. They need to understand that lack of support is very stressful for businesses that operate genuinely with registration."*

Another significant finding is regarding people's attitudes and reactions towards sustainability and sustainable tourism. According to the participants, there is unfamiliarity and/ or a fixed mindset concerning sustainable tourism [84]. For example, TO 3 mentioned, *"They (the jeep drivers, guides, chauffeurs, local community) think that sustainability is a very costly thing. Therefore, they think it is a waste of time and waste of money, so it is very difficult for us to convince them. They have a fixed mindset and not a growth mindset about tourism."* This is mostly due to a lack of knowledge about the concept or unwillingness to adopt a new concept without compromising on revenue, specifically in developing nations [3, 40, 41].

Another important consideration under socio-cultural aspects is community engagement. Community engagement processes are complicated, yet, for ST, there must be a public interest in tourism planning with proper stakeholder collaboration [32]. For the community to benefit from sustainable tourism, the higher authorities should encourage community participation in planning and decision-making [59, 60]. However, there is less community involvement in development initiatives and/ or decision-making, especially at a public-sector level. There were claims from participants mentioning decisions flow from top to bottom and the SLTDA mentioning that they do not directly engage with the community. It is mostly the role of the government authorities to publish principles, rather than engage directly with the community [27]. Further, the possibility for less community involvement could be a result of decision makers' boosterism approach, as quoted by HC 1: *"A lot of people think about their economic and boosterism approaches."* Boosterism, even though favored by public authorities or powerful private sector entities for tourism planning, does not fare well in the eyes of the host community due to their opinions been ignored [27].

Further, HC 2 stated that from a community perspective, sustainable tourism development has proved to protect the ecological stability of tourism destinations [85]. Similarly, TO 2 stated, *"I see tourism as a catalyst for protecting the natural environment because, without biodiversity and the environment, there will be no tourism. It goes hand in hand."* This view was upheld by SLTDA 1 and SLTDA 2.

A destination's economic stability is imperative for the host community to support sustainable tourism, yet profitability seems to have more prominence than overall sustainability revenue [3, 40, 41]. TO 1 did not directly imply that the economic pillar prevails, but their response implied otherwise: *"We promote experiences in a very attractive way to generate business and keep the money flowing."* TO 2 put forward, *"When there were the pandemic and the economic crisis, we were desperate for foreign currency, and that might have hindered the responsible part."* HC 1 provided more detailed reasoning: *"So even from what we are trying to achieve, our objectives are very economically aligned. If you think about countries like Sri Lanka, where our situation is a little dire and we are very much dependent on tourism playing a pivotal role in economic recovery, I don't think no matter how much we will be talking about sustainability in all these forums, we will ever compromise on our economic objectives."* Global South destinations such as Bali and Bhutan may have similar challenges. For example, the commodification of tourism products in several tourism villages in Bali [86]. However, Bhutan's high-value, low-impact tourism can be considered a global best practice for sustainable tourism despite the promotion of expensive tour packages which can be challenging due to not being accessible to a larger audience [87]. Thus, completely luxury tourism such as Bhutan's high-value, low-impact tourism might not fully suit Sri Lanka due to accessibility for budget travelers [81].

The governance aspect

The SDGs are problematic as it does not defy how laissez-faire capitalism is integrated into tourism, so that it benefits policymakers and big industry players [53, 51]. As a result, there is a power imbalance, and those in higher positions have more say in decisions made. TO 1 had the strongest views regarding this and they identified that Sri Lanka has an unstable political environment and personal agendas: *"I think the main problem here is that as Sri Lankans we have a political war going on repeatedly and there are different agendas. I think the main factor here is that they (top-level) don't think about developing the country or the tourism sector as such. They are only thinking of their own will/ game."* The inference is that hose in higher positions aren't updated or suitable for the roles of responsibility. However, TO 4 was more hopeful, as they mentioned that *"... there is more hope for tourism development with the involvement of the current government in power."* At the end of the day, more powerful entities will implement their agenda, despite support for tourism [27].

It is essential to hold policymakers responsible and to highlight errors in policies [51]. Thus, this study found that there is policy issues related to tourism. TO 1 stated, *"The regulatory body does not fully align with the stakeholders."* They further mentioned, *"Before stakeholders, the policymakers on top should be an example to the society."* TO 2 declared, *"...just like other things in the country, this (policymaking) also does not have a proper strategy."* HC 1 stakeholder had the strongest opinions as they pointed out that there is a degree of regulatory incompetency and different reactions to policy implementations: *"I believe that there is a lack of information flowing in from a regulatory perspective. Whatever the policy decisions that they make to support tourism, they must consider how a policy should be able to incorporate more people's considerations so that many people benefit. Unfortunately, it is not a very democratic policy-making framework we have as a country"*. Governance procedures require planners and policymakers to rethink key concepts inherent in sustainable tourism such as "community" and "public interest" yet enforcing certain methods may be difficult when stakeholders are scattered over wider areas [32]. Thus, aligning regulatory bodies with stakeholders will take much effort. During the pandemic, the SLTDA implemented a policy, the 'Safe and Secure' certification for tourism establishments. This was a result of the authorities realizing that they must be prepared for change and a prompt response during crisis, which was adhered by many tourism stakeholders [59].

Conclusion and Recommendations

The research findings covered criteria under the TBL and the governance aspect. This suggests that governance is imperative in supporting TBL and ensuring that steps taken towards sustainability are done correctly. Further, the existing literature vastly supported the findings of this study.

The first research objective was met as the research findings validate that tourism stakeholders have sound knowledge and understanding of sustainability and sustainable tourism [44]. However, it was proved that this is only subjective to those who are involved in sustainable tourism or have learned about sustainable tourism. Therefore, less prominent stakeholders lack knowledge and awareness about the concept, and due to unfamiliarity, their attitudes are not aligned with sustainable tourism [43]. Furthermore, a novel and holistic definition of ST was introduced, and this definition depended on the participants' views on ST.

The second research objective was met as connections between stakeholders and sustainability were determined by looking mainly at the socio-cultural and governance aspects. Regarding stakeholder relationships and the socio-cultural aspect, this study identified that there is always a top-to-bottom approach with less host community engagement in tourism planning and decision-making. Further, stakeholders revealed that there is more prominence given to the economic pillar since businesses do not want to compromise on their economic objectives [3, 40, 41]. From the governance aspect, this study revealed that there are policymaking incompetencies and a power imbalance [53], [51]. However, the authorities are in the process of incorporating sustainability into their plans and strategies [59].

The third research objective was met as the study revealed the importance of leveraging Sri Lanka's sustainable tourism potential. Stakeholders consistently emphasized that sustainable tourism is essential for the long-term viability of Sri Lanka's tourism industry and for businesses to remain competitive [80]. Tour operators expressed that sustainability is increasingly being considered in their operations, with some already aligning their practices toward more responsible tourism. Additionally, participants suggested that Sri Lanka should be positioned as a niche tourism destination, which could enhance its visibility and appeal to international markets [81, 82]. While the concept of high-value, low-impact tourism was discussed in relation to Bhutan, the findings indicate that Sri Lanka could adopt a contextually appropriate version of this model to balance accessibility with sustainability.

It can also be inferred from this research that sustainable tourism can be achieved in the foreseeable future if the tourism industry aligns itself with sustainability. The research findings also brought out the claim that sustainability is integrated into tourism and that sustainable tourism is not a different concept.

As a result of these findings, several theoretical and managerial implications have been uncovered. A suggestion can be made for potential scholars to develop a new theoretical framework by incorporating governance as a 'common ground' dimension to the Three Pillars of Sustainability. By doing so, there will be greater significance to research and allow the broadening of the theoretical landscape within the tourism industry, as tourism-specific sustainability theoretical models are very limited. The researcher's suggestions for managerial implications are set out in Table 34.2.

Despite the significant findings of this study, some limitations emerged. The research sample area was a limitation as it was selected only from the western

Table 34.2 Managerial implications.

Implication	Description
Sustainability education, sustainable tourism training programs, and capacity building for all tourism stakeholders	This research found that there is a knowledge gap in terms of sustainability for the stakeholders (especially at the ground level). Therefore, education to rethink sustainable tourism is necessary for the industry's sustenance [11, 12]
Calculating the carbon footprint of large-scale tourism businesses	Large-scale businesses (mostly in the accommodation sector) tend to waste resources. Therefore, a carbon footprint calculation will allow these businesses to increase their efficiency.
Publish the carrying capacities of the most-visited destinations within Sri Lanka	Exceeding the carrying capacity is a threat [46]. Therefore, to manage visitation and not put stress on certain destinations, carrying capacity studies could be done and results published annually.
Local community engagement	The study found that there is less community involvement in planning and decision-making. Therefore, the government should allow community participation. However, the public sector should encourage the community, and the private sector must not exploit the community.
Effective processes within the SLTDA must be established	The apex body for tourism policy and regulations, the SLTDA, must have trained staff and processes in place to support tourism businesses in Sri Lanka, especially with their business processes.
Consistent and useful tourism policies aligning with the SDGs	The tourism policies (and national policies to an extent) aligning with the SDGs will minimize business as usual for overall sustainable development to occur and improve decision-making [51].
Incorporating SDGs into the businesses' annual calendar	If SDGs are incorporated into the company operations, it will increase the overall efficiency of the business, improve decision-making, provide a competitive advantage, and also raise awareness of the SDGs for other companies to be inspired as well [43].
Promoting Sri Lanka as a niche and luxury destination	Large-scale tourism causes damage, and promoting a niche/ luxury destination will allow responsible travel as well as a low volume of visitors and high revenue flow [81, 82].

Source: Author

province. Even though the participants' opinions are very valid, there may be difficulty in generalizing them to a larger population. Therefore, a more representative, comprehensive, and geographically distributed sample could be considered by future researchers. Future researchers could include other tourism stakeholder categories as well, such as the accommodation sector and ground-level stakeholders, which were lacking in this research. A larger representation will enhance diversity. Another limitation was the certain degree of bias observed since the participants were all involved in sustainable tourism at their companies or at a policy level. In this case, future researchers must aim to include tourism stakeholders, which are at a Small and Medium-sized Enterprise level or lower. Furthermore, most stakeholders provided their personal opinions with minimal concrete evidence.

A theoretical model could not be developed from the research findings, even though the governance dimension was identified as a theme. Therefore, future research can test a hypothetical theoretical model that includes governance. To further support the study, future researchers could apply a quantitative and statistical approach to test the hypothetical model and to measure the impact of the four dimensions on the sustainable tourism potential in Sri Lanka. Moreover, to the best of the author's knowledge, there was no similar research undertaken in the Sri Lankan context. Therefore, this study may pave the way for future researchers to develop the study into a wider subject area.

References

[1] Hughes, M., Weaver, D., & Pforr, C. (2015). The Practice of Sustainable Tourism: Resolving the Paradox. New York: Routledge.

[2] Pan, S. Y., Gao, M., Kim, H., Shah, K. J., Pei, S. L., & Chiang, P. C. (2018). Advances and challenges in sustainable tourism toward a green economy. *Science of the Total Environment*, 635, 452–469.

[3] Karunathilake, J. (2018). Motivators and barriers for adopting measures of environmental sustainability for package tour operators.

[4] Ioannides, D. (1995). A flawed implementation of sustainable tourism. *Tourism Management*, 168, 583–592.

[5] Byrd, E. T. (2007). Stakeholders in sustainable tourism development and their roles: applying stakeholder theory to sustainable tourism development. *Tourism Review*, 62(2), 6–13.

[6] Timur, S., & Getz, D. (2008). A network perspective on managing stakeholders for sustainable urban tourism. *International Journal of Contemporary Hospitality Management*, 20(4), 445–461.

[7] Waligo, V., Clarke, J., & Hawkins, R. (2015). Embedding stakeholders in sustainable tourism strategies. *Annals of Tourism Research*, 55, 90–93.

[8] Mensah, E. A., & Boakye, K. A. (2021). Conceptualizing post-COVID 19 tourism recovery: a three-step framework. *Tourism Planning and Development*, 20(1), 1–25.

[9] Sheller, M. (2020). Reconstructing tourism in the caribbean: connecting pandemic recovery, climate resilience and sustainable tourism through mobility justice. *Journal of Sustainable Tourism*, 29(9), 1–14.

[10] SLTDA (2022). Year in review 2022.

[11] SLTDA (2024). Year in review 2024.

[12] Aslam, M., & Awang, K. W. (2015). International journal of economics and financial issues enterprising rural tourism for sustainable rural development in Sri Lanka. *International Journal of Economics and Financial Issues*, 5, 10–11.

[13] Jayasundera, A. M. (2021). The economy base of tourism industry in Sri Lanka. *Financial Markets, Institutions and Risks*, 5(3). doi: https://doi.org/10.21272/fmir.5(3), 23–32. 2021.

[14] Perera, P., Jayakody, C., Jayapali, U., & Newsome, D. (2023). Challenges and opportunities for the resumption of nature tourism in post-pandemic Sri Lanka. *International Journal of Geoheritage and Parks*, 11(2), 234–246. doi: https://doi.org/10.1016/j.ijgeop.2023.03.001.

[15] SDGs (2015). THE 17 GOALS | Sustainable Development. [Online]. Available from: https://sdgs.un.org/goals#history.

[16] Pathirana, M. T. (2024). Potentiality of developing mountain tourism in Sri Lanka: case of central province Sri Lanka. *Journal on Tourism and Sustainability*, 7 (1 and 2), 78–91. doi: https://doi.org/10.5281/zenodo.12599119.

[17] Donaldson, T., & Preston, L. E. (1995). The stakeholder theory of the corporation: concepts, evidence and implications. *Academy of Management Review*, 20(1), 65–91.

[18] Neville, B. A., Bell, S., & Menguc, B. (2005). Corporate reputation, stakeholders and the social performance-financial performance relationship. *European Journal of Marketing*, 39(9-10), 1184–1198.

[19] Sheehan, L. R., Ritchie, J. R. B., & Hudson, S. (2007). Destination stakeholders, exploring identity and salience. *Annals of Tourism Research*, 32(3), 711–734.

[20] Polonsky, M. J., & Scott, D. (2005). An empirical examination of the stakeholder strategy matrix.

European Journal of Marketing, 39(9-10), 1199–1215.

[21] Savage, G. T., Nix, T. W., Whitehead, C. J., & Blair, J. D. (1991). Strategies for assessing and managing organisational stakeholders. *Academy of Management Executives*, 5(2), 61–75.

[22] Freeman, R. E. (1984). Strategic management: A Stakeholder Approach. Boston: Pitman.

[23] Butler, R. W. (1999). Sustainable tourism: a state of the art review. *Tourism Geographies*, 1(1), 7–25.

[24] Getz, D., & Timur, S. (2005). Stakeholder Involvement in Sustainable Tourism: Balancing the Voices. Oxford: Butterworth–Heinemann.

[25] Mason, P. (2003). Tourism impacts, Planning and Management. Oxford: Butterworth-Heinemann.

[26] Bramwell, B., & Sharman, A. (2000). Approaches to Sustainable Tourism Planning and Community Participation: The Case of the Hope Valley. London, New York: Routledge.

[27] Hall, C. M. (2008). Tourism planning: Policies, Processes and Relationships. Harlow: Pearson Prentice Hall.

[28] Nguyen, T. Q. T., Young, T., & Johnson, P. (2019). Conceptualizing networks in sustainable tourism development. *Tourism Management Perspectives*, 32, 1–11.

[29] Byrd, E. T. (2003). An analysis of variables that influence stakeholder participation and support for sustainable tourism development in rural North Carolina.

[30] Gossling, S., Hall, C. M., & Weaver, D. B. (2009). Sustainable Tourism Futures: Perspective on Systems, Restructuring and Innovations. Abingdon: Routledge.

[31] Bramwell, B., & Lane, B. (2011). Critical research on the governance of tourism and sustainability. *Journal of Sustainable Tourism*, 19(4-5), 411–421.

[32] Dredge, D., & Jamal, T. (2013). Mobilities on the gold coast, Australia: implications for destination governance and sustainable tourism. *Journal of Sustainable Tourism*, 21(4), 557–579.

[33] Ladkin, A., & Bertramini, A. M. (2002). Collaborative tourism planning: a case study of Cusco, Peru. *Current Issues in Tourism*, 5(2), 71–93.

[34] Marwick, M. C. (2000). Golf tourism development, stakeholders, differing discourses and alternative agendas. *Tourism Management*, 21(5), 515–524.

[35] Hardy, A., Beeton, R., & Pearson, L. (2002). Sustainable tourism: an overview of the concept and its position in relation to conceptualisations of tourism. *Journal of Sustainable Tourism*, 10(6), 475–496.

[36] Currie, R. R., Seaton, S., & Wesley, F. (2009). Determining stakeholders for feasibility analysis. *Annals of Tourism Research*, 36(1), 41–63.

[37] Byrde, E. T., & Gustke, L. D. (2004). Identifying tourism stakeholder groups based on support for sustainable tourism development and participation in tourism activities. *Sustainable Tourism*. Volume 76 / 97–108.

[38] Yarcan, S., & Çetin, G. (2021). Tour Operating Business. Turkey: Istanbul University Central Campus.

[39] Mihalic, T. (2016). Sustainable-responsible tourism discourse - towards "responsustable" tourism. *Journal of Cleaner Production*, 111, 461–470.

[40] Khairat, G., Maher, A., & Nations, U. (2012). Integrating sustainability into tour operator business : an innovative approach in sustainable tourism. *Tourismos Journal*, 7(1), 213–233.

[41] Lee, S. W., & Xue, K. (2020). Model of destination loyalty: integrating destination image and sustainable tourism sustainable tourism. *Asia Pacific Journal of Tourism Research*, 25(4), 393–408.

[42] Buckley, R. (2012). Sustainable tourism: research and reality. *Annals of Tourism Research*, 39(2), 528–546.

[43] Pattanaro, G., & Donato, S. (2018). Sustainable development goals: a business opportunity for tourism companies?. *Ekonomiczne Problemy Turystyki*, 43, 21–27.

[44] Księżak, P., & Fischbach, B. (2018). Triple bottom line: the pillars of CSR. *Journal of Corporate Responsibility and Leadership*, 4(3), 95.

[45] Hamid, M. C., Isa, S. M., & Kiumarsi, S. (2021). Sustainable tourism practices and business performance from the tour operators' perspectives. *Anatolia*, 32(1), 23–32.

[46] GSTC (2025). Global sustainable tourism council. [Online]. Available from: https://www.gstc.org/.

[47] Edgell, D. L., Allen, M. D. M., Smith, G., & Swanson, J. R. (2008). Tourism Policy and Planning: Yesterday, Today, and Tomorrow. London: Routledge.

[48] Gössling, S., Ring, A., Dwyer, L., Andersson, A. C., & Hall, C. M. (2016). Optimizing or maximizing growth? a challenge for sustainable tourism. *Journal of Sustainable Tourism*, 24(4), 527–548.

[49] Hall, C. M. (2011). Policy learning and policy failure in sustainable tourism governance: from first- and second-order to third-order change?. *Journal of Sustainable Tourism*, 19(4-5), 649–671.

[50] Rasoolimanesh, S. M., Ramakrishna, S., Hall, C. M., Esfandiar, K., & Seyfi, S. (2020). A systematic scoping review of sustainable tourism indicators in relation to the sustainable development goals. *Journal of Sustainable Tourism*, 31(7), 1497–1517.

[51] Hall, C. M. (2019). Constructing sustainable tourism development: the 2030 agenda and the managerial ecology of sustainable tourism. *Journal of Sustainable Tourism*, 27(7), 1044–1060.

[52] Hall, C. M., & Williams, A. M. (2019). Tourism and Innovation. London: Routledge.

[53] Higgins-Desbiolles, F. (2018). Sustainable tourism: sustaining tourism or something more?. *Tourism Management Perspectives*, 25, 157–160.

[54] Aall, C. (2014). Sustainable tourism in practice: promoting or perverting the quest for a sustainable development?. *Sustainability*, 6(5), 2562–2583.

[55] Bramwell, B., Higham, J., Lane, B., & Miller, G. (2017). Twenty-five years of sustainable tourism and the journal of sustainable tourism: looking back and moving forward. *Journal of Sustainable Tourism*, 25(1), 1–9.

[56] GSTC (2020). Costa Rica CST Standard is a GSTC-Recognized Standard. GSTC. https://www.gstc.org/costa-rica-cst-standard-gstc-recognized-standard/.

[57] Usman, O. (2019). Environmental performance and tourism development in EU-28 Countries: the role of institutional quality. *Current Issues in Tourism*, 23(17), 2103–2108.

[58] Slivar, I. (2018). Stakeholders in a tourist destination – matrix of possible relationships towards sustainability. *Open Journal for Research in Economics*, 1(1), 1–10.

[59] Boukas, N., & Ziakas, V. (2014). A chaos theory perspective of destination crisis and sustainable tourism development in Islands: the case of Cyprus. *Tourism Planning and Development*, 11(2), 191–209.

[60] Gursoy, D., Ouyang, Z., Nunkoo, R., & Wei, W. (2019). Residents' impact perceptions of and attitudes towards tourism development: a meta-analysis. *Journal of Hospitality Marketing and Management*, 28(3), 306–333.

[61] Gannon, M., Rasoolimanesh, S. M., & Taheri, B. (2021). Assessing the mediating role of residents' perceptions toward tourism development. *Journal of Travel Research*, 60(1), 149–171.

[62] Budeanu, A., Miller, G., Moscardo, G., & Ooi, C. S. (2016). Sustainable tourism, progress, challenges and opportunities: an introduction. *Journal of Cleaner Production*, 111, 285–294.

[63] Law, A., De Lacy, T., Lipman, G., & Jiang, M. (2016). Transitioning to a green economy: the case of tourism in Bali, Indonesia. *Journal of Cleaner Production*, 111, 295–305.

[64] Saunders, M., Lewis, P., & Thornill, A. (2007). Research Methods for Business Students. Harlow: Prentice Hall.

[65] Sandelowski, M. (2004). Using qualitative research. *Qualitative Health Research*, 14(10), 1366–1386.

[66] Chowdhury, M. F. (2014). Interpretivism in aiding our understanding of the contemporary social world. *Open Journal of Philosophy*, 4(3), 432–438.

[67] Saunders, M. N. K., Lewis, P., & Thornhill, A. (2019). Research Methods for Business Students. Harlow: Pearson.

[68] Cornelisse, M. (2020). Peru case study: power relations in community-based tourism. *Journal of Tourism and Cultural Change*, 18(4), 437–454.

[69] Jordan, E. J., Vogt, C. A., & Kruger, L. E. (2013). The interplay of governance, power, and citizen participation in community tourism planning. *Journal of Policy Research in Tourism Leisure and Events*, 5(3), 270–288.

[70] Samarathunga, W. H. M. S., Cheng, L., & Weerathunga, P. (2021). Buddhist gaze and power in a post-war destination: case study of Jaffna, Sri Lanka. *Journal of Tourism and Cultural Change*, 19(5), 654–680.

[71] Saito, H., & Ruhanen, L. (2017). Power in tourism stakeholder collaborations: power types and power holders. *Journal of Hospitality and Tourism Management*, 31, 189–196.

[72] DCS (2024). Statistical Pocket Book 2024. Department of Census and Statistics Sri Lanka.

[73] Banister, P., Burman, E., Parker, I., Taylor, M., & Tindall, C. (2011). Qualitative Methods In Psychology: A Research Guide: A Research Guide. Berkshire: Open University Press.

[74] Bryman, A., & Bell, E. (2011). Business Research Methods. Oxford: Oxford University Press.

[75] Feilzer, M. Y. (2010). Doing mixed methods research pragmatically: implications for the rediscovery of pragmatism as a research paradigm. *Journal of Mixed Methods Research*, 4(1), 6–16.

[76] Yin, R. K. (2014). Case Study Research: Design and Methods. Thousand Oaks, CA: SAGE.

[77] Howell, K. E. (2015). An Introduction to the Philosophy of Methodology. London: SAGE.

[78] Birks, M., & Mills, J. (2011). Grounded Theory: A Practical Guide. SAGE.

[79] Clarke, V., & Braun, V. (2017). Thematic analysis. *Journal of Positive Psychology*, 12(3), 297–298.

[80] Moscardo, G., & Murphy, L. (2014). There is no such thing as sustainable tourism: re-conceptualizing tourism as a tool for sustainability. *Sustainability*, 6(5), 2538–2561.

[81] Gamage, D., & Samarathunga, M. (2020). Alternative tourism as an alternate to mass tourism during the post-COVID-19 recovery phase. *Sunday Times, Sri Lanka.*

[82] Ranasinghe, R. (2015). Strategic myopia of tourism development in Sri Lanka; a critique. *International Journal of Multidisciplinary Research and Development*, 2(2), 604–609.

[83] BBC Travel (2025). The 25 best places to travel in 2025. Bbc.com. https://www.bbc.com/

travel/article/20250115-the-25-best-places-to-travel-in-2025.

[84] Cavagnaro, E., Staffieri, S., & Ngesa, F. (2015). Looking from a local lens: Inbound tour operators and sustainable tourism in Kenya. *Research in Hospitality Management*, 5(2), 135–145.

[85] Cucculelli, M., & Goffi, G. (2016). Does sustainability enhance tourism destination competitiveness? evidence from Italian destinations of excellence. *Journal of Cleaner Production*, 111, 370–382.

[86] Prasiasa, D. P. O., Karmini, N. W., & Widari, D. A. D. S. (2024). Challenges of strengthening culture in the development of sustainable tourism Villages in Bali. *Journal Seni Budaya*, 39(1), 34–44. doi: https://doi.org/10.31091/mudra.v39i1.2554.

[87] Tenzin, K., Mee-Udon, F., & Prampesit, R. (2019). Community opinion towards a village homestay program in Soe, a small nomadic community in the North-West of bhutan community opinion towards a village homestay program in Soe, a small nomadic community in the North-West of Bhutan. *African Journal of Hospitality, Tourism and Leisure*, 8(3), 1–10.

35 Fostering writing autonomy in ESL learners: self-directed learning with ChatGPT in large-class settings

Ashani Jayasundara[1,a] *and Fairoza Fairooz*[2,b]

[1]NSBM Green University, Pitipana, Homagama, Sri Lanka

[2]Oklahoma State University, United States

Abstract

Large undergraduate ESL classes often struggle to provide timely, individualized writing feedback, hindering students' writing development and autonomy. The integration of Generative AI tools like ChatGPT in undergraduate education is gaining momentum as they offer instant, personalized support, however their role in facilitating self-directed learning and writing autonomy remains under-explored. This study explores how ChatGPT can support self-directed writing in an under-resourced, large ESL writing classrooms setting. Conducted with 150 undergraduates following a mandatory English course at a private university in Sri Lanka, the research adopts a qualitative approach by deriving data from student interviews, focus groups, and error analysis of student writing. Findings indicate that AI-generated feedback significantly improves lower-order writing skills, such as grammar and mechanics, by offering immediate, consistent suggestions. In contrast, teacher feedback is more effective for higher-order aspects like idea development, coherence, and organization, due to its personalized and context-sensitive nature. Students reported increased confidence and motivation when using ChatGPT, citing its instant explanations and capacity for supporting self-correction. In large ESL classes, ChatGPT can significantly support learner autonomy by offering scaffolded, real-time feedback and idea support. To maximize its benefits, instructors should integrate ChatGPT with traditional instruction: leveraging AI for routine corrections while focusing teacher feedback on higher-order concerns. However, the study also emphasizes the continuous need for teacher guidance in managing content and structure.

Keywords: AI tools, ChatGPT, error analysis, ESL writing, feedback, learner autonomy, self-directed learning

Introduction

English writing instruction in large university classes faces persistent challenges in providing individualized feedback as it traditionally relies on teacher feedback to guide students through content development, organization, grammar, and style. Students in English as a Second Language (ESL) contexts often encounter a range of linguistic challenges such as limited vocabulary, unfamiliarity with academic discourse, and difficulties with grammar and cohesion which hinder their academic success. In large-class environments, however, individualized feedback is scarce due to limited instructor time and resources. Specifically, in developing countries like Sri Lanka, writing courses often has more than hundred undergraduates, making regular formative feedback from instructors impractical. This often leads to unaddressed writing issues and low student confidence. In such settings, AI tools present a promising avenue to provide instant, individualized feedback that will help students improve their writing outside the constraints of classroom time. Autonomous, self-directed learning in writing is therefore, desirable as learners will be able to independently identify and correct errors by themselves.

With the increasing accessibility of AI-powered platforms educators and researchers are beginning to explore how these tools can be harnessed to enhance English writing skills. Large Language Models (LLMs) such as OpenAI's ChatGPT have emerged as promising solutions [1]. These tools aim to automate certain aspects of providing feedback, offering immediate and consistent revisions that could potentially reduce teacher workload and enable more frequent and personalized feedback for learners [2]. Early research suggests AI tutoring can double learning efficiency and that hybrid human-AI approaches leverage both rapid AI feedback and teacher guidance.

[a]ashani.J@nsbm.ac.lk, [b]fairoza.fairooz@okstate.edu

DOI: 10.4324/9781003739920-35

However, concerns remain about AI's role. In the literature on writing feedback, a clear distinction exists between lower-order concerns (LOC) which includes grammar, vocabulary, mechanics and higher-order concerns (HOC) which refers to content, coherence, idea development. Human instructors typically emphasize HOC, offering conceptual guidance, whereas automated tools excel at LOC. ChatGPT, as an AI-powered feedback tool, is reputed to provide detailed grammar corrections and explanations however, its capacity to address complex HOC issues or promote genuine learner autonomy remains uncertain. This paper explores the role of ChatGPT in supporting writing autonomy among ESL learners in large classes specifically, (1) how students perceive ChatGPT as a self-directed learning aid, (2) in which aspects of writing ChatGPT feedback is most and least effective, and (3) how it complements teacher feedback. The study investigates how ChatGPT reliably fixes grammar and mechanics, boosting learner confidence, while human instructors are still crucial for advising on structure and content.

Learner autonomy and self-directed learning

Learner autonomy refers to students' ability to take charge of their own learning, including goal setting, strategy use, and self-assessment. In language education, promoting autonomy has been linked to higher motivation and better long-term outcomes. AI-driven feedback has been proposed to encourage students to explore language forms and content independently. ChatGPT fosters personalized and interactive learning, thereby promoting SDL, as students can input their own questions and research topics through the AI [3]. Similarly, automated writing evaluation (AWE) systems like Pigai have been reported to increase autonomy when students engage in multiple revision cycles at their own pace. These studies suggest that AI tools can complement autonomy by providing flexible, on-demand support. However, autonomy does not emerge automatically; it depends on how learners engage with feedback.

AI feedback and writing skill development

Prior studies show that AI-driven writing tools can positively impact L2 writing accuracy and learner attitudes. One study conducted a large-scale intervention with undergraduates and found a significant positive impact of ChatGPT on students' academic writing skills [4]. Students in the study overwhelmingly viewed ChatGPT as a helpful, reliable grammar aid. Similarly, a recent TESL forum review reports empirical evidence that ChatGPT aids learners in "enhancing their acquisition of grammar, vocabulary, and writing skills"; participants noted marked improvements in grammar scores after sustained ChatGPT use. In aggregate, these findings suggest ChatGPT is a potent automated writing evaluator (AWE) for certain writing dimensions.

Notably, systematic reviews conclude that ChatGPT and related AI tools can "boost learners' motivation, automating instructional tasks, and offering instantaneous, personalized feedback to learners". By tailoring corrections to individual errors and immediately responding to queries, ChatGPT functions as a 24/7 writing coach, potentially increasing learner engagement. It was found that Korean EFL students using ChatGPT reported high confidence and a "shift toward metacognitive awareness", attributing improved writing to the tool's feedback [5]. These studies highlight ChatGPT's role in building learner autonomy: by providing on-demand explanations and suggestions, students can practice self-editing without waiting for a teacher. ChatGPT increases learning autonomy by providing tailored language support, promoting self-reflection and self -evaluation, enabling practice in language skills, and offering instant feedback [6]. In short, AI feedback seems especially effective at reinforcing LOC issues and giving learners agency.

Teacher feedback and higher-order concerns

Several studies have compared ChatGPT-generated feedback to teacher or peer feedback. Conversely, much literature emphasizes that human teachers excel at higher-order writing feedback. According to writing pedagogy, LOC (spelling, tense) is separate from HOC (idea quality, coherence). In ESL contexts, teachers often place a strong emphasis on content development and organizational coherence which are areas where AI tools still face limitations. Experienced ESL instructors offer nuanced, context-sensitive feedback on elements such as clarity, the strength and relevance of supporting evidence, and the overall unity of the text. According to research in writing assessment, this kind of interactive and dialogic teacher feedback plays a crucial role in fostering students' reasoning skills and critical thinking. These HOC tasks remain largely beyond the current capabilities of AI writing tools.

Writing autonomy and large classes

Teaching writing in large ESL classes is often constrained by class size and resource limitations. Learner autonomy is a core goal in L2 writing students to monitor and correct their own errors and learn more effectively. ChatGPT's interactive nature encourages students to ask questions and reflect, fostering autonomy. In crowded classrooms where teachers cannot address every student individually, ChatGPT can break the barrier by offering tailored feedback that goes beyond the barriers of language, time, and place [4]. ChatGPT and similar AI tools strengthen self-directed L2 writing by improving accuracy and motivation, while traditional teacher feedback remains indispensable for deeper conceptual learning.

Materials and Methodology

This study employed a qualitative, exploratory design to investigate ESL learners' experiences with ChatGPT in a large class writing context. The participants were 150 undergraduate students enrolled in mandatory English writing courses in the faculty of Computing at a private Sri Lankan university. The students represented various proficiency levels and academic majors, but all had foundational writing instruction. Over one semester, ChatGPT was integrated into the writing curriculum as a supplementary feedback tool. The ESL instructor demonstrated how to use the ChatGPT chatbot for drafting and revising essays and provided guidelines on posing effective prompts. Students were then assigned writing tasks including short essays and paragraphs for which they could consult ChatGPT. They were instructed to use ChatGPT's suggestions to refine their drafts and to keep track of how they incorporated AI feedback.

Multiple qualitative data sources captured student perspectives. First, semi-structured focus group discussions (total 5 groups of 6–8 students, selected to represent various proficiency levels) probed how students used ChatGPT, compared it to teacher feedback, and what outcomes they perceived. Second, in-depth interviews (15 participants, purposively chosen for active ChatGPT users) explored individual experiences, autonomy in writing, and attitudes toward AI feedback.

For each assignment, students first drafted essays and then received feedback in two ways: (a) automated feedback from ChatGPT (in a guided self-review exercise) and (b) conventional teacher comments (on a separate draft). To ensure consistency, teacher feedback was provided according to a rubric covering both content, organization and language accuracy. After receiving feedback and revising their drafts, students faced semi-structured interviews to gain deeper insights into attitudes and learning processes. Interview questions probed how students used ChatGPT, what kinds of errors it helped with, and how it affected their self-editing strategies.

Additionally, an error analysis was performed on a stratified sample of 45 student writing samples. Rather than quantifying frequency, the analysis focused on how students responded to different types of errors (e.g., grammar, vocabulary, coherence) and how they used ChatGPT feedback to revise them. A qualitative error analysis of students was conducted by asking them to annotate their drafts with reflections on how they used ChatGPT (e.g., which suggestions they accepted, ignored, or modified), offering insights into their reasoning and decision-making. These annotated drafts were treated as artifacts of learner thinking, aligning with qualitative traditions in writing research.

Thematic analysis was complemented by an interpretive error analysis, where errors were categorized into LOC and HOC, and then linked to student reflections and interview data. Rather than tracking correction rates, it was observed how learners understood the nature of their errors, how ChatGPT helped or failed to resolve them and how students' revision strategies reflected growing autonomy. This approach allowed to explore the relationship between error awareness, AI feedback, and learner agency which are central themes in self-directed writing development.

Results and Discussion

A large majority of students reported that ChatGPT helped them correct grammar (89%) and vocabulary usage (81%) in their essays, compared to fewer for teacher feedback on these issues. In contrast, most students found teacher feedback more helpful for content and organization: 77% said teacher comments improved the coherence of their ideas versus only 22% for ChatGPT. Students' responses illustrate a clear split: ChatGPT was valued for fixing mechanical errors, while teachers guided higher-order improvement.

Lower-order feedback and learning

Interviews revealed that ChatGPT's detailed explanations empowered students to self-correct and learn rules. One student remarked, "I've been using Grammarly, but ChatGPT explains grammar queries with examples… you learn the details about sentence structure". Many students appreciated that ChatGPT would not only mark an error but also describe why it was wrong and how to fix it. Several interviewees said ChatGPT acted like a tutor, allowing them to ask follow-up questions ("Why is this wrong?") in real time. In reflective annotations, students often quoted ChatGPT's suggestions and explained why they accepted or modified them. For example:

> *"ChatGPT said 'has went' is wrong and should be 'has gone.' I checked online, and yes, it's past participle. Now I remember that rule."*

Students actively engaged with feedback, asking follow-up questions or trying out different prompts to verify their understanding. This self-questioning behavior aligns with principles of metacognitive development. Importantly, students began noticing patterns in their own writing:

> *"I always forget to add articles. After ChatGPT corrected me three times, I realized I do this a lot."*

This iterative self-correction process was seen as building confidence and autonomy where students took ownership of learning by experimenting with prompts and explanations. For instance, after revising with ChatGPT, one student reported double-checking and understanding new concepts, saying they felt "less dependent" on the teacher for spotting minor mistakes.

Higher-order feedback limitations

A second theme concerned ChatGPT's limitations. Students acknowledged that while ChatGPT polished grammar and style, it often missed deeper issues. One participant noted that ChatGPT tended to "focus on individual sentences" without considering the essay's overall logic. In several annotated essays, students noted: "ChatGPT says 'your argument is strong,' but I'm not sure. It didn't tell me what part is strong". Some students copied vague suggestions like "Consider improving the organization" without understanding how to act on them. Others ignored ChatGPT's higher-order advice altogether, relying instead on teacher input or peer feedback.

Several students remarked they preferred teacher feedback for organization: "The teacher noticed that my conclusion didn't follow from the introduction," one said, a connection ChatGPT never highlighted. This suggests that current AI lacks the true understanding of ideas needed to mentor higher-order concerns.

Autonomy and motivation

Across interviews, students expressed that using ChatGPT made them more engaged and self-motivated. The ability to get instant feedback "24/7" meant they could revise drafts late at night or on weekends without waiting, which is critical in large classes where teacher availability is limited. The interviews revealed deeper autonomy gains: students reported that after interacting with ChatGPT, they more actively reflected on their choices ("I now always ask ChatGPT why I chose that word"). This aligns with the theory that tailored feedback lowers affective barriers and fosters self-regulation. By prompting self-reflection and offering alternative wordings or sentence structures, ChatGPT seems to encourage an internalized learning process, with one student commenting, "It shows me mistakes, then I think 'How can I avoid that next time?'".

Student preferences

Over one semester, students used ChatGPT alongside regular writing instruction. Students overwhelmingly reported that ChatGPT's immediate feedback and idea-generation support empowered them to revise drafts autonomously, especially for surface-level issues. Many saw ChatGPT as a non-judgmental tutor that enhanced their motivation and confidence. However, students also noted ChatGPT's limitations in addressing the need to verify its suggestions. When comparing feedback sources, students found ChatGPT excelled at rapid surface-level corrections, whereas teacher feedback was preferred for deeper content and structural guidance. Importantly, combining AI and teacher feedback yielded the most comprehensive revisions. In large ESL classes, ChatGPT can significantly support learner autonomy by offering scaffolded, real-time feedback and idea support.

When asked to compare, 83% of students said they would continue using ChatGPT for grammar and editing homework, whereas only 30% felt confident using it to develop essay ideas. Almost all students still valued teacher input on content. Many suggested a hybrid workflow: use ChatGPT for initial draft revision, then discuss substance with the instructor. This preference supports a blended approach: leverage AI for efficiency on repetitive tasks, while dedicating scarce teacher time to critical thinking and creativity. As one student summarized, "ChatGPT is great for drills; the teacher is great for discussion." These perceptions mirror recommendations in literature for combining AI and human instruction.

Findings highlight both opportunities and challenges. One of the key highlights is that ChatGPT can scale feedback in large classes. Instructors in the study noted that with ChatGPT handling most grammar checks, they had more time to address global issues during class. This addresses a key gap in crowded ESL settings. ChatGPT's multilingual support also helped students with weaker English: some asked questions in their first language and received explanations in English, a strategy impossible with one teacher. However, in terms of challenges, overreliance and accuracy were concerns. A few students admitted to depending on ChatGPT too much, sometimes accepting its corrections without critical thought. Instances of ChatGPT providing an incorrect suggestion, for example, and odd synonym, made students cautious. Teachers must therefore train students to verify AI feedback, treating it as a second opinion. It should be encouraged as a pedagogical tool instead of a shortcut. Another issue is motivation drift: while most were engaged, a small minority became complacent, skimming suggestions rather than grappling with their own mistakes. There is also the risk of students using ChatGPT inappropriately (e.g., generating content instead of editing it). Pedagogically, clear guidelines are needed: instructors in this study began requiring students to submit a list of "questions asked to ChatGPT" as proof of active use.

Overall, the results suggest a hybrid feedback model. Teachers can continue to evaluate essays holistically and address thesis, support, and organization tasks where AI feedback is limited. Meanwhile, curricula can incorporate ChatGPT-based exercises: for example, low-stakes drafts could be submitted to ChatGPT first, allowing students to learn from mistakes. This frees teacher time to focus on higher-order conferences or group workshops.

Conclusion

In large-lecture ESL writing classes, fostering student autonomy is a cornerstone of effective instruction. Our study reveals that ChatGPT-assisted self-directed learning offers a promising strategy for addressing the challenge of providing timely and individualized feedback in such settings. ChatGPT functioned as an accessible and responsive tool for students to engage in self-assessment, particularly in addressing lower-order concerns such as grammar, vocabulary, and mechanics. Students were able to act immediately on AI-generated corrections, resulting in measurable reductions in mechanical errors, as supported by our error analysis.

The pedagogical implications of these findings are significant. Educators should consider integrating ChatGPT into their instruction as part of a blended feedback model, in which AI offers continuous, low-level support while teachers concentrate on complex, conceptual aspects of writing. Adopting this approach can help mitigate the feedback bottleneck commonly experienced in large ESL classes while empowering learners to become more independent, reflective writers. Moreover, fostering critical digital literacy around tools like ChatGPT is an essential skill for 21st century learners navigating increasingly AI-integrated academic and professional environments.

The findings suggest that a blended feedback model where AI supports routine corrections and teachers address conceptual development can enhance learner autonomy in large-class ESL settings. This model offers practical implications for educators and curriculum designers seeking to integrate AI tools into academic writing instruction while maintaining the essential role of human feedback. Future work could explore long-term effects of ChatGPT use on writing proficiency and autonomy, as well as optimal ways to train teachers and learners for this new paradigm. Despite initial challenges, our evidence indicates that self-directed use of ChatGPT boosts writing autonomy and skill in ESL learners, making it a valuable tool in the modern classroom.

References

[1] Makwana, R. (2025). A comparative analysis of AI-powered and teacher-led feedback. *Journal of*

English Language Teaching and Innovation (JELTI), 6(1), 14–29.

[2] Nassar, H. M. (2025). Comparing the quality of AI-generated and instructor feedback in a university writing program. M.A. thesis, Dept. of Applied Linguistics, American Univ. in Cairo, Cairo, Egypt.

[3] Li, Z., Wang, C., & Bonk, C. J. (2024). Exploring the utility of ChatGPT for self-directed online language learning. *Online Learning*, 28(3), 159–172.

[4] Mahapatra, S. (2024). Impact of ChatGPT on ESL students' academic writing skills: a mixed methods intervention study. *Smart Learning Environments*, 11(1), 9. doi: 10.1186/s40561-024-00295-9.

[5] Van Horn, K. R. (2024). ChatGPT in English language learning: exploring perceptions and promoting autonomy in a university EFL context. *TESL-EJ*, 28(1), 1–26.

[6] Agustini, H., et al. (2023). Improving language abilities, learning autonomy and motivation through ChatGPT. *Studies in Applied Linguistics*, 24(1), 24–37.

36 The impact of gamification in enhancing user engagement and motivation for learning management platforms

U.P.D.P. Maduranga[1,a], *J.P.D. Wijesekara*[2,b], *H.P. Dissanayake*[1,c], *M.G. Tharaka Nayanapriya*[1,d] *and P.S. Kankanamge*[3,e]

[1]Department of Marketing and Tourism Management , NSBM Green University, Homagama, Sri Lanka

[2]Department of Computer and Data Science, NSBM Green University, Homagama, Sri Lanka

[3]Department Software Engineering and Computer Security, NSBM Green University, Homagama, Sri Lanka

Abstract

The integration of gamification in learning management systems (LMS) has emerged as a transformative strategy. Especially to address persistent issues of learner disengagement and motivation decline in digital education environments. This study investigates the effectiveness of game-based elements such as points, badges, leaderboards, and adaptive feedback in fostering user engagement and motivation within LMS platforms. This study is grounded in established motivational frameworks, including Self-Determination Theory and Flow Theory. The research employs a mixed-methods approach to analyze how learners respond to various gamification features and how these responses differ across both traditional and adaptive gamification on user engagement and motivation. The findings reveal that traditional gamification techniques can significantly boost short term engagement. Whereas they often suffer from sustainability challenges such as gamification fatigue. In contrast to that adaptive gamification where content and rewards are tailored to individual user profiles demonstrates stronger potential in promoting long term motivation and inclusive learning experiences. The study concludes with practical recommendations for LMS developers and educators on implementing effective, personalized gamification strategies to enhance learning outcomes and user satisfaction.

Keywords: Adaptive gamification, educational technology, gamification, learning management systems, motivation, user engagement

Introduction

The growth of learning management systems (LMS) has transformed educational delivery in academic and corporate settings by enabling accessible, scalable, and asynchronous learning experiences. Contrast to their widespread adoption, LMS platforms frequently encounter challenges in maintaining consistent learner engagement and motivation, leading to reduced course completion rates, diminished learning outcomes, and overall dissatisfaction among users [1].

In order to address these challenges, gamification of the application of game design elements in non-game contexts has emerged as a promising pedagogical strategy. Elements such as points, badges, leaderboards, and progress tracking are integrated into LMS platforms. This is led with the goal of fostering a more interactive, rewarding, and motivating learning environment [3]. Gamification draws on motivational theories such as Self-Determination Theory (SDT), which emphasizes autonomy, competence, and relatedness as key drivers of intrinsic motivation [4], and Flow Theory, which posits that optimal learning occurs when individuals are fully immersed in appropriately challenging tasks [5].

Recent studies indicate that gamification can improve user participation and engagement in LMS contexts. Especially in the early stages of course interaction [6]. However, concerns persist regarding the long-term effectiveness of static gamified elements. Repeated exposure to fixed rewards can result in "gamification fatigue". Where learners become desensitized to stimuli such as badges and points, thereby weakening their intrinsic motivation over time [7]. Gamification outcomes are not uniformly positive across all learners. Some users respond negatively to competitive mechanisms like leaderboards [8].

[a]dpmaduranga.info@gmail.com, [b]dulanjali.w@nsbm.ac.lk, [c]hasantha.d@nsbm.ac.lk, [d]tharaka.n@nsbm.ac.lk, [e]pavithras@nsbm.ac.lk

DOI: 10.4324/9781003739920-36

For the purpose of mitigating these limitations adaptive gamification has gained attention. This approach involves dynamically adjusting gamified elements based on individual learner profiles, performance data, and preferences. This offers a personalized motivational experience [9]. Adaptive gamification seeks to sustain user interest by providing contextually relevant challenges and feedback tailored to individual progress and behavior patterns.

This study investigates the impact of both traditional and adaptive gamification on user engagement and motivation within LMS platforms. Further this study evaluates how different gamification strategies influence learning behavior and satisfaction. The findings aim to inform educators and LMS developers about effective, sustainable gamification practices that can enhance digital learning outcomes and learner well-being.

Literature Review

Gamification which is called the application of game design elements in non-game contexts. This has become a widely adopted strategy in digital education to enhance learner engagement and motivation. This section synthesizes the theoretical foundations of gamification, explores the effects of specific game elements, and also examines emerging trends in adaptive gamification.

Theoretical foundations of gamification

Gamification is conceptually grounded in self-determination theory (SDT). This is put forward that learners are more intrinsically motivated when their psychological needs. Such as autonomy, competence, and relatedness are fulfilled [1]. Game elements such as points, badges, and feedback mechanisms address these needs by offering structured rewards, recognition, and opportunities for meaningful progress [15].

Flow theory, which was introduced by Csikszentmihalyi, further explains how learners achieve optimal engagement when tasks are matched to their skill levels and present meaningful challenges [2]. In gamified LMS platforms, tasks such as progressively difficult quizzes or time-based challenges help maintain this balance [16].

Behavioral reinforcement theory supports the notion that positive reinforcement. Through rewards also can shape learner behavior and enhance motivation. Research shows that immediate feedback from gamification leads to faster and more persistent learner engagement in online platforms [3].

Gamification in learning management systems

Gamification has demonstrated a significant impact on student performance and learning management systems (LMS) interaction [17]. In a study conducted by Hamari, gamified LMS platforms incorporating points, badges, and leaderboards (PBL) reported a 30 to 40% increase in engagement metrics compared to non-gamified systems [4]. As well as that Domínguez found that gamification improved task completion rates and fostered a sense of achievement which is leading to better academic outcomes [5].

A systematic review by Zainuddin concluded that gamification improves retention and enjoyment in online learning. This made students 33% more likely to complete their courses [6]. More recent studies have echoed these findings. In a 2021 study, Mora analyzed gamification interventions across 25 European universities and found statistically significant improvement in student engagement across STEM disciplines. Sailer emphasized that properly aligned gamified elements enhance students' emotional and cognitive involvement, particularly when paired with formative feedback [22]. These findings reinforce the potential of gamification to address core challenges in online education.

Impact of core gamification elements

The most common gamification framework points, badges, and leaderboards (PBL) have diverse effects on learners [14]

- Points serve as immediate feedback mechanisms that reward task completion and reinforce positive behavior. Points-based systems in LMS like Moodle have been linked to increased assignment submissions and participation rates [4].
- Badges function as symbols of mastery. Research indicates that they improve learner confidence and satisfaction when tied to meaningful achievements [7].
- Leaderboards promote competition and visibility of performance. While effective for competitive students, they may demotivate others, leading to the need for optional or team-based ranking systems [8].

Additional features such as progress bars, quests, and collaborative missions have been found to stimulate long-term cognitive engagement and group interaction in blended and STEM-focused environments [9].

Adaptive gamification and personalization

To overcome the limitations of static gamification, such as "gamification fatigue," where learners become desensitized to repetitive rewards, researchers have advocated for adaptive gamification—the tailoring of game mechanics based on learner behavior and performance data [19].

Studies by Alomari [10] demonstrated that adaptive systems dynamically adjust challenge levels and feedback frequency, resulting in 20% higher satisfaction and 15% better retention rates compared to standard gamified platforms [10]. These systems personalize rewards and learning paths based on real-time learner data, improving inclusivity and long-term motivation.

While traditional gamification often uses static features, adaptive gamification personalizes the learning experience by adjusting challenges and rewards based on learner data. Alomari in their research found that adaptive systems led to a 20% increase in learner satisfaction and higher knowledge retention. Through tailoring content to users' skill levels, adaptive gamification fosters inclusivity and reduces disengagement.

Artificial intelligence (AI)-driven gamification systems are gaining traction, with recent models capable of real-time content adaptation, sentiment analysis, and predictive motivation tracking [21]. These intelligent systems are particularly valuable in large-scale MOOCs, where learner heterogeneity is high.

However, implementing adaptive gamification presents challenges, including the need for sophisticated algorithms, real-time analytics, and ethical concerns related to user data privacy [11].

Critical reflections on the drawbacks of gamification

Though gamification is widely recognized for its ability to enhance engagement, several drawbacks must be critically considered. One such issue is gamification fatigue, where learners become desensitized to repetitive rewards like points and badges, reducing their long-term motivational value [23]. This effect can undermine sustained learning by shifting focus away from intrinsic goals.

Furthermore, over-reliance on extrinsic motivators may erode intrinsic motivation. Hanus and Fox found that students exposed to gamification often performed worse in the long term due to diminished self-directed learning, especially when rewards overshadowed content relevance [24].

Equity and inclusivity concerns have also been raised. Competitive elements such as leaderboards can demotivate learners who consistently rank lower, especially those with lower self-efficacy or from non-competitive cultural backgrounds [25]. This makes gamification potentially exclusionary if not carefully designed [18].

Moreover, the effectiveness of gamification is highly context-dependent. Elements that resonate with younger learners may appear trivial or patronizing to adult or professional learners [26]. Adaptive gamification offers a partial solution, but introduces new challenges related to privacy, data ethics, and algorithmic bias, particularly when systems personalize content based on behavioral tracking [27].

These limitations underscore the need for thoughtful, learner-centered design and careful alignment between gamified elements and pedagogical goals.

Case studies of gamified LMS implementations

Several case studies further demonstrate gamification's effectiveness

- Classcraft, used in UI/UX design courses, assigns learners roles like Wizard or Warrior and involves quests that increase collaborative learning and student motivation [12].
- Moodle, integrated with PBL mechanics, saw a significant rise in course completion rates and student satisfaction through competitive ranking and immediate feedback [6].
- SEP-CyLE, a gamified platform for STEM education, used points and social collaboration to increase engagement, especially in teamwork-driven modules [13].

Methodology

Research design

This study adopted a mixed-methods research design to examine how gamification influences user engagement and motivation in Learning Management Systems (LMS), specifically within programing language and technical content learning contexts.

Combining quantitative and qualitative methods enabled a robust analysis of learner behavior and perceptions in response to gamified features.

Due to limitations in accessing institutional LMS platforms, a mock LMS interface was custom developed to simulate key LMS functionalities using backend logs, embedded with gamification elements such as points, badges, leaderboards, and progress tracking. This allowed for controlled testing while closely replicating a real-world LMS experience. A mock LMS interface was custom developed to simulate key functionalities (see Figure 36.1 for the student dashboard, Figure 36.2 for course overview, and Figure 36.3 for course content display.

Study duration and experimental setup

The experimental study was conducted over a four-week period and followed a structured A/B testing methodology with standardization measures such as Same lab, same task order, no external materials. Initially, a mock Learning Management System (LMS) was custom developed to simulate realistic academic tasks, such as quizzes, exercises, and content review in modules. Two versions of the LMS were created, one using static gamification elements (fixed badges, leaderboards, etc.) and the other incorporating adaptive gamification (tailored difficulty levels, personalized feedback).

Participants (n = 48) were randomly assigned into two equal groups. Group A (static gamification) and Group B (adaptive gamification). Each group participated in scheduled, supervised lab sessions twice a week, ensuring consistency in environmental conditions and task access. Each session lasted 60 minutes, during which participants interacted with the LMS while all activity (logins, completions, time-on-task) was recorded via backend logs.

Pre-study surveys were conducted to assess baseline motivation and engagement levels, and post-study surveys captured changes in learner perception, motivation, and usability. A subgroup from each group also participated in follow-up interviews to gain deeper qualitative insights. This controlled setup allowed for accurate comparison of gamification types on learner behavior and motivation.

Participants

The study involved 48 undergraduate students enrolled in programming languages and technical content learning courses across three different universities in Sri Lanka. Participants were selected to represent a diversity of academic disciplines, digital proficiency levels, and motivational profiles. All participants engaged with the mock LMS interface under supervised conditions.

A purposive sampling method ensured the inclusion of learners from faculties such as business, engineering, and humanities, thereby increasing the external validity of the study findings.

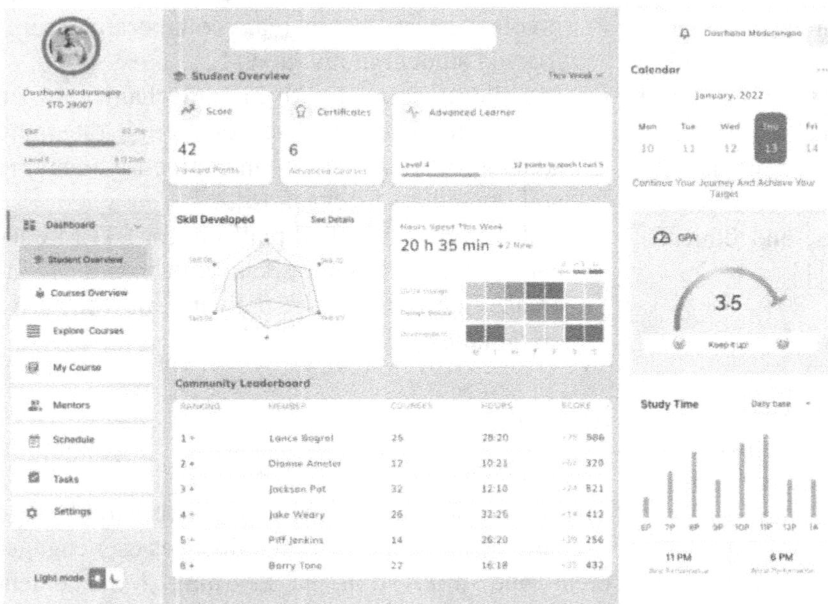

Figure 36.1 Student dashboard suggested for the learning management platform
Source: Author

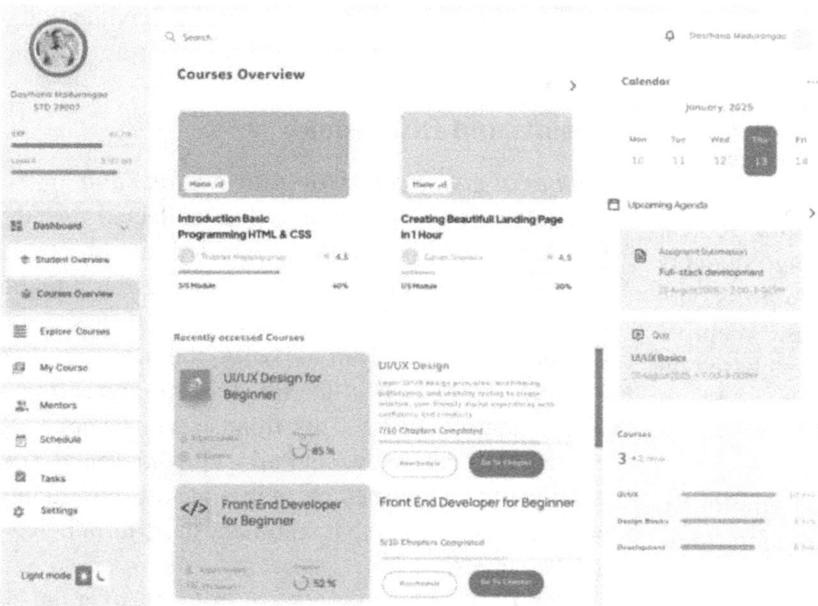

Figure 36.2 Course overview
Source: Author

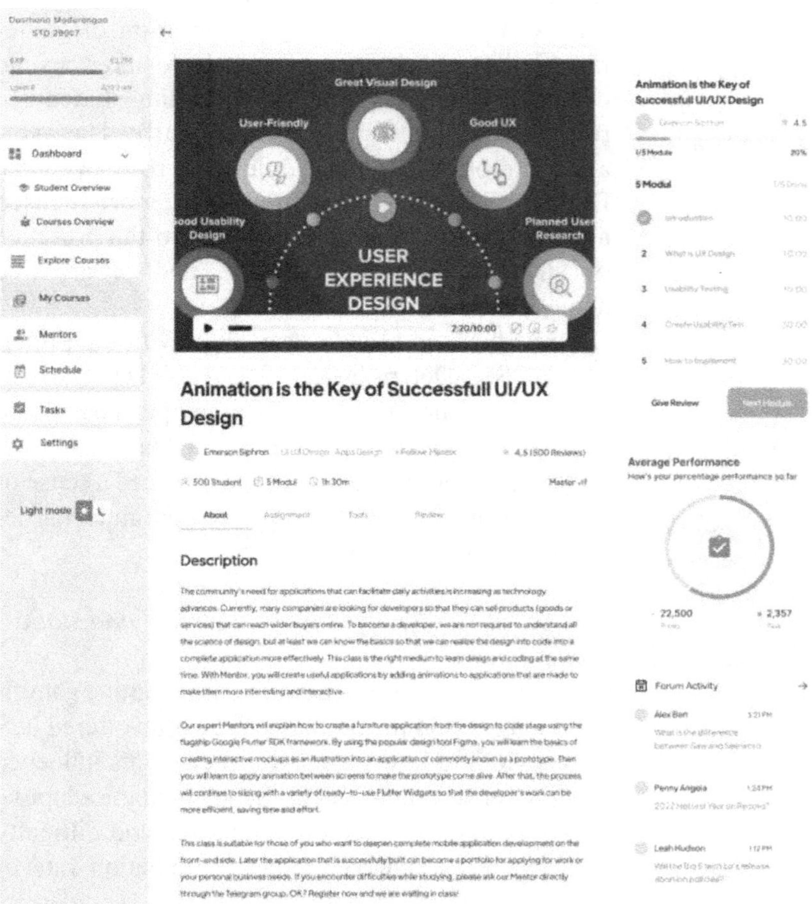

Figure 36.3 Course content display page
Source: Author

Gamification elements implemented

The mock LMS was designed with the following gamification components based on Self-Determination Theory and Flow Theory. Points for completing vocabulary, grammar, and comprehension exercises. Badges are awarded for milestones such as consistent attendance or high quiz scores. Leaderboards displaying top-performing students weekly to foster positive competition. Progress bars to indicate individual completion status. Adaptive feedback and bonus challenges for learners based on real-time performance.

Data collection methods

For this research quantitative data was employed. The mock LMS recorded user interaction logs, including login frequency, task completions, and time-on-task. Data were analyzed pre- and post-gamification exposure to observe behavioral changes.

Qualitative Data was gathered using interviews. Participants responded to a structured questionnaire consisting of Likert-scale items and open-ended prompts that explored engagement, motivation, and usability. Learner reflections on the gamified experience, particularly in relation to learnings, were gathered. A subgroup of 20 participants interacted with an adaptive version of the gamified interface where task difficulty and feedback were customized based on learner inputs. Comparative analysis was conducted against a non-adaptive group to assess differences in motivation and completion rates.

Data analysis techniques

Quantitative data were analyzed using SPSS, with paired t-tests and ANOVA used to identify statistically significant differences in engagement levels and learning outcomes. Qualitative data were analyzed using NVivo for thematic coding and interpretation of learners' motivational patterns, emotional responses, and design feedback. Correlation analysis was employed to explore the relationship between gamification exposure and self-reported motivation metrics.

Ethical considerations

Ethical clearance was obtained from relevant undergraduates to conduct this research. All participants were informed of their rights and voluntarily consented to participate. Data anonymity and confidentiality were strictly maintained, with all digital records stored in encrypted repositories.

Results and Discussion

Impact of gamification on user engagement

The analysis of quantitative data collected through the mock LMS interface revealed a substantial increase in user engagement following the integration of gamified features. The average task completion rate rose from 64% in the non-gamified interface to 88% post-gamification, representing a 37.5% improvement. This trend is consistent with previous research by Hamari [1] who found that gamification increases participation by introducing extrinsic motivators that stimulate short-term behavioral changes.

Login frequency increased from an average of 4.1 sessions per week to 7.2 sessions per week. This indicates heightened platform interaction and suggests that gamified features promoted more regular engagement with learning materials. In line with Flow Theory [2] the addition of game-like challenges and rewards likely fostered a state of immersive involvement, encouraging students to return to the platform more frequently. The average time-on-task per module also rose by 21%. Further reinforcing the learners were more focused and invested in their activities due to the presence of structured goals, feedback, and progressive achievement.

These behavioral indicators align with the principles of Self-Determination Theory (SDT) particularly the psychological need for competence. When students received immediate feedback through points and progress bars, they experienced a sense of accomplishment, which reinforced continued participation and persistence.

Comparative effectiveness of adaptive and static gamification

A comparative analysis between the adaptive gamification group and the non-adaptive group offered better insight into how personalized elements influence motivation and engagement. Learners in the adaptive group who received tailored feedback and difficulty adjusted tasks achieved a task completion rate of 92%. This is significantly higher. 81% recorded by their peers in the static gamification group. This supports recent findings by Alomari [3] which suggest that adaptive gamification enhances engagement by aligning challenge levels with learner ability, a core component of Flow Theory.

Self-reported motivation scores which were captured via post-activity Likert-scale surveys shows averaged 4.3/5 for the adaptive group compared to 3.7/5 in the control group. This statistically significant difference demonstrate that adaptive systems not only improve behavioral metrics but also positively affect learners' affective experiences. The personalization of gamification elements contributed to enhanced perceptions of autonomy and relatedness two other fundamental needs identified by SDT. Learners perceived the system as responsive and context-aware, which validated their efforts and reduced anxiety associated with rigid progression standards.

Learner perceptions and affective responses

Thematic analysis of open-ended questionnaire responses revealed several affective benefits associated with gamified learning environments. Most participants described game elements such as badges and progress bars as motivational and enjoyable. These features provided learners with clear, tangible indicators of success which fostered a sense of competence and goal orientation. As Bandura's Social Cognitive Theory posits, perceived self-efficacy plays a central role in motivation [4]. The recognition of achievement through visual elements helped reinforce learners' belief in their abilities.

However, the responses regarding leaderboards were mixed. While some learners found them exciting and motivating others reported feelings of stress and performance anxiety when consistently ranked low. These reactions highlight the importance of designing leaderboards with caution. The dual impact supports prior findings by Hanus and Fox [5], who emphasized the psychological risks of competitive gamification, particularly for learners less inclined toward performance-based motivation.

The most important factor is students from the adaptive group frequently noted that the system felt "less repetitive" and "more intuitive." The personalization of content and feedback reduced the sense of mechanical progression and supported sustained cognitive engagement. These responses support the proposition that gamification systems should evolve from static mechanics to responsive ecosystems capable of meeting diverse learner needs.

Observed improvements in language learning attitudes

More than the behavioral and emotional engagement the study also documented perceptual shifts in learners' attitudes toward learning. Several participants noted that the gamified LMS made practice "less intimidating" and "more fun." One student stated "It didn't feel like studying; it felt like completing missions, and I ended up practicing more." This suggests that gamification helped to lower the affective filter a key barrier in language acquisition theory and contributed to increased confidence and voluntary engagement with learning materials.

With repeated exposure and active recall through gamified quizzes and exercise tasks, learners engaged more frequently with the target content. This observation aligns with the Constructivist perspective which emphasizes that learning is most effective when it is active, contextual, and learner centered [6]. The structured challenges embedded in the LMS created low-pressure opportunities for students to apply knowledge in iterative cycles, reinforcing mastery through practice.

Methodological implications and research value

Although the study relied on a mock LMS interface due to institutional access constraints, the outcomes underscore the value of simulation in educational technology research. The controlled environment allowed for the systematic observation of user behavior while preserving core dynamics of gamified learning. This methodology also proved useful in isolating the effects of individual gamification features, which can be difficult to assess in large-scale LMS deployments with multiple confounding variables.

The findings support the broader argument that gamification particularly when enhanced with adaptive mechanisms can address persistent issues of learner disengagement in digital environments. However, the differential impact of specific elements (e.g., badges versus leaderboards) reinforces the need for customizable gamification configurations. This flexibility would allow educators and system designers to accommodate diverse learner profiles and prevent unintended negative outcomes.

Conclusion

This study explored the impact of gamification on learner engagement and motivation within Learning

Management Systems, using a controlled mock LMS environment with embedded game elements such as points, badges, leaderboards, and adaptive feedback mechanisms. The results confirmed that gamification has a significant positive effect on user behavior, increasing task completion rates, login frequency, and time-on-task. The findings are aligned with existing motivational theories, particularly Self-Determination Theory and Flow Theory which suggest that satisfaction of psychological needs (competence, autonomy, and relatedness) and optimal challenge levels enhance intrinsic motivation and cognitive engagement.

Notably, the comparative analysis between adaptive and static gamification groups revealed that personalization further amplifies the motivational impact of gamified environments. Learners exposed to adaptive game elements demonstrated higher performance, deeper emotional engagement, and more positive perceptions of the learning process. These results emphasize the importance of tailoring gamified content and feedback to individual learner profiles, learning paces, and preferences, especially in diverse academic settings such as language learning.

The affective and attitudinal data collected from learners reinforce the view that gamification not only boosts participation but also contributes to positive learner identity and confidence particularly in technical subjects where psychological barriers (e.g., fear of failure, low self-efficacy) are common. Thus, gamification presents a dual benefit: enhancing behavioral engagement and supporting effective and cognitive development in digital learning contexts.

However, this study also highlighted that the effectiveness of gamification is not uniform among all learners. Elements like leaderboards were found to produce both motivational and demotivational outcomes depending on the user's disposition toward competition. This underscores the need for modular and configurable gamification strategies that allow learners to engage with features that align with their motivational styles.

Future Work

Building on the results of this research, several avenues for future work are proposed. Longitudinal studies should be conducted to assess the sustainability of gamification's motivational effects over extended academic terms. While this study captured short-term gains, the risk of gamification fatigue remains a critical consideration, especially in systems that rely heavily on extrinsic motivators.

Future implementations should explore integration with AI-driven learning analytics to enhance adaptivity. Machine learning algorithms could refine personalization strategies in real time, ensuring that feedback, challenge levels, and rewards evolve in response to learner behavior and performance [20].

Research could extend to different academic subjects and diverse learner populations, including secondary and postgraduate learners, to examine the generalizability of gamification models across disciplines and cognitive maturity levels. Additionally, the intersection of gamification with immersive technologies such as virtual reality (VR) and augmented reality (AR) presents promising opportunities for multi-sensory, experiential learning environments.

Ethical considerations and learner agency should be central to future gamification frameworks. As adaptive systems become more complex, ensuring transparency, data privacy, and learner consent in the use of behavioral analytics will be essential to maintaining trust and academic integrity.

In conclusion this study contributes valuable empirical evidence and theoretical insight to the growing field of gamified digital learning. It underscores the potential of gamification, especially when adaptive—to transform LMS platforms into dynamic, learner-centered environments that foster deeper motivation, engagement, and educational success.

References

[1] Deci, E. L., & Ryan, R. M. (2017). Self-Determination Theory: Basic Psychological Needs in Motivation, Development, and Wellness. New York, NY, USA: Guilford Press.

[2] Csikszentmihalyi, M. (1990). Flow: The Psychology of Optimal Experience. New York, NY, USA: Harper & Row.

[3] Skinner, B. F. (1953). Science and Human Behavior. New York, NY, USA: Macmillan.

[4] Hamari, J., Koivisto, J., & Sarsa, H. (2014). Does gamification work?—a literature review of empirical studies on gamification. In Proceedings of 47th Hawaii International Conference on System Sciences, Waikoloa, HI, USA, (pp. 3025–3034). doi: 10.1109/HICSS.2014.377.

[5] Domínguez, A., Saenz-de-Navarrete, J., de-Marcos, L., Fernández-Sanz, L., Pagés, C., & Martínez-Herráiz, J. (2013). Gamifying learning experiences:

practical implications and outcomes. *Computers and Education*, 63, 380–392. doi: 10.1016/j.compedu.2012.12.020.

[6] Zainuddin, M., Chu, M., Shujahat, R., & Perera, M. (2020). The impact of gamification on learning outcomes in e-learning: a meta-analysis and systematic review. *Sustainability*, 12(12), 2213. doi: 10.3390/su12062213.

[7] Deterding, S., Dixon, D., Khaled, R., & Nacke, L. (2011). From game design elements to gamefulness: defining gamification. In Proceedings of the 15th International Academic MindTrek Conference, Tampere, Finland, (pp. 9–15). doi: 10.1145/2181037.2181040.

[8] Hanus, M. D., & Fox, J. (2015). Assessing the effects of gamification in the classroom: a longitudinal study on intrinsic motivation, social comparison, satisfaction, effort, and academic performance. *Computers and Education*, 80, 152–161. doi: 10.1016/j.compedu.2014.08.019.

[9] Caponetto, L., Earp, J., & Ott, M. (2014). Gamification and education: a literature review. In Proceedings of European Conference Games Based Learning, Berlin, Germany, (pp. 50–57).

[10] Alomari, I., Davies, M., & Zainuddin, F. (2020). Adaptive gamification in education: a review of literature. *International Journal of Emerging Technologies in Learning*, 15(22), 72–90. doi: 10.3991/ijet.v15i22.15015.

[11] Koivisto, J., & Hamari, J. (2019). The rise of motivational information systems: a review of gamification research. *International Journal of Information Management*, 45, 191–210. doi: 10.1016/j.ijinfomgt.2018.10.013.

[12] Bandura, A. (1977). Social Learning Theory. Englewood Cliffs, NJ, USA: Prentice-Hall.

[13] Classcraft Studios, Classcraft reimagines the classroom to make learning fun—and accelerates growth as a Google for Education Build Partner, Google Cloud Customers, [Online]. Available: https://cloud.google.com/customers/classcraft [Accessed: Sep. 22, 2025].

[14] Handayani, S., & Mustofa, A. (2021). Gamification in cyberlearning environment: a case study on SEP-CyLE platform. *Journal of e-Learning and Knowledge Society*, 17(1), 45–54.

[15] Piaget, J. (2001). The Psychology of Intelligence. London, U.K.: Routledge. (Original work published 1950).

[16] Ryan, R. M., & Deci, E. L. (2000). Intrinsic and extrinsic motivations: classic definitions and new directions. *Contemporary Educational Psychology*, 25(1), 54–67. doi: 10.1006/ceps.1999.1020.

[17] Kapp, A. (2013). The gamification of learning and instruction: game-based methods and strategies for training and education. *International Review of Research in Open and Distributed Learning*, 14(4), 248–250.

[18] Seaborn, K., & Fels, D. I. (2015). Gamification in theory and action: a survey. *International Journal of Human-Computer Studies*, 74, 14–31. doi: 10.1016/j.ijhcs.2014.09.006.

[19] Wouters, L. P., & van Oostendorp, R. (2013). A meta-analytic review of the role of instructional support in game-based learning. *Computers and Education*, 60(1), 412–425. doi: 10.1016/j.compedu.2012.07.018.

[20] Nah, A., Lee, D., & Kim, U. Y. (2016). Gamification in education: a literature review and future research directions. In Proceedings of 18th International Conference on Human-Computer Interaction, Los Angeles, CA, USA, (pp. 401–409). doi: 10.1007/978-3-319-39396-4_38.

[21] Capano, G., Taddei, F., & Moroni, A. (2023). AI-driven gamification in digital education: promise and perils. *British Journal of Educational Technology*, 54(2), 293–308.

[22] Sailer, M., Homner, L., & Uhl, L. (2022). Learning with digital badges: evidence from a large-scale experiment. *British Journal of Educational Technology*, 53(1), 94–110.

[23] Koivisto, J., & Hamari, J. (2019). The rise of motivational information systems: a review of gamification research. *International Journal of Information Management*, 45, 191–210.

[24] Hanus, M. D., & Fox, J. (2015). Assessing the effects of gamification in the classroom: a longitudinal study. *Computers and Education*, 80, 152–161. doi: 10.1016/j.compedu.2014.08.019.

[25] Xu, B., Chen, N. S., & Chai, C. S. (2021). Gamification in online learning: a gender-based analysis. *Educational Technology Research and Development*, 69(3), 1651–1670.

[26] Seaborn, K., & Fels, D. I. (2015). Gamification in theory and action: a survey. *International Journal of Human–Computer Studies*, 74, 14–31.

[27] Zhu, X., Lin, Y., & Guo, H. (2023). Ethical dilemmas in personalized education systems. *Computers and Education: Artificial Intelligence*, 4, 100102.

37 Equipping arbitration to seize the future and not fall behind: a roadmap for Sri Lanka in the wake of the era of artificial intelligence

M.D. Chavindri Chiranga Perera[a]

Department of Legal Studies, Faculty of Business, NSBM Green University, Sri Lanka

Abstract

Artificial intelligence (AI), commonly understood as the ability of machines to mimic human intelligence and perform tasks such as learning, reasoning, and decision-making, is the buzzword of the day. It is permeating every facet of society, and arbitration has not evaded this trend. Arbitration, a prominent mechanism of Alternative Dispute Resolution (ADR), is increasingly influenced by AI-driven tools that assist with legal research, procedural strategy, and even decision-making. This paper explores the evolving role of AI in international arbitration by examining recent global trends and soft law instruments that shaped its adoption. It seeks to determine whether AI will merely serve as a tribunal secretary or take a more significant leap toward acting as an arbitrator, potentially replacing human arbitrators. In doing so, it critically analyzes the potential of AI to augment and possibly replace functions traditionally performed by human arbitrators, raising questions about fairness, disclosure, confidentiality, credibility, and party autonomy. Although the Arbitration Act No. 11 of 1995 forms the statutory framework for arbitration in Sri Lanka, it has not undergone any amendments since its inception, despite frequent criticisms of its obsolescence and repeated calls for reform. As existing literature has extensively addressed these legislative deficiencies and the need for statutory reform, this paper shifts focus to examine practical limitations within Sri Lanka's arbitration landscape, in the context of integrating AI and emerging technologies. To this end, the study critically assesses initiatives adopted by other jurisdictions and leading arbitration seats, and evaluates the effectiveness of guidelines issued by institutions such as the Silicon Valley Arbitration and Mediation Center (SVAMC), JAMS, and the Chartered Institute of Arbitrators (CIArb). The paper ultimately argues for a balanced, human-centered integration of AI into Sri Lanka's arbitration framework, among other recommendations, in order to modernize its dispute resolution landscape while preserving essential legal values and positioning the country as a competitive arbitration hub in South Asia.

Keywords: Artificial intelligence arbitrators, AI in dispute resolution, arbitration reform in Sri Lanka, artificial intelligence (AI), emerging technologies in ADR, international arbitration

Introduction

"Cost savings? Astronomical. A preliminary decision? Within one month. The AI judge's eye for 1970 case law? Well, he's not hungry or tired like your articling student."

- Tara Vasdani, Principal Lawyer at Remote Law Canada, commenting on China's 'No Court Room'-Internet Courts. First established in 2017, these courts operate 24 hours a day, 7 days a week, with AI generated- holographic judges who set schedules, question litigants, take evidence and issue dispositive rulings. They have heard over millions of legal disputes related to intellectual property, e-commerce, online financial transactions, product liability from online purchases and certain administrative disputes. Remarkably, around 98% of the rulings have been accepted without an appeal to a human judge in a traditional courtroom. Additionally, Estonia has implemented an AI-judge to resolve small claims disputes, and eBay has reported that its online processes resolve approximately 60 million matters annually [1].

Artificial intelligence (AI) is the new normal. From automation, facial recognition technologies to virtual assistants like Siri and Alexa and advanced tools such as Open AI's Chat GPT, Google's Gemini and Deepseek, etc., AI has now declared itself a "cannot do without" in our daily lives. In this context, it is

[a]ccpact.law@gmail.com

DOI: 10.4324/9781003739920-37

now poised to transform the dispute resolution mechanisms. Having aided legal professionals with their research and preparation of submissions, and tribunals to assess and analyze the merits, AI is now making inroads to the sphere of international arbitration, showing promising results to disputants speedier and with more uniformity.

Nevertheless, whilst a few jurisdictions have provided limited guidelines on the use of AI in arbitration, international treaties and domestic legislations continue to remain silent on the same. The European Union's Regulation 2024/1689, also referred to as the 'Artificial Intelligence Act', adopted in March, last year is the only notable exception. This regulation, directly applicable to all member countries requiring no domestic ratification, provides for rules on AI use in arbitral proceedings effective from 02nd August 2026. Hence, scholars and experts await its practical impact to comment on its effectiveness.

Few other arbitration institutions such as the London Court of International Arbitration(LCIA) Rules by its Art. 14(6)(iii) and HongKong International Arbitration Centre(HKIAC) Rules by its Art. 13(1) encourage the adoption of technology for speedier and cost-effective proceedings. Regardless, promoting technology use does not automatically equate to authorizing AI use by tribunals [2]. However, Art. 17(1) of UNCITRAL Arbitration Rules stipulates that a tribunal may conduct the arbitration 'in such manner as it considers appropriate'...and that the tribunal in exercising its discretion, 'shall conduct proceedings so as to avoid unnecessary delay and expense and to provide a fair and efficient process for resolving the dispute'. Although these Rules predate the modern AI era, this broad discretion could arguably encompass the use of emerging technologies and AI in the arbitration process.

Despite its vision of becoming a prominent commercial hub in South Asia, Sri Lanka's arbitration regime remains hamstrung by an outdated legal framework, the Arbitration Act no.11 of 1995. A comprehensive reform of this statutory framework is essential, along with a necessary shift in mindset among Arbitrators and legal professionals, to align with the realities of the AI era and emerging technologies [3]. Accordingly, beyond those statutory deficiencies, this paper addresses limitations encountered in practice within the Arbitration landscape of Sri Lanka, through a critical analysis of recent trends in International Arbitration involving AI. It explores how these developments could be integrated into Sri Lanka's legal system to drive a paradigm shift in its arbitration landscape and position the country as a premier international arbitration seat in South Asia.

While extensive literature has highlighted the outdated nature of Sri Lanka's Arbitration Act No. 11 of 1995 and repeatedly called for its reform, there remains a noticeable gap in scholarship concerning the practical integration of AI tools and global arbitration trends into Sri Lanka's dispute resolution landscape. Much of the existing discourse focuses on statutory shortcomings, with limited attention paid to how soft law instruments, institutional guidelines, and emerging international practices, particularly those involving AI in arbitration, can be adapted to the Sri Lankan context. This paper aims to bridge that gap by shifting the focus from legislative reform alone to a broader, practice-oriented approach that considers how Sri Lanka can proactively incorporate evolving global standards and technological innovations to remain competitive as an international arbitration venue.

Methodology

This paper primarily adopts a doctrinal legal research methodology within the qualitative research paradigm. Rather than focusing on statutory analysis alone, it critically evaluates the practical and institutional limitations within Sri Lanka's arbitration landscape in the context of integrating artificial intelligence (AI) and emerging technologies. The research draws on non-binding instruments and soft law frameworks such as the Silicon Valley Arbitration & Mediation Center (SVAMC) Guidelines, the Chartered Institute of Arbitrators (CIArb) Framework Guideline on the Use of Technology in International Arbitration, and the JAMS Rules Governing Disputes Involving Artificial Intelligence Systems, which increasingly inform arbitral practices globally.

A comparative approach is employed to examine these developments across leading arbitration jurisdictions and institutions, aiming to identify adaptable best practices for Sri Lanka. While the Arbitration Act No. 11 of 1995 remains the governing legal framework, the paper does not center on its statutory provisions; instead, it contextualizes Sri Lanka's challenges within a broader, practice-driven discourse. Through this analysis, the study offers normative recommendations for integrating AI into the arbitration process in a balanced and human-centered manner, enhancing Sri Lanka's competitiveness as a potential international arbitration hub.

Results and Discussion

Undue delays in arbitral proceedings due to arbitration being dominated by legal counsels and retired judges is found to be a major challenge in Sri Lanka. Fleeting arbitral sitings that last around 2-3 hours at most, habitually commencing at 3 or 4pm after court work and adjourned to afford them time to prepare for court work on the following day or postponements that are readily granted to accommodate the busy schedules of the practitioners, necessitating a greater number of sittings defies the very purpose of arbitration as an alternative dispute resolution(hereinafter referred to as 'ADR') mechanism. On top of the delays, hefty fees charged by counsels, arbitrators and the institutions for these numerous sittings further discourage disputants in resorting to arbitration.

Although it is proposed to raise awareness among disputants of their rights and entitlements to fix time limits or other flexible procedures for expedited dispute resolution, practically it cannot be readily expected that these counsels would advise their clients that such time limits could be imposed, where they would be required to strictly commit to the said timeframes regardless of their demanding schedules. Despite further proposals for institutional rules to be updated with a binding code of ethics for arbitrators and counsels, facilitating daily hearings of at least 8 hours, it must be pointed out that the 1995 Act already provides statutory recognition for the importance of faster dispute resolution, beside the strong calling of attitudinal change towards an arbitration-friendly atmosphere among the said stakeholders. In spite of this, we still witness hearings dragging for over months or even years [3]. It also entails practical difficulties such as making available each day's proceedings the very same evening for the counsel to prepare for the following day's sittings. Although one may argue that this is already adopted in Dubai and Singapore, there's always a question on part of the accuracy of proceedings prepared by exhausted stenographers and on part of the efficiency of the exhausted counsels over long consecutive hearings. Another question is the affordability of the costs and expenses of such a mechanism, by the client, as it would entail significant labor fees, on top of the fees for counsels, arbitrators and institutional charges, payment of which may be required either upfront or daily.

This is where AI, if welcome in the arbitration landscape of Sri Lanka, can run for its rescue. It comes with promising potential to enhance the quality, efficiency and speed of dispute resolution. AI-based research tools outshine the traditional search engines with increased adaptability and consistent improvement, and assist in drafting legal documentation minimizing errors. This will enable counsels to effortlessly prepare for the next hearing effectively and arbitrators too to analyze all information and verify that an informed decision has been reached. For instance, in *Loomis v Wisconsin* [4], the judge having used the state's proprietary risk assessment software when deciding the prison sentence for Loomis was found to have not infringed the due process as he had not been entirely reliant on the software, but had only used it to verify his decision and other factors too had supported the decision. This case has since heightened the confidence of tribunals on the use of technology, allowing arbitrators to stress-test their findings effortlessly. AI tools with robust text mining and text generation features could analyze complex information including witness examinations and instantly generate proceedings hassle-free. Even in cross-border disputes where the hearings may involve the use of multiple languages, AI-based translation tools can facilitate coherent communication and document exchange flexibly and readily make available the proceedings at the end of that day's sitting. As such, AI could undoubtedly assist in accelerating the arbitral process and that too, at a fraction of the costs for human translators and stenographers. AI can also support virtual hearings and facilitate remote proceedings, which would be quite beneficial if the hearings involve witness testimonies from overseas or if the disputants themselves should travel a distance to attend the sittings. In other words, provided that the right tools are made accessible for under-resourced parties at reasonable costs of course, AI may emerge victorious in remedying 'inequality of arms' among disputants. Moreover, AI detection tools can verify the authenticity of evidence presented by detecting if other AI tools or deepfakes have been utilized, thus instilling public faith and confidence in the tribunal. Most prominently, AI tools can go beyond merely analyzing data or conducting legal research. They can predict and forecast probable outcomes of disputes and share insights into possible responses to specific procedural approaches or arguments. This enables parties to strategize and cut down unnecessary delays by selecting appropriate procedures at no extra cost, or even take the time to reach a mutually beneficial settlement, reflecting the very objectives of ADR mechanisms [5].

Integration of AI into international arbitration also encourages not only stakeholders, but also respective legislators to formulate guidelines standardizing the involvement of AI in arbitration in their jurisdictions, such as the guidelines presented by Silicon Valley Arbitration and Mediation Centre (hereinafter referred to as 'SVAMC') and the Chartered Institute of Arbitrators ((hereinafter referred to as 'CIArb'). These guidelines are supplementary international standards, intended to serve as a common denominator providing for ethical and effective use of AI in arbitration.

Having analyzed the pros of AI in Arbitration, this paper shall now analyze its cons and assess whether these international guidelines could remedy or mitigate their risks. The challenge at the forefront is the risk of bias. Since, AI tools are reliant on the data they are fed and trained on, biased training data would be reflected in their output. This is particularly critical in international arbitrations where apart from legal considerations, cultural and social differences among jurisdictions also affect the dispute at hand. Besides, it is doubtful as to who would be held accountable for errors by the AI tool. It is noteworthy in this instance that SVAMC guidelines requires participants to arbitral proceedings to understand the intended uses of the relevant AI tools used and their limitations, biases and risks if any which should then be mitigated to possible extents. This is so because such knowledge enables participants to adapt their use suitably and thus would be ultimately held responsible for erroneous AI-generated outputs. It further provides that the name and version of the relevant tool, which of its settings and how it was utilized, prompt given and the output may be disclosed. This information allows the output to be reproduced and evaluated for accuracy. Concurrently, it imposes a duty of diligence or competence on the user to ensure that errors or inaccuracies of the respective output are corrected.

It is a known fact that arbitration often deals with confidential information, and one may argue that employment of AI involves the risk of data breaches. Once data is inputted, it is unclear where the data will be stored as the relevant tool may use multiple platforms to generate results and may also store such data for machine learning purposes and potentially present them to other users of the tool. SVAMC guidelines require assuring that materials submitted to these AI tools are redacted, where there is no appropriate scrutiny or approval including use of data and retention policies. Whilst integrity is to be always upheld, wherein, AI shall not be used to falsify evidence or mislead tribunals, it further requires that no arbitrator shall delegate his personal judgment to any AI tool, as such mandate must entail an independent analysis of evidence, facts and the law [6]. Judicial Arbitration and Mediation Services. Inc, (hereinafter referred to as JAMS), a US based organization offering ADR services, also had released certain rules governing disputes involving AI systems. The rules provide for the establishment of a protective order for sensitive data and Intellectual Property rights it may encompass, that limits access for the relevant data only to the party's counsel in some cases and further mandates for expert involvement for AI-related disputes assuring such sensitive data is allowed the highest standards of security and expertise [7].

Participants also should be vigilant about any increased vulnerability to cybersecurity threats from AI use. Besides, since AI is still an emerging technology, certain jurisdictions may ban or restrict the use of specific AI tools in view of regulatory concerns. In such an event, participants should be mindful of the choice of technology, since the conduct of proceedings should not clash with mandatory rules and regulations, applicable laws or policies of the respective country or institutional rules of the respective seat thereto [8]. Another aspect to this is, the New York Convention providing for the recognition of foreign arbitral awards as well as the Washinton Convention on Settlement of Investment Disputes between State and Nationals of Other States (ICSID) too do not explicitly stipulate that arbitral awards must be issued by humans, though it could be argued upon the analysis of underlying requisites of the arbitral process and the award may mean that awards issued by machines are not enforceable, thus posing difficulties when such an award is sought to be enforced in the respective party's home country.

Nevertheless, it is suggested that integration of AI into arbitration potentially bridges the gap between various jurisdictions and their local laws on the use of AI, thereby overcoming uncertainties and complexities that may arise in cross-border disputes. Coincidentally, supplementary guidelines such as those from the aforesaid SVAMC and CIArb also encourage domestic legal systems to embrace emerging technologies, which is crucial for the country's economic growth. In turn, such harmonized frameworks for use of AI shall ensure fair arbitrations by maintaining consistency while upholding confidentiality principles and set the stage for arbitration seats to achieve international standards in AI arbitration [9].

However, it is argued that such guidelines are not foolproof. For instance, uncertainty looms around the necessity and scope of disclosures, as both guidelines provide for different thresholds. CIArb ties disclosure to the result of the arbitration or to the impact on evidence whilst SVAMC leaves it to the tribunal's discretion. Also, unlike SVAMC requires the name, version, settings and prompts given to the relevant AI tool to be disclosed as mentioned earlier, CIArb doesn't specify what exact information must be disclosed- whether they are to simply mention that AI was used or detailed information is to be given. Moreover, both these guidelines, in respect of disclosure of AI tool used, are also silent on the form and timing of disclosure- whether it ought to be disclosed proactively at the commencement of arbitral proceedings or only when AI-generated materials are submitted- allowing the counsel or the tribunal to take the call [10].

Some experts comment that AI-arbitrators are better positioned than human-arbitrators, in tackling the risk of bias. As discussed earlier, these tools are as good as the data trained on. However, it is a common view that AI-arbitrators will outperform its human counterparts with not just the superior capabilities of digesting and analyzing massive volumes of factual data, but also zero risk of personal agendas, prejudices or poor decisions made over tired or cranky moods. Yet, its decisioning will not only lack a vital characteristic of sound human judgment formed by real-world experience coupled with empathy, but also pose many other intricacies upon uncertainties as reflected above. Especially, tribunals often deal with confidential materials and trade secrets and no tribunal will publicize the full picture of issues dealt. This problem is more prominent in investment arbitration as the overall number of awards issued per year is low. This absence of a reliable guidepost for the AI arbitrator to train on questions its suitability and credibility. It may then be argued that it could be trained on respective domestic judicial decisions. Nevertheless, judgments especially from lower courts may not always be readily available in every jurisdiction. Besides, arbitration is supposed to be more liberal and flexible, deviating from the rigid application of rules pertaining to procedural and evidentiary issues. Hence, there remains a danger of training AI arbitrators in judgments as it may eliminate the flexibility and defy the whole purpose of Arbitration as a resolution mechanism alternative to litigation.

Selection and appointment of arbitrators is also an integral part of the arbitral process where the 2 arbitrators appointed by the parties shall nominate and appoint the chair in the traditional context. But, in the context of an AI-arbitrator, would a party have to code their own arbitrator? And be allowed to examine and scrutinize the co-arbitrator coded by the other party? Would the chair be jointly programmed and if so, at which step would they agree on the code? These obscurities would have to be necessarily clarified with the assistance of a programming expert on top of the legal fees for the counsels. In the event, the parties choose to proceed with an AI-arbitrator created by a third party or offered by the institution, how may potential disagreements as to the proposed code be handled among the parties? These anonymities may always be possible to be raised by the losing party as evidence of the tribunal not being constituted appropriately, which then would jeopardize enforceability of the award, rendering all effort, time and money spent during the arbitral process in vain.

Another challenge that has come to light in this context is the use of guerilla tactics in arbitration. These abusive practices are rarely recorded or follow well-established tracks. The offending party would gamble on its ability to persuade the tribunal that its respective situation is genuinely exceptional. However, whether AI-arbitrators, designed to reply to specific prompts in predetermined ways or as it may have learnt from previous similar scenarios (machine learning) would be able to differentiate genuinely exceptional situations from such non-linear abusive tactics and follow the due process free from adverse inferences is doubtful.

The Black Box problem is another hurdle that has not yet seen an appropriate solution. This refers to the path followed by the AI tool in reaching a decision being unidentifiable. It is particularly observable in machine learning models that automatically draw connections and patterns among large volumes of data and reach a result. As per Art. 31(2) of UNCITRAL Model law, it is true that reasons need not be given for decisions where the parties have settled the matter on agreed terms, which otherwise would be a mandatory requirement. This is because parties are entitled to know the reasoning, which will not only keep arbitrariness in check, but also enable a losing party to seek an appeal or resist enforcement. With the path leading to the decision is unidentifiable, there is no possibility of giving reasons for decisions reached by AI arbitrators. In such situations, there is a risk of 'hallucinations'. These are fictitious information generated using mathematical probabilities presented as factually accurate and coherent by AI tools when they lack information to provide a response. Wording the query in a manner that is likely to generate a better reply, also termed as 'prompt engineering' or providing the AI tool with source material together with the query, referred to as 'retrieval-augmented generation' might help in tackling hallucinations but, may not be capable of complete elimination [7]. On the other hand, 'Explainable AI' will be a potential solution as it explains how it generated its output, but that too is not without any trade-offs. In that, complete AI system may not be comprehendible by non-tech experts, and the more the explainability of the AI model is, the more the precision and reliability may be compromised in the name of transparency. At the end of the day, critics argue that human arbitrators/judges decide the result first and form the justifications later. In other words, it is suggested that in certain scenarios, their reasons may not truly reflect the decision, and hence, human arbitrators may be bigger black boxes than AI serving adjudicatory roles [11].

The claimant in *LaPaglia v Valve Corp.* [12] petitioned to vacate an arbitral award on grounds of arbitrator allegedly depending on AI to the extent of 'having outsourced his adjudicative role'. This matter, currently pending before US Federal Court posed a revolutionary question on the possibility and admissibility of AI arbitrators. In the said matter, the claimant also referred to *Move Inc. v Citigroup Global Markets Inc.*, [13] where the Court had vacated an arbitral award over arbitrators falsifying their credentials or made other false representations. Therein, the award had been vacated due to the absence of any way of deciding whether an imposter; whom in this instance was the person who appeared as a qualified arbitrator, influenced the decision of the other members of the panel.

On those lines, a duty is imposed on arbitrators to independently verify the awards. The disputed award in his matter may be vacated as the adjudication and decision making is 'outsourced' to AI other than the appointed Arbitrator. Legal experts also points out that in the event the AI employed by the arbitrator referred to both untrue facts that were not submitted during the trial or present in the record, a duty lies on the arbitrator to verify those for its accuracy. This is enshrined in SVMAC and CIArb guidelines as discussed above, a failure of which would be declared as an inappropriate use of AI. These arguments in *LaPaglia* spotlights a chain of other doubts:

- How can the claimant prove that the award/ part of it was drafted by AI?
- Are AI detection tools reliable and to what extent can such reliability be guaranteed in a court of law?
- How should Courts treat such evidence?
- What if an arbitrator uses AI simply to enhance clarity rather than to substitute reasoning? [14]

Whilst it is plausible to believe that this fourth question above, on the use of AI for clarity, as raised in *LaPaglia*, would be justifiable as already analyzed in this paper, it is opined that the first three questions are yet to be discussed in global forums. All in all, AI is indeed the buzzword of the day, and would not be practical to imagine a future for arbitration in the absence of these emerging technologies.

Way Forward

Artificial intelligence (AI) holds the potential to streamline arbitration processes and redefine the boundaries of dispute resolution. As we move toward an AI-augmented future, the role of arbitrators is not diminished but rather enhanced, equipped with advanced tools to better address the evolving needs of participants in the global commercial arena. In this light, AI in arbitration should be seen as a complement, not a threat or replacement to specialized human expertise.

While these technological advancements are promising, they must be embraced with caution and guided by judicial balance. The essence of human judgment, shaped by empathy, ethics, and flexibility, remains a cornerstone of effective arbitration. The risks inherent in AI must be acknowledged, and the question of whether AI should ever fully replace human arbitrators remains open to debate.

Fundamentally, arbitration is rooted in party autonomy. Parties retain the freedom to determine the extent to which AI may be used, the specific tools employed, and any limitations on their application. The inclusion of model clauses in arbitration agreements should be encouraged, allowing tribunals and disputants to adopt soft law instruments, such as those issued by the Silicon Valley Arbitration and Mediation Center (SVAMC), JAMS, or the Chartered Institute of Arbitrators (CIArb) as guiding principles throughout proceedings.

For parties and tribunals open to AI-led arbitration, such innovation should not be discouraged. AI-driven tribunals may prove particularly valuable in emergency arbitrations or where urgent matters require swift resolution. However, to preserve fairness and trust, it could be recommended that awards rendered by AI arbitrators should be subject to appeal before human-led tribunals.

Ultimately, AI is not a force to be resisted but a tool to be responsibly harnessed. Sri Lanka must proactively position itself to accommodate these emerging technologies to establish itself as a competitive international arbitration seat in South Asia.

References

[1] Vasdani, T. (2020). Robot Justice: China's use of Internet Courts. Lexisnexis Canada. Available from: https://www.lexisnexis.ca/en-ca/ihc/2020-02/robot-justicechinas-use-of-internet-courts.page (Accessed Jun. 9, 2025).

[2] Eftekhar, R. (2025). The legal framework applicable to using AI by an arbitral tribunal. Daily Jus. Available from: https://dailyjus.com/legal-tech/2025/03/the-legal-framework-applicable-to-using-ai-by-an-arbitral-tribunal. Accessed on Jun. 9, 2025.

[3] Perera, C. C. (2023). Sri Lanka on its pursuit to becoming an international arbitration centre: lessons learnt and way forward. The Bar Association Law Journal 2021/2022, XXVI(1), 297–311. Available from: https://www.researchgate.net/publication/390582360_Sri_Lanka_on_its_pursuit_to_becoming_an_international_arbitration_centre_Lessons_learnt_and_way_forward. Accessed on Jun. 9, 2025.

[4] Loomis v. Wisconsin 881 N.W. 2d 749 (Wis. 2016).

[5] Guideline on the Use of AI in Arbitration (2025). Chartered Institute of Arbitrators. Available from: https://www.ciarb.org/media/m5dl3pha/ciarb-guideline-on-the-use-of-ai-inarbitration-2025-_final_march-2025.pdf Accessed on Jun. 9, 2025.

[6] Mills T. & Shanker M. (2024). New frontiers: Regulating artificial intelligence in international arbitration, Norton Rose Fulbright Available: https://www.nortonrosefulbright.com/en/knowledge/publications/3cb82b55/new-frontiers-regulating-artificial-intelligence-in-international-arbitration. [Accessed: Jun. 09, 2025].

[7] Staff, N. JAMS Sets New Standard with AI-Specific Arbitration Rules, Newsline, May 13, 2024. Available: https://newsline.haystackid.com/jams-sets-new-standard-with-ai-specific-arbitration-rules/. Accessed on Jun. 11, 2025.

[8] Fatayri, L. A. (2024). AI in international arbitration: what is the big deal? American Review of International Arbitration- ARIA Blog, Available from: https://aria.law.columbia.edu/ai-in-international-arbitration-what-is-the-big-deal/. [Accessed on Jun. 10, 2025].

[9] SVAMC (2024). Guidelines on the Use of Artificial Intelligence in Arbitration. Silicon Valley Arbitration & Mediation Center, Inc. Available from: https://svamc.org/wp-content/uploads/SVAMC-AIGuidelines-First-Edition.pdf. Accessed on Jun. 09, 2025.

[10] Vagenheim, A., & Abouellail, Z. (2025). Navigating AI disclosure in arbitration: practical steps for transparency. Daily Jus. Available from: https://dailyjus.com/news/2025/06/navigating-ai-disclosure-in-arbitration-practical-steps-for-transparency. Accessed on Jun. 09, 2025.

[11] Praštalo, B. (2024). 'Arbitration tech toolbox: AI as an arbitrator: overcoming the "black box" challenge? Kluwer Arbitration. Available from: https://arbitrationblog.kluwerarbitration.com/2024/08/23/arbitration-tech-toolbox-ai-as-an-arbitrator-over-

coming-the-black-box-challenge/> Accessed on Jun. 09, 2025.

[12] LaPaglia v. Valve Corp., No. 3:25-cv-00833 (S.D. Cal. Apr. 8, 2025).

[13] Move, Inc. v. Citigroup Global Markets, Inc., 840 F.3d 1152, 1159 (9th Cir. 2016).

[14] Aceris Law (2025). When Arbitrators Use AI: LaPaglia v. Valve and the Boundaries of Adjudication. Aceris Law. Available from: https://www.acerislaw.com/when-arbitrators-use-ai-lapaglia-v-valve-and-the-boundaries-of-adjudication/. Accessed on Jun. 09, 2025.

38 Tackling the abuse of the doctrine of Fair use training Gen-AI models; a study through an analysis of the US and Indian legal frameworks

H.M Oshan N. Piumantha[1,a], *S. A. Wanniachy*[2,b] *and*
M.D. Chavindri Chiranga Perera[2,c]

[1]Department of Marketing and Tourism Management, NSBM Green University, Sri Lanka

[2]Department of Legal Studies, Faculty of Business, NSBM Green University, Sri Lanka

Abstract

The rapid advancement of generative artificial intelligence (Gen AI) has led to unparalleled opportunities for creativity, especially in the production of audiovisual content. Nevertheless, this technological evolution raises complex legal questions, especially regarding the use of copyrighted materials in the process of training AI. In Sri Lanka, the key legal framework, the Intellectual Property Act No. 36 of 20media [s enacted before the upsurge of AI and lacks specific provisions addressing such matters. Whilst Section 6 of the Intellectual Property Act provides protection for original works, including audiovisual media, by granting authors both economic and moral rights, it does not lucidly regulate whether such copyrighted content can be used for machine learning purposes without explicit authorization. This research investigates the legal status of training Generative AI models using audiovisual content which may be copyright protected within the framework of Sri Lankan copyright law. A comparative legal analysis is adopted based on the copyright regimes of the United States and India, where evolving doctrines of fair use and fair dealing respectively, provide varying thresholds for the use of such content for training AI models. Findings reveal that under existing Sri Lankan law, the use of copyrighted works for AI training is likely to constitute infringement due to the absence of relevant exceptions or licensing mechanisms. This creates legal uncertainty and may smother local innovation in AI. The study concludes with a call for urgent legal reform, recommending the introduction of statutory exceptions or licensing regimes tailor-made to AI technologies. Such reforms are necessary to balance creators' rights with technological advancement, guaranteeing that Sri Lanka remains competitive and ethically grounded in the global AI arena.

Keywords: Audio-visual content, copyright law, fair use, generative artificial intelligence, training AI dataset

Introduction

The swift progression of generative artificial intelligence (AI) technologies has steered into a new era of innovation and creativity. These AI systems, adept at generating convincing audiovisual content, have raised noteworthy issues regarding the legality of using copyrighted materials for training purposes. The Intellectual Property Act No. 36 of 2003 serves as the cornerstone of copyright law in Sri Lanka, providing safeguards to creators of original works, including audiovisual content. Nevertheless, the Act was enacted before the emergence of AI technologies, leading to a legal framework that may not sufficiently address the intricacies introduced by AI-generated works. Original works in the literary, artistic, and scientific domains are protected under Section 6 of the Intellectual Property Act with explicit reference to audiovisual works. These protections consist of both economic rights, permitting authors to benefit financially from their creations, and moral rights, protecting the personal and reputational interests of authors.

Notwithstanding robust fortifications, there are many challenges with regard to the application of the Act to training Generative AI models. AI systems often train on many datasets that include copyrighted audiovisual materials, which raises concerns about impending infringements of the exclusive rights of copyright holders. The process of training AI models encompasses reproducing and transforming these works, activities that typically entail authorization under copyright law. Moreover, the outputs that are generated by AI models, while novel, may still be

[a]oshan.p@nsbm.ac..lk, [b]samithri.w@nsbm.ac.lk, [c]ccpact.law@gmail.com

DOI: 10.4324/9781003739920-38

considered derivative works, depending on their similarity to the original materials used in training. This blurs the lines between permissible use and infringement, generating a legal grey area that is not explicitly addressed by the current legislation.

Internationally, the juncture of AI and copyright law has been a topic of intense debate. Courts in many jurisdictions are grappling with whether the use of copyrighted materials to train AI models comprises fair use or fair dealing, with exceptions that allow limited use of copyrighted works without permission. These legal doctrines are devised to balance the interests of copyright holders with the public benefit resultant from certain uses of works. However, the application of these exceptions to AI training is complex and varies across different legal systems. In Sri Lanka, the absence of clear guidelines on this matter necessitates a careful examination of the existing legal framework to determine its adequacy in addressing the challenges posed by AI technologies.

The implications of AI-generated works encompass beyond legal considerations. Ethical concerns ascend regarding the attribution of authorship and the potential displacement of human creators. Furthermore, the use of copyrighted materials without authorization may undermine the economic interests of content creators, affecting industries reliant on the protection of intellectual property. These issues emphasize the need for a comprehensive approach that ponders not only the legal aspects but also the broader societal impacts of AI technologies.

All in all Copyright law of Sri Lanka has no distinctive provisions pertaining to the application of copyrighted materials in training Gen- AI models which creates ambiguity concerning copyright infringement, fair use and authorship. This gap gives rise to ethical and economic concerns for human creators and challenges the balance between creations and intellectual property rights.

Considering these challenges, there is a persistent necessity for reform in Sri Lanka's copyright laws to address the nuances encountered when training generative AI. This research aims to explore the legality of training generative AI models using audiovisual media under the current legal framework, identify gaps and ambiguities, and propose possible avenues for legislative reform. By examining the intersection of AI and copyright law, this study seeks to contribute to the development of a legal framework that balances the protection of creators' rights alongside the promotion of technological innovation.

Literature Review

Introduction to generative AI

Technology is constantly evolving and changing, and artificial intelligence has become a technology that can impact many fields. Emeritus professor John McCarthy, who is known as the father of AI, stated that [1]. "It is the science and engineering of making intelligent machines, especially intelligent computer programs. It is related to the similar task of using computers to understand human intelligence, but AI does not have to confine itself to methods that are biologically observable". Generative AI is a branch of artificial intelligence (AI) that emphasizes using patterns found in existing data to create new content, like text, audio, images, or videos. Generative AI was introduced in the 1960s in chatbots. But it was not until 2014, with the introduction of generative adversarial networks, or GANs, a type of machine learning algorithm that generative AI could create convincingly authentic images, videos, and audio of real people [2]. Generative Adversarial Networks (GANs), diffusion models, and large vision-language models are among the models that are trained on large datasets that are frequently scraped from the internet to understand compositional techniques, visual elements, and artistic styles. Generative AI is transforming the way people work in creative fields and opening up new artistic possibilities. According to Moses Alabi, the capabilities of generative AI have the potential to significantly transform creative industries such as art, design, music, film, and media production [3]. Generative AI can enhance productivity by automating certain tasks, expand the range of creative possibilities, and provide unique tools for innovation and experimentation. This technology has seen widespread adoption, especially for the creation of audiovisual media platforms.

Applications in audiovisual media

The two fundamental components of sound and visual must be used in accordance with the intended aim when creating a piece for audiovisual media. It is also important to prepare creations with an understanding of the capabilities, limitations, and technical and artistic spaces of audiovisual media. Audio Visual media, also termed as 'Audio visual design', plays a vital part in augmenting the user experience in modern media [4]. It integrates sound and visual elements to create a more immersive and engaging environment, making content more memorable and impactful. Audio-visual media serves as a tool for communication and has several functions, including educational, social, cultural, and economic functions. It can make it the conveyance of information, expand understanding, convey values, preserve cultural heritage, and achieve goals effectively [5]. AI plays a significant and multifaceted role in the production of audio-visual contents. Content creators may now concentrate on more creative areas of the production process because this automation saves them a significant amount of time and work.

According to literature, generative AI technology is used to generate a wide range of audiovisual content. The capability of generative AI models to produce realistic images and videos has clear and noteworthy practical implications across a multitude of domains, such as art [6], entertainment [7], gaming [8], design [9, 23], medicine [10–13], and data augmentation [12] for machine learning tasks. Legal researchers throughout the world are currently debating whether using copyrighted images to train AI is against the law. According to the research conducted by Adam Buick [14], to fully grasp the significance of the debate around copyright and training data, it is necessary to first understand how such data is used to train a modern generative AI model. While AI models that could be described as 'generative' in some senses have existed for decades, the current wave of popular generative AI models such as OpenAI's GPT series or Stability AI's image generators are based on a subtype of machine learning known as 'deep learning'. As generative AI reshapes creative expression, it also fuels legal discussions about the implications and enforcement of copyright law.

Legal debates on AI and copyright

Generative AI models must be trained utilizing existing audio and visual works in compliance with copyright laws and can be seen that legal issues have arisen regarding existing data that was trained without following that legal procedure.

Various cases of copyright infringement of original works are being discovered when training datasets for AI models. For example, an influential case currently in litigation between stock photo provider Getty Images and Generative AI company Stability AI centers on the alleged misuse of copyrighted works in generative AI development [15, 21]. Internationally, several countries are currently formulating legal policies related to artificial intelligence. The U.S. Copyright Office (USCO) has recently published its anticipated Report on Generative AI Training, which constitutes the third and final installment in the USCO's series on AI and copyright, in a pre-publication version. It further states Using copyrighted works to train AI models may constitute prima facie infringement of the right to reproduce such works [16]. The Indian Intellectual Property Act also contains provisions to protect existing works used to train AI models through copyright provisions. The Indian Intellectual Property Act, No. 14 of 1957, provides that original literary, dramatic, musical and artistic works, cinematograph films; and sound recordings are protected works under the copyright provisions, and this law applies to the use of any work for AI training datasets [17].

The primary approach to addressing this issue in the Sri Lankan context is the copyright provisions of the Sri Lanka Intellectual Property Act, No. 36 of 2003. The 6th section of the Act mentions 11 works protected by copyright in Sri Lanka and these protected works cover literary, artistic, and scientific work, including computer programs, books, speeches, stage production, musical compositions, audiovisual works, architecture, fine art, photography, applied art, and different kinds of maps or scientific representations [18]. The Act guarantees that original works in these disciplines are afforded legal protection, providing a favorable climate for innovation and creative expression in the nation. Sri Lankan copyright law contains clear provisions to protect data used to feed an AI model.

Although previous research emphasized the revolutionary effects of generative AI on creative industries, specifically in the fields of art, design, film, and audiovisual media, the majority of these studies have focused on the technology's technical capabilities and innovative uses in international contexts. The copyright implications of employing copyrighted content(data) to train AI models have started to be examined by legal scholarship, particularly in countries like the US and India. However, there is still a remarkable lack of targeted scholarly research about the legal status of such acts in relation to Sri Lankan copyright law, more especially the Intellectual Property Act No. 36 of 2003.

Few research have examined whether training generative AI with unlicensed works(data) infringes Sri Lankan copyright laws. Although incidents from throughout the world demonstrate the importance of the problem, nothing is known about how well Sri Lanka's IP framework can handle issues unique to AI. There is also an absence in comparative legal analysis. By analyzing the legality of such approaches in Sri Lanka, comparing global legal developments, and evaluating the preparedness of current legislation to control AI training practices, this paper fills this void.

Methodology

This study employs the Doctrinal Research method of the qualitative research paradigm. The authors have adopted this method to thoroughly examine legal documents and judicial rulings alongside academic analysis because they are fundamental to understanding how copyright laws interact with artificial intelligence technology. Hence, under this method, the legal status of Copyrighted works in Sri Lanka shall be analyzed in terms of the Intellectual Property Act No. 36 of 2003, in respect of audio-visual media for training generative AI models.

A comparative legal analysis of Sri Lankan copyright law in respect of this context is then carried out against the legal frameworks in India and the United States of America to enable a critical assessment of those jurisdictional approaches to copyright ownership as well as fair use and liability matters in training generative AI applications.

The main data sources consist of statutory provisions pertaining to copyright in Sri Lanka under the Intellectual Property Act No.36 of 2003 of Sri Lanka, the US Copyright Act of 1976, and Indian Copyright Act No 14 of 1957 together with key judicial decisions. *Getty Images v. Stability AI* case from the US and the *Suryas AI image* case from Sri Lanka were chosen as case studies to explore judicial approaches to copyright infringement claims linked to AI training datasets. These cases demonstrate how courts reason through legal issues and address challenges in this new field of law. The analysis of findings draws context from secondary sources like academic articles and legal commentaries along with official reports by embedding the results in broader scholarly and policy discussions.

The study offers a thorough legal analysis of the concepts of authorship, originality, and fair use in relation to artificial intelligence-generated works. The legal evaluation identifies the advantages and disadvantages of Sri Lanka's legal system while highlighting the differences and similarities among jurisdictions through comparative analysis. This method makes it possible to create recommendations for legal reform that are intended to solve the challenges posed by generative artificial intelligence technologies.

A comprehensive and rigorous analysis of the subject is ensured by the use of this qualitative, comparative methodology, which offers a strong basis for understanding the existing legal framework and guiding future legislative developments. This strategy supports the goals of the study and enables careful examination of complex legal problems related to AI and copyright.

Results and Discussions

The study discloses that Sri Lankan law, as established by the Intellectual Property Act No. 36 of 2003, is not adequately equipped at present to handle the multifaceted and developing legal issues arising from using copyrighted audio-visual content to train generative AI (GenAI) models. A blackletter reading of the Act reveals a strict, rights-holder-focused perspective that does not obviously allow for intermediate or transformative uses of copyrighted material in AI or machine learning model building. This part discusses the applicable legal provisions in this area, identifies gaps in legislative transparency, and compares Sri Lanka's experience with that of other nations, like India and the United States, where similar problems are being addressed and debated more intensively.

Copyright protection under Sri Lankan law automatically exists in original literary, artistic, dramatic, musical, and audio-visual works, among others. The Act expressly confers authors exclusive economic and moral rights, including the right of reproduction, communication to the public, distribution, adaptation, and transformation. Within the scope of Generative AI training, a series of operations undertaken by developers' reproduction of audio-visual content, conversion into data vectors, and utilization within neural network models have a direct nexus to the economic rights under the law. As provided under

Section 9 and clarified in Part II, the reproduction, albeit as part of data management or algorithmic training processes, without authorization constitutes a copyright infringement. Furthermore, moral rights of authors, including the right to prevent derogatory treatment of work (Section 10), also render any technical transformation or non-human intervention defense more challenging.

The legal system in Sri Lanka does not have a broad fair use defense. Rather, it spells out specific exceptions as stated in Sections 12 to 15 of the said Act. These are geared towards private study, educational use, and limited quotation for the purpose of review and criticism, none of which evidently support or approve extensive automated use of copyrighted works to train AI models. This legislative lacuna creates essentially all unlicensed GenAI system training on Sri Lankan audio-visual works illegal. In contrast to legal systems where "intermediate copying" is potentially fair in specific technological contexts, Sri Lankan copyright law is untested on these facts.

This legal strictness is further evident when it is compared to India and the United States. In India, a "fair dealing" provision in the Copyright Act of 1957 under Section 52(1) is functionally narrower than the U.S. "fair use" doctrine [19]. Fair dealing is primarily for personal use, criticism, review, and reporting current events. There is no specific legal exception mentioned to permit the use of copyright works for AI training. As was brought to light in the case of *ANI Media v. OpenAI*, Indian authorities have demanded that licenses are required for AI developers in using protected material to train datasets [20]. The ambiguity of law, coupled with the growing rate of litigation, signals a period of transition for Indian copyright law in its treatment of artificial intelligence.

In the United States, the doctrine of fair use under Section 107 of the Copyright Act provides a more flexible but contentious approach [22]. Judicial bodies consider four factors: the purpose and character of the use (including its commercial or transformative nature), the nature of the copyrighted work, the amount and substantiality of the material used, and the effect on the potential market. Several prominent lawsuits, *New York Times v. OpenAI*, *Getty Images v. Stability AI*, and *Sarah Silverman et al. v. Meta* challenge the legitimacy of scraping and training on copyrighted work by AI companies. Defendants routinely argue that AI training is "transformative" because it gleans statistical relationships, rather than expressive content. Yet this argument is not always accepted, particularly where the model outputs substantially replicate the original works or function as market substitutes.

The ongoing U.S. debates demonstrate the complexity of the fair use doctrine in the age of AI. While a number of people believe that training data must be considered non-expressive and intermediate use, others believe that this can destroy the market for original works and infringe on both reproduction and derivative rights. The *Warhol v. Goldsmith* ruling recently underscored that even extensive transformation of a work may be infringing if the new work is to the same purpose as the original, a principle that would constrain most GenAI fair use arguments.

The implications are deep. Sri Lanka can fall behind in global AI advancements if it fails to establish a legal framework for training models on domestically generated audio-visual content. Producers essentially have a choice between completely avoiding the use of local content or risking legal exposure, unless there is a change in legislation. Such is the situation that not only hinders local technological innovation but also deprives the country of the capacity to build AI competencies grounded in its linguistic and cultural context.

In conclusion, the findings of this legal analysis highlight the imperative of urgent reform of Sri Lanka's copyright law to keep abreast of the contemporary trends in generative AI. The necessity exists to develop a structural legal framework through amendment of the current legislation or by judicial interpretation to demarcate the allowable uses of copyrighted work for training AI models. Possible reforms involve creating a fair use or fair dealing regime specially tailored for artificial intelligence, building a system of licensing for large training datasets, and creating regulatory controls that safeguard the interests of both creators and developers. In the absence of such reforms, the present blackletter law is a brake both on technological advancement and legal certainty.

Conclusion

The rapid advancement of Gen AI technologies has unleashed new boundaries of innovation and creativity while restricting conventional axioms of copyright legislation simultaneously. This research opines that the legal framework governing the utilization of copyrighted audiovisual content in training AI models, as envisioned in Sri Lanka's Intellectual Property Act No. 36 of 2003, is characterized by limitations along with ambiguity. The law, although comprehensive in the protection it offers for creators' economic and moral rights, was envisioned prior to the advent of artificial intelligence and does not make allowances for the transformative, intermediary, or large-scale automated uses of copyrighted work necessary to enable the creation of generative AI technologies.

Blackletter reading of the Sri Lankan legal system indicates that reproduction and adaptation of copyrighted material integral practices in artificial intelligence training are under specific authorization unless expressly excepted. Legislative exceptions under the Act, however, are not exhaustive, limited mostly to private use, educational purpose, and criticism or analysis. The provisions do not extend to automated, bulk, and often commercial uses typical of AI training. Thus, in the absence of explicit authorization from rights holders, the training of generative AI models on copyrighted audio-visual works amounts to copyright infringement under existing Sri Lankan law.

By contrast with India and the United States, Sri Lanka's IP regime is further exposed by its limitations. Indian copyright law is equally devoid of explicit provisions for AI use but is in transition through policy discussion and court testing. Under United States law, fair use is a more permissive standard but one that remains contentious and fact-specific, particularly where commercial GenAI uses are at issue. These jurisdictions are having active discussions both legislative and judicial in nature on the balance between innovation accommodation and copyright protection, a conversation that is conspicuously lacking in the Sri Lankan system.

Moreover, this research recognizes that the ambiguity in legal systems not only exposes Sri Lankan developers and researchers to the risk of legal lacunae but also impedes the country's potential to position itself effectively in the global AI ecosystem. In a context where the availability of data is one of the decisive factors for the competitiveness of AI solutions, restrictive and obsolete intellectual property legislation can quite significantly impinge on innovation, collaboration, and knowledge sharing.

It is evident that there is a pressing need for legislative reform. This reform must start by acknowledging the unique features of generative AI, which is both a consumer and creator of copyrightable content. Sri Lanka can potentially learn from comparative regimes, such as the text and data mining (TDM) exceptions in the European Union, Japanese provisions for AI training, and the balanced application of fair use in the United States. Any reform proposal needs to consider introducing a statutory exception or licensing regime for AI training that is respectful of authors' rights but also encourages responsible technological innovation. Rules or guidelines also need to be drafted with a view to governing the output of AI models, particularly where they risk encroaching on the derivative rights of the original creators.

Lastly, Sri Lanka stands at a legal and technological juncture. Regardless of whether it opts to keep its strict copyright regime or shift towards a more innovative-based legal system, the decision will influence not only the size of its artificial intelligence industry but also its role in influencing future intellectual property standards in the age of information.

Sri Lanka should amend its copyright legislation in order to define how AI systems utilize creative works. It is imperative to strike a balance between limited content use for AI training and respecting the rights of creators. Licenses which enable developers to access the necessary content in a legal and safe manner assists in content creation. The European Union and the United States provide useful examples for Sri Lanka with their text-and-data mining provisions which support innovation alongside copyright. Specialists in the law, information technology, creators, and the general public should all be included in these conversations. Such collaboration will enable Sri Lanka safeguard innovation and new technologies beside respecting creative works with a comprehensive legal framework.

This research calls on policymakers, legal scholars, and media stakeholders to embark on an ambitious reform agenda that grasps both the economic potential and the ethical imperatives of the era of generative artificial intelligence.

References

[1] McCarthy, J. (2007, November 12). What is artificial intelligence? Stanford University, Computer Science Department. http://www-formal.stanford.edu/jmc/whatisai.html.

[2] Lawton, G. (2023). What is generative AI? Everything you need to know. TechTarget. https://www.

techtarget.com/searchenterpriseai/definition/generative-AI.

[3] Alabi, M. (2024, October 25). Generative AI and its applications in creative industries. ResearchGate. https://www.researchgate.net/publication/385508903_Generative_AI_and_its_Applications_in_Creative_Industries.

[4] Applied Global Technologies (2025). Why Audiovisual Design Design Matters. Applied Global Technologies. https://www.appliedglobal.com/why-audiovisual-design/.

[5] Surya, J. (2023). Audiovisual: Definition, Characteristics, Functions, Benefits, and Purpose. Sinaumedia. https://sinaumedia.com/audiovisual-definition-characteristics-functions-benefits-and-purpose/.

[6] Elgammal, A., Liu, B., Elhoseiny, M., & Mazzone, M. (2017). CAN: Creative Adversarial Networks, Generating "Art" by Learning About Styles and Deviating from Style Norms. arXiv (Cornell University). Https://doi.org/10.48550/arxiv.1706.07068.

[7] Li, Y., Fang, C., Yang, J., Wang, Z., Lu, X., & Yang, M.-H. (2017). Universalstyle transfer via feature transforms. *Advances in Neural Information Processing Systems*, 30.

[8] Liu, R., Nageotte, F., Zanne, P., de Mathelin, M., & Dresp-Langley, B. (2021). Deep reinforcement learning for the control of robotic manipulation: a focussed mini-review. *Robotics*, 10, 22.

[9] Gatys, L. A., Ecker, A. S., & Bethge, M. (2016). Image style transfer usingconvolutional neural networks. In Proceedings of the IEEE Conference on Computer Vision and Pattern Recognition, (pp. 2414–2423).

[10] Pinaya, W. H. L., Graham, M. S., Kerfoot, E., Tudosiu, P., Dafflon, J., Fernandez, V., Sanchez, P., Wolleb, J., F, D. C. P., Patel, A., Chung, H., Zhao, C., Peng, W., Liu, Z., Mei, X., Lucena, O., Ye, J. C., Tsaftaris, S. A., Dogra, Cardoso, M. J. (2023). Generative AI for Medical Imaging: extending the MONAI Framework. arXiv (Cornell University). https://doi.org/10.48550/arxiv.2307.15208.

[11] Jing, B., Erives, E., Pao-Huang, P., Corso, G., Berger, B., & Jaakkola, T. (2023). Eigenfold: generative protein structure prediction with diffusion mod-els. arXiv preprint arXiv:2304.02198.

[12] Shokrollahi, Y., Yarmohammadtoosky, S., Nikahd, M. M., Dong, P., Li, X., & Gu, L. (2023). A comprehensive review of generative AI in healthcare. arXiv preprint arXiv:2310.00795.

[13] Ktena, I., Wiles, O., Albuquerque, I., Rebuffi, S. A., Tanno, R., Roy, A. G., ... & Gowal, S. (2024). Generative models improve fairness of medical classifiers under distribution shifts. Nature Medicine, 30(4), 1166–1173.

[14] Buick, A. (2024). Copyright and AI training data—transparency to the rescue? *Journal of Intellectual Property Law and Practice*, 20(3), 182–192. doi: https://doi.org/10.1093/jiplp/jpae102.

[15] Coulter, M. (2024). Aiming for fairness: an exploration into getty images v. stability AI and its importance in the landscape of modern copyright law. *DePaul Journal of Art, Technology and Intellectual Property Law*, 34(1), 124–126. Available from: https://via.library.depaul.edu/jatip/vol34/iss1/4.

[16] U.S. Copyright Office. (2025). Copyright and artificial intelligence, part 3: Generative AI training (Pre-publication version). U.S. Copyright Office. https://www.copyright.gov

[17] Government of India (1957). The Copyright Act, 1957 (Act No. 14 of 1957). New Delhi: Ministry of Law and Justice. Available from: https://copyright.gov.in/Documents/CopyrightRules1957.pdf.

[18] Parliament of the Democratic Socialist Republic of Sri Lanka. (2003). Intellectual Property Act, No. 36 of 2003. Department of Government Printing.

[19] (2025). AI-generated work and its implications on copyright law in India. *Journal of Intellectual Property Rights (JIPR)*, 30(1). https://doi.org/https://doi.org/10.56042/jipr.v30i1.5862.

[20] ANI Media (P) Ltd. v. Open AI Inc, 2024 SCC OnLine Del 8120.

[21] Smith, J., et al. (2025). Getty Images v Stability AI Ltd. Available from: https://www.judiciary.uk/wp-content/uploads/2025/01/Getty-Images-and-others-v-Stability-AI-14.01.25.pdf.

[22] (2025). Copyright and Artificial Intelligence part 3: Generative AI Training. United States Copyright Office. https://www.copyright.gov/ai/Copyright-and-Artificial-Intelligence-Part-3-Generative-AI-Training-Report-Pre-Publication-Version.pdf.

[23] Oshan, P. H. M. N. (2024). Harnessing generative AI for production design in audio-visual creations: exploring opportunities, overcoming challenges, and shaping the future. In Conference-Proceeding.

39 The role of credit risk management strategies in achieving sustainable competitive advantage

C. H Adhikari[1,a], A.B.S. Tharaka[2,b] and A.A.M.A.K. Panamaldeniya[1,c]

[1]Department of Management and Business Studies, Faculty of Management and Social Science, CINEC Campus, Sri Lanka

[2]Department of Accounting and Finance, Faculty of Business, NSBM Green University, Sri Lanka

Abstract

In today's dynamic financial environment, achieving a sustainable competitive advantage has become essential for businesses to sustain in the long run. This objective is increasingly being impacted by the effectiveness of credit risk management strategies in the banking industry. Strategic risk management has become crucial as banks navigate a competitive market where private institutions frequently top performance rankings. In the context of banks operating in Sri Lanka, this study assesses how credit risk management strategies can achieve sustainable competitive advantage. A structured questionnaire was distributed to 146 senior banking professionals and credit risk officers as part of the quantitative method used in the study to gather primary data. With a 77% response rate, the findings demonstrate a strong positive association between a bank's capacity to maintain a competitive edge and well-structured credit risk procedures. The results set a foundation for future study in risk-driven strategic management and offer practitioners helpful information.

Keywords: Credit risk, risk absorption, risk mitigation, risk transferring, sustainable competitive advantage

Introduction

The Banking Sector is a major component of any country's financial service sector. It plays a vital role in the corporate world by significantly contributing to the country's economy. Banks perform different functions, and the main function is to take money from people with surplus funds and lend money to people who have a shortage of funds. This process is the financial intermediation in a country's economy [1][2].

Risk can be defined as the inevitability of future earnings within various circumstances or outcome deviations from future expectations. Banks also face different kinds of risks and external events that are out of direct control, which may also cause risk in the banking industry [3][4]. Several types of risk have been identified and classified as credit risk, market risk, operational risk, liquidity risk, reputational risk, technology risk, risk of financial stability, regulatory compliance & legal risk, risk of reputation management, risk of customer retention and risk of gaining competitive advantage [5][6][7].

Risk management involves detecting, estimating, controlling, and mitigating loss exposure [8]. Compared to the other industries, the banking industry is adversely involved in risk management practices. Reducing the negative effects of risks on a bank's operations, finance, and reputation is the main objective of risk management in the banking industry. So, a deeper comprehension of risk management and its significance is necessary to gain the best risk management in the Banking industry [5].

However, a bank is unable to eliminate risks; therefore, banks must identify and assess the risks in each division or department. As a result, the risk management department serves as the foundation for every bank or other financial institution. Generally, the Chief Risk Officer (CRO), the regulatory authorised person, should be accountable to the board to evaluate the risks of a bank [9]. Establishing and maintaining an adequate internal audit and risk management system compatible with banks' activities and structure. In accordance with changing conditions and reporting to the board of directors within the established framework and principles necessary for the banks to monitor and control the risks [10][11].

As demonstrated by the financial crises of 2007 and 2008, poor risk management in the national and

[a]hansic624@gmail.com, [b]sachini.a@nsbm.ac.lk, [c]ashvini.panamaldeniya@cinec.edu

DOI: 10.4324/9781003739920-39

global banking systems is widespread, since governments had to band together to bail out banks [12] But in the present scenario, banks and financial institutions have grown and become more controlled on a national and international level, making a huge contribution to money creation. In short, Banks execute frameworks of rules, procedures and controls to manage risks [13]. To overcome some of these obstacles, most global and local banks have embraced industry-standard frameworks such as ISO 31000:2008 or COSO ERM-Integrated Framework [3] Currently, most banking and financial sectors follow four main risk management strategies to handle risk.

- Risk avoidance strategies
- Risk minimisation strategies
- Risk acceptance or absorption strategies
- risk transferring strategies [6].

Among various kinds of risks, credit risk or default risk is the major risk in the banking and financial sector and is common for local and global financial platforms. Credit risk is a possible loss from a counterparty or borrower who cannot fulfil their commitments or obligations according to the factors agreed upon with the bank [14]. Credit risk management is about managing the operating risk faced by the banking sector. Banks' credit risk management is directly impacted by their entire procedure, especially for the bank's operating performance, and it also affects the financial sector of an economy [14]. The Central Bank of Sri Lanka (CBSL) have proposed a separate credit risk management process for the banking sector, including finance companies. According to the CBSL, credit risk management and its guidance must be modified to comply with other standards such as accounting standards, evolving global best practices from the Basel Committee on Banking Supervision and local and global developments in the banking industry [15].

The concept of competitive advantage is considered to have a moderating role of managerial expertise. Organisations can gain a competitive advantage by creating one or more activities than competitors [16] [17] The term "Sustainable" can be defined according to the different frameworks [2][18]. To efficiently gain a competitive advantage, a sustainable concept must be developed. According to the matrix formed by [19], cost leadership, the advantage of differentiation and a strict focus on identifying strategies can be used to pursue and create a sustainable competitive advantage. This study focuses on how credit risk management strategies such as risk avoidance, risk absorption and transfer strategies impact the sustainable competitive advantage in the banking industry [7][18].

Materials and Methodology

Brief methodology

The study was used a quantitative approach to identify credit risk management strategies by obtaining the opinions of managerial-level or above officers and credit officers or credit underwriters in Sri Lanka [15][20][21]. The study population would not be exactly calculated because it had confidential information. So, the target population was unknown, and a useful and appropriate sampling frame was unavailable for this study. Top-level officers, managers, and above-level personnel who have knowledge of credit risk management and are employed in Sri Lanka's western province's banking industry were considered the population of this study to resolve the issue.

The CRO, Chief Managers and Senior Managers were the managerial and above-level or top-level officers assigned to oversee circulating credit risk management strategies. In addition, assistant managers, executive-level officers, credit officers, and branch managers assigned to the head of the risk department or bank branches were considered middle-level officers. In this research, respondents viewed from many angles across the head of the department and several branches of the bank [21].

The sample was selected using the purposive sampling technique known as judgment sampling from the previously mentioned demographic. Due to the unknown sample size, a maximum of 385 credit officers or the officers above were included in this study's sample [22]. Certainly, it was essential to consider candidates with a strong background in credit risk management, banking operations and financial analysis. On the other hand, ideal candidates should possess relevant experience in assessing and mitigating credit risk, as well as a through understating of banking strategies and regulatory framework. Additionally, candidates were considered as the main decision makers in managing credit risk in a bank and who with a strategic mindset and familiarity with how risk management contributes to competitive advantage provided a valuable insights for the study. The data was gathered by surveying the chosen sample. The surveys were created with an emphasis on previous research and professional judgment. Construct validity and reliability tests were conducted to verify the accuracy and consistency of the data analysis [23][24][25][26].

Sample collection

The target audience of commercial banks performing in the Western Province of Sri Lanka was selected as the geographical area, and it consisted of three main districts: Colombo, Gampaha, and Kalutara [20][21]. The people with managerial, executive, or above-level expertise, i.e. assistant managers, managers, credit officers, or credit underwriters employed in all branches of commercial banks actively performing in selected provinces, were considered the population.

Conceptual framework

Hypotheses have been developed.

H1: There is a significant relationship between the CRMS and SCA.
H2: There is a significant relationship between the CRTS and SCA.
H3: There is a significant relationship between the CRAS and SCA.

The purposive sampling method was used to distribute questionnaires, and the demographic data was collected through the survey by distributing it among the selected sample. After collecting data through the self-administrative questionnaire, it was analyzed using IBM Statistical Package for Social Sciences (SPSS 22). The data was analyzed using descriptive

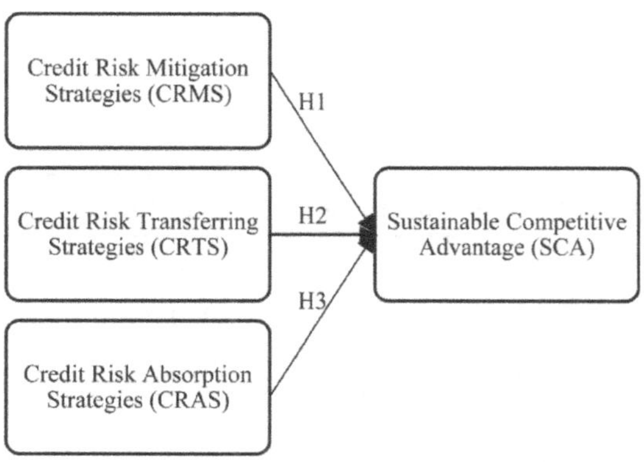

Figure 39.1 Conceptual framework
Source: Developed by Author referring [29]

and inferential statistics and validity and reliability tests [27][28][29].

Discussion

Validity and reliability statistics

To evaluate the validity and reliability, the Cronbach Alpha value for each independent and dependent variable exceeded the benchmark value/ threshold limit of 0.7. This means that the independent and dependent variables were in an acceptable range and their items were sufficiently consistent to indicate that the measure was reliable. The benchmark range of Kaiser-Meyer-Olkin (KMO) value was located between 0 and 1, and the KMO of this study was greater than 0.6 and close to 1. Table 39.1 shows the Cronbach and KMO values, indicating the target population's credit risk management.

One sample statistics for the elements of credit risk management strategies

As per the analysis results obtained from the Table 39.2, all elements are important at the significant level of 1%. However, as stated by CRAS, these were the most important strategies among the above-mentioned variables, representing the mean value of 4.14. The lower standard deviation level represented

Table 39.1 Reliability and validity measures.

Factors	Cronbach's alpha	Cronbach alpha based on SD	KMO Value
CRMS	.702	.703	.711
CRAS	.736	.734	.750
CRTS	.758	.761	.808
SCA	.838	.836	.828

[A]No failure occurred
Source: Author

Table 39.2 One sample statistics for overall elements.

Places	Mean	SD	Std. error mean
CRMS	4.1115**	.485	.046
CRAS	4.1451**	.482	.045
CRTS	4.0832**	.533	.050

[A]No failure occurred
Source: Author

the highest mean value and the lowest dispersion from the generated results. The standard deviation of all strategies below one that defined those with a lower dispersion from the given mean values. So, as the target population or participants, credit risk officers and those above expertise should consider all these strategies.

Regression analysis

According to the R value greater than 0.5, the model predicts that some portion of the relationship and data better fit each other. The researcher had concluded a positive relationship and strong joint correlation between three independent variables and the dependent variable (R value of this study is greater than 0.7. The regression model has explained that R^2 was 0.572 (57%), which can be used for further studies. There was a small gap between R2 and adjusted R2 (1.2%). It indicated that no unnecessary independent variables in the model. The standard error of estimate was reached at 0.357, which denoted that the model has a low number of errors. If another model had the highest volume compared to this one, the researcher may select the model with the lowest standard error of estimate (Table 39.3).

HA: Model is valid

The researcher concluded that the study was valid, reliable, and jointly correlated with each variable to conduct further studies. An ANOVA computation had been developed to check the validity of the model (Table 39.4). CRMS and CRTS obtained significant values, and CRAS was indicated as insignificant in obtaining a 0.544 value (0.5 < 0.544). Considering the three independent variables, CRAS has negatively impacted the SCA, while the other two independent variables have a positive (Table 39.5).

Table 39.3 Model summary[b].

Model	R	R Square	Adjusted R square	Std. error of the estimate
1	.756[a]	.572	.560	.357

[A]No failure occurred.
[a]Predictors: (Constant) CRTS, CRMS, CRAS
[b]Dependent Variable: SCA
Source: Author

Inferential statistics analysis

Karl Pearson's correlation analysis depicts the relationship between two variables. This analysis was considered bivariate because it identified the relationship between two variables. According to that, with the r value exceeding 0.5 (r > or = to 0.5), CRMS and CRTS had an average positive relationship with the dependent variable. Although those two variables had an average positive relationship with the

Table 39.4 ANOVA[a].

Model	Sum of square	df	Mean square	F	Sig
Regression	18.617	3	6.206	48.609	.000[b]
Residual	13.916	109	.128		
Total	32.533	112			

[A]No failure occurred.
[a]Dependent Variable: SCA
[b]Predictors: (Constant) CRTS, CRMS, CRAS
Source: Author

Table 39.5 Coefficients[a].

	Unstandardized coefficients		Standardized coefficients	t	Sig
	B	Std. Error	Beta		
Constant	.506	.325		1.553	.123
CRMS	.494	.096	.445	5.127	.000
CRAS	-.059	.097	-.053	-.609	.544
CRTS	.431	.093	.426	4.644	.000

[A]No failure occurred.
[a]Dependent Variable: SCA
Source: Author

Table 39.6 Correlation Analysis.

Variable	Pearson correlation	Sig (2 tailed)
CRMS	.691**	.000
CRAS	.495**	.000
CRTS	.682**	.000

[A]No failure occurred.
[a]Dependent variable: SCA
[b]Predictors: (Constant) CRTS, CRMS, CRAS.
Source: Author

dependent variable, the relationship between CRAS and SCA was indicated as a weak positive relationship (Table 39.6).

Results and Findings

Most of the past researchers have conducted different studies covering credit risk management. Their results differed from the current study due to variations among selected dependent and independent variables or indicators.

Examine the impact of credit risk management strategies on the sustainable competitive advantage of Commercial Banks.
The first objective was to examine the impact of credit risk management strategies on SCA of commercial banks within the Sri Lankan banking sector. To achieve this objective, the study conducted a regression analysis. In addition, each variable's t-test was performed to identify the experience, knowledge of credit risk officers and above-level expertise.

Identify the relationship between credit risk management strategies and the sustainable competitive advantage of Commercial Banks.
The study was conducted a hypothesis test for correlation analysis to identify the relationship between independent and dependent variables. This analysis was implemented separately for the three independent variables. According to the above table, the P value is significant, lower than 0.05 ($P < 0.05$) at the 95% confidence level. A hypothesis was tested by using the coefficient of correlation to make appropriate decisions.

Hypothesis for CRMS
H1: There was a significant relationship between the CRMS and the SCA.

Therefore, H1 was accepted. This result indicates that there was a significant relationship between CRMS and SCA. That means effective credit risk mitigation strategies positively influence a bank's competitive advantage.

Hypothesis for CRTS
H2: There was a significant relationship between the CRTS and the SCA.

Therefore, H2 was accepted. This indicates that there was a significant relationship between CRTS and SCA. That means effective credit risk transferring strategies positively influence a bank's competitive advantage.

Hypothesis for CRAS
H3: There was a significant relationship between the CRAS and the SCA.

Therefore, H3 was accepted. This indicates that there was a significant relationship between CRAS and SCA. That means effective credit risk absorption strategies positively influence a bank's competitive advantage.

The study suggested the following based on the obtained results.

There was a significant relationship among the variables studied. A stronger association was identified between credit risk mitigation strategies and competitive advantage. Based on this, the researcher recommended that banks focus on credit risk mitigation or avoidance strategies to enhance their competitive positioning and achieve sustainability within the banking sector.

The results indicated that both credit risk mitigation and transferring strategies significantly impact competitive advantage in the Sri Lankan banking sector. Among these, credit risk mitigation strategies exhibited a higher effect. Consequently, the researcher suggests that these strategies should be implemented efficiently and appropriately to maximise benefits from competitive advantages.

Conclusion

Despite the contribution and implications of this study, there were some limitations. Though the study provided theoretical, empirical, and practical implications for the banking and finance sector, both aspects had some limitations. A dearth of past studies relating to this research area was noted when considering the empirical aspects. Further, the researcher has collected data from credit risk officers and above-level expertise to conduct this analysis. This target population was assigned to operational, middle, and overseeing level credit risk management activities. However, some other parties were assigned to other risk management activities, such as market and operational risk, and have experience, knowledge, and ideas about credit risk management.

Considering the practical scenario, the conclusion was based on providing further insight about overall credit risk management strategies, which was vital for the regulators, practitioners and other academic researchers who expect to use this study area. Credit risk management strategies were circulated and implemented by the operational, middle, and overseeing management level experts related to credit risk management activities. For this reason, the data was collected from the above target population. Considering the practical aspect, this study's final result would benefit their circulation and recommendations. This study created a platform to identify currently applicable new credit risk management strategies and assessed the reliability and validity of those strategies in the Sri Lankan context. In addition, this study guided gaining a competitive advantage by enhancing their performance and implementing the best credit risk management strategies within the banking sector.

References

[1] Gobat, Jeanne, "What Is a Bank? Institutions that match up savers and borrowers help ensure that economies function smoothly," *Finance & Development,* vol. 49, no. 001, p. 60, 14 March 2012.

[2] S. F. Ratna Wardhani, "The effect of enterprise risk management and sustainability reporting quality on performance: evidence from Southeast Asia countries," *International Journal of Economic Policy in Emerging Economies,* vol. 13, no. 4, pp. 344–355, 9 September 2020.

[3] CFI Team, 2015. [Online]. Available: https://corporatefinanceinstitute.com/resources/career-map/sell-side/risk-management/risk-transfer/.

[4] M. M. K. Thirupathi Kanchu, "Risk Management in Banking Sector," *International Journal of Marketing, Financial Services & Management Research,* vol. 2, no. 2, p. 102, 2013.

[5] G. I. R. Assessment, "Intone.com," Understand What is Risk Management and its importance, 3 February 2023. [Online]. Available: https://intone.com/understand-what-is-risk-management-and-its-importance/.

[6] V. Vicente, "Types of Risk Management Strategies to Follow," Auditboard, 14 June 2024. [Online]. Available: https://auditboard.com/blog/10-risk-management-strategies. [Accessed 21-23 October 2025].

[7] S. A. S. M. Waqas Ali, "Effect of Risk Management Practices on Banks Performance Moderating Role of Managerial Expertise as a Competitive Edge," *IBT Journal of Business Studies (IBT-JBS),* vol. 16:01, no. 88-100 (2020), p. 13, October 2020.

[8] PUSAT, "Risk Assessment," 25 October 2024. [Online]. Available: https://riskassessmentt.info/risk-management-process/.

[9] H. M. K. Salitha, "Credit Risk and Profitability of Banking Sector in Sri Lanka," *Journal of Economics, Finance and Accounting Studies,* vol. 3, no. 1, pp. 65–71, 2017.

[10] I. Županović, "Sustainable Risk Management in the Banking Sector," *Journal of Central Bnaking Theory and Practice,* vol. 3, no. 1, p. 20, 13 November 2013.

[11] J. D. S. A. S. Boahene, "Credit Risk and Profitability selected banks in Ghana," *Research Journal of Finance and Accounting,* vol. 3, no. 7, pp. 6–15, 2012.

[12] W. S. L. N. T. and K. P. E., "The determinants of bank risks: Evidence from the recent financial crisis," *Journal of International Financial Markets, Institutions and Money,* vol. 34, pp. 277–293, January 2015.

[13] M. J. Zeidan, "The effects of violating banking regulations on the financial performance of the US banking industry," *Journal of Financial Regulation and Compliance,* vol. 20 (1), pp. 56-71, February 2012.

[14] Jiongyong Chen, "Bank Credit Risk Avoidance and Countermeasures," *Hindawi,* p. 7, 2022.

[15] Central Bank, Sri Lanka, "Proposed new direction on Credit Risk Management for Licensed Finance Companies (LFCs)," *Direction for Commercial Banks,* p. 25, 16 October 2019.

[16] M. R. Oyeyo, "Sources of Sustainable competitive advantage in the banking industry in Kenya," April 2008.

[17] S. Claessens, "Competition in the Financial Sector: Overview of Competition Policies," *IMF Working Paper,* March 2009.

[18] A. M. H. Hari Tohar Muljono, "[26] Tohar, H., Abdul, M. and Hasyim, M. (2023) 'Strategies for Achieving Sustainable Competitive Advantage to Enhance Company Performance," *Journal Ilmu Management Profitability,* vol. 7(2), p. 172, August 2023.

[19] Michael Porter, Competitive Advantage: Creating and Sustaining Superior Performance, Reprint ed., Simon and Schuster, 2008, p. 592.

[20] Bank of Ceylon, "Bank of Ceylon Annual Report 2023," Public Finance, Colombo, Sri Lanka, 2023- 24.

[21] Sampath Bank PLC, "Sampath Bank Annual report 2024," Kites Global, Colombo, Sri Lanka, 2024.

[22] Calculator.net, "Sample SIze Calculator," Calculator.net, 2008. [Online]. Available: e=1&cl=95&ci=5&pp=50&ps=250&x=Calculate. [Accessed 2008].

[23] H. M. K. S. B. A. L. M. J. and H. A., "Credit Risk and Profitability of Banking Sector in Sri Lanka,"

Journal of Economics Finance and Accounting Studies, vol. 3(1), pp. 65-71, April 2021.

[24] K.-E. Sveiby, "Knowledge based theory of the firm to guide strategy formulation," *Journal of intellectual capital,* vol. 2(4), p. 15, December 2001.

[25] M. Sammy, "Relationship between financial risk management and financial performance of commercial banks in Kenya," *University of Nairobi,* 2014.

[26] R. Wardhani, "The effect of enterprise risk management and sustainability reporting quality on performance: evidence from Southeast Asia countries," *International Journal of Economic Policy in Emerging Economies,* p. 13, January 2020.

[27] J. Chen, "Bank Credit Risk Avoidance and Countermeasures Based on Wireless Communication," *Hindawi Scientific Programming,* vol. 2022, no. 7793088, p. 7, March 2022.

[28] M. A. Idowu, "Impact of Credit Risk Management on Performance of Microfinance Banks in Akure, Ondo State," *International Journal of Financial Res and Business Development,* vol. 06 (7), p. 10, October 2024.

[29] M. M. K. -. U. o. Nairobi, "The Effect of Risk Management Strategies on the Sustainable Competitive Advantage of Commercial Banks in Kenya," vol. 7, no. 2, p. 63, 2017.

40 Investigating operational drivers of the bullwhip effect in the upstream supply chain of the FMCG industry

Ashani Galagedara[1,a] *and Shaja M.M.M.*[2,b]

[1]CBL Foods International (Pvt) Ltd., Sri Lanka

[2]Department of Operations and Logistics, Faculty of Business, NSBM Green University, Sri Lanka

Abstract

This study investigates the factors influencing the Bullwhip Effect (BWE) in the upstream supply chain of the Fast-Moving Consumer Goods (FMCG) industry, with particular emphasis on operational drivers such as price variations, lead time, and Minimum Order Quantities (MOQs). The BWE refers to the phenomenon where demand variability increases as orders move upstream in the supply chain, often leading to inefficiencies such as excess inventory, stockouts, and increased operational costs. Despite extensive research on the BWE, there remains a notable gap in understanding how specific operational factors like price fluctuations, lead time variability, and MOQs contribute to demand amplification in FMCG supply chains. This study aims to address this gap by providing empirical evidence and analytical insights into the complex relationships among these variables. Data were collected through a structured questionnaire administered to supply chain professionals within the FMCG sector. The collected data were analyzed using a combination of descriptive and inferential statistical methods to ensure a comprehensive understanding of the underlying dynamics. The results demonstrate that price variations, extended lead times, and rigid MOQs significantly exacerbate the Bullwhip Effect in upstream supply chain stages. Furthermore, the study highlights the critical role of advanced information systems and collaborative planning mechanisms in mitigating these effects. By improving communication, demand forecasting accuracy, and inventory management practices, supply chain partners can reduce demand variability and enhance overall supply chain performance. These findings offer valuable insights for supply chain professionals and policymakers seeking to optimize FMCG supply chains.

Keywords: Bullwhip effect, FMCG industry, operational drivers, upstream supply chain

Introduction

Efficient supply chain management is fundamental to the success of modern enterprises, as it ensures the seamless flow of goods from suppliers to end consumers. In a typical supply chain, suppliers provide raw materials to manufacturers, who then produce finished goods for distribution through wholesalers and retailers before reaching the final customer. The coordination of information and material flows across these stages is critical, yet disruptions often arise due to variations in ordering patterns between different supply chain phases. One significant phenomenon resulting from such disruptions is the bullwhip effect (BWE), where demand fluctuations amplify as they move upstream from consumers to producers.

The bullwhip effect has been extensively documented in supply chain literature, notably by Forrester [1] and later by Buffa and Taubert [2], who highlighted how demand variability intensifies as it propagates through the supply chain. Contributing factors include demand fluctuations, inaccurate forecasts, lead time uncertainties, batch ordering, supply shortages, price changes, backorder policies, and misinterpretation of time delays. These factors can be categorized into operational and behavioral tactics, both of which exacerbate demand volatility within the supply chain [3].

The impact of the bullwhip effect is particularly pronounced in the fast-moving consumer goods (FMCG) industry, where it leads to increased inventory costs, reduced efficiency, and suboptimal alignment between supply and demand [3]. While numerous studies have investigated the causes and consequences of the BWE [1, 4–6], there remains a notable gap in understanding how price volatility and minimum order quantities (MOQs) in the upstream supply chain encompassing manufacturers and suppliers contribute to this phenomenon. Most existing

[a]ashanig.cblf@cbllk.com, [b]shaja.m@nsbm.ac.lk

DOI: 10.4324/9781003739920-40

research has focused on the downstream supply chain, such as retail and distribution, leaving the upstream dynamics underexplored.

This study aims to address this gap by examining the influence of price volatility, lead time, and MOQ regulations on the bullwhip effect in the FMCG industry's upstream supply chain. By analyzing collected data, this research seeks to provide deeper insights into the mechanisms driving demand fluctuations and to propose strategies for mitigating the bullwhip effect in FMCG supply chains.

Literature Review

The Bullwhip Effect (BWE) is a well-documented phenomenon in supply chain management characterized by the amplification of demand variability as orders move upstream from retailers to manufacturers and suppliers. Initially conceptualized by [1] in the late 1950s and early 1960s, the term "Bullwhip Effect" was popularized by [3], who described how small fluctuations in consumer demand at the retail level led to much larger fluctuations in orders placed upstream in the supply chain. This amplification causes significant inefficiencies such as excess inventory, stockouts, increased operational costs, and reduced customer satisfaction, making it one of the most critical challenges in supply chain management [7].

Several causes contribute to the bullwhip effect. demand signal processing is a primary factor where supply chain members forecast demand based on orders from their immediate downstream partners rather than actual consumer demand, leading to distorted and amplified signals [3]. Order batching, where companies place large orders at set intervals rather than continuously, creates artificial peaks and troughs in demand, exacerbating variability [7]. Price fluctuations and promotional activities encourage forward buying and stockpiling, which further distort demand patterns and increase variability [7]. Other causes include rationing and shortage gaming, where downstream partners inflate orders anticipating supply shortages, long and variable lead times that increase uncertainty, and behavioral factors such as cognitive biases and overreaction to demand changes [3]. Additionally, poor communication and lack of transparency among supply chain partners contribute to delayed and inaccurate information flow, worsening the effect [7].

The consequences of the Bullwhip Effect are substantial. Excess inventory held to buffer against perceived demand uncertainty leads to increased holding costs and risks of obsolescence [7]. Paradoxically, despite high inventory levels, stockouts and delayed deliveries frequently occur, damaging customer satisfaction and brand loyalty [7]. Fluctuating order patterns disrupt production schedules and increase setup, labor, and transportation costs, collectively eroding profitability [8]. The environmental impact of overproduction and waste is an emerging concern, as excess inventory often results in spoilage or disposal [7]. These inefficiencies highlight the urgent need for effective mitigation strategies.

Measuring the Bullwhip Effect often involves analyzing the variance amplification ratio, which compares the variance of orders at different supply chain stages to the variance of actual demand [8]. Simulation tools such as the Beer Game have been widely used to illustrate behavioral causes and effects [9]. Advances in computational intelligence, including genetic algorithms and fuzzy logic, have enhanced modelling capabilities for understanding and predicting demand amplification [10].

Mitigation strategies focus on improving information transparency and collaboration across the supply chain. Sharing point-of-sale (POS) data, inventory levels, and forecasts enables partners to base decisions on actual demand rather than distorted order signals, significantly reducing variability [1, 3]. Electronic supply chain management systems and collaborative planning, forecasting, and replenishment (CPFR) initiatives facilitate this transparency [10]. Reducing lead times through process improvements and supplier development decreases uncertainty and lowers safety stock requirements [3]. Encouraging smaller, more frequent orders instead of large batch orders smooths demand signals; vendor-managed inventory (VMI) and continuous replenishment programs exemplify this approach [3]. Price stabilization strategies, such as everyday low pricing (EDLP), discourage forward buying and reduce order variability caused by promotions [1]. Aligning incentives through coordinated contracts, like buy-back agreements and quantity flexibility contracts, helps reduce gaming behaviors, and fosters cooperation [9]. The use of advanced analytics, including demand sensing and predictive modelling, further enhances forecasting accuracy and supply chain responsiveness [10, 11].

The Fast-Moving Consumer Goods (FMCG) sector is particularly vulnerable to the Bullwhip Effect due to its high-volume, low-margin products, frequent promotions, and complex supply chains [3]. Rapid product innovation and short product life cycles complicate demand forecasting and inventory management [9]. Information technology integration, including enterprise resource planning (ERP) and electronic data interchange (EDI), plays a crucial role in mitigating the BWE by enabling real-time data sharing and coordinated decision-making [3]. Retailer ordering behavior, influenced by promotions and price changes, often leads to irregular and amplified order patterns that propagate upstream [3]. Moreover, FMCG companies expanding into emerging markets face additional challenges such as infrastructure constraints and volatile demand, which can exacerbate the BWE [9].

Price variations and promotional activities are major contributors to demand variability and the BWE. Empirical studies confirm that frequent price changes increase order variability and inventory costs [1, 3, 12, 13]. The adoption of EDLP strategies by retailers has been shown to reduce these effects by stabilizing order patterns [1]. Minimum order quantities (MOQs) also influence inventory management and the BWE. High MOQs can force larger-than-necessary orders, increasing inventory holding costs and demand amplification, while flexible MOQs adjusted based on real-time demand forecasts help align supply with actual consumption [3]. Advanced inventory models incorporating stochastic demand, lead time variability, and service level requirements optimize safety stock levels and minimize the BWE [10].

Lead time management remains critical for mitigating the Bullwhip Effect. Shorter and more reliable lead times allow supply chains to respond rapidly to demand changes, reducing the need for excess safety stock and dampening order variability [3]. Supplier development, process standardization, and logistics optimization are key strategies for lead time reduction [9]. Behavioral factors such as cognitive biases and risk aversion also influence the persistence of the BWE. Training, decision support systems, and organizational learning can improve ordering decisions and reduce variability [9]. Organizational culture promoting trust, transparency, and collaboration is essential for successful mitigation [10].

Recent technological advances such as the Internet of Things (IoT), blockchain, and artificial intelligence (AI) offer promising avenues for further reducing the Bullwhip Effect. Real-time tracking of inventory and shipments, automated replenishment, and predictive analytics enhance supply chain responsiveness and resilience [10, 14–16]. Blockchain technology provides secure, transparent, and tamper-proof information sharing, reducing information asymmetry and building trust among supply chain partners [10, 17, 18]. Despite these advances, research gaps remain, particularly in understanding BWE dynamics in emerging markets and integrating sustainability considerations into supply chain practices [9]. Behavioral interventions and gamification also represent promising but underexplored areas for reducing demand variability [10].

In conclusion, the bullwhip effect continues to pose significant challenges for supply chain efficiency, profitability, and sustainability. While substantial progress has been made in understanding its causes and developing mitigation strategies—from enhanced information sharing and lead time reduction to advanced analytics and behavioral interventions—ongoing innovation is essential to address evolving supply chain complexities. The FMCG sector, with its unique characteristics and rapid growth in emerging markets, exemplifies the critical need for integrated, technology-enabled, and collaborative approaches to managing demand variability. As global supply chains become more interconnected and dynamic, leveraging lessons from decades of BWE research will be vital for building resilient, responsive, and competitive supply networks.

Materials and Methodology

Research philosophy and approach

This study adopted a positivist research philosophy, emphasizing objectivity and empirical observation to investigate the bullwhip effect (BWE) in the Fast-Moving Consumer Goods (FMCG) industry. The positivist paradigm facilitated the development and testing of hypotheses using quantitative methods, ensuring the reliability and generalizability of the findings.

A deductive research approach was employed, beginning with hypotheses derived from existing theories regarding the influence of price fluctuations and minimum order quantities (MOQs) on the BWE. These hypotheses were tested through statistical analysis of the collected data. Although deductive reasoning provided a systematic framework for testing, it inherently limited the exploration of unanticipated phenomena.

Research design

Quantitative, mono-method research design was used, relying primarily on structured surveys for data collection. This approach ensured consistency and allowed robust statistical analysis. The study focused on three independent variables: price variations (fluctuations in raw material or product prices), MOQs, and lead time. The dependent variable was the bullwhip effect observed in the upstream supply chain of the FMCG industry.

Data were collected using a cross-sectional time horizon, capturing information at a single point in time. While this approach provided immediate insights, it did not account for temporal dynamics or establish causality.

Unit of analysis and scope

The unit of analysis was the upstream supply chain of the FMCG industry, including sourcing, procurement, and raw material production activities. This focus allowed the study to identify specific factors contributing to the bullwhip effect in this segment of the supply chain.

Conceptual framework

The conceptual framework (Figure 40.1) illustrated the hypothesized relationships between price variations, MOQs, lead time, and the bullwhip effect.

Hypotheses

The study tested the following hypotheses:

H0: There is no significant relationship between price variations and the bullwhip effect in the upstream supply chain of the FMCG industry.

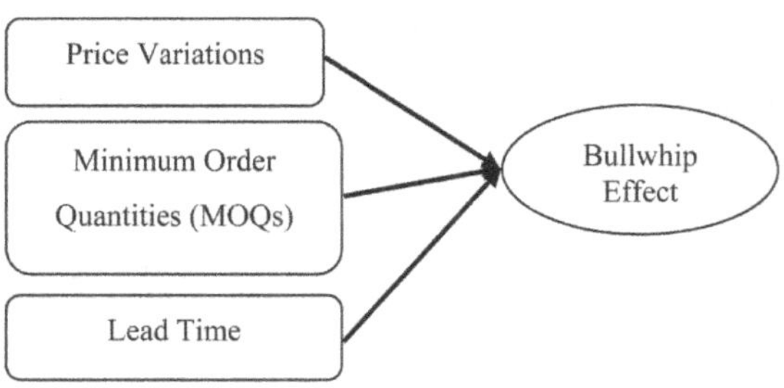

Figure 40.1 Conceptual framework
Source: Author

H1: There is a significant relationship between price variations and the bullwhip effect.

H0: There is no significant relationship between MOQs and the bullwhip effect.

H2: There is a significant relationship between MOQs and the bullwhip effect.

H0: There is no significant relationship between lead time and the bullwhip effect.

H3: There is a significant relationship between lead time and the bullwhip effect.

Data collection and analysis

Structured surveys were distributed to supply chain professionals within the FMCG sector. The collected data were analyzed using statistical techniques, including correlation and regression analysis, to test the stated hypotheses.

Data analysis and Results

This section presents a comprehensive analysis of the data collected through a self-administered survey, focusing on the upstream supply chain of the FMCG industry. The analysis is divided into reliability assessment, correlation analysis, and regression modeling to explore the relationships between price variations, minimum order quantities (MOQs), lead time, and the Bullwhip Effect (BWE).

Reliability analysis

Reliability analysis was conducted using Cronbach's alpha to assess the internal consistency of the survey scales. As shown in Table 40.1, all variables demonstrated high reliability, with Cronbach's alpha values exceeding the acceptable threshold of 0.7. Specifically, price variations scored 0.828, MOQs 0.898, lead time 0.876, and the bullwhip effect 0.873. These values indicate that the survey items consistently measured their respective constructs, ensuring the dependability of the data.

Table 40.1 Summary of reliability analysis.

Variable	Cronbach's Alpha	Reliability
Price variations	0.828	Good
Minimum order quantity (MOQ)	0.898	Good
Lead Time	0.876	Good
Bullwhip effect	0.873	Good

Source: Author

Correlation analysis

Pearson correlation analysis (Table 40.2) was performed to examine the relationships between the independent variables (price variations, MOQs, lead time) and the dependent variable (Bullwhip Effect).

Price variations and bullwhip effect: The analysis revealed a strong positive correlation ($r = 0.624$, $p < 0.01$), indicating that increased price fluctuations are associated with a higher Bullwhip Effect. This suggests that frequent changes in prices lead to unpredictable ordering behaviors, amplifying demand variability and supply chain inefficiencies.

Minimum order quantities and bullwhip effect: A very strong positive correlation was found ($r = 0.791$, $p < 0.01$), showing that higher MOQs significantly contribute to the Bullwhip Effect. Larger, less frequent orders stemming from high MOQs distort demand signals and increase inventory holding costs.

Lead time and bullwhip effect: The strongest correlation was observed between lead time and the Bullwhip Effect ($r = 0.808$, $p < 0.01$). Longer lead times were associated with greater demand variability, as firms tend to place larger orders to buffer against delays, further amplifying the BWE.

Multiple regression analysis

A multiple regression analysis was conducted to determine the combined effect of price variations, MOQs, and lead time on the bullwhip effect.

The model (Table 40.3) demonstrated a high explanatory power, with an R Square of 0.720, indicating that approximately 72% of the variance in the Bullwhip Effect can be explained by the three predictors.

Table 40.2 Summary of correlation analysis.

_Bullwhip Effect		
Price variations	Pearson correlation	.624**
	Sig. (2-tailed)	.000
	N	250
Minimum order quantities	Pearson correlation	.791**
	Sig. (2-tailed)	.000
	N	250
Lead time	Pearson correlation	.808**
	Sig. (2-tailed)	.000
	N	250

**. Correlation is significant at the 0.01 level (2-tailed).

Source: Author

The ANOVA results (Table 40.4) ($F = 210.470$, $p < 0.001$) confirm that the regression model is statistically significant. The regression equation is:

$$\text{Bullwhip effect} = 0.588 + 0.083(\text{price variations}) + 0.307(\text{MOQ}) + 0.460(\text{lead time})$$

All predictors were found to have a significant positive effect on the bullwhip effect. Lead time had the highest standardized effect (Beta = 0.481), followed by MOQs (Beta = 0.338) and price variations (Beta = 0.101) (Table 40.5).

These findings highlight the critical importance of managing lead times, optimizing MOQs, and stabilizing prices to mitigate the Bullwhip Effect and enhance supply chain efficiency in the FMCG industry.

Table 40.3 Regression model summary.

Model	R	R Square	Adjusted R square	Std. Error of the Estimate
1	0.848	0.720	0.716	0.30069

Source: Author

Table 40.4 ANOVA summary.

Model	Sum of Squares	df	Mean Square	F	Sig.
Regression	57.088	3	19.029	210.470	.000
Residual	22.242	246	0.090		
Total	79.329	249			

Source: Author

Table 40.5 Regression coefficients.

Predictor	B	Std. Error	Beta	t	Sig.
(Constant)	0.588	0.139		4.223	.000
Price Variations	0.083	0.039	0.101	2.095	.037
Minimum Order Quantities	0.307	0.058	0.338	5.296	.000
Lead Time	0.460	0.053	0.481	8.691	.000

Source: Author

Discussion

This study underscores the significant impact of three critical factors such as price variations, minimum order quantities (MOQs), and lead times on the bullwhip effect within the upstream supply chain of the FMCG sector. Gaining a clear understanding of how these elements interact is essential for managing variability and improving supply chain performance.

Price variations have a profound influence on the bullwhip effect. When prices fluctuate frequently, they create uncertainty that disrupts accurate demand forecasting. Buyers often respond to such fluctuations by stockpiling inventory when prices fall, anticipating future price increases. This behavior, commonly referred to as forward buying, distorts real demand signals and causes amplified order variability further up the supply chain. Previous research has consistently shown that pricing strategies like promotions and discounts can significantly increase order variability and exacerbate the bullwhip effect [3, 8, 19, 20].

Minimum order quantities (MOQs) also contribute to the problem by encouraging buyers to order in large batches instead of aligning orders with actual consumption patterns. This batching leads to irregular ordering cycles, which create artificial spikes and troughs in demand. As these fluctuations ripple upstream, they increase overall supply chain instability. Studies have highlighted that MOQs can intensify this order amplification by forcing buyers into irregular purchasing patterns, thereby increasing variability within the supply chain [21, 22].

Lead Time, defined as the period between placing an order and receiving it, plays a crucial role as well. Longer and unpredictable lead times delay the flow of information, creating a mismatch between actual demand and inventory decisions. When suppliers base their orders on outdated or incomplete information, they tend to overcompensate by increasing order sizes or reducing them abruptly, which further amplifies the bullwhip effect. Research suggests that reducing lead times and making them more consistent can substantially mitigate these order variabilities, enabling smoother and more responsive supply chains [1, 2, 23, 24].

In conclusion, this analysis confirms that price fluctuations, MOQs, and lead times individually and collectively contribute to demand amplification in the FMCG upstream supply chain. Addressing these challenges through more coordinated pricing approaches, flexible ordering policies, and targeted lead time reductions can help alleviate the bullwhip effect, fostering greater supply chain stability and overall efficiency [3, 20].

Conclusion

The findings of this study demonstrate that price variations, minimum order quantities, and lead time are critical drivers of the bullwhip effect in the upstream supply chain of the FMCG sector. Managing these factors by stabilizing prices, minimizing MOQs, and reducing lead times can help mitigate the bullwhip effect and enhance overall supply chain efficiency.

Furthermore, the research suggests that the adoption of advanced technologies, such as artificial intelligence (AI) and the Internet of Things (IoT), can improve demand forecasting, supply chain visibility, and decision-making, thereby reducing the impact of these variables. Future research could expand on these results by exploring additional factors, such as behavioral aspects and collaborative supply chain practices, to further understand and manage the bullwhip effect in dynamic market environments.

References

[1] Forrester, J. W. (1961). Industrial Dynamics. Cambridge, MA: MIT Press.

[2] Buffa, E. S., & Taubert, J. F. (1972). Production-Inventory Systems: Planning and Control. Homewood, IL: Richard D. Irwin.

[3] Lee, H. L., Padmanabhan, V., & Whang, S. (1997). The bullwhip effect in supply chains. *MIT Sloan Management Review*, 38(3), 93–102.

[4] Chen, Y., Liu, Y., & Li, X. (2022). Pricing strategies and bullwhip effect in supply chains with consumer price forecasting behavior. *RAIRO - Operations Research*, 56(4), 2873–2890.

[5] van Donselaar, J. J. J., van Woensel, T., Fransoo, J. C., & van Houtum, G. J. A. (2006). The Impact of Store Order Batching on the Bullwhip Effect in Supply Chains. Eindhoven University of Technology.

[6] Pastore, S., Alfieri, G., Pinto, A., & Vocaturo, A. V. (2017). The bullwhip effect in supply chains: a review of methods, components and drivers. *International Journal of Production Research*, 55(1), 1–17.

[7] Inbound Logistics. (2023). Bullwhip Effect: Example, Causes, and Impact on Supply Chain. Inbound Logistics. https://www.inboundlogistics.com/articles/bullwhip-effect/.

[8] Chen, F., Drezner, Z., Ryan, J., & Simchi-Levi, D. (2000). Quantifying the bullwhip effect in a simple supply chain: the impact of forecasting, lead times, and information. *Management Science*, 46(3), 436–443. doi: 10.1287/mnsc.46.3.436.12069.

[9] Kumar, S., & Saini, R. (2023). The bullwhip effect: causes, intensity, and mitigation. *Journal of Industrial and Production Engineering*, 34(2), 124–134. doi: 10.1080/21693277.2020.1862722.

[10] Varma, D. A. K. (2009). An Experience with Bullwhip Effect in a Supply Chain - A Case Study. SSRN: https://ssrn.com/abstract=1506871 or http://dx.doi.org/10.2139/ssrn.1506871.

[11] Rahman, M. H., Rahman, M. A., & Talapatra, S. (2020). The bullwhip effect: causes, intensity, and mitigation. *Production and Manufacturing Research*, 8(1), 406–426. doi: 10.1080/21693277.2020.1862772.

[12] Sabbaghnia, M., Gholamian, M. R., & Fathi, M. (2018). Optimal control of supply chain dynamics: minimizing inventory propagation. *Mathematics*, 6(11), 251. doi: 10.3390/math6110251.

[13] Ahmed, M. H., & Hussain, S. (2019). Analysis of bullwhip effect: a behavioral approach. *Supply Chain Forum: An International Journal*, 12, 102–112. doi: 10.1080/16258312.2019.1617566.

[14] O'Donnell, F. J., Wood, R. J., & Power, D. M. (2006). Optimisation of supply chain management using computational intelligence techniques. *International Journal of Production Research*, 44(9), 1839–1852. doi: 10.1080/00207540500442492.

[15] Aminnoust, A., Fatemi Ghomi, S. M. T., & Zandieh, M. (2013). A multi-objective genetic algorithm for solving a fuzzy multi-period and multi-product supply chain network design problem. *International Journal of Production Economics*, 145(1), 53–64. doi: 10.1016/j.ijpe.2012.10.003.

[16] Campuzano-Bolarín, A., Pliego, F. J. C., & Mula, J. (2019). A rolling horizon approach for the supply planning problem in supply chains. *Computers and Industrial Engineering*, 137, 106036. doi: 10.1016/j.cie.2019.106036.

[17] Hill, A., Hill, J., & Chinda, T. (2018). Lean six sigma: a literature review and future directions. *International Journal of Lean Six Sigma*, 9(3), 389–398. doi: 10.1108/IJLSS-02-2017-0017.

[18] Trapero, J. R., & Pedregal, D. J. (2016). Improving the bullwhip effect in supply chains using optimal transfer functions. *International Journal of Production Economics*, 181, 145–156. doi: 10.1016/j.ijpe.2016.08.017.

[19] Zhai, X. (2013). The bullwhip effect in supply chain management, MSc Thesis, University of Gothen burg, School of Business, Economics and Law.

[20] Disney, S. M., Towill, D. R., & Riddalls, C. (2011). The impact of vendor managed inventory on the bullwhip effect in supply chains. *International Journal of Production Economics*, 71(3), 265–272.

[21] Zhang, R. Q. (2004). Impact of order batching on supply chain performance. *International Journal of Production Economics*, 88(2), 179–192.

[22] Cachon, G. P., & Fisher, M. (2000). Supply chain inventory management and the value of shared information. *Management Science*, 46(8), 1032–1048.

[23] Sterman, J. D. (1989). Modeling managerial behavior: misperceptions of feedback in a dynamic decision making experiment. *Management Science*, 35(3), 321–339.

[24] Croson, R., & Donohue, K. (2006). Impact of POS data sharing on supply chain management: an experimental study. *Production and Operations Management*, 15(1), 1–11.

For Product Safety Concerns and Information please contact our EU
representative GPSR@taylorandfrancis.com
Taylor & Francis Verlag GmbH, Kaufingerstraße 24, 80331 München, Germany

www.ingramcontent.com/pod-product-compliance
Lightning Source LLC
LaVergne TN
LVHW080805011026
849160LV00015B/1542
9781041240679